Frommer's®

Austria

14th Edition

254   273

by Dardis McNamee & Maggie Childs

SALZ CARD
PJ 230

- FASTIES
- ZIPFER
- SPAR MARKET
- MIRABEL

MAP
296-247

WILEY

A John Wiley and Sons, Ltd, Publication

Published by:

WILEY PUBLISHING, INC.

Copyright © 2011 John Wiley & Sons Ltd, The Atrium, Southern Gate, Chichester, West Sussex PO19 8SQ, UK

Telephone (+44) 1243 779777

Email (for orders and customer service enquiries): cs-books@wiley.co.uk. Visit our Home Page on www.wiley.com

UK Publisher: Sally Smith

Project Manager: Daniel Mersey

Commissioning Editor: Mark Henshall

Development Editor: Caroline Sieg

Content Editor: Erica Peters

Cartography: Andrew Dolan

Photo Editor: Jill Emeny

Front cover photo: Village of Neustift, Tyrol, Austria. © LOOK Die Bildagentur der Fotografen GmbH / Alamy. Back Cover photo: The Bad Blumau Spa Hotel in Styria. © Walter Bibikow / awl-images.

For information on our other products and services or to obtain technical support, please contact our Customer Care Department within the U.S. at 877/762-2974, outside the U.S. at 317/572-3993 or fax 317/572-4002.

British Library Cataloguing in Publication Data

A catalogue record for this book is available from the British Library

ISBN 978-0-470-97595-4 (pbk)

ISBN 978-1-119-97253-2 (ebk)

ISBN 978-1-119-99451-0 (ebk)

ISBN 978-1-119-99467-1 (ebk)

Typeset by Wiley Indianapolis Composition Services

Printed and bound in the United States of America

5 4 3 2 1

CONTENTS

FASTIES — 252

LIST OF MAPS

ABOUT THE AUTHORS

Dardis McNamee is Editor in Chief of the English-language monthly, *The Vienna Review* and on the research faculty in Media Communications at Webster University Vienna. In her long career in journalism she has been a correspondent for, among others, *The New York Times* and *Condé Nast Traveler* in New York, and for the *Wall Street Journal Europe* and *Die Zeit* in Vienna, as well as a speech writer to two US ambassadors to Austria. She has lived in Vienna for 15 years.

Maggie Childs is a journalist and travel writer for publications such as *Condé Nast Traveler US*, *The Vienna Review*, *Gig Magazine*, and various in-flight magazines. She has lived in Vienna for 14 years and also works for the Vienna bureau of the Associated Press. She is also the author of the Austria Chapter of *Europe For Dummies* and the Co-Author of *Frommer's Vienna & the Danube Valley*.

ACKNOWLEDGMENTS

The authors wish to thank the following for their contributions:
Christopher Anderson (Upper Austria, Salzburg, Salzburgerland)
Austin Childs (Lower Austria, Carinthia, Styria)
Jessica Spiegel (Burgenland, Innsbruck-Tyrol, Voralberg)

HOW TO CONTACT US

In researching this book, we discovered many wonderful places—hotels, restaurants, shops, and more. We're sure you'll find others. Please tell us about them, so we can share the information with your fellow travelers in upcoming editions. If you were disappointed with a recommendation, we'd love to know that, too. Please email frommers@wiley.com or write to:

Frommer's Austria, 14th Edition
Wiley Publishing, Inc. • 111 River St. • Hoboken, NJ 07030-5774

AN ADDITIONAL NOTE

Please be advised that travel information is subject to change at any time—and this is especially true of prices. We therefore suggest that you write or call ahead for confirmation when making your travel plans. The authors, editors, and publisher cannot be held responsible for the experiences of readers while traveling. Your safety is important to us, however, so we encourage you to stay alert and be aware of your surroundings. Keep a close eye on cameras, purses, and wallets, all favorite targets of thieves and pickpockets.

FROMMER'S STAR RATINGS, ICONS & ABBREVIATIONS

Every hotel, restaurant, and attraction listing in this guide has been ranked for quality, value, service, amenities, and special features using a **star-rating system.** In country, state, and regional guides, we also rate towns and regions to help you narrow down your choices and budget your time accordingly. Hotels and restaurants are rated on a scale of zero (recommended) to three stars (exceptional). Attractions, shopping, nightlife, towns, and regions are rated according to the following scale: zero stars (recommended), one star (highly recommended), two stars (very highly recommended), and three stars (must-see).

In addition to the star-rating system, we also use **seven feature icons** that point you to the great deals, in-the-know advice, and unique experiences that separate travelers from tourists. Throughout the book, look for:

special finds—those places only insiders know about

fun facts—details that make travelers more informed and their trips more fun

kids—best bets for kids and advice for the whole family

special moments—those experiences that memories are made of

overrated—places or experiences not worth your time or money

insider tips—great ways to save time and money

great values—where to get the best deals

The following **abbreviations** are used for credit cards:

AE	American Express	DISC Discover	V Visa
DC	Diners Club	MC MasterCard	

TRAVEL RESOURCES AT FROMMERS.COM

Frommer's travel resources don't end with this guide. Frommer's website, **www.frommers. com**, has travel information on more than 4,000 destinations. We update features regularly, giving you access to the most current trip-planning information and the best airfare, lodging, and car-rental bargains. You can also listen to podcasts, connect with other Frommers. com members through our active-reader forums, share your travel photos, read blogs from guidebook editors and fellow travellers, and much more.

THE BEST OF AUSTRIA

From soaring alpine peaks in the west to the seemingly endless valleys and lowlands in the east, Austria's natural beauty is breathtaking. For over a millennium the region has been at the center of European history and culture. Its lively historic cities, like the capital Vienna, Graz, Innsbruck, and Salzburg are as aesthetically pleasing as their dramatic settings. In summer, Austria's lakes, rivers, and hiking paths come to life, while the winter months are interwoven with hot-spiced wine and ski excursions.

The Austrians are elegant and cultured people with a dark, yet resilient sense of humor and a knack for fashioning lifestyle to fit their needs. From 5th generation country farmers to middle class city dwellers to members of the faded aristocracy, sophistication, beauty, and good food are of the utmost importance.

For such a small country, Austria has made more than its fair share of global impact. Besides exports like Linzer Torte, Manner wafers, and Red Bull, Vienna is the third UN headquarters' city, along with New York and Geneva. With some 17,000 diplomats in residence and conveniently located at the crossroads of eastern and western Europe, Austria has the highest density of foreign intelligence agents in the world.

Once the seat of the Austro-Hungarian Empire, today's Austrian capital Vienna is a bustling metropolis with a strong commitment to the good life, and the city is consistently ranked number 1 in quality of life worldwide.

Throughout this book, you'll find Austria's choice sights, restaurants, and hotels, and this chapter gives you a glimpse of the very best. Some are classics, like Vienna's opera or Tyrol's Kitzbühel, others are less well known. However, surely you'll add your own bests to this list. The same applies for this whole book of candid recommendations: Hopefully you'll benefit from the inside pointers, but you'll surely discover favorites of your own. When places change significantly, for better or worse, you'll find it on Frommers.com—feel free to join in the conversation there.

THE best TRAVEL EXPERIENCES

- **Skiing in the Alps:** Skiing is the Austrian national sport, bringing thousands of visitors to Austria. The country abounds in ski slopes, with the best ones in Tyrol, Land Salzburg, and Vorarlberg, although most parts of Carinthia, western Styria, and Lower Austria also have slopes. The season lasts from late November to April, depending on snow conditions. At 1,739m (5,705 ft.), the Obertauern region extends its ski season until May. Adventurers can ski glaciers at 3,355m (11,010 ft.), even in summer. See "The Best Ski Areas," later in this chapter.

- **Savoring *Tafelspitz,* the "Emperor's Dish":** No Austrian dish is more typical than the fabled *Tafelspitz,* favored by Emperor Franz Joseph. Boiled beef sounds dull, but *Tafelspitz* is far from bland. A tender delicacy, the cut absorbs a variety of flavors, including juniper berries, celery root, and onions. Apple-and-horseradish sauce further enlivens the dish, which is usually served with fried grated potatoes. For Vienna's best *Tafelspitz,* try **Plachutta,** on the Wollzeile in Vienna (*©* **01/5121577**). See p. 127.

- **Taking the Cure at a Spa:** Few things touch the beauty of taking time to recharge your batteries. In Austria, it is seen as part of a balanced lifestyle. Sauna landscapes, lakeside spa treatments with local mineral muds, and herbal treatments from the rich natural resources on offer will keep you purring. If you really want to get a taste of Austria, make sure you plan at least one day of rest and rejuvenation at an alpine or thermal spa. See chapters 10, 12, and 13 for high-altitude pampering and chapters 7, 8, 11, 14, and 15 for thermal springs.

- **Listening to Mozart:** It's said that at any time of the day or night in Austria, someone, somewhere is playing the music of Wolfgang Amadeus Mozart. You might hear it at an opera house; a church; a festival; an open-air concert; or, more romantically, in a Belle Epoque cafe, performed by a Hungarian orchestra. Regardless, "the sound of music" drifting through Vienna is likely the creation of this child prodigy. Try to hear Mozart on his home turf, especially in Vienna and Salzburg. See chapters 6 and 9.

- **Watching the Lipizzaner Stallions (Vienna):** Nothing evokes the heyday of imperial Vienna more than the Spanish Riding School. The sleek white stallions and their expert riders demonstrate the classic art of dressage in choreographed leaps and bounds. The stallions are the finest equestrian performers on earth. You can watch the performances, but you'll need to make reservations 6 to 8 weeks in advance. See p. 151.

- **Cruising the Danube (Donau):** Johann Strauss used a bit of poetic license when he called it *The Blue Danube*—it's only really blue on the sunniest of days. Cruising the river is nevertheless a highlight of any Viennese holiday. The legendary DDSG, Blue Danube Shipping Company, Handelskai 265, A-1020 Vienna (*©* **01/588800;** www.ddsg-blue-danube.at), offers 1-day trips. On board, you'll pass some of the most famous sights in eastern Austria, including Krems and Melk. See p. 170.

- ***Heuriger* Hopping in Grinzing:** The *Heuriger* are rustic wine taverns that celebrate the arrival of each year's new vintage (*heurig*) by placing a pine branch over the door. The Viennese rush to the taverns to taste the new local wines and feast on country buffets. Some *Heuriger* have garden tables with sweeping views of the

Danube Valley; others provide shaded, centuries-old courtyards where revelers enjoy live folk music. See "The *Heuriger*," in chapter 6.

- **Reliving *The Sound of Music:*** In 1964, Julie Andrews, Christopher Plummer, and a gaggle of kids imitating the von Trapp family filmed one of the world's great musicals. The memory of that Oscar-winning movie lingers on, as a steady stream of visitors head to Salzburg just to take *The Sound of Music* tour. You visit the Nonnberg Abbey and that little gazebo where Rolf and Liesl danced in the rain. There's also a stop at the Felsenreitenschule (Rock Riding School), where the von Trapps gave their final performance. See p. 268.

- **Driving on Top of the World on the Grossglockner Road (Land Salzburg):** For the drive of a lifetime, you can take Europe's longest and most panoramic alpine highway, with hairpin turns and bends around every corner. It begins at Bruck an der Grossglocknerstrasse at 757m (2,484 ft.); continues through the Hochtortunnel, where the highest point is 2,507m (8,225 ft.); and ends in the province of Carinthia. The mountain part of the road, stretching some 22km (14 miles), often at 1,983m (6,506 ft.), has a maximum gradient of 12%. You can drive this stunning engineering feat from mid-May to mid-November, although the road is safest from mid-June to mid-September. The views are among the greatest in the world, but keep your eyes on that curvy road! See "Land Salzburg," in chapter 10.

- **Exploring the Alps:** There are few places in the world that are as splendid as the limestone alpine mountains shared between Austria and Bavaria. Moving toward the East, the Alps slope away to the Great Hungarian Plain. The Austrian Alps break into three chains, including the High or Central Alps, the Northern Limestone Alps, and the Southern Limestone Alps. In the west, you discover untouched Tyrolean villages, the Holy Roman Empire attractions of Innsbruck, and some of the world's greatest ski resorts, including St. Anton, Zürs, Lech, and Kitzbühel. Filled with quaint little towns, the eastern Alps sprawl across the Tyrolean country, west Styria, and Land Salzburg. Castles and stunning views await you at every turn. See chapters 10, 12, 13, and 15.

THE most romantic GETAWAYS

- **Hof bei Salzburg (Land Salzburg):** Lying on Lake Fuschl (Fuschlsee), this chic resort is only a 15-minute ride from Salzburg; it boasts a breathtaking alpine backdrop of blue clear, but chilly, waters, mountains, and evergreen forests. Based here, you can also easily get to Fuschlsee, Wolfgangsee, and Mondsee. The town offers some romantic places to stay, notably the **Hotel Schloss Fuschl** (✆ 06229/22530; www.starwoodhotels.com). See p. 308.

- **St. Wolfgang (Upper Austria):** On the Wolfgangsee, one of Austria's loveliest lakes, St. Wolfgang lies in the mountains of the Salzkammergut. It's the home of the **White Horse Inn** (✆ 06138/23060; www.weissesroessl.at), which served as the setting for Ralph Benatzky's operetta of the same name. Lying 50km (32 miles) east of Salzburg, the resort is a summer paradise, with lakefront beaches and cafes, hiking opportunities in all directions, and skiing in winter. See "St. Wolfgang & Bad Ischl," in chapter 11.

- **Mutters (Tyrol):** On a sunny plateau above Innsbruck, this small resort is one of the most quaint and beautiful villages in Tyrol (quite a compliment). Mutters attracts visitors year-round, and a cable car will take you to the Muttereralm where skiing, hiking, and mountain biking are possible. The most romantic place to stay is the **Hotel Altenburg** (✆ 0512/548524; www.altenburg.com), which was a restaurant in 1622 and later a farmhouse before it converted into an elegant hotel. See p. 375.

o **Stuben (Vorarlberg):** The rich and famous might flock to Vorarlberg's stellar ski resorts, Zürs or Lech, but a stay in the village of Stuben, 10km (6 miles) north of Lech on the west side of the Arlberg Pass, may be a lot cozier. A way station for Alpine travelers for centuries, Stuben was the birthplace of the great ski instructor Hannes Schneider. In winter, you can take a horse-drawn sleigh from Lech to Stuben. Once here, stay at **Hotel Mondschein** (✆ 05582/511; www. mondschein.com), a 1739 house converted to a hotel. See p. 418.

o **Pörtschach (Carinthia):** Many wealthy Viennese have lavish summer homes in this resort town on the northern perimeter of Lake Wörther (p. 447). Known for its lakeside promenade, it attracts a sports-oriented crowd who want to hike, play golf, ride, sail, water-ski, or just enjoy scenic drives through the countryside. Lake Wörther is Carinthia's largest alpine lake, yet its waters are warm, often going above 27°C (80°F) in summer. We recommend staying and dining at the romantic **Hotel Schloss Leonstain** (✆ 04272/2816; www.leonstain.at), where Johannes Brahms composed his Violin Concerto and Second Symphony.

o **Bad Aussee (Styria):** An old market town and spa, in the "green heart" of the Salzkammergut, Bad Aussee is 80km (50 miles) southeast of Salzburg. In the Valley of Traun, it's set against the backdrop of Totes Gebirge and the Dachstein massif. June is a lovely time to visit, when fields of narcissus burst into bloom. Bad Aussee lies only 5km (3 miles) north of the lake, Altausee, and is situated in one of the most beautiful parts of Austria. Long known as a summer spa resort, it's also developing into a winter ski center. The best place to stay is the **City Hotel Erzherzog Johann** (✆ 031622/52507; www.erzherzog-johann.com). See "Bad Aussee," in chapter 15.

THE best CASTLES & PALACES

o **Schönbrunn Palace (Vienna):** This palace of 1,441 rooms was the summer residence of the powerful Habsburg family. The great baroque architect J. B. Fischer von Erlach modeled his plans on Versailles, though he ultimately surpassed the French palace in size. Even so, Maria Theresa spoke of the palace as "cozy," where she could retreat with her many children and paint watercolors or work on her embroidery. The Habsburg dynasty came to an end here when Karl I signed his Act of Abdication on November 11, 1918. See p. 157.

o **Hofburg (Vienna):** The winter palace of the Habsburgs, Hofburg was the seat of an imperial throne that once governed the mighty Austro-Hungarian Empire. The sprawling palace reads like an architectural timeline of the Habsburg family, dating from 1279 with subsequent additions continuing until 1918. Today the Hofburg houses everything from the offices of the president of Austria to the Spanish Riding School with its Lipizzaner stallions—even the Vienna Boys' Choir. See chapter 6.

o **Österreichische Galerie Belvedere (Belvedere Palace; Vienna):** On a slope above Vienna, this palace was designed by Johann Lukas von Hildebrandt, the last major architect of the baroque in Austria. Belvedere served as a summer home for Prince Eugene of Savoy, the country's greatest military hero. The palace was a gift from the imperial throne in recognition of the prince's military achievements, although he was (at the time) richer than the Habsburgs. Not exactly pleased with his "gift," the hero made stunning baroque additions and improvements. As a collector and patron of the arts, he filled the palace with *objets d'art*. See p. 156.

o **Schloss Esterházy (Eisenstadt):** This castle in Eisenstadt, capital of Burgenland, was the seat of the Esterházy princes, a great and powerful Hungarian family who helped the Habsburgs gain control of Hungary. The seat of their power was built around an inner courtyard and designed by Carlone, the Italian architect. Work started on the castle in 1663, but the design was subsequently altered over the years and later received the baroque treatment. The family invited Haydn here to work on his music, and in the Haydnsaal, the great composer conducted an orchestra for the family's entertainment. See p. 216.

o **Residenz (Salzburg):** The seat of the Salzburg prince-bishops, this opulent palace dates from 1120. Over the years, newer palaces were added to form an ecclesiastical complex. On the palace's second floor is a 15-room art gallery filled with the works of 16th- to 18th-century European masters. You can also walk through more than a dozen richly decorated staterooms. The Residenz fountain, which dates from the 1660s, is one of the largest and most impressive baroque fountains north of the Alps. See p. 259.

o **Hofburg (Innsbruck):** This imperial palace, built in the 14th to 16th centuries, was the seat of Emperor Maximilian I, and the center of the Habsburg Empire during his reign. In the 18th century, Empress Maria Theresa made major structural changes, giving it a rococo appearance; the Giant's Hall is an architectural marvel of 18th-century Austrian architecture. In the palace's main hall hangs a portrait of Maria's famous youngest daughter, Marie Antoinette—with her head. See p. 354.

THE best CATHEDRALS & ABBEYS

o **Domkirche St. Stephan (Vienna):** Crowned by a 137m (450-ft.) steeple, St. Stephan's, the Cathedral of Vienna, is one of Europe's great Gothic structures. The Austrian writer Adalbert Stifter claimed that its "sheer beauty lifts the spirit." The Viennese regard this monument with great affection, calling it Der Steffl. Intricate altar pieces, stone canopies, and masterful Gothic sculptures are just some of the treasures that lie within. Climb the spiral steps to the South Tower for a panoramic view of the city. See p. 159.

o **Melk Abbey (Melk):** This abbey church, situated on a promontory above the Danube, is one of the world's finest baroque buildings. Melk figures in the Nibelungenlied, the great German epic poem, as well as Umberto Eco's best-selling The Name of the Rose. The view from here is one of the most panoramic in a country known for its views. This baroque masterpiece has burned many times, the first time in 1297 and then in 1683 and 1735, but each time it has risen from the ashes. After a 1947 fire, the golden abbey church was restored yet again, including the regilding of statues and altars with gold bullion. See p. 212.

o **Salzburger Dom (Salzburg):** World renowned for its 4,000-pipe organ, this cathedral is the "most perfect" Renaissance structure in the Germanic countries, with a rich baroque interior and elaborate frescoes. It towers 76m (249 ft.) into the air and holds 10,000 worshippers. The present cathedral was consecrated with great ceremony in 1628, although records show a cathedral on this spot since the 8th century. In 1756, Mozart was baptized in the Romanesque font. See p. 262.

o **Abbey of St. Florian (St. Florian, Near Linz):** Austria's largest abbey is a towering example of the baroque style. On a site occupied by the Augustinians since the 11th century, the present structure was constructed mainly from 1686 to 1751. Honoring a 4th-century Christian martyr and saint, the abbey has as its chief treasure the Altdorfer Gallery, whose most valuable pictures are those by Albrecht Altdorfer, master of the Danubian school. Anton Bruckner, Austria's greatest composer of church music in the 1800s, became the organist at St. Florian as a young man and composed many of his masterpieces here. See p. 319.

THE best MUSEUMS

o **Kunsthistorisches Museum (Vienna):** This art gallery, across from Hofburg Palace, houses the stellar art collection of the Habsburg dynasty. It's especially strong in the Flemish, Dutch, and German schools, with works ranging from Rubens and Dürer to Pieter Bruegel the Elder and Van Dyck. Also strong are the Italian, Spanish, and French collections, with works by Veronese, Caravaggio, and Tintoretto. See p. 153.

o **MuseumsQuartier (Vienna):** Vienna launched its new millennium with one of the major cultural centers to open in Middle Europe in some 2 decades. Architecturally stunning, this complex contains a treasure trove of art, being especially strong in modern works. The three major museums to visit here are Kunsthalle Wien, Leopold Museum, and MUMOK (Museum of Modern Art Ludwig Foundation). See p. 151.

o **Mozart's Geburtshaus (Salzburg):** Music pilgrims flock to see the typical old burgher's house where Mozart was born. You can still see many of his childhood belongings, including a lock of his hair, his first viola, and a pair of keyboard instruments. Mozart's first violin is also displayed. Even at the age of 4, he was a musical genius. See p. 262.

o **Mauthausen (Upper Austria):** You can make a sobering outing 29km (18 miles) down the Danube from Linz. Mauthausen was a Nazi concentration camp and extermination center, where Austria's Jews and other so-called undesirables were tortured and killed during World War II. Estimates by historians of the number of deaths vary considerably, ranging from a low of 35,000 deaths in the main camp to a high of over 2 million; while records at the main camp were intact at the liberation, they were incomplete. Visitors today can bear witness to this scene of Nazi atrocities. See p. 326.

o **Landeszeughaus (Graz):** This armory, built between 1642 and 1645, displays 3 centuries of weaponry, one of Europe's great collections. Here you'll see some 30,000 harnesses, coats of mail, helmets, swords, pikes, and muskets of various kinds, along with pistols and harquebuses. There are richly engraved and embossed jousting suits and a parade of armor. See p. 464.

o **Österreichisches Freilichtmuseum (Outside Graz):** Just 16km (10 miles) from Graz, in a wooded valley, is one of Austria's great open-air museums. This museum of vernacular architecture, spread across 50 hectares (120 acres), features some 80 rural homes with ancillary buildings that have been reassembled. The site presents an excellent overview of the country's rural heritage, from a Carinthian farmstead to alpine houses from the Tyrol.

THE best HISTORIC TOWNS

- **Krems (Lower Austria, Outside Vienna):** In the eastern part of the Wachau, on the river's left bank, this 1,000-year-old town incorporates the little village of Stein, with narrow streets terraced above the river. Many houses date from the 16th century. See p. 206.
- **Hallstatt (Salzburg):** With a history stretching back 2,200 years, you can't get more historic than Hallstatt. As an added plus, this lakeside village dwarfed by a curtain of mountainpeaks also offers a scenic backdrop for exploration of history. See p. 337
- **St. Christoph (Tyrol):** St. Christoph, the mountain way station of St. Anton in Tyrol, sits at an elevation of 1,784m (5,853 ft.). It was a famous settlement on the road to the Arlberg Pass, and was the site of a fabled hospice established in 1386. Members patrolled the pass looking for frozen bodies and assisting wayfarers in trouble. See p. 383.
- **Lienz (East Tyrol):** Not to be confused with Linz in Upper Austria, Lienz, is the capital of remote East Tyrol. Set at the junction of three valleys, this colorful town stretches along the banks of the Isel River. In summer, mountain climbers use it as a base to scale the Dolomites. The town is presided over by Schloss Bruck, the fortress of the counts of Gorz. See p. 406.
- **Mariazell (Styria):** Pilgrims come here to see the Mariazell Basilica, dating from the early 1200s, and its trio of prominent towers. Both Fischer von Erlachs, senior and junior, the famed baroque architects, helped transform the church. The Chapel of Grace inside is the national shrine of Austria, Hungary, and Bohemia. If you're exploring Styria, this old town, both a winter playground and a summer resort, is worth a stop. See p. 472.

THE best OUTDOOR ADVENTURES

Skiing is the name of the game in Austria. See below, for a list of the best ski areas.

- **Biking Along the Danube:** The Lower Danube Cycle Track is a biker's paradise. The most exciting villages and stopovers along the Danube, including Melk and Dürnstein, are linked by a riverside bike trail between Vienna and Naarn. As you pedal along, you'll pass castles, medieval towns, and latticed vineyards. You can rent bikes from the train or ferry stations, and all tourist offices provide route maps. See chapters 6 and 7.
- **Ballooning over Styria:** Styria has some of the best alpine ballooning in Europe, as experienced by participants who have sailed over the alpine ranges of the Salzkammergut and a steppe-like landscape that evokes the Great Hungarian Plain. A typical ballooning excursion will cross river valleys, mountain peaks, glaciers, and vineyards. For outfitters, see p. 457.
- **Canoeing & Rafting in the Salzburg Alps (Land Salzburg):** Known for their beautiful alpine lakes and roaring white-water streams, the lakes in and around Salzburg are some of the most ideal in Europe for canoeing, rafting, and kayaking. Waters aren't polluted and powerboats are restricted, making these safe and idyllic adventures. See p. 278.

- **Hiking in the Zillertal Alps (Tyrol):** This mountain paradise is the best place to hike in western Austria. Instead of roads, you'll find footpaths winding through the scenic Ziller Valley, east of Innsbruck. Guides will lead you through stunning scenery, where green pastures end at the feet of jagged peaks. It becomes more impressive the deeper you travel into the valley and hike across mountain trails or ascend on lifts to higher elevations. You can even find year-round skiing at Tuxer Gletscher, a glacier. See "The Ziller Valley," in chapter 12.

- **Traversing Ice Age Valleys:** No scenic thrill in all of Europe quite matches that available in the Hohe Tauern National Park, Europe's largest national park. Part of the Austrian Central Alps, the Hohe Tauern range cuts across Land Salzburg, Tyrol, and Carinthia. Molded during the Ice Age, these valleys are filled with pastureland, alpine heaths, vast expanses of snow and ice, forested bulwarks, fields of rock, and gargantuan alluvial and mudflow cones. The park is also home to numerous nearly extinct species. Much of this vast and remote area has never been explored, but parts are accessible by car or government-owned Bundesbus (the route goes from Böckstein to Badgastein and from Zell am Ziller to Krimml). You can get car or bus information from the local tourist offices. See chapter 10.

THE best SKI AREAS

- **Innsbruck:** Tyrol's capital Innsbruck is set against a scenic backdrop of daunting snow-capped peaks, with good skiing in virtually all directions. Two Olympic Winter Games have been staged in the Innsbruck area. It's somewhat inconvenient to get to the slopes, but it's worth the effort. There are five ski resorts around Innsbruck. Hungerburg is the local favorite, because a funicular from the city heads directly to the base station at Höch Innsbruck at 300m (984 ft.). Nearby Igls also enjoys great popularity, with its extensive slopes under the Patscherkofel peak. Although it's the farthest from Innsbruck, Axamer Lizum offers the most extensive all-around skiing. Good snow conditions are generally the rule. See chapter 12.

- **St. Anton am Arlberg:** This picture-postcard Tyrolean village sits at 1,304m (4,278 ft.), although its upper slopes climb to more than 2,801m (9,190 ft.). Massive snowfalls attract intermediate and expert skiers from all over. St. Anton lies at the eastern base of the Arlberg Pass. St. Christoph, 10km (6 miles) west, lies almost on the Arlberg Pass and is another chic winter enclave. Four major ski areas at St. Anton (Galzig, Valluga, St. Christoph, and Gampen/Kapall) form one big ski circuit. See p. 377.

- **Seefeld (Tyrol):** Seefeld is one of the major international ski resorts of Europe, and hosted the Nordic events for the 1964 and 1976 Olympic Winter Games and the 1985 Nordic Ski World Championships. On a sunny plateau at 1,052m (3,451 ft.), it has prime skiing conditions and a network of surface lifts, chairlifts, and cable cars that bring skiers of all levels to excellent slopes. In addition, there are 200km (124 miles) of prepared cross-country tracks. Seefeld is also known for its other winter sports, including curling and outdoor skating. See "Seefeld," in chapter 12.

- **Kitzbühel:** This home of the world's original lift circuit is a medieval walled city and regal resort that, in the 1960s, blossomed into a premier international spot. Visitors flock here in winter to ski forested trails and broad ridges. The Hahnenkamm ski circus has more than 50 lifts at elevations of 800 to 2,000m (2,625–6,566 ft.). The main season runs from Christmas to mid-March. See "The Kitzbühel Alps," in chapter 12.

- **Lech & Zürs:** In Vorarlberg, these neighboring resorts feature some of the best skiing in Austria. They are also among Europe's most exclusive ski resorts, drawing the rich and famous from across Europe. Both resorts cater to novice and intermediate skiers, with broad boulevards winding between peaks and runs that fall straight back to the resorts. The resorts also offer high altitudes and good snow conditions, plus a high-tech lift system. Huge chunks of skiable terrain above both resorts provide a 20km-long (12-mile) circuit. See p. 412 for Lech; p. 419 for Zürs.

THE best LAKE RESORTS & SPAS

- **Baden bei Wien (Lower Austria):** Developed by the ancient Romans, and then studded with ocher-colored Biedermeier buildings during the early 19th century, this was once known as the "dowager empress" of Austrian spas. Today, frequent chamber concerts and elaborate flowerbeds keep the aura of old-fashioned grandeur alive. See "The Spa Town of Baden bei Wien," in chapter 7.
- **Bad Hofgastein (Land Salzburg):** A select annex of the larger, better-known resort of Badgastein, Bad Hofgastein appeals to anyone in search of peace, healing, and quiet. Civic architecture and hotels are appropriately grand and solemn. See "Bad Hofgastein," in chapter 10.
- **Badgastein (Land Salzburg):** This is Austria's premier spa, with a resort industry dating from the 1400s. Hotels are almost universally excellent, offering the densest concentration of fine lodgings in Land Salzburg. See chapter 10.
- **St. Wolfgang (Upper Austria):** The landscapes around this lake are so lovely that they served as the setting for the popular musical work *The White Horse Inn*, by Ralph Benatzky. Adjacent to the grander and somewhat more formal resort of Bad Ischl, St. Wolfgang offers ample options for outdoor diversions. See chapter 11.
- **Bad Ischl (Upper Austria):** For more than 60 years, Franz Josef selected Bad Ischl as the summer holiday seat of the Habsburg Empire. No other Austrian resort captures the glamour of the long-departed empire quite like this one. See chapter 11.
- **Velden (Carinthia):** The region's most sophisticated resort, Velden is the heart of the so-called "Austrian Riviera." Despite the traffic, it offers a convenient combination of bucolic charm and Viennese style. See p. 447.
- **Villach (Carinthia):** The second-largest town in the province, it's the gateway to Austria's lake district, northeastern Italy, and Slovenia. The nearby village of Warmbad-Villach offers warm springs, favored by the ancient Romans. See "Villach," in chapter 14.
- **Bad Gleichenberg (Styria):** Set within one of the most undiscovered regions of Austria, near the Slovenian border, this is the most important summer spa in Styria. It stands among rolling hills and vineyards, and is an area rich in history, natural beauty, and imperial nostalgia. See "Bad Gleichenberg," in chapter 15.
- **Bad Aussee (Styria):** Lying at the junction of two tributaries of the region's most important river, Bad Aussee is known for its verdant beauty, healthful waters, and bracing climate. It's also the center of a network of hiking and cross-country ski trails. See "Bad Aussee," in chapter 15.

THE best LUXURY HOTELS

o **Goldener Hirsch** (Salzburg; © 800/325-3535 in the U.S., or 0662/8084; www.goldenerhirschsalzburg.com): For some 6 centuries, this mellow old hostelry has been welcoming guests to its patrician precincts. With the city's best and most professional staff, the Goldener Hirsch is the finest hotel in Salzburg. In the Old Town, near Mozart's birthplace, the building is a historical monument, rich in legend and lore. Although rooms vary, all are furnished with antiques, in traditional taste, but have modern plumbing and appointments. See p. 233.

o **Palais Coburg** (Vienna; © 518-180; www.palais-coburg.com): A stone's throw away from the Stadtpark, this former palace is now a Viennese haven of luxury and class. From the seductive bathrobes to the full-out pampering spa to the largest and most comprehensive wine collections in Europe, this place is the stuff of magnificence. Enjoy! See p. 108.

o **Hotel Grüner-Baum** (Badgastein; © 06434/25160; www.hoteldorf.com): A veritable village has grown up around this converted hunting lodge. The family-run hotel has sheltered everybody from Toscanini to the Shah of Iran. Scattered chalets house some of the finest rooms at this fashionable spa—each in the typical alpine style. The hospitality is unequaled in the area. See p. 290.

o **Hotel Imperial** (Vienna; © 800/325-3589 in the U.S., or 01/501100; www.luxury collection.com/imperial): Once a ducal palace, and now Vienna's most glamorous hotel, the Imperial is a landmark two blocks east of the Staatsoper. Built in 1869, it's Austria's official "guesthouse," often hosting visiting musicians (Wagner stayed here long ago). A wealth of antiques adorns the gracious public areas, and everything is gilt-edged, from the polished marble to the glittering chandeliers. Opulently appointed rooms vary in size but are generally regal. See p. 107.

o **Hotel Schloss Dürnstein** (Dürnstein, on the Danube; © 02711/212; www.schloss.at): Near the medieval village in Wachau, this fairy-tale castle is perched above a bend in the river. The ruins of Dürnstein castle, where Richard the Lion-Hearted was imprisoned on his return from the Crusades, sit on a hillside above the hotel. This gem of a place brims with history, class, and traditional Austrian hospitality. See p. 211.

o **Hotel Schloss Fuschl** (Hof bei Salzburg; © 06229/22530; www.schlossfuschl resort.at): East of Salzburg, this medieval castle and its outbuildings have origins dating from 1450. Everybody from Eleanor Roosevelt to Khrushchev has stayed in this rich, lush setting of oriental rugs, antiques, fine art, and vaulted ceilings. Diners sit on a terrace taking in panoramic lake and alpine views. The spacious rooms are beautifully furnished and well maintained. Sports lovers feel at home with a 9-hole golf course, indoor pool, and Turkish bath and sauna. See p. 309.

o **Grand Hotel** (Zell am See; © 06542/788-0; www.grandhotel-zellamsee.at): Three "grand hotels" have stood on this site over the years, and the latest incarnation is the grandest of them all. Windows open onto incredible views of the lake and the Alps. Flanked by pillars, the glassed-in pool also offers lake views, and the hotel has an array of facilities ranging from a gym to a sauna. The contemporary rooms, which vary in size and design, are the best in town. See p. 306.

o **Romantik Hotel Post** (Villach; © 04242/261010; www.romantik-hotel.com): With architectural origins from 1500, this is the most fabled hotel in Carinthia. A hotel since the 1730s, it's a cozy and charming retreat on the town's main square. A pianist plays on the terrace in summer. Rooms are richly furnished, often with oriental rugs on parquet floors, including the suite where Emperor Charles V once slept in the 1500s. A solarium, gym, and sauna keep the hotel up to date. See p. 452.

THE best AFFORDABLE HOTELS

- **Hotel Alte Post-Wrann** (Velden; ℂ **04274/2141;** www.wrann.at): In the sophisticated summer resort of Carinthia, at the western end of the Wörther See, this is an ideal choice for an "Austrian Riviera" trip. Once the headquarters of a postal route station, it was long ago renovated, enlarged, and turned into this welcoming hotel. Rooms are sunny and traditionally furnished. The restaurant, with its massive ceiling beams, is very good. There's also a Viennese-style *heuriger* (rustic wine tavern) serving the finest local wines. See p. 448.

- **Hotel & Villa Auersperg** (Salzburg; ℂ **0662/889440;** www.auersperg.at): A traditional family-run hotel with generously sized rooms, this charmer has an old-fashioned atmosphere but is still beautifully maintained, from its antiques-filled drawing room to its convivial library bar. It's a warm, inviting, and cozy place to base yourself in the city of Mozart. See p. 239.

- **Hotel Goldener Adler** (Innsbruck; ℂ **0512/571111;** www.goldeneradler.com): This hotel, which has hosted everyone from Goethe to Paganini, has a history spanning 6 centuries. Genuine art decorates the public areas, and the four dining rooms (including a Tyrolean cellar) are local favorites for eating and drinking. Rooms vary in size but are nicely appointed. The place isn't luxurious, but it's historic and comfortable. See p. 360.

- **Hollmann Beletage** (Vienna; ℂ **01/9611960;** www.hollmann-beletage.at): This hidden treasure only has 24 rooms smack in the center of town. In modern Austrian style, the rooms are comfortable and classy. The spa and in-house cinema will be welcome distractions after a long day on Vienna. See p. 111.

- **Hotel-Restaurant Sänger Blondel** (Dürnstein; ℂ **02711/253;** www.saengerblondel.at): Along the Danube sits this charmingly old-fashioned place, painted a bright lemon and accented with green shutters. It's named after the faithful minstrel who searched the countryside for the imprisoned Richard the Lion-Hearted. Today guests are housed in traditionally styled and cozy rooms; if your windows are open, you can sometimes hear zither music drifting in from the courtyard. See p. 210.

- **Hotel Seehof** (Goldegg; ℂ **06415/8137-0;** www.seehof-goldegg.com): This hotel, on a small alpine lake south of Salzburg, dates from 1449. Rustic artifacts and local painted furnishings add to its old-fashioned charm. In summer, guests can enjoy the outdoor terrace, but in winter, they come here for skiing. The hotel rents ski equipment and directs guests to the nearby slopes. See p. 283.

- **Romantik Hotel Traube** (Lienz; ℂ **04852/64444;** www.hoteltraube.at): Deep in the heart of east Tyrol, this classic hotel, rebuilt after World War II damage, is the most desirable in this remote and offbeat part of Austria. Its prices are reasonable, and the hotel also offers one of the most reputable restaurants in east Tyrol. See p. 408.

- **Schlosshotel Freisitz Roith** (Gmunden; ℂ **07612/64905;** www.freisitzroith.at): Built as a summer house by the Habsburg Emperor Rudolf II in 1597, this castle hotel, in one of the most popular summer resorts in the Salzkammergut, is now open to the masses. Converted into a hotel in 1965, it's a winning combination of a baroque private residence and a Victorian hotel. See p. 343.

THE best RESTAURANTS

- **Europastüberl** (Innsbruck; ✆ **0512/593-01**): Head here for spectacular food served among meticulously recreated traditional Tyrolean decor. Its setting manages to be simultaneously rustic and sumptuous, and its kitchen was recently awarded two *Toques* from Gault Millau. See p. 363.
- **Motto am Fluss** (Vienna; ✆ **01/25255-10**): Newly opened in 2010, this restaurant is housed in a boat-like structure along the Danube Canal and has quickly become a local favorite. It may be hard to get a table, but a wait at the bar looking out onto the canal is worth it. Make sure you dress tres chic as the media, business, and fashion world use this as their second living room. See p. 129.
- **Goldener Hirsch** (Salzburg; ✆ **0662/80840**): Hospitality has been served up within its thick walls since 1407, but today the victuals are vastly improved, and the clientele is a little more refined. Few other places are as elegant, and during the Salzburg Music Festivals, this is definitely the place to be. The chef prefers the *grand bourgeois* tradition, and prepares meals with both a jeweler's precision and a poet's imagination. See p. 233.
- **Maria Loretto** (Klagenfurt; ✆ **0463/24465**): This is the premier restaurant in the capital of Carinthia, site of Austria's summer lake district. A specialist in seafood, the restaurant hauls in raw ingredients from the Mediterranean and Atlantic, and its chefs fashion them into delectable platters. See p. 443.
- **Restaurant Ferwall** (St. Anton; ✆ **05446/3249**): Set in the high Alps near the Arlberg Pass, this place attracts some of the most discerning palates in Europe. Since 1972, the restaurant has been serving some of the finest fare in Tyrol, with a traditional Austrian and international menu taking on innovative modern twists. The restaurant celebrates Tyrolean country life. See p. 381.
- **Steirereck Vienna** (Vienna; ✆ **01/7133168**): If you feel the need to lighten your wallet for some of the best food you will ever eat anywhere, this is where to go. Local recipes and treats from all over the globe are served here in inspired fashion, but with a matter-of-course attitude that make the experience all the more enjoyable. See p. 139.

THE best CLASSIC CAFES

- **Café Bazar** (Salzburg; ✆ **0662/874278**): This cafe has been a local favorite since 1906, enjoying a palatial pink stucco setting across the river from the Old Town. It's been fashionable since the days of Franz Josef and the menu never changes—only the prices. See p. 248.
- **Café Demel** (Vienna; ✆ **01/5351717**): This most famous cafe in Vienna has a long-standing feud with the Sacher Hotel (p. 107) as to who has the right to sell the legendary and original Sachertorte. Demel claims that the chef who invented the torte left the Sacher to work for Demel, bringing his recipe with him. See p. 134.
- **Café Frauenschuh** (Mondsee; ✆ **06232/2312**): Deliciously loaded with every imaginable kind of high-calorie pastry, this time-honored place is a cliché of old-fashioned Austrian charm. See p. 332.

- **Café Tirolerhof** (Vienna; ✆ **01/5127833**): At a prime location right across from the Albertina, this cafe is dripping with tradition and charm. This place is in no way passé. The art, music, and literary crowd sip java next to time-honored eccentrics and university professors. A true *Wiener Melange*. See p. 135.
- **Café Landtmann** (Vienna; ✆ **01/241000**): The newspapers it provides for its patrons are tattered by the end of every day, and a haze of smoke evokes the backroom machinations of a meeting of political cronies from another era. Sigmund Freud claimed it as his favorite cafe; and after your first 15 minutes inside, you might, too. See p. 134.
- **Café Munding** (Innsbruck; ✆ **0512/584118**): Plushly decorated and upholstered, this cafe offers a setting from 1720, torrents of Tyrolean color, unusual murals, and platters of food followed by a scrumptiously fattening array of creamy pastries. See p. 369.
- **Café Tomaselli** (Salzburg; ✆ **0662/844488**): Established in 1705, it provides a rich atmosphere as well as delectably fattening pastries and endless cups of coffee. See p. 248.
- **Konditorei Zauner** (Bad Ischl; ✆ **06132/2331020**): It's the oldest pastry shop in Austria and the emporium that satisfied the long-ago sugar cravings of such Habsburg monarchs as Franz Josef. Today, it trades heavily on the aristocratic associations of yesteryear, attracting droves of tourists to its baroque-inspired setting in the resort's center. See p. 337.

THE best OF AUSTRIA ONLINE

- **www.austria.info**: By far the most helpful site when planning your trip through Austria. **The Austria Tourism Board** is the place to start, no matter if you plan to be snowboarding in Tyrol, spending Christmas in Vienna, or need to find a hotel on the Wörthersee, this site will point you in the right direction.
- **Austria by Region:** Each region has its own tourist website, which are detailed, informative, and in English. They cover sightseeing, music and stage shows, shopping, wining and dining, as well as hotels and travel information. The site for Carinthia is **www.kaernten.at**, Upper Austria is **www.oberoesterreich.at**, for Salzburg city go to **www.salzburg.info**, for the lake district Salzkammergut go to **www.salzkammergut.at**, for insight into traveling in Styria it's **www.steiermark.com**, for Tyrol go to **www.tirol.at**, the site for the country's capital, Vienna is **www.wien.info**, and for Vorarlberg it's **www.vorarlberg.travel**. All of these sites include a search engine.
- **www.wien.gv.at/english/**: Here you'll find the official stats on the city of Vienna. The site provides up-to-date information on what to do in and around Vienna, as well as general information for visitors like a calendar of events and a hotel and sightseeing guide.
- **www.virtualvienna.net**: This is an English-language guide to life in Vienna; information services provided on the website range from a general living guide and an event calendar, to a property and relocation section, as well as a web directory.
- **www.falter.at**: Only helpful if you speak a little German, this is a high-quality Austrian weekly "Falter," featuring an extensive list of events ("Event Programm") and movie theaters ("Kino Programm") as well as restaurant reviews ("Wien wie es isst") and a shopping guide ("Best of Vienna").

o **http://tupalo.com**: An international social networking site that allows users to find, review, and share local businesses with others. The Vienna section is quite well frequented. Categories include food and beverages, art and entertainment, nightlife, local services, and shopping in Vienna.

o **www.vienna-expats.net**: The online forum on the website of Vienna's ex-pat community provides a meeting place for English-language people in Vienna. The site also includes a directory of bars and cafes, services, shops, restaurants, nightlife, cinemas, and property in the city.

o **www.viennareview.net**: This is the website of The Vienna Review, a monthly publication and Austria's only English-language newspaper, covering international as well as local events including an "Event Calendar" that can be accessed on the website.

o **www.wanderdoerfer.at**: You'll find all the information here is first hand and constantly updated. Check out this site if you plan on undertaking hiking trips during your stay. There are entries, photos, and descriptions of hiking trails all over the country, just to whet your appetite.

o **www.wetter.at**: This site will help you be in the know about weather conditions all over the country. Make sure to check for icy roads, especially before you drive in Tyrol and Vorarlberg.

AUSTRIA IN DEPTH

The Austrian lives in two worlds at the same time—one of graces and entertainments, the other of dark realism, where contradictions are not resolved, but absorbed into a way of seeing the world. Austrians enjoy the best and expect the worst, insist on comfort but also the right to complain! They are often gruff but dislike confrontation, enforcing civil manners with a grimace rather than the law. They relish tales of a glorious past, convinced it never happened. Here imagination is fired by ambiguity rather than idealism—an ambivalence with deep roots that lives on in the Austria of today, to be encountered by a traveler in countless ways.

But let us begin with the magic of mask and music. No one conjures up these images of the *fin de siecle* empire more than Johann Strauss, Jr. (1825–99), whose *Blue Danube Waltz* still rings out over Vienna rooftops each New Year's Eve, music so lovely that Brahms wished he had written it. Yet Strauss's music, like that of the other quintessentially Viennese composer Franz Schubert, carried within it the ineffable mix of joy and melancholy. In the glittering life of Austria's imperial heyday, a society of romance and gaiety lived side by side with a culture of frustration at a world of artifice; in the coffeehouses and artists' studios, in lecture halls and at writing desks, new ideas were emerging that would shape the future.

"It was in Habsburg Austria and its successor states that many, perhaps even most, of the seminal thinkers of the twentieth century emerged," wrote intellectual historian William Johnston, made possible through the peculiar combination of bureaucratic formalism and laissez-faire, an obsession with high culture and a love of pleasure, of conservatism and imagination.

As Austria moves deeper into a new millennium, it's good to look back at its rich cultural legacy to appreciate its present. What is now a small social democracy in the middle of Central Europe had been the heart of the Habsburg Empire for over 600 years, a center of art and music, as well as architecture, science, and ideas. It was the birthplace of Mozart, Freud, Kafka, and Hitler, as well as public education, alternating current, Porsche, and Red Bull. From the Congress of Vienna through the Cold

DID YOU know . . . ?

- Seventy percent of Austria is covered by the mountains and foothills of the Alps.
- After the 1683 siege of Austria, the retreating Turks left behind sacks of coffee, giving birth to the Viennese coffeehouse.
- Viennese composer Franz Schubert's work was never performed in public during his lifetime, his "rediscovery" and fame is due to tireless promotion by Robert Schumann, as Felix Mendelssohn did for the forgotten J. S. Bach.
- The 1913 premier of George Bernard Shaw's play *Pygmalion*, on which *My Fair Lady* was based, was not in London, but in German at the Hofburgtheater in Vienna.
- The first woman to win the Nobel Peace Prize was a Viennese aristocrat, Baroness Bertha von Suttner, awarded in 1905 for her book *Lay Down Your Arms*.
- The young artist Adolf Hitler was rejected from the Viennese Academy of Fine Arts, leaving him very bitter. Later he insisted: "I feel that I have it in my soul to become one of the great artists of the age and that future historians will remember me not for what I have done for Germany, but for my art."

War, and even today, its arts of diplomacy and disguise have earned Vienna the exotic distinction of spy capital of the world.

Visitors today will find all of Austria's cities livelier and brighter than at any time since before World War II. Throughout the regions, in Graz, Klagenfurt, Linz, Innsbruck, and Bregenz, a lively cultural scene is in full swing, in between outings into the mountains or cycling by the rivers. In the capital of Vienna, cafes, clubs, theaters, and concert halls are everywhere, open nightly and sold out. Among the proud cityscapes and lovely old squares, each season hosts festivals and open markets that bring the streets alive. In spite of two world wars, much of the empire's glory remains, its treasures now glistening in museum galleries, its parks and palaces the daily settings of city life.

In 2010, more than 70 years after the *Anschluss,* time has begun to heal many of Austria's old wounds. For better and for worse, few witnesses to the horrors and denials, the tyrannies and resistance of World War II are still alive, which has allowed public acknowledgment and reconciliation in many settings, and the cultural devastation of the country's creative class to gradually be repaired. Much property has gone through restitution, and émigrés now seem to feel comfortable in a country that welcomes them once again. Today they find an Austria alive with the energy of cutting-edge art and ideas, and yet that knows in its deepest heart how to live well.

AUSTRIA TODAY

Austria is a parliamentary democracy, and the head of the state is the federal president. The parliament is made up of the *Nationalrat,* the primary legislate body, and the *Bundesrat,* that gives "advice and consent" on the approval of a new president and for acts of war. Together they form what is known as the federal assembly. The federal government is headed by a chancellor, who, along with cabinet members appointed from members of the *Nationalrat,* conducts any activities of government not the responsibility of the president. In today's Austria, personal liberty is guaranteed, and the federal constitution prohibits discrimination on the grounds of sex, birth, class, religion, race, status, or language.

With the expansion of the E.U., Vienna is now again at the center and crossroads of an open and reunited Europe, just as it was as the Habsburg capital of the vast Austro-Hungarian Empire. During the Cold War, the government adopted a position of diplomatic neutrality, as Austrian leaders feared the return of the Russians, who left peacefully in 1955. But, since the collapse of the Iron Curtain, Austria has been moving toward greater cooperation and unity with the western powers—that is, until 2000 when an estrangement between Austria and its fellow E.U. members over a coalition with the far–right Freedom Party briefly made world headlines.

As it has always been, Austria today is a city of hospitality, and tourism a mainstay of its thriving economy. In spite of the world financial crisis, visitors continue to fill Vienna's hotels, restaurants, theaters, and museums, helping to keep unemployment here among the lowest in Europe.

In 1998, continuing the effort to lay the past to rest, Austrian officials agreed to return to their rightful owners works of art confiscated by the Nazis. The Austrian minister of culture, Elisabeth Gehrer, said she wanted to correct what she termed "immoral decisions" made at the end of World War II. This bold move sent reverberations throughout the museum world of Europe and the U.S.

In one of the most famous cases, Maria Altmann won the restitution of five paintings by Gustav Klimt that had belonged to her uncle Ferdinand Bloch, including two portraits of his wife Adele Bloch-Bauer. It was the largest restitution of Nazi art ever, and when "Adele" left Austria in 2006, reproductions of the painting filled billboards around the city, with the text, "Adele is leaving." The painting was later purchased by the cosmetics heir Ronald Lauder for $135 million, at the time the highest sum ever paid for a painting. It is on display at Lauder's Neue Galerie in New York.

As a center of European culture, Vienna has more than 100 art museums, attracting eight million visitors annually. In 2001 Vienna was designated a UNESCO World Heritage Site. In both 2009 and 2010, it was ranked first in the world in quality of life.

The entrance of the far-right Freedom Party into a coalition government in 2000 brought Austria widespread condemnation, and battles over immigration policy continue to dominate public debates. In contrast, many citizens of the Austrian capital are among the most liberal, advanced, well-informed, and tolerant. As one example of the more left-wing Austria, environmental awareness is strong. Recycling is more evident in Vienna than most other European capitals—in fact, recycling bins are commonplace on the city's streets. The Viennese are often seen sorting their paper, plastic, and aluminum and steel cans, and people may scowl at passersby who toss a heedless wrapping.

In 2004, recognition came on two fronts that seemed to capture the continuing ambivalence about the past: Elfriede Jelinek, a controversial writer of lyric beauty and persistent voice of conscience, won the Nobel Prize for literature. Elsewhere, Charles I, the last Habsburg to rule as emperor, was beatified by the Pope, leaving many scratching their heads in puzzled surprise.

Today, as it was under the empire, Vienna is again a city of immigration. In 2010, 16% of Austrians were foreign born, and 32.8% of Vienna's residents, most from another E.U. country (11.1%), followed by the former Yugoslavia (10.2%), and then Turkey (4.3%). The largest number of new residency permits in Austria now goes to Germans, a point of some pride to Austrians, who knew they had a better thing going all along.

SINGING A NEW song

When you hear the moving strains of the magnificent imperial hymn *Gott erhalte*—known to many as the slow movement of Haydn's *Emperor String Quartet*—it is hard to understand how the Austrian Republic could have allowed it to be stolen by the Germans. This was a cultural end run that had actually begun as far back as 1841, when August Heinrich Hoffmann von Fallersleben wrote the text *Das Lied der Deutschen* to the tune and again in 1922, when president Frederick Ebert cornered it for the Weimar Republic. And again as all stood by and watched the melody's heroic power abused under National Socialism. This last was a legacy no one wanted.

But in Austria there is lots of wonderful music to go around, and the anthem of the postwar Austrian Republic is set to another fine tune, this one from an opera by Mozart (possibly based on a tune of fellow Free Mason Johann Baptist Holzer), inaugurated in 1947 with a text by novelist and poet Paula von Preradović. The new Austrian national hymn sings of mountains and rivers, meadows and cathedrals, and the energy of industry looking toward the future.

"Having shouldered many burdens since honored days gone by," the lyrics continue, "much praised and much tested, Austria beats like a strong heart at the center of Europe"—which is, after all, not a bad description.

And the Germans? Well, in 1952, they took up the wondrous Haydn tune once again as their official national anthem, managing to salvage it from its Nazis' taint by switching the text from the *Deutschland über alles* of verse one, to verse three, about "unity, law, and freedom." Which left the Austrians muttering under their breath that those Germans had, once again, made off with an important piece of Austria's cultural heritage. There were lively discussions about taking formal action at the time of the State Treaty in 1955. A last plea for the Haydn hymn was made in 1959 by a group of musicians, artists, and writers. But the government was no longer listening.

Austria is considered one of the most successful social democracies in Europe. The SPÖ has dominated Austrian politics since 1918, except when it was banned under the Austro Fascists and then the Nazis between 1934 and 1945, and in Vienna, free elections have always voted in a social democratic mayor. The result has been a history of citizen-friendly politics, including excellent health care (rated no. 2 in the world after France by the WHO), wonderful public recreation, free universities, and a pioneering program of low-cost residential housing estates called *Gemeindebauten.*

Built in response to a massive housing shortage after World War I, these "palaces of the people" were financed by luxury and "sin" taxes plus a dedicated housing tax, and designed by some of Austria's most famous architects—attractive spaces, beautifully landscaped and full of light, and built to last. Between 1926 and 1934, Vienna built some 380 *Gemeindebauten,* that provided over 64,000 apartments to people of all social classes. The program picked up again after World War II, and today, the city of Vienna manages over 220,000 of these desirable *Gemeindebau* apartments, housing some 500,000 people—about a quarter of the city's population—making it the largest property manager in Europe.

Vienna is also the home base of major charitable organizations, including SOS Kinderdorf, or "Children's Village" founded in 1949, that today serves 132 countries and territories worldwide.

But it was the U.S./Russian spy swap in the summer of 2010 that reminded East and West that Vienna was still the world center of espionage. The third UN headquarters city after New York and Geneva, as well as home to energy and security organizations like OPEC and the OSCE, Vienna is host to some 17,000 diplomats, "around half of whom have some connection to the intelligence agencies," according to Graz scholar Siegfried Beer, making Austria the country with the highest density of foreign intelligence agents in the world.

LOOKING BACK AT AUSTRIA

Austria's history has been heavily influenced by its location along the Danube. Its position at the crossroads of three great European cultures—Roman, Germanic, and Slavic—transformed the country into a melting pot, and more often than not, a battlefield.

By 100 B.C., the Romans had begun making military excursions into Austria; by 15 B.C., they had conquered the entire country. Valued as an alpine outpost of the frontier, it remained under the control of Rome for more than 500 years. Roads were built, vineyards and wine-making introduced, and Roman law instituted. The spread of Christianity began around A.D. 300. Germanic tribes weakened the Romans' hold and the region was eventually taken over by the Bavarians from the northwest, under Frankish leadership. When Charlemagne became king of the Franks in A.D. 768, he brought peace and a more civilized culture.

After Charlemagne's death, the region again became a battleground, with a staggering number of claimants. The Babenbergs won out, and ruled over Austria from 976 to 1246, gaining more territory by treaty, inheritance, marriage, and politics than through war, so the region grew, and farms, towns, and cities thrived. By the end of the 10th century, the region was already being mentioned as Ostarrichi, which evolved into the German name, Österreich (Austria).

The Habsburg Reign

The first Habsburg, Rudolph I, was crowned in 1273, inaugurating a dynasty that would last more than 600 years as Holy Roman Emperors and rulers of Austria, Hungary, Germany, Bohemia, Italy, Belgium, Spain, the Netherlands, and other territories; their troops were involved in every conflict in Europe, and neighboring nations moved from ally to adversary and back again. In all there were 20 emperors and kings, and at its height, the sun never set on the Habsburg Empire.

Of these many Habsburg rulers, Rudolf IV (1339–65) is remembered as "The Founder," who laid the cornerstone of St. Stephan's Cathedral and founded the University of Vienna following the one in neighboring Prague.

In 1453, at the close of the 100 Years War, Friedrich II was elected Holy Roman Emperor, ruling from Vienna. However, he lost control of both Bohemia and Hungary, each electing a king, and in 1485, he was driven from the capital by the Hungarian King Matthias Corvinus, who ruled for 5 years from Vienna's Hofburg. At his death in 1490, a civil war broke out in Hungary, allowing Friedrich's son Maximilian I (1459–1519) to regain most of the lost territory.

But the Habsburgs were not warriors. In fact, the family's motto became: "Let others wage wars, but you, happy Austria, marry!" Over the years they added Spain, Burgundy, and the Netherlands to their empire. In 1496, just after Columbus discovered America, a Habsburg, Phillip the Fair, married the Spanish *infanta* (heiress), whose son Charles became ruler of Spain and its New World holdings in 1516, and 3 years later was crowned Holy Roman Emperor as Charles V, ceding Austria to his younger brother Ferdinand who married Anna Jagiello, heiress to Hungary and Bohemia, adding those countries to the empire.

In 1526, civil war broke out in Vienna, leading to brutal repression and a new city charter that placed the city directly under Habsburg control. In the following decades, incursions into the Balkans by Ottoman Turks continued to upset the balance of power in Central Europe, while outbreaks of the Black Death spread over Europe; in 1679, between 75,000 and 150,000 died in Vienna alone. Leopold I commemorated the city's deliverance with the famous *Pestaule,* the Plague Column, that stands on the Graben, like many smaller ones across the empire.

The final defeat of the Turks came in September 1683. And with the passing of the plague, the victory revitalized Vienna and Austria emerged as a major European power. The Treaty of Karlowitz in 1699 brought most of Hungary under Habsburg domination, a union that lasted until 1918.

Under Charles VI (1711–40) and his daughter, Maria Theresa, Austria thrived and Vienna became a mecca of the arts. Architects like Johann Bernhard Fischer von Erlach and Johann Lukas von Hildebrandt designed lavish buildings, and composers and musicians flooded into the city from the imperial provinces. When Charles II, last of the Spanish Habsburgs, died without an heir, Austrian emperor Charles VI established the Pragmatic Sanction, which ensured that his daughter would follow him. Maria Theresa ascended to power in 1740 at the age of 23, waged and won a 7-year War of the Austrian Succession (1741–48) and reigned for 40 years, launching an era of prosperity and a golden age of baroque. During Maria Theresa's long reign, the population of Vienna almost doubled, from 88,000 to 175,000. Her architectural legacies include sections of Vienna's Hofburg and her beloved Schönbrunn Palace, completed in 1769.

Maria Theresa is credited with extensive reforms, including unifying the National Army, strengthening the economy through more effective tax collection, establishing a civil service, and founding the first national public education system, required for both sexes for ages 6 to 12. With her chief advisor, the Dutch physician Gerard van Swieten, she founded the Vienna General Hospital and Europe's first medical research university and had all her 13 children inoculated against smallpox. Her reforms laid the foundations of many Austrian institutions, its intellectual life and traditions that have characterized the country ever since.

Maria Theresa's son, Joseph II, was justifiably called "The Enlightened Despot." An enlightened monarch who eschewed ritual, he abolished serfdom and introduced freedom of religion—and made himself available to the people, issuing an "Edict of Tolerance" that heavily influenced succeeding Habsburg rulers. Among his many generous acts, Joseph II opened both the Prater and the Augarten parks to the public for their "pleasure and recreation" and issued the Law of the *Heuriger,* that gave any Austrian the right to sell his own wine on his own premises to the public without a restaurant license, establishing the tradition of the family wine taverns that are a fixture of Austrian life to this day.

The 19th century had a turbulent start, with Napoleon's incursions onto Habsburg territories beginning in 1803 and culminating in the French occupation of Vienna in 1805 and 1809. Napoleon ordered Franz I to abdicate his position as Holy Roman Emperor, ultimately causing a collapse of Austria's banking system. In one of the 19th century's more bizarre marriages, Napoleon married the Habsburg archduchess

Marie-Louise by proxy in 1810. He was finally defeated at the "Battle of Nations" in Leipzig in 1813 and abdicated the following year.

Organized to reorder European boundaries after Napoleon's defeat, the pivotal Congress of Vienna (1814–15) included representatives of all Europe's major powers. The Congress was a showcase for the brilliant diplomacy and intrigue of Austria's foreign minister, Klemens von Metternich, who restored Austria's pride and influence within a redefined confederation of German-speaking states.

Metternich's dominance of Austria between 1815 and 1848, repressive as it was, ushered in another golden age of sorts. The Biedermeier period was an era of increased prosperity of the bourgeoisie. Virtually excluded from politics, they concentrated on culture, building villas and the first big apartment houses, and encouraging painting, music, literature, and design. The first steamship company on the Danube was established in 1832, and Austria's first railway line opened in 1837, one of the Continent's first, between Vienna and Wagram.

In the meantime, Metternich's domestic policies almost guaranteed civil unrest, eradicating many civil rights with a near police state, and creating an economic climate that favored industrialization at the expense of wages and workers' rights. In March 1848, events exploded not only in Vienna and Hungary, but also across most of Europe. Metternich was ousted and fled the city, hidden in a laundry cart, while some of his not-so-lucky colleagues were hanged. Faced with the threat of revolution, the Austrian army imposed new controls, and Franz Joseph I came to a secure throne in 1848, at the age of 18, beginning a 68-year autocratic rule.

Franz Joseph's austere civility created the perfect foil for the cultural explosion of the newly revitalized city and during his reign the cultural life of Vienna and its other regional capitals—Prague, Budapest, and others—blossomed as never before or since. The unification with Hungary was enshrined in a new constitution in 1867, which also made Jews full citizens, with all civil and political rights, thus releasing a flood tide of creative energy and helping to usher in a half century of prosperity and the flowering of art and ideas that shaped the modern era.

Franz Joseph transformed the city with the Ringstrasse, built from 1857 to 1909 on the site of the old city walls that became a work of homogeneous civic architecture unparalleled throughout Europe, while advancing technology helped transform the city into a glittering showcase. The empire's vast resources were used to keep theaters, coffeehouses, concert halls, palaces, and homes well lit, cleaned, and maintained. A state-of-the-art water supply was installed, and the Danube regulated. A new town hall was built, and the Stadtpark opened.

During the Belle Epoque, Europe sat on a powder keg of frustrated socialist platforms, national alliances, and conflicting colonial ambitions. When a Serbian nationalist assassinated Franz Joseph's nephew and designated heir, the Archduke Franz Ferdinand, and his wife, Sophie, in Sarajevo on June 28, 1914, the Austro-Hungarian Empire, in a Triple Alliance with Germany and Italy, leapt headfirst into armed conflict. An embittered Franz Joseph died in 1916, midway through the conflict. His successor, Charles I, the last of the Habsburgs, abdicated in 1918.

The punitive Versailles Treaty in 1919 broke up the vast Austro-Hungarian territories into the nations of Hungary, Poland, Yugoslavia, and Czechoslovakia—a decision Winston Churchill described in his memoirs as "a cardinal tragedy." After the boundaries were redrawn, tiny Austria was what French Prime Minister Clemenceau called "that which is left over." This overnight collapse of the empire caused profound dislocations of populations and trade patterns. Some of the new nations refused to deliver raw materials to Vienna's factories or, in some cases, food to Vienna's markets. Coupled with the reparations and the massive loss of manpower and resources in a war where 80% of the Austrian army had died, Vienna soon found itself on the brink of starvation.

Against staggering odds, the new government—assisted by a massive loan in 1922 from the League of Nations—managed to stabilize the currency while Austrian industrialists hammered out new sources of raw materials. A democratic socialist "Red Vienna" also undertook pioneering experiments in public works and high-quality public housing that characterize Viennese life to this day.

Anschluss & World War II

In 1934, social tensions broke out in civil war, Europe's first confrontation between fascism and democracy. Authoritarian nationalism under Engelbert Dollfuss put an end to progressive policies, until his assassination later that year by Austrian Nazis who were included in a coalition government. In 1938, Austria was joined to Germany (the *Anschluss*) and Hitler marched triumphantly to Vienna, several decades after he had lived there as an impoverished and embittered artist. In a referendum, 99.75% of Austrians voted their support.

The rise of Austria's Nazis devastated Vienna's academic and artistic communities. Many, including Sigmund Freud, fled to safety elsewhere. About 60,000 Austrian Jews were sent to concentration camps, of whom an estimated 2,000 survived; Austria's homosexual and gypsy populations too were decimated.

Beginning in 1943, Allied bombing raids damaged many Austrian cities, particularly Vienna. The roof of the city's most prominent landmark, St. Stephan's Cathedral, collapsed and there were fires in both towers; the city's death rate was one of the highest in Europe. The war ended abruptly on April 11, 1945, when Russian troops marched in from bases in Hungary.

During a confused interim that lasted a decade, Austria was divided into four zones of occupation, each controlled by one of the four Allies (the United States, the Soviet Union, Britain, and France). Vienna, deep within the Soviet zone, was also divided, with control of the inner city alternating every month. It was a dark and depressing time, particularly in Vienna; rubble was slowly cleared away from bomb sites, but some of the most glorious public buildings in Europe lay in ruins. Espionage, black-market profiteering, and personal betrayals proliferated, poisoning the memories of many older Viennese even today. In 1950, Allied commanders were replaced by diplomats. The Russian military occupation remained, stripping assets and hampering recovery until the State Treaty in 1955.

Postwar Austria

Occupation forces withdrew in 1955, marking the beginning of coalition governments and a stable economy. The Soviets returned property that had been seized as German assets—major industrial plants, oil fields and installations, and the Danube Steamship Company—in return for money and goods as reparation.

In the Austrian State Treaty, signed by the United States, Britain, France, and the Soviet Union in 1955, Austria was recognized as a sovereign, independent, and democratic state. The pre-1938 frontiers were guaranteed, political or economic union with Germany was prohibited, human rights and the rights of the Slovene and Croat minorities and of democratic institutions were pledged, and all National Socialist and Fascist organizations were dissolved.

Although not mentioned in the treaty, the Allied powers also guaranteed Austrian neutrality, which was declared in an amendment to the country's constitution, along with a rejection of all military alliances or the establishment of military bases by foreign states on its territory.

Recent History

Once again part of a republic, the Viennese actively sought to restore their self-image as cultural barons. Restoring the State Opera House and other grand monuments became a top priority. As a non-aligned capital, Vienna became the obvious choice for meetings between John Kennedy and Nikita Khrushchev (in 1961), and Leonid Brezhnev and Jimmy Carter (in 1979).

In 1970 the election of Bruno Kreisky, the republic's longest-serving chancellor, began a 12-year "golden age" in Austrian politics and culture, with full employment, a solid social state, an influential foreign policy, and a "Sun-King" chancellor who appeared with a solid socialist majority—never repeated—that allowed him to push through reforms. Many international organizations (including OPEC and the International Atomic Energy Agency) established offices there.

However, Vienna's self-image suffered a blow with Austria's president and former UN Secretary General Kurt Waldheim, elected in 1986, who as an officer in the Wehrmacht had been aware of the deportation of Jews to extermination camps. Although never convicted of direct guilt, the United States declared him persona non grata. Many Austrians stood by Waldheim; others were deeply embarrassed. Waldheim did not seek re-election, and in May 1992, Thomas Klestil, a career diplomat of the center right Austrian People's Party, was elected.

In 1989, Empress Zita of Bourbon-Parma, in exile since 1919 where she had raised Crown Prince Otto, was buried in one of the most lavish and emotional funerals ever held in Vienna. Dying aged 96, this last empress of Austria and queen of Hungary had been revered as a symbol of the glorious days of the empire.

In the spring of 1998, the Austrian government stunned the art world by agreeing to return artworks confiscated by the Nazis. Many prominent Jewish families had fled into exile in 1938, and nearly all postwar claims had been unsuccessful. "The art was stolen by the Nazis and stolen a second time by the Austrian government," wrote journalist Hubertus Czernin. One museum director claimed Austria had "a specific moral debt," which it was now repaying.

In 1999, the far-right Freedom Party (FPÖ) won notoriety—and 27% of the vote—by denouncing the presence of foreigners in Austria. Echoing Nazi rhetoric, the party blames foreigners for drugs, crime, welfare abuse, and the spread of tuberculosis. The party remains racist in spite of the death in a car accident of its charismatic leader, Jörg Haider. After first announcing punishing sanctions against Austria for its tilt to the far right, the European Union back-pedaled in September 2000, while vowing to keep an eye on Austrian right-wing politics. In spite of earlier defiance, the Austrian government had taken "concrete steps to fight racism, xenophobia, and anti-Semitism," E.U. officials decided.

In 2002, Austria faced one of its worst disasters in decades, when crippling floods along the Danube overflowed through Central Europe, leaving billions of euros in damage to homes, farms, buildings, and businesses.

In 2004 Elfriede Jelinek, the controversial feminist writer and outspoken critic of the far-right Freedom Party, won the Nobel Prize for literature. On another front, Charles I, the last Habsburg to rule as emperor, was beatified by the Pope.

News of an expat Austrian from Graz made the biggest headlines in 2004. Their homegrown son, muscleman/movie star Arnold Schwarzenegger, swept into the governor's office in California in a recall vote. Even though he's married to a Kennedy, Maria Shriver, Schwarzenegger is a Republican, and lent his name to George W. Bush's campaign for re-election. He was defeated in 2010.

In October 2006, Austria's opposition Social Democrats (SPÖ) won nationwide elections, swinging the country back center-left after more than 6 years of far-right influence. Immigration was a central theme in the campaign, and the FPÖ hoped to reduce foreigners in Austria by 30%. The SPÖ countered with job creation and the closing of the gender gap in salaries. The politics of resistance have not worked: By 2010, Vienna's foreign-born population had risen to 32.8% (from 23% in 2001), and in Austria as a whole, 16% up from 9%.

Record warmth in recent years—with autumn (fall) temperatures prevailing even in winter—has brought the profound threat of climate change to the country's ski industry. Climatologists announced in 2008 that the warming trend would become drastic by 2020. In reports filed, these experts said that the Austrian Alps are warming twice as fast as the average in the rest of the world. They claimed that in 1980, 75% of alpine glaciers were advancing. By 2010, over 90% were retreating.

AUSTRIA'S ART & ARCHITECTURE

Austria's location at the intersection of Germanic, Mediterranean, and eastern European worlds contributed to a rich and varied artistic heritage. Here the delicate curves of 18th-century Theresian churches are topped with oriental onion domes, neoclassical columns support designs in Moorish mosaic under a soaring Gothic arch. In a visual metaphor for the city's complex cultural roots, Austria embraces styles from Romanesque through rococo, baroque to Biedermeier, from medieval to modern, blending together into a consciously unified urban landscape.

Art

EARLY ECCLESIASTICAL ART

Most art in the early medieval period was church art. From the Carolingian period, the only survivors are a handful of **illuminated manuscripts,** now in Vienna's National Library. The most famous is the *Cutbercht Evangeliar* from around 800, a richly illuminated copy of the four gospels.

The Romanesque period reached its peak between 1000 and 1190. Notable from this time is the *Admont Great Bible*, crafted around 1140, one of the prized treasures of Vienna's National Library. In 1181, the famous goldsmith Nicolas de Verdun produced one of the finest **enamel works** in Europe for the pulpit at Klosterneuburg Abbey. Verdun's 51 small panels, crafted from enamel and gold, depict scenes from the religious tracts of the Augustinians. After a fire in the 1300s, the panels were repositioned onto an altarpiece, the Abbey's Verdun Altar.

THE GOTHIC AGE

The Gothic age in Austria is better remembered for its architecture than its painting and sculpture. Early Gothic sculpture was influenced by the **Zachbruchiger Stil** (zigzag style), identified by vivid angular outlines of forms against contrasting backgrounds. The era's greatest-surviving sculptures date from around 1320 and include the *Enthroned Madonna of Klosterneuburg* and the *Servant's Madonna,* showcased in Vienna's St. Stephan's Cathedral.

By the late 1300s, Austrian sculpture was strongly influenced by Bohemia. The human form became elongated and idealized, often set in graceful but unnatural S curves. Wood became popular as a medium, often painted in vivid colors. A superb example of **Gothic sculpture** is the *Servant's Madonna* in St. Stephan's, from about 1320, depicting Mary enthroned and holding a standing Christ child.

FROM THE RENAISSANCE TO THE 18TH CENTURY

During most of the Renaissance, Vienna was too preoccupied with invasions, sieges, and plagues to produce the kind of painting and sculpture that flowered in other parts of Europe. As a result, in the 17th and 18th centuries, Vienna struggled to keep up with such cities as Salzburg, Munich, and Innsbruck. What was produced was for the baroque churches and palaces, and artists were imported from Italy; one, **Andrea Pozzo** (1642–1709), produced the masterpiece *The Apotheosis of Hercules,* which appears on the ceilings of Vienna's Liechtenstein Palace. Baroque painting emphasized symmetry and unity, and *trompe l'oeil* was used to give extra dimension to a building's sculptural and architectural motifs.

The first noteworthy Austrian-born baroque painter was **Johann Rottmayr** (1654–1730), the preferred decorator of the two most influential architects of the age, von Hildebrandt and Fischer von Erlach. Rottmayr's works adorn some of the ceilings of Vienna's Schönbrunn Palace and Peterskirche. Countless other artists contributed to the Viennese baroque, including **Daniel Gran** (1694–1754), whose frescoes decorate the Hofbibliothek and an altarpiece in the Karlskirche.

Vienna emerging from muddy fields into a majestic fantasy of baroque architecture was captured in the landscapes of **Bernardo Bellotto** (1720–80), nephew and pupil of the Venetian painter Canaletto. Brought to Vienna by Maria Theresa, Bellotto managed to bathe the city in a flat but clear light of arresting detail. His paintings today are valued for their historical as well as artistic value.

Dutch-born, Swedish-trained **Martin van Meytens** (1695–1770), court painter to Maria Theresa, captured the lavish balls and assemblies of Vienna's aristocracy. His canvases, though awkwardly composed and overburdened with detail, are the best visual record of the Austrian court's balls and receptions. In 1730, van Meytens was appointed director of Vienna's Fine Arts Academy.

Sculptors also made their contribution to the baroque style. **Georg Raphael Donner** (1693–1741) is best known for the remarkable life-size bronzes of the Fountain of Providence in the Neuer Markt. **Balthasar Permoser** (1651–1732) is responsible for the equestrian statues of Prince Eugene of Savoy in the courtyard of the Belvedere Palace. The famous double sarcophagus in the Kapuzinerkirche, designed for Maria Theresa and her husband, Francis Stephen, is the masterpiece of **Balthasar Moll** (1717–85).

Equally influential was **Franz Xaver Messerschmidt** (1737–83), the German-trained resident of Vienna, who became famous for his portrait busts. His legacy leaves accurate and evocative representations of Maria Theresa, her son Joseph II, and other luminaries.

THE REVOLT AGAINST "OFFICIAL ART"

In rebellion against "official art," a school of **Romantic Realist** painters emerged, drawing on biblical themes and Austrian folklore. Scenes from popular operas were painted lovingly on the walls of the Vienna State Opera. The 17th-century Dutch masters influenced landscape painting.

Georg Waldmüller (1793–1865), a self-proclaimed enemy of "academic art" and an advocate of realism, created one of the best pictorial descriptions of Viennese Biedermeier society in his *Wiener Zimmer* (1837). More than 120 of his paintings are on display at the Upper Belvedere museum.

The second most influential portraitist of this era was renowned court painter **Friedrich von Amerling** (1803–87), several of whose extraordinarily vivid portraits of actors at the Burgtheater are on view at the Liechtenstein Museum.

Another realist was **Carl Moll** (1861–1945), painting graceful and evocative scenes of everyday life. **Joseph Engelhart** (1864–1941) gave voluptuous renderings of Belle Epoque coquettes flirting with Viennese gentlemen.

THE SECESSIONIST MOVEMENT

Young painters, decorators, and architects from Vienna's Academy of Fine Arts founded the Wiener Secession in 1897. The name captures their retreat (secession) from the Künstlerhaus (Artists' Association), which they considered pompous, artificial, mediocre, and mired in the historicism favored by Emperor Franz Joseph. Their artistic statement was similar to that of the Art Nouveau movement in Paris and the Jugendstil movement in Munich.

The Secession headquarters, on the Friedrichstrasse, at the corner of the Naschmarkt was inaugurated in 1898 as an exhibition space for avant-garde artists. Foremost among the group was **Gustav Klimt** (1862–1918), whose work developed rapidly into a highly personal and radically innovative form of decorative painting based on the sinuous curved line of Art Nouveau. His masterpieces include a mammoth frieze, 33m (110 ft.) long, encrusted with gemstones, and dedicated to Beethoven. Executed in 1902, it's one of the artistic focal points of the Secessionist Pavilion. Other pivotal works include *Portrait of Adele Bloch-Bauer* (1907), an abstract depiction of a prominent Jewish Viennese socialite. Its gilded geometric form is reminiscent of ancient Byzantine art.

THE MODERN AGE

Klimt's talented disciple was **Egon Schiele** (1890–1918). Tormented, overly sensitive, and virtually unknown during his brief lifetime, he is now considered a modernist master whose work can stand alongside that of van Gogh and Modigliani, granting a kind of anthropomorphic humanity to landscape painting. One of his most disturbing paintings is the tormented *The Family* (1917), originally conceived as decoration for a mausoleum.

Modern sculpture in Vienna is inseparable from the international art trends that dominated the 20th century. **Fritz Wotruba** (1907–75) introduced a neo-cubist style of sculpture. Many of his sculptural theories are in his Church of the Most Holy Trinity, erected toward the end of his life in Vienna's outlying 23rd District. Adorned with his sculptures and representative of his architectural theories in general, the building is an important sightseeing and spiritual attraction.

Oskar Kokoschka (1886–1980) was one of Vienna's most important contemporary painters. Kokoschka expressed the frenzied psychological confusion of the years before and after World War II. His portraits, like that of artist Carl Moll, are studies in psychological realism and violent emotion.

Architecture

GOTHIC

Although Vienna holds no remains of early medieval buildings, a number of Gothic buildings rest on older foundations. During the 1300s, ecclesiastical architecture was based on the Hallenkirche (hall church), a model that originated in Germany. These buildings featured interiors that resembled enormous hallways, with nave and aisles of the same height. The earliest example of this style was the choir added in 1295 to an older Romanesque building, the abbey church of Heiligenkreuz, 24km (15 miles) west of Vienna.

During the late 1400s, Gothic architecture retreated from the soaring proportions of the Hallenkirche style, and focus turned to more modest buildings with richly decorated interiors. Stonemasons added tracery (geometric patterns) and full-rounded or low-relief sculpture to ceilings and walls. Gothic churches continued to be built in Austria until the mid-1500s.

FROM GOTHIC TO BAROQUE

One of the unusual aspects of Vienna is its lack of Renaissance buildings. The Turks besieged Vienna periodically from 1529 until the 1680s, forcing planners to use most of their resources to strengthen the city's fortifications. Late in the 16th century, many Italian builders settled in the regions of Tyrol, Carinthia, and Styria. In these less-threatened regions of Austria, Italian influence produced a number of country churches and civic buildings in the Renaissance style, with open porticoes, balconies, and loggias.

THE FLOWERING OF THE BAROQUE

The 47-year rule of Leopold I (1658–1705) witnessed the beginning of the golden age of Austrian baroque architecture. Italian-born Dominico Martinelli (1650–1718) designed the **Liechtenstein Palace,** built between 1694 and 1706 and inspired by the Renaissance-era Palazzo Farnese in Rome.

Austria soon began to produce its own architects. **Johann Bernhard Fischer von Erlach** (1656–1723) trained with both Bernini and Borromini in Rome. His style was restrained but monumental, drawing richly from the great buildings of antiquity. Fischer von Erlach knew how to transform the Italianate baroque of the south into a style that suited the Viennese. His most notable work is the **Karlskirche,** built in 1713. He also created the original design for Maria Theresa's **Schönbrunn Palace.** He had planned a sort of super-Versailles, but the project turned out to be too costly. Only the entrance facade remains of Fischer von Erlach's design. The **Hofbibliothek (National Library),** on Josephsplatz, and the **Hofstalungen** are other notable buildings he designed.

Fischer von Erlach was succeeded by another great name in the history of architecture: **Johann Lukas von Hildebrandt** (1668–1745). Von Hildebrandt's design for Prince Eugene's **Belvedere Palace**—a series of interlocking cubes with sloping mansard-style roofs—is the culmination of the architectural theories initiated by Fischer von Erlach. Other von Hildebrandt designs in Vienna include the **Schwarzenberg Palace** (now a hotel) and **St. Peter's Church.**

The **rococo style** developed as a more ornate, somewhat fussier progression of the baroque. Gilt stucco, brightly colored frescoes, and interiors that drip with embellishments are its hallmarks. Excellent examples include the **Abbey of Dürnstein** (1731–35) and **Melk Abbey,** both in Lower Austria. One of the most powerful proponents of rococo was Maria Theresa, who used its motifs so extensively within Schönbrunn Palace during its 1744 renovation that the school of Austrian rococo is sometimes referred to as "late-baroque Theresian style."

In response to the excesses of rococo, architects eventually turned to classical Greece and Rome for inspiration. The result was a restrained neoclassicism that transformed the skyline of Vienna and lasted well into the 19th century.

ECLECTICISM & VIENNA'S RING

As Austria's wealthy bourgeoisie began to impose their tastes on public architecture, 19th-century building grew more solid and monumental. The neoclassical style remained the preferred choice for government buildings, as evidenced by Vienna's **Mint** and the **Palace of the Provincial Government.**

The 19th century's most impressive Viennese architectural achievement was the construction of the **Ringstrasse** (1857–91). The medieval walls were demolished, and the Ring was lined with showcase buildings. This was Emperor Franz Joseph's personal project and his greatest achievement. Architects from all over Europe answered the emperor's call, eager to seize the unprecedented opportunity to design a whole city district. Between 1850 and the official opening ceremony in 1879, the Ring's architecture became increasingly eclectic: French neo-Gothic (the Votivkirche), Flemish neo-Gothic (the Rathaus), Greek Revival (Parliament), French Renaissance (Staatsoper), and Tuscan Renaissance (Museum of Applied Arts).

SECESSIONIST & POLITICAL ARCHITECTURE

By the late 19th century, younger architects were in rebellion against the pomp and formality of older architectural styles. In 1896, young **Otto Wagner** (1841–1918) published a tract called *Moderne Architektur,* which argued for a return to more natural and functional architectural forms. The result was the establishment of **Art Nouveau (Jugendstil).** The Vienna Secession architects used new building materials to great effect, as in Wagner's **Kirche am Steinhof** and the city's **Postsparkasse** (Post Office Savings Bank).

Joseph Hoffman (1870–1955) and **Adolf Loos** (1870–1933) promoted the use of glass, newly developed steel alloys, and aluminum. In the process, they discarded nearly all ornamentation, a rejection that contemporary Vienna found profoundly distasteful and almost shocking. Loos's most controversial design is the **Michaelerplatz Building.** Sometimes referred to as "the Loos House," it was erected on Michaelerplatz in 1908. The streamlined structure was bitterly criticized for its similarities to the "gridwork of a sewer." The emperor found it so offensive that he ordered his drivers to avoid the Michaelerplatz gate altogether.

Architects during the "Red Vienna" period were much affected by the socialist reformers' desire to alleviate public housing shortages, a grinding social problem of the years between the wars. The SPÖ began erecting "palaces for the people," among the most famous, the **Karl-Marx-Hof** (Heiligenstadterstrasse 82–92, A-1190), which includes 1,600 apartments and stretches for more than half a mile.

TO THE PRESENT DAY

After World War II, much of Vienna's resources went toward restoring older historic buildings to their prewar grandeur. New buildings were streamlined and functional; much of Vienna today features the same kind of neutral modernism you're likely to find in postwar Berlin or Frankfurt.

Postmodern masters, however, have broken the mold of the 1950s and 1960s. They include the iconoclastic mogul Hans Hollein, designer of the silvery, curved-sided **Haas Haus** (1990) adjacent to St. Stephan's Cathedral. The self-consciously avant-garde **Friedensreich Hundertwasser** is a multicolored, ecologically inspired apartment building at the corner of Löwengasse and Kegelgasse that appears to be randomly stacked.

Lately, **Hermann Czech** has been stirring architectural excitement, not so much by building new structures as developing daring interiors for boutiques and bistros;

examples are the **Kleines Café** (Franziskanerplatz 3) and **Restaurant Salzamt** (Ruprechtsplatz 1).

THE LAY OF THE LAND

Except for the fertile valleys of the Danube and the eastern and southeastern sections that border on Moravia and the great Hungarian plain, almost three-quarters of the country is mountainous, an average of 915m (3,000 ft.) above sea level. It marks the eastern terminus of the Alps that cover about two-thirds of the country, the rest the ancient granite mass of the Bohemian massif.

Geologists divide the alpine regions of Austria into the central, southern, and northern districts. All three are naturally beautiful. The highest peaks and longest glaciers are in the central region, in the region of the Ötztal; Silvretta; the Stubai Alps; and the Hohe Tauern, site of the country's most powerful glaciers.

A large belt along the eastern slopes of the Grossglockner and a section of the Schobergruppe Massif have been earmarked as the Hohe Tauern National Park, which features some of the most dramatic landscapes in the country. Lakes, forests, and alpine pastures—set against a backdrop of powerful and protecting glaciers—riddle the park. These glaciers advanced north at least 10,000 years ago, spreading across the Bavarian plateau, almost to the border of what today is the city of Munich. All this movement created natural amphitheaters called "cirques" and what geologists call "hanging valleys," marked by towering waterfalls.

The season for mountain wildflowers varies depending on spring temperatures and snowpack; expect most to have blossomed by the end of July or early August. In autumn, the perennial changing of the leaves is another colorful and splendid sight. If you're interested in learning more about high-altitude flora, visit an alpine garden or walk down an instructional guided path.

You might even find wild berries or (if you know what you are doing) mushrooms. Wild raspberries, strawberries, blackberries, cranberries, flap mushrooms, chanterelles, and parasol mushrooms quell a hiker's hunger with exotic tastes, particularly when hand-picked. Nearly half of the vegetation is remnants of deciduous forests, such as mixed mountain forests. Most alpine forests consist of conifers, including the spruce, the larch (the only European conifer to lose its needles in winter), the Austrian pine (with a darkly fissured bark), and the arolla pine, with upward-curving branches that evoke candelabra.

Nearly a third of the vegetation sprouts on rock debris and in alpine meadows. A mixed mountain forest thrives below 1,372m (4,500 ft.), whereas a coniferous forest exists at an altitude of 1,678m (5,500 ft.). Above that, wind-dwarfed bushes and alpine meadows predominate.

In spring, summer, and autumn, many different rare species of plants flower. They don't live long once picked, so please leave them for the next person to enjoy. The flora coexist with a variety of alpine animals such as the chamois, ibex (reintroduced in 1930), marmot, snow hare, alpine salamander, golden eagle, ptarmigan, black grouse, capercaillie, alpine chough, black woodpecker, and three-toed woodpecker. Other animals, such as the wolf, lynx, bear, and golden vulture, once thrived in the Alps but have not survived.

After its mountains, Austria's great defining feature is the Danube. With the exception of a handful of streams in the country's west that flow to the Rhine, and a few in the north that empty into the Moldau (a tributary of the Elbe), all of Austria's creeks, streams, and rivers empty into the Danube. This, Europe's longest river, originates in

THE wild ALPS

Many alpine animals such as the lynx, otter, and alpine ibex have all but disappeared during this century in the Alps. Other animals are endangered, including wildcats, susliks, certain nesting birds, toads, and fish.

An effort to reintroduce over-hunted species has been successful on the whole. Brown bears have been sighted in recent years, along with migrating elk. Although wolves were killed off by ranchers in the 1950s, the deer and stag population has flourished, so that hunting is again necessary to keep the natural balance.

Other species continue to thrive in the alpine environment, and unobtrusive hikers will find the Alps teeming with creatures. You might behold the chamois gracefully bounding up alpine trees or watch a golden eagle in circling flight above. The griffon vulture's 2.7-m (9-ft.) wingspan may intimidate even the most seasoned hiker. A hiker might even be befriended by a marmot or an alpine chough basking in a sunny meadow. The hill country and lower mountain ranges are often home to badgers, martens, and hares. Hedgehogs are rare, one of the endangered species of rodents.

Ornithologists have a field day in the Alps. Great white herons guide you down the Danube like a teasing trail of gingerbread crumbs; they pause for respite along the banks long enough for you to catch up with them by riverside trail, only to depart in flight to another sanctuary 20m (66 ft.) downstream. Storks, marsh warblers, gray geese, spoonbills, and terns can also be spotted or a diving blue kingfisher, particularly its extended underwater search for insects below ripples of streams and rivers.

The distinctive red-and-black wings of the gray alpine wall creeper set it apart from its cliff habitat. The spotted woodpecker, the goldfinch, the redstart, the thrush, and the blue lit sing for wintertime food from nearby human settlements, but the finch, the lark, and the song thrush save their voices for spring. Keen eyes may spot falcons, buzzards, and other birds of prey, and at night, the tawny owl.

The creation of national parks has helped protect this fauna from the detrimental effects of mass tourism yet keep them accessible to respectful admirers. Water lilies, flowering meadow shrubs, patches of moss and fern that grow in the dank darkness of forests, the snowdrop, and the pink hues of meadow saffron, even the gorgeous colors of the mountain rose and gentian—which punctuate the flowering alpine meadows—are finest in their natural setting, not wilting in a makeshift bouquet. But the bluebells, pinks, cornflowers, buttercups, daisies, and primroses blossom in such abundance that they can be picked at will.

Germany's Black Forest and enters Austria near Passau. A few miles from the Austrian border the Danube is joined by the Inn River (from which comes the name Innsbruck); the water provided by this great tributary, which flows from the Bernina and the Tauern Alps, is what makes the Danube navigable. One of the most important watercourses in European history, the Danube runs west to east across the Vienna basin, as the fertile plains of central Austria are called. The river bisects both Vienna and Budapest (capital of Austria's historic partner, Hungary), and links together in navigable form many towns and settlements of south-central Europe.

Austria is also graced with many freshwater lakes that are beautiful and draw sports enthusiasts to their shores.

AUSTRIA IN POPULAR CULTURE: BOOKS, FILM & MUSIC

Books

HISTORY

The Austrians: A Thousand-Year Odyssey, Gordon Brook-Shepherd: Historian Brook-Shepherd looks at Austria's long history to explain its people: Who they are, how they got there, and where they're going.

The Austrian Mind, an Intellectual and Social History 1848 to 1938, William M. Johnston: Wide-ranging and wonderfully lucid, the thinkers, artists, politicians, academics, and literati of the end of the monarchy and foundations of the republic.

Danube, Claudio Magris: A discursive portrait of the Danube valley, from Bavaria through Austro-Hungary and the Balkans to the Black Sea, a blend of observation and cultural history, philosophy and reflection, and wonderful storytelling.

The Paradoxical Republic: Austria 1945–2005, Oliver Rathkolb (Otmar Binder trans.): Decoding the contradictions, Rathkolb leads the reader through the labyrinth of Austria. Always critical, very readable—and enlightening.

The Struggle for Democratic Austria, Bruno Kreisky on Peace and Social Justice, by Bruno Kreisky, Ed. Matthew Paul Berg (trans.), Jill Lewis, Oliver Rathkolb. Foreword by John Kenneth Galbraith. Fascinating annotated memoirs.

The Viennese: Splendor, Twilight and Exile, Paul Hofmann: A masterful social history of the city by a Vienna-born political journalist and Rome bureau chief for the *New York Times,* illuminating the city's genius and the contradictions with affection and insight. Also, *The Spell of the Vienna Woods.*

Fin-de-Siecle Vienna: Politics and Culture, Carl E. Schorske: This landmark book takes you into the political and social world of Vienna during the late 19th and early 20th centuries.

A Nervous Splendor: Vienna 1888–1889, Frederic Morton: Morton uses the mysterious deaths of Archduke Rudolf and Baroness Marie Vetsera at Mayerling as a point of departure to capture in detail the life of imperial Vienna at its glorious height. In a second book, *Thunder at Twilight,* Morton recreates the intense confluence of events in Vienna on the eve of World War I, when Stalin, Trotsky, Lenin, Freud and Jung, Klimt, Kafka, and Karl Kraus were all haunting the coffeehouses of Vienna, conceiving the ideas that became the 20th century.

ART, ARCHITECTURE & MUSIC

Vienna 1900: Art, Architecture, and Design, Kirk Varnedoe: During the late 19th century, Vienna's artistic genius reached dazzling heights of modernity. These movements are explored in this appealing primer.

A Short History of Art in Vienna, Marina Pippl: A well-told survey of art and architecture in Vienna from Roman times to the present; full of good stories, in a graceful translation by Michael Foster.

On Mozart, Anthony Burgess: Set in heaven, amid a reunion of the greatest composers of all time, this controversial book creates debates about music that never occurred but should have. Condemned by some critics as gibberish and praised by others as brilliant and poetic, Burgess's work is highly recommended for musical sophisticates with a sense of humor.

BIOGRAPHY

Bruno Kreisky, Chancellor of Austria: A Political Biography, by H. Pierre Secher: Long the only book in English on Austria's legendary chancellor.

J. B. Fischer von Erlach, Hans Aurenhammer: This entertaining volume illuminates the life, times, and aesthetic vision of the court-appointed architect who transformed the face of 18th-century Vienna and Salzburg.

Freud: A Life for Our Times, Peter Gay: Gay's biography is a good introduction to the life of one of the seminal figures of the 20th century. Freud, of course, was a Viennese until he fled from the Nazis in 1938, settling with his sofa in London.

Haydn: A Creative Life in Music, Karl and Irene Geiringer: This is the best biography of composer Franz Josef Haydn, friend of Mozart, teacher of Beethoven, and court composer of the Esterházys.

Mozart: A Cultural Biography, Robert W. Gutman: Music historian Gutman places Mozart squarely in the cultural world of 18th-century Europe.

Empress Maria Theresa, Robert Pic: The life and times of the greatest, most colorful Habsburg monarch is richly treated in this engrossing biography.

Wittgenstein: The Duty of Genius, Ray Monk: A brilliant personal and intellectual portrait of the 20th century's most influential philosopher, as well as of his roots in the Jewish haute Bourgeoisie in pre-World War I Vienna.

Film

Though Austrians have played a major role in world cinema, most have made their movies in Berlin or Hollywood. Austrians who went on to international film fame have included Erich von Stroheim, Josef von Sternberg (who masterminded the career of Marlene Dietrich), G. W. Pabst, legendary director Max Reinhardt, Curd Jurgens, Hedy Lamar, Oscar Werner (*Jules et Jim*), Romy Schneider (*The Trial*), Maximilian Schell (*Judgment at Nuremburg*), and Klaus Maria Brandauer. The World War II Oscar-winning classic *Casablanca* was awash with Austrians, from director **Michael Curtiz** and composer **Max Steiner** (also *Gone with the Wind*), to co-star Paul Henreid as the resistance leader Victor Lazlo, Peter Lorre as the black marketer Ugarte, and S. Z. Sakall as the waiter Carl.

Among the other distinguished émigré directors, **Billy Wilder** made some of the most classic Hollywood pictures of all time, such as *Sunset Boulevard* (1950) with Gloria Swanson and *Some Like It Hot* (1959) with Marilyn Monroe. **Fred Zinnemann** directed some 21 feature films, including *The Men* (1949), *High Noon* (1951), and *Julia* (1976).

A first-rate film that hauntingly evokes life in postwar Vienna is *The Third Man* (1949), starring Joseph Cotton and Orson Welles. And who could visit Austria without renting a copy of *The Sound of Music* (1965)? The film won several Academy Awards, including Best Picture. Starring Julie Andrews, it was filmed in the lovely city of Salzburg.

Fritz Lang (1890–1976) was an Austrian-born director whose success was proven in Europe before emigrating to the United States. Often developing themes of fatalism and terror, his films were hailed for their intellectualism and visual opulence. His European films included *Metropolis* (1924), a stark and revolutionary portrayal of automated urban life, and, on the eve of the Nazi rise to power, the eerily clairvoyant *Das Testament des Dr. Mabuse* (1933). Welcomed into Hollywood, his credits included *Fury* (1936) and *Western Union* (1941).

Erich von Stroheim (1886–1957) was the pseudonym of Oswald von Nordenwald. He was one of the most innovative and exacting film directors in the history of

THE VIENNA–HOLLYWOOD sound

The legends of Hollywood are full of stories about Erich Wolfgang Korngold and Max Steiner, the two Viennese composers who dominated film music for nearly 3 decades from its beginning with Steiner's score for *King Kong* and Korngold's minor masterpiece the *Sea Hawk* that was held on a par with Wagner.

Korngold the "serious" composer, Steiner the entertainer, they liked and respected each other.

> "So Korngold, all your music has gotten a lot worse since you've been in Hollywood," Steiner teased him. "While mine has gotten a lot better."

> "Of course!" said Korngold. "You have been stealing from me, and I have been stealing from you."

By most measures, Erich Wolfgang Korngold was a fortunate man. Born into the Jewish intelligentsia during Vienna's glory years, he was a child prodigy whose adoring father was also the leading music critic. At 11, Korngold wrote his first ballet performed at the Court Opera. At 13, he wrote his first full-length piano sonata, and many successes later, his opera *Die Tote Stadt* premiered in 1920 when he was 23—that made him, along with Richard Strauss, the most performed composer in Vienna.

Steiner too was blessed. His grandfather Maximillian was the manager of Theater an der Wien and his father Gabor impresario at the Prater. He studied piano with Johannes Brahms and composition with Gustav Mahler, and Richard Strauss was his godfather. Arriving in New York in 1914, he worked on the Broadway musicals of Victor Herbert, Jerome Kern, and George Gershwin. He left for Hollywood in 1929 and never looked back. By 1935, he had won his first Oscar for *The Informer*.

In 1931 Korngold followed director Max Reinhardt (and Steiner) to Hollywood to arrange the film score for a *Midsummer Night's Dream*. He won Oscars in 1936 for *Anthony Adverse* and in 1938 for *The Adventures of Robin Hood*. Unable to return to Vienna after the rise of Hitler, he became the most successful composer in Hollywood.

Or was it Max Steiner? Over the next decade Steiner won two more Oscars for *Now Voyager* and *Since You Went Away,* and failed to win them for two of the best-loved movie sound tracks of all time: *Casablanca* and *Gone With the Wind*. He continued writing into his 70s, including the score for John Ford's the *Searchers,* considered the greatest western ever made. He died in 1971 at the age of 83—with a star on the Walk of Fame, a Hollywood man to the end.

And Korngold? After dozens of brilliant scores, he tried to return to "serious" music. But his violin concerto, written for Jascha Heifitz, was dismissed as "more 'Korn' than 'gold,'" and gurus of the new atonal world condemned his music as "sounding like Hollywood." Except, of course, that it was Hollywood that sounded like Erich Korngold, whose music had created the range and flexibility of the Hollywood score, bringing the tools of opera to the screen, telling a story in sound.

The audiences knew Korngold's idiom so well, they had forgotten where it came from. So in the end, he was condemned for being himself.

cinema. Born in Vienna, he served in the ranks of the Habsburg cavalry before rising within the ranks of Berlin's golden age of silent films. Reaching Hollywood in 1914, he worked for legendary director D. W. Griffith, becoming noted for his obsessive realism. His directing credits included the epic masterpiece *Greed* (1928), and the spectacularly expensive flop that almost ended Gloria Swanson's film career, *Queen Kelly* (1928). As an actor, he played stiff-necked but highly principled Prussian military officers as in Jean Renoir's *Grand Illusion* (1937), and the loyal valet in Billy Wilder's 1950 classic, *Sunset Boulevard.*

Hedy Lamarr (1915–2000), born in Vienna into the Jewish haute Bourgeoisie, studied with Max Reinhart, who described her as "the most beautiful woman in Europe," and became one of the shining lights in MGM mogul Louis B. Mayer's cavalcade of stars. Achieving world notoriety for her nude scenes in *Ecstasy,* she later played opposite Clark Gable in *Comrad X* and made such films as *White Cargo* and the Cecil B. DeMille epic *Samson and Delilah.* She was also a gifted mathematician, and together with *avant garde* composer George Antheil, a neighbor, Lamarr developed a frequency-hopping technology for the animated control of musical instruments, patented in 1941. Later this idea was revived as the basis for modern spread-spectrum communication used in Wi-Fi networks, for which she was honored in 1997 by the Electronic Frontier Foundation.

A more recent Austrian actor to achieve world fame is **Klaus Maria Brandauer,** who appeared in *Russia House* and *White Fang.* Born in 1944 in Austria, Brandauer attracted the attention of Hollywood as protagonist Hendrik Hofgen in the 1982 film version of Klaus Mann's novel *Mephisto,* directed by famed Hungarian Iztvan Szabo (*Being Julia*), winning the Oscar for best foreign film. This stocky, balding, and short actor—not your typical leading man—is however best remembered in America as the villain in the James Bond thriller *Never Say Never Again* and as the husband of Meryl Streep in *Out of Africa,* for which he was nominated for a second Oscar as best supporting actor in 1985.

Some film critics have hailed Austria today as "the world capital of feel-bad cinema," whose most recent high-profile director is **Michael Haneke,** who came to prominence with *The Seventh Continent* in 1989, followed by *The Piano Teacher* in 2001 (based on a novel of Austrian Nobel laureate Elfriede Jelenek), *Cache* in 2005 (with Juliette Binoche), and *The White Ribbon* in 2009 (winning the Palm d'Or at Cannes).

Austria has won further Oscars: Best foreign film in 2007 for **Stefan Ruzowitzky's** *The Counterfeiters* and best supporting actor in 2009 for **Christoph Waltz** playing the creepy Nazi general (in three languages) in Quentin Tarantino's *Inglourious Basterds.*

The best-known Austrian actor—now a governor—is, of course, **Arnold Schwarzenegger.** This son of a policeman from Graz became a multimillionaire superstar in America, from bodybuilder to world-class action star; from *The Terminator* to political life as the governor of California.

However, the Austrian émigré with the biggest footprint in Hollywood history is probably **Eric Pleskow,** former president of United Artists and Orion Pictures, and producer of a long list of greats including *One Flew Over the Cuckoo's Nest, Rocky, Annie Hall, Amadeus, Dances with Wolves,* and *Silence of the Lambs.* Since 1998, Pleskow has spent time here again as president of the Vienna International Film Festival, the Viennale.

Music

Music is central to Austrian life. From the concert hall to the opera house, from cabaret to *Hausmusik,* people are making and listening to music at every turn. You might encounter an accordion band in a Styrian *Gasthaus* or *Wienerlieder* at a *Heuriger* (see box, below) in the *Weinviertl,* a Klezmer band at a local *Beisl* or a piano player at a Viennese cafe or hotel bar. Or jazz, or pop, musical comedy or alternative rock. It's all there. The works of the musicians mentioned below are available on classical CDs.

SHALL WE waltz?

Dictionaries define the waltz as a form of "round dance," but anyone who has ever succumbed to its magic remembers it as pure pleasure, akin to falling in love—an intoxicating, romantic whirling of women in long gowns, men in tails, gliding across gilded ballrooms in the shimmer of refracted light from crystal chandeliers.

Many people think that the Strausses—father and son—invented the waltz, but its roots are actually much older, from peasant polkas and line dances, in theaters and country inns. Fashionable hostesses considered it vulgar. At court, the stylized minuet and the gavotte—more detached, more controlled—were the rule. The waltz began to bring a greater naturalism and zest to grand parties, with its rhythmic lilt and uninhibited spinning, throwing body against body, in dizzying abandon.

A violinist and composer of dance music, Johann Strauss the Elder (1804–49) introduced his famous *Tauberlwalzer* in Vienna in 1826. As a dance musician for court balls, he became indelibly associated with the social glitter of the Austrian court. His fame grew to such an extent that he began a series of tours (1833–40) that took him to England, where he conducted his music at Queen Victoria's coronation.

His famous son, Johann Strauss the Younger, was "the King of the Waltz." He formed his own dance band and met with instant success. He toured Europe and even went to America, playing his waltzes to enthusiastic audiences. By 1862, he relinquished the leadership of his orchestra to his two brothers and spent the rest of his life writing music. He brought the waltz to such a high degree of technical perfection that eventually he transformed it into a symphonic form in its own right.

The waltz lives on today in his most famous pieces, *The Blue Danube* (1867), *Tales from the Vienna Woods* (1868), *Weiner Blut* (1899), and the *Emperor Waltz* (1889). His genius ushered in the "golden age of operetta." Every New Year's Eve the Vienna State Opera schedules a splendid performance of perhaps the best beloved of his operettas, *Die Fledermaus* (1874), that begins the celebrations. The heritage of "the Waltz King" forms a vital part of Austria's cultural self-image.

THE CLASSICAL PERIOD

The classical period was a golden age in Viennese musical life. Two of the greatest composers of all time, Mozart and Haydn, lived and worked in Vienna. Maria Theresa herself trilled arias on the stage of the Schlosstheater at Schönbrunn, and with her children and friends, performed operas and dances.

Classicism's first great manifestation was the development of *Singspiele,* a reform of opera by **Christoph Willibald Ritter von Gluck** (1714–87). Baroque opera had become overburdened with ornamentation, and Gluck introduced a more natural musical form. In 1762, Maria Theresa presented Vienna with the first performance of Gluck's innovative opera *Orpheus and Eurydice.* It and *Alceste* (1767) are his best-known operas, regularly performed today.

Franz Joseph Haydn (1732–1809) is the creator of the classical sonata, which is the basis of classical chamber music. Haydn's patrons were the rich and powerful Esterházy family, whom he served as musical director. His output was prodigious. He wrote chamber music, sonatas, operas, and symphonies. His strong faith is in evidence in his oratorios; among the greatest are *The Creation* (1798) and *The Seasons* (1801). He is also the composer of the Austrian national anthem (1797), which he later elaborated in his quartet, Opus 76, no. 3.

The most famous composer of the period was **Wolfgang Amadeus Mozart** (1756–91). The prodigy from Salzburg charmed Maria Theresa and her court with his playing when he was only 6 years old. His father, Leopold, exploited his son's talent— "Wolferl" spent his childhood touring all over Europe. Later, he went with his father to Italy, where he absorbed that country's fertile musical traditions. Leaving Salzburg, he settled in Vienna, at first with great success. Eccentric and extravagant, he was unable to keep patronage or land any lucrative post; he finally received an appointment as chamber composer to the emperor Joseph II at a minimal salary. Despite hard times, Mozart refused the posts offered him elsewhere, possibly because in Vienna he found the best of all musical worlds—the best instrumentalists, the finest opera, the most talented singers. He composed more than 600 works in practically every musical form known to the time and his greatest are unmatched in beauty and profundity. He died in poverty, buried in a pauper's grave, the whereabouts of which are uncertain.

THE ROMANTIC AGE

Franz Schubert (1797–1828), the only one of the great composers born in Vienna, was also one of the most Viennese of musicians. He turned *lieder,* popular folk songs often used with dances, into an art form. He was a master of melodic line, and he created hundreds of songs, chamber music works, and symphonies. At 18, he set the words of German poet Goethe to music in *Margaret at the Spinning Wheel* and *The Elf King.* While his *Unfinished Symphony* remains best known to many concert goers, connoisseurs consider his greatest achievement in chamber music pieces like the C Major Strings Quintet (with two cellos) and the song cycles, performed at home soirees called Schubertiades. None of his music was ever performed in public in his lifetime.

THE 19TH CENTURY

After 1850, Vienna became the world's capital of light music, exporting it to every corner of the globe. The **waltz,** originally developed as a rustic Austrian country dance, was enthusiastically adopted by Viennese society.

Johann Strauss (1804–49), composer of more than 150 waltzes, and his talented and entrepreneurial son, **Johann Strauss the Younger** (1825–99), who developed the art form further, helped spread the stately and graceful rhythms of the waltz across Europe. The younger Strauss also popularized the operetta, the genesis of the Broadway musical.

The tradition of Viennese light opera continued to thrive, thanks to the efforts of **Franz von Suppé** (1819–95) and Hungarian-born **Franz Lehár** (1870–1948). Lehár's witty and mildly scandalous *The Merry Widow* (1905) is the most popular light opera ever written.

Vienna did not lack important serious music in the late 19th century. **Anton Bruckner** (1824–96) composed nine symphonies and a handful of powerful masses. **Hugo Wolf** (1860–1903), following in Schubert's footsteps, reinvented key elements of the German lieder with his five great song cycles. Most innovative of all was **Gustav Mahler** (1860–1911). A pupil of Bruckner, he expanded the size of the orchestra, often added a chorus or vocal soloists, and composed evocative music, much of it set to poetry.

THE NEW VIENNA SCHOOL

Mahler's musical heirs forever altered the world's concepts of harmony and tonality, and introduced what were then shocking concepts of rhythm. **Arnold Schoenberg** (1874– 1951) expanded Mahler's style in such atonal works as *Das Buch der Hangenden Garten* (1908) and developed a 12-tone musical technique referred to as "dodecaphony" (*Suite for Piano,* 1924). Later, he pioneered "serial music," series of notes with no key center,

WIENERLIEDER—DEATH IS viennese

Vienna is proud of its obsessions—or are they love affairs?—with music, with nostalgia, and most of all, with death. As cabaretist Georg Kreisler sang, "Death must surely be a Viennese, as love is a *femme fatale*."

Thus the annual celebration of Viennese song, the Wienerlied Festival each autumn goes by the name of "Wean hean"—dialect for "Vienna is a goner." Of course this prediction of doom is meant with affection, as in the famed Austrian saying that "The situation is hopeless, but not serious."

There are few cities, great or small, where music and song are as much a part of daily life as they are in Vienna. Perhaps it was the convergence of cultures of the old empire—where song may have helped bridge the barriers of language and culture—that nurtured the *Wienerlied*. Or maybe it was simply the chronically overcast sky.

"The every day reality of the present (or of *any* present!) is gray enough, that you need *something* to help you escape from it from time to time," wrote the famed chronicler of *Wienerlieder*, Stasi Lohr. In Vienna, this escape is most often into the past, where experience can be transformed in memory.

"Even suffering, when reflected upon, can be transformed into a bit of happiness," Lohr wrote. "That is where the truly Viennese art comes in."

Many devotees of *Wienerlieder*—these Viennese songs of the *Heuriger,* the cabaret and the street—claim that with all the city's charms, things are not what they once were. Well, maybe. But in Vienna they probably never were to begin with.

"When a song goes: 'It will never be as beautiful again as it once was,' it also means, as beautiful as it could have been—because it never actually was," wrote Lohr.

"But," he adds, "what difference does that make?"

You can hear *Wienerlieder* at many Viennese *Heuriger,* for example the Zwölfapostelkeller on 1., Sonnenfelsgasse 3 (📞 01/512-6777), or *Heuriger* Reinprecht on 19., Coblenzlgasse 22, in Grinzing (📞 01/321-471 0). Or on cabaret evenings at Theater L.E.O., 3., Ungargasse 18 (📞 01/712-1427).

shifting from one tonal group to another. **Anton von Webern** (1883–1945) and **Alban Berg** (1885–1935), composer of the brilliant but esoteric opera *Wozzeck*, were pupils of Schoenberg's. They adapted his system to their own musical personalities.

Finally, this discussion of Viennese music would not be complete without mention of the vast repertoire of folk and tavern songs, the *Wienerlieder* (see box, below), Christmas carols, and country dances that have inspired both professional musicians and ordinary folk for generations. The most famous Christmas carol in the world, **Stille Nacht, Heilige Nacht** (*Silent Night, Holy Night*), was composed and performed for the first time in Oberndorf, near Salzburg in 1818 and heard in Vienna for the first time that year.

EATING & DRINKING IN AUSTRIA

It's pointless to argue whether a Viennese dish is of Hungarian, Czech, Austrian, Slovenian, or even Serbian origin. All were part of the Empire and in Vienna, all count as local cuisine. Our palates respond well to *Wienerküche* (Viennese cooking), a centuries-old blend of foreign recipes and homespun concoctions.

From Wiener Schnitzel to Salzburger Knockerl

Of course everyone knows Wiener Schnitzel, the breaded veal cutlet that has achieved popularity worldwide. The most authentic local recipes call for the Schnitzel to be lightly fried in lard, and when done properly, it is light and tender.

Another renowned meat specialty is boiled beef, or *Tafelspitz*, said to reflect "the soul of the empire." This was Emperor Franz Joseph's favorite dish. If you're in Vienna, try it at Plachuta on Wollzeile (**ℂ 512-1577**), or for the humble, at the *Beisl* Reinthaler on Gluckgasse (**ℂ 512-3366**) around the corner, where whatever you order, you can be sure it's the real thing.

Roast goose is served on festive occasions, such as Christmas, or in autumn the Martinigansl, special for the feast day of St. Martin on November 11. But goose is a favorite at any time of the year, because *eine gut gebratene Gans ist eine gute Gabe Gottes* (a well-roasted goose is a gift from God!). After such a rich dinner, you might want to relax over some strong coffee, followed by a *Schnapps* to help the digestion.

For a taste of Hungary, order a goulash. Goulashes (stews of beef or pork with paprika) can be prepared in many different ways. The local version, *Wiener Gulasch,* is lighter on the paprika than most Hungarian versions. And don't forget *Gulyassuppe* (a Hungarian goulash soup), which can be a meal in itself.

Viennese pastry is probably the best in the world, both rich and varied. The familiar strudel comes in many forms; *Apfelstrudel* (apple) is the most popular, but you can also order cherry and other flavors. Viennese cakes defy description—look for *Gugelhupf, Wuchteln,* and *Mohnbeugerl*. Many of the *Torten* are made with ground hazelnuts or almonds in place of flour. You can put whipped cream on everything. Don't miss *Rehruken,* a chocolate "saddle of venison" cake that's studded with almonds.

Even if you're not addicted to sweets, there's a gustatory experience you mustn't miss: The Viennese Sachertorte. Many gourmets claim to have the authentic, original recipe for this "king of tortes," a rich chocolate cake with a layer of apricot jam. Master pastry baker Franz Sacher created the Sachertorte for Prince von Metternich in 1832, and it is still available in the Hotel Sacher. Outstanding imitations can be found throughout Vienna.

Coffee

Although it might sound heretical, the Ottoman Turks are credited with establishing the famous Viennese coffeehouse. Legend holds that while retreating from the siege of Vienna they abandoned several sacks of coffee, which, when brewed by the victorious Viennese, established the Austrian passion for coffee for all time. The first *Kaffeehaus* was established in Vienna in 1683.

In Vienna, *Jause* is a 4pm coffee-and-pastry ritual that is practiced daily in the city's coffeehouses. You can order your coffee a number of different ways—everything from the ubiquitous *Melange* (cappuccino), to *verkehrt* (cafe latte), to *Mocca* (ebony black). Note that in Vienna, only strangers ask for *einen Kaffee* (a coffee). If you do, you'll be asked what kind. Your safest choice is a *grosser* (large) or *kleiner* (small) *Brauner*—coffee with milk. *Kaffee mit Schlagobers* (with whipped cream) for a sweet tooth. You can even order eine *doppelte Portion Schlagobers* (double whipped cream).

Beer, Wine & Liqueurs

Vienna imposes few restrictions on the sale of alcohol, so you should be able to order beer or wine with your meal—even if it's 9am. Many Viennese have a first strong drink in the morning, preferring beer over coffee to get them going.

More than 99% of all **Austrian wine** is produced in vineyards in eastern Austria, principally Vienna, Lower Austria, Styria, and Burgenland. Traditionally, Austrian wines were served when new, and consumed where produced. This has changed in recent years, however, with some of the best widely available abroad. Following the 1985 revelation that some vintners had been adulterating their wine with diethylene glycol (antifreeze), the industry went through a wrenching overhaul of methods and standards, resulting in a rebirth, and Austrian wines now regularly win in blind competitions against leading wines worldwide.

The most popular Austrian white wine varieties are the Grüner Veltliner and the Welchriesling, the best of which grow primarily in the Wachau region west of Vienna. The leading reds, the Blauer Zweigelt and Blaufränkish, come from Burgenland and Styria to the south. Most astonishing to a visitor, 700 of the country's 49,000 hectares (121,000 acres) of vineyards are within the city limits.

Austrian beers are relatively inexpensive and quite good, and they're sold throughout Vienna. Vienna is home to the excellent Schwechater as well as Ottakringer, brewed locally in the 16th District and widely sold in Vienna's bars and taverns. Gösser, from Styria, is also popular and comes in both light and dark, as with the more robust Stiegl from Salzburg. And a local brew, Null Komma Josef, for those who prefer alcohol-free beer.

Two of the most famous and favored **liqueurs** among Austrians are any of a long list of sorts of Schnapps or Obstbrand, or fruit brandies, primarily apple, pear, or apricot. *Slivovitz* (a plum brandy that originated in Croatia) is also popular, as is the Slovak Borovicka.

Imported whisky and bourbon may be pricey, depending on where you buy. When you're in Vienna, it's a good rule of thumb to drink the "spirit of the land."

The most festive drink is ***Bowle*** (pronounced *bole*), which is often served at parties, prepared by soaking berries and sliced peaches or apricots overnight in brandy, adding three bottles of dry white wine, and letting it stand for another 2 to 3 hours. Before serving, pour over a bottle of champagne. *Prost!*

The *Heuriger*

In 1784, Joseph II decreed that each vintner in the suburbs of Vienna could sell his own wine along with a cold menu right on his own premises without a restaurant license, launching a tradition that continues today. *Der heurige Wein* refers to the "new wine" or, more literally, "of this year."

The *Heuriger,* or wine taverns, lie on the outskirts of Vienna, principally in Grinzing, Nussdorf, Neustift am Walde, and Stammersdorf, and throughout the Weinviertl and Wachau areas of Lower Austria and in Burgenland. In summer, in fair weather, much of the drinking takes place in vine-covered gardens. In some on a nippy night, you'll find a crackling fire in a flower-bordered ceramic stove. There's likely to be a gypsy violinist, an accordionist, or perhaps a zither player entertaining with Viennese songs, the *Wienerlieder* (see box, above). Most *Heuriger* are rustic, with wooden benches and tables, and it's perfectly acceptable to bring your own snacks. Today most serve warm buffets as well—of meats, cheeses, breads, and vegetables. Because many Viennese visiting the *Heuriger* outside the city didn't want to get too drunk, they started diluting the new wine with club soda or mineral water. Thus the *Spritzer* was born. The mix is best with a very dry white wine. For more information, see chapter 6.

PLANNING YOUR TRIP TO AUSTRIA

3

or such a small country, Austria is quite a handful—much more than you could possibly cover in one visit. Many of the things for which Austria is world famous are seasonal activities and public festivals (opera, jazz, dance, skiing, boating, hiking, etc.), so it pays to read up ahead of time. Vienna, Mozart, and the Alps alone could keep you busy for weeks. But Austria has a lot more under the surface, a richness of experience that only gets better. While much of the country exudes an echo of the stately elegance of the Habsburg Dynasty, Vienna and Graz boast cutting-edge contemporary construction—in short, imperial palaces and art museums mingle with the avant garde in music, theater, art, and design, with the energy of modernism in architecture and ideas.

Gourmets will find themselves overwhelmed by the quality and variety of good food in Austria—especially Vienna—and wine connoisseurs will be kept busy for as long as they can manage to stay. Vienna has all the charm of any European capital but much less grime. Even other Austrians—not to mention the rest of the German-speaking world—see Vienna as very laissez-faire. In general, Austria is a country that respects the good life, and its ski resorts, spas, and wineries spell comfort at every turn.

So don't rush through Austria—take in the sights but find time to walk, strike up a conversation with a native, sample delectable pastries, and people-watch in a country for connoisseurs.

VISITOR INFORMATION

TOURIST OFFICES Before you book your tickets, we recommend you contact a local Austrian tourism agency at one of these locations.

In the United States Contact the Austrian National Tourist Office, P.O. Box 1142, New York, NY 10108-1142 (© **212/944-6880;** www. austriainfo.com).

In Canada   You'll find offices at 2 Bloor St. E., Suite 3330, Toronto, ON M4W 1A8 (☎ **416/967-3381**).

In the U.K.   Contact the Austrian National Tourist Office at 14 Cork St., London, W1X 1PF (☎ **0845/101-1818**).

WEBSITES   The **Austrian National Tourist Office** (www.austria.info) and the **Vienna Tourist Board** (www.wien.info) are good places to begin your Web search. Their local affiliates in your home country can be found online. They will not only be able to help with hotel bookings, but also with deals on private home rentals or rooms in farmhouses in the countryside.

When in Austria, you'll see signs with a fat "i" symbol. Most often that stands for "information," and you'll be directed to a local tourist office. Chances are the office staff can help you obtain maps of the area and even assist in finding a hotel, or getting tickets for various events.

MAPS   Some of the most useful maps for touring the countryside include Michelin's *Austria* (no. 426) and Freytag & Berndt's *Autokarte Austria.* Even more detailed is Freytag & Berndt's *Grosse Strassenkarte,* which covers Austria in three separate breakdowns, with the enlargement of certain regions of Land Salzburg available on a fourth. Some visitors find it more convenient to buy these same four maps in the form of the 12-page atlas, *Grosser Auto Atlas Österreich.* It includes helpful blowups of the centers of many of the country's large and medium-size cities.

Freytag & Berndt also publish detailed maps (in either atlas or foldaway form) of *Grossraum Wien* (Greater Vienna). Maps of Vienna's public transport system are available from the city's tourist offices.

Hill-climbers and trekkers appreciate Freytag & Berndt's detailed topographical maps known as the *Wanderkarten (W.K.).* The company also publishes canoeing maps of specific regions, including the Carinthian lakes.

Most of the maps mentioned above are available in bookstores throughout Austria and in larger bookstores in Europe and North America. Freytag & Berndt's shops are at Kohlmarkt 9, in Vienna, and at Wilhelm-Greil-Strasse 15, in Innsbruck.

WHEN TO GO

The Austrian capital of Vienna experiences its high season from April through October, with July and August the less crowded times. Bookings around Christmas are also heavy because many Austrians visit the capital during this festive time. The winter months are also the high tourist season for ski regions like Tyrol, Vorarlberg, and the ski resorts in Salzburg. Basically, though, the country is popular year-round so always arrive with reservations.

Climate

In Austria, the temperature varies greatly depending on your location. The national average ranges from a low of 15°F (–9°C) in January to a high of 68°F (20°C) in July. However, in Vienna, the January average is 32°F (0°C); for July, it's 66°F (19°C). Snow falls in the mountainous sectors by mid-November. Road conditions in winter can be very dangerous in many parts of the country. And snow fall very heavy. The winter air is usually crisp and clear, with many sunny days. The winter snow cover lasts late December through March in the valleys, November through May at about 1,830m (6,004 ft.), and all year at 2,592m (8,504 ft.) or higher. The ideal times for visiting Vienna are spring through autumn. Even in spring and autumn, there are many mild, sunny days. By the end of July, alpine wildflowers are in full bloom.

Vienna's Average Temperature & Rainfall

	JAN	FEB	MAR	APR	MAY	JUNE	JULY	AUG	SEPT	OCT	NOV	DEC
Temp. (°F)	32	33	42	49	59	64	68	68	61	51	40	34
Temp. (°C)	0	1	5	9	15	17	20	20	16	10	4	1
Rainfall (in.)	1.2	1.9	3.9	1.3	2.9	1.9	.8	1.8	2.8	2.8	2.5	1.6

Salzburg's Average Temperature & Rainfall

	JAN	FEB	MAR	APR	MAY	JUNE	JULY	AUG	SEPT	OCT	NOV	DEC
Temp. (°F)	30	31	40	47	56	61	64	64	59	49	39	31
Temp. (°C)	-1	0	4	8	13	15	17	17	15	9	3	0
Rainfall (in.)	2.5	2.6	2.8	3.5	5.3	6.8	7.5	6.4	3.6	2.9	2.7	2.7

Innsbruck's Average Temperature & Rainfall

	JAN	FEB	MAR	APR	MAY	JUNE	JULY	AUG	SEPT	OCT	NOV	DEC
Temp. (°F)	27	32	41	49	57	63	66	65	59	49	39	30
Temp. (°C)	-2	0	5	9	13	17	18	18	14	9	3	-1
Rainfall (in.)	3.4	2.5	3.2	4.1	4.5	5.4	5.8	5.3	4.2	3.5	3.3	3.7

Austria Calendar of Events

For more information about these and other events, contact the various tourist offices throughout Austria. For an exhaustive list of events beyond those listed here, **check http://events.frommers.com**, where you'll find a searchable, up-to-the-minute roster of what's happening in cities all over the world.

JANUARY

New Year's Eve/New Year's Day. A performance of **Die Fledermaus** by Johann Strauss launches Vienna's biggest night, followed by a city-wide celebration, with live music and dancing and hot mulled wine through the streets of the 1st District, crowned at midnight with the popping of corks and bear-hug waltzes to the strains of **The Beautiful Blue Danube** wafting from synchronized radios on every rooftop. However late, struggle to be up for the famed **New Year's Concert** of the Vienna Philharmonic, nearly impossible to get tickets for, but shared by all on big screens outside, or at home on TV or radio. For the determined, contact the Wiener Philharmoniker for tickets and information: Bösendorferstrasse 12, A-1010 Vienna (© **01/505-6525;** www.wiener philharmoniker.at).

The **Imperial Ball** in the Hofburg follows the concert. For information and tickets, contact the Hofburg Kongresszentrum, Hofburg, Heldenplatz, A-1014 Vienna (© **01/587-3666;** www.hofburg.com). December 31/January 1.

Bergisel Ski Jumping Competition, Innsbruck. One of the country's most daredevil ski-jump competitions kicks off the New Year at a platform built for the 1964 Olympics. First week in January.

Hahnenkamm World Cup Ski Race, Kitzbühel. Since 1931, this major sporting event has drawn world-class skiers from around the globe to compete for the prestigious World Cup. Skiers compete over 2 days, but the whole town parties for a week. Tickets are available at the gate. For information, contact the Kitzbühel Tourist Office (© **05356/777;** www.kitzbuehel.com). Mid-January.

Eistraum (Dream on Ice). During the coldest months of Austrian winter, the monumental plaza between the Town Hall and the Burgtheater is flooded and frozen; lights, loudspeakers, and a stage are hauled in, and the entire civic core is transformed into a gigantic ice-skating rink. Sedate waltz tunes accompany the skaters during the day, and DJs spin rock, funk, and reggae after the sun goes down. At the rink, dozens of kiosks sell everything from hot chocolate and snacks to wine and beer. For information, call ((C)) **01/4090040,** or visit **www.wienereistraum.com**. Last week of January to mid-March.

Mozart Week, Salzburg. This festival features opera, orchestral works, and chamber music. Get tickets at the Mozarteum, Schwarzstrasse 26, A-5024 Salzburg ((C)) **0662/873154;** www.mozarteum.at). Late January to early February.

FEBRUARY

Opera Ball. Vienna's high society gathers at the Staatsoper for the grandest ball of the season, on the last Thursday before *Fasching* in either February or March. The evening opens with a performance by the Opera House Ballet. You don't need an invitation, but you do need a ticket, which, as you might guess, isn't cheap. But worth it. For information, call the Wiener Staatsoper ((C)) **01/514-44-2250;** www.staatsoper.at).

Ski Festival. Gaschurn, in the heart of Vorarlberg (9.6km/6 miles from Schruns), is the resort that lies closest to the downhill runs of the Silvretta-Nova subdivision of the Montafon Valley. It's the site of a 1-week ski festival sponsored by the Belgian–Austrian chocolate manufacturer Suchard. The men's and women's events are the Montafon Valley's most important ski competition. For information, contact the Vorarlberg Tourist Office ((C)) **05574/ 425250;** www.vorarlberg.cc). Late February to early March.

MARCH

Bregenz Spring Festival. The Vienna Symphony Orchestra usually appears at these concerts, which usher in the greening of the surrounding Alps. For information, contact the Bregenz Festival, Platz der Wiener Symphoniker 1, A-6900 Bregenz ((C)) **0557/ 4076;** www.bregenzerfestspiele.com). First 3 weeks of March.

Osterklang. At this **(Sound of Easter)** festival in Vienna you can always count on music by the world's greatest composers, including Mozart and Brahms and also lesser-known greats from the period ((C)) **01/58885;** www.osterklang.at). From the end of March through the April 9.

MAY

International Music Festival. This traditional highlight of Vienna's concert calendar features top-class international orchestras, distinguished conductors, and classical greats. You might hear Beethoven's *Eroica* as it was meant to be played, Mozart's *Jupiter* Symphony, and perhaps Bruckner's *Romantic*. The list of conductors and orchestras reads like a who's who of the international world of music. The venue and booking address is the Wiener Konzerthaus, Lothringerstr. 20, A-1030 ((C)) **01/ 242002;** www.konzerthaus.at). Early May through late June.

Vienna Festival (Wiener Festwochen). An exciting array of operas, operettas, musicals, theater, and dances, this festival presents new productions of classics alongside avant-garde premieres, all staged by international leading directors. Celebrated productions from renowned European theaters offer guest performances. Expect such productions as Mozart's *Così Fan Tutte*, Alban Berg's *Wozzek* or *Lulu; fresh* staging of classics on the same stage as ruthless *theatre avant-garde*. For bookings, contact Wiener Festwochen, Lehárgasse 11, A-1060 Vienna ((C)) **01/589-2222;** www.festwochen.at). Second week of May until mid-June.

JUNE

Midsummer Night Celebration. This celebration is held all over Austria, with bonfires and folkloric events. The liveliest observances are in the Tyrolean valley towns and in the Wachau region along the Danube in Austria. June 20.

Styriarte Graz. This grand annual cultural celebration features a different theme every year. For tickets and information, contact Styriarte Graz, Palais Attems, Sackstrasse 17, A-8010 Graz ((C)) **0316/8129410;** www.styriarte.com). Late June to mid-July.

Vienna Jazz Festival. This is one of the world's top jazz events, using the Vienna State Opera as its central venue. The program calls for appearances by more than 50 international and local stars. For information and bookings, contact the Verein Jazz Fest Wien, Lammgasse 12 ((C)) **01/7124224;** www. viennajazz.org). Late June to mid-July.

Life Ball. Since 1993 the city of Vienna has hosted this colossal AIDS gala, the largest of its kind. The motto is "Fighting AIDS and celebrating Life." The dress code: No tie at all, since the guests of this ball are meant to look as crazy and colorful as they please. Amazing dancers, performers, and hoards of international celebrities flock to this annual celebration in Vienna's City Hall (℃ **01/5955600;** www.Lifeball.org).

JULY

Vienna Summer of Music. This premier event fills the cultural calendar with concerts at City Hall, Schönbrunn Palace, and many landmark homes of great 19th-century Viennese musicians. Densely packed with options, the festival often features a series of different musical events on any given night. For tickets, schedules, and information, contact the Wiener Musiksommer, Laudongasse 4, A-1010 Vienna (℃ **01/ 400084722**). July 1 to late August.

Festival of Early Music, Innsbruck. Everything from baroque operas to recitals featuring historical instruments characterizes this annual event. Concerts are presented at the Hofburg, the Tiroler Landestheater, and the Castle Ambras. For tickets and information, contact the Innsbruck Festival, Burggraben 3, A-6020 Innsbruck (℃ **0512571032;** www.altemusik.at). Mid-July into August.

Bregenz Summer Festival. The cultural highlight of the summer is the appearance once again of the Vienna Symphony Orchestra and a world-class opera production on a stage floating the Bodensee. For information, contact the Bregenz Tourist Office, Platz der Wiener, Symphoniker 1, A-6900 Bregenz (℃ **05574/407;** www.bregenzerfestspiele.com). Mid-July to mid-August.

Salzburg Festival. Since the 1920s, this has been one of the premier cultural events of Europe, sparkling with opera, chamber music, plays, concerts, appearances by world-class artists, and many other cultural presentations. Always count on stagings of Mozart operas. Performances are held at various venues throughout the city. For tickets, write several months in advance to the Salzburg Festival, Postfach 140, A-5010 Salzburg

(℃ **0662/8045500;** www.salzburgfestival. at). Late July to late August.

Summer Stage, Vienna. Along the quays of the Donau Inlet, adjacent to the Friedensbrücke, midsummer is celebrated by hundreds of the young, the upwardly mobile, and the trendy who converge on the Danube Canal to enjoy the night air and one another's company. Temporary stages present a revolving program of live music and contemporary art installations. Adding to the revelry are the 20 or so seasonal bars that open their doors to the milling summer crowd every night from 5pm to 2am. July and August.

Music Film Festival. Opera, operetta, and masterful concert performances captured on celluloid are enjoyed free under a starry sky in front of the neo-Gothic City Hall on the Ringstrasse. Programs focus on works by Franz Schubert, Johannes Brahms, or other composers. For more information, contact Ideenagentur Austria, Opernring 1R, A-1010 Vienna (℃ **01/40008100;** www.wien-event.at). Mid-July to mid-September.

SEPTEMBER

Haydn Days, Eisenstadt, in Burgenland. Held in Eisenstadt, where Haydn lived for 40 years, this festival presents the composer's trios, quartets, symphonies, operas, and choral works. Venues include the Esterházy castle, local churches, and even the city's public parks. For tickets and information, contact the Burgenländische Haydn Festspiele, Schloss Esterházy, A-7000 Eisenstadt (℃ **02682/61866;** www.haydn festival.at). Early to mid-September.

International Bruckner Festival, Linz. This month-long festival features concerts, theatrical presentations, art exhibits, and fireworks. For tickets and information, contact Festspiele, Untere Donaulände 7, A-4010 Linz (℃ **0732/76122124;** www.brucknerhaus.linz. at). Mid-September to early October.

OCTOBER

Viennale. This film festival shows everything from the most daringly avant-garde to golden oldies of the (mostly European) silver screen. Check the program to see which films will be in English or have English subtitles. For tickets and information, contact the Wiener Festwochen Viennale,

Stiftgasse 6, A-1070 Vienna (© **01/ 5265947;** www.viennale.at). Throughout October.

Wien Modern, in its 22nd year in 2009, was founded by Claudio Abbado and is devoted to the performance of contemporary works in music. The emphasis is not just on Austrian composers—it has included works from Scandinavian and Baltic countries, Iceland, Romania, Portugal, and other nations. Some of the composers make live appearances and discuss their compositions. Concerts usually last 1½ to 2 hours. Performances are at Verein Wien Modern, Lothringerstrasse 20, A-1030 Vienna (© **01/242000**). For tickets (© **01/ 242002;** www.konzerthaus.at). Late October to late November.

NOVEMBER

Vienna Schubert Festival. This all-Schubert celebration marked its 27th annual observance in 2009. For information, contact Wiener Musikverein, Karlsplatz 6, A-1010 Vienna (© **01/5058190;** www.musikverein-wien.at). Third week of November.

DECEMBER

Christmas Markets. Between late November and New Year, look for pockets of folk charm (and, in some cases, kitsch), associated with the Christmas holidays. The so-called *Weihnachtsmärkte* consist of small outdoor booths, usually adorned with evergreen boughs, red ribbons, and, in some cases, religious symbols and sprout up in clusters around the city. They sell old-fashioned toys, *Tannenbaum* (Christmas tree) decorations, and gift items. Food vendors offer sausages, cookies and pastries, candied fruit, roasted chestnuts, *Kartoffelpuffer* (charcoal-roasted potato slices), and of course hot *Punsch* and mulled wine (*Glühwein*). The greatest concentration of open-air markets is in front of the Rathaus, the famous **Christkindlmarkt.** Other good ones are in the Spittelberg Quarter (7th District), at Freyung, the historic square in the northwest corner of the Inner City, or on the university campus grounds called *Altes AKH* (Old General Hospital).

ENTRY REQUIREMENTS

Passports

Citizens of the United States, Canada, the United Kingdom, Australia, Ireland, and New Zealand need only a valid passport to enter Austria. No visa is required for stays up to 90 days. If you lose your passport, visit the nearest consulate of your native country for a replacement as soon as possible. It's always a good idea to have a photocopy of your passport to expedite replacement.

Customs

WHAT YOU CAN BRING INTO AUSTRIA

Visitors who live outside Austria in general are not liable for duty on personal articles brought into the country temporarily for their own use, depending on the purpose and circumstances of each trip. Customs officials have great leeway. Travelers 17 years of age and older may carry up to 200 cigarettes, 50 cigars, or 250 grams of tobacco; 1 liter of distilled liquor; and 2 liters of wine or 3 liters of beer duty-free. Also cash amounts above 10,000 € must be declared at customs.

WHAT YOU CAN TAKE HOME FROM AUSTRIA

U.S. CITIZENS   Returning U.S. citizens who have been away for 48 hours or more are allowed to bring back, once every 30 days, $800 worth of merchandise duty-free. You'll pay a flat rate of 10% duty on the next $1,000 worth of purchases. Be sure to have your receipts handy. On gifts, the duty-free limit is $200. For more specific guidance, contact the **Customs & Border Protection (CBP)** (© **877/287-8667;**

www.cbp.gov), and request the free pamphlet "Know Before You Go." Download the pamphlet from the Internet at **www.cbp.gov**.

U.K. CITIZENS United Kingdom citizens can buy wine, spirits, or cigarettes in an ordinary shop in Austria and bring home almost as much as they like. But if you buy goods in a duty-free shop, the old rules still apply—the allowance is 200 cigarettes and 2 liters of table wine, plus 1 liter of spirits or 2 liters of fortified wine. If you're returning home from a non-European Union country, the same allowances apply, and you must declare any goods in excess of these allowances. British Customs tends to be strict and complicated. For details, get in touch with **H.M. Revenue & Customs** (© **0845/010-9000;** www.hmrc.gov.uk).

CANADIAN CITIZENS For a clear summary of Canadian rules, write for the booklet "I Declare," issued by **Canada Border Services Agency** (© **800/461-9999** in Canada, or 204/983-3500; www.cbsa-asfc.gc.ca). Canada allows its citizens a C$750 exemption, and you're allowed to bring back, duty-free, 200 cigarettes, 200 grams of tobacco, 1.5 liters of liquor, and 50 cigars. In addition, you may mail gifts to Canada from abroad at the rate of C$60 a day, provided they are unsolicited and aren't alcohol or tobacco (write on the package: "Unsolicited gift, under $60 value"). Before departure from Canada, declare all valuables on the Y-38 form, including serial numbers of, for example, expensive foreign cameras that you already own. *Note:* The C$750 exemption can be used only once a year and only after an absence of 7 days.

AUSTRALIAN CITIZENS The duty-free allowance in Australia is A$900 or, for those under age 18, A$450. Personal property mailed back from Austria should be marked "Australian goods returned" to avoid duties. Upon returning to Australia, citizens can bring in 250 cigarettes or 250 grams of loose tobacco, and 2.25 liters of alcohol. If you're returning with valuable goods you already own, such as foreign-made cameras, you should file form B263. A brochure, available from Australian consulates or customs offices, is "Know Before You Go." For more information, contact **Australian Customs Services,** GPO Box 8, Sydney NSW 2001 (© **1300/363-263** in Australia; www.customs.gov.au).

NEW ZEALAND CITIZENS The duty-free allowance for New Zealand is NZ$700. Citizens over 17 years of age can bring in 200 cigarettes, 50 cigars, or 250 grams of tobacco (or a mixture of all three if their combined weight doesn't exceed 250 grams), plus 4.5 liters of wine and beer or 1.125 liters of liquor. New Zealand currency does not carry import or export restrictions. Fill out a certificate of export, listing the valuables you are taking out of the country; that way, you can bring them back without paying duty. Ask for the free pamphlet available at New Zealand consulates and customs offices, "New Zealand Customs Guide for Travellers, Notice no. 4." For more information, contact **New Zealand Customs Services** (© **0800/428-786** or 04/473-786; www.customs.govt.nz).

GETTING THERE & GETTING AROUND

Getting There

BY PLANE

As a gateway between western and eastern Europe, Vienna International Airport (VIE) has seen an increase in air traffic. Although a number of well-respected European airlines serve Vienna, many flights from America or Canada require a transfer in another European city, such as Paris, London, Zurich, or Frankfurt. Flights from Australia and New Zealand often have two stops, one in Asia and one in a larger European capital.

If you're planning to travel to western Austria—Innsbruck, Salzburg, Tyrol, Vorarlberg, and parts of Land Salzburg—keep in mind that these destinations are closer to Munich than to Vienna. It might be easier to fly to Munich and then rent a car or take a train to your final destination.

Also, if your destination lies somewhat off the beaten track, note that more connections are possible into the secondary airports of Austria from Frankfurt than from any other non-Austrian city. These connections are usually made by Lufthansa, Austrian Airlines, or Tyrolean Air, or on flights maintained cooperatively by some combination of those three.

Most flights from London to Vienna depart from London's Heathrow Airport. The flight takes 2 hours and 20 minutes.

The Major Airlines

FROM THE UNITED STATES   You can fly directly to Vienna on **Austrian Airlines** (𝄢 **800/843-0002** in the U.S. and Canada; www.austrianair.com), the national carrier of Austria. There are nonstop services from New York, Washington, and Toronto (approximately 9 hr.). Austrian's partner, United Airlines, also serves this route (𝄢 **800/UNITED 1;** www.united.com).

British Airways (𝄢 **800/AIRWAYS** in the U.S. and Canada; www.british airways.com) provides excellent service to Vienna via London.

Flights on **Lufthansa** (𝄢 **800/645-3880** in the U.S. and Canada; www. lufthansa.com), the German national carrier, depart from North America for Frankfurt and Düsseldorf, with frequent connections to Vienna.

American Airlines (𝄢 **800/433-7300** in the U.S. and Canada; www.aa.com) funnels Vienna-bound passengers through Zurich or London.

FROM CANADA   You can usually connect from your hometown to **British Airways** (𝄢 **800/AIRWAYS** in Canada; www.britishairways.com) gateways in Toronto, Montreal, and Vancouver. Nonstop flights from both Toronto's Pearson Airport and Montreal's Mirabelle Airport depart every day for London; flights from Vancouver depart for London three times a week. In London, you can stay for a few days (arranging discounted hotel accommodations through the British Airways tour desk) or head directly to Vienna on any of the two to five daily nonstop flights from either Heathrow or Gatwick.

FROM THE U.K.   There are frequent flights to Vienna, the majority of which depart from London's Heathrow Airport. Flight time is 2 hours and 20 minutes.

   Security Measures

Because of increased security measures, the Transportation Security Administration has made changes to the prohibited items list. All liquids and gels—including shampoo, toothpaste, perfume, hair gel, suntan lotion, and all other items with similar consistency— are limited to 100 ml containers packed in a separate clear bag within your carry-on baggage at the security checkpoint. Check the **Transportation Security Administration** site, www.tsa. gov, for any updates.

Austrian Airlines (② **0870/124-2625** from the U.K.; www.austrianair.com) has four daily nonstop flights into Vienna from Heathrow.

British Airways (② **0870/850-9850** in London; www.britishairways.com) offers three daily nonstops from Heathrow and two from Gatwick, with easy connections through London from virtually every other part of Britain.

BY CAR

If you're already on the Continent, you might want to drive to Austria. That is especially true if you're in a neighboring country, such as Italy or Germany; however, international arrangements should be made in advance with your car-rental company.

Inaugurated in 1994, the Chunnel running under the English Channel cuts driving time between England and France to 35 minutes. Passengers drive their cars aboard the Eurostar at St. Pancras, or Le Shuttle, at Folkestone in England, and vehicles are transported to Calais, France. Your continuing journey to Austria can also be partly covered by train. The auto accommodations are reasonably priced and easy to use.

Vienna can be reached from all directions on major highways called *Autobahnen* or by secondary highways. The main artery from the west is Autobahn A-1, coming in from Munich (466km/291 miles), Salzburg (334km/207 miles), and Linz (186km/115 miles). Autobahn A-2 runs from the south, from Graz and Klagenfurt (both in Austria). Autobahn A-4 comes in from the east, connecting with route E-58, which runs to Bratislava and Prague. Autobahn A-22 takes traffic from the northwest, and Route E-10 brings you to the cities and towns of southeastern Austria and Hungary.

Unless otherwise marked, the speed limit on *Autobahnen* is 130km/h (81 mph); however, when estimating driving times, figure on 80–100km/h (50–62 mph) because of traffic, weather, and road conditions.

When you arrive in the capital, park your car or find a garage (p. 99), because in Vienna decoding the one-way streets and sorting out parking is no fun at all.

BY TRAIN

If you plan to travel a lot on the European or British railroads on your way to or from Austria, you'd do well to secure the latest copy of the *Thomas Cook European Timetable of Railroads*. It's available exclusively online at **www.thomascooktime tables.com**.

Vienna has rail links to all the major cities of Europe. From Paris, a daily train leaves the Gare de l'Est at 7:49am, arriving in Vienna at 9:18pm. From Munich, a train leaves daily at 9:24am, arriving in Vienna at 2:18pm, and at 11:19pm, arriving in Vienna at 6:47am. From Zurich, a 9:33pm train arrives in Vienna at 6:45am.

Rail travel in Austria is superb, with fast, clean trains taking you just about anywhere in the country and through some incredibly scenic regions.

Train passengers using the **Chunnel** under the English Channel can go from London to Paris in just 3 hours and then on to Vienna (see above). Le Shuttle covers the 50-km (31-mile) journey in just 35 minutes. The train also accommodates passenger cars, charter buses, taxis, and motorcycles through a tunnel from Folkestone, England, to Calais, France. Service is year-round, 24 hours a day.

Rail Passes for North American Travelers

EURAILPASS If you plan to travel extensively in Europe, the **Eurail Global Pass** might be a good bet. It's valid for first-class rail travel in 20 European countries. With one ticket, you travel whenever and wherever you please; more than 100,000 rail miles are at your disposal. Here's how it works: The pass is sold only in North

America. A Eurailpass good for 15 days costs $669, a pass for 21 days is $869, a 1-month pass costs $1,085, a 2-month pass is $1,529, and a 3-month pass goes for $1,889. Children under 4 travel free if they don't occupy a seat; all children under 12 who take up a seat are charged half-price. If you're under 26, you can buy a **Eurail Global Pass Youth,** which entitles you to unlimited second-class travel for 15 days ($435), 21 days ($565), 1 month ($705), 2 months ($995), or 3 months ($1,229). Travelers considering buying a 15-day or 1-month pass should estimate rail distance before deciding whether a pass is worthwhile. To take full advantage of the tickets for 15 days or a month, you'd have to spend a great deal of time on the train. Eurailpass holders are entitled to substantial discounts on certain buses and ferries as well. Travel agents in all towns and railway agents in such major cities as New York, Montreal, and Los Angeles sell all of these tickets. For information on Eurailpasses and other European train data, call **RailEurope** at ✆ **877/272-RAIL,** or visit it on the Web at **www.eurail.com**.

Eurail Global Pass Saver offers a 15% discount to each person in a group of three or more people traveling together between April and September, or two people traveling together between October and March. The price of a Saverpass, valid all over Europe for first class only, is $569 for 15 days, $739 for 21 days, $919 for 1 month, $1,299 for 2 months, and $1,609 for 3 months. Even more freedom is offered by the **Saver Flexipass,** which is similar to the Eurail Saverpass, except that you are not confined to consecutive-day travel. For travel over any 10 days within 2 months, the fare is $675; for any 15 days over 2 months, the fare is $889.

The **Eurail Select Pass** offers unlimited travel on the national rail networks of any three, four, or five bordering countries out of the 23 Eurail nations linked by train or ship. Two or more passengers can travel together for big discounts, getting 5, 6, 8, 10, or 15 days of rail travel within any 2-month period on the national rail networks of any three, four, or five adjoining Eurail countries linked by train or ship. A sample fare: For 5 days in 2 months you pay US$425 for three countries. **Eurail Select Pass Youth** for travelers under 26 allows second-class travel within the same guidelines as Eurail Selectpass, with fees starting at US$275. **Eurail Select Pass Saver** offers discounts for two or more people traveling together, first-class travel within the same guidelines as Eurail Select Pass, starting at US$359.

Rail Passes for European Travelers

If you plan to do a lot of exploring, you might prefer one of the three rail passes designed for unlimited train travel within a designated region during a predetermined number of days. These passes are sold in most European countries and can be used only by European residents.

The **InterRail Global Pass** (www.interrail.net) allows unlimited travel through 30 European countries, including non-E.U. members Switzerland, Norway, and the Balkans, excepting Albania. Adults purchasing an InterRail Global Pass can travel first or second class. In first class, prices are 374€ for 5 days in 10 days; 539€ for 10 days in 22 days; 704€ for 22 days continuous; or 899€ for 1 month. In second class, the cost is 249€ for 5 days in 10 days; 359€ for 10 days in 22 days; 469€ for 22 days continuous; and 599€ for 1 month continuous.

An **InterRail Global Youth Pass** is also sold and is available only in second class. A youth is defined as from age 12 up to and including 25 years of age. The cost is 159€ for 5 days in 10 days; 239€ for 10 days in 22 days; 309€ for 22 days continuous; and 399€ for 1 month continuous.

For information on buying individual rail tickets or any of the just-mentioned passes, contact any larger train station in Europe or simply the Austria ÖBB (Österreichische

Bundesbahn). Tickets and passes are also available at any of the larger railway stations, as well as selected travel agencies throughout Europe. For more savings ask for any special rates and accommodations on Euro city or inter-city trains that go from capital city to capital city.

BY BUS

Because of the excellent rail service funneling from all parts of the Continent into Vienna, bus travel is limited and not especially popular. **Eurolines,** part of National Express Coach Lines (© **0871/781-8181;** www.nationalexpress.com), operates two express buses per week between London's Victoria Coach Station and Vienna. The trip takes about 29 hours and makes 45-minute rest stops en route about every 4 hours. Buses depart from London at 8:15am every Friday and Sunday, traverse the Channel between Dover and Calais, and are equipped with reclining seats, toilets, and reading lights. The one-way fare is 52€ to 72€; a round-trip ticket costs 80€ to 104€. You won't need to declare your intended date of return until you actually use your ticket (although advance reservations are advisable), and the return half of your ticket will be valid for 6 months. The return to London departs from Vienna every Sunday and Friday at 7:45pm, arriving at Victoria Coach Station about 29 hours later.

Getting Around

BY TRAIN

Rail travel is superb in Austria, with fast, clean trains taking you through scenic regions. Trains will take you nearly every place in Austria except to remote hamlets tucked away in almost inaccessible mountain districts. Many other services tie in with railroad travel, among them car or bicycle rental at many stations, bus transportation links, and package tours, including boat trips and cable-car rides. Inter-City Express trains connect Vienna with all major cities in the country, including Salzburg, Klagenfurt, Graz, and Linz. A train trip from Salzburg to Vienna takes about 3 hours.

Rail Passes

See "Getting There," earlier in this chapter, for information on the **Eurail** and **Inter-Rail** passes, which are valid in Austria.

Other Railway Data

For information on short-distance round-trip tickets, cross-country passes, and passes for all lines in the individual provinces, as well as piggyback transportation for your car through the Tauern Tunnel, check with the **Austrian Federal Railways** (Österreichische Bundesbahn, ÖBB; © **01/930-000;** www.oebb.at).

BY CAR

Driving, of course, is the best way to crisscross Austria, going up and down its scenic mountain valleys and along its vast mountain passes. It's one of the greatest countries in the world for scenery. That applies only to the summer months. Driving conditions in Austria can be difficult in winter.

Renting a car is not the most economical way to see the country; by train or bus is cheaper.

Some mountain roads require a toll. The good news is that there is almost no delay at border crossings. Motorists zip about casually—say, between Germany and Austria—but in the wake of worldwide terrorism, conditions can often change at a moment's notice for reasons you will not be aware of.

All main roads in Austria are hard-surfaced. There's a four-lane Autobahn between Salzburg and Vienna; and between Vienna and Edlitz the Autobahn has six lanes. Part of the highway system includes mountain roads; and in the alpine region drivers face gradients of 6 to 16%, or even steeper in some places. When driving in Austria, always plot your course carefully. If you have had no experience in mountain driving—much less alpine mountain driving—you might want to take a train or a bus to get to the loftier alpine retreats.

In summer, driving conditions are good, but in winter, December through March, motorists must reckon with snow on the roads and passes at higher altitudes. Roads at altitudes of up to 1,700m (5,577 ft.) are kept open in winter, although they can be temporarily closed because of heavy snowfall or avalanche danger. If you're planning to drive in Austria in winter, you'll need snow tires or chains.

Don't take chances. Ask about road conditions before you start on a trip. This information is available in English 7 days a week from 6am to 8pm from the **Österreichischer Automobil-, Motorrad- und Touringclub (ÖAMTC),** Schubertring 1–3, Vienna (✆ **0810/120-120;** www.oeamtc.at).

Rentals

Drivers in Austria must have been in possession of a valid driver's license for at least 1 year before renting a vehicle. They must also present a valid passport when they sign the rental agreement. Drivers not in possession of a major credit card must pay in advance a minimum deposit, plus the estimated rental cost and the estimated tax. Cars rented from most rental companies can be dropped off in major cities of Germany for no additional charge. Drop-offs in Switzerland or Italy require an extra charge, which can be quite high.

Be aware that car rentals in Austria are taxed at a whopping rate of 21.2%. This is in addition to a 15% municipal airport tax added to the cost of any car rented at an airport. Clarify in advance whether the rates you're quoted include the taxes. *Tip:* You might consider taking a taxi to your hotel upon arrival and then renting your vehicle from an inner-city location to avoid the 15% airport surcharge.

When you reserve a car, be sure to ask if the price includes insurance. The rental outfits offer an optional insurance policy known as a loss-damage waiver (LDW). If you accept it, you'll be charged from 25€ per day. It allows you to waive all financial responsibility for any damage to your car, even if it's eventually determined that you were the driver at fault. In some instances, certain credit card companies offer free insurance if you use their card to pay for the rental. Check directly with your credit card issuer to see if you are covered.

Budget Rentacar (✆ **800/472-3325;** www.budget.com) is among the least expensive options in Austria. It maintains more than a dozen locations throughout the country, including branches at all the major airports and at downtown locations in most of the provincial capitals.

Hertz Care Hire (✆ **800/654-3001;** www.hertz.com) maintains offices in about 18 cities throughout Austria. During limited periods, it sometimes publicizes price promotions worth inquiring about, depending on the season, as well as discounts to employees of some large North American corporations.

Avis Car Rental (✆ **800/331-1084;** www.avis.com) operates offices in 19 Austrian cities, at airports and downtown, as well as at some of the country's larger ski resorts. Avis usually offers 10% discounts for members of such organizations as AAA and AARP. Like Budget and Hertz, it offers seasonal price promotions.

Kemwel Drive Europe (✆ **877/820-0668;** www.kemwel.com) has offices in about 10 cities throughout Austria.

AutoEurope (✆ **888/223-5555;** www.autoeurope.com) operates 12 offices in Austrian cities as well as airports.

Gasoline

A gas (petrol) station is a *Tankstelle*, in German. They sell super, normal, and diesel. Prices per liter range from .85€ to 1.50€, so it pays to shop around for gas and the farther from the city center the lower the price. Taxes are already included in the printed price. One U.S. gallon equals 3.8 liters, and 1 imperial gallon equals 4.4 liters.

Driving Rules

Traffic regulations are similar to those in other European countries, where you *drive on the right*. Driving under the influence of alcohol is severely punished. The permissible blood-alcohol level is very low—two beers or 8 ounces of wine can put you over the mark. The *minimum* fine is 350€ and possible loss of a driver's license. Hence public transit, the salvation of lovers of the good life! If you drink, just take the tram!

Use of seat belts is compulsory, and children under 12 may not sit in the front passenger seat unless a child's seat belt or a special seat has been installed. The use of hand-held cellphones is prohibited while driving, and a right turn at a red light is **not** permitted. Effective from late 2005, headlights must be on at all times of day in bad weather.

Automobile Clubs

The leading auto club of Austria is the **ÖAMTC** (Österreichischer Automobil-, Motorrad- und Touringclub), Schubertring 1–3, A-1010 Vienna (✆ **0810/120-120;** www.oeamtc.at), in association with AAA. **ARBÖ** (✆ **050/123-123;** www.arboe.at) is another.

Breakdowns/Assistance

If your car breaks down, foreign motorists can call the two auto clubs mentioned above. Call **ARBÖ** (✆ **123**) or **ÖAMTC** (✆ **120**) anywhere in Austria. You don't need to use an area code for either number. However, if you're not a member of either of these clubs, you'll pay for emergency road service.

Motorcycles

The same requirements for operating cars in Austria hold for operating motorcycles. Both drivers and passengers of motorcycles must wear crash helmets. Lights must be kept on in bad weather, even in the daytime.

BY TAXI

Taxis are easy to find in Vienna. Taxi stands are marked by signs, or you can call ✆ **01/31300,** 01/60160, 01/713-7196, or 01/40100. The basic fare is 2.50€, plus 1.20€ per kilometer. The fare for trips to or from the airport is 33€ from anywhere in Vienna.

Each other region will have its own taxi companies, but in general fare prices are the same. There are extra charges of 1€ for luggage in the back of the car. For night rides after 11pm, and for trips on Sunday and holidays, there is a surcharge of 2.50€. There is an additional charge of 2.50€ if ordered by phone, however you avoid this by walking to a taxi stand, which you can find in almost any neighborhood. Otherwise the fare for longer trips should be agreed upon in advance, and a 10% tip is the norm.

BY PLANE

Austrian Airlines (✆ **800/843-0002** in the U.S. and Canada; www.austrianair.com) offers flights that link Vienna to the country's leading cities. Outgoing flights from Vienna are carefully timed to coincide with the arrivals of most of the company's transatlantic flights.

Getting There & Getting Around | PLANNING YOUR TRIP TO AUSTRIA

Tyrolean Airways (same telephone number and website as Austrian Airlines) is a wholly owned subsidiary of Austrian Airlines, and offers a very useful airborne network whose home base is the Tyrolean capital of Innsbruck. Its regular flight network consists of up to four flights per day between Vienna and Innsbruck, and four flights each between Innsbruck and both Frankfurt and Zurich. The airline also offers about five flights a week between Innsbruck and the Styrian capital of Graz. Reservations on Tyrolean Airways can be made through Austrian Airlines. Its fleet consists almost entirely of turbo-prop planes containing no more than 49 seats. The airline specializes in domestic flights and commuter runs to destinations close to the border, including Munich and Budapest.

BY BUS

It's easiest to get around Austria on the country's excellent rail network, but many Austrian villages are not near rail lines. Reaching some of these areas can be best accomplished by car or bus. To facilitate travel, the Austrian government maintains two different bus networks: Those maintained by the **Austrian Postal Service** (whose vehicles, in most cases, are painted a reddish-orange) and those maintained by the **Austrian Federal Railways** (Bundesbus, which have numbers ending in B, i.e. 22B). In recent years, efforts have been made to merge both of these systems into one overall administration identified as the **Bundesbus System,** but they still service slightly different routes. There are also a limited number of privately owned bus companies that specialize in long-haul transits to major cities outside Austria.

Buses (some of which also carry mail) cover a network of almost 30,500km (18,952 miles) of often very remote secondary roads. One of their primary functions involves retrieving passengers at railway stations for the continuation of journeys. Bus departures are usually timed to coincide with the arrival of trains from other parts of Austria. Buses are particularly helpful at the bottom of alpine valleys, where transit is needed to carry passengers from the local railway station up toward ski resorts and hamlets at higher altitudes. Children under 6 travel free on many of these buses, and children under 15 usually receive a 50% discount.

Information about bus schedules and routings is available at most post offices, at the reception desks of most hotels whose business relies on clients arriving by bus, and at travel agencies. Specifics about routes and schedules are in the *Kursbuch* (Austrian Motor Coach Schedule), a timetable that is usually updated annually and that forms part of the basic library maintained by virtually every tourist office in Austria. Bus information is usually also merged into the thousands of railway timetables that are posted at train stations throughout the country. An especially convenient way to find out about bus schedules, if you're heading to a hotel in a remote area, is to call the hotel and ask.

BY BICYCLE

From April to the beginning of November, you can rent a bicycle at some 120 rail stations across Austria. Charges vary but are nominal, with a 50% discount if you present a rail ticket for the day that you're renting a bike. Photo ID must be presented at the time of rental. You can reserve a bicycle in advance, but you can almost always get a bike without making reservations. The vehicle can be returned to where it was rented or to any other Austrian railroad station during business hours.

MONEY & COSTS

Foreign currency and euros can be brought in and out of Vienna under the amount of 10,000€ without any restrictions. Although there are many ways to change currency, nowadays it can also be simplest and cheapest to get euros from an ATM using your debit or credit card from home.

The **euro,** the single European currency, is the official currency of Austria and 15 other participating countries. The symbol of the euro is a stylized E: €. Exchange rates of participating countries are locked into a common currency. For more details and exchange rates with the euro, check out **www.europa.eu.int**.

The relative value of the euro fluctuates against the world's other currencies, therefore its value might not be the same by the time you travel to Vienna. We advise a last-minute check before your trip.

Exchange rates are more favorable at the point of arrival than at the point of departure. Nevertheless, it's often helpful to exchange at least some money before going abroad (standing in line at the exchange bureau in the Vienna airport isn't fun after a long overseas flight). Check with any of your local American Express or Thomas Cook offices or major banks. Or, order in advance from **American Express** (ⓒ **800/221-7282,** cardholders only; www.americanexpress.com) or **Thomas Cook** (ⓒ **800/223-7373;** www.thomascook.com).

It's best to exchange currency or traveler's checks at a bank, not at a currency service, hotel, or shop. Currency and traveler's checks (for which you'll receive a better rate than cash) can be changed at all principal airports and at some travel agencies, such as American Express and Thomas Cook; **www.europa.eu.int/euro**.

ATMs

ATMs are prevalent in all Austrian cities and even smaller towns. ATMs are linked to a national network that most likely includes your bank at home. Though there will be small fees for extracting money in a foreign country, the fees will not be as high as when changing cash anywhere but an Austrian bank. Both the **Cirrus** (ⓒ **800/424-7787;** www.mastercard.com) and the **PLUS** (ⓒ **800/843-7587;** www.visa.com) networks have automated ATM locators listing the banks in Austria that'll accept your card. Or, just search out any machine with your network's symbol emblazoned on it.

Traveler's Checks

You can buy traveler's checks at most banks. In the United States they are offered in denominations of $20, $50, $100, $500, and sometimes $1,000. Generally, you'll pay a service charge ranging from 1 to 4%.

The most popular traveler's checks are offered by **American Express** (ⓒ **800/528-4800** or 800/221-7282 for cardholders—this number accepts collect calls, offers

---

Emergency Cash—The Fastest Way

If you need emergency cash over the weekend, when all banks and American Express offices are closed, you can have money wired to you from **Western Union** (ⓒ **800/325-6000;** www.westernunion.com). You must present valid ID to pick up the cash at the Western Union office. However, in most countries, you can pick up a money transfer even if you don't have valid identification, as long as you can answer a test question provided by the sender. Be sure to let the sender know in advance that you don't have ID. If you need to use a test question instead of ID, the sender must take cash to his or her local Western Union office rather than transfer the money over the phone or online. However, this can also make the transaction safer.

THE EURO, THE U.S. & CANADIAN DOLLAR & THE BRITISH POUND

The U.S. Dollar and the Euro: At the time of writing, US$1 was worth approximately .764€. Inversely stated, 1€ was worth approximately US$1.35.

The British Pound, the U.S. Dollar, and the Euro: At the time of writing, £1 equaled approximately US$1.60, and approximately 1.19€.

The Canadian Dollar, the U.S. Dollar, and the Euro: At the time of writing, C$1 equaled approximately US$1 and approximately .714€.

The chart inserted below reflects the figures in the paragraphs above, but because international currency ratios can and almost certainly will change prior to your arrival in Europe, you should confirm up-to-date currency rates shortly before you go.

Euro	US$/C$	Can$	UK£	Aus$	NZ$
1	1.35	1.38	0.85	1.40	1.80
2	2.60	2.75	1.70	2.80	3.60
3	4.00	4.10	2.60	4.20	5.50
4	5.40	5.50	3.40	5.60	7.30
5	6.70	6.90	4.30	7.00	9.20
6	8.00	8.30	5.10	8.40	11.00
7	9.40	9.70	6.00	9.80	12.85
8	10.70	11.00	6.80	11.20	14.70
9	12.00	12.40	7.70	12.60	16.50
10	13.00	14.00	9.00	14.00	18.00
15	20.00	21.00	13.00	21.00	28.00
20	27.00	28.00	17.00	28.00	37.00
25	34.00	35.00	21.00	35.00	46.00
50	67.00	69.00	43.00	70.00	92.00

service in several foreign languages, and exempts Amex gold and platinum cardholders from the 1% fee); **Visa** (℃ **800/732-1322**)—AAA members can obtain Visa checks for a $9.95 fee (for checks up to $1,500) at most AAA offices or by calling ℃ **866/339-3378**; and **MasterCard** (℃ **800/223-9920**).

American Express, Thomas Cook, Visa, and **MasterCard** offer **foreign currency traveler's checks,** which are useful if you're traveling to one country, or to the Euro zone; they're accepted at locations where dollar checks may not be.

If you carry traveler's checks, keep a record of their serial numbers separate from your checks in the event that they are stolen or lost. You'll get a refund faster if you know the numbers.

Credit Cards

Credit cards are invaluable when traveling—they're a safe way to carry money and a convenient record of all your expenses. You can also withdraw cash advances from

WHAT THINGS COST IN VIENNA	EURO€	US$/C$	UK£
Bus from the airport to the city center	6.00	7.85	5.00
U-Bahn (subway) from St. Stephan's to Schönbrunn Palace	1.80	2.35	1.50
Double room at das Triest (expensive)	289.00	377.80	241.45
Double room at the Am Parkring (moderate)	133.00	174.00	111.00
Double room at the Pension Dr. Geissler (inexpensive)	65.00	104.00	52.00
Lunch for one, without wine, at König von Ungarn (expensive)	40.00	52.00	33.50
Lunch for one, without wine, at Griechenbeisl (moderate)	30.00	39.20	25.00
Dinner for one, without wine, at Plachutta (expensive)	40.00	52.00	33.50
Dinner for one, without wine, at Motto am Fluss (moderate)	28.00	36.60	23.40
Dinner for one, without wine, at Café Leopold (inexpensive)	12.00	15.60	10.00
Glass of wine	2.50	3.25	2.00
Half-liter of beer in a *beisl*	3.50	7.00	3.50
Coca-Cola in a cafe	3.00	3.90	2.50
Cup of coffee (*ein kleiner Brauner*)	3.00	3.90	2.50
Movie ticket	10.00	13.00	8.30
Admission to Schönbrunn Palace	12.90	17.00	10.80

your cards at any bank (although this should be reserved for dire emergencies only, because you'll start paying hefty interest the moment you receive the cash).

Note, however, that many banks, including Chase and Citibank, charge a 2 to 3% service fee for transactions in a foreign currency.

STAYING HEALTHY

You'll encounter few health problems while traveling in Austria. The tap water is generally safe to drink, the milk is pasteurized, and health services are good. And the food supply is the most fiercely protected in Europe. Occasionally, simply the change in diet and water could cause some minor disturbances, so you might want to talk to your doctor.

There is no need to get any shots before visiting Austria. Just to be prepared, you might pack some anti-diarrhea medications. It's not that the food or water in Austria is unhealthy; it's just different and might cause digestive problems for the unfamiliar.

It's easy to get over-the-counter medicine. Fortunately, generic equivalents of common prescription drugs are available at most destinations in which you'll be traveling. It's also easy to find English-speaking doctors and to get prescriptions filled at all cities, towns, and resorts. In addition, pharmacists are licensed to recommend many treatments that might require prescriptions in other countries. So ask. However, you might experience some inconvenience, of course, if you travel in the remote hinterlands.

Regional Health Concerns

Some concerns might arise if you're planning strenuous activities at higher altitudes. All of us, of course, are affected by a lack of oxygen at altitudes more than 2,500m (8,202 ft.). Symptoms of **altitude sickness** are often a severe headache, a feeling of nausea, dizziness, loss of appetite, and lack of sleep.

In a nutshell, high-altitude sickness most often occurs when you go too high too fast. The body needs time to acclimatize itself as you climb to higher regions. This is an extremely complicated subject, and if you plan to climb the high peaks, you may want to read the Princeton University study at **www.princeton.edu/~oa/safety/altitude.html**.

In winter, higher elevations might also cause **frostbite.** Wet clothes, the wind chill factor, and extreme cold can cause frostbite. Some people with poor circulation, such as those who suffer from diabetes, are particularly vulnerable. Precautions are advised—no smoking, no drinking, good food, and rest. As you proceed higher and higher, wear multiple layers of clothing, especially waterproof synthetics. Survive Outdoors Inc. has frostbite prevention advice at **www.surviveoutdoors.com/reference/frostbite.asp**.

Snow blindness is caused by the exposure of your unprotected eyes to the ultraviolet rays of the sun. This often happens in conditions of great snow or ice, mostly at higher altitudes. It is usually prevented by wearing dark-lensed "glacier glasses," of the wraparound, side-shielded variety. Wear these glasses even if the sky is overcast, as ultraviolet rays can pass through masses of cloud formations.

If You Get Sick

Nearly all doctors in Austria speak English. If you get sick, consider asking your hotel concierge to recommend a local doctor—even his or her own. You can also try the emergency room at a local hospital. Many hospitals also have walk-in clinics for emergency cases that are not life-threatening; you may not get immediate attention, but you won't pay the high price of an emergency room visit. We list hospitals and emergency numbers under the "Fast Facts" section in the various city chapters.

If you worry about getting sick away from home, consider purchasing **medical travel insurance,** and carry your ID card in your purse or wallet. In most cases, your existing health plan will provide the coverage you need. See the section on insurance, above, for more information.

If you suffer from a chronic illness, consult your doctor before you depart. For conditions such as epilepsy, diabetes, or heart problems, wear a **MedicAlert Identification Tag** (℃ **888/633-4298;** www.medicalert.org), which will immediately alert doctors to your condition and give them access to your records through MedicAlert's 24-hour hotline.

Contact the **International Association for Medical Assistance to Travelers** (**IAMAT**; ☎ **716/754-4883** or 416/652-0137; www.iamat.org) for tips on travel and health concerns in the countries you're visiting and lists of local, English-speaking doctors. The U.S. **Center for Disease Control and Prevention** (☎ **800/311-3435** or 404/498-1515; www.cdc.gov) provides up-to-date information on necessary vaccines and health hazards by region or country. In Canada, check **Health Canada** at ☎ **613/957-2991**; www.hc.sc.gc.ca.

Travel Health Online (www.tripprep.com), sponsored by a consortium of travel medicine practitioners, may also offer helpful advice on traveling abroad. You can find listings of reliable medical clinics overseas at the **International Society of Travel Medicine** (www.istm.org).

U.K. nationals will need a **European Health Insurance Card** (**EHIC**; ☎ **0845/606-2030**; www.ehic.org.uk) to receive free or reduced-cost health benefits during a visit to a European Economic Area (EEA) country (European Union countries plus Iceland, Liechtenstein, and Norway) or Switzerland.

We list **hospitals** and **emergency numbers** under "Fast Facts: Austria," p. 478.

CRIME & SAFETY

Austria has a low crime rate, and violent crime is rare. However, travelers can become targets of pickpockets and purse-snatchers who operate where tourists tend to gather. Some of the most frequently reported spots include Vienna's train stations, the plaza around St. Stephan's Cathedral, and the nearby pedestrian shopping areas (in Vienna's 1st District). Just pay attention, keep your bag zipped or closed, and the thieves won't have a chance.

Mostly, however, Vienna is a very safe city and even at night there is little to worry about in the center of town, or where most of tourist life takes place.

Report the loss or theft of your passport immediately to the local police and the nearest embassy or consulate. The same is true when you have been a victim of crime overseas. The embassy/consulate staff, for example, can assist you in finding appropriate medical care, contacting family members or friends, and explaining how funds could be transferred. Although the investigation and prosecution of the crime is solely the responsibility of local authorities, consular officers can help you understand the local criminal justice process and find a lawyer, if needed.

MOUNTAIN SAFETY   For information and safety tips for hikers and others planning to venture into the mountains, see "Hiking & Mountaineering," under "Special Interest & Escorted Trips," below.

SPECIALIZED TRAVEL RESOURCES

Travelers with Disabilities

Laws in Austria compel rail stations, airports, hotels, and most restaurants to follow strict regulations about **wheelchair accessibility** for restrooms (toilets), ticket counters, and the like. Museums and other attractions conform to the regulations. However, old buildings with historic preservation laws may not be equipped. Call ahead to check on accessibility in hotels, restaurants, or sights you want to visit.

Organizations that offer assistance to travelers with disabilities include **Moss-Rehab** (✆ **800/CALL-MOSS;** www.mossresourcenet.org), which provides a library of accessible-travel resources online; **SATH** (**Society for Accessible Travel & Hospitality;** ✆ **212/447-7284;** www.sath.org), which offers a wealth of travel resources for all types of disabilities and informed recommendations on destinations, access guides, travel agents, tour operators, vehicle rentals, and companion services; and the **American Foundation for the Blind** (AFB; ✆ **800/232-5463** or 212/502-7600; www.afb.org), a referral resource for the blind or visually impaired that provides information on traveling with Seeing Eye dogs.

AirAmbulanceCard.com (✆ **877/424-7633**) is now partnered with SATH and allows you to preselect top-notch hospitals in case of an emergency.

Access-Able Travel Source (✆ **303/232-2979;** www.access-able.com) offers a comprehensive database on travel agents from around the world with experience in accessible travel; destination-specific information; and links to such resources as service animals, equipment rentals, and access guides.

Many travel agencies offer customized tours and itineraries for travelers with disabilities. Among them are **Flying Wheels Travel** (✆ **507/451-5005;** www.flying wheelstravel.com) and **Accessible Journeys** (✆ **800/846-4537** or 610/521-0339; www.disabilitytravel.com).

Flying with Disability (www.flying-with-disability.org) is a comprehensive information source on airplane travel.

Also check out the quarterly magazine *Emerging Horizons* (www.emerginghorizons. com), available by subscription (US$17 year U.S.; US$22 outside U.S.).

The "Accessible Travel" link at **Mobility-Advisor.com** (www.mobility-advisor. com) offers a variety of travel resources to persons with disabilities.

British travelers should contact **Holiday Care** (✆ **0845-124-9971** in the U.K. only; www.holidaycare.org.uk) to access a wide range of travel information and resources for disabled and elderly people.

For more on organizations that offer resources to travelers with disabilities, go to frommers.com.

Gay & Lesbian Travelers

Austria's acceptance of homosexuals varies depending on the area. While bigger cities like Vienna and Graz are not only tolerant, but have constantly growing gay scenes in the form of bars, clubs, and restaurants, in smaller cities and more rural areas there is no outright gay-bashing, but people may look down on same-sex public displays of affection. The annual Life Ball is the biggest AIDS gala in Europe and also is a global symbol for gay rights and tolerance.

For information about gay-related activities in Vienna, go to **Rainbow Online** (www.gay.or.at).

Most famous gay bars are in the 6th District close to the MuseumsQuartier and Karlsplatz. For more information see "Gay & Lesbian Bars" in chapter 6.

In Austria, the minimum age for consensual homosexual activity is 18.

The International Gay and Lesbian Travel Association (IGLTA; ✆ **800/448-8550** or 954/776-2626; www.iglta.org) is the trade association for the gay and lesbian travel industry, and offers a directory of gay- and lesbian-friendly travel businesses; go to its website and click "Members." In Canada, contact **Travel Gay Canada** (✆ **416/761-5151;** www.travelgaycanada.com).

Many agencies offer tours and travel itineraries specifically for gay and lesbian travelers, such as **Above and Beyond Tours** (© 800/397-2681; www.abovebeyond tours.com). **Now, Voyager** (© 800/255-6951; www.nowvoyager.com) is a well-known San Francisco-based gay travel service. **Olivia Cruises & Resorts** (© 800/ 631-6277; www.olivia.com) charters entire resorts and ships for exclusive lesbian trips and offers smaller-group experiences for both gay and lesbian travelers. **Gay. com Travel** (© 800/929-2268 or 415/834-6500; www.gay.com/travel or www.out andabout.com) is an excellent online successor to the popular *Out & About* print magazine. It provides regularly updated information about gay-owned, gay-oriented, and gay-friendly lodging, dining, sightseeing, nightlife, and shopping establishments in every important destination worldwide. It also offers trip-planning information for gay and lesbian travelers for more than 50 destinations, along various themes, ranging from Sex & Travel to Trips for Couples.

The following travel guides are available at many bookstores, or you can order them from any online bookseller: *Spartacus International Gay Guide* (Bruno Gmünder Verlag; www.spartacusworld.com/gayguide) and *Odysseus: The International Gay Travel Planner* (www.odyusa.com), both good, annual, English-language guidebooks focused on gay men; and the *Damron* guides (www.damron.com), with separate, annual books for gay men and lesbians. For more gay and lesbian travel resources, visit frommers.com.

Senior Travel

Many Austrian hotels offer discounts for seniors. Mention the fact that you're a senior citizen when you make your travel reservations.

Members of **AARP**, 601 E St. NW, Washington, DC 20049 (© 888/687-2277; www.aarp.org), get discounts on hotels, airfares, and car rentals. AARP offers members a wide range of benefits, including *AARP: The Magazine* and a monthly newsletter. Anyone over 50 can join.

Many reliable agencies and organizations target the 50-plus market. **Elderhostel** (© 800/454-5768; www.elderhostel.org) arranges study programs for those aged 55 and over (and a spouse or companion of any age) in the U.S. and in more than 80 countries around the world, including Austria. Most courses last 2 to 4 weeks abroad, and many include airfare, accommodations in university dormitories or modest inns, meals, and tuition.

Recommended publications offering travel resources and discounts for seniors include: The quarterly magazine *Travel 50 & Beyond* (www.travel50andbeyond. com); *Travel Unlimited: Uncommon Adventures for the Mature Traveler* (Avalon); and *Unbelievably Good Deals and Great Adventures That You Absolutely Can't Get Unless You're Over 50* (McGraw-Hill), by Joann Rattner Heilman.

Frommers.com also offers information and resources on travel for seniors.

Family Travel

If you have enough trouble getting your kids out of the house in the morning, dragging them thousands of miles away may seem like an insurmountable challenge. But family travel can be immensely rewarding, and Austria is a great place to take your kids. The pleasures available for children in Vienna (which most adults enjoy just as much) range from watching the magnificent Lipizzaner stallions at the Spanish Riding School to exploring the region's many castles and dungeons.

One outstanding children's attraction is the Prater amusement park, with its giant Ferris wheel, roller coasters, merry-go-rounds, arcades, and Lilliputbahn (tiny railroad).

Even if your kids aren't very interested in touring palaces, take them to the hands-on roman city of Carnuntum (see chapter 7), where kids discover history playfully. In summer, beaches along the lakes in the Salzkammergut and Carinthia (Wörthersee) are popular swimming, windsurfing, and boating retreats (see "Special Interest & Escorted Trips" later in the chapter). And don't forget the lure of the *Konditorei*, little bakeries that sell scrumptious Austrian cakes and pastries.

Babysitting services are available through most hotel desks or by applying at the tourist information office in the town where you're staying. Many hotels have children's game rooms and playgrounds.

Throughout this guide, look for the "Kids" icon, which highlights child-friendly destinations.

Recommended family travel Internet sites include **Family Travel Forum** (www.familytravelforum.com), a comprehensive site that offers customized trip planning; **Family Travel Network** (www.familytravelnetwork.com), an award-winning site that offers travel features, deals, and tips; **Traveling Internationally with Your Kids** (www.travelwithyourkids.com), a comprehensive site offering sound advice for long-distance and international travel with children; and **Family Travel Files** (www.thefamilytravelfiles.com), which offers an online magazine and a directory of off-the-beaten-path tours and tour operators for families.

For a list of more family-friendly travel resources, turn to the experts at frommers.com.

RESPONSIBLE TOURISM

If you're arriving from elsewhere in Europe, the best way to be a responsible tourist when visiting Austria is to consider catching the **train** rather than flying. Highspeed trains now crisscross much of the continent, making travel by rail a serious alternative to flying. See "Getting There & Getting Around" above.

Since so much of Austria's tourism is due to the **natural beauty** of the Alps and the sustainability of ski resorts, the country takes the environment very seriously. Although the country has no coastline, Austria is covered in water. The country is somewhat spoiled by the quality and abundance of it. This gift is not taken for granted, however. **Waterpower** has become a main energy source. In the countryside many make their own energy with solar paneling, and various companies offer green electricity from water, wind, and solar power.

Austria is number five on the *Reader's Digest* green list of countries, after Finland, Iceland, Norway, and Sweden. Sustainability and respect for nature, preservation, and organic food are very important to Austrians. You won't find off-season fruits and vegetables in a normal supermarket as Austria adheres to strict transportation laws.

Although there is not a deposit on all glass and plastic bottles, when there is, it's around .25€, so with four bottles you'd get a euro back from the machines in supermarkets. Otherwise the Austrians recycle at every open market in the city. You'll also find recycling containers in groups in every small neighborhood, mostly on street corners.

When in Austria and Vienna, the main thing is that waste is looked down on in general, as is littering. Besides the occasional cigarette butt and dog dropping, the streets are very tidy. Also look in to bike rentals and bike tours for fun outings that are not only sustainable but also easy to use on the multitude of bike paths throughout the city. (See "Getting Around," By Bicycle, above.)

IT'S EASY BEING green

In addition to the resources for Austria listed above, the following websites provide valuable wide-ranging information on sustainable travel.

o **Responsible Travel** (www.responsibletravel.com) is a great source of sustainable travel ideas; the site is run by a spokesperson for ethical tourism in the travel industry. **Sustainable Travel International** (www.sustainabletravelinternational.org) promotes ethical tourism practices, and manages an extensive directory of sustainable properties and tour operators around the world.

o In the U.K., **Tourism Concern** (www.tourismconcern.org.uk) works to reduce social and environmental problems connected to tourism. The **Association of Independent Tour Operators (AITO)** (www.aito.co.uk) is a group of specialist operators leading the field in making holidays sustainable.

o In Canada, **www.greenlivingonline.com** offers extensive content on how to travel sustainably, including a travel and transport section and profiles of the best green shops and services in Toronto, Vancouver, and Calgary.

o In Australia, the national body which sets guidelines and standards for ecotourism is **Ecotourism Australia** (www.ecotourism.org.au). **The Green Directory** (www.thegreendirectory.com.au), **Green Pages** (www.thegreenpages.com.au), and **Eco Directory** (www.ecodirectory.com.au) offer sustainable travel tips and directories of green businesses.

o **Carbonfund** (www.carbonfund.org), **TerraPass** (www.terrapass.org), and **Cool Climate** (http://coolclimate.berkeley.edu) provide information on "carbon offsetting," or offsetting the greenhouse gas emitted during flights.

o **Greenhotels** (www.greenhotels.com) recommends green-rated member hotels around the world that fulfill the company's stringent environmental requirements. **Environmentally Friendly Hotels** (www.environmentallyfriendlyhotels.com) offers more green accommodation ratings. The **Hotel Association of Canada** (www.hacgreenhotels.com) has a Green Key Eco-Rating Program, which audits the environmental performance of Canadian hotels, motels, and resorts.

o **Sustain Lane** (www.sustainlane.com) lists sustainable eating and drinking choices around the U.S.; also visit **www.eatwellguide.org** for tips on eating sustainably in the U.S. and Canada.

o For information on animal-friendly issues throughout the world, visit **Tread Lightly** (www.treadlightly.org). For information about the ethics of swimming with dolphins, visit the **Whale and Dolphin Conservation Society** (www.wdcs.org).

o **Volunteer International** (www.volunteerinternational.org) has a list of questions to help you determine the intentions and the nature of a volunteer program. For general information on volunteer travel, visit **www.volunteerabroad.org** and **www.idealist.org**.

Here are a few tips on how to be a green tourist and respect Austria's natural beauty:

- Whenever possible, choose **nonstop flights;** they generally require less fuel than indirect flights that stop and take off again. Try to fly during the day—some scientists estimate that night-time flights are twice as harmful to the environment. And pack light—each 15 pounds of luggage on a 5,000-mile flight adds up to 50 pounds of carbon dioxide emitted.

- At hotels, request that your sheets and towels not be changed daily. (Many hotels already have programs like this in place.) Turn off the lights and air-conditioner (or heater) when you leave your room.

- Use **public transport** where possible—trains, buses, and even taxis are more energy-efficient forms of transport than driving. Even better is to walk or cycle; you'll produce zero emissions and stay fit and healthy on your travels.

- If renting a car is necessary, ask the rental agent for a **hybrid,** or rent the most fuel-efficient car available.

- Eat at **locally owned** and operated restaurants that use produce grown in the area. This contributes to the local economy and cuts down on greenhouse gas emissions by supporting restaurants where the food is not flown or trucked in across long distances.

PACKAGES FOR THE INDEPENDENT TRAVELER

Before you start your search for the lowest airfare, you may want to consider booking your flight as part of a travel package. Package tours are not the same thing as escorted tours. Package tours are simply a way to buy the airfare, accommodations, and other elements of your trip (such as car rentals, airport transfers, and sometimes even activities) at the same time and often at discounted prices—kind of like one-stop shopping. Packages are sold in bulk to tour operators—who resell them to the public at a cost that usually undercuts standard rates.

A sampling of some well-recommended tour operators follows, but you should always consult a good travel agent for the latest offerings.

British Airways Holidays (© **800/AIRWAYS;** www.britishairways.com) offers a far-flung and reliable touring experience. Trips usually combine Vienna and other Austrian attractions with major sights in Germany and Switzerland. BA can arrange a stopover in London en route for an additional fee and allow extra time in Vienna before or after the beginning of any tour for no additional charge.

Other attractive options are North America's tour-industry giants. They include **Delta Vacations** (© **800/221-6666;** www.deltavacations.com), **American Express Travel** (© **800/297-2977;** www.americanexpress.com), and an unusual, upscale (and very expensive) tour operator, **Abercrombie & Kent** (© **800/554-7016;** www.abercrombiekent.com), long known for its carriage-trade rail excursions through Eastern Europe and the Swiss and Austrian Alps.

Ask for a copy of the brochure "Nature the Healer: Spas and Health Resorts in Austria." You can also learn about "Kneipp Cures," a method developed in the 19th century as a restorative treatment and still hailed as "a magic formula in the world of natural medicine." This cure, popular among seniors with limited circulation, involves simple stretching exercises and moderate amounts of low-impact aerobics. The exercise session is followed by a footbath in icy, non-sulfurous water.

Several big **online travel agencies**—Expedia.com, Travelocity, Orbitz, Site59, and Lastminute.com—also do a brisk business in packages. If you're unsure about the pedigree of a smaller packager, check with the Better Business Bureau in the city where the company is based, or go online to **www.bbb.org**. If a packager won't tell you where it's based, don't fly with it.

Travel packages are also listed in the travel section of your local Sunday newspaper. Or check ads in national travel magazines such as *Arthur Frommer's Budget Travel Magazine, Travel & Leisure, National Geographic Traveler,* and *Condé Nast Traveler.*

ESCORTED GENERAL-INTEREST TOURS

Escorted tours are structured group tours with a group leader. The price usually includes everything from airfare to hotels, meals, admission costs, and local transportation.

Many people derive a sense of ease and security from escorted trips. Escorted tours—whether by bus, train, or boat—let travelers sit back and enjoy the trip without having to spend lots of time behind the wheel or worrying about details. You know your costs up front, and there are few surprises. Escorted tours can take you to the maximum number of sights in the minimum amount of time with the least amount of hassle—you don't have to sweat over the plotting and planning of a trip schedule. Escorted tours are particularly convenient for people with limited mobility. They can also be a great way to meet people.

On the downside, an escorted tour often requires a big deposit up front, and lodging and dining choices are predetermined. You'll have few opportunities for serendipitous interactions with locals. The tours can be jam-packed with activities, leaving little room for individual sightseeing, whim, or adventure—plus they also often focus only on the heavily touristy sites, so you miss out on lesser-known gems.

American Express Vacations (© 800/335-3342; www.americanexpress vacations.com) is one of the biggest tour operators in the world. Its offerings are comprehensive, and unescorted customized package tours are available, too.

Brendan Vacations (© 800/421-8446; www.brendanvacations.com) has a selection of 8- to 16-day tours. Accommodations are at the better hotels, and rates include everything except airfare. **Collette Vacations** (© 800/340-5158; www. collettevacations.com) has 14 tours that cover Austria and various other European cities. **Globus & Cosmos Tours** (© 800/338-7092; www.globusandcosmos.com) offers 9- to 16-day escorted tours of various parts of Austria. It also has a budget branch that offers tours at lower rates. **Maupintour** © 800/255-4266; www.mau pintour.com) has a selection of upscale tours, such as a 14-day Blue Danube Discovery Tour, which take in such cities as Vienna, Linz, Dürnstein, Melk, and Salzburg, and an unusual, upscale (and very expensive) tour operator, **Abercrombie & Kent** (© 800/554-7016; www.abercrombiekent.com), known for its carriage-trade rail excursions through eastern Europe and the Swiss and Austrian Alps.

The oldest travel agency in Britain, **Cox & Kings,** 30 Millbank, London SW1P 4EE (© 020/7873-5000; www.coxandkings.co.uk), specializes in unusual, if pricey, holidays. Offerings in Austria include organized tours through the country's many regions of natural beauty and tours of historic or aesthetic interest. Also available are opera tours to Salzburg and Vienna.

Other companies featuring offbeat adventure travel include **HF Holidays,** Catalyst House, 720 Centennial Ct., Elstree, Hertfordshire WD6 3SY (☏ **020/8732-1220;** www.hfholidays.co.uk). It offers a range of 1- to 2-week packages to Austria. **Sherpa Expeditions,** 131A Heston Rd., Hounslow, Middlesex TW5 0RF (☏ **020/8577-2717;** www.sherpaexpeditions.com), offers treks through off-the-beaten-track regions of Europe, especially the Alps.

Travel packages are also listed in the travel section of your local Sunday newspaper. Or check ads in the national travel magazines such as *Arthur Frommer's Budget Travel Magazine, Travel & Leisure, National Geographic Traveler,* and *Condé Nast Traveler.*

Package tours can vary by leaps and bounds. Some offer a better class of hotels than others. Some offer the same hotels for lower prices. Some offer flights on scheduled airlines, while others book charters. Some limit your choice of accommodations and travel days. You are often required to make a large payment up front. On the plus side, packages can save you money, offering group prices but allowing for independent travel. Some even let you add on a few guided excursions or escorted day trips (also at prices lower than if you booked them yourself) without booking an entirely escorted tour.

Before you invest in a package tour, get some answers. Ask about the **accommodations choices** and prices for each. Then look up the hotels' reviews in a Frommer's guide, and check their rates online for your specific dates of travel. You'll also want to find out what **type of room** you get. If you need a certain type of room, ask for it; don't take whatever is thrown your way. Request a nonsmoking room, a quiet room, a room with a view, or whatever you fancy.

Finally, look for **hidden expenses.** Ask whether airport departure fees and taxes, for example, are included in the total cost.

SPECIAL INTEREST & ESCORTED TRIPS

Besides the performing arts, Austrians love sports and the outdoors and, although skiing is a national obsession, there are opportunities to participate in a variety of activities. Here we outline the best places to go and who can guide you there. You'll find specific information in each regional chapter.

Music Tours

For the Mozart and Strauss lover, there are an abundance of escorted tours which can take anywhere from a few hours to a few days.

There are a variety of tours from Vienna to Salzburg, stopping at historical or musical sites along the way. For Mozart, Haydn, Schubert, Bruckner, and Gustav Mahler tours contact **Herzerltours** (☏ **914/771-8558;** 800-684-8488 toll free in the U.S.; www.herzerltours.com).

Ballooning

Hot-air ballooning over the dramatic landscapes of Austria, including alpine terrain, can be a real thrill ride. One of the best centers for this is Ballooning Vorarlberg in western Austria. The balloon specialist here is **Günter Schabus,** Bruderhof 12A, A-6833 (☏ **05523/51121;** www.ballooning.at), which features ballooning 7 days a week from April to September—weather permitting, of course—near the German and Swiss borders. The cost of ballooning is 220€ per person for up to five people.

Biking

Hindriks European Bicycle, P.O. Box 7010, citrus Heights, CA 95621 (*©* **800/852-3258;** fax 916/729-2181; www.hindrikstours.com), is the North American representative for a Dutch-based company that leads 10-day bicycle tours in Austria. You'll bike along well-laid-out paths and quiet country roads, which are thankfully flat and mostly downhill. The cost of this tour is 1,625€ per person based on double occupancy.

Backroads, 801 Cedar St., Berkeley, CA 94710 (*©* **800/GO-ACTIVE** in the U.S., or 510/527-1555; www.backroads.com), offers 6-day, 5-night trips that take you from Prague to Vienna going along the Danube. Lodging is either in castles or first-class country inns. The trip also includes most meals.

David Zwilling, Waldhof 64, A-5441 Abtenau (*©* **06243/30690;** fax 06243/306917; www.zwilling-resort.at), organizes Austria's best mountain-biking trips, as well as other adventure activities such as rafting, rock climbing, and paragliding.

For a wide variety of shorter, themed, and family-based bike tours check out the website of Austria Bike tours (**www.radtouren.at**).

Fishing

Austria is an angler's paradise, with many clear, unpolluted streams and deep rivers and lakes. You can try for trout, char, pike, sheatfish (monster catfish), and pikeperch in well-stocked mountain streams. In the right tributaries of the Danube, you might catch a *Huchen,* a landlocked salmon that's an excellent fighter and a culinary delight, usually fished for in late autumn. The Wörther See in Carinthia sometimes yields the North American big-mouth black bass, which once stocked the lake because of an accident by an owner of Velden Castle—intended for a pond on his estate, one barrel fell into the lake and burst, introducing the immigrants from America to a new happy home. The local tourist office in each province offers information about local fishing conditions and can advise you of the best local outfitters. Fishermen generally need two permits—a general license issued by the state and a private permit from the local owner of the land. Fishing is also possible in Vienna, on the same terms; just call or write for information from the **Österreichischen Arbeiter-Fischerei-Verein,** Lenaugasse 14, A-1080 Vienna (*©* **01/4032176;** www.fischerei.or.at).

Golf

One of the country's most outstanding 18-hole courses is at the Murhof in Styria, near Frohnleiten. Others are the Igls/Rinn near Innsbruck; Seefeld-Wildmoos in Seefeld; Dallach on the shores of the Wörther See in Carinthia; Enzesfeld and Wiener Neustadt-Foehrenwald in Lower Austria; and the oldest of them all, Vienna-Freudenau, founded in 1901. There are numerous 9-hole courses throughout the country. The season generally extends from April to October or November. For more information, contact **Österreichischer Golf-Verband,** Prinz Eugen-Strasse 12, A-1040 Vienna (*©* **01/505324519;** www.golf.at).

Hiking & Mountaineering

More than 70% of Austria's total area is covered by mountains of all shapes and sizes, and the rugged beauty of the Alps demands exploration. Walking, hiking, or mountain climbing across these hills and glaciers is an unforgettable experience. Paths and trails are marked and secured, guides and maps are readily available, and there's an

Staying Healthy in the Mountains

For information on altitude sickness, frostbite, and snow blindness—conditions with which visitors unfamiliar with mountainous terrain should become familiarized—see the "Staying Healthy" section earlier in this chapter.

outstanding system of huts to shelter you. Austria has more than 450 chairlifts or cable cars to open up the mountains for visitors.

Certain precautions are essential, foremost being to inform your innkeeper or host of your route. Also, suitable hiking or climbing shoes and protective clothing are imperative. Camping out overnight is strongly discouraged because of the rapidly changing mountain weather and the established system of keeping track of hikers and climbers in the mountains. More than 700 alpine huts—many of which are really full-service lodges with restaurants, rooms, and dormitories—are spaced about 4 to 5 hours apart so that you can make rest and lunch stops. Hikers are required to sign in and out of the huts and to give their destination before setting off. If you don't show up as planned, search parties go into action.

If you're advised that your chosen route is difficult, hire a mountain guide or get expert advice from some qualified local person before braving the unknown. Certified hiking and climbing guides are based in all Austrian mountain villages and can be found by looking for their signs or by asking at the local tourist office.

Above all, *obey signs.* Even in summer, if there's still snow on the ground, you could be in an area threatened by avalanches. There are other important rules to follow for your own safety, and you can obtain these from the Austrian National Tourist Offices, bookstores, branches of various alpine clubs, or at local tourist offices in villages throughout the Alps.

For information about alpine trekking, contact **Österreichischer Alpenverein (Austrian Alpine Club),** Olympia-Strasse 37, A-6020 Innsbruck (𝄢 **0512/59547;** www.alpenverein.at). Membership costs 49€. Members receive 50% off overnight stays in mountain refuges. There is an English-speaking branch in Vienna, **The Alpine Club** Vienna, at Rotenturmstr. 14, A-1010 Vienna; www.alpineclubvienna.org; group leader, Jack Curtain (𝄢 **0699 1155 1111**). One of the best trekking adventure companies in Austria is **Exodus,** 1311 63 St., Suite 200, Emeryville, CA 94608 (www.exodus.co.uk). Run by avid naturalists and mountaineers, it offers hiking tours through Austria for moderately experienced hikers in good physical condition. Tours usually last 8 to 15 days.

The most cutting-edge sporting outfit in Austria, the kind of place that merges California cool with alpine adventure, is **David Zwilling,** Waldhof 64, A-5441 Abtenau (𝄢 **06243/30690;** fax 06243/306917; www.zwilling-resort.at). It organizes the best mountain-biking trips in Austria and is also the front-runner in mountain- and rock-climbing tours. This outfitter also arranges paragliding adventures over nerve-jangling cliffs and some incredible whitewater rafting trips.

There are summer and winter mountaineering schools in at least 3 dozen resorts in all Austrian provinces except Burgenland, with regular courses, mountain tours, and camps for all ages.

Skiing

Austria is world renowned for its downhill skiing facilities. Across the country, some 3,500 lifts transport skiers and sightseers to the summits of approximately 20,113km

(12,498 miles) of marked runs. Don't forget to look around on the way up; the view above is as amazing as the runs below.

Ski "circuses" allow skiers to move from mountain to mountain, and ski "swings" opening up opposite sides of the same mountain tie villages in different valleys into one big ski region. Shuttle buses, usually free for those with a valid lift ticket, take you to valley points where you board funiculars, gondolas, aerial trains, or chairlifts. Higher up, you can leave the larger conveyance and continue by another chairlift or T-bar. Because competition among ski resorts is so fierce, you'll probably find roughly equivalent prices at many resorts for 1-, 2-, and 3-day passes. For example, at the Arlberg in Tyrol, one of the most famous ski areas of Europe, a 1-day pass costs 42.50€ to 44.50€. Discounts are granted for longer stays. A 6-day pass ranges from 202€ to 212€ per person. Prices for skiing in other regions of Austria, such as the area around Lech and Zürs in the Vorarlberg, and the Ötzal region of the Tyrol, tend to be similar. And skiers who buy passes valid for more than 2 days are rewarded with a much wider diversity of skiing options. The Austrian Ski School is noted for its fine instruction and practice techniques, available in many places: Arlberg; the posh villages of Zürs and Lech am Arlberg, where the rich and famous gather; the Silvretta mountains; and Hochgurgl, Obergurgl, Hochsölden, and Sölden in the Tyrolean Ötzal, to name a few. Year-round skiing is possible in the little villages of the Stubaital through use of a cableway on the Stubai glacier, more than 3,050m (10,007 ft.) above sea level. Kitzbühel is known to all top skiers in the world, while Seefeld lures the trendy.

Skiing is a family sport in Austria, and ski centers usually have bunny slopes and instruction for youngsters, plus babysitting services for very small children. Many of these areas offer more than just fine powder. The Valley of Gastein was known for its medicinal thermal springs long before it became a ski center. The people of Schladming, in the Dachstein Mountains, continued to preserve local traditions even after cross-country skiers discovered the high plateau surrounding the small, unspoiled village of Ramsau.

Among the most attractive large-scale skiing areas are the Radstädter Tauern region and Saalbach/Hinterglemm in Salzburg province. Here, as in most of the winter-sports areas, you can rest your tired legs by the crackling fire of a ski hut while enjoying hot spiced wine or a Jägertee, hot tea heavily laced with rum.

Snowboarding, whose popularity is spreading each year, is making inroads in Austria. The best outfitter is **Ski Europe** (© **800/333-5533** or 713/960-0900; www.ski-europe.com). They can arrange all sorts of trips focused on skiing and snowboarding, as well as winter hiking.

Cross-country skiing is popular among those who want to quietly enjoy the winter beauty and get a great workout. Many miles of tracks are marked for this sport, and special instructors are available.

In the summer, you can give skiing on glaciers a try. Some of the best glacier skiing is found in the peaks that rise from the Ziller Valley in Tyrol. Ask the Austrian National Tourist Office for a list of resorts providing this sport, as well as for details about areas offering summer skiing.

For information about the best skiing in Austria, contact **Österreichischer Skiverband** (Austrian Ski Federation), Olympiastrasse 10, A-6020 Innsbruck (© **0512/33501;** www.oesv.at).

Spas & Health Resorts

As part of the good life, Austrians have long been aware of the therapeutic faculties of mineral water, thermal springs, and curative mud in their own country. More than

100 spas and health resorts are found here, including the Oberlaa Spa Center on the southern hills of Vienna. These institutions not only use the hidden resources of nature to prevent physical ailments, but they offer therapy and rehabilitation as well.

You can "take the waters" at Baden (baths), with springs ranging from thermal brine to thermal sulfur water, some rich in iodine or iron and some rich in radon. (Many hot-water springs in Europe contain trace amounts of radon, which is not harmful in the doses that doctors prescribe.) Users of these facilities have found them an effective treatment for digestive troubles, rheumatism, cardiac and circulatory diseases, and gynecological and neurological ills, to name just a few.

Information about these spas and treatments is available from **Österreichischer Hellbäder- und Kurotelverband,** Josefsplatz 6, A-1010 Vienna (*©* **01/5121904**). Ask for a copy of the brochure "Nature the Healer: Spas and Health Resorts in Austria." See p. 63.

Watersports

Austria has no seacoast, but from Bodensee (Lake Constance) in the west to Neusiedlersee (Lake Neusiedl) in the east, the country is rich in lakes and boasts some 150 rivers and streams.

Swimming is, of course, possible year-round if you want to use an indoor pool or swim at one of the many health clubs in winter. Swimming facilities have been developed at summer resorts, especially those on the warm waters of Carinthia, where you can swim from May to October, and in the Salzkammergut between Upper Austria and Land Salzburg.

The beauty of Austria underwater is attested to by those who have tried diving in the lakes. Most outstanding are the diving and underwater exploration possibilities in the Salzkammergut and in Weissen See in Carinthia. You can receive instruction and the necessary equipment at both.

If you prefer to remain on the surface, you can go sailing, windsurfing, or canoeing on the lakes and rivers.

The boating (*Yachtklub*) season lasts from May to October, with activity centered on the Attersee in the Salzkammergut, on Lake Constance out of Bregenz, and on Lake Neusiedl, a large shallow lake in the east. Winds on the Austrian lakes can be treacherous, but a warning system and rescue services are alert. For information on sailing, contact **Österreichischer Segel-Verband,** Seestrasse 17b, A-7100 Neusiedl am See (*©* **02/167402430;** www.segelverband.at).

Most resorts on lakes or rivers where windsurfing can be safely enjoyed have equipment and instruction available. This sport is increasing in popularity and has been added to the curriculum of several sailing schools, especially in the area of the Wörthersee in Carinthia, the warmest of the alpine lakes.

If you're interested in riding the rapids of a swift mountain stream or just paddling around on a placid lake, don't miss the chance to go canoeing in Austria. You can canoe down slow-flowing lowland rivers such as the Inn or Mur, or tackle the wild waters of glacier-fed mountain streams suitable only for experts. Special schools for fast-water paddling operate May through September in the village of Klaus on the Steyr River in Upper Austria, in Opponitz in Lower Austria on the Ybbs River, and in Abtenau in Salzburg province.

STAYING CONNECTED
Telephone

The country code for Austria is 43. To call Austria from the United States, dial the international access code 011, then 43, then the city code, then the regular phone number. To call inside Europe just replace the 011 with 00 or +. *Note:* The phone numbers listed in this book are to be used within Austria; when calling from abroad, omit the initial 0 in the city code.

For directory assistance: Dial ✆ **118877** if you're looking for a number inside Austria, and dial ✆ **1613** for numbers to all other countries.

For operator assistance: If you need operator assistance in making a call, dial ✆ **0180/200-1033.**

Local and long-distance calls may be placed from all post offices and from most public telephone booths, about half of which operate with phone cards, the others with coins. Phone cards are sold at post offices and newsstands in denominations of 6€ to 25€. Rates are measured in units rather than minutes. The farther the distance, the more units are consumed. Telephone calls made through hotel switchboards can double, triple, or even quadruple the base charges at the post office, so be alert to this before you dial. In some instances, post offices can send faxes for you, and many hotels offer Internet access—for free or for a small charge—to their guests.

Austrian phone numbers are not standard. In some places, numbers have as few as three digits. In cities, one number may have five digits, whereas the phone next door might have nine. Austrians also often hyphenate their numbers differently. But since all the area codes are the same, these various configurations should have little effect on your phone usage once you get used to the fact that numbers vary from place to place.

Be careful dialing **toll-free numbers.** Many companies maintain a service line beginning with 0180. However, these lines might appear to be toll free but really aren't, costing .12€ per minute. Other numbers that begin with 0190 carry a surcharge of 1.85€ per minute—or even more. Don't be misled by calling a 1-800 number in the United States from Austria. This is not a toll-free call but costs about the same as an overseas call.

To call the U.S. or Canada from Austria, dial 01, followed by the country code (1), then the area code, and then the number. Alternatively, you can dial the various telecommunication companies in the States for cheaper rates. From Austria, the access number for **AT&T** is ✆ **0800/8880010,** for **MCI** ✆ **0800/8888000. USA Direct** can be used with all telephone cards and for collect calls. The number from Austria is ✆ **013/00010. Canada Direct** can be used with Bell Telephone Cards and for collect calls. This number from Austria is ✆ **013/00014.**

If you're calling from a public pay phone in Austria, you must deposit the basic local rate.

Toll-free numbers: Numbers beginning with 08 and followed by 00 are toll-free. But be careful. Numbers that begin with 08 followed by 36 carry a .35€ surcharge per minute.

Cellphones (Mobiles)

The Austrian cellphone network is quite state of the art. Although there are holes in reception, the service is mostly constant. You even have reception in the U-Bahn. In order to have a local number, you'll need a SIM Card (Scriber Identity Module Card).

This is a small chip that gives you a local phone number and plugs you into a regional network. If your cellphone is locked to your home provider, you can use an Austrian card from that provider, or get it unlocked at specialty stores. In the U.S., T-Mobile, AT&T Wireless, and Cingular use this quasi-universal system; in Canada, Microcell and some Rogers customers are GSM, and all Europeans and most Australians use GSM.

For many, **renting** a phone is a good idea. While you can rent a phone from any number of overseas sites, including kiosks at airports and at car-rental agencies, we suggest renting the phone before you leave home. North Americans can rent one before leaving home from **InTouch USA** (☎ **800/872-7626** or 703/222-7161; www.intouchglobal.com); they can also advise you on whether your existing phone will work overseas.

Buying a phone can be economically attractive, as many nations have cheap prepaid phone systems. Once you arrive at your destination, stop by a local cellphone store and get the cheapest package; you'll probably pay less than 60€ for a phone and a starter calling card. Local calls may be as low as .10€ per minute and incoming calls are free.

Internet & E-mail
WITH YOUR OWN COMPUTER

More and more hotels, cafes, and retailers have Wi-Fi (wireless fidelity) "hotspots," or free wireless. Mac owners have their own networking technology: Apple AirPort. **T-Mobile Hotspot** (www.t-mobile.com/hotspot or www.t-mobile.co.uk) serves up wireless connections at coffee shops nationwide. **Boingo** (www.boingo.com) and **Wayport** (www.wayport.com) have set up networks in airports and high-class hotel lobbies. iPass providers (see below) also give you access to a few hundred wireless hotel lobby setups. To locate other hotspots that provide **free wireless networks** in cities in Austria, go to **www.jiwire.com**.

For dial-up access, most business-class hotels offer dataports for laptop modems, and a few thousand hotels in Austria now offer free high-speed Internet access. In addition, major Internet service providers (ISPs) have **local access numbers** around the world, allowing you to go online by placing a local call. The **iPass** network also has dial-up numbers around the world. You'll have to sign up with an iPass provider, who will then tell you how to set up your computer for your destination(s). For a list of iPass providers, go to www.ipass.com and click on "Individuals Buy Now." One solid provider is **i2roam** (☎ **866/811-6209** or 920/233-5863; www.i2roam.com).

Wherever you go, bring a **connection kit** of the right power and phone adapters, a spare phone cord, and a spare Ethernet network cable—or find out whether your hotel supplies them to guests.

WITHOUT YOUR OWN COMPUTER

Cybercafes are found in all large Austrian cities, especially. But they do not tend to cluster in any particular neighborhoods because of competition. They are spread out, but can be found on almost every business street in large cities. For locations check www.bignet.at.

Aside from formal cybercafes, most **youth hostels** and **public libraries** have Internet access. Most **hotel business centers** don't charge for guest usage anymore, but it's good to check before you log on.

Vienna International airport now has free **Internet kiosks** scattered throughout their gates. These give you basic Web access for a per-minute fee that's usually higher than cybercafe prices.

TIPS ON ACCOMMODATIONS

Austrian hotels, inns, and pensions (boardinghouses) are classified by the government into five different categories and are rated with stars. A five-star rating is deluxe, while one star designates a simple inn or hotel; there's a chance that not all rooms have private bathrooms. One-star hotels are most often clean and decent establishments where you get more value for your euro than anywhere else in the country.

Reservations are advised, especially if you're visiting in high season, which varies in different parts of the country. Summer is high season in Salzburg and Vienna, while Innsbruck enjoys a great deal of summer tourist business but is also the center of the bustling Tyrolean ski industry in winter. High season at ski resorts is usually from Christmas to mid-April; most resorts actually lower their prices in summer. Sometimes hotels offer a "shoulder" rate in spring and autumn when business lessens; sometimes these hotels close if business is slow.

The local tourist office in any Austrian city or resort can assist you in making the necessary reservations. If a certain hotel is booked and cannot accept your reservation, the tourist office will be able to make an alternative reservation in a hotel of comparable price and character. Regional service organizations are your best bet if you want to visit several towns or resorts in one Austrian province or one of Austria's major cities. These addresses are available from the Austrian National Tourist Office abroad (www.austria.info).

Bed & Breakfasts

Look for the signs that say ZIMMER FREI (Vacancy - Room Available) attached to the front of a house or to a short post at the front-yard gate or driveway. This means that the proprietors rent rooms on a bed-and-breakfast basis to travelers. You'll encounter these signs along Austria's country roads and along some main streets in small towns.

Such accommodations have hot and cold running water in the bedrooms, although private bathroom and toilet facilities are rare. (There's usually a toilet on every floor and one bathroom in the house.) A continental breakfast will nearly always be served.

Few homes accept advance reservations, so just stop in and inquire. When the rooms are filled, the sign is taken down or covered. The **local tourist office** can also help you find B&B accommodations.

You might need a few words of basic German to converse with the owner, as only a few of these proprietors will speak English. If you're staying for only 1 night, you might be asked to pay your bill in advance, and it must be paid in euros.

Farmhouse Accommodations

Groups or whole families can stay on a farm, renting several rooms or even a wing of the house. This can be a great money-saving opportunity for larger groups. However, a stay of at least a week is generally required, and advance reservations through a local tourist office or regional tourist board are necessary. Get in touch with the tourist office of the region for a reliable booking at a farmhouse in the area.

Schlosshotels (Castle Hotels)

Graced with a rich and ornate imperial tradition, Austria poured funds and resources throughout its history into constructing palaces and castles. Many of these ancestral buildings have been transformed into hotels. Information on these hotels can be obtained through **Euro-Connection,** 7500 212th St. SW, Suite 103, Edmonds, WA

98026 (© **800/645-3876;** www.euro-connection.com), which represents castle hotels throughout Europe.

Chalets, Villas & Apartments

Many cottages, chalets, and condominiums are available for short-term rentals to qualified visitors. These rental properties are usually at or near sites of natural or historic beauty or in ski or lakeside resorts.

Pego Leasing Centre, Rathausgasse 11, A-6700 Bludenz (© **05552/65666;** www.pego.at), inventories more than 1,000 rental properties in Austria. The company arranges rentals of 1 week to a year or more for 1 to 30 occupants at a time; rentals traditionally begin and end on a Saturday. Pego usually collects most of its fee from the owners of the rental property, but the tenant usually pays an agency fee to Pego of around 10% for each booking.

Pensions

A pension is generally more intimate and personal than a hotel. Of course, the nature and quality of the welcome depends largely on the host or hostess, who might also be the cook and chief maid. The host is however invariably a local and can help you plan your day excursions with insider information. As a general rule, a first-class pension in Austria is equal in services to a second-class hotel; a second-class pension is equal to a third-class hotel. Usually a continental breakfast is served; some pensions also offer dinner. Expect to be on your own for lunch.

Home Exchanges

You can arrange a home exchange—swapping your home with that of an Austrian family, often with a car included—through several U.S.-based organizations. **Intervac U.S. & International,** P.O. Box 590504, San Francisco, CA 94159 (© **800/756-home;** www.intervacus.com), publishes three catalogs a year containing listings of more than 9,000 homes in more than 36 countries. Members contact each other directly. Depending on your type of membership, fees begin at 59€.

Youth Hostels

Austria has 108 youth hostels distributed throughout the provinces. Rates for a bed-and-breakfast run from 15€ per person daily. Some hostels lock their doors between 10pm and 6am to discourage late arrivals. Dormitories must be empty between 10am and 5pm. You must have an International Youth Hostel Federation membership card to use Austria's youth hostels, and advance reservations are recommended. In Austria, you can get information about hostels from any branch of the Austrian National Tourist Office. A detailed brochure is available. For information on finding a hostel worldwide, visit **www.hostels.com**.

SUGGESTED AUSTRIAN ITINERARIES

4

For any traveler, discovering Austria through its famous landmarks, its rich culture, and dramatic landscapes is a pleasure not soon to be forgotten. If you have more time, you may also begin to uncover another Austria, the one of the artists' studios and the rehearsal halls, vineyards and coffeehouses where patterns of life make beauty possible.

You'll need a "lean-and-mean" attitude if you want to experience the best of Austria in a relatively small amount of time. An alpine country, Austria is small, but because of its mountains and backcountry roads—and most definitely winter driving conditions—getting around and seeing everything can take a while. All the major cities are linked by express highways called *Autobahnen,* but due to soundproofing, you don't see Austria from these arteries. If you're pressed, you'll find the 1- or 2-week itineraries helpful in getting you around quickly to the highlights.

Feel free to drop a place or two, though, to save a day to relax, to just take a stroll around town, to sit in a cafe and read or write some letters, to walk in the countryside and pass a slow afternoon at a *Heuriger,* to lose your sense of time—a vital part of your Austrian experience. One week provides just barely enough to see a good bit of Vienna and some memorable highlights of the rest of the country. There are those who will argue that the glory of Austria lies in its mountain landscapes and small villages. That is true to some extent. But if you're skimming, Austria has two of the most historic attractions in Europe: The Imperial capital of **Vienna** and the baroque jewel of **Salzburg,** the graces of past alive in the modern world that few first-time visitors will want to miss.

The Tyrolean capital of alpine **Innsbruck** is also a potent lure. This trip takes in all those three cities, but allows some time for drives along the **Danube** and an invasion of the **Salzkammergut,** the famous lake district around Salzburg where *The Sound of Music* was filmed.

THE REGIONS IN BRIEF

The forests, mountains, and lowlands of the Austrian landscape were divided early in their history into nine distinctly different regions (see the map on the inside back cover of this guide). In addition to their topographical diversities, each region has its own history, cultural identity, and—in some cases—oddities of language and dialect.

Vienna

Austria's capital, the former hub of a great empire, and a province in its own right, Vienna is one of Europe's most beautiful cities. Images spring to mind of imperial palaces, the angelic voices of the **Vienna Choirboys, the Spanish Riding School,** and *Heuriger* wine restaurants and the *Kaffeehäuser.* In this former seat of the Habsburg dynasty, you follow in the footsteps of Mozart, Beethoven, Schubert, Strauss, Brahms, and Mahler, but also Freud, Wittgenstein, Kafka, Krauss, and Klimt, who, along with Leon Trotzky, could all be found in the coffeehouses of Vienna on the eve of World War I.

One channel of the Danube used to cut through the city until flooding forced Vienna to divert the river, creating a broad central flow and the smaller Danube Canal that runs along the boundary of the 1st and 2nd Districts. The inner city is the oldest part of Vienna, the imperial capital of the Habsburgs who controlled a great deal of Europe for more than 6 centuries until it suffered humiliating defeats in both world wars of the 20th century.

Visitors today will find a newer and brighter Vienna, a city with more *joie de vivre* than it's had since before World War II; cafes, clubs, theaters, and concert halls are everywhere, open nightly and sold out. Among its grand cityscapes and lovely old squares, each season hosts festivals and open markets that bring the streets alive. In spite of two world wars, much of the empire's glory remains, its treasures now glistening in museum galleries, its parks and palaces the daily settings of city life. Today's Vienna is alive with the energy of cutting-edge art and ideas, and yet knows in its deepest heart how to live well.

Lower Austria

Set at Austria's northeastern corner, bordering the Czech Republic and Slovakia, this is Austria's largest province. Known for its fertile plains, renowned vineyards, and prosperous bourgeoisie, it's very different from the alpine regions of western Austria. Although the administrative capital is the culturally ambitious city of **St. Pölten,** most of the region directs its focus toward Vienna, which it completely surrounds. Visitors to Lower Austria typically come on a day trip from Vienna to explore the **Wienerwald (Vienna Woods),** romanticized in operetta, literature, and the famous Strauss waltz. One of the best places to explore the Vienna Woods is **Klosterneuburg,** a major wine-producing center. Other places to explore include **Mayerling,** in the heart of the woods, and **Heiligenkreuz,** one of Austria's oldest Cistercian abbeys. The district's leading spa is **Baden bei Wien,** a lively casino town in the eastern sector of the Vienna Woods.

The other major attraction of Lower Austria is the **Wachau–Danube Valley,** rich in scenic splendor and castles. In the valley, you can visit the ancient town of **Tulln,** the early-12th-century **Herzogenburg Monastery,** the 1,000-year-old city of **Krems,** and the lovely town of **Dürnstein. Melk Abbey** is one of the world's finest baroque buildings.

Burgenland

The newest of the Austrian provinces was formed in 1921 from the German-speaking region of what had once been part of the Hungarian half of Austria–Hungary. Located at Austria's southeastern tip, its plains, reef-fringed lakes, and abundant bird life

Suggested Austrian Itineraries

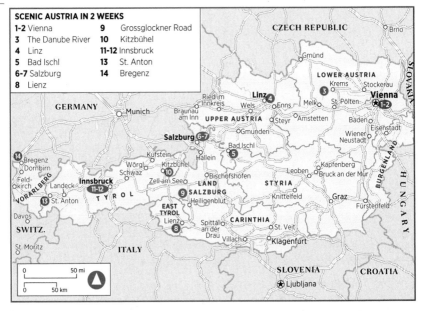

HIGHLIGHTS OF AUSTRIA IN 1 WEEK

1-2 Vienna
3 The Danube River
4 Salzkammergut
5-6 Salzburg
7 Innsbruck

SCENIC AUSTRIA IN 2 WEEKS

1-2 Vienna
3 The Danube River
4 Linz
5 Bad Ischl
6-7 Salzburg
8 Lienz
9 Grossglockner Road
10 Kitzbühel
11-12 Innsbruck
13 St. Anton
14 Bregenz

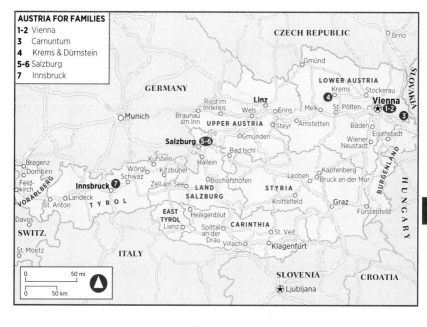

AUSTRIA FOR FAMILIES

1-2 Vienna
3 Carnuntum
4 Krems & Dürnstein
5-6 Salzburg
7 Innsbruck

THE SALZKAMMERGUT LAKE DISTRICT IN 1 WEEK

1 Salzburg
2 Mondsee
3 St. Wolfgang
4 Bad Aussee
5 Villach
6-7 Klagenfurt

resemble the landscapes of Hungary. Its capital is **Eisenstadt,** the native city of composer Franz Josef Haydn. Largely agricultural, with an unusual demographic mixture of Hungarians, Croats, and German-speaking Austrians, Burgenland lacks the visual drama and grand alpine scenery of other parts of Austria. Lakes, like the **Neusiedlersee,** and the surrounding vineyards and wineries remain its primary attraction, and they are best visited in summer.

Salzburg

A city rich with the splendors of the baroque age and the melodies of Mozart, Salzburg is one of Europe's premier architectural gems. It's also the setting for Austria's most prestigious music festival. Its natural setting is panoramic—hugging both banks of the Salzach River and "pinched" between two mountains, Mönchsberg and Kapuzinerberg.

Although the film took many liberties with the geography and history of the real Austria—to the frustration of the locals—many travelers come here to follow in the footsteps of Julie Andrews in the fabled 1965 musical *The Sound of Music*. The von Trapps and Mozart have put Salzburg on international tourist maps.

Land Salzburg

The only area of Austria that can compare with Tyrol in outdoor activities and scenic grandeur alike is Land Salzburg, which lies at the doorstep of Salzburg. It's easy to spend weeks in this mountainous area. In summer, the greatest attraction is the **Grossglockner Hochalpenstrasse** (Grossglockner Alpine Road), Europe's longest and most splendid highway. In winter, **Zell am See** is the most popular resort in the region, located on a lake against a mountain backdrop, but there are many other options to consider. **Golling,** in the Salzach Valley, south of Salzburg, is one of the most inviting. Visitors frequently visit the winter and summer spa resorts of **Badgastein** and **Bad Hofgastein** in the Gastein Valley. Two major ski resorts are **Saalbach** and **Hinterglemm.**

Upper Austria

Tied to the Danube's fertile plains, which straddle that famous river, this region produces much of Austria's agricultural bounty. Its capital is the historic but heavily industrialized city of **Linz,** famous for a raspberry-chocolate concoction known as the Linzer torte, and a vibrant university town with the **University of Art and Design, Johann Keppler Universität** business school, the **Anton Bruckner Privatuniversität** for music and the performing arts, and now a dazzling new **Ars Electronica Center** that has set off an explosion of energy in creative technologies. Upper Austria boasts charming scenery, especially in summer at **Attersee,** the largest lake in the Austrian Alps. Another major summer resort is **Mondsee (Moon Lake),** the warmest lake in the Salzkammergut. Also in the Salzkammergut, **Wolfgangsee,** one of Austria's most romantic lakes, draws visitors to its White Horse Inn, of the fabled operetta. **Bad Ischl,** once the summer retreat of Emperor Franz Josef, is one of the country's most fashionable spas. Hallstatt is the best center for exploring the province's major attractions: The salt mines of **Salt Mountain** and the spectacular **Dachstein Caves.**

Tyrol

One of Austria's most historic and colorful provinces, this breathtaking mountainous district was once the medieval crossroads between the Teutonic world and Italy. Its capital is the beautiful city of **Innsbruck,** both a summer resort and a winter ski center. Filled with attractions, it's the place to be in ski season. But the glories of Tyrol hardly end in Innsbruck. The province is a weave of valleys, lakes, and streams, whose resorts draw summer and winter visitors alike. These lush valleys include the beautiful Stubai and Wipp, where the major resorts of **Fulpmes** and **Neustift** offer vistas of glacier tops and alpine peaks.

The **Upper Inn district** is also worth a visit. The old market town of **Imst** makes a good stop along the Upper Inn. On the eastern side of the Arlberg are the resorts of **St. Anton am Arlberg,** an old village on the Arlberg Pass, and **St. Christoph,** the mountain way station of St. Anton. **Seefeld** and **Ischgl** are also great ski resorts, offering both summer and winter outdoor activities. In the Ziller Valley is another sophisticated resort, **Zell am Ziller.** The **Kitzbühel Alps** offer some of Austria's best skiing. If you have time, journey to **East Tyrol** to **Lienz,** a rich, folkloric town on the Isel River with romantic old inns and guesthouses.

Vorarlberg

Vorarlberg, located at the country's westernmost tip, shares most of its borders with the wild and mountainous eastern border of Switzerland; it's home to some of Austria's most sophisticated ski resorts, highest alpine peaks, and much of its most beautiful scenery. Its capital is **Bregenz,** a pleasant town at any time of the year, although it hardly competes with the scenic grandeur of the province's resorts, such as **Lech** and **Zürs.** In winter, Lech and the even more elegant Zürs, on the western side of the Arlberg, are among Europe's leading ski resorts.

The **Montafon Valley,** known for its powdery snow and sun, has been called a winter "ski stadium." The best places for skiing here are the hamlets of **Schruns** and **Tschagguns.** If you're here in summer, you might want to explore the **Bregenz Forest (Bregenzerwald),** although it's hardly the Black Forest in Germany. The northern part of the Vorarlberg alpine range is a prime place for outdoor activities. You'll want to dine and stay at **Bezau.** If you have time, the towns of **Dornbirn, Feldkirch,** and **Bludenz** are interesting to explore.

Carinthia

Noted for its forests, rolling hills, and hundreds of freshwater lakes, Carinthia shares most of its border with Slovenia. Although landlocked, the province has just a hint of Mediterranean flavor, which permeates its gardens, lakeside resorts, and the verdant capital city, **Klagenfurt.** Outside the capital is the striking hilltop **Hochosterwitz Castle.** The province's biggest alpine lake is **Wörther See,** where you can stay at the idyllic summer resorts of **Krumpendorf** or **Pörtschach.** The sophisticated resort of **Velden,** at the western end of Wörther See, is called the heart of the "Austrian Riviera." In the center of the lake district, **Villach,** with its nearby warm springs, is another major destination.

Styria

One of the most heavily forested of the Austrian provinces, Styria has landscapes that rise from lush valleys to towering alpine peaks. With a strong medieval tradition, this area originated the Loden-colored jackets and felt hats with feathers that many newcomers assume are the Austrian national costume. The district's capital is **Graz,** the second largest city in Austria, boasting an array of galleries and modern art museums as well as one of the best-preserved medieval cores of any Austrian city—a World

Heritage site. You'll also want to visit **Bad Gleichenberg,** the province's most important summer spa, and **Mariazell,** a major pilgrimage site because of its Mariazell Basilica. Another spa, **Bad Aussee,** is in the "green heart" of the Salzkammergut, in an extremely beautiful part of Austria. You'll find the area's best skiing in the **Dachstein-Tauern,** where you can stay at the twin resorts of **Schladming** and **Rohrmoos.**

THE HIGHLIGHTS OF AUSTRIA IN 1 WEEK

Days 1 & 2: Vienna ★★★: Gateway to Austria

Most tours of Austria begin in Vienna, unless you're coming in from the west— say, after a visit to Switzerland. If so, you can use Innsbruck as your gateway and take this highlight tour in reverse.

Starting in Vienna on **Day 1,** check into your hotel and enjoy a hearty Austrian breakfast of fresh bread with farmer's ham and local cheeses, or perhaps an *Eierspeis* of scrambled eggs and some of the fabled Viennese pastries. You might get a good enough "tuck in" that you'll skip lunch.

It would take a few weeks to see all of Vienna's major sights, but you can skim the highlights in 2 days by concentrating on **St. Stephan's Cathedral** (p. 159) in the heart of the Altstadt (Old Town). Climb its south tower for the most panoramic view. Later that morning visit the once imperial **Schönbrunn Palace** (p. 157), summer seat of the Habsburgs. In the afternoon walk over to the **Hofburg** (p. 145), visiting its major attractions such as the Imperial Crown Jewels. As the sun sets, you can doll up for an evening of delicious excess at the opera or make your own drama at a Viennese tavern, bar, or club (see chapter 6).

On **Day 2,** take in the wonders of the **MuseumsQuartier** (p. 151), stopping at the **Leopold Museum** and the **Kunsthalle Wien.** And then wander through the nearby **Burggarten** and **Volksgarten** (p. 165), or take in a performance of the **Vienna Boys' Choir** (p. 147). Try for an afternoon visit to the **Belvedere Palace** (p. 156) and its fine art galleries. For a typically Viennese experience, spend your final night at one of the *Heuriger* wine taverns on the outskirts of the city. Some of the best are found in the suburbs of **Grinzing, Neusdorf,** or **Neustift am Walde.** Our *Heuriger* recommendations begin on p. 186.

Day 3: The Danube River ★★★

On **Day 3,** head off to Salzburg. If you only have a day or two, you can take the Autobahn straight to Salzburg. But you'd miss a lot. We suggest a more leisurely, 2-day journey, with stops in the Danube Valley and the Salzkammergut.

Instead of the Autobahn, take Route 3, called the "Austrian Romantic Road," west from Vienna. On the north of the river you can follow this lovely old road into **Krems** (80km/50 miles west of Vienna; p. 206), among the most rewarding stopovers in the Danube Valley, with its old churches, ancient houses, covered *passages,* and cobblestone streets. You can use Krems as a base and set out on two side trips; first to the medieval wine town of **Dürnstein,** 8km (5 miles) west of Krems, where the English King Richard the Lion-Hearted was imprisoned on his way back from the Third Crusade. In summer this is a great area to go biking in, since it is quite flat and the cascading vineyards and Roman ruins greet you at every turn. From Dürnstein, follow Route 33 along the south bank of the Danube to **Stift Melk** (p. 212), a magnificent Benedictine monastery, and surrounding Renaissance town in parts dating back to the 15th century. The distance is 31km (19 miles). You can double back along the road leading northeast into Krems for the night, or book a room in Dürnstein, even more romantic than Krems.

Day 4: Salzkammergut ★★★: Salzburg's Lake District

On the morning of **Day 4,** leave Krems and drive south to the Autobahn (E60) that runs west to Salzburg. At the junction with Route 145, head south into Bad Ischl, your best base for touring the Salzkammergut. The driving distance between Krems and Bad Ischl is 224km (139 miles).

Check into a hotel in the fashionable spa of Bad Ischl and stroll its Esplanade, where the Emperor Franz Josef used to walk with his mistress, court actress Katharina Schratt. You can see the **Kaiservilla** (p. 335) where the emperor lived for 60 summers, and a short walk away, Katharina's "Villa Felicitas" (now Villa Schratt). If time remains, you can also check out the sumptuous **Villa Léhar** (p. 336), home of *Merry Widow* composer Franz Léhar, where he spent each summer from 1912 until his death in 1948 and, he claimed, got his best ideas.

After lunch, drive down to **Hallstatt,** 19km (12 miles) south of Bad Ischl, where you'll discover one of the most beautiful villages in Austria. It is on the narrow Hallstättersee, and takes roughly 2 hours to see. Northwest of Hallstatt you can also visit the **Salzwelten/Hallstatt Salt Mines** (p. 339), one of the area's most distinctive geological formations. Return to Bad Ischl for a relaxing night.

Days 5 & 6: Salzburg ★★★: Birthplace of Mozart

On the morning of **Day 5,** hop on the train to Salzburg, or by car head south of Dürnstein to the Autobahn (A1), which will carry you directly into **Salzburg,** 245km (152 miles) to the west. Check into a hotel for 2 nights, then set about exploring the city. Head for the Mozartplatz to hear the **Glockenspiel** (p. 259) or carillon, the 35 bells that ring from the Residenz. While here, stroll through the **Salzburger Dom** (p. 262), or cathedral, on the south side of the Residenzplatz. In the afternoon, book tickets for the whole family for *"The Sound of Music* Tour," named after the 1965 film that still enjoys worldwide success.

Sit at a cafe on **Mozartplatz** for a coffee and a pastry before taking the funicular gondola to the **Hohensalzburg Fortress** (p. 271) for a tour. After lunch, you can see **Mozart's birthplace** (p. 262) on Getreidegasse. Allow time in the afternoon for a visit to the **Residenzgalerie** (p. 259), the opulent palace and former seat of the ruling Salzburg prince-archbishops. Treat yourself to a midday or evening concert at the **Mozarteum** conservatory (✆ **0662 873154;** Theatergasse 2; www.mozarteum.at) and if the **Salzburg Festival** is taking place at the time of your visit, reserve ahead for concerts, theater, or opera.

On **Day 6,** set out to see the sights you missed the day before, including the **Dom** or cathedral (p. 262) and **Stiftskirche St. Peter** (p. 265), as well as **Petersfriedhof** (p. 259), the cemetery of St. Peter's. Wander through the **Mirabell Gardens** (p. 267), and spend at least 2 or 3 hours in the **Altstadt**

The Highlights of Austria in 1 Week

(p. 350), the Old Town, where you can shop for local specialties and enjoy just walking the streets.

Day 7: Innsbruck ★★★: Capital of Tyrol

On the morning of **Day 7,** leave Salzburg and drive 190km (118 miles) southwest to Innsbruck, arriving in time for lunch. Check into a hotel for your final night. Set out on foot to explore the **Altstadt** (Old Town) for at least 2 hours, and stroll **Maria-Theresien-Strasse,** the main street. You can also see the **Golden Roof** (Goldenes Dachl), the magnificent covered balcony from which the Kaiser Maximilian I could watch the goings on in the square below (p. 354).

In the afternoon, visit **Hofkirche** (p. 355). If time remains, take in the exhibits of the **Tiroler Volkskunst Museum** (p. 356).

After Innsbruck, you discover the glories of the Tyrol, its plunging mountains carved out of a brilliant blue sky. See chapter 12 for complete coverage. When time's up, head back to your transportation hub. If that's Vienna, go by train to indulge yourself in a scenic and very relaxing end to your travels. Or head west into Switzerland for yet another adventure (see *Frommer's Switzerland* for complete coverage).

SCENIC AUSTRIA IN 2 WEEKS

It may seem an unlikely undertaking, but it's possible to take in "Essential Austria" in just 2 weeks with some fast footwork. If you start in **Vienna** and head west, via **Linz** and **Salzburg,** you can see a lot of the beauty that spans the country, all the way to Vorarlberg in the west at the gateway to Switzerland.

Highlights of this vast panoramic trip include not only Vienna and Salzburg, but the other two major centers: Linz and Innsbruck. The most spectacular highlights are the lake district at Salzkammergut and the fabled Grossglockner Road. In winter the roads can be quite precarious, in which case ask at the Austrian National Railway (http://www.oebb.at/en/index.jsp) or a travel agency for the simplest train route to reach these destinations. The only site you'll miss is the Grossglockner Road. From Innsbruck onwards the train is recommended—the vistas are missed if you have to drive.

Days 1 & 2: Vienna ★★★: The Launch Pad

Follow the same itinerary as outlined in the 1-week tour of Austria (see above).

Day 3: The Danube River ★★★

Explore the beautiful Danube Valley west of Vienna as described in **Day 3** above.

Day 4: Linz ★★

Instead of heading on to the Salzkammergut, as we did in **Day 4** (see above), we suggest you leave Krems in the morning and take the scenic Route 3, which meanders along the north of the Danube into Linz, where you can overnight. The distance from Krems to Linz is 254km (158 miles).

After checking into a hotel, set out to explore the attractions of this city, including its newest sights, the **Ars Electronica Center** (p. 318) and **Lentos Kunstmuseum Linz** (p. 318). In the afternoon, take an excursion from Linz to that baroque masterpiece, the **Abbey of St. Florian** (p. 319). Since Linz is celebrated for its Linzer torte, sample the delicacy in one of the cafes we recommend on p. 323

Day 5: Salzkammergut's Bad Ischl ★★★

On the morning of **Day 5,** leave Linz and head south to the Autobahn (E55), which you can follow to the junction with Route 145, leading south into the spa of **Bad Ischl,** a good overnight base and a place for rest and relaxation before you press on to Salzburg. Take in its attractions as outlined under Day 4 in the tour above.

Days 6 & 7: Salzburg ★★★

Spend **Days 6 and 7** here in the birthplace of Mozart, site of the most famous musical festival in Europe. Occupy your time here as outlined under Days 5 and 6 in the 1-week tour of Austria (see above).

Day 8: South to Lienz ★: Capital of East Tyrol

Leave Salzburg on the morning of **Day 8.** Head south on Route 150 to the junction with Route 159. Follow this highway south until it merges with Route 311 going west toward **Zell am See,** a distance of 85km (53 miles) southwest of Salzburg. Make this your luncheon stopover (for recommendations, see p. 305). If you have time, ascend the mountain plateau of **Schmittenhöhe** (p. 305) for one of the best panoramic views of Land Salzburg.

After lunch, continue south along Route 107 into Lienz for the night, a distance of 92km (57 miles). Not to be confused with Linz (capital of Upper Austria), the Tyrolean city of Lienz lies at the junction of three valleys. You can spend the rest of the afternoon wandering its old streets and visiting Schloss Bruck (p. 407).

Day 9: Grossglockner Road ★★★: The Great Alpine Highway

On the morning of **Day 9,** leave Lienz and head for the most scenic drive on this tour, the legendary **Grossglockner Road.** There are several approaches to this magnificent mountain road; for details, our coverage begins on p. 302. From our starting position in Lienz, you can drive north on Route 107 to the town of **Heiligenblut,** where you might stop for a coffee before climbing the mountain in your car. Driving distance between Lienz and Heiligenblut is 48km (30 miles).

The road will lead you to **Bruck an der Grossglocknerstrasse** in Land Salzburg, near the **Zell am See** ski area. From here follow the signs to the famed ski resort of **Kitzbühel** along Routes 168 and 161, where you can overnight. From the Zell am See area to Kitzbühel is a distance of 55km (34 miles).

Day 10: Kitzbühel ★★★: Ski Circus

Kitzbühel has earned its fame for its winter Ski Circus, but if you're a motorist on a driving tour, chances are you'll be here in fairer weather, when there are a different set of attractions, including the **Alpine Flower Garden** (p. 397). See "More Winter & Summer Pursuits" (p. 397) for a range of other activities. We suggest that you spend the best part of the day in Kitzbühel, enjoying the stunning scenery of this resort before heading out to Innsbruck for a stop of 2 nights (see below). To reach Innsbruck, a distance of 100km (62 miles) to the west, we recommend a cross-country scenic road, Route 170, cutting through the mountains until it links with the E45/A12 going southwest into Innsbruck.

Days 11 & 12: Innsbruck ★★★: Fun in Tyrol

On the morning of **Day 11,** follow the same general plan as outlined for Day 7 in our 1-week tour of Austria (see above). As **Day 12** begins, leave Innsbruck altogether to see some major Tyrolean attractions in the environs. Visits are possible to **Hungerburg** (p. 357), a plateau that's the most beautiful spot in the Tyrol, and to the renaissance palace of **Schloss Ambras** (p. 357). In 1 day, you can also work in a visit to the **Wiltener Basilica** (p. 357), which is one of the loveliest churches in Tyrol, dating from the 18th century. When you return to Innsbruck for a final overnight, catch an orchestra concert, opera, musical, or dance, Tuesday to Sunday at the **Tiroler Landestheater** (p. 350). If possible, leave your car in Innsbruck for the remainder of your trip. The train ride to Bregenz is breathtaking and stops in St. Anton, right at the foot of the mountain. With a standard open ticket, you can stop for lunch and continue on a later train. Much more fun if you don't have to drive!

Day 13: West to St. Anton am Arlberg ★★★

On the morning of **Day 13,** either hop on the train heading to Bregenz or if you are driving head west out of Innsbruck along 171 to the junction with Route 186, at which point you can go south in the **Ötz Valley,** arguably the most scenic and panoramic in Tyrol both by car and by train. You'll see many waterfalls and snow-covered mountains as you dip past the glaciers and peaks of the **Ötzal Alps.** The road takes you deep into the heart of what is known as the "Tyrolean Arctic," a glacier region that is among the most beautiful in Austria. You can also stop at **Ötztal,** the main town for refueling and for lunch. It lies on a sunny slope at 822m feet (2,697 ft.). If you're driving, you might go as far as Sölden, climbing to 1,342m (4,403 ft.). It is a quaint old village of folkloric charm. After a stopover, head back to the main highway and continue west in the opposite direction of Innsbruck. Hop off the train or exit the highway in **St. Anton** for the night, a distance of 100km (62 miles) west of Innsbruck, and reached along Route 171. St. Anton was once an important trade center crossing the Alps and is one of the great ski resorts of Austria. Overnight here before you begin your crossing of the **Arlberg Pass** in the morning.

Day 14: The Final Scenic Route West to Bregenz ★★

For **Day 14,** your final day in Austria, get a morning train to Vorarlberg's capital, **Bregenz** or head across the **Arlberg Pass** by car, a scenic drive of panoramic beauty. Leave St. Anton, heading for St. Christoph at 1,784m (5,853 ft.). It's reached from St. Anton by following Route 316. The location is 8km (5 miles) away. Continue west into the province of Vorarlberg (westernmost in Austria) until you arrive at its Vorarlberg's capital, Bregenz. Follow S19 west until you hook up with the A14 Autobahn heading north. Bregenz lies 150km (90 miles) northwest of Innsbruck along the southeastern shore of the Bodensee (Lake Constance). You can spend 2 or 3 days here taking in both mountain and lakeside attractions, or even rent a boat or take a tour of the Bodensee as a Dreiländereck (Three Country Corner: Austria, Germany and Switzerland) but you may have run out of time. If so, you are only 130km (81 miles) a short train ride east of Zurich, which, of course, is one of the transportation hubs of Europe if you want to end your Austrian journey, or just head back to Vienna on a train and catch some shut-eye.

AUSTRIA FOR FAMILIES

In addition to its majestic alpine peaks and fabulous natural wonders, Austria also has many manmade attractions for kids. Your main concern with children along is pacing yourself for the right mix of museum, adventure, and leisure time. After all, it's your trip too. Our suggestion is to combine city attractions found in Vienna and Salzburg with some trips into the countryside. Although you can take a car for any of these, most people find they are more stress-free by train.

Days 1 & 2: Vienna ★★★: Getting Started

Your child has probably been held captive on a long jet plane ride and will be eager for exercise. Get the legs moving on **Day 1** by climbing the **Domkirche St. Stephan** (p. 159), the historic cathedral of Vienna, for a panoramic view. Later, plan on spending 2 hours at the grand Habsburg palace, **Schönbrunn** (p. 157), where special 60- to 90-minute tours are conducted by guides through rooms that offer hands-on displays for children. If the weather is fair, get the makings of a picnic and wander into **Stadtpark** (p. 165) for a place to enjoy it. Spend the afternoon visiting the amusements, including a famous Ferris wheel, the **Riesenrad** in the **Prater** (see "The Prater", p. 165).

On the morning of **Day 2,** try to schedule your day around two performances—that of the concert by the **Vienna Boys' Choir** (p. 147) and a visit to see the horses at the **Spanische Hofreitschule** (p. 151), which kids always enjoy. Because of scheduling problems, you may not always get to hear the choir, but the whole family can see the Lipizzaners prance to the music of Johann Strauss. Spend the afternoon touring the **Hofburg Palace Complex** (p. 145), where children are generally fascinated by the Kaiserappartements, especially the splendid sections where the royal children lived. Cap the afternoon off with a stroll down the bustling Graben and Kärntnerstrasse to the Haus der Musik, where the kids can test their musical skill with hands-on exhibitions and even record their own CD.

Day 3: The Danube Valley pt. 1: Carnuntum ★★★

Keep your Vienna hotel for one more night as this trip is not far off. Take the Train S7 from Landstrasse/Wien-Mitte to Petronell-Carnuntum or Bad Deutsch-Altenburg. The ride takes about an hour and on weekends and public holidays a shuttle bus is available to take you from the station to the **Carnuntum Open Air Museum.** By car take the A4 (toward Budapest/Airport)—exit Fischamend/Bratislava, then take the B9 (main road to Bratislava) to Petronell-Carnuntum or Bad Deutsch-Altenburg (about 35 min.). Once you've arrived you can spend some 3–6 hours exploring, depending on the weather, at this former Roman fortress town. The small museum will take about an hour and the open-air museum takes as long as you want. The main attractions for kids are in summer, when there are Roman games and gladiator re-enactments and theatrical productions. When all are spent, head back to Vienna for your last night.

Day 4: The Danube Valley pt. 2 ★★★: Krems & Dürnstein

Before leaving Vienna, pack a picnic to enjoy later at a secluded spot. Either take the train from Franz-Josephs Bahnhof or take the "Austrian Romantic Road" (Route 3) west from Vienna along the more scenic northern banks of the Danube. Your first stopover can be at **Krems,** 80km (50 miles) west of Vienna. You don't want your child to think Austria is all about cities, and Krems is a perfect town for exploring. Kids often take it for a set from Harry Potter, with its arched gateways, narrow cobbled lanes, hidden staircases, and ancient town walls. You can spend at least 2 hours simply wandering. A part of Krems called Stein is best for exploring, a village-like section of narrow streets terraced above the river.

For your overnight stopover, we suggest you continue 8km (5 miles) west of Krems to the romantic medieval wine town of **Dürnstein.** Richard the Lion-Hearted of England was held prisoner here in 1193. Check into one of the old inns for the night and set about exploring. The whole family can delight in wandering the town's castle fortress 159m (522 ft.) above the town. Later explore the Hauptstrasse and the many little streets that branch off from it.

If you have time, continue along Route 3 north of the Danube to the city of Linz, a distance of 158km (98 miles) from Dürnstein. Plan an overnight here. After checking into a hotel, pick up the brochure, "A Walk Through the Old Quarter," and do what it says; this attraction could take up to 2 hours of your time. For children, the most intriguing attraction is the **Ars Electronica Center** (p. 318), with its hands-on exhibits and its dancing marionettes for the digital age. Kids go on a trip "to the outer reaches of space." As a reward for taking the kids here, make a visit to the **Lentos Kunstmuseum Linz** (p. 318) to see some great art. Children are often mesmerized by some of the paintings here.

Days 5 & 6: Salzburg ★★★: It's Not All Mozart

On the morning of **Day 5,** hop on the train to Salzburg, or by car head south of Linz to the Autobahn (E55/E60), which will carry you directly into **Salzburg,** 130km (82 miles) to the west. Check into a hotel for 2 nights, then set about exploring the city. Head for the Mozartplatz to hear the **Glockenspiel** (p. 259) or carillon, the 35 bells that ring from the Residenz. While here, stroll through the **Salzburger Dom** (p. 262), or cathedral, on the south side of the Residenzplatz. In the afternoon, book tickets for the whole family for "*The Sound of Music* Tour," named after the 1965 film that still enjoys worldwide success.

On **Day 6,** take the family up to the impressive **Hohensalzburg Fortress,** which is reached by a funicular ride. Allow 1½ hours for this. After a visit, head for **Schloss Hellbrunn** (p. 274) in the environs. Although it's only a 20-minute drive, the boat ride from the center of town is much more fun (ask at hotel for details). After a visit, call on the 800 zoo animals at the **Salzburger Tiergarten Hellbrunn** (p. 275). Following lunch, there's still time to go to Hallein and the **Dürrnberg Salt Mines** (p. 275). Hallein lies only 15km (9 miles) from the center of Salzburg and if you buy your tickets for the mines at the train station there is a discount on the rail ride and the ticket. For many kids, a trip aboard an electric mine train, the **Salzbergwerkbahn,** going deep into the caverns will be the highlight of their visit to Salzburg.

Day 7: In Winter: Innsbruck ★★★: Center of the Tyrol In Summer: Wörthersee ★★: Watersport Oasis

For a final look at Austria, head out from Salzburg on the morning of **Day 7** for Innsbruck, and the most spectacular train ride on this trip. Check into a hotel for your final night. Innsbruck is reached by Autobahn A8, which joins Autobahn A93 (later A12) for its final descent 190km (118 miles) to the southwest.

In Innsbruck, spend at least 2 hours traversing the Old Town on foot. Stroll along the main street, **Maria-Theresien-Strasse,** and visit the **Goldenes Dachl,** or golden roof (p. 354). After lunch, pay a visit to the 15th-century imperial palace, **Hofburg** (p. 354), and try to budget time for the **Alpenzoo** (p. 353), on the southern slope of the Hungerburg plateau. Not only can you see mammals indigenous to the Alps, but you will also be rewarded with one of the most panoramic views in Tyrol.

If it's hot outside, a dip into the waters of the Wörthersee may be just the ticket. Take a train to **Klagenfurt,** the capital of Carinthia. The kids will love the **Minimundus,** a microcosm of famous structures from all over the world. The minute Taj Mahal is only a stone's throw away from Rome's St. Peter's Cathedral. Then it's off to the famous lake, either to one of the many resorts like **Maria Wörth** or **Velden** (p. 447), or just ask at your hotel for nearby beaches, there are so many. From Klagenfurt you can either return to Vienna or continue your trip in the Mediterranean Slovenia, directly south.

THE SALZKAMMERGUT LAKE DISTRICT ★★★ IN 1 WEEK

Fleeing the alpine peaks, we descend on the southern lake district to wind up our final tour of Austria. Of course, this tour is recommended during the all-too-short summer months. Instead of Vienna, we suggest using Salzburg as our gateway to the lakes, which begins in the province of Land Salzburg and ends in the summer resorts of the southeastern province of Carinthia. This trip does require a car, as lake-hopping involves back roads and windy coastlines.

Day 1: Salzburg ★★★: Gateway to the Lakes

Salzburg lies at the door to some of the greatest natural attractions in Europe, found in the province of Land Salzburg. After driving or flying to Salzburg, you'll have just enough time to walk the ancient streets of its Old Town (allow 2 or 3 hr.) and visit the **Residenzgalerie** (p. 259) and the **Hohensalzburg Fortress** (p. 271).

Day 2: Mondsee ★: Austria's Moon Lake

On the morning of **Day 2,** leave Salzburg and head east on the A-1 until you see the turnoff to **Mondsee,** 27km (17 miles) to the east. Check into a hotel for the night and visit **Schloss Mondsee** (p. 331), where Maria married Captain von Trapp in *The Sound of Music.* Stroll along the lovely Marktplatz, a square filled with lively cafes. Arrangements can be made to go sailing (check with the tourist office—see p. 331), or you can just enjoy the lakefront beaches. "Moon Lake" (Mondsee in German) is the warmest of Land Salzburg's bodies of water.

Day 3: St. Wolfgang ★: The Romantic Lake

For **Day 3** you can still use Mondsee as a base or transfer over to **St. Wolfgang** so you won't have to make the 40-minute drive back at night. The easiest way to get here without taking difficult roads is to head southeast along Route 154, following it around the southern rim of Wolfgangsee, then cutting back west at the signposts into St. Wolfgang, which lies on the northern tier of Wolfgangsee, arguably known as the most romantic lake in Austria. It was the setting for the popular operetta *The White Horse Inn,* written by Oscar Blumenthal Gustav Kadelburg in 1896, but still performed all over Austria annually and in the light opera repertoire worldwide. Swimming and watersports dominate the lakefront beach life, and you can also plan visits to the **Pfarrkirche St. Wolfgang** (p. 333), a pilgrimage church since the 12th century. It's also possible to take an excursion to **Schafberg** (p. 334) for the most panoramic views in Upper Austria. On a clear day, you can see 13 lakes in Land Salzburg from here.

Day 4: Bad Aussee ★: The Green Heart

On the morning of **Day 4,** head east from St. Wolfgang, retracing your steps to the main road at the junction with Bad Ischl. From here, follow Route 145 southeast to **Bad Aussee,** a distance of only 34km (22 miles). Check in for the night.

The old spa of Bad Aussee is called the "green heart" of the Salzkammergut. At Bad Aussee you'll have crossed over from the province of Land Salzburg in Syria. Its lake, **Altaussee,** is one of the most beautiful bodies of water in that province. The resort, lying 650m (2,133 ft.) above sea level, is set in a network of other lakes in the Traun Valley. Drop in at the tourist office to hook up with any activities offered at the time of your visit. Hiking through this mini lake district is one of the joys of coming here, and it breaks up all that time at the wheel.

Day 5: Villach ★: Heart of the Carinthian Lake District

On the morning of **Day 5,** leave Bad Aussee, heading for **Villach,** 206km (128 miles) to the southeast. Follow Route 145 southwest to the junction with the highway A10 heading south to Spittal. Once here, continue southeast on the Autobahn (E55/E66) into Villach. After checking into a hotel for the night, explore on foot its **Altstadt** (Old Town) out from the **Hauptplatz** (Main Square). With a map from the tourist office, set out into the **Villacher Alps** (p. 450), one of the most scenic drives in Carinthia, taking you for an 18-km (11-mile) journey via the **Villacher Alpenstrasse Toll Road** with panoramic views in all directions.

Days 6 & 7: Klagenfurt ★: Carinthia's Capital

On the morning of **Day 6,** leave Villach on the A2 for **Klagenfurt,** 56km (35 miles) away. Anchor into Klagenfurt for 2 nights. After a tour of the Old Town and a visit to its **Domkirche** (p. 440) and **Diözesanmuseum** (p. 440), you can head for nearby **Wörthersee** for sailing and swimming in the mild lake water.

After a day on the water, plan to take a nearby excursion on **Day 7,** your final day in Austria. In a period of a single day, you can drive to **Maria Saal** (p. 446), a pilgrimage church outside Klagenfurt; **Hochosterwitz Castle,** whose origins go back to 860; and to **St. Veit an der Glan** (p. 444), the old capital of Carinthia back in 1170. After Klagenfurt, it's a 309-km (192-mile) northeast drive to Vienna. Or you can drop off your rental car and indulge in the luxury of a train ride north through the Alps.

SETTLING INTO VIENNA

Vienna is a romantic city of music, cafes, waltzes, art and design, parks, pastries, and wine, a true cosmopolitan center. Over the last decade Vienna has morphed from a traditional city with a visible and turbulent past to a modern metropolis in which the new compliments the old.

Vienna has always been a cosmopolitan city. From its place as the Roman Celtic settlement on the Danube River and their most important central European forts, "Vindobona," the city we now know as Vienna, has been the meeting place of the nations and cultures. Today, the many-peopled city of the Habsburgs is again at the center of a borderless Europe, as its imperial palaces and art museums mingle with modern installations and the challenge of cultural encounter. The result is a creative explosion on the stages and in the streets, in clubs and cabarets, in the open markets and on the menus: When it comes to dining, Vienna today is a gourmet's paradise. Having lived through war, siege, victory, defeat, the death of an empire and the birth of a republic, foreign occupation, independence, and the new internationalism of the European Union, fortunately, the Viennese character—a devotion to the good life—has endured.

ORIENTATION
Arriving
BY PLANE
As a gateway between western and eastern Europe, **Vienna International Airport (VIE)** (© **01/70070;** www.viennaairport.com) has seen an increase in air traffic. Although a number of well-respected European airlines serve Vienna, many flights from North America require a transfer in another major European city. Flights from Australia or New Zealand usually require a transfer in Asia and/or a larger European Airport.

One of the official **Vienna Tourist Information Offices** is in the arrival hall of the airport, open daily 6am to 11pm.

There's a regular, high-speed City Airport Train (CAT) service between the airport and the **City Air Terminal,** adjacent to the Vienna Hilton and directly across from the **Wien Mitte/Landstrasse** rail station, where you can easily connect with subway and tram lines. Trains run every 30 minutes from 6:05am to 11:35pm. The trip takes 16 minutes and costs 19€

per person. There's also a bus service between the airport and other destinations: Schwedenplatz, Westbahnhof, the UN Complex, and Südtirolerplatz, leaving every 30 minutes to an hour. Fares are 6€. Tickets are sold on the bus and must be purchased with euros.

There's also a local train service, Schnellbahn (S-Bahn), between the airport and the Wien Nord and Wien Mitte rail stations. Trains run every half hour from 5am to 11:40pm and leave from the basement of the airport. Trip time is 25 to 30 minutes, and the fare is 3.60€. This ticket can also be used for your further travel by public transportation within Vienna. In general, ticket prices vary for children, students, and seniors.

BY TRAIN

Vienna is connected to all Austrian cities and towns and to all major European cities. For train information for all stations, call ☎ **05/1717.**

Westbahnhof (West Railway Station), on Europaplatz, is currently under construction, but most trains from western Austria, France, Germany, Switzerland, and some eastern European countries arrive here nonetheless. It also has frequent links to major Austrian cities such as Salzburg. Westbahnhof connects with local trains, the U3 and U6 underground lines, and several tram and bus routes.

Südbahnhof (South Railway Station), at Südtirolerplatz, still services southern and eastern Austria. It's linked with the local rail service and tram and bus routes. At the time this was published the train station was being transformed to the new **Hauptbahnhof,** which should open by 2012/13. In the meantime trains are deferred to Westbahnhof or Matzleinsdorferplatz in the 10th District.

Other stations in Vienna include **Franz-Josef Bahnhof,** on Franz-Josef-Platz, used mainly by local trains, although connections are made here to Prague and Berlin. You can take the D-tram line to the city's Ringstrasse from here. **Wien Mitte,** at Landstrasser Hauptstrasse 1, is also a terminus for local trains, plus a depot for trains to the Czech Republic and to Vienna International Airport.

BY BUS

Because of the excellent rail service funneling from all parts of the Continent into Vienna, bus transit is limited and not especially popular. **Eurolines,** part of National Express Coach Lines (☎ **0871/781-8181**) is a 29-hour option from London costing 52€ to 72€ one way. The **City Bus Terminal** is at the Wien Mitte rail station, Landstrasser Hauptstrasse 1. This is the arrival depot for Post and Bundesbuses from points all over the country, as well as the arrival point for private buses from various European cities. The terminal has lockers, currency-exchange kiosks, and a ticket counter open daily from 6:15am to 6pm. For bus information, call ☎ **01/71101** daily from 6:15am to 6pm.

BY CAR

Vienna can be reached from all directions via *Autobahnen* (major highways) or by secondary highways. The main artery from the west is Autobahn A1, coming in from Munich (468km/291 miles), Salzburg (336km/209 miles), and Linz (186km/116 miles). Autobahn A2 arrives from the south, from Graz (200km/124 miles) and Klagenfurt (308km/191 miles). Autobahn A4 comes in from the east, connecting with Route E58, which runs to Bratislava and Prague. Autobahn A22 takes traffic from the northwest, and Route E10 connects to the cities and towns of southeastern Austria and Hungary.

Visitor Information

Once you've arrived safely in Vienna, head for either of two information points that make it their business to have up-to-the-minute data about what to see and do in Vienna. The more centrally located of the two is the **Wien Tourist-Information** office at Albertinaplatz (© **01/211140;** tram: 1 or 2). Located directly behind the Vienna State Opera, on the corner of Philharmoniker Strasse, in the heart of the Innere Stadt (Inner City), it's open daily from 9am to 7pm. The staff will make free hotel reservations for anyone in need of accommodations. Larger and more administrative, but also willing to handle questions from the public, is the headquarters of the **Vienna Tourist Board,** Obere Augartenstrasse (© **01/21114412;** tram: 31), open Monday to Friday 8am to 4pm. Both branches stock free copies of a tourist magazine, **Wien Monatsprogramm,** which lists what's going on in Vienna's concert halls, theaters, and opera houses. Also worthwhile here is *Vienna A to Z,* a general, pocket-size guide with descriptions and locations for a slew of attractions. This booklet is also free, but don't rely on its cluttered map.

For information on Vienna and Austria, including day trips from the city, visit the **Austrian National Tourist Office,** Margaretenstrasse 1, A-1040 (© **01/588660;** www.austria.info). For a rundown on the Wachau (Danube Valley) and the Wienerwald (Vienna Woods), you might want to contact **Niederösterreich Information,** Fischhof 3/3, A-1010 (© **01/536106200;** www.niederoesterreich.at).

City Layout

From its origins as a Roman village on the Danubian plain, Vienna had become one of the great capitals of Europe by the 15th century, grew to a city of over 2 million on the eve of World War I, and today numbers about 1.8 million, of whom 32% are foreign born. It is also one of the largest capitals of central Europe, with a surface area covering 414 sq. km (160 sq. miles), reputed to have a greater percentage of green space within the city limits than any other city in Europe. That city has been divided into 23 *Bezirke* (districts), each with its own character and reputation; for example, the 9th District is known as Vienna's academic quarter, whereas the 10th, 11th, and 12th Districts are home to blue-collar workers and are the most densely populated.

The 1st District, known as the **Innere Stadt (Inner City),** is where most foreign visitors first flock. This compact area is Vienna at its most historic; with St. Stephans at its core, it boasts the city's astounding array of monuments, churches, palaces, parks, and museums, in addition to its finest hotels and restaurants. Its size and shape roughly correspond to the original borders (then walls) of the medieval city.

The Inner City is surrounded by the **Ring or Ringstrasee,** a circular boulevard about 4km (2½ miles) long. Constructed between 1859 and 1888, it's one of the most ambitious examples of urban planning and restoration in central European history. Built over the foundations of Vienna's medieval fortifications, the Ring opened new urban vistas for the dozens of monumental 19th-century buildings that line its edges today. The name of this boulevard changes as it moves around the Inner City, which can get confusing. Names that correspond with the boulevard end in *ring:* Schottenring, Dr.-Karl-Lueger-Ring, Burgring, Opernring, Kärntner Ring, Stubenring, Parkring, and Schubertring.

Ironically, the river for which Vienna is so famous, the **Danube,** doesn't really pass through the center of the city at all. Between 1868 and 1877, the river was channeled into its present muddy banks east of town, and was replaced with a small-scale substitute, the **Donaukanal (Danube Canal),** which was dug for shipping food and other supplies to the Viennese and is now lined with cafes, clubs, and restaurants. The canal is set against Ringstrasse's eastern edge, and is traversed by five bridges in the 1st District alone.

Surrounding the Ring and the Inner City, in a more or less clockwise direction, are the inner suburban districts (2–9), which contain many hotels and restaurants popular for their proximity to the city center. The 5th District is an exception, as it squeezes in between the 4th and 6th, not touching the Inner City. The villas and palaces of Vienna's 18th-century aristocrats can be found in the first 9 districts, as well as modern apartment complexes and the homes of 19th-century middle-class entrepreneurs. These districts are profiled below under "Neighborhoods in Brief."

The outer districts (10–23) form another concentric ring of suburbs, comprising a variety of neighborhoods from industrial parks to rural villages. **Schönbrunn,** the Habsburg's vast summer palace, is located in these outlying areas in the 13th District, **Hietzing.** Also noteworthy is the 19th District, **Döbling,** with its grand villas and famous *Heuriger* villages, such as Grinzing and Sievering (see "*Heuriger*," p. 186), and the 22nd District, **Donau-stadt,** home to the verdant Donauinsel (Danube Island) and the adjoining UNO-City, an impressive modern complex of United Nations' agencies.

FINDING AN ADDRESS

Street addresses are written with the street name first and then the house number (i.e. Postgasse 5), followed by a four-digit postal code, or sometimes a Roman numeral, that identifies the district in which the address is located. Often the code is preceded by the letter "A." The district number is coded in the two middle digits, so if an address is in the 1st District ("01"), the postal code would read A-1010; in the 7th District, A-1070; and in the 13th District, A-1130.

A rule of thumb used by hotel concierges and taxi drivers involves the following broad-based guidelines: Odd street numbers are on one side of the street, and even numbers are on the other. The lowest numbers are usually closest to the city's geographic and spiritual center, Stephansplatz, and get higher as the street extends outward. Naturally, this system won't work on streets running parallel to the cathedral, so you'll have to simply test your luck.

What about the broad expanses of Vienna's Ring? Traffic always moves clockwise on the Ring, and any backtracking against the direction of the traffic must be done via side streets that radiate from the general traffic flow. Numeration on the Ring always goes from high numbers to lower numbers, as determined by the direction of the prevailing traffic (odd street numbers appear on a driver's left, and even numbers appear on the right).

STREET MAPS

You'll need a very good and detailed map to explore Vienna, as it has some 2,400km (1,491 miles) of streets (many of them narrow). As so many places, including restaurants and hotels, lie in these alleyways, routine overview maps that are given away at hotels or the tourist office won't do. You'll need the best city map in Vienna, which is called **Streetwise Vienna,** and is pocketsized and laminated to survive your trip. It is sold at major newsstands, bookstores, and in many upscale hotels.

Neighborhoods in Brief

Many of Vienna's hotels and restaurants are conveniently located within or just outside the 1st District. In this section, we profile the Inner City, or Innere Stadt, and the adjacent districts.

Innere Stadt (1st district) This compact area is the oldest part of Vienna, bounded on all sides by the legendary Ring, the street tracing the former city walls. This

Vienna Neighborhoods

Währing
XVIII

↑ To Grinzing

Alsergrund
IX

Allgemeines
Krankenhaus

Schumanng.

Währinger Gürtel

Währinger Gürtel

Spitalgasse

Währinger Str.

Porzellangasse

Liechtensteinstr.

Bergg.

Hernals
XVII

Jörger Str.

221

Altes
Allgemeines
Krankenhaus

Türkenstr.

Hörlgasse

Maria-Theresien-

Börse

Ottakringer Str.

Hernalser Gürtel

Hernalser Gürtel

Skodagasse

Ledererg.

Lange Gasse

Alser Str.

Universitätsstr.

Schottenring

Universität

Dr.-K.-Lueger-Ring

Herren-
gasse

Ottakring
XVI

Thaliastr.

Lerchenfelder Gürtel

Lerchenfelder Gürtel

Florianigasse

Josefstadt
VIII

Josefstädter

Strozzigasse

Lange Gasse

Strasse

Rathaus

ℹ

Burg-
theater

A1 223

Koppstr.

223 Gablenzgasse

Lerchenfelder Strasse

Neustiftgasse

Burggasse

Parlament

Dr.-K.-
Renner-
Ring

Burgring

Hofburg
Complex

Neubau Gürtel

Neubau Gürtel

Schottenfeldgasse

Neubau-

gasse

Neubau
VII

Westbahn- str.

Siebensterngasse

Kirchengasse

Museumstr.

Museums-
Platz

Museums-

MuseumsQuartier

Seidengasse

Hütteldorfer Str.

Linden- gasse

Mariahilfer Str.

Opern-

Rudolfsheim
XV

ℹ Westbahnhof

Felberstr.

Kaiserstr.

Mariahilfer Str.

Linke Wienzeile

Rechte Wienzeile

221

Mariahilf
VI

Gumpendorfer Str.

Margaretenstr.

Mariahilfer Str.

Mariahilfer Gürtel

Mariahilfer Gürtel

Sechshauser Gürtel

Linke Wienzeile

Schönbrunner Str.

Sechshauser Str.

Margareten
V

Margaretenstr.

Reinprechtsdorfer Str.

Wiedner Hauptstr.

To
← Schönbrunn

Linke Wienzeile

Schönbrunner Str.

Meidling
XII

Margareten Gürtel

Gaudenzdorfer Gürtel

1

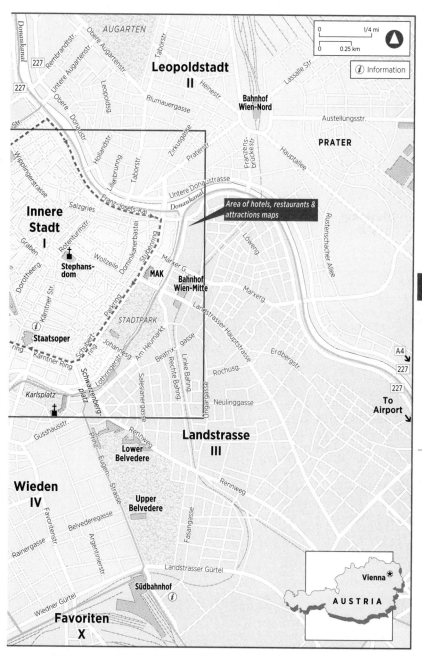

district remains at the center of Viennese life. The Inner City has dozens of streets devoted exclusively to pedestrian traffic, including **Kärntnerstrasse,** which leads from the Vienna State Opera House, to the **Graben,** which it meets at Stephansplatz, home to the famous cathedral. Competing with both the cathedral and the Opera House as the district's most famous building is the **Hofburg,** the Habsburg palace that's now a showcase of attractions, including the National Library, the Spanish Riding School, and six museums. Other significant landmarks include the Rathaus (City Hall), Parlament (Parliament), the Universität Wien (University of Vienna), the Naturhistorisches (Natural History), and the Kunsthistorisches (Art History) museums, and Stadtpark.

Leopoldstadt (2nd district) Once inhabited by Balkan traders and later by Vienna's Jewish community, this area doesn't physically border the Ringstrasse, but lies on the eastern side of the Danube Canal, across from Schwedenplatz or Schottenring. The district boasts lots of green and some of the only kosher restaurants and shops in the city. In addition to the tree-lined gravel paths of the Augarten, this is where you'll find the massive **Prater Park,** which boasts an amusement park, miles of tree-lined walking paths and numerous sports facilities, including a large stadium. At the far end of the park is Vienna's renowned trade-fair exhibition site. After a spree of development along the canal in recent years, Leopoldstadt has experienced a real revival.

Landstrasse (3rd district) The stately **Stadtpark** spreads into this district, where you'll see more streets dotted with churches, monuments, and palaces. One is the grand **Schwarzenberg Palace** and the looming **Konzerthaus** (concert house). However, the top attraction remains Prince Eugene Savoy's **Belvedere Palace,** an exquisite example of baroque architecture. Several embassies are in a small section of Landstrasse that's known as Vienna's diplomatic quarter. The **Wien Mitte rail station** and the **City Air Terminal** are also here.

Wieden (4th district) This small neighborhood extends south from Opernring and Kärntnering, and is almost as fashionable as the 1st District. Most activity centers on **Karlsplatz,** a historic square with its domed namesake, Karlskirche. Also nearby are Vienna's **Technical University** and the **Historical Museum of the City of Vienna.** Kärntnerstrasse, the main boulevard of the city center, turns into **Wiedner-Hauptstrasse** as it enters this district, and the **Südbahnhof,** one of the two main train stations, lies at its southern tip.

Margareten (5th district) Southwest of the 4th District, Wieden, this area does not border the Ring and thus lies a bit farther from the Inner City. You'll start to see more residential neighborhoods, representing the continual growth of Vienna's middle class. The historic homes of composers Franz Schubert and Christoph Gluck still stand here among modern apartment complexes and industrial centers.

Mariahilf (6th district) One of Vienna's busiest shopping streets, **Mariahilferstrasse,** runs through this bustling neighborhood. The sprawling, lively **Naschmarkt** (produce market), selling fresh fruits, vegetables, breads, cheeses, and more, is ideal for people-watching. On Saturdays, the adjacent **Flohmarkt** (flea market) adds to the lively but sometimes seedy atmosphere as vendors sell antiques and junk. In the surrounding streets you'll find the occasional Beisl (small pub/eatery), theater, cafe, and tavern. Farther from the city center, you'll find that the landscape becomes more residential.

Neubau (7th district) Bordering the expansive MuseumsQuartier, this is an ideal place to stay, as it's easily accessible by public transportation. The picturesque and once neglected **Spittelberg quarter** lies atop a hill just beyond Vienna's most famous museums. The vibrant cultural community is popular with both young and old visitors. The old Spittelberg houses have been renovated into boutiques, restaurants, theaters, and art galleries—a perfect backdrop for an afternoon stroll.

Josefstadt (8th district) The smallest of Vienna's 23 districts is named after Habsburg Emperor Joseph II and was once home to Vienna's civil servants. Like Neubau, this quiet, friendly neighborhood sits behind the City Hall and the adjacent grand museums of the Ringstrasse. Here you'll find secluded parks, charming cafes, and elaborate monuments and churches. Vienna's oldest and most intimate theater, **Theater in der Josefstadt,** has stood here since 1788. Shops and restaurants in the 8th district have a varied clientele, from City Hall lawmakers to university students.

Alsergrund (9th district) This area is often referred to as the Academic Quarter, not just because of housing a campus of the University of Vienna, but also because of its many hospitals and clinics. This is Freud territory, and you can visit his home, now the **Freud Museum,** on Berggasse. Here you'll also stumble upon the **Liechtenstein Palace,** one of Vienna's biggest and brightest, which today houses the family's collection from over 4 centuries.

GETTING AROUND
By Public Transportation

Whether you want to visit the Inner City's historic buildings or the outlying Vienna Woods, *Wiener Linien* (Vienna Public Transport) can take you there. This vast transit network—U-Bahn (subway), Strassenbahn (streetcar/tram), or bus—is safe, clean, and easy to use. If you plan on taking full advantage of it, pay the 1€ for a map that outlines the U-Bahn, buses, streetcars, and *Schnellbahn*, or S-Bahn (local trains). It's sold at *Informationdienst der Wiener Verkehrsbetriebe* (the Vienna Public Transport Information Center), which has five locations: Karlsplatz, Stephansplatz, Schottentor, Westbahnhof, Landstrasse (Wien Mitte), and Praterstern (Wien Nord). For information about any of these outlets, call © **01/7909100.** These offices are open Monday to Friday 6:30am to 6:30pm.

Vienna maintains a uniform fare that applies to all forms of public transport. A ticket for the bus, subway, or tram costs 1.80€ if you buy it in advance at one of the automated machines in U-Bahn stations, or at a *Tabac-Trafik* (a store or kiosk selling tobacco products and newspapers) or 2.20€ if you buy it onboard. Smart Viennese buy their tickets in advance, usually in blocks of at least five at a time, from any of the city's thousands of *Tabac-Trafiken* or at any vending machine. No matter what vehicle you decide to ride within Vienna, remember that once a ticket has been stamped (validated) by either a machine or a railway attendant, it's valid for one trip in one direction, anywhere in the city, including transfers. For other options see the "Transportation for Less" box, below.

U-BAHN (SUBWAY) Most of the top attractions in the Inner City can be seen by foot, tram, or bus, but the U-Bahn is your best bet to get across town quickly or reach the suburbs. It consists of five lines labeled U1, U2, U3, U4, and U6 (there is no U5). Stephansplatz, in the heart of the Inner City, and Karlsplatz are the most important underground stations for visitors, as the U1, U2, U3, and U4 stop at either of them. From Karlsplatz U2 traces part of the Ring and continues across the Danube, the U4 goes to Schönbrunn, and the U1 stops at both Stephansplatz and Karlsplatz. The U3 also stops at Stephansplatz and connects with Westbahnhof. The U-Bahn runs daily 6am to midnight and all night on Fridays and Saturdays.

TRANSPORTATION FOR less

The **Vienna Card** is the best ticket when using public transportation within the city limits. It's extremely flexible and functional for tourists because it allows unlimited travel, plus various discounts at city museums, restaurants, and shops. You can purchase a Vienna Card for 18.50€ at tourist information offices, public transport centers, and some hotels, or order one over the phone with a credit card (☎ **01/7984400148**).

A ticket valid for unlimited rides during any 24-hour period on the public transport system costs 5.70€; an equivalent ticket valid for any 72-hour period goes for 13.60€. There's also a green ticket, priced at 28.80€, that contains eight individual partitions. Each of these, when stamped, is good for 1 day of unlimited travel. An individual can opt to reserve all eight of the partitions for his or her own use, thereby gaining 8 days of cost-effective travel on the city's transport system. Partitions can be subdivided among a group of several riders.

These tickets are also available at *tabac-trafiks,* vending machines in underground stations, the airport's arrival hall (next to baggage claim), the *Reichsbrücke* (DDSG landing pier), and the *Österreichisches Verkehrsbüro* (travel agencies) of the two main train stations.

STRASSENBAHN (STREETCAR/TRAM)   Riding the trams (*Strassenbahn*) is not only a practical way to get around, but it's also a great way to see the city. Tram stops are well marked and lines are labeled as numbers or letters. Lines 1 and 2 will bring you to all the major sights on the Ringstrasse, but not all the way around. There is also a yellow Ring Tram that circles the Ring and costs 6€ for adults and 4€ for children.

BUS   Buses with hybrid engines have traversed Vienna in all directions since 1972, operating daily, including at night (but with more limited service then). Night buses leave every 10 to 30 minutes from Schwedenplatz, fanning out across the city. It is usually not necessary to change lines more than once. Normal tickets are valid aboard these late-night buses (no extra charge). On buses you can buy tickets from the driver.

By Taxi

Taxis are easy to find within the city center, but be warned that fares can quickly add up. Taxi stands are marked by signs, or you can call ☎ **01/31300,** 01/60160, 01/713-7196, or 01/40100. The basic fare is 2.50€, plus 1.20€ per kilometer. There are extra charges of 1€ for luggage in the trunk. For night rides after 11pm, and for trips on Sunday and holidays, there is a surcharge of 2.50€. There is an additional charge of 2€ if ordered by phone. The fare for trips to or from the airport is 33€ to or from anywhere in Vienna. Otherwise the fare for trips outside the city should be agreed upon in advance, and a 10% tip is the norm.

By Car

When in Austria use a car only for excursions outside Vienna's city limits; don't try to drive around the city. Parking is a problem; the city is a maze of one-way streets; and the public transportation is too good to endure the hassle of a car.

If you do venture out by automobile, information on road conditions is available in English (and French) on the radio station FM4 (103.8) and also 7 days a week from

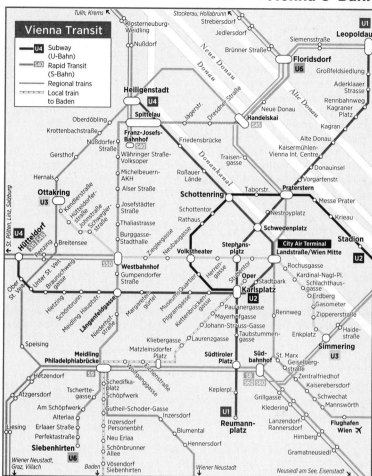

6am to 8pm from the **Österreichischer Automobil-, Motorrad- und Touringclub (ÖAMTC),** Schubertring 1–3, A-1010 Vienna (*©* **01/711-990**). This auto club also maintains a 24-hour emergency road service number (*©* **120** or 0810/120-120).

RENTALS It's always best to reserve rental cars in advance (p. 51), but you can rent a car once you've arrived in Vienna. You'll need a passport and a driver's license that's at least 1 year old. Avoid renting a car at the airport, where there's an extra 15% tax, in addition to the 21% value-added tax on all rentals.

Major car-rental companies include **Avis,** Opernring 3–5 (*©* **01/5876241**); **Budget Rent-a-Car,** Laaer Berg Strasse 43 (*©* **01/601870**); and **Hertz,** Kärntner Ring 17 (*©* **01/5128677**).

PARKING Curbside parking in Vienna's 1st District, site of most of the city's major monuments, is extremely limited—almost to the point of being nonexistent. When

5

SETTLING INTO VIENNA | Getting Around

curbside parking is available at all, it's within one of the city's "blue zones," and is usually restricted to 90 minutes or less from 8am to 6pm. If you find an available spot within a blue zone, you'll need to display a *scheine* (parking voucher) on the dashboard of your car. Valid for time blocks of only 30, 60, or 90 minutes, they're sold at branch offices of Vienna Public Transport Information Center (see above) and, more conveniently, within tobacco/news shops. Write in the date and time of your arrival before displaying the voucher on the right side of your car's dashboard. Be warned that towing of illegally parked cars is not an uncommon sight here. Frankly, it's easier to go to parking garages and avoid searching for curbside parking spots.

Underground parking garages are scattered throughout the city, and most of them charge between 3.50€ and 6€ per hour. Every hotel in Vienna is acutely aware of the location of the nearest parking garage—if you're confused, ask. Some convenient 24-hour garages within the 1st District include **Parkgarage,** Am Hof (*©* **01/5335571**); **Parkgarage Freyung,** Freyung (*©* **01/5350450**); and **APCOA,** Cobdengasse 2 (*©* **01/5125554**).

DRIVING & TRAFFIC REGULATIONS In general, Austria's traffic regulations do not differ much from those of other countries where you *drive on the right.* In Vienna, the speed limit is 50km/h (about 30 mph). Out of town, in such areas as the Wienerwald, the limit is 130km/h (81 mph) on motorways and 100km/h (62 mph) on all other roads. Honking car horns is forbidden in the city.

By Horse-Drawn Carriage

A *Fiaker* (horse-drawn carriage) has been used as a form of transportation in the Inner City for some 3 centuries. You can clip-clop along in one for about 20 minutes at a cost of about 40€. Prices and the length of the ride must be negotiated in advance. In the 1st District, you'll find a *Fiaker* for hire at the following sites: On the north side of St. Stephan's, on Heldenplatz near the Hofburg, and in front of the Albertina on Augustinerstrasse. There is also a 40-minute tour, and it costs 65€.

By Bike

Vienna has more than 1,000km (620 miles) of marked bicycle paths within the city limits. In the summer, many Viennese leave their cars in the garage and ride bikes. You can take bicycles on specially marked U-Bahn train carriages for free, but only Monday through Friday from 9am to 3pm and 6:30pm to midnight. On weekends in July and August, bicycles are carried free from 9am to midnight.

There is a virtually free way to wheel it in Vienna, which is to use a **Citybike** (www.citybikewien.at). The kiosks are all over the city and the bikes can be rented with a visa or maestro card from which 1€ is booked. After registering you can ride your city bike for free for the first hour of every rental and then simply return it to any other kiosk. The second hour costs 1€, the third 2€, and every further hour 4€. For a more comfortable or high-tech bike try rental stores around the Prater (see chapter 6) and along the banks of the Danube Canal, which is the favorite bike route for most Viennese. One of the best of the many sites specializing in bike rentals is **Pedalpower,** Ausstellungsstrasse 3 (*©* **01/7297234**), which is open March through October from 8am to 7pm. The Vienna Tourist Board (p. 92) can also supply a list of rental shops and more information about bike paths. Bike rentals begin at about 27€ per day.

[FastFACTS] VIENNA

American Express
The office at Kärntner-strasse 21–23 (📞 **01/5124004**), near Stock-im-Eisenplatz, is open Monday to Friday 9am to 5pm and Saturday 9am to noon.

Babysitters Most hotels will provide you with names of babysitters if they do not provide their own service. Sitters charge roughly 8€ to 12€ per hour, and you'll need to provide transportation home, via a cab, if they sit beyond 11pm.

Business Hours Most shops are open Monday to Friday from 9am to 6pm and Saturday from 9am to noon, 12:30, or 1pm, depending on the store. On the first Saturday of every month, shops customarily remain open until 4:30 or 5pm. The tradition is called *langer Samstag.*

City Code The telephone city code for Vienna is **01.** It's used only when you're calling from outside Vienna.

Dentists For dental problems, call 📞 **01/5122078,** where the staff can tell you about availability of dentists in the area.

Doctors A list of physicians can be found in the telephone directory under "Arzte." If you have a medical emergency at night, call 📞 **141** daily from 7pm to 7am.

Drug Laws Penalties are severe and could lead to either imprisonment or deportation. Selling drugs to minors is dealt with particularly harshly.

Drugstores *Apotheken* (chemist's shops/pharmacies) are open Monday to Friday from 8am to noon and 2 to 6pm, and Saturday from 8am to noon. At night and on Sunday, you'll find the names of the nearest open shops on a sign outside every Apotheke.

Electricity Vienna operates on 220 volts AC (50 cycles). This means that U.S.-made appliances without a 200/110 switch will need a transformer (sometimes called a converter). Many Viennese hotels stock adapter plugs but not power transformers. Electric clocks, CD players, and voice recorders, may not work well, even with transformers. Laptops generally adjust automatically with the proper power cord.

Emergencies Call 📞 **122** to report a fire, **133** for the police, or **144** for an ambulance.

Hospitals The major hospital is **Allgemeines Krankenhaus,** Währinger Gürtel 18–20 (📞 **01/40400**). The **Krankenhaus der Barmherzigen Brüder,** Johannes von Gott Platz 1 (📞 **01/21121-1100;** www.barmherzige-brueder.at; U-Bahn: Nestroyplatz, tram:

2 Karmeliterplatz), is in the 2nd District and run by a catholic order and will accept all emergency cases without insurance at no charge.

Internet Access Many hotels, coffeehouses, and other businesses offer Internet access, either Wi-Fi or with online computers. The dedicated Internet cafe business seems to be dying out. Many cafes around the city offer free Wi-Fi.

Luggage Storage & Lockers All four main train stations in Vienna have lockers available on a 24-hour basis, costing 3€ for 24 hours. It's also possible to store luggage at these terminals daily from 4am to midnight (1:15am at the Westbahnhof) at a cost of 2.50€.

Money During off-hours, you can exchange money at *bureaux de change* (exchange bureaus) throughout the Inner City (there's one at the intersection of Kohlmarkt and the Graben), as well as at travel agencies, train stations, and at the airport. There's also a 24-hour exchange service at the post office at Fleischmarkt 19.

Newspapers & Magazines Most newsstands at major hotels or news kiosks along the streets sell copies of the *International Herald Tribune* and *USA Today,* and also carry copies of the European editions of *Time* and *Newsweek*.

Police The emergency number is ☏ **133**.

Post Offices Post offices in Vienna can be found in the heart of every district. Addresses for these can be found in the telephone directory under "Post." Post offices are generally open for mail services Monday to Friday 8am to noon and 2 to 6pm. The *Hauptpostamt* (central post office), Fleischmarkt 19 (☏ **01/5138350**), and most general post offices are open 24 hours a day, 7 days a week. Postage stamps are available at all post offices and at tobacco shops, and there are stamp-vending machines outside most post offices.

Safety In recent years, Vienna has been plagued by purse-snatchers in tourist areas. Around St.

Stephan's Cathedral, signs (in German only) warn about pickpockets. Small children often, part of organized begging rings, approach sympathetic adults asking for money. As the adult goes for the wallet, full-grown thieves rush in and grab the money. As in many cities, anyone with a lot to carry should hold purses, computers or briefcases tightly and avoid opening them in public.

Taxes Vienna imposes no special city taxes, other than the national value-added tax that's tacked on to all goods and services.

Telegrams, Money-grams, Telexes & Faxes The central telegraph office is at Börse-platz 1. Faxes and wire transfers can be sent from any post office.

Transit Information Information, all types of

tickets, and maps of the transportation system are available at Vienna Transport's main offices on Karlsplatz or at the Stephansplatz underground station Monday to Friday 8am to 6pm and Saturday, Sunday, and holidays from 8:30am to 4pm. Alternatively, you can call ☏ **0810/222324** 24 hours a day for information in German and English about public transport anywhere within greater Vienna.

Useful Telephone Numbers Dial ☏ **05/1717** for rail information, ☏ **0810/222324** for bus schedules, and ☏ **01/211140** for tourist information daily from 9am to 7pm. For hotel reservations, call the Vienna Tourist Board's room reservations system (☏ **01/24555**) daily from 9am to 7pm.

WHERE TO STAY

Vienna has some of the greatest hotels in Europe and a long-standing tradition of service that has set a standard worldwide. But be warned: Finding a room can be a problem if you arrive without a reservation, especially in August and September. During these peak months, you might have to stay on the outskirts, in the Grinzing or the Schönbrunn districts, for example, and commute to the Inner City by streetcar, bus, or U-Bahn. Not that this is difficult, as Vienna's public transport is the envy of other cities even in Europe. And if you're looking to cut costs, staying outside the center makes sense, as you can pay 20 to 25% less for a hotel outside the Ringstrasse.

High season in Vienna encompasses most of the year: From May to October or early November, and during some weeks in midwinter, when the city hosts major trade fairs, conventions, and other cultural events. If you're planning a trip around Christmas and New Year's Day, room reservations should be made *at least* 1 month in advance. Some rate reductions (usually 15–20%) are available during slower midwinter weeks—it always pays to ask.

Note: A new antismoking ban went into effect throughout Austria on January 1, 2009, transforming all hotel rooms to nonsmoking. The smoking ban encompasses all public spaces, so the lobby is now off limits to smokers as well.

Any branch of the **Austrian National Tourist Office** (☏ **01/588-660**), including the Vienna Tourist Board, will help you book a room. They have branch offices in the arrival halls of the airport, train stations, and major highways that access Vienna. However, they will not reserve a room in advance for you.

If you prefer to deal directly with an Austrian travel agency, three of the city's largest are **Austropa,** Friedrichsgasse 7, A-1010 (☏ **01/588-00510**); **Austrobus,** Dr.-Karl-Lueger-Ring 8, A-1010 (☏ **01/534-110**); and **Blaguss Reisen,** Wiedner Hauptstrasse 15, A-1040 (☏ **01/50180**). Any of them can reserve hotel space, sell airline tickets, and procure hard-to-get tickets for music festivals. Many of their employees speak English fluently.

Innere Stadt (Inner City)
VERY EXPENSIVE

Do & Co. Hotel ★★   In 2006, one of Vienna's most consistently high-profile restaurants commandeered four floors of the Haas Haus and transformed it into a stylish hotel. The result is a quirky but relentlessly upscale and obsessively design-conscious venue that some find pretentious and others love. You take an elevator from an impersonal ground-floor entryway up to the registration area on level six, somewhat awkwardly positioned within a busy area that otherwise functions as a vestibule for the stylish **Onyx Bar.** The rooms, however, are artfully minimalist and very comfortable, with yummy but hard-to-define colors of toffee and putty. Sybaritic details include showers with visible interiors. Bedrooms have mahogany louvered doors, lots of polished travertine, dark-grained hardwoods, and floor plans that follow the curved walls and tucked-away balconies of the Haas Haus. Views from your windows encompass the crowds scurrying around the all-pedestrian Graben and the Stephansplatz.

In the Haas Haus, Stephansplatz 12, A-1010 Vienna. ☏ **01/24188.** Fax 01/24188444. www.doco.com. 43 units. 165€–350€ double; from 740€–1,550€ suite. AE, DC, MC, V. Valet parking. U-Bahn: Stephansplatz. **Amenities:** Restaurant; bar; dry cleaning; laundry service; room service. *In room:* A/C, TV, hairdryer, minibar, safe, free Wi-Fi.

Grand Hotel Wien ★★   Some of the most discerning hotel guests in Europe, from visiting soloists to diplomats, prefer this seven-story deluxe hotel to the more traditional and famous Imperial or Bristol (see below). Only a block from the Staatsoper, the spacious soundproof accommodations are posh, with all the modern luxuries, such as heated floors, beverage makers, and phones in marble bathrooms (which contain tub/shower combinations and even antifogging mirrors). Silk wallpaper, marble, and mahogany woodwork envelop bed, bath, and mini-bar. The more expensive units have more elaborate furnishings and decoration, including ornamental plaster molding. The main dining room specializes in Austrian and international dishes, and there's also a Japanese restaurant that serves the town's best sushi brunch on Sunday. High standards and taste are satisfied at every turn—excepting the tiny fitness center and absent pool and sauna.

Kärntner Ring 9, A-1010 Vienna. ☏ **01/515800.** Fax 01/5151310. www.grandhotelwien.com. 205 units. 211€–299€ double; from 765€–1,000€ suite. AE, DC, MC, V. Parking 28€. U-Bahn: Karlsplatz. **Amenities:** 3 restaurants; 2 bars; health club; boutiques; salon; room service; massage; babysitting; laundry service; dry cleaning; rooms for those w/limited mobility. *In room:* A/C, TV, coffeemaker, hairdryer, minibar, trouser press, safe, free Wi-Fi.

Hotel Ambassador ★   Until it became a hotel in 1866, the six-story Ambassador was a warehouse for wheat and flour, a far cry from its status today as one of Vienna's refined contemporary hotels. Much more modern than the Bristol or Imperial, it

Hotels in Vienna

5

Where to Stay

SETTLING INTO VIENNA

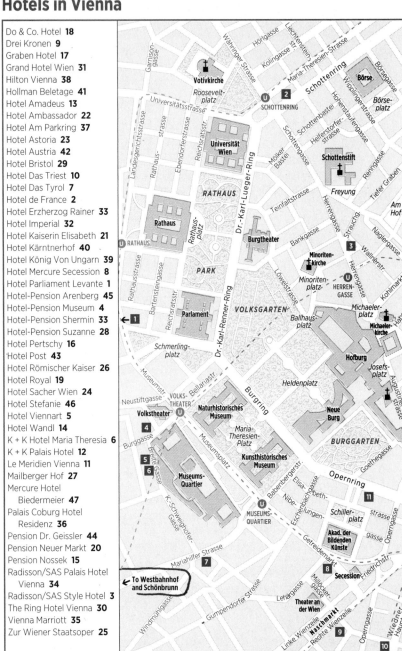

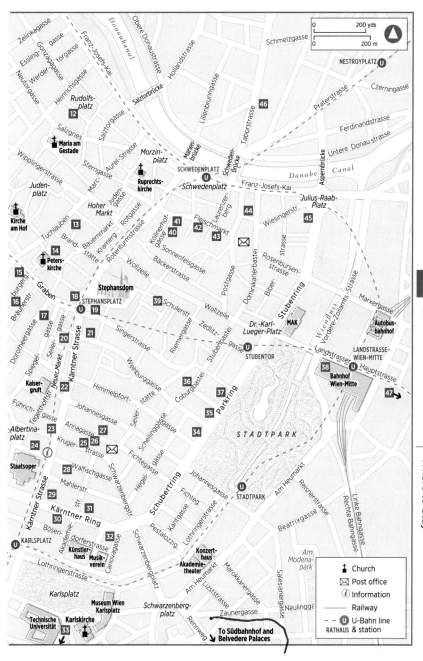

remains upscale and has the advantage of a great location, between the Vienna State Opera and St. Stephan's Cathedral, on the Neuer Markt square facing the Donner Fountain. Shop-lined Kärntnerstrasse is on the other side. Mark Twain stayed here, as have a host of diplomats and celebrities, including Theodore Roosevelt. Bedrooms are furnished with Biedermeier and Art Nouveau period pieces. The quieter rooms open onto Neuer Markt, although you'll miss the view of lively Kärntnerstrasse. Comfortable beds, marble bathrooms with tub/shower combinations and toiletries, and ample closet space add to the hotel's allure. The restaurant, Léhar, serves high-quality Austrian and international cuisine.

Kärntnerstrasse 22, A-1010 Vienna. © **01/961610.** Fax 01/5132999. www.ambassador.at. 86 units. 220€–404€ double; 700€ junior suite. AE, DC, MC, V. Parking 30€. U-Bahn: Stephansplatz. **Amenities:** Restaurant; bar; room service; laundry service; dry cleaning. *In room:* A/C, TV, minibar, hairdryer, safe, Wi-Fi: 1hr 8€, 3hr 15€, 24hr 18€.

Hotel Astoria   A first-class hotel, the Astoria has an eminently desirable location on the shopping center near St. Stephan's Cathedral and the Vienna State Opera. Decorated with a tasteful, understated elegance that honors turn-of-the-20th-century Vienna, the hotel offers well-appointed traditional bedrooms where comfort is not just on the surface. The interior rooms tend to be too dark, and singles are a little too cramped. Rooms contain built-in armoires, well-chosen linens and duvets on good beds, and bathrooms that, for the most part, are spacious and have such extras as dual basins, heated racks, and bidets. A recent renovation has left the old style unharmed; and management seems genuinely concerned about offering high-quality service.

Kärntnerstrasse 32–34, A-1010 Vienna. © **01/515770.** Fax 01/5157782. www.austria-trend.at. 118 units. 158€–450€ double; 650€ suite. Rates include breakfast. AE, DC, MC, V. Parking 22€–32€. U-Bahn: Stephansplatz. **Amenities:** Restaurant; bar; room service; babysitting; laundry service; dry cleaning. *In room:* TV, minibar, hairdryer, safe.

Hotel Bristol   Connoisseurs maintain that for service, comfort, and convenience, this is a superb choice. Constructed in 1894 next to the Vienna State Opera, it has been updated to provide guests with black-tiled bathrooms and other modern conveniences. Each bedroom includes a living area, and many have a small balcony providing a rooftop view of the Vienna State Opera and Ringstrasse.

Many of the hotel's architectural embellishments rank as *objets d'art* in their own right, including the black carved-marble fireplaces and the oil paintings in the salons. The Bristol Club Rooms in the tower offer comfortable chairs, an open fireplace, a self-service bar, library, stereo, deck, and sauna. Corkscrew columns of rare marble grace the Korso, Bristol's restaurant, which is one of the best in Vienna.

Kärntner Ring 1, A-1015 Vienna. © **888/625-5144** in the U.S., or 01/515160. Fax 01/51516550. www. westin.com/bristol. 146 units. 271€–439€ double; from 526€ suite. Rates include breakfast. AE, DC, MC, V. Parking 30€. U-Bahn: Karlsplatz. Tram: 1 or 2. **Amenities:** 2 restaurants; bar; business center; babysitting; dry cleaning; free access to nearby fitness center; laundry service; rooms for those w/limited mobility; room service; sauna. *In room:* A/C, TV, hairdryer, minibar, safe, Wi-Fi: 1hr 9€, 24hr 19€.

Hotel de France   Right on the Ring, the Hotel de France has long been a popular choice with international visitors. Its central location makes it a neighbor to the university and the Votivkirche. Its chiseled gray facade is little changed from when it was first erected in 1872. Recast as a hotel after World War II, its modern elements and unobtrusively conservative decor are the result of extensive renovation. In such a subdued undemanding atmosphere, you often encounter businesspeople from all over the world, appreciate the dignity of the high-ceilinged public rooms and oriental carpets, the generously padded armchairs, yet without the pretense of a celebrity hotel. The bedrooms are among the finest for their price range in Vienna. The best units are on the fifth floor, although too high to offer the view unless you're very tall! Schottenring 3, A-1010 Vienna. © **01/31368.** Fax 01/3195969. www.hoteldefrance.at. 212 units. 185€– 330€ double; from 495€ suite. Rates include buffet breakfast. AE, DC, MC, V. Parking 20€. U-Bahn: U2 or Schottentor. Tram: 1, 2, 37, or D. Bus: 1A. **Amenities:** 2 restaurants; 3 bars; dry cleaning; laundry service; room service; sauna. *In room:* A/C, TV, hairdryer, minibar, safe, trouser press, free Wi-Fi.

Hotel Imperial ★★★   Listed by Relais et Chateaux as among the most beautiful hostelries in the world, this hotel of princes has been the host of Austria's visitors of state since it reopened in 1955. Here in the former home of the Prince of Wüttemberg you are afforded the essence of royalty in every velvet brocade curtain and cherry wood cabinet, and your butler serves a hand-ironed newspaper with your morning coffee. It also has perhaps the sweetest period cocktail bar in town, where Thomas at the Bösendorfer plays everything from Hungarian polkas to Cole Porter.

Some of the most desirable rooms are on the 4th and 5th floor, on a more human scale than the overwhelming "state" suites. As you go higher, life becomes more "bourgeois"; appointments diminish, as do bathroom sizes. If this marvelous five star hotel has a weakness, it is in the fitness rooms and despite the lovely sauna, there is no spa. Kärntner Ring 16, A-1015 Vienna. © **800/325-3589** in the U.S., or 01/501100. Fax 01/50110410. www. luxurycollection.com/imperial. 138 units. 700€ double; from 1,000€ suite. AE, DC, MC, V. Parking 32€. U-Bahn: Karlsplatz. **Amenities:** 2 restaurants; bar; babysitting; dry cleaning; health club; massage; laundry service; rooms for those w/limited mobility; room service; salon; sauna. *In room:* A/C, TV, hairdryer, minibar, safe, Wi-Fi: 1hr 9€, 24hr 19€.

Hotel Sacher Wien ★★★   The fame of the 152-room privately owned hotel could just as well be due to the luscious brocade drapes and attentive service, but for most people, it's all about chocolate cake. The Café Sacher Wien, where the world-famous delicacy with its apricot middle and shiny near-black top was invented, is still going strong (and still guarding its recipe jealously), but there's also an enchanting hotel attached—a centerpiece of Viennese life since 1876. Recently renovated, this hotel opposite the Staatsoper couldn't be more central, with all the silk wallpaper, 19th-century oils, and Biedermeier furniture you could wish for. Nine suites have adjoining 23-sq. m (250-sq.-ft.) terraces with stunning views. The spa offers "hot chocolate treatments" that follow the Sachers' sweet tradition. Along with the confiserie and cafe, there's the Anna Sacher Restaurant, the post-opera favorite the Blaue Bar, and the sexy Rote Bar, with its charming winter garden. Philharmonikerstrasse 4, A-1010 Vienna. © **01/514560.** Fax 01/51256810. www.sacher.com. 152 units. 299€–464€ double; from 650€ junior suite; from 720€ executive suite. AE, DC, MC, V. Parking 32€. U-Bahn: Karlsplatz. Tram: 1, 2, 62, 65, D, or J. Bus: 4A. **Amenities:** 2 restaurants; bar; babysitting; dry cleaning; hairdryer; room service; laundry service; massage; spa. *In room:* A/C, TV, minibar, safe, Wi-Fi: 1hr 6€, 24hr 36€.

Le Meridien Vienna   Located directly on the famous Ringstrasse, this is a true "glam" hotel, a five-star, high-shine hostelry next to the Academy of Fine Arts and only a short stroll from the Vienna State Opera. Extensive renovations converted an apartment block of turn-of-the-20th-century Viennese architecture into this new city landmark, the first here for this popular French chain. Luscious maple wood and satin-chrome steel and glass create an aura of understated elegance in public rooms, and special illuminations and lighting effects are used dramatically. The midsize-to-spacious bedrooms feature designer beds, parquet floors, warm carpeting, and "sink-in" armchairs. Windows were designed to capture the most light possible, and decorators created drama using pinks and blues accented by earth tones.

Opernring 13-A, A-1010 Vienna. ☎ **01/588900.** Fax 01/588909090. http://vienna.lemeridien.com. 294 units. 170€–385€ double; from 655€ suite. AE, DC, MC, V. U-Bahn: Karlsplatz. **Amenities:** Restaurant; 2 bars; babysitting; dry cleaning; gym; laundry service; indoor heated pool; room service; rooms for those w/limited mobility; sauna. *In room:* A/C, TV, beverage maker, hairdryer, iron, minibar, safe, free Wi-Fi.

Palais Coburg Hotel Residenz ★★

Originally built in 1846 by August von Sachsen-Coburg-Saalfeld (whose family managed to sire the House of Windsor and most of the monarchs of western Europe) as the dynasty's Vienna residence. This magnificent, sprawling palace, vandalized by the occupying Russian army, was rebuilt during a 6-year renovation completed in 2006, and all traces of the mundane have been banished. The smaller and less expensive suites are contemporary, intensely design-conscious, and very comfortable. The more expensive are high-end posh, with many pale satin upholsteries and valuable antiques. All this grandeur is the personal property of an (individual) Austrian investor, whose stated ambition involves the on-site compilation of the largest and most comprehensive wine collection in Europe. A full-service spa is reserved only for residents of the hotel.

Coburgbastei 4, A-1010 Vienna. ☎ **01/518-180.** Fax 01/518-181. www.palais-coburg.com. 35 suites. 560€–1,900€ suites. Rates include breakfast. Parking 40€. AE, DC, MC, V. **Amenities:** 2 restaurants; dry cleaning; health club; indoor pool; laundry service; room service; sauna; spa. *In room:* A/C, TV, full kitchen w/bar, safe, free Wi-Fi.

Radisson/SAS Palais Hotel Vienna ★

This is one of Vienna's grandest renovations, converted to a hotel in 1985 by SAS, the Scandinavian airline; in 1994, another palace next door was added, allowing the hotel to double in size. Near Vienna's gracious Stadtpark, the hotel boasts facades accented with cast-iron railings, reclining nymphs, and elaborate cornices. The interior is lushly outfitted with 19th-century architectural motifs, all impeccably restored and dramatically illuminated. The lobby contains arching palms, a soaring ceiling, and a bar with evening piano music. The result is an uncluttered, tastefully conservative, and well-maintained hotel that is managed in a breezy, highly efficient manner. Bedrooms are outfitted in either soothing pastels or, in the new wing, in summery shades of green and white. The hotel also offers several duplex suites, or *maisonettes;* conventional suites; and rooms in the Royal Club, which has upgraded luxuries and services.

Parkring 16, A-1010 Vienna. ☎ **800/333-3333** in the U.S., or 01/515170. Fax 01/5122216. www.radisson. com. 247 units. 169€–284€ double; from 334€ junior suite. AE, DC, MC, V. Parking 30€. U-Bahn: Stadtpark. Tram: 2. **Amenities:** Restaurant; 2 bars; babysitting; dry cleaning; fitness center; Jacuzzi; laundry service; 1 room for those w/limited mobility; sauna; room service; spa. *In room:* A/C, TV, hairdryer, minibar, safe, free Wi-Fi.

Radisson/SAS Style Hotel ★

In the early 1900s, this building was the headquarters of an Austrian bank, but in 2005 it was converted into an elegant, neo-*Jugendstil* hotel. The result is a quirky and somewhat eccentric design with an enviable facade that's embellished with gilded, Secessionist-era bas-reliefs; virtually no signage in front; and a style-conscious, avant-garde interior that takes the era's design elements and adapts them with just enough swagger to pull it off. Right across the street from the famed Café Central, the hotel offers bedrooms that are comfortable, and angular-minimalist, with warm earth tones and at their best, cozy. The dramatic lounge has oversized, high-backed chairs that define the space and the most appealing public area is perhaps the H-12 wine bar, a long, narrow space with hard metallic surfaces, and an alabaster bar surface that's illuminated from within.

Herrengasse 12, A-1010 Vienna. ☎ **01/22780-0.** Fax 01/22780-77. www.style.vienna.radissonsas. com. 78 units. 199€–310€ double; 555€–585€ suite. AE, DC, MC, V. U-Bahn: Herrengasse. **Amenities:**

Restaurant; wine bar; health club; laundry service; room service; dry cleaning; sauna. *In room:* A/C, TV, minibar, safe, free Wi-Fi.

The Ring Hotel Vienna ★★ Vienna's self-dubbed "Casual Luxury Hotel" opened in 2006 and has quickly become a favorite for touring musicians and fashion icons, but better still, it's warm and inviting. Color-coordinated prints hang instead of oil originals, toning down the opulence, and the designer decor is stylish but cozy. Visit the delicious spa for a massage—and a seductive glimpse of the Karlskirche from the sauna. The restaurant "at eight" has little to boast for atmosphere but the food is great. Best of all, the impeccable service adds the finishing touch of personal luxury and the casual theme does not diminish the five-star quality of the accommodations. It is a welcome and less expensive alternative to the usual Imperial or Art Deco styles.

Kärntnerring 8, A-1010 Vienna. ✆ **01/122-122.** Fax 01/221-22-900. 68 units. 200€–420€ double; from 500€ suite. Rates include buffet breakfast. AE, DC, MC, V. Valet parking 26€. U-Bahn: Karlsplatz. **Amenities:** Restaurant; bar; fitness room; massage; babysitting; laundry service; dry cleaning; rooms for those w/limited mobility; room service; sauna; solarium; spa. *In room:* A/C, TV, hairdryer, iron, Nespresso machine, minibar, safe, free Wi-Fi.

Vienna Marriott This Marriott is popular because of the service and convenience rather than the decor, which is one grade above an airport. Opposite the Stadtpark, the location is great and with the American consulate in the same building, a good place to be if things get complicated. The lobby culminates in a stairway whose curved sides frame a splashing waterfall surrounded with plants. Many of the comfortably modern bedrooms are larger than those in the city's other contemporary hotels, although furnishings are a bit commercial. The British Bookshop is around the corner on Weihburggasse, also a distinct plus.

Parkring 12A, A-1010 Vienna. ✆ **888/236-2427** in the U.S., or 01/515180. Fax 01/515186736. www. marriott.com. 313 units. 229€–294€ double; 429€–690€ suite. AE, DC, MC, V. Parking 32€. Tram: 1 or 2. **Amenities:** 3 restaurants; 3 bars; indoor heated pool; fitness center; Jacuzzi; sauna; car-rental desk; salon; room service; massage; babysitting; laundry service; dry cleaning; solarium; rooms for those w/ limited mobility. *In room:* A/C, TV, minibar, hairdryer, iron, trouser press, safe, free Wi-Fi for executive lounge guests, DSL (for large data files): 1hr 6€.

EXPENSIVE

Hotel Kaiserin Elisabeth This yellow-stoned hotel is conveniently located near the cathedral. The interior is decorated with oriental rugs on well-maintained marble and wood floors. The main salon has a pale-blue skylight suspended above it, with mirrors and half-columns in natural wood. The small, quiet rooms have been considerably updated since Wolfgang Mozart, Richard Wagner, Franz Liszt, and Edvard Grieg stayed here, and their musical descendants continue to patronize the place. Polished wood, clean linens, and perhaps another oriental rug grace the rooms. Bathrooms are a bit cramped, with not enough room for your toiletries; but they are tiled and equipped with tub/shower combinations, vanity mirrors, and, in some cases, bidets.

Weihburggasse 3, A-1010 Vienna. ✆ **01/515260.** Fax 01/515267. www.kaiserinelisabeth.at. 63 units. 216€–245€ double. Rates include buffet breakfast. AE, DC, MC, V. Parking 30€. U-Bahn: Stephansplatz. **Amenities:** Restaurant; bar; dry cleaning; laundry service; room service. *In room:* A/C (in most units), TV, hairdryer, minibar, safe, free Wi-Fi.

Hotel König Von Ungarn ★ On a narrow street near St. Stephan's, this hotel occupies a dormered building that dates back to the early 17th century and is Vienna's oldest continuously operated hotel. In all, this is an evocative, intimate, and cozy retreat. It was once a *pied-à-terre* for Hungarian noble families during their stays in the Austrian capital. In 1791, Mozart reportedly resided and wrote some of his immortal music in the upstairs apartment that's now a Mozart museum. A mirrored solarium/bar area boasts a glass roof over the atrium and a tree growing out of the sidewalk. Tall, hinged windows overlook the Old Town, and Venetian mirrors adorn some walls. Everywhere you look, you'll find low-key luxury, tradition, and modern convenience. Try for the two rooms with balconies. Guest rooms have been newly remodeled with Biedermeier accents and traditional furnishings. Some rooms—and you should try to avoid these—lack an outside window.

Schulerstrasse 10, A-1010 Vienna. ✆ **01/515840.** Fax 01/515848. www.kvu.at. 33 units. 215€ double; 295€–345€ apt. Rates include breakfast. AE, DC, MC, V. U-Bahn: Stephansplatz. **Amenities:** Restaurant; bar; babysitting; dry cleaning; laundry service; room service. *In room:* A/C, TV, hairdryer, minibar, safe, free Wi-Fi.

Hotel Römischer Kaiser ★ ☺   A Best Western affiliate, this hotel is housed in a National Trust building that has seen its share of transformations. It's located in a traffic-free zone between St. Stephan's Cathedral and the Vienna State Opera, on a side street off Kärntnerstrasse. It was constructed in 1684 as the private palace of the imperial chamberlain; it later housed the Imperial School of Engineering before becoming a hostelry at the turn of the 20th century. The hotel rents romantically decorated rooms; our favorite has red satin upholstery over a chaise lounge. Double-glazed windows keep down the noise, and baroque paneling is a nice touch. Some rooms—notably nos. 12, 22, 30, and 38—can accommodate three or four beds, making this a family-friendly place. The red-carpeted sidewalk cafe has bar service and tables shaded with flowers and umbrellas.

Annagasse 16, A-1010 Vienna. ✆ **800/528-1234** in the U.S., or 01/51277510. Fax 01/512775113. www. bestwestern.com. 23 units. 132€–229€ double; 195€ suite. Rates include buffet breakfast. AE, DC, MC, V. Parking 21€. U-Bahn: Stephansplatz. **Amenities:** Restaurant; bar; dry cleaning; laundry service; room service. *In room:* A/C, TV, hairdryer, minibar, safe, free Wi-Fi.

K + K Palais Hotel ★   This hotel, with its severely dignified facade, sheltered the affair of Emperor Franz Josef and his celebrated mistress, Katherina Schratt, in 1890. Occupying a desirable position near the river and a 5-minute walk from the Ring, it remained unused for 2 decades until it was renovated in 1981. Vestiges of its imperial past remain, in spite of the contemporary but airy lobby and the lattice-covered bar. The public rooms are painted a shade of imperial Austrian yellow, and one of Ms. Schratt's antique secretaries occupies a niche near a white-sided tile stove. The bedrooms are comfortably outfitted and stylish. Rooms have a certain Far East motif, with lightwood, wicker, and rattan.

Rudolfsplatz 11, A-1010 Vienna. ✆ **01/5331353.** Fax 01/533135370. www.kkhotels.com. 66 units. 185€–255€ double. Rates include buffet breakfast. AE, DC, MC, V. No parking. U-Bahn: Schottenring. **Amenities:** Bistro; bar; babysitting; dry cleaning; laundry service; room service. *In room:* A/C, TV, hairdryer, minibar, safe, Wi-Fi.

MODERATE

Graben Hotel   Back in the 18th century, this was called Zum Goldenen Jägerhorn; over the years, it has attracted an array of Bohemian writers and artists. The poet Franz Grillparzer was a regular guest; and during the dark days of World War II, it was a gathering place for writers like Franz Kafka, Max Brod, and Peter Altenberg. The hotel stands on a narrow street off the Kärntnerstrasse, in the very center of the city. Guests gather around the stone fireplace in winter and look at fascinating memorabilia, including original postcards left by Altenberg. Rooms are high-ceilinged but rather cramped. Although there are some Art Nouveau touches, much of the furniture is simple and will feel spartan to someone looking for luxury. Sunlight streams into the front rooms, but not the darker havens at the rear.

Dorotheergasse 3, A-1010 Vienna. ℰ **01/51215310.** Fax 01/512153120. www.kremslehnerhotels.at. 41 units. 160€–195€ double. Rates include buffet breakfast. AE, DC, MC, V. Parking 27€. U-Bahn: Karlsplatz. **Amenities:** Restaurant; lounge; babysitting; room service (7am–10pm). *In room:* TV, hairdryer, minibar, safe, Wi-Fi: 30min 3€, 24hr 12€.

Hollman Beletage ★★ 👜 This discovery, smack in the center of town, has beautifully designed rooms in a typically modern Austrian style. The waterfall showers and spa area will pamper after long eventful days. The rooms have beautiful bath facilities, the breakfast is opulent, and the staff prides itself in being hosts rather than just employees. The in-house cinema shows three films a day, all relating somehow to Vienna, for instance Orson Welles' *The Third Man.* This establishment is small, sophisticated, and simple, while esteeming to be the best and perhaps only place of its kind. Since it only has 24 rooms make sure you book ahead.

Köhlnerhofgasse 6. A-1010 Vienna. ℰ **01/9611960.** Fax 01-513-9698. www.hollmann-beletage.at. 24 units. 140€–250€ double. Rates include breakfast. AE, DC, MC, V. U-Bahn: Stephansplatz. **Amenities:** Breakfast room; restaurant; cinema; fitness center; games room; garden; spa. *In room:* TV, hairdryer, minibar, safe, free Wi-Fi.

Hotel Amadeus Cozy and convenient, this boxlike hotel is only 2 minutes away from Stephansdom and within walking distance of practically everything of musical or historical note in Vienna. It was built on the site of a once-legendary tavern (Zum roten Igel), a haunt of Johannes Brahms and Franz Schubert. Behind a dull 1960s' facade, the bedrooms and carpeted public rooms are pleasant, furnished in a comfortable, modern style, many with views of the cathedral. Ceilings are uncomfortably low, and the double-glazing on the windows quiets but does not obliterate street noise. Tiled bathrooms are midsize, but there's not enough room to lay out your toiletries. Eight rooms have showers but no tubs. It's good value for the money, but don't expect warm fuzzies from the reserved staff.

Wildpretmarkt 5, A-1010 Vienna. ℰ **01/5338738.** Fax 01/533-87383838. www.hotel-amadeus.at. 30 units. 178€–203€ double. Rates include buffet breakfast. AE, DC, MC, V. U-Bahn: Stephansplatz. **Amenities:** Breakfast room; lounge; babysitting; dry cleaning; laundry service; rooms for those w/limited mobility. *In room:* A/C, TV, hairdryer, minibar, safe, free Wi-Fi. Parking with advance reservation.

Hotel Am Parkring This well-maintained hotel occupies the top three floors of a 13-story office building near the edge of Vienna's Stadtpark. A semiprivate elevator services only the street-level entrance and the hotel's floors. There are sweeping views of the city from all of its bedrooms, which are furnished in a conservative but comfortable style. Business travelers and tourists alike patronize this hotel, although the atmosphere is a bit sterile if you're seeking nostalgic Vienna. Rooms here are a standard, reliable choice. This hotel is not the kindest to the lone tourist, as single accommodations tend to be small, often using sofa beds.

Parkring 12, A-1015 Vienna. ℰ **01/514800.** Fax 01/5148040. www.bestwestern.com. 64 units. 149€–230€ double; 360€ suite. Rates include buffet breakfast. AE, DC, MC, V. Parking 19€. U-Bahn: Stadtpark or Stubentor. Tram: 1 or 2. **Amenities:** Restaurant; bar; babysitting; dry cleaning; laundry service; room service. *In room:* A/C, TV, hairdryer, minibar, Wi-Fi.

Hotel-Pension Arenberg ★ This genteel but unpretentious hotel-pension, a Best Western, occupies the second and third floors of a six-story apartment house that was built at the turn of the 20th century. On the Stubenring across from the Stadtpark and the Museum of Applied Arts, it offers small, soundproof bedrooms outfitted in old-world style with oriental carpets, conservative furniture, and intriguing artwork. The hotel appeals to those with a sense of history, and has a helpful English-speaking staff.

Stubenring 2, A-1010 Vienna. © **800/528-7234** in the U.S., or 01/5125291. Fax 01/5139356. www.best western.com. 23 units. 158€–208€ double; 293€ triple. Rates include breakfast. AE, DC, MC, V. Parking 15€. U-Bahn: Schwedenplatz. **Amenities:** Lounge; babysitting; dry cleaning; laundry service; rooms for those w/limited mobility; breakfast-only room service. *In room:* A/C, TV, hairdryer, minibar, safe, free Wi-Fi.

Hotel Royal ★   This dignified, nine-story hotel on Singerstrasse is <u>less than a block from St. Stephan's</u> Cathedral, with a piano in the lobby that Wagner used to compose *Die Meistersinger von Nürnberg*. Each of the ample rooms is furnished differently, with some good reproduction antiques and even an occasional original. Opened in 1931, the hotel was rebuilt in 1982. Try for a room with a balcony and a view of the cathedral. Corner rooms have spacious foyers, although those facing the street tend to be noisy.

Singerstrasse 3, A-1010 Vienna. © **01/515680.** Fax 01/513-9698. www.kremslehnerhotels.at. 81 units. 140€–200€ double. Rates include breakfast. AE, DC, MC, V. U-Bahn: Stephansplatz. **Amenities:** 2 restaurants; bar; wine bar; dry cleaning; laundry service; room service. *In room:* TV, hairdryer, minibar, Wi-Fi: 30min 3€, 24hr 12€.

Hotel Viennart ★ 📖   This fully renovated, six-story hotel is a choice for lovers of modern art and convenient to the many enticements of the MuseumsQuartier (see chapter 6). The location is at the edge of the Spittelberg, a district locals call "the Montmartre of Vienna." The decor is sock-it-to-you modern, in red, white, orange, and black. Rooms are outfitted in a functional style, with details nicer than necessary.

Breite Gasse 9, A-1070 Vienna. © **01/523-13-450.** Fax 01/523-13-45-111. www.austrotel.at. 56 units. 100€–170€ double; 246€ suite. Children under 12 stay free in parent's room. Rates include buffet breakfast. AE, DC, MC, V. U-Bahn: Volkstheater. **Amenities:** Breakfast room; babysitting; dry cleaning; laundry service. *In room:* TV, hairdryer, minibar, free Wi-Fi.

Mailberger Hof ★   This old palace was built in the 14th century as a mansion for the knights of Malta and was converted into a hotel in the 1970s and a Maltese cross still hangs over the two large wooden entry doors. The vaulted ceiling, the leather armchairs, and marbleized walls are about all that would remind the knights of their former home. All is new, although a cobblestone courtyard, set with tables in fair weather, remains. A cozy family-run establishment, the hotel features moderate-size bedrooms often brightened with pastels. In general, though, public rooms beat private.

Annagasse 7, A-1010 Vienna. © **01/5120641.** Fax 01/512064110. www.mailbergerhof.at. 40 units. 180€–260€ double; 210€–280€ suite. Rates include buffet breakfast. AE, DC, MC, V. Parking 29€. U-Bahn: Karlsplatz. **Amenities:** Bar; babysitting; laundry service; dry cleaning; room service (7am–10pm). *In room:* A/C, TV, hairdryer, minibar, safe, free Wi-Fi.

INEXPENSIVE

Drei Kronen 🍴   The "three crowns" in the German name Drei Kronen refer to Austria, Hungary, and Bohemia from the old Austro-Hungarian Empire, displayed on top of the building. The hotel enjoys one of Vienna's best locations, right next to the Naschmarkt. Built in 1894, the five-story hotel was completely renovated in 1999, but while comfortable, the rooms are small and many of the smaller courtesies, like storage space or toiletries, are missing. Some of the rooms are large enough to contain full-size "house" beds, but only some. Best to ask.

Schleifmuehlgasse 25, A-1040 Vienna. © **01/5873289.** Fax 01/587328911. www.hotel3kronen.at. 41 units. 75€ double; 85€ triple. AE, DC, MC, V. Parking 15€. U-Bahn: Karlsplatz. **Amenities:** Breakfast room; lounge; babysitting. *In room:* TV, safe (some), free Wi-Fi.

Hotel Austria   This unpretentious, family-owned hotel sits on a small, quiet cul de sac, a corner building on the adjoining street, Fleischmarkt 20. The comfortable furnishings in the lobby and in the chandeliered breakfast room are beautifully cared for, and every detail of service carried out with style. Every year one of the four floors of the hotel is completely renovated with new wallpapering, furniture, and bedding, and reproduction period furniture accents a stylish modern decor. The staff is knowledgeable about goings on in the neighborhood for a good meal or a glass of wine, and offers printouts explaining the neighborhood's medieval origins.

Am Fleischmarkt 20, A-1011 Vienna. © **01/51523.** Fax 01/51523506. www.hotelaustria-wien.at. 46 units, 42 w/bathroom. 69€–90€ double w/no bathroom; 115€–178€ double w/bathroom. Rates include buffet breakfast. AE, DC, MC, V. Parking 19€. U-Bahn: Schwedenplatz. Tram: 1 or 2. **Amenities:** Breakfast room; lounge; massage; babysitting; dry cleaning; laundry service; breakfast-only room service. *In room:* TV, hairdryer, minibar, free Wi-Fi.

Hotel Kärntnerhof ★ ☺   Only a 4-minute walk from the cathedral, the Kärntnerhof has been refurbished and renovated, and is now more comfortable and just as friendly. The decor of the public rooms is tastefully arranged around oriental rugs, well-upholstered chairs and couches with cabriole legs, and an occasional 19th-century portrait. The midsize to spacious units are up-to-date, usually with the original parquet floors and striped or patterned wallpaper set off by curtains. Many of the guest rooms are large enough to handle an extra bed, making this a family favorite. The owner is also helpful, directing guests to nearby services and Vienna landmarks.

Grashofgasse 4, A-1011 Vienna. © **01/5121923.** Fax 01/513222833. www.karntnerhof.com. 44 units. 110€–175€ double; 180€–280€ suite. Rates include buffet breakfast. AE, DC, MC, V. Parking 17€. U-Bahn: Stephansplatz. **Amenities:** Breakfast room; lounge; room service; laundry service; dry cleaning. *In room:* TV, free Wi-Fi.

Hotel-Pension Shermin 🗝   This small, inviting family-run boardinghouse in the city center is much nicer than its price would suggest. Bedrooms are big and comfortable, and the details are chosen with taste; the owners do a lot with less. The location is central, with most attractions a 5-minute walk away. Furnishings are modern and without much flair, but are exceedingly comfortable, attracting many repeat guests.

Rilkeplatz 7, A-1040 Vienna. © **01/58661830.** Fax 01/586618310. www.hotel-pension-shermin.at. 11 units. 72€–114€ double. Rates include buffet breakfast. AE, DC, MC, V. Parking 7€ Mon–Fri, free Sat–Sun. U-Bahn: Karlsplatz. **Amenities:** Breakfast room; lounge; breakfast-only room service. *In room:* TV, hairdryer, free Wi-Fi.

Hotel-Pension Suzanne ★ ☺   Only a 45-second walk from the opera house, this is a real discovery. Once you get past its postwar facade, the interior warms considerably; it is brightly decorated in comfortable, Viennese turn-of-the-20th-century style with antique beds, plush chairs, and the original molded ceilings. Now into its second generation of managers, the hotel-pension is run by the welcoming Strafinger family. Rooms are midsize and exceedingly well maintained, facing either the busy street or a courtyard. Some of the rooms contain three beds, making the hotel suitable for families. Some bedrooms are like small apartments, with kitchenettes.

Walfischgasse 4. A-1010 Vienna. © **01/5132507.** Fax 01/5132500. www.pension-suzanne.at. 26 units. 100€–112€ double; 135€–145€ triple. Rates include buffet breakfast. AE, DC, MC, V. U-Bahn: Karlsplatz. **Amenities:** Breakfast room; lounge; babysitting; breakfast-only room service; free Wi-Fi at reception. *In room:* TV, hairdryer.

Hotel Pertschy ★   These apartment-like digs are a more affordable inner city alternative to the classic hotel experience. Several rooms overlook a central courtyard

From July to September, a number of student dormitories in Vienna are transformed into fully operational hotels. Three of the most viable and popular of these are the **Academia Hotel,** Pfeilgasse 3A; the **Avis Hotel,** Pfeilgasse 4; and the **Atlas Hotel,** at Lerchenfelderstrasse 1. All are within a block of one another, and each is a rather unimaginative-looking, angular, 1960s-style building. They're comfortable and reasonably priced alternatives, only a 20-minute walk west of St. Stephan's. The lodgings will definitely take you back to your dorm days, though each room has a phone and a private bath. Many groups book well in advance, but individual travelers are welcome if space is available.

Depending on the hotel, doubles cost from 80€ to 108€ a night, and triples range from 105€ to 130€ each. Breakfast is included in the rates. Bookings at all three hotels are arranged through the Academia Hotel, which functions as the headquarters for the entire Academia chain.

For reservations and information, call ☎ **01/401-76-55,** or fax 01/401-76-20; www.reservation@academiahotel.at. To get to the Academia and Avis hotels, take the U-Bahn to Thaliastrasse, and then transfer to tram no. 46 and get off at Strozzigasse. For access to the Atlas Hotel, take the U-Bahn to Volkstheater or Rathaus. These hotels accept American Express, Diners Club, MasterCard, and Visa for payment.

and are scattered among six or seven private apartments, whose residents are used to foreign visitors roaming through the building. The recent renovations have left the quarters elegant and simple, without losing the old Vienna touch. This family-run establishment exudes comfort and right off the Graben it's hard to out-bid.

Habsburgergasse 5, A-1010 Vienna. ☎ **01/534490.** Fax 01/5344949. www.pertschy.com. 50 units, 2 w/ kitchen. 119€–151€ double. AE, DC, MC, V. Parking 16€. U-Bahn: Stephansplatz. **Amenities:** Breakfast room; lounge. *In room:* TV, hairdryer, minibar, free Wi-Fi.

Hotel Post ◢ Hotel Post lies in the medieval slaughterhouse district, just above Schwedenplatz and backing onto the Vienna Chamber Opera and the tiny theater Drachengasse, which hosts English-language Improv Theater every other Friday night (p. 180). Following a major renovation, the hotel has been reopened with a bright, airy feel to the modest to midsize rooms that makes this even better value for money. The manager is quick to tell you that both Mozart and Haydn frequently stayed in a former inn at this address, and their music is still played in the coffeehouse, Le Café, just renovated, below the hotel.

Fleischmarkt 24, A-1010 Vienna. ☎ **01/515830.** Fax 01/51583808. www.hotel-post-wien.at. 107 units, 77 w/bathroom. 76€ double w/no bathroom; 125€ double w/bathroom; 100€ triple w/no bathroom; 152€ triple w/bathroom. Rates include buffet breakfast. AE, DC, MC, V. Parking 18€. Tram: 1 or 2. **Amenities:** Restaurant; lounge; dry cleaning; laundry service; 1 room for those w/limited mobility; salon; free Wi-Fi in lobby. *In room:* TV, DSL cable, hairdryer.

Hotel Wandl ★ Under the same ownership for generations, the Wandl lies in the Inner City behind the Peterskirche and around the corner from the famed literary Café Korb, haunt of journalists and theater people. Many of the rooms offer views of the steeple of St. Stephan's Cathedral from windows that often open onto small balconies. The breakfast room is a high-ceilinged, two-toned room with hanging chandeliers and ceiling medallions. The bedrooms are spacious and comfortable, many with sitting room space to entertain. Beds are frequently renewed. All in all, this is a comfortable choice if you don't need luxury.

Petersplatz 9, A-1010 Vienna. © **01/534550.** Fax 01/5345577. www.hotel-wandl.com. 138 units. 158€–205€ double; 220€ suite. Rates include breakfast. AE, DC, MC, V. U-Bahn: Stephansplatz. **Amenities:** Breakfast room; lounge; dry cleaning; laundry service; room service. *In room:* TV, hairdryer, safe, DSL cable: 24hr 5€.

Pension Dr. Geissler 🗡 Unpretentious lodgings at extremely reasonable prices are offered here by Schwedenplatz at the edge of the Danube Canal. The bedrooms in this attractive, informal guesthouse are furnished with simple blond headboards and a few utilitarian pieces. Hallway bathrooms are generous. Most units have their own private bathrooms, which are tiled and well maintained but a bit cramped.

Postgasse 14, A-1010 Vienna. © **01/5332803.** Fax 01/5332635. www.hotelpension.at. 35 units, 21 w/ bathroom. 65€ double w/no bathroom; 95€ double w/bathroom. Rates include buffet breakfast. AE, DC, MC, V. U-Bahn: Schwedenplatz. **Amenities:** Breakfast room; bar; babysitting; dry cleaning; laundry service; breakfast-only room service. *In room:* TV, Wi-Fi on the top 2 floors: 1hr 1€.

Pension Neuer Markt 🛉🛏 Near the cathedral, in the heart of Vienna, this pension is housed in a white baroque building that faces a square with an ornate fountain. The carpeted but small rooms are clean and well maintained in an updated motif of white walls and strong colors, with large windows in some. Some of the comfortable, duvet-covered beds are set into niches. Each of the units has central heating. Bathrooms with tub/shower combinations are small, seemingly added as an afterthought; but for Vienna the price is delicious. We recommend reserving 30 days in advance.

Seilergasse 9, A-1010 Vienna. ©**01/5122316.** Fax 01/5139105. www.hotelpension.at. 37 units. 80€–135€ double. Rates include buffet breakfast. AE, DC, MC, V. Parking 4.60€. U-Bahn: Stephansplatz. **Amenities:** Breakfast room; bar; babysitting; dry cleaning; laundry service; breakfast-only room service. *In room:* TV, safe, free Wi-Fi.

Pension Nossek Here where Mozart lived from 1781–82, and wrote the *Haffner* symphony and *The Abduction from the Seraglio,* you can walk out your front door into the heart of Vienna. The pension lies on one of Vienna's best shopping streets, just blocks away from all the major sights. In 1909, the building was converted into a guesthouse and has always been a good bet for clean, comfortable accommodations with decent (mostly comfortable) beds. Most of the bedrooms have been renovated, and all but a few singles contain small private bathrooms with tub/shower combinations.

Graben 17, A-1010 Vienna. © **01/53370410.** Fax 01/5353646. www.pension-nossek.at. 30 units. 110€–115€ double; 143€ suite. Rates include breakfast. No credit cards. Free parking. U-Bahn: Stephansplatz. **Amenities:** Breakfast room; lounge; dry cleaning; laundry service. *In room:* TV, hairdryer (some), minibar, Wi-Fi: 24hr 5€.

Zur Wiener Staatsoper 🛉🛏 This simple but well-run family hotel has a facade that's more evocative of Vienna's late 19th-century golden age than any equivalently rated hotel in town. Built in 1896 as a private home, it retains some of the charm—and the drawbacks—of its origins. Don't expect grandeur: Other than some elaborate plasterwork in the entryway, the decor is simple. You'll register within a cubbyhole-style office near the entrance, then take an elevator to any of the six floors. Rooms are high-ceilinged, functional, relatively comfortable, and, other than small bathrooms (with showers only), adequate for most needs. Literary fans appreciate that this hotel provided the inspiration to John Irving for one of the settings (a run-down hotel that had evolved into a whorehouse) in his novel *Hotel New Hampshire.*

Krugerstrasse 11, A-1010 Vienna. ℂ **01/513-12-74.** www.zurwienerstaatsoper.at. 22 units. 113€–150€ double; 135€–175€ triple. Rates include buffet breakfast. DC, MC, V. U-Bahn: Karlsplatz. *In room:* TV, safe, free Wi-Fi.

Leopoldstadt (2nd District)
EXPENSIVE
Austria Trend Hotel Messe Wien ★   Located directly across from the Messe Wien, Vienna's premier trade fair and convention center, this hotel is brand new high shine and, if you need to be there, unbeatably convenient. A convex shape and an inclining facade makes all the rooms flooded with light and some of the architectural features continue through the hotel's corridors and private bedrooms. The well-appointed bedrooms feature French windows with a view of the fairgrounds. The top two levels house business rooms and suites that offer panoramic views of the city.

Messestrasse 2, A-1020 Vienna. ℂ **01/727270.** Fax 01/72727-100. www.austriatrend.at. 243 units. 250€–270€ double; 400€ suite. AE, DC, MC, V. U-Bahn: Praterstern. **Amenities:** Restaurant; bar; business center; dry cleaning; laundry service; room service; sauna. *In room:* A/C, TV, hairdryer, minibar, safe, free Wi-Fi on 6th and 7th floors, DSL cable available.

Hilton Vienna Danube ★★   Vienna has yet a third Hilton hotel, this one lying on the Danube River next to the trade fair and convention center, Messezentrum Wien, a 10-minute ride from the city center (free shuttle service), and a short walk to the Prater park. Business people like its proximity to international companies, although it's equally suitable for vacationers with a stunning setting on the river with a bike path to Klosterneuburg and the Wachau in one direction and Hungary in the other. The hotel has the largest guest rooms of any hotel in Vienna. Dining is a special feature here; the Symphony Donau Restaurant serves international and Austrian cuisine on a beautiful terrace opening onto views of the river. The chef is famous for his Sunday (noon–3pm) Royal Swedish Smörgasbord, a buffet of Swedish specialties. There is also an attractive traditional coffee shop with excellent coffee, pastries, and international newspapers.

Handelskai 269, A-1020 Vienna. ℂ **800-HILTONS** or 01/727770. Fax 01/7277782200. www.vienna-danube.hilton.com. 367 units. 125€–205€ double; 250€–295€ suite. AE, DC, MC, V. U-Bahn: U1 to Praterstern and then tram 21 to Meiereistrasse. **Amenities:** Restaurant; bar; dry cleaning; gym; laundry service; rooms for those w/limited mobility; outdoor pool; room service; sauna; tennis court. *In room:* A/C, TV, beverage maker (some), hairdryer (some), minibar, trouser press, safe, Wi-Fi: 1hr 10€, 24hr (limited download) 17€, 24hr (unlimited) 22€, free for gold and diamond customers.

MODERATE
Hotel Stefanie   This well-regarded traditional hotel is just across the Danube Canal from Schwedenplatz, a short walk to the rest of the city. A hotel since the 1700s, it was renamed in 1870 by the Schick family in honor of the marriage of the Crown Prince Rudolf to the Princess Stefanie. Over the past 20 years, all the bedrooms have had major renovations and today are well furnished in sleek Viennese styling. Some are a bit small but all are beautifully maintained. The small tiled bathrooms contain tub/shower combinations but not enough shelf space. And while the furnishings and decor are reproductions rather than antique, the effect works, successfully maintaining the period feel. The bar is more modern, with black leather armchairs on chrome swivel bases, and the concealed lighting throws an azure glow over the artfully displayed bottles.

Taborstrasse 12, A-1020 Vienna. ℂ **800/528-1234** in the U.S., or 01/211500. Fax 01/21150160. www.schick-hotels.com. 131 units. 149€–211€ double. Rates include buffet breakfast. AE, DC, MC, V. Parking

19€. U-Bahn: Schwedenplatz. Tram: 21. **Amenities:** Restaurant; bar; dry cleaning; laundry service; room service. *In room:* A/C, TV, hairdryer, minibar, safe, free Wi-Fi.

Landstrasse (3rd District)
VERY EXPENSIVE

Hilton Vienna ★★ This 15-story box overlooks the Wienfluss and offers plush accommodations and elegant public areas. Despite the hotel's slick modernity, it manages to provide plenty of Viennese flavor, with attractive cafe-lounge and bar areas that are a popular daytime meeting place for business people and the local after-work crowd. And its soaring atrium and bustling nightlife make it a vibrant spot for business travelers. The hotel offers well-appointed bedrooms in a range of styles, including Biedermeier, contemporary, baroque, and Art Nouveau. Towering over the city skyline, it also affords great views from the upper floors. All bedrooms include tub/shower combinations, with extra features in the suites. The lovely Stadtpark is across the street and connected by a footbridge, which strollers and joggers use during excursions into the landscaped and bird-filled park.

Am Stadtpark, A-1030 Vienna. © **800/445-8667** in the U.S., or 01/717000. Fax 01/7130691. www. hilton.com. 579 units. 205€–310€ double; from 355€ suite. AE, DC, MC, V. Parking 27€. The Hilton is at the City Air Terminal and the City Airport Train takes 17 minutes to Schwechat. U-Bahn: Landstrasse. **Amenities:** Restaurant; bar; babysitting; business center; dry cleaning; car rental desk; fitness center; Jacuzzi; laundry service; rooms for those w/limited mobility; children's playground; indoor heated pool; room service; sauna. *In room:* A/C, TV, hairdryer, minibar, safe, Wi-Fi: 1hr 10€, 24hr (limited download) 22€, 24hr (unlimited) 27€, free for gold and diamond customers.

EXPENSIVE

Mercure Hotel Biedermeier ★★ ☺ This hotel, established in 1983, is in a very attractively renovated late-18th-century Biedermeier apartment house enclosing a charming narrow cobblestone walk, "Zinnhofpassage." Here service is a source of pride and the staff is particularly friendly and accommodating. Although the hotel is near the Wien Mitte train and subway station, most bedrooms overlook the pedestrian-only walkway lined with shops and cafes that is another world altogether. Duvets cover the firm beds, and double glazing on the windows minimizes the noise. Bathrooms are small and tiled, and mostly tub/shower combinations. On the premises are the formal restaurant Zu den Deutschmeistern and the very appealing Weissgerberstube, also a favorite of locals. For families, one child stays free with parents. For German speakers, the delightful cabaret Theater L.E.O. is right around the corner.

Landstrasser Hauptstrasse 28, A-1030 Vienna. © **800/780-5734** in the U.S., or 01/716710. Fax 01/ 71671503. www.dorint.de. 203 units. 180€–233€ double; 315€–350€ suite. Rates include breakfast. AE, DC, MC, V. Parking 15€. U-Bahn: Rochusgasse. **Amenities:** 2 restaurants; 2 bars; room service; babysitting; laundry service; dry cleaning; rooms for those w/limited mobility. *In room:* A/C, TV, minibar, hairdryer, trouser press, safe, free DSL connection.

Wieden & Margareten (4th & 5th Districts)
EXPENSIVE

Hotel Das Triest ★★ 🎁 Sir Terence Conran, the famous English restaurant owner and designer, created the interior for this contemporary hotel in the center of Vienna, a 5-minute walk from St. Stephan's Cathedral. An emerging favorite with artists and musicians, this hip hotel has such grace notes as a courtyard garden. The building was originally used as a stable for horses pulling stagecoaches between Vienna and Trieste—hence its name, "City of Trieste." Its old cross-vaulted rooms, which give the structure a distinctive flair, have been transformed into lounges and suites. Bedrooms are midsize to spacious, tastefully furnished, and comfortable.

Wiedner Hauptstrasse 12, A-1040 Vienna. (✆ **01/589180.** Fax 01/5891818. www.dastriest.at. 73 units. 273€ double; 338€–556€ suite. Rates include buffet breakfast. AE, DC, MC, V. Parking 25€. U-Bahn: Stephansplatz. **Amenities:** Restaurant; bar; babysitting; dry cleaning; fitness center; laundry service; massage; room service; salon; sauna; solarium. *In room:* A/C, TV, hairdryer, minibar, trouser press, safe, free Wi-Fi.

MODERATE

Hotel Erzherzog Rainer   Popular with groups and business travelers, this very appealing family-run hotel was built just before World War I by a frustrated court framer who decided a hotel was the only business where you could get carriage trade customers to "pay as you go." A short subway or tram ride takes you to the Vienna State Opera, the Musikverein or Kärntnerstrasse, with a U-Bahn stop just steps away. The bedrooms are well decorated and come in a variety of sizes; you'll find telephones and good beds, but not always soundproofing. The singles are small; and like many traditional hotels in Austria, there is no air-conditioning, although it's fair to say that in Vienna's temperate climate, this is rarely an issue. An informal brasserie serves Austrian specialties, and the cozy bar is modishly decorated with black and brass.

Wiedner Hauptstrasse 27–29, A-1040 Vienna. (✆ **01/22111.** Fax 01/22111-350. www.schick-hotels.com. 84 units. 135€–203€ double. Rates include breakfast. AE, MC, V. Parking 18€. U-Bahn: Taubstummengasse; tram 61, 62, on the Wiedner Hauptstrasse. **Amenities:** Restaurant; bar; babysitting; dry cleaning; laundry service; rooms for those w/limited mobility; room service. *In room:* TV, hairdryer, minibar, safe (some), free Wi-Fi.

Mariahilf (6th District)

EXPENSIVE

Hotel Das Tyrol ★★ 🏨   It's friendly, fairly priced, loaded with charm, and lies within a 7-minute walk of one of the densest concentrations of museums in Europe. The hotel's only drawback is that it's so good that it's often booked weeks in advance. It occupies what was originally built 175 years ago as a convent, which later functioned as a simple hotel. In 1999, it was bought by an Austrian Member of Parliament, Helena von Ramsbacher, who, at the time of her election, was one of the youngest women ever to become an MP. After pouring money into the building's restoration, she justifiably defines it as a boutique-style luxury hotel. Don't expect a scaled-down version of, say, the Imperial or the Bristol. What you get are high ceilings, a comfortable mix of *Jugendstil* and contemporary furnishings, a fascinating collection of contemporary art, a sense of uncluttered spaciousness, a lovely glassed, period elevator, and a winding central staircase that preserve the building's timeless feel—all a short walk from the Ring.

Mariahilferstrasse 15, A-1060 Vienna. (✆ **01/587-54-15.** Fax 01/587-54-15-49. www.das-tyrol.at. 30 units. 185€–239€ double; 259€ junior suite. Rates include breakfast. Parking 18€. U-Bahn: U2 MuseumsQuartier, Volkstheater, or U3 Neubaugasse. **Amenities:** Sauna and wellness center; room service; laundry service; dry cleaning. *In room:* A/C, TV, minibar, Nespresso machine, safe, free Wi-Fi.

Hotel Kummer   Established by the Kummer family in the 19th century, this hotel was built in response to the growing power of the railways as they forged new paths of commerce and tourism through central Europe, but has all the dignity of a palace in the 1st District. The facade is richly embellished with Corinthian capitals on acanthus-leaf bases, urn-shaped balustrades, and representations of four heroic demigods staring down from under the building's eaves. A short walk from Vienna's Westbahnhof, the hotel lies at a busy intersection, but the bedrooms have soundproof windows and often come with stone balconies with a fine view over the comings and goings below. Not all rooms are alike—some feature superior appointments and deluxe furnishings. If possible, opt for a corner room—they have better light and are more spacious.

Mariahilferstrasse 71A, A-1060 Vienna. ℰ 01/588950. Fax 01/5878133. www.hotelkummer.at. 100 units. 95€–255€ double. Rates include buffet breakfast. AE, DC, MC, V. Parking 15€. U-Bahn: Neubaugasse. Bus: 13A or 14A. **Amenities:** Restaurant; bar; dry cleaning; laundry service; room service; salon. *In room:* TV, hairdryer, minibar, safe, trouser press, Wi-Fi: 1hr 12€, 24hr 27€.

MODERATE

Fürst Metternich Hotel ★ 🛍 Pink-and-gray walls and ornate stone window trims identify this handsome, solidly built 19th-century hotel, formerly an opulent private home. It's located between the Ring and the Westbahnhof near Mariahilferstrasse, about a 20-minute walk to the center. Many of the grander details have been retained, including a pair of red stone columns in the entranceway and an old-fashioned staircase guarded with griffins. The high-ceilinged bedrooms are relatively neutral and not all that roomy, although they do have lovely feather pillows. Windows in the front units are only partially soundproof, so if you are a light sleeper, opt for a room in the rear. The Barfly's Club, a popular hangout open daily, offers 120 different exotic drinks.

Esterházygasse 33, A-1060 Vienna. ℰ 01/58870. Fax 01/5875268. www.austrotel.at. 55 units. 100€–170€ double. Rates include buffet breakfast. AE, DC, MC, V. Parking 17€. U-Bahn: Zieglergasse. **Amenities:** Breakfast room; bar; babysitting; dry cleaning; laundry service. *In room:* TV, minibar, free Wi-Fi.

Golden Tulip Wien City This seven-story concrete-and-glass hotel was designed in 1975 with enough angles in its facade to give each bedroom an irregular shape. Usually the units have two windows that face different skylines. Aside from the views, bedrooms are a good size with comfortable furnishings. Opt for a studio with a terrace on the seventh floor, if one is available. The hotel also has a public rooftop terrace where guests sip drinks in summer.

Wallgasse 23, A-1060 Vienna. ℰ 01/599900. Fax 01/5967646. www.goldentulipwiencity.com. 77 units. 150€–230€ double; from 270€ suite. Rates include buffet breakfast. AE, DC, MC, V. Parking 15€. U-Bahn: Gumpendorfer. Bus: 57A. **Amenities:** Breakfast room; bar; babysitting; dry cleaning; laundry service; breakfast-only room service. *In room:* A/C, TV, hairdryer, minibar, safe, free Wi-Fi.

Hotel Mercure Secession ★ Sitting at the corner of Lehárgasse and the Getreidemarkt just behind Olbrich's stunning gold-domed Secession, this hotel is in the center of Vienna between Karlsplatz and the Naschmarkt. It's a modern five-story building with panoramic windows on the ground floor, warmly decorated with some 19th-century antiques and comfortably upholstered chairs. And while not the cheapest, the friendly service added to the location near theaters, concert halls, and galleries makes it a favorite of musicians, singers, actors, and other artists who join a loyal clientele; families are especially fond of the place as many rooms contain kitchenettes.

Getreidemarkt 5, A-1060 Vienna. ℰ 01/588380. Fax 01/58838212. www.mercure.com. 68 units. 150€–175€ double. Rates include buffet breakfast. AE, DC, MC, V. Parking 18€. U-Bahn: Karlsplatz. **Amenities:** Breakfast room; bar; room service; babysitting; dry cleaning; laundry service. *In room:* A/C, TV, hairdryer, minibar, safe, free Wi-Fi.

Neubau (7th District)
EXPENSIVE

K + K Hotel Maria Theresia ★ The hotel's initials are a reminder of the empire's dual monarchy (*Kaiserlich und Königlich*—imperial and royal, i.e. "by appointment to the Emperor of Austria and King of Hungary"). Even the surrounding neighborhood, home to some major museums and many buildings from the late 19th century *Grunderzeit,* is reminiscent of the days of the monarchy. The hotel is in the artists' colony of Spittelberg, within an easy walk of the Art History and Natural History Museums, the Volkstheater, and the shopping street Mariahilferstrasse. Rebuilt as a hotel in the late 1980s, this sleek example of contemporary Vienna offers ample, well-appointed rooms, with ample, tiled baths.

Kirchberggasse 6–8, A-1070 Vienna. ✆ **800/537-8483** in the U.S., or 01/52123. Fax 01/5212370. www. kkhotels.com. 123 units. 230€ double; from 280€ suite. Rates include buffet breakfast. AE, DC, MC, V. Parking 16€. U-Bahn: Volkstheater. Tram: 49. **Amenities:** Restaurant; bar; babysitting; dry cleaning; fitness center; laundry service; massage; room service; sauna. *In room:* A/C, TV, hairdryer, minibar, safe, free Wi-Fi.

MODERATE

Altstadt Vienna ★★ 🏨
Otto Ernst Wiesenthal knows what it means to feel at home abroad. The *créateur* of "your personal residence in Vienna," as he calls it, takes pride in finding each guest the right room—all uniquely and stylishly quirky—with big patrician windows, parquet floors, vivid wall colors, mismatched upholstery fabrics, and original art. The internationally renowned architect Matteo Thun designed the 17 new rooms, each of which has books, art magazines, and CDs to go with them, and the hotel boasts the best collection of lamps in Austria. The hotel now offers apartments for longer stays (prices on request). Not only is a hearty breakfast included, but also tea and cakes in the afternoon. To complete the artistic atmosphere, guests can also use the Bösendorfer in the cafe. Besides the affordability of the hotel's magnificent rooms, Wiesenthal prides himself on his employees' heartfelt service.

Kirchengasse 41, A-1070 Vienna. ✆ **01/5226666.** Fax 01/5234901. www.altstadt.at. 47 units. 119€–200€ double; 169€–369€ suite. AE, DC, MC, V. Parking 18€. U-Bahn: Volkstheater. **Amenities:** Breakfast room; bar; babysitting; dry cleaning; laundry service; room service; salon. *In room:* TV, hairdryer, minibar, safe, free Wi-Fi.

Falkensteiner Hotel Am Schottenfeld ★ ☺
The design of the hotel is young, modern, and chic, just like many of its guests. A skillful use of light combines the contemporary with selected Biedermeier fabrics and accent pieces of 1900s' *Jugendstil* for a successful reinvention of Wien Modern. Rooms offer contemporary comfort and tasteful appointments, and bathrooms with marble floors, an image of elegance. Outside the hotel is a wide range of small bars and restaurants, along with antique and junk shops, trendy boutiques, and antiquarian booksellers.

Schottenfeldgasse 74, A-1070 Vienna. ✆ **01/5265181.** Fax 01/5265181-160. www.falkensteiner.com. 95 units. 157€–249€ double; 50€ extra for junior suite. AE, DC, MC, V. U-Bahn: Volkstheater. **Amenities:** Bistro; bar; babysitting; dry cleaning; Turkish bath; kids' club; laundry service; room service; sauna; solarium. *In room:* A/C, TV, hairdryer, minibar, safe, Wi-Fi: 15min 2€, 1hr 4€, 3hr 8€, 24hr 15€.

INEXPENSIVE

Hotel-Pension Museum 🏨 🗝
Originally a private home dating from the 1600s, the exterior of this gracious hotel was transformed around 1890 into the elegant Art Nouveau facade it has today. Right behind the Volkstheater and across from the Imperial Museums, there is little you will want to do that is more than a pleasant walk away. Bedrooms vary, with some spacious and others a bit cramped. However, the rates are very modest, particularly for the quality, making many guests loyalists.

Museumstrasse 3, A-1070 Vienna. ✆ **01/52344260.** Fax 01/523442630. www.tiscover.com/hotel. museum. 15 units. 70€–135€ double. Rates include breakfast. AE, DC, MC, V. Parking 22€ Mon–Fri, free Sat–Sun. U-Bahn: Volkstheater. **Amenities:** Breakfast room; lounge; room service. *In room:* TV, hairdryer, free Wi-Fi.

Hotel Savoy Built in the 1960s, this well-managed hotel rises six stories above one of Vienna's busiest shopping districts and just opposite the Neubaugasse entrance to U-Bahn line U3. Decorations are tasteful and most units offer picture-window views of the neighborhood. The hotel serves breakfast and the neighborhood offers the rest.

Lindengasse 12, A-1070 Vienna. (€) **01/5234646.** Fax 01/5234640. www.hotelsavoy.at. 43 units. 83€–150€ double; 121€–180€ triple. Rates include buffet breakfast. AE, DC, MC, V. Parking 16€. U-Bahn: Neubaugasse. **Amenities:** Breakfast room; babysitting; dry cleaning; laundry service. *In room:* TV, hairdryer, minibar, safe, free Wi-Fi.

Josefstadt (8th District)
EXPENSIVE

Cordial Theaterhotel Wien Radically modernized in the late 1980s, this 19th-century hotel right by the Theater an der Josefstadt is a favorite of Austrian business travelers, who profit from the hotel's proximity to the city's wholesale buying outlets. Each simply furnished room contains its own small but efficient kitchenette. The on-site Theater-Restaurant is especially busy before and after performances.

Josefstadter Strasse 22, A-1080 Vienna. (€) **01/4053648.** Fax 01/4051406. www.cordial.at. 54 units. 107€–194€ double; 174€–317€ suite. Rates include buffet breakfast. AE, DC, MC, V. Parking 15€. U-Bahn: Rathaus. **Amenities:** Restaurant; bar; babysitting; business center; dry cleaning; fitness center; massage; laundry service; room service; sauna. *In room:* TV, hairdryer, minibar, Wi-Fi: 1hr 1€.

Hotel Parliament Levante ★ This is a good example of the wave of new, design-conscious hotels that opened in Vienna during 2006. It sits behind a rectilinear, five-story facade of distressed concrete, which, in 1908, was chiseled into a Bauhaus-inspired design—a radical departure from the neo-Gothic facade of the nearby Rathaus (City Hall) and the cool, elegant Greek Revival style of the Austrian Parliament. After a radical reconfiguration, the hotel gives the impression that every interior angle and every interior line was meticulously plotted into a postmodern, avant-garde design. The decor includes lots of white Turkish travertine and marble, dark-grained wood, and a (sometimes excessive) use of the photos of Austrian photographer Curt Themessl and the free-form glass vases and sculptures of Romanian glass-blower Ioan Nemtoi. Most of the rooms face a quiet but dull inner courtyard, and each is comfortable, decoratively neutral, and postmodern.

Auerspergstrasse 15, A-1080 Vienna. (€) **01/228-280.** Fax 01/228-2828. www.thelevante.com. 70 units. 280€ double; 355€ suite. Extra bed 45€. Rates include breakfast. AE, DC, MC, V. Parking 22€. U-Bahn: Rathaus. **Amenities:** Dry cleaning, fitness room w/sauna; room service; laundry service; free Wi-Fi in lobby. *In room:* A/C, TV, minibar, Wi-Fi: 1hr 3€, 24hr 9€.

INEXPENSIVE

Hotel Graf Stadion ★ ☺ This is one of the few genuine Biedermeier-style hotels left in Vienna right behind the Rathaus, a 10-minute walk from most of the central monuments. The facade evokes early-19th-century elegance, with triangular or half-rounded ornamentation above many of the windows. The refurbished bedrooms are comfortably old-fashioned, and many are spacious enough to accommodate an extra bed for people traveling with small children.

Buchfeldgasse 5, A-1080 Vienna. (€) **01/405-5284.** Fax 01/4050111. www.graf-stadion.com. 40 units. 105€–150€ double. Rates include buffet breakfast. AE, DC, MC, V. Parking 15€. U-Bahn: Rathaus. **Amenities:** Breakfast room; bar; babysitting; dry cleaning; laundry service. *In room:* TV, hairdryer, Wi-Fi: 1hr 1€, 6hr 5€.

Hotel-Pension Zipser A 5-minute walk from the Rathaus, this pension offers rooms with wall-to-wall carpeting and central heating, many overlooking a private garden. Much of the renovated interior is tastefully adorned with wood detailing. Generous-size bedrooms are furnished in a functional, modern style, with some opening onto balconies above the garden. The staff is very friendly and it is a favorite of locals for friends or relatives who are staying longer than a few days.

Lange Gasse 49, A-1080 Vienna. ✆ **01/404540.** Fax 01/4045413. www.zipser.at. 47 units. 85€–165€ double. Rates include buffet breakfast. AE, DC, MC, V. Parking 14€. U-Bahn: Rathaus. Bus: 13A. **Amenities:** Breakfast room; bar; lounge. *In room:* TV, hairdryer, safe, free Wi-Fi.

Alsergrund (9th District)

MODERATE

Austria Trend Hotel Albatros   A 10-minute ride from the city, the Trend is dull on the outside but lively inside. Well-furnished rooms are medium in size and fitted with comfortable upholstery and small but efficient bathrooms (shower only).

Liechtensteinstrasse 89, 1090 Vienna. ✆ **01/317-35-08.** Fax 01/317-35-08-85. www.austria-trend.at. 70 units. 128€–248€ double. Rates include buffet breakfast. AE, DC, MC, V. Parking: 17€ U-Bahn: Friedensbrücke. **Amenities:** Breakfast room; bar; sauna. *In room:* A/C, TV, minibar, hair dryer, free Wi-Fi.

Hotel Bellevue   This hotel was built in 1873, at about the same time as the Franz-Josefs Bahnhof, a short walk away, whose passengers it was designed to house. Its wedge shape on the acute angle of a busy street corner is reminiscent of the Flatiron Building in Manhattan. Unfortunately most of the old details have been stripped from the public rooms, although renovation has left clean lines and a handful of antiques. Some 100 guest rooms are in a wing added in 1982. All rooms are functional and well maintained, and contain comfortable low beds and utilitarian desks and chairs.

Althanstrasse 5, 1091 Vienna. ✆ **01/313-480.** Fax 01/3134-8801. www.hotelbellevue.at. 173 units. 210€–240€ double; from 250€ suite. Rates include buffet breakfast. AE, DC, MC, V. Parking 19€. U-Bahn: Friedensbrücke. Tram: 5 or D. **Amenities:** Restaurant; bar; sauna; room service; babysitting. *In room:* TV, minibar, hair dryer, Wi-Fi: 30mins free in Deluxe rooms, otherwise .35€/min, 24hr 17€.

Hotel Regina   Established in 1896 next to the Votivkirche, this hotel was built in the "Ringstrasse" style. The facade is appropriately grand, reminiscent of a French Renaissance palace, while inside it is unashamedly an old-world hotel with red salons and interminable corridors. Guest rooms are well maintained and traditionally furnished; some have canopied beds and elaborate furnishings. Room sizes vary, but it all works. The tree-lined street is usually calm.

Rooseveltplatz 15, A-1090 Vienna. ✆ **01/404-460.** Fax 01/408-8392. 128 units. 107€–250€ double; 185€–300€ deluxe double. Rates include buffet breakfast. AE, DC, MC, V. Parking 20€. U-Bahn: Schottentor. Tram: 1, D, 37, 38, 40, 41, or 42. **Amenities:** Restaurant; cafe; bar; room service. *In room:* TV, minibar, hair dryer, Wi-Fi: 30mins 3€, 1hr 6€, 24hr 12€.

Rathaus Wein & Design Hotel ★★ 🎁   From the outside, this government-rated four-star hotel has a glowing 18th-century facade in Schönbrunner yellow. Inside, photographs record the building's radical upgrade, a minimalist and very tasteful contemporary design, a glistening white-with-touches-of-alabaster wine bar that doubles as a breakfast room, and one of the most unusual blends of hotel and wine-industry marketing in Austria. Bedrooms, scattered over five floors, are each dedicated to an Austrian vintner, each entryway has a door-size wine label identifying that room's allegiance to, say, the Triebaumer or Jamek wineries, or to any of 31 other vintners. Bedrooms are comfortable, high-ceilinged, and large, with a palette of neutral earth tones, stylish bathroom fixtures, and a sense of postmodern hip.

Lange Gasse 13, 1080 Vienna. ✆ **01/400-11-22.** Fax 01/400-11-22-88. www.hotel-rathaus-wien.at. 33 units. 148€–198€ double. Parking 15€. AE, DC, MC, V. U-Bahn: U3 or U4 to Volkstheater. **Amenities:** Wine bar; breakfast room; limited room service; babysitting. *In room:* TV, minibar, hair dryer, safe, free Wi-Fi.

WHERE TO EAT

In Vienna, dining out is a local pastime; while there are pricey restaurants, many are not and you can eat out very well for little more than what you might have spent for a good meal at home. And there are so many restaurants to choose from: Along with Austrian and Mediterranean cuisine, you'll find fine restaurants serving Croatian, Serbian, Slovenian, Slovak, Hungarian, and Czech food, as well as Asian, French, and Russian. Although traditional Viennese *Gasthaus* meals are simple and filling, international influences—principally from Italy, the Balkans, and Turkey—have long influenced Austrian cuisine. Today, this trend toward internationalism is even stronger, and innovative chefs throughout the city now turn out lighter versions of the classics along with new combinations of old and new. And in spite of the myths, this pleases the health-conscious and environmentally aware Viennese who like to eat well in both senses of the word.

Unlike those in many western European capitals, Vienna's restaurants still heed Sunday closings (marked by SONNTAG RUHETAG signs). Also, beware of those summer holiday closings, when chefs would rather rush to nearby lake resorts than cook for Vienna's visiting hordes. However, post-theater dining is fashionable in this city, and many restaurants and cafes stay open late.

Innere Stadt (Inner City)
VERY EXPENSIVE

Fabios ★★ INTERNATIONAL/MEDITERRANEAN   This is one of the trendiest restaurants in Vienna, with considerable jockeying for a table among the city's glitterati. The creation of the young and fun Fabio Giacobello, the space is bigger inside than you might think. Most of the visual distraction in this mostly black but plush and artfully lit environment comes from its fashion-conscious (and usually good-looking) clients. The menu might include warm octopus marinated with olive oil and parsley served on a bed of cold gazpacho cream sauce, and roasted rack of lamb with cold marinated eggplant and tomatoes served with deep-fried polenta *gnocchetti*. Incidentally, don't overlook the wine bar as a nightlife option. Enough drama unfolds around its rectangular surface to keep a few tabloid writers busy, and someone famous within the inner workings of Vienna's media and politics always seems to be popping up for air and a drink or two.

Tuchlauben 6. ✆ **01/532-2222.** www.fabios.at. Reservations recommended. Main courses 29€–32€. AE, MC, V. Mon–Sat 10am–1am. U-Bahn: Stephansplatz.

Julius Meinl ★ CONTINENTAL   This upscale and appealingly formal restaurant is the most sought-after of the three elements within the Julius Meinl trio, which includes, on the same premises, one of the most comprehensive delicatessens and wine shops in Austria, as well as a cellar-level wine bar. The restaurant is upstairs with big-windowed views that sweep out over the all-pedestrian grandeur of the Graben. With dark paneling and touches of gilt, a voluptuous-looking service bar is positioned within a few steps of the bustling and brightly illuminated premises of its delicatessen. Restaurant choices might include tuna with avocado cream and a carrot and ginger-flavored vinaigrette, or marinated gratin of lobster with fennel. For dessert

Restaurants in Vienna

Abend-Restaurant
  Feuervogel **2**
Akakiko **51**
Alfi's Goldener Spiegel **16**
Altes Jägerhaus **40**
Altwienerhof **13**
Amerlingbeisl **10**
Augustinerkeller **21**
Bauer **38**
Bohème **10**
Buffet Trzésniewski **50**
Café Central **23**
Café Cuadro **19**
Café Demel **22**
Café Diglas **47**
Café Dommayer **16**
Café Frauenhuber **56**
Café Landtmann **6**
Café Leopold **11**
Café Phil **14**
Café Restaurant Halle **11**
Café Sperl **15**
Café Tirolerhof **54**
Cantinetta Antinori **36**
Danieli **55**
Demmers Teehaus **5**
Do & Co. **49**
DOTS **12**
Dubrovnik **42**
Esterházykeller **25**
Fabios **28**
Figlmüller **37**
Finkh **13**
Fischrestaurant Kaj **31**
Gasthaus Ubl **18**
Gräfin vom Naschmarkt **17**
Griechenbeisl **32**
Gulaschmuseum **45**
Hansen **3**
Hietzinger Bräu **16**
Hollerei **12**
Julius Meinl **26**
Kardos **39**
Kervansaray und
  Hummer Bar **57**
Leopold **31**
Leupold's Kupferdachl **4**
Mörwald im Ambassador **53**
Motto **19**
Motto am Fluss **33**
Motto am Fluss Café **33**
Niky's Kuchlmasterei **34**
Ofenloch **27**
Österreicher im MAK **43**
Palmenhaus **20**
Piaristenkeller **9**
Plachutta **44**
Plutzer Bräu **10**
Restaurant Salzamt **29**
Schnattl **9**
Schweizerhaus **34**
Silberwirt **19**
Simchas **31**

← To Westbahnhof
and Schönbrunn

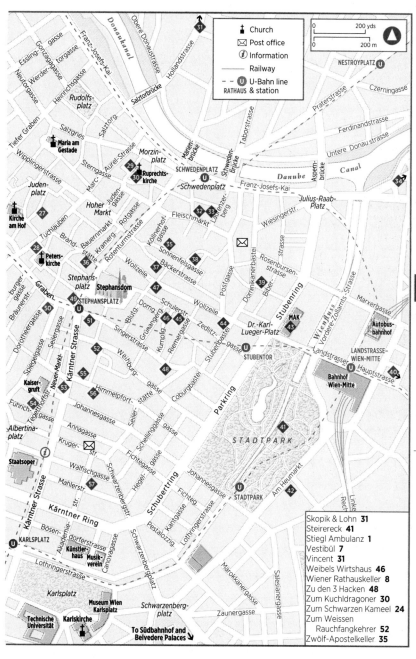

Skopik & Lohn **31**
Steirereck **41**
Stiegl Ambulanz **1**
Vestibül **7**
Vincent **31**
Weibels Wirtshaus **46**
Wiener Rathauskeller **8**
Zu den 3 Hacken **48**
Zum Kuchldragoner **30**
Zum Schwarzen Kameel **24**
Zum Weissen
   Rauchfangkehrer **52**
Zwölf-Apostelkeller **35**

consider a praline mousse with raspberries and tonka-bean ice cream, or a semolina soufflé with plums and elderberries. And then there's the cheese trolley, a movable feast and a work of art in its own right.

Graben 19. ℂ **01/5323334.** www.meinl.at. Reservations recommended. Main courses 24€–35€. Mon-Sat 8am–midnight. U-Bahn: Stephansplatz.

Kervansaray und Hummer Bar ★★ SEAFOOD   Here you'll sense the historic link between the Habsburgs and their 19th-century neighbor, the Ottoman Empire. On the restaurant's ground floor, polite waiters announce a changing array of daily specials and serve tempting salads from an hors d'oeuvre table. Upstairs, guests enjoy the bounties of the sea at the Lobster Bar. There's also a deli. A meal often begins with a champagne cocktail, followed by one of many appetizers, including a lobster and salmon caviar cocktail. The menu has a short list of such meat dishes as filet mignon with Roquefort sauce, but it specializes in seafood, including grilled filet of sole with fresh asparagus, Norwegian salmon with a horseradish-and-champagne sauce, and, of course, lobster. If shellfish is your weakness, be prepared to pay for your indulgence.

Mahlerstrasse 9. ℂ **01/5128843.** www.hummerbar.at. Reservations recommended. Main courses 25€–50€. AE, DC, MC, V. Restaurant Mon–Sat noon–midnight. U-Bahn: Karlsplatz. Tram: 1 or 2. Bus: 3A.

Mörwald im Ambassador ★★★ VIENNESE   Views from its greenhouse-style windows, two floors above street level, sweep out over the Neumarkt and one of Vienna's most memorable outdoor fountains. Bankers, diplomats, and what one local food critic called "Helmut Lang-clad hipsters" show up for the sophisticated twists on classic Viennese cuisine. Menu items change with the seasons, but are likely to include tartar of French-derived Limousin beef with rosemary toasts and cocktail sauce; foie gras with kumquats and a sauce made from sparkling wine; ravioli stuffed with pulverized lamb, artichoke hearts, and mint sauce; and roasted loin of veal with chanterelles and a spicy potato-based cream sauce.

On the second floor of the Hotel Ambassador, Kärntner Strasse 22. ℂ **01/961610.** Reservations required. Main courses 24€–34€; set-price lunches 29€–39€; set-price dinners 75€–110€. AE, DC, MC, V. Daily noon–3pm and 6–11pm. U-Bahn: Stephansplatz.

EXPENSIVE

Bauer ★★ AUSTRIAN/CONTINENTAL   It's upscale, it's *gemütlich*, and it's on the shortlist of restaurants that concierges at some of Vienna's most upscale hotels recommend to their clients. You'll find it on a narrow street a few blocks northeast of the cathedral, beneath 500-year-old ceiling vaults, now painted a dark shade of pink, that evoke a venue that's more folksy and rustic than this sophisticated restaurant really is. The fact that there are only 30 seats enhances the coziness of a venue that was established in its present format in 1989. Expect glamorous food. The finest examples include carpaccio of beef with mustard sauce; sweetbreads with vanilla sauce and braised chicory; and stuffed squid with lemon sauce and pepper-flavored cream sauce.

Sonnenfelsgasse 17. ℂ **01/5129871.** Reservations recommended. Main courses 26€–32€; 4-course set-price menu 62€. AE, DC, MC, V. Mon 6–11pm, Tues-Fri noon–2pm and 6–11pm. Closed Sat and Sun, 1 week at Easter, and mid-July to mid-Aug. U-Bahn: Stephansplatz, Schwedenplatz, or Stubentor.

Do & Co. ★ INTERNATIONAL   Positioned on the 7th floor of a radically angular hypermodern building of the also-recommended hotel, across from St. Stephan's, this restaurant is in demand. It's difficult to overstate its fame within the complicated but steely hierarchy of fine and/or stylish Viennese dining. If you didn't reserve, or your table isn't ready, consider a pre-dinner cocktail at the stylish Onyx Bar on the building's 6th floor, then climb a circular staircase to the 7th-floor dining room. Here, *if you've reserved,* you'll be presented with a slightly claustrophobic table and a confusingly diverse set of menu items. Dishes are divided into categories that include "Tastes of the World" (Tataki of Atlantic tuna or sushi), "Catch of the Day" (potpourri of scallops), "Beef & Co." (French breast of duck with green beans and creamy kumquat polenta), "Kebab, Wok & Curries" (dishes inspired by Asia, especially Thailand), "Austrian Classics" (deep-fried monkfish with potato salad).

In the Haas Haus, Stephansplatz 12. ⓒ **01/24188.** www.doco.com. Reservations required. Main courses 18€–26€. AE, DC, MC, V. Daily noon–3pm and 6–11:45pm. U-Bahn: Stephansplatz.

Plachutta ★ VIENNESE   Few restaurants have built such a fetish around one dish as Plachutta has done with *Tafelspitz,* offering 10 variations of the boiled beef dish, which was the favorite of Emperor Franz Josef throughout his prolonged reign. The differences between the versions are a function of the cut of beef you request. We recommend *Schulterscherzel* (shoulder of beef) and *Beinfleisch* (shank of beef), but if you're in doubt, the waiting staff is knowledgeable about one of the most oft-debated subjects in Viennese cuisine. Hash brown potatoes, chives, and an appealing mixture of horseradish and chopped apples accompany each order. Other Viennese staples, such as goulash soup, calf's liver, and braised pork with cabbage, are also available.

Wollzeile 38. ⓒ **01/5121577.** www.plachutta.at. Reservations recommended. Main courses 18€–26€. DC, MC, V. Daily 11:30am–midnight. U-Bahn: Stubentor.

Weibels Wirtshaus ★ 🍴AUSTRIAN   Don't be fooled by the unpretentious and cozy feel to this place, which at first glance might look like a simple tavern. Food is considerably better than the *Wirtshaus* (tavern) appellation implies, and the clientele is a lot more upscale than the usual wurst-with-potatoes-and-beer crowd. There are only two rooms (and about 40 seats) within this wood-paneled restaurant, each on a separate floor of a building whose age is estimated to be around 400 years old. During clement weather, another 30 seats become available within a garden at the back. The wine list, with more than 250 varieties of Austrian wine, looks like a patriotic, pro-Austrian statement in its own right. Menu items include pumpkinseed soup, sliced breast of duck with lentils, well-prepared schnitzels of veal and chicken, and a superb saddle of lamb with polenta and spinach.

Kumpfgasse 2. ⓒ **01/5123986.** www.weibel.at. Reservations recommended. Main courses 14€–19€; fixed-price menu 36€. AE, MC, V. Daily 11:30am–midnight. U-Bahn: Stephansplatz.

Wiener Rathauskeller ★★ INTERNATIONAL/VIENNESE   City halls throughout the Teutonic world have traditionally maintained restaurants in their basements, and Vienna is no exception. Although Vienna's famous Rathaus was built between 1871 and 1883, its cellar-level restaurant wasn't added until 1899. Today, in half a dozen richly atmospheric dining rooms, with high-vaulted ceilings and stained-glass windows, you can enjoy good and reasonably priced food. The chef's specialty is a *Rathauskellerplatte* for two, consisting of various cuts of meat, including a veal schnitzel, lamb cutlets, and pork medallions. One section of the cellar is devoted every evening to a Viennese musical soiree beginning at 8pm. Live musicians ramble through the world of operetta, waltz, and *Schrammel* (traditional Viennese music) as you dine.

Rathausplatz 1. ⓒ **01/405-1210.** www.wiener-rathauskeller.at. Reservations required. Main courses 11€–39€. AE, DC, MC, V. Mon–Sat 11:30am–3pm and 6–11pm. U-Bahn: Rathaus.

5

SETTLING INTO VIENNA | Where to Eat

Zum Schwarzen Kameel ★★ INTERNATIONAL This Jugendstil restaurant has remained in the same family since 1618. A delicatessen against one of the walls sells wine, liquor, and specialty meat items, although most of the action takes place among the chic clientele in the cafe. On Saturday mornings, the cafe is packed with locals trying to recover from a late night. Uniformed waiters will bring you a beverage here, and you can select open-face sandwiches from the trays on the black counter-tops. The specialty is a rosy hand-carved *Beinschinken* (boiled ham with freshly grated horseradish).

Beyond the cafe is a perfectly preserved Art Deco dining room, where jeweled copper chandeliers hang from beaded strings. The walls are a combination of polished paneling, yellowed ceramic tiles, and a dusky plaster ceiling frieze of grape leaves. The restaurant has just 11 tables, and it's the perfect place for a nostalgic lunch in Vienna. The hearty and well-flavored cuisine features herring filet Oslo, potato soup, tournedos, Roman saltimbocca (veal with ham), and an array of daily fish specials.

Bognergasse 5. ⓒ **01/5338125.** Main courses 19€–37€. AE, DC, MC, V. Mon–Sat 8am–midnight. U-Bahn: Schottentor. Bus: 2A or 3A.

MODERATE

Cantinetta Antinori ★ ITALIAN This is one of three European restaurants run by the Antinori family, who own Tuscan vineyards and whose name is nearly synonymous with Chianti. The traditions and aesthetics of the original restaurant, in Florence, have been reproduced here to showcase Antinori wines and the culinary zest of Tuscany. Within a 140-year-old building overlooking the Stephansplatz and the cathedral, you'll find a high-ceilinged dining room, as well as a greenhouse-style "winter garden" that transports you straight to Tuscany. Start off with an order of *antipasti tipico*, a medley of marinated vegetables and seafood arranged by the staff. This might be followed by sumptuous ravioli stuffed with porcini mushrooms and summer truffles, or perfectly grilled lamb steaks with sun-dried tomatoes and Mediterranean herbs. *Panna cotta*, a creamy flan, is a simple but flavorful way to finish a meal. A large selection of wines is served by the glass.

Jasomirgottstrasse 3–5. ⓒ **01/5337722.** www.antinori.it. Reservations required. Main courses 19€–29€. AE, DC, MC, V. Daily 11:30am–11pm. U-Bahn: Stephansplatz.

Danieli ★★ ITALIAN This is one of Vienna's premier Italian restaurants. Located near St. Stephan's on a side street of Kärntnerstrasse, it has a red brick interior with chandeliers and cushioned leather seating. The kitchen specializes in high-end versions of time-honored Italian classics. Start with antipasti, served on a tower of plates and then choose from the classical pasta variations or one of their delicious wood stove pizzas. The fish and meat dishes are inspired and loyal to Italian cooking traditions. Their wine list is overwhelming, but the attentive staff will help you choose a suitable accompaniment. Upstairs is great for a romantic table for two.

Himmelpfortgasse 3. ⓒ **01/5137913.** Reservations recommended. Main courses 10€–26€. AE, DC, MC, V. Daily 10am–midnight. U-Bahn: Stephansplatz.

Griechenbeisl ★ AUSTRIAN Astonishingly, Griechenbeisl was established in 1450 and is still one of the city's leading restaurants. There's a maze of dining areas on three different floors, all with low-vaulted ceilings, smoky paneling, and wrought-iron chandeliers. Watch out for the Styrian-vested waiters who scurry around with large trays of food. As you enter, look down at the grate under your feet for an illuminated view of a pirate counting his money. Inside, check out the so-called inner sanctum, with signatures of former patrons such as Mozart, Beethoven, and Mark

Twain. The beer is well chilled, and the food is hearty and ample. Menu items include fried breaded filet of chicken with cucumber–potato salad; and roast filet of pikeperch with almonds. As an added treat, the restaurant features nighttime accordion and zither music.

Fleischmarkt 11. ⓒ **01/5331941.** www.griechenbeisl.at. Reservations required. Main courses 16€–23€. AE, DC, MC, V. Daily 11am–1am (last order at 11:30pm). Tram: N, 1, 2, or 21.

Hansen ★ 🏛AUSTRIAN/INTERNATIONAL/MEDITERRANEAN   One of the most intriguing and stylish restaurants in Vienna opened as a partnership between a time-tested culinary team and the downtown showrooms of one of Austria's most famous horticulturists and gardening stores (Lederleitner, GmbH). You'll find them cheek-by-jowl in the vaulted cellars of Vienna's stock exchange, a Beaux Arts pile designed in the 1890s by the restaurant's namesake, Theophile Hansen. Part of the charm of this place involves trekking through masses of plants and elaborate garden ornaments on your way to your dining table. Expect to be joined by the movers and shakers of corporate Vienna at lunch and at relatively early dinners, when the place is likely to be very busy. Choose from a small but savory menu that changes weekly. Examples include a spicy bean salad with strips of chicken breast served in a summer broth, risotto with cheese and sour cherries, and poached *Saibling* (something akin to trout from the coldwater streams of the Austrian Alps) with a potato and celery puree and watercress.

In the cellar of the Börse (former Vienna Stock Exchange), Wipplingerstrasse 34 at the Schottenring. ⓒ **01/5320542.** www.vestibuel.at. Reservations recommended. Main courses 8€–20€. AE, DC, MC, V. Mon–Fri 9am–8pm (last order); Sat 9am–3:30pm (last order). U-Bahn: Schottenring.

Leupold's Kupferdachl ★ VIENNESE/AUSTRIAN   Run by the Leopold family since the 1950s, this restaurant is known for "new Austrian" cuisine, although the chef does prepare traditional dishes. Recommended menu items include beef tenderloin (Old Viennese style) with dumplings boiled in a napkin, lamb loin breaded and served with potatoes, and chicken breast Kiev. The interior is both rustic and elegant, decorated with oriental rugs and cozy banquettes with intricate straight-back chairs. The restaurant operates a beer pub, with good music and better prices. The pub is open daily from 10am to midnight.

Schottengasse 7. ⓒ **01/5339381.** www.leupold.at. Reservations recommended. Main courses 10€–20€. AE, DC, MC, V. Mon–Fri 10am–3pm; Mon–Sat 6pm–midnight. U-Bahn: Schottentor. Tram: 2, 37, 38, 43, or 44.

Motto am Fluss ★★ INTERNATIONAL/CONTINENTAL   In a boat-like structure that functions as the docking station for passenger ships along the Danube and canal, this new addition to the Schwedenplatz neighborhood is a welcome change from the present concentration of *Beisl* and bars. The famous mother restaurant in the 5th District (see Motto below) is a long-time favorite and has now come downtown. Upstairs at the cafe, the breakfast and burgers are spectacular, with light fare and hearty sausage-slathered inspirations (see Coffeehouses & Cafes, below). Downstairs at the cafe the menu is eclectic and somewhat confusing, with starters and main courses all in one list, however the prices make the portions clear. Marinated tuna and yellowtail on a lime onion with sesame dressing and sprout salad, or goose liver terrine with ginger plums and Bali pepper are good examples of this varied selection. Sip and nibble as you gaze at the urban waterfront.

Schwedenplatz 2. ⓒ **01/25-255-10.** www.motto.at. Reservations recommended. Main courses: 10€–26€. AE, DC, MC, V. Mon–Fri 6pm–2am. Closed Sat–Sun. U-Bahn: Schwedenplatz.

Ofenloch VIENNESE   Viennese have frequented this spot since the 1600s, when it functioned as a simple tavern. The present management dates from the mid-1970s and maintains a well-deserved reputation for its period charm and old-fashioned courtesies. Waitresses wear classic Austrian dress and will give you a menu that looks more like a magazine, with some amusing archival illustrations inside. The hearty soup dishes are popular, as is the schnitzel. For smaller appetites, the menu offers salads and cheese platters, plus an entire page devoted to one-dish meals. For dessert, choose from old-style Viennese specialties.

Kurrentgasse 8. ✆ **01/5338844.** www.ofenloch.at. Reservations required. Main courses 10€–19€. AE, DC, MC, V. Tues–Sat 11am–midnight. U-Bahn: Stephansplatz. Bus: 1A.

Österreicher im MAK ★★ VIENNESE/AUSTRIAN   The oft-decorated star chef of the Steirereck, Helmut Österreicher, opened a new restaurant in 2006, in the Museum of Applied Arts. The "Österreicher" has quickly become *the* place to go for anyone who is anybody in the art, architecture, and design world. The decor mixes classical art with modern. The enormous chandelier above the well-equipped bar is a collage of wine bottles, the original parquet floor and impossibly high, panelled ceilings inset with paintings are themselves a design event. The menu reflects this stylistic dissonance, offering artistic renditions of classical Austrian dishes alongside Österreicher's own creations such as a white-wine calf stew with a dark bread omelet followed by salmon trout in a muesli crust and sweetened with chestnut cream on fruit salad. Sample the Austrian wine list: The Knoll Riesling or the Nittnaus Pinot Noir. For intimacy, take the back room—more floral and modern but less noisy.

In the MAK (Museum für Angewante Kunst), Stubenring 5. ✆ **01/714-0121.** www.oesterreicherimmak. at. Reservations recommended. Main courses 8€–22€. AE, DC, MC, V. Daily 8:30am–1am. U-Bahn: Stubentor or Schwedenplatz.

Restaurant Salzamt ★ AUSTRIAN   This is the best restaurant in a neighborhood—the "Bermuda Triangle"—that's loaded with less desirable competitors. It evokes a turn-of-the-20th-century Viennese bistro, replete with Wiener Werkstätte-inspired chairs and lighting fixtures, cream-colored walls, and dark tables and banquettes where you're likely to see an arts-involved, sometimes surprisingly prominent clientele of loyal repeat diners, including Karl Lagerfeld and the Prince of Monaco. Sit within its vaulted interior or—if weather permits—move out to any of the tables on the square that overlook Vienna's oldest church, St. Ruprecht. Well-prepared items include a terrine of broccoli and artichoke hearts, light-textured pastas, filets of pork with a Gorgonzola-enriched cream sauce, several kinds of goulash, and fresh fish. One of the most noteworthy of these is fried filets of *Saibling,* a fish native to the coldwater streams of western Austria, served with lemon or tartar sauce.

Ruprechtsplatz 1. ✆ **01/5335332.** Reservations recommended. Main courses 8€–19€. V. Daily 5pm–midnight. U-Bahn: Schwedenplatz.

Vestibül ★ 🏛 AUSTRIAN   For theater buffs in particular, this is a real discovery. The restaurant entrance originally existed for the emperor's coach. Architect Luigi Blau took the basic structure and enlarged it, creating a setting that is both antique and modern. Before or after the theater, guests gather in the elegant bar for an aperitif, digestif, or coffee. Tapas are also served here, with tables opening onto a view of the City Hall and Ringstrasse. Beginning on the first warm spring day and lasting until the mild afternoons of autumn, tables are also placed outside in the garden. A team of skilled chefs present classic cuisine with market-fresh ingredients. An appetizer of fresh oysters might be followed by such main dishes as traditional paprika chicken (inspired by nearby Hungary) or a traditional *Beuschel* (a Viennese-style hash made of heart and lung). Styrian beef is also a local favorite.

Dr.-Karl-Lueger-Ring 2. ✆ **01/5324999.** www.vestibul.at. Reservations recommended. Main courses 14€–24€. AE, DC, MC, V. Mon–Fri 11am–midnight; Sat 6pm–midnight, July–Aug closed Sat. U-Bahn: Schottentor or Herrengasse.

Zum Weissen Rauchfangkehrer VIENNESE   Established in the 1860s, this dinner-only place is the former guildhall for Vienna's chimney sweeps. In fact, the restaurant's name (translated as the "white chimney sweep") comes from the story of a drunken and blackened chimney sweep who fell into a kneading trough and woke up the next day covered in flour. The dining room is rustic, with deer antlers, fanciful chandeliers, and pine banquettes that vaguely resemble church pews. A piano in one of the inner rooms provides nighttime music and adds to the comfortable ambiance. Big street-level windows let in lots of light. The hearty, flavorful menu offers Viennese fried chicken, both Tyrolean and Wiener schnitzel, wild game, veal goulash, brat-wurst, and several kinds of strudel. You'll certainly want to finish with the house specialty, a fabulously rich chocolate cream puff.

Weihburggasse 4. ✆ **01/5123471.** Reservations required. Main courses 15€–26€. DC, MC, V. Tues–Sat 6pm–midnight. Closed July and Aug. U-Bahn: Stephansplatz.

INEXPENSIVE

Akakiko 🍴 ASIAN   It's busy and loaded with Asians living permanently or tempo-rarily within Vienna. And as a member of a chain with eight equivalent branches throughout Vienna, it boasts a carefully rehearsed and inexpensive formula for Asian food within an otherwise very expensive neighborhood. To reach its dining room, you'll pass by an open kitchen, where everything gives the impression of wholesome-ness and a recent scrubbing. Within the brightly lit modern dining room, outfitted in tones of white and bamboo green, you'll pick from menu items that include sushi, sashimi, teppanyaki, bento boxes, and wok versions of duck, chicken, beef, fish, and vegetarian dishes inspired by the cuisines of China.

Singerstrasse 4. ✆ **057/333-140.** www.akakiko.at. Reservations not accepted. Main courses 8.95€–14€. MC, V. Daily 10:30am–11:30pm. U-Bahn: Stephansplatz.

Augustinerkeller AUSTRIAN   Since 1857, the Augustinerkeller has served wine, beer, and food from the basement of one of the grand Hofburg palaces. It attracts a lively and diverse crowd that gets more boisterous as the *Schrammel* (traditional Vien-nese music) is played late into the night. The vaulted brick room, with worn pine-board floors and wooden banquettes, is an inviting place to grab a drink and a simple meal. Be aware that this long and narrow dining room is usually as packed with people as it is with character. An upstairs room is quieter and less crowded. This place offers one of the best values for wine-tasting in Vienna. The ground-floor lobby lists prices of vintage local wines by the glass. Tasters can sample from hundreds of bottles near the stand-up stainless-steel counter. Aside from the wine and beer, the kitchen serves simple food, including roast chicken, schnitzel, and *Tafelspitz*.

Augustinerstrasse 1. ✆ **01/5331026.** Main courses 9€–17€. AE, DC, MC, V. Daily 10am–midnight. U-Bahn: Stephansplatz.

Buffet Trzésniewski ★ SANDWICHES   Everyone in Vienna, from the most hurried office worker to the most elite hostess, knows about this spot. Franz Kafka lived next door and used to come here for sandwiches and beer. It's unlike any buffet you've seen, with six or seven cramped tables and a rapidly moving line of people, all jostling for space next to the glass counters. Indicate to the waitress the kind of sandwich you want (if you can't read German, just point). Most people hurriedly devour the delicious finger sandwiches, which come in 18 different combinations of cream cheese, egg, onion, salami, herring, tomatoes, lobster, and many other tasty ingredients. You can also order small glasses of fruit juice, beer, or wine with your snack. If you do order a drink, the cashier will give you a rubber token, which you'll present to the person at the far end of the counter.

Dorotheergasse 1. ℂ **01/5123291.** Reservations not accepted. Sandwiches .90€. No credit cards. Mon–Fri 8:30am–7:30pm; Sat 9am–5pm. U-Bahn: Stephansplatz.

Café Leopold ★ 👔 INTERNATIONAL   Set one floor above street level in the Leopold Museum, and with a schedule that operates long after the museum is closed for the night, it's sheathed in the same pale-pink sandstone as the museum's exterior. The marble walls and huge windows accent the touches of Jugendstil in the establishment, rounded off by a chandelier shaped like a UFO. During the day, the place functions as a conventional cafe and restaurant, serving a postmodern blend of central European and Asian food. Examples include roasted shoulder of veal with Mediterranean vegetables, Thai curries, Vietnamese spring rolls, and arugula-studded risottos. Several nights a week, however, from around 10pm till at least 3am, any hints of kitsch and coziness are banished as soon as a DJ begins cranking out dance tunes for hard-drinking night owls. For more on this cafe's role as a nightclub, see "Vienna After Dark," in chapter 6.

In the Leopold Museum, Museumsplatz 1. ℂ **01/5236732.** www.cafe-leopold.at. Main courses 5.90€–11€. AE, DC, MC, V. Sun–Wed 10am–2am; Fri–Sat 10am–4pm. U-Bahn: Volkstheater or MuseumsQuartier.

Café Restaurant Halle INTERNATIONAL   Set within the Kunsthalle, this is the direct competitor of the also-recommended Café Leopold (see above). Larger and with a more sophisticated menu than the Leopold, but without any of its late-night emphasis on dance music, this is a postmodern, airy, big-windowed quartet of wood-trimmed, cream-colored rooms. The menu changes every 2 weeks, and service is efficient, conscientious, and in the old-world style. The first thing you'll see when you enter is a Spartan-looking cafe area, with a trio of more formal dining rooms at the top of a short flight of stairs. Despite the commitment of its staff to changing the *carte* very frequently, the menu always contains a half-dozen meal-size salads, many garnished with strips of steak, chicken, or shrimp; two daily homemade soups; and a rotating series of platters that might include tasty braised filets of shark and roasted lamb, prepared delectably in the Greek style, with yogurt-and-herb dressing.

In the Kunsthalle Wien, Museumsplatz 1, in the MuseumsQuartier. ℂ **01/5237001.** Main courses 8€–17€. MC, V. Daily 10am–2am. U-Bahn: MuseumsQuartier.

Dubrovnik BALKAN/CROATIAN/VIENNESE   Dubrovnik's allegiance is to the culinary (and cultural) traditions of Croatia. The restaurant, founded in 1965, consists of three dining rooms on either side of a central vestibule filled with busy waiters in Croat costume. The menu lists a lengthy choice of Balkan dishes, including goose liver pâté; stuffed cabbage; and filet of veal with boiled potatoes, sour cream, and sauerkraut. Among the fish dishes, the most exotic is *Fogosch* (a whitefish) served with potatoes and garlic. For dessert, try baklava or an assortment of Bulgarian cheeses. The restaurant schedules live piano entertainment nightly from 7:30 to 11pm. On site is an unconventional-looking cafe (the Kono-Bar) that serves drinks and many of the main courses available during the grander restaurant's daily mid-afternoon closing.

Am Heumarkt 5. ☎ **01/713-7102.** Reservations recommended. Main courses 8€–18€. AE, DC, MC, V. Daily 11am–3pm and 6pm–midnight; cafe Mon–Fri 11am–midnight. U-Bahn: Stadtpark.

Esterhàzykeller ☺AUSTRIAN   It is a local favorite and a very well kept secret with occasional live gypsy music. This underground beer hall and buffet-style eatery also serves a la carte, but the real fun is choosing from the cutlets, spreads, and salads at the bar. The network of caves and long rooms gives it a very personal feel despite the vastness of the cellar. No one will mind if children want to explore the various caves, and they'll have fun sampling the finger food and Almdudler (herbal soda, a local favorite). This is a good inner-city alternative to the more rural *Heuriger* (see *"Heuriger"* in chapter 6).

Haarhof 1, off Naglergasse around the corner from the Graben. ☎ **01/5333482.** Reservations not necessary. U-Bahn: Stephansplatz. Main courses: 6.50€; buffet 15€. AE, DC, MC, V. Daily 11am–11pm. U-Bahn: Stephansplatz

Figlmüller AUSTRIAN   This is the latest branch of a wine tavern whose original home, established in 1905, lies only a few blocks away. This new branch, thanks to a location on three floors of a thick-walled 200-year-old building and lots of old-world memorabilia attached to the walls, evokes Old Vienna with style and panache. Austrian Airlines referred to its black-and-white uniformed waiters as "unflappable," and we believe that its schnitzels are the kind of plate-filling, golden-brown delicacies that people always associate with schmaltzy Vienna. Menu items include goulash soup, onion-flavored roast beef, Vienna-style fried chicken, and strudels. During mushroom season (autumn and early winter), expect many variations, perhaps most deliciously served in a herbed cream sauce over noodles. This restaurant's nearby twin, at Wollzeile 5 (☎ **01/5126177**; www.figlmueller.at), offers basically the same menu, prices, and richly nostalgic wine-tavern ambiance.

Bäckerstrasse 6. ☎ **01/5121760.** Reservations recommended. Main courses 11€–15€. AE, DC, MC, V. Daily 11:30am–midnight. Closed Aug. U-Bahn: Stephansplatz.

Gulaschmuseum ★ ☺AUSTRIAN/HUNGARIAN   If you thought that goulash was available in only one form, think again. This restaurant celebrates at least 15 varieties of it, each an authentic survivor of the culinary traditions of Hungary, and each redolent with the taste of the national spice, paprika. The Viennese adopted goulash from their former vassal centuries ago, and have long since added it to their culinary repertoire. You can order versions of goulash made with roast beef, veal, pork, or even fried chicken livers. Vegetarians rejoice: Versions made with potatoes, beans, or mushrooms are also available. Boiled potatoes and rough-textured brown or black bread usually accompanies your choice. An excellent starter is the Magyar national crepe, *Hortobágy Palatschinken,* stuffed with minced beef and paprika-flavored cream sauce. If you prefer an Austrian dish, there are *Tafelspitz,* Wiener schnitzel, fresh fish from Austria's lakes, and such dessert specialties as homemade *Apfelstrudel* and *Sachertorte.*

Schulerstrasse 20. ☎ **01/5121017.** www.gulasch.at. Reservations recommended. Main courses 8€–16€. MC, V. Mon–Fri 9am–midnight; Sat–Sun 10am–midnight. U-Bahn: Wollzeile or Stephansplatz.

Kardos AUSTRIAN/HUNGARIAN/SLOVENIAN   This folkloric restaurant specializes in the strong flavors and potent traditions that developed in different parts of what used to be the Austro-Hungarian Empire. Similarly, the setting celebrates the idiosyncratic folklore of various regions of the Balkans and the Great Hungarian Plain. Newcomers are welcomed with piquant little rolls known as *Grammel,*

COFFEEHOUSES & cafes

Café Central ★, Herrengasse 14 (📞 01/ 5333764; www.palaisevents.com; U-Bahn: Herrengasse), stands in the center of Vienna across from the Hofburg and the Spanish Riding School. This grand cafe offers a glimpse into 19th-century Viennese life—it was once the center of Austria's literati. Even Lenin is said to have met his colleagues here. The Central offers a variety of Viennese coffees, a vast selection of pastries and desserts, and Viennese and provincial dishes. It's a delightful spot for lunch. Open Monday to Saturday from 7:30am to 10pm, Sunday 10am to 10pm.

The windows of the venerated 1888 **Café Demel** ★★, Kohlmarkt 14 (📞 01/ 5351717; U-Bahn: Herrengasse; Bus: 1A or 2A), are filled with fanciful spun-sugar creations of characters from folk legends. Inside you'll find a splendidly baroque landmark where dozens of pastries are available daily, including the *Pralinen,* Senegal, truffle, *Sand,* and *Maximilian* tortes, as well as *Gugelhupfs* (cream-filled horns). Demel also serves a luscious variety of tea sandwiches of smoked salmon, egg salad, caviar, or shrimp. To be traditional, ask for a Demel-Coffee, which is filtered coffee served with milk, cream, or whipped cream. It's open daily from 10am to 7pm.

Café Diglas, Wollzeile 10 (📞 01/ 5125765; www.diglas.at; U-Bahn: Stubentor), evokes prewar Vienna better than many of its competitors, thanks to a decor that retains some of the accessories from 1934, when it first opened. The cafe prides itself on its long association with composer Franz Léhar. It offers everything in the way of run-of-the-mill caffeine fixes, as well as more elaborate,

liqueur-enriched concoctions such as a Biedermeier (with apricot schnapps and cream). If you're hungry, ask for a menu (foremost among the platters is an excellent Wiener schnitzel). The cafe is open daily from 7am to 11pm.

Café Dommayer, Auhofstrasse 2 (📞 01/8775465; U-Bahn: Schönbrunn), boasts a reputation for courtliness that goes back to 1787. In 1844, Johann Strauss, Jr., made his musical debut here, and beginning in 1924, the site became known as *the* place in Vienna for tea dancing. During clement weather, a garden with seats for 300 opens at the back. The rest of the year, the venue is restricted to a high-ceilinged black-and-white old-world room. Every Saturday from 2 to 4pm, a pianist and violinist perform; and every third Saturday, an all-woman orchestra plays mostly Strauss. Most patrons come for coffee, tea, and pastries, but if you have a more substantial appetite, try the platters of food, including Wiener schnitzel, *Rostbraten,* and fish. It's open daily from 7am to 10pm.

Even the Viennese debate the age of **Café Frauenhuber,** Himmelpfortgasse 6 (📞 01/5125353; http://café-frauenhuber. at; U-Bahn: Stephansplatz). But regardless of whether its opening fell in 1788 or 1824, it has a justifiable claim to being the oldest continuously operating coffeehouse in the city. The old-time decor is a bit battered and more than a bit smoke-stained. Wiener schnitzel, served with potato salad and greens, is a good bet, as are any of the ice cream dishes and pastries. It's open daily Monday to Saturday 8am to 11pm.

One of the Ring's great coffeehouses, **Café Landtmann** ★, Dr.-Karl-Lueger-Ring 4 (📞 01/241000; www.cafe-wien.

seasoned with minced pork and spices, and a choice of grilled meats. Other specialties include Hungarian *Fogosch* (a form of pikeperch) that's baked with vegetables and at; Tram: 1, 2, or D), has a history dating to the 1880s and has long drawn a mix of politicians, journalists, and actors. It was also Freud's favorite. The original chandeliers and the prewar chairs have been refurbished. We highly recommend spending an hour or so here, perusing the newspapers, sipping on coffee, or planning the day's itinerary. The cafe is open daily from 7:30am to midnight (lunch is served 11:30am to 3pm and dinner, 5 to 11pm).

Part of the success of **Café Sperl,** Gumpendorferstrasse 11 (✆ **01/5864158;** www.cafesperl.at; U-Bahn: Karlsplatz), is surely due to the Gilded Age paneling and accessories, installed in 1880, that are still in place. These, plus the attentive service, contributed to Sperl's designation in 1998 as "Austria's best coffee-house of the year." So if you order black coffee, you'll be in good company. Platters include salads; toast; baked noodles with ham, mushrooms, and cream sauce; omelets; steaks; and Wiener schnitzels. The staff evokes a bemused kind of courtliness, and an enduring respect for the timeless pastimes of billiards (two excellent tables), chess, and darts. It's open Monday to Saturday 7am to 11pm and Sunday 11am to 8pm (closed Sun July–Aug).

Café Tirolerhof, Fürichgasse 8 (✆ **01/5127833;** U-Bahn: Stephansplatz or Karlsplatz), which has been under the same management for decades, makes for a convenient sightseeing break, particularly from a tour of the nearby Hofburg complex. One coffee specialty is the Maria Theresia, a large cup of mocha flavored with apricot liqueur and topped with whipped cream. You can also order a Viennese breakfast of coffee, tea, hot

chocolate, two Viennese rolls, butter, jam, and honey. And their Apfelstrudel is one of the best in town. Another curiosity: An old wood and glass phone booth, with working pay phone. Open Monday to Saturday 7:30am to 10pm.

Thirty kinds of tea are served at **Demmers Teehaus,** Mölker Bastei 5 (✆ **01/5335995;** www.demmer.at; U-Bahn: Schottentor), along with dozens of pastries, cakes, toasts, and English sandwiches. Demmers is managed by the previously recommended restaurant, Buffet Trzésniewski (p. 131); however, the teahouse offers you a chance to sit down, relax, and enjoy your drink or snack. It's open Monday to Friday from 9am to 6pm.

Motto am Fluss Café, Schwedenplatz 2 (✆ **01/35355-11;** www.motto.at; U-Bahn: Schwedenplatz), is a more modern version of the Viennese sit and sip tradition. Above the restaurant (p. 129), this cafe is refined and modern, with all the great offerings of the traditional establishments. In warm weather try for outdoor seating by the left entrance where the sun shines longest. The in-house patisserie is also a great place for a baked pick-me-up to go.

Café Phil, Gumpendorferstrasse 10–12 (✆ **01/5810489;** www.phil.info; U-Bahn: MuseumsQuartier). This cafe-bookshop has become a live-in reading room for an entire generation of university students and theater people. With a mix of easy chairs, upholstered benches, and tavern booths in and around several rooms of bookshelves, plus public readings, and the required assortment of newspapers on hand to soak up at your leisure, the place can be habit-forming. Open Tuesday to Sunday 9am to 1am.

parsley potatoes, Hungarian goulash, and braised cabbage. The cellar atmosphere is gypsy schmaltz—pinewood accents and brightly colored Hungarian accessories.

During the winter, you're likely to find a strolling violinist. To begin, try a glass of *Barack,* an aperitif made from fermented apricots.

Dominikaner Bastei 8. ℭ **01/5126949.** www.restaurantkardos.com. Reservations recommended. Main courses 8€–20€. AE, DC, MC, V. Mon–Sat 11:30am–2:30pm and 6–11pm. U-Bahn: Schwedenplatz.

Palmenhaus ★ AUSTRIAN   Many architectural critics consider the Jugendstil glass canopy of this greenhouse the most beautiful in Austria. Overlooking the formal terraces of the Burggarten, it was built between 1901 and 1904 by the Habsburgs' court architect Friedrich Ohmann as a graceful architectural transition between the Albertina and the National Library. Damaged during wartime bombings, it was restored in 1998. Today, its central section functions as a chic cafe and, despite the lavishly historic setting, an appealingly informal venue. No one will mind if you drop in for just a drink and one of the voluptuous pastries displayed near the entrance. But if you want a meal, there's a sophisticated menu that changes monthly and might include fresh Austrian goat's cheese with stewed peppers and zucchini salad; young herring with sour cream, horseradish, and deep-fried beignets stuffed with apples and cabbage; and squash blossoms stuffed with salmon mousse.

In the Burggarten. ℭ **01/5331033.** www.palmenhaus.at. Reservations recommended for dinner. Main courses 15€–18€. AE, DC, MC. V. Daily 10am–2am. U-Bahn: Opera.

Zu den 3 Hacken (at the Three Axes) ★ AUSTRIAN   Cozy, small-scale, and charming, this restaurant was established 350 years ago and today bears the reputation as the oldest *Gasthaus* (tavern) in Vienna. In 1827, Franz Schubert had an ongoing claim to one of the establishment's tables as a site for entertaining his cronies. Today, the establishment maintains midsummer barriers of green-painted lattices and potted ivy for tables that jut onto the sidewalk. During inclement weather, head for one of three paneled dining rooms, each evocative of an inn high in the Austrian Alps. Expect an old-fashioned menu replete with the kind of dishes that fueled the Austro-Hungarian Empire. Examples include *Tafelspitz,* beef goulash, mixed grills piled high with chops and sausages, and desserts that include Hungarian-inspired *Palatschinken* (crepes) with chocolate-hazelnut sauce. The Czech and Austrian beer here seems to taste especially good when it's dispensed from a keg.

Singerstrasse 28. ℭ **01/5125895.** www.vinum-wien.at. Reservations recommended. Main courses 7.50€–18€. AE, DC, MC, V. Mon–Sat 11am–11pm. U-Bahn: Stephansplatz.

Zum Kuchldragoner AUSTRIAN   Some aspects of this place will remind you of an old-fashioned Austrian tavern, perhaps one that's perched high in the mountains, far from any congested city neighborhood. The feeling is enhanced by the pine trim and the battered *Gemütlichkeit* of what you'll soon discover is a bustling, irreverent, and sometimes jaded approach to feeding old-fashioned, flavorful, but far-from-cutting-edge cuisine to large numbers of urban clients, usually late into the night after everyone has had more than a drink or two. You can settle for a table inside, but our preferred venue is an outdoor table, immediately adjacent to the Romanesque foundation of Vienna's oldest church, St. Ruprechts. Come here for foaming steins of beer and such Viennese staples as Wiener schnitzel, schnitzel cordon bleu, baked eggplant layered with ham and cheese, and grilled lamb cutlets.

Seitenstettengasse 3 or Ruprechtsplatz 4–5. ℭ **01/5338371.** www.kuchldragoner.at. Reservations recommended. Main courses 7.80€–15€. MC, V. Mon–Thurs 11am–2am; Fri–Sun 11am–4am. U-Bahn: Schwedenplatz.

Zwölf-Apostelkeller VIENNESE   For those seeking a taste of old Vienna, this is the place. Sections of this wine tavern's walls predate 1561. Rows of wooden tables stand under vaulted ceilings, with lighting partially provided by streetlights set into the masonry floor. It's so deep that you feel you're entering a dungeon. Students love this place for its low prices and proximity to St. Stephan's. In addition to beer and wine, you can get hearty Austrian fare. Specialties include Hungarian goulash soup, meat dumplings, and a *Schlachtplatte* (a selection of hot black pudding, liverwurst, pork, and pork sausage with a hot bacon and cabbage salad). The cooking is hardly refined, but it's very well prepared.

Sonnenfelsgasse 3. (℗) **01/5126777.** www.zwoelf-apostelkeller.at. Main courses 6.50€–12€. AE, DC, MC, V. Daily 11am–midnight. Closed July. U-Bahn: Stephansplatz. Tram: 1, 2, 21, D, or N. Bus: 1A.

Leopoldstadt (2nd District)

EXPENSIVE

Vincent ★ CONTINENTAL   Once a bohemian hangout for left-wing intellectuals who appreciated fine cooking, Vincent has evolved into a stylish restaurant that is both chic and cozy. Here guests can opt for a seat in three different dining rooms, any of which might remind you of a richly upholstered, carefully decorated private home that's accented with flickering candles, flowers, and crystal. The set menus change with the season and the current fascinations of the chef, reinventing traditional dishes with imagination and finesse. The finest examples include a well-prepared rack of lamb flavored with bacon; whitefish or pikeperch in white-wine sauce; turbot with saffron sauce; filet of butterfish with tiger prawns served with a consommé of shrimp; and, in season, many different game dishes, including quail and venison.

Grosse-Pfarrgasse 7. (℗) **01/2141516.** www.restaurant-vincent.at. Reservations required. 5-course menu 50€; 7-course menu 69€; 10-course menu 95€. AE, DC, MC, V. Mon–Sat 5:30pm–1am. U-Bahn: Schwedenplatz.

MODERATE

Altes Jägerhaus ★ AUSTRIAN/GAME   Little about the decor here has changed since this place opened in 1899. Located 1.5km (1 mile) from the entrance to the Prater in a verdant park, it's a welcome escape from the more crowded restaurants of the Inner City. Grab a seat in any of the four old-fashioned dining rooms, where the beverage of choice is equally divided between beer and wine. Seasonal game like pheasant and venison are the house specialty, but you'll also find an array of seafood dishes that might include freshwater and saltwater trout, zander, or salmon. The menu also features a delicious repertoire of Austrian staples such as *Tafelspitz* and schnitzel.

Freudenau 255. (℗) **01/72895770.** Reservations recommended. Main courses 13€–25€. AE, DC, MC, V. Daily 10am–11pm. U-Bahn: Schlachthausgasse, then bus 77A.

Leopold 🏠 ☺ AUSTRIAN/CONTINENTAL   This simplistic and modern atmosphere is home to a sophisticated kitchen, with a menu that will make your mouth water. Besides the usual schnitzel and *Eiernockerl* (dumpling noodles), the hip bohemian clientele enjoy a monthly menu of local and seasonal dishes with such temptations as ginger-lime chicken with lychees and basmati rice or a simpler local catfish served with olives, capers, and mashed potatoes. The food is always inspired, light, and delectable. This is only a dinner restaurant except on Sundays, when there is a vast brunch buffet from 10am to 3pm that is all you can eat for 13€. Dig in!

Große Pfargasse 11. (℗) **01/2182281.** Main courses 7€–14€. AE, DC, MC, V. Daily 5–11pm. U-Bahn: Taborstrasse. Tram: 2.

Simchas ★ JEWISH/BULGARIAN   One of Vienna's few kosher restaurants, the Natanov family prides itself on mixing Jewish cooking traditions from around the world. They were part of the Jewish Diaspora and fled to Bulgaria and Uzbekistan, making the cuisine a many-cultured product of the generation who returned to Vienna. In the tastefully modern interior, the friendly staff serve delicious specialties such as hummus and eggplant starters, luscious meat and fish skewers, samosa, and borscht, and five varying small salads are served with your main course. The food is top-notch, but starters are quite large so to leave room for your main dish, it may make sense to share. The culinary mixture is well thought through and this is definitely one of the finest kosher restaurants in the city.

Taborstrasse 47. ℂ **01/2182833.** Main courses 12€–25€. AE, DC, MC, V. Daily 10am–11pm. U-Bahn: Taborstrasse. Tram: 2.

Skopik & Lohn ★ AUSTRIAN/INTERNATIONAL   Here, a charismatic ex-New Yorker of Viennese decent serves up his twin cultures with a nod to his in-laws from Tuscany and Provence. The interior is striking, with wild scribblings of black paint writing an attitude of edgy originality all over the white ceilings, and turning a traditional restaurant space into a place of well-chosen and tasteful surprises. Try a traditionally Hungarian paprika chicken with *Topfenspätzle* (curd cheese pasta) and chive sauce or an Italian *Buratta* with pepperonatta sauce. The food is inspired and very artfully served in a place that may be only the first bite of the Big Apple feeling in Vienna's trendy Leopoldstadt.

Leopoldgasse 17. ℂ **01/2198977.** Main courses 10€–22€. AE, DC, MC, V. Daily 6pm–1am. U-Bahn: Shottenring. Tram: 2.

INEXPENSIVE

Fischrestaurant Kaj ★★ CROATIAN   Simple and intimate, this captivating little bistro is a quick side trip to the Dalmatian coast. Fresh fish arrives each morning by train to the South Station and finds its way to Kaj, where it will be carried out on a platter for you to examine, and make your selection. Everything is cooked fresh; while you're waiting, order an antipasto platter, and in minutes an extravagance of delicious seafood and roasted veggies will appear, served cold and perfectly spiced—which makes you glad the main course will take a while. The Balkan wines are also fun to try; let yourself be advised. This is a pauper's feast, hard to duplicate anywhere. Reserve 2 days ahead.

Fugbachgasse 9. ℂ **01/2166495.** Main courses 6.50€–15€. AE, DC, MC, V. Daily 11am–3pm, 5:30–11pm. U-Bahn: Praterstern.

Schweizerhaus ★ AUSTRIAN   This place is legend. Not only does it seat what seems like millions, it has been a beer hall for centuries and was re-opened in 1868 as the Schweizer Meierei, or Swiss Dairy, hence it's current name. Today though, it has nothing to do with the Swiss: The Kolarik family, which now runs the place, calls it Vienna's biggest beer barrel and although that may be accurate—endless numbers of *Krügerl* (large beers) are hauled past on massive trays—the eatables are no trifle either. The *Schweinsstelzen* (leg of pork) is served on the bone with a knife and cutting board as your only aid. Other favorites include schnitzel, goulash, and *Kartoffelpuffer* (fried potato medallions), as well as homemade beer chocolate. A visit is in order after romping through the Prater. You'll find it at the far end of the amusement park, or just ask anyone.

Prater 116. ℂ **01/7280152-13.** Main courses 5€–16€. AE, DC, MC, V. Daily 11am–11pm. U-Bahn: Praterstern or Stadion.

Landstrasse (3rd District)
VERY EXPENSIVE

Steirereck ★★★ AUSTRIAN/VIENNESE *Steirereck* means "corner of Styria," which is exactly what Heinz and Birgit Reitbauer have created in this intimate and rustic restaurant. Traditional Viennese dishes and "new Austrian" selections appear on the menu. Begin with a caviar–semolina dumpling or roasted turbot with fennel (served as an appetizer), or opt for the most elegant and expensive item of all, goose-liver Steirereck. Some enticing main courses include asparagus with pigeon, saddle of lamb for two, prime Styrian roast beef, and red-pepper risotto with rabbit. The menu is wisely limited and well prepared, changing daily depending on what's fresh at the market. The restaurant is popular with after-theater diners, and the large wine cellar holds some 35,000 bottles.

Am Heumarkt 2A. ✆ **01/7133168.** www.steirereck.at. Reservations required. Main courses 15€–25€; 5-course fixed-price dinner 100€. AE, DC, MC, V. Mon–Fri 11:30am–2:30pm and 6:30–11pm. Closed holidays. U-Bahn: Stadtpark.

EXPENSIVE

Dining Room ★★★ 🍴 INTERNATIONAL On a quiet lane outside the center of town, this little restaurant has only four tables, seating 12 guests. It's in a private home and follows a European trend of opening little hideaway restaurants for those who appreciate great food served in a very intimate and personal atmosphere. The owner and chef, Angelika Apfelthaler, prepares each meal herself, offering a set menu. Each night's menu is dedicated to a special theme, including, perhaps, white truffles in Piedmont, Moroccan nights, or cooking with spices from around the world. Top-quality products go into every menu; and not only is the bread homemade, but the jams and chutneys are as well. You might begin with a chestnut and hazelnut soup, followed by an arugula salad with sautéed porcini mushrooms. A main course might be a juicy duck breast with a creamy saffron-laced risotto.

Maygasse 31. ✆ **01/804-8586.** Reservations required. Fixed-price menu 44€. DC, MC, V. 7:30pm (but confirm exact time when you call for a reservation). U-Bahn: Hietzing, then tram 60 to Riedelgasse/ Orthopädisches Krankenhaus (a 5-min. walk from here).

Niky's Kuchlmasterei ★ INTERNATIONAL/VIENNESE The decor features old stonework with some modern architectural innovations, and the extensive menu boasts well-prepared food. The lively crowd of loyal habitués adds to the welcoming ambiance, making Niky's a good choice for an evening meal, especially in summer when you can dine on its unforgettable terrace. After a long and pleasant meal, your bill will arrive in an elaborate box suitable for jewels, along with an amusing message in German that offers a tongue-in-cheek apology for cashing your check.

Obere Weissgerberstrasse 6. ✆ **01/7129000.** www.kuchlmasterei.at. Reservations recommended. Main courses 18€–20€; 3-course fixed-price lunch 19€; 7-course fixed-price dinner 51€. AE, DC, MC, V. Mon–Sat noon–midnight. U-Bahn: Schwedenplatz.

Wieden & Margareten (4th & 5th Districts)
MODERATE

Motto AUSTRIAN/INTERNATIONAL This is the premier gay-friendly restaurant of Austria, with a cavernous red-and-black interior, a busy bar, and a clientele that has included many of the glam figures (Thierry Mugler, John Galliano, and lots of theater people) of the international circuit. Even Helmut Lang worked here briefly as a waiter. It's set behind green doors and a sign that's so small and discreet as to be nearly invisible. In summer, it's enhanced with tables set up in a garden. No one will mind if you pop in just to chat, as it's a busy nightlife entity in its own right. But if you're hungry, cuisine is about as eclectic as it gets, ranging from sushi and Thai-inspired curries to *gutbürgerlich* (home and hearth) food like grandma used to make.

Schönbrunnerstrasse 30 (entrance on Rudigergasse). ✆ **01/5870672.** www.motto.at. Reservations recommended. Main courses 7€–21€. MC, V. Daily 6pm–4am. U-Bahn: Pilgrimgasse.

Silberwirt VIENNESE   Despite the fact that it opened a quarter of a century ago, this restaurant oozes with Old Viennese style and resembles the traditional *Beisl* (bistro) with its copious portions of conservative, time-honored Viennese food. You can dine within a pair of dining rooms or move into the beer garden. Menu items include stuffed mushrooms, *Tafelspitz,* schnitzels, and filets of zander, salmon, and trout.

Schlossgasse 21. ✆ **01/5444907.** www.schlossquadr.at. Reservations recommended. Main courses 9€–22€. V. Daily noon–10pm. U-Bahn: Pilgrimgasse.

INEXPENSIVE

Café Cuadro INTERNATIONAL   Trendy, countercultural, and arts-oriented, this cafe and bistro is little more than a long, glassed-in corridor with vaguely Bauhaus-inspired detailing. There are clusters of industrial-looking tables, but many clients opt for a seat at the long, luncheonette-style counter above a Plexiglas floor with four-sided geometric patterns illuminated from below. In keeping with the establishment's name (Cuadro), the menu features four of everything—salads (including a very good Caesar option), juicy burgers, homemade soups, steak, and—if you're an early riser—breakfasts.

Margaretenstrasse 77. ✆ **01/5447550.** Breakfast 4€–8€; main courses 5€–12€. V. Mon–Sat 8am–midnight; Sun 9am–11pm. U-Bahn: Pilgramgasse.

Gasthaus Ubl ★ 🍴 AUSTRIAN   This closely guarded Viennese secret is where locals go when they want to enjoy some of the famous dishes enjoyed by their last great emperor, Franz Josef. This is an authentic guesthouse-like atmosphere with an old Viennese stove. Three sisters run it, and the whole place screams Old Vienna—nothing flashy or touristy here. Begin with one of the freshly made salads or soups, then follow with the classics—the best *Tafelspitz* in the area or such old favorites as *Schweinsbraten* (a perfectly roasted pork). Desserts are old-fashioned and yummy. The staff is most welcoming.

Pressgasse 26. ✆ **01/5876437.** Reservations recommended. Main courses 10€–15€. AE, DC, MC, V. Daily noon–2pm and 6–10pm. U-Bahn: Karlsplatz. Bus: 59A.

Mariahilf (6th District)
MODERATE

Finkh ★ 🍴 AUSTRIAN/VIENNESE   This dwarf of a restaurant resembles a radically minimalist work of art in some Berlin gallery. Unobtrusively modern, this newly opened gem is a bit off the beaten path but well worth the search. The menu is small and consists of genuinely good and simple versions of Austrian classics and mirrors the wine list which is also select, but sufficient. The menu changes weekly and is always fresh, seasonal, local, and organic. The owner Fridolin Fink and cook Elias Zenzmaier are both young, inspired souls who have already received much acclaim in local circles. The schnitzel is grandiose as is the *Blunzengröstl* (Blutwurst speciality), taking even the Viennese's breath away.

Esterhazygasse 12. ✆ **01/913-8992.** Reservations not necessary. Main courses 7€–29€. MC, V. Tues–Sat 3pm–midnight, Sun 10am–3pm. U-Bahn: Neubaugasse. Bus: 13A.

Gräfin vom Naschmarkt AUSTRIAN/CONTINENTAL   For night owls, this restaurant is almost immediately adjacent to the Naschmarkt. This all-day, all-night 125-year-old restaurant seems very far removed from the Habsburg grandeur of central Vienna. The clientele is people whose business or hobby is to be out past their bedtime. Early-morning truckers loading and unloading at the nearby market drop in for beer and schnitzel, next to soggy insomniacs from the neighborhood's many straight and gay bars. It also does a roaring business from the after-theater crowd at the nearby Theater an der Wien, and by 4am the place is usually packed. Menu items are *Hausmannskost*, substantial, traditional, and comfort food. Examples include Styrian-style chicken salad with pine nuts, bacon-studded dumplings with green salad, pork cutlets with potato salad, and what a local paper (*Kurier*) defined as "Vienna's best *Gulaschsuppe*."

Linke Wienzeile 14. ⓒ **01/5863389.** Reservations not necessary. Main courses 7€–29€. MC, V. 24 hours a day, although service and menu items are reduced as the restaurant is cleaned, every morning between 2–4am. U-Bahn: Karlsplatz or Kettenbrückengasse.

INEXPENSIVE

Alfi's Goldener Spiegel VIENNESE   By everyone's account, this is the most prominent gay restaurant in Vienna, where the majority gay clientele enjoys food and ambiance that might remind you of a simple Viennese *beisl* in a working-class district. If you do decide to sit down for a meal, expect large portions of traditional Viennese specialties such as Wiener schnitzel, roulade of beef, filet steaks with pepper sauce, and *Tafelspitz*. Its position near Vienna's Naschmarkt, the city's biggest food market, ensures that the food served is impeccably fresh.

Linke Wienzeile 46 (entrance on Stiegengasse). ⓒ **01/5866608.** www.goldenerspiegel.com. Main courses 6.50€–15€. No credit cards. Daily 7pm–2am. U-Bahn: U4 to Kettenbruckengasse.

Neubau (7th District)
MODERATE

Bohème ★ INTERNATIONAL/VIENNESE   This one-time bakery dating from 1750 is in a historic pedestrian streetscape of unspoiled baroque facades, friendly taverns, and funky shops. Since opening in 1989, Bohème has attracted a crowd that's knowledgeable about the nuances of wine, food, and the opera music that reverberates throughout the two dining rooms. Even the decor is theatrical; it looks like a cross between a severely dignified stage set and an artsy, turn-of-the-19th-century cafe. Menu items are listed as movements in an opera, with overtures (aperitifs), prologues (appetizers), and first and second acts (soups and main courses). As you'd guess, desserts provide the finales. Some tempting items include Andalusian gazpacho, platters of mixed fish filets with tomato risotto, and *Tafelspitz* with horseradish.

Spittelberggasse 19. ⓒ **01/5233173.** www.boheme.at. Reservations recommended. Main courses 10€–23€. AE, DC, MC, V. Mon–Sat 11am–midnight. Closed Jan 7–23. U-Bahn: Volkstheater.

DOTS ★ 🍴 ASIAN   This "experimental sushi" restaurant is a joy for the gums. Inhabiting a hidden area only reachable through a passageway off Mariahilferstrasse, the interior is all in white. The business, nightlife, and fashion community fill the clear plastic chairs and elegant waiters are skilled at coping with the pickiest of clientele. From octopus and salmon teppanyaki to traditional sushi and maki and inspired creations like truffle–asparagus maki, this cuisine is beautiful, tasty, and fun to eat. The staff will be glad to help you choose.

Mariahilferstrasse 103. *©* **01/920-9980.** www.dots-lounge.com. Reservations recommended. Main courses 11€–23€. DC, MC, V. Mon–Sat noon–midnight; Sun 3pm–midnight. U-Bahn: Zieglergasse.

INEXPENSIVE

Amerlingbeisl AUSTRIAN   The hip clientele, occasionally blasé staff, and minimalist, somewhat industrial-looking decor give Amerlingbeisl a modern sensibility. If you get nostalgic, you can opt for a table out on the cobblestones of the early-19th-century building's glassed-in courtyard, beneath a grape arbor, where horses used to be stabled. Come to this neighborhood spot for simple but good food and a glass of beer or wine. The menu ranges from simple sandwiches and salads to more elaborate fare, such as Argentinean steak with rice, turkey, or pork schnitzels with potato salad, and dessert crepes stuffed with marmalade.

Stiftgasse 8. *©* **01/5261660.** www.amerlingbeisl.at. Main courses 7.60€–8.70€. DC, MC, V. Daily 9am–2am. U-Bahn: Volkstheater.

Plutzer Bräu ★ 🍴AUSTRIAN   This is one of the best examples in Vienna of the explosion of hip and trendy restaurants within the city's 7th District. Maintained by the Plutzer Brewery, it occupies the cavernous cellar of an imposing 19th-century building. Any antique references are quickly lost once you're inside, thanks to an industrial-looking decor with exposed heating ducts, burnished stainless steel, and accessories that might remind you of the cafeteria in a central European factory. You can stay at the long, accommodating bar and drink fresh-brewed Plutzer beer, but if you're hungry (and this very good beer will probably encourage an appetite), head for the well-scrubbed dining room, where the menu reflects Old Viennese traditions. Food is excellent and includes veal stew in beer sauce with dumplings, "brewmaster's-style" pork steak, and pasta with herbs and feta cheese. Dessert might include curd dumplings with poppy seeds and sweet bread crumbs.

Schrankgasse 2. *©* **01/5261215.** www.plutzerbrau.at. Main courses 6.90€–17€. MC, V. Daily 10am–midnight. U-Bahn: Volkstheater.

Josefstadt (8th District)

EXPENSIVE

Schnattl ★ AUSTRIAN   Even the justifiably proud owner of this place, Wilhelm (Willy) Schnattl, dismisses its decor as a mere foil for the presentation of his sublime food. Schnattl is near Town Hall, in a location that's convenient for most of the city's journalists and politicians, and features a cozy bar area and a medium-size dining room, an inviting, intimate, green-painted and wood-paneled space of enormous comfort and charm. Menu items show intense attention to detail and—in some cases—a megalomaniacal fervor from a chef whom the press has called a "mad culinary genius." Roasted sweetbreads are served with a purée of green peas; marinated freshwater fish (a species known locally as *Hochen*) comes with a parfait of cucumbers. Wild duck and a purée of celery are perfectly cooked, as is a celebrated parfait of pickled tongue—a terrine of foie gras and a mousse, wrapped in strips of tongue and served with a toasted corn brioche.

40 Lange Gasse. *©* **01/405-3400.** www.schnattl.com. Reservations required. Main courses 17€–26€. AE, DC, MC, V. Mon–Fri 6–11pm. Closed weekends and for 2 weeks at Easter, 2 weeks late Aug. U-Bahn: Rathaus.

MODERATE

Piaristenkeller AUSTRIAN   Erich Emberger has successfully renovated and reassembled this wine tavern with centuries-old vaulted ceilings in a vast cellar room. The place was founded in 1697 by Piarist monks as a tavern and wine cellar. The kitchen, which once served the cloisters, still dishes out traditional Austrian specialties based on original recipes. Zither music is played beginning at 7:30pm, and in summer the garden at the church square is open from 11am to midnight. Wine and beer are available whenever the cellar is open. Advance booking is required for a guided tour of the cloister's old wine vaults.

Piaristengasse 45. ℰ **01/4059152.** Reservations recommended. Main courses 14€–22€. AE, DC, MC, V. Mon–Sat 6pm–midnight. U-Bahn: Rathaus.

Alsergrund (9th District)

Abend-Restaurant Feuervogel RUSSIAN   Since World War I, this restaurant has been a Viennese landmark, bringing Russian cuisine to a location across from the palace of the Prince of Liechtenstein. You'll eat in romantically Slavic surroundings with gypsy violins playing Russian and Viennese music. Specialties include chicken Kiev, beef Stroganoff, veal Dolgoruki, borscht, and many other dishes that taste as if they came right off the steppes. For an hors d'oeuvre try *sakkuska,* a variety platter that's popular in Russia. You can also order a gourmet fixed-price dinner with five courses. Be sure to sample the Russian ice cream known as *plombier.*

Alserbachstrasse 21. ℰ **01/3175391.** www.feuervogel.at. Reservations recommended. Main courses 11€–16€. AE, DC, MC, V. Mon–Sat 6pm–midnight. Closed July 20–Aug 8. U-Bahn: Friedensbrücke. Bus: 32.

Stiegl Ambulanz AUSTRIAN/VIENNESE   Smack in the middle of the university campus at the old general hospital (Altes AKH), the Austrian beer brewery Stiegl has opened a modern *Gasthaus* that translates as "Stiegl emergency room." In summer the outdoor beer garden is always full of students, professors, and the general public from the neighborhood. Inside, one room has lines of long tables and a lounge area with sofas is slightly separate. The food is simple and tasty and the establishment makes a point of always ensuring organic, free range, and local ingredients.

40 Lange Gasse. ℰ **01/402-1150.** www.stiegl.com. Main courses 7€–15€. AE, DC, MC, V. Mon–Fri 11am–midnight, Sun 11am–9pm. U-Bahn: Schottentor. Tram: 5.

Near Schönbrunn (5th & 13th Districts)
MODERATE

Altwienerhof ★★★ AUSTRIAN/FRENCH   A short walk from Schönbrunn Palace lies one of the premier dining spots in Vienna. The building is completely modernized, but it was originally designed as a private home in the 1870s. Mr. Günter brings sophistication and charm to the dining rooms, which retain many Biedermeier embellishments from the original construction. The chef prepares nouvelle cuisine using only the freshest and highest-quality ingredients. The menu changes frequently, and the maître d' is always willing to assist with recommendations. Each night the chef prepares a tasting menu, which is a sampling of the kitchen's best nightly dishes. The wine list consists of more than 700 selections, each of which is chosen by Mr. Günter himself. The cellar below houses about 18,000 bottles.

In the Altwienerhof Hotel, Herklotzgasse 6. ℰ **01/8926000.** www.altwienerhof.at. Reservations recommended. Main courses 12€–21€. AE, DC, MC, V. Mon–Sat 5–11pm. Closed first 3 weeks in Jan. U-Bahn: Gumpendorferstrasse.

Hietzinger Bräu AUSTRIAN   Established in 1743, this is the most famous and best-recommended restaurant in the vicinity of Schönbrunn Palace. Everything about it evokes a sense of bourgeois stability—wood paneling, a staff wearing folkloric costume, and platters heaped high with *gutbürgerlich* cuisine. The menu lists more than a dozen preparations of beef, including the time-tested favorite, *Tafelspitz,* as well as mixed grills, all kinds of steaks, and fish that includes lobster, salmon, crab, and zander. Homage to the cuisine of Franz Josef appears in the form of very large Wiener schnitzels, a creamy goulash, and even a very old-fashioned form of braised calf's head. Wine is available, but the most popular beverage here, by far, is a foaming stein of the local brew, Hietzinger.

Auhofstrasse 1. ✆ **01/87770870.** Reservations not necessary. Main courses 16€–23€. DC, MC, V. Daily 11:30am–3pm and 6–11:30pm. U-Bahn: Hietzing.

Hollerei ★ VEGETARIAN   This fresh, bright addition to the neighborhood is the place to go for delectable vegetarian and vegan cuisine. Only 10 minutes from Schönbrunn, the stylish interior is only topped by the overgrown garden seating area, which is a great place to take a veggie date. The food has Asian and Mediterranean influences, prepared in a style all its own. Eggplant and mozzarella strudel, gnocchi with mushrooms over cranberries and root vegetables, or red Thai curry with sweet potatoes, ginger, and tofu over coconut rice are just a few tasty options. The clientele is not even all vegetarian, but like this chic alternative to *Wurst* and schnitzel.

Hollergasse 9. ✆ **01/8923356.** www.hollerei.at. Reservations recommended. Main courses 11€–15€. MC, V. Mon–Sat 11:30am–3pm and from 6pm onwards; Sun 11:30am–afternoon. U-Bahn: Hütteldorf. Bus: 57A.

EXPLORING VIENNA

B e warned that it's possible to spend a week here and only touch the surface of this multifaceted city. In this chapter, we'll explore the many sights of this vibrant and storied capital, including its palaces, museums, churches, parks, attractions for kids, and many more for those with the special curiosities only satisfied here. We'll take you through the highlights, but try to set aside some time for wandering and taking in the street life. We'll also take you shopping, and into the glittering world of Vienna after dark, including a look at its rich cultural life and world-class performing-arts scene.

THE HOFBURG PALACE ★★★

Once the winter palace of the Habsburgs, the Hofburg sits in the heart of Vienna and is a warren of vast courtyards and narrow passages, grand halls, apartments, ballrooms, and museums. To reach it, you can also take the U-Bahn to Stephansplatz, Herrengasse, or MuseumsQuartier, or else tram no. 1, 2, D, or J to Burgring. Or you head on foot up Kohlmarkt to Michael-erplatz 1, Burgring (✆ **01/5875554**), where a pair of baroque giants in stone stand guard with the eagle, snake, and sword of the monarchy at the gate, the waters of life bubbling up from the sea monsters at their feet.

This complex of imperial edifices, the first of which was constructed in 1279, grew with the empire, so today the palace is virtually a city within a city. The earliest parts were built around a courtyard, the **Swiss Court,** named after the Swiss mercenaries who performed guard duty here, thought to be at least 700 years old.

The Hofburg's complexity of styles, which are not always harmonious, is the result of each emperor or empress opting to add to or take away some of the work done by his or her predecessors. This sprawling palace, which has withstood three major sieges and a great fire, is simply called *die Burg* by the Viennese. Of its more than 2,600 rooms, some two-dozen are open to the public.

Albertina ★   A Hofburg museum, named after a son-in-law of Maria Theresa, houses one of the world's great graphic art collections, spanning 6 centuries. The museum was transformed in 2000–2003, restoring the magnificent statuary, fountain, and facade supporting the terrace bastion and entryway, opening three major exhibition spaces for rotating that have made the Albertina one of the most exciting museums in Europe. Its permanent collection includes Dürer's *Hare* and *Clasped Hands,* as well as some 60,000 drawings and one million prints, the best known include Ruben's children's studies. In addition, the museum owns masterpieces of Schiele, Cézanne, Klimt, Kokoschka, Picasso, and Rauschenberg. The collection was threatened in 2008 in the unprecedented flooding that submerged towns all along the Danube, when its high-security depot, thought to be waterproof, began leaking. Some 950,000 artworks were evacuated to another location until the damage could be repaired and the site dried out. The Albertina is also considered one of the most beautiful classical palaces in the world, its state apartments among the most admired examples of classical architecture.

Albertinaplatz 1. ℰ **01/534830.** www.albertina.at. Admission 9.50€ adults, 7€ students, 8€ senior citizens, free for children and those under 19. Thurs–Tues 10am–6pm; Wed 10am–9pm. U-Bahn: U1, U2, U4 Karlsplatz/Oper, U3 Stephansplatz.

Augustinerkirche (Church of the Augustinians) ★ The 14th-century Church of the Augustinians was built within the Hofburg complex to serve as the parish church for the imperial court. In the latter part of the 18th century, it was stripped of its baroque embellishments and returned to the original Gothic features. The Chapel of St. George, dating from 1337, is entered from the right aisle. The **Tomb of Maria Christina** ★, the favorite daughter of Maria Theresa, is near the rear entrance, but there's no body in it. The princess was actually buried in the imperial crypt, described later in this section. But the magnificent ornamental carvings by Antonio Canova more than make up for it. A small room in the Loreto Chapel is filled with urns containing the hearts of the imperial Habsburgs that can be viewed through a window in an iron door. The Chapel of St. George and the Loreto Chapel are open to the public by prearranged tour.

The Augustinerkirche was also where Maria Theresa married her beloved François of Lorraine in 1736, with whom she had 16 children. Other royal weddings included Marie Antoinette to Louis XVI of France in 1770, Marie-Louise of Austria to Louis Napoleon in 1810 (by proxy—he didn't show up), and Franz Joseph to Elisabeth of Bavaria in 1854.

The best time to visit the church is on Sunday at 11am, when a High Mass is of Mozart, Haydn, Schubert, Gounod, Kodaly, or Faure, with full choir and orchestra.

Augustinerstrasse 3. ℰ **01/533-70-99.** Free admission. Daily 6:30am–6pm. U-Bahn: Stephansplatz.

Burgkapelle (Home of the Vienna Boys' Choir) Construction of this Gothic chapel began in 1447 during the reign of Emperor Frederick III, but it was later massively renovated. Beginning in 1449, it was the royal family's private chapel. Today the Burgkapelle hosts the **Hofmusikkapelle** ★★, an ensemble of current and former members of the Vienna Boys' Choir and of the Vienna State Opera chorus and orchestra, which performs works by classical and modern composers. Written applications for reserved seats should be sent at least 8 weeks in advance, to Verwaltung der Hofmusikkapelle, Hofburg, A-1010 Vienna. Use a credit card; do not send cash or checks. If you failed to reserve in advance, you might be lucky enough to secure tickets from a block sold at the Burgkapelle box office every Friday from 11am to 1pm or 3 to 5pm. The line starts forming at least half an hour before that. If you're willing to settle for standing room, it's free. The Choir Boys' school is at Palais Augarten, Obere Augartenstrasse.

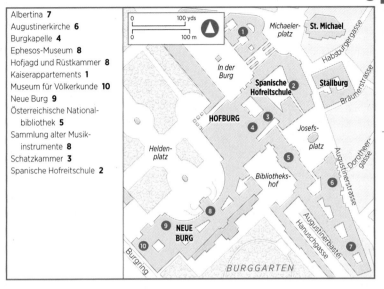

Albertina **7**
Augustinerkirche **6**
Burgkapelle **4**
Ephesos-Museum **8**
Hofjagd und Rüstkammer **8**
Kaiserappartements **1**
Museum für Völkerkunde **10**
Neue Burg **9**
Österreichische National-
bibliothek **5**
Sammlung alter Musik-
instrumente **8**
Schatzkammer **3**
Spanische Hofreitschule **2**

Hofburg (entrance on Schweizerhof). ⓒ **01/5339927.** Mass: Seats and concerts 5€–29€; standing room free. Masses held only Jan–June and mid-Sept to Dec, Sun and holidays 9:15am. Concerts May–June and Sept–Oct Fri 4pm. U-Bahn: Stephansplatz or Herrengasse.

Kaiserappartements (Imperial Apartments) ★★   This was the imperial family residence of Franz Joseph and Elisabeth and their children, reached through the rotunda of Michaelerplatz. Here you can see reception, dining and living rooms, bedrooms and private studies, the nursery, and even bathrooms. In the reception rooms, wall panels are filled with huge oil paintings of life at court; the more private rooms, however, are covered with deep red moiré, which also helped insulate against the cold. The court tableware and silver is of breathtaking opulence, reflecting the pomp and splendor of a court whose lands included two-thirds of all Europe. You'll see the narrow "iron bed" of Franz Joseph, sleeping "like his own soldiers," and the Empress's exercise equipment, to stay fit for the horsemanship she loved. A separate

---

  The Vienna Boys' Choir

In 1498, Emperor Maximilian I decreed that 12 boys should be included among the official court musicians. Over the next 500 years, this group evolved into the world-renowned *Wiener Sängerknaben* (Vienna Boys' Choir). They perform in Vienna at various venues, including the Staatsoper, the Volksoper, and Schönbrunn Palace and at Sunday and Christmas Masses with the *Hofmusikkapelle* (Court Musicians) at the Burgkapelle (see above for details). The choir's boarding school is at Augarten-palais, Obere Augartenstrasse. For more information on where they are performing and how to get tickets, go to the choir's website (www.wsk.at).

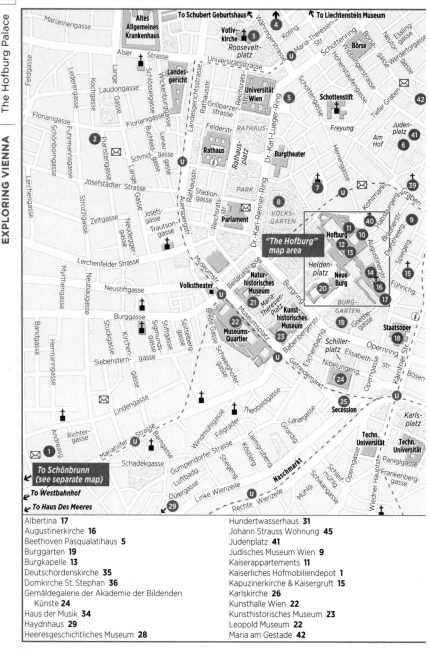

Albertina **17**
Augustinerkirche **16**
Beethoven Pasqualatihaus **5**
Burggarten **19**
Burgkapelle **13**
Deutschordenskirche **35**
Domkirche St. Stephan **36**
Gemäldegalerie der Akademie der Bildenden
   Künste **24**
Haus der Musik **34**
Haydnhaus **29**
Heeresgeschichtliches Museum **28**

Hundertwasserhaus **31**
Johann Strauss Wohnung **45**
Judenplatz **41**
Judisches Museum Wien **9**
Kaiserappartements **11**
Kaiserliches Hofmobiliendepot **1**
Kapuzinerkirche & Kaisergruft **15**
Karlskirche **26**
Kunsthalle Wien **22**
Kunsthistorisches Museum **23**
Leopold Museum **22**
Maria am Gestade **42**

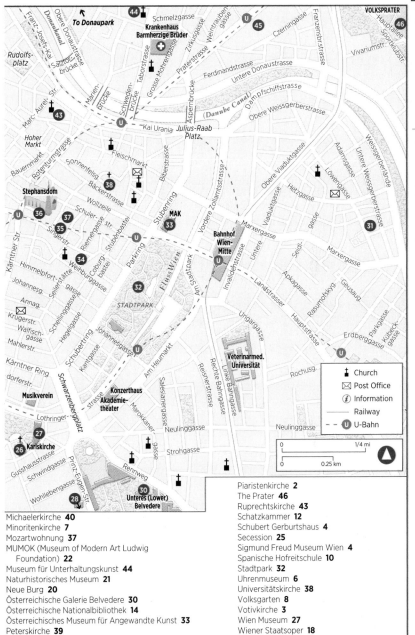

"Sissi Museum" opened in 2004 devoted to the life and complex personality of this famous, tragic empress.

The remaining imperial quarters once occupied by the Empress Maria Theresa are now the rooms used by the president of Austria, and are not open to the public. However, the **Imperial Silver and Porcelain Collection** from the 18th and 19th centuries provides a window into court etiquette of Maria Theresa's time.

Michaeler Platz 1 (inside the Ring, about a 7-min. walk from Stephansplatz; entrance via the Kaisertor in the Inneren Burghof). ℰ **01/533-7570.** www.hofburg-wien.at. Admission 9.90€ adults, 5.90€ children 6–18, free for children 5 and under, students and seniors 8.90€. Open daily, Sept–June 9am–5.30pm, July–Aug 9am–6pm. U-Bahn: U1 or U3 to Stephansplatz. Tram: 1, 2, 3, or J to Burgring.

Neue Burg   The most recent addition to the Hofburg complex is the Neue Burg. Construction was started in 1881 and continued through 1913. The palace was the residence of Archduke Franz Ferdinand, the nephew and heir apparent of Franz Joseph, whose assassination at Sarajevo by Serbian nationalists set off the chain of events that led to World War I.

The Arms and Armor Collection, said to be second only to the Metropolitan Museum in New York, is in the **Hofjagd und Rüstkammer ★★**, on the second floor. On display are crossbows, swords, helmets, pistols, and other armor, mostly of emperors and princes, some disarmingly small. Some of the items, such as scimitars, were captured from the Turks as they fled their unsuccessful siege.

The **Sammlung alter Musikinstrumente ★** is devoted to old instruments of the 17th and 18th centuries, some as early as the 16th century. There are pianos and harpsichords played by Brahms, Schubert, Mahler, Beethoven, and a few Austrian emperors, several of whom, like Joseph II, were also devoted musicians.

In the **Ephesos-Museum (Museum of Ephesian Sculpture),** with an entrance behind the Prince Eugene monument, you'll see finds from Ephesus in Turkey and the Greek island of Samothrace. The Parthian monument is one of the most important relief frieze from Roman times ever found in Asia Minor, erected to celebrate Rome's victory in the Parthian wars (A.D. 161–65).

Visit the **Museum für Völkerkunde (Museum of Ethnology)** for no other reason than to see the only original Aztec feather headdress in the world. Also on display are Benin bronzes, Cook's collections of Polynesian art, and Indonesian, African, Eskimo, and pre-Columbian exhibits.

Heldenplatz 1. ℰ **01/525-24-0.** Admission 12€ adults, children and those under 19 free, students and seniors 9€. Sammlung alter Musikinstrumente and Ephesos-Museum: Wed–Sun 10am–6pm. Museum für Völkerkunde: Wed–Mon 10am–6pm. Admission 8€ adults, 6€ students and seniors, children and young people under 19 free. U-Bahn: Volkstheater; Tram, Kunsthistorisches Museum.

Österreichische Nationalbibliothek (Austrian National Library)   The royal library of the Habsburgs dates from the 14th century; and the library building, developed on the premises of the court from 1723 on, is still expanding to the Neue Burg. The **Great Hall ★★** of the present-day library was ordered by Karl VI and designed by those masters of the baroque, the Fischer von Erlachs, father and son. The complete collection of Prince Eugene of Savoy is the core of the holdings. With its manuscripts, rare autographs, globes, maps, and other historic memorabilia, this is among the finest libraries in the world.

Josefsplatz 1. ℰ **01/53410.** www.onb.ac.at. Admission 7€, students and seniors 4.50€. Thurs 10am–9pm; Fri–Sun and Tues–Wed 10am–6pm. U-Bahn: Stephansplatz, Oper.

Schatzkammer (Imperial Treasury) ★★★   Reached by a staircase from the Swiss Court, the Schatzkammer is the greatest treasury in the world. It's divided into two sections: The Imperial Worldly and the Sacred Treasuries. The first displays the crown jewels and an assortment of imperial riches, while the other contains ecclesiastical treasures.

The most outstanding exhibit in the Schatzkammer is the imperial crown, which dates from 962. It's so big that, though padded, it probably slipped down over the ears of many a Habsburg at his coronation. Studded with emeralds, sapphires, diamonds, and rubies, this 1,000-year-old symbol of sovereignty is a priceless treasure. That fact was not lost on Adolf Hitler, who had it taken to Nürnberg in 1938. Be sure to have a look at the coronation robes of the imperial family, some dating from the 12th century, which are depicted in a marvelous portrait of Francis I with the robes and insignia themselves glistening in the glass case beside it.

You can also view the 9th-century saber of Charlemagne and the 8th-century holy lance, a sacred emblem of imperial authority, that was thought in medieval times to be the weapon that pierced the side of Christ on the cross. Among the great Schatzkammer prizes is the Burgundian Treasure. Seized in the 15th century, it is rich in vestments, oil paintings, and gems. Highlights are the artifacts connected with the Order of the Golden Fleece, the medieval order of chivalry.

Hofburg, Schweizerhof. ✆ **01/525-240.** www.khm.at. Admission 12€ adults, students and seniors 9€, children and people under 19 free. Wed–Mon 10am–6pm. U-Bahn: Herrengasse; Tram, Kunsthistorischesmuseum.

Spanische Hofreitschule (Spanish Riding School) ★
The Spanish Riding School is housed in a white, crystal-chandeliered ballroom in an 18th-century building. You'll marvel at the skill and beauty of the sleek Lipizzaner stallions as their adept trainers put them through their paces in a show that hasn't changed for 4 centuries. These are the world's most famous classically styled equine performers. Many North Americans have seen them in the States, but to watch the Lipizzaners prance to the music of Johann Strauss or a Chopin polonaise in their home setting is a pleasure you shouldn't miss.

Reservations for performances must be made in advance, as early as possible. Order your tickets for the Sunday and Wednesday shows by writing to Spanische Reitschule, Hofburg, A-1010 Vienna (fax 01/533903240), or through a travel agency in Vienna. Tickets for the Saturday shows must be ordered from travel agencies. Tickets for training sessions can be purchased at the entrance.

Michaelerplatz 1, Hofburg. ✆ **01/5339032.** www.srs.at. Regular performances 40€–135€ seats, 25€ standing room. Classical art of riding w/music 13€–26€. Regular shows Mar–June, Sept–Oct, and Dec, most Sun at 11am and some Fri at 6pm. Classical dressage w/music performances Apr–June and Sept, Tues–Sat 10am–noon. U-Bahn: Herrengasse; Tram, Kunsthistorischesmuseum.

Exploring the MuseumsQuartier ★★★

The giant modern art complex **MuseumsQuartier** (www.mqw.at; U-Bahn: MuseumsQuartier), installed in former Habsburg stables, opened in 2001. Art critics proclaimed that it tipped the city's cultural center of gravity from Habsburg pomp into the new millennium. One of the largest cultural complexes in the world, it is like combining New York's Guggenheim Museum, Museum of Modern Art, and Brooklyn Academy of Music, plus a children's museum, an architecture and design center, theaters, video workshops, an ecology center, and a museum of digital culture. Take the U-Bahn (U2) to the MuseumsQuartier stop.

Kunsthalle Wien ★
This is a showcase for cutting-edge contemporary and classic modern art. You'll find works by Picasso, Joán Miró, and Jackson Pollock to Paul Klee,

Andy Warhol, and Yoko Ono. From expressionism to cubism, exhibits reveal the major movements in contemporary art of the mid-20th century. Exploring the five floors takes 1 to 2 hours, depending on what interests you.

Museumsplatz 1. ☏ **01/521-89-33.** Admission 11.50€ adults, 9.50€ students and seniors, 4.60€ students, 2€ 10–18, children under 10 free. Fri–Wed 10am–7pm; Thurs 10am–9pm. U-Bahn Museums-Quartier, Volkstheater.

Leopold Museum ★★ This extensive collection of Austrian art includes the world's largest collection of Egon Schiele (1890–1918), who now stands alongside Gustav Klimt and Oskar Kokoschka as the pre-eminent artist of the Wiener Modern. The collection includes more than 2,500 Schiele drawings and watercolors and 330 oil canvases. Other Austrian modernists include Kokoschka, Klimt, Anton Romaki, and Richard Gerstl, and Klimt's Secessionist colleagues Josef Hoffmann, Kolo Moser, Adolf Loos, and Franz Hagenauer.

Museumsplatz 1. ☏ **01/525-700.** www.leopoldmuseum.org. Admission 11€ adults, 7€ students and children over 7, 7€ students and seniors, 8€ senior citizens. Fri–Wed 10am–6pm; Thurs 10am–9pm. U-Bahn: MuseumsQuartier, Volkstheater.

MUMOK (Museum of Modern Art Ludwig Foundation) ★ This gallery presents one of the most outstanding collections of contemporary art in central Europe. It exhibits mainly American pop art, mixed with concurrent Continental movements such as hyperrealism of the 1960s and 1970s. The museum features five exhibition levels (three above ground, two under ground).

Museumsplatz 1. ☏ **01/525-00.** www.mumok.at. 9€ adults, 7.20€ students and seniors. Free admission for those under 19 and students up to 27. Fri–Wed 10am–6pm; Thurs 10am–9pm. U-Bahn Museums-Quartier, Volkstheater.

OTHER TOP ATTRACTIONS
The Inner City

Gemäldegalerie der Akademie der Bildenden Künste (Painting Gallery of the Academy of Fine Arts) ★ This gallery is home to the *Last Judgment* ★★ triptych by Hieronymus Bosch. In this masterpiece, the artist conjured up all the demons of hell and the suffering and sins that humankind must endure. You'll see many Dutch and Flemish paintings, some from as far back as the 15th century, plus leading 17th-century art including Van Dyck, Rembrandt, and others. There are several works by Lucas Cranach the Elder, the most outstanding his *Lucretia* from 1532, as enigmatic as *Mona Lisa*. Rubens is represented here by more than a dozen oil sketches. You can see Rembrandt's *Portrait of a Woman* and scrutinize Guardi's scenes from 18th-century Venice.

Schillerplatz 3. ☏ **01/58816-2222.** www.akademiegalerie.at. Admission 8€ adults, 5€ students and seniors, those up to 19 free. Tues–Sun 10am–6pm. U-Bahn: Karlsplatz.

Haus der Musik ★ This full-scale museum devoted to music is both hands-on and high-tech. Wandering the building's halls and niches, you encounter reminders of the great composers who have lived in Vienna—not only Mozart, but also Beethoven, Schubert, Brahms, and others. You can listen to your favorite renditions of their works or explore memorabilia. You can even take to the podium and conduct the Vienna Philharmonic that responds to your baton. A memorial, *Exodus*, pays tribute to the Viennese musicians driven into exile or murdered by the Nazis. At the rooftop Musicantino Restaurant, enjoy a panoramic view of the city and good food. There's a coffeehouse at street level.

Seilerstätte 30. ℰ **01/5134850.** www.hdm.at. Admission 10€ adults, 8.50€ students and seniors, 5.50€ children 3–12, children 0–3 free. Open daily 10am–10pm. UBahn: Oper.

Hundertwasserhaus   In a city filled with baroque palaces and numerous architectural adornments, this sprawling public-housing project in the rather bleak 3rd District is visited—or at least seen from the window of a tour bus—by about a million visitors annually. Completed in 1985, it was the work of self-styled "eco-architect" Friedensreich Hundertwasser. The facade, like a gigantic black-and-white game board, is relieved with scattered splotches of red, yellow, and blue. Trees stick out at 45-degree angles from apartments among the foliage. There are 50 apartments here, and signs warn not to go inside. There's a tiny gift shop (ℰ **01/715-15-53**) at the entrance where you can buy Hundertwasser posters and postcards, plus a coffee shop on the first floor.

Löwengasse and Kegelgasse 3. ℰ **01/715-15-53.** www.hundertwasserhaus.info. U-Bahn: Landstrasse. Tram: 1.

Kunsthistorisches Museum (Museum of Art History) ★★★   Across from Hofburg Palace, this huge building houses many of the truly fabulous art collections gathered by the Habsburgs as they added new territories to their empire. One highlight is the fine collection of ancient Egyptian and Greek art. The museum also has works by many of the great European masters, such as Velásquez and Titian.

On display here are Roger van der Weyden's *Crucifixion* triptych, a Memling altarpiece, and Jan van Eyck's portrait of Cardinal Albergati. The museum is renowned for the works of **Pieter Bruegel the Elder,** known for his sensitive yet vigorous landscapes and lively studies of peasant life. Don't leave without a glimpse of Bruegel's *Children's Games* and his *Hunters in the Snow,* one of his most celebrated works, and those of Van Dyck, especially his *Venus in the Forge of Vulcan.* The collection of Peter Paul Rubens includes his *Self-Portrait* and *Woman with a Cape,* for which he is said to have used the face of his second wife, Helen Fourment. From Rembrandt you can see some of the master drawings and two remarkable self-portraits, as well as a moving portrait of his mother and one of his sons, Titus.

A highlight of any trip to Vienna is the museum's **Albrecht Dürer** collection. The Renaissance German painter and engraver (1471–1528) is known for his innovative art and his painstakingly detailed workmanship. *Blue Madonna* is here, as are some of his landscapes, such as *Martyrdom of 10,000 Christians.*

Maria-Theresien-Platz, Burgring 5. ℰ **01/52524-4025.** www.khm.at. Admission 12€ adults, 9€ students and seniors, free for those under 19. Tues–Sun 10am–6pm; Thurs 10am–9pm. U-Bahn: Mariahilferstrasse. Tram: 1, 2, D, or J.

Secession ★   Come here if for no other reason than to see Gustav Klimt's *Beethoven Frieze,* a 30m-long (98-ft.) visual interpretation of Beethoven's Ninth Symphony. This building—a virtual art manifesto proclamation—stands south of the Opernring, beside the Academy of Fine Arts. The Secession was the home of the Viennese avant-garde, which extolled the glories of Jugendstil (Art Nouveau). A young group of painters and architects launched the Secessionist movement in 1897 in rebellion against the strict, conservative ideas of the official Academy of Fine Arts. Gustav Klimt was a leader of the movement, which defied the historicism favored by the Emperor Franz Joseph. The works of Kokoschka were featured here, as was the "barbarian" Paul Gauguin.

Today many of the greatest works by the Secessionist artists are on display in the Belvedere Palace, and the Secession building itself by Josef Maria Olbrich, as much a work of art as any of the paintings, is used for significant contemporary exhibits. It was constructed in 1898 and is crowned by a magnificent dome once called "outrageous in its useless luxury." The empty dome—covered in triumphal laurel leaves—echoes that of the Karlskirche on the other side of Vienna.

Friedrichstrasse 12 (on the western side of Karlsplatz). ⓒ **01/587-530711.** www.secession.at. Admission 5€ adults, 4€ students and seniors, children under 10 free. Tues–Sun 10am–6pm; Thurs 10am–8pm. U-Bahn: Karlsplatz.

Wiener Staatsoper (Vienna State Opera) ★   This is one of the most important opera houses in the world. When it was built in the 1860s, critics apparently upset one of the architects, Eduard van der Null, so much that he killed himself. Heavily damaged by Allied bombing in the last months of World War II, restoration work on the opera house began soon afterward; while there were many other pressing needs such as public housing, the spiritual need to return the opera to the center of the city's life was considered essential to restoration of morale. It was finished in time to celebrate the country's independence from the four-power occupation in 1955. (See "Vienna After Dark" later in this chapter.)

Opernring 2. ⓒ **01/5144-42250.** www.staatsoper.at. Tours daily year-round, 2–5 times a day, depending on demand. Tour times are posted on a board outside the entrance. Tours 6.50€ per person, 5.50€ senior citizens, 3.50€ students. U-Bahn: Karlsplatz.

Ringstrasse ★★★

In 1857, Emperor Franz Josef ordered that all the foundations of the medieval fortifications around the Altstadt (Old Town) be removed and that a grand circular boulevard or belt of boulevards replace them. This transformation, which rivaled Paris under Baron Haussmann, created the Vienna we know today. Work on this ambitious project began in 1859 and stretched on to 1888 when the grand boulevard reached a distance of 4km (2½ miles).

Taking the streetcar around the Ring takes you past a dozen monumental public buildings constructed in those 29 years. There are several options: The simplest is the yellow Ring Tram that circles the Ring and costs 6€ for adults and 4€ for children. Other lines include the D (from Nussdorf hedging around part of the Ring before veering off to Südbahnhof), and 1 and 2 (each do a half circle of the Ring and continue into outer districts—1 to the west, 2 to the east). The 1 takes you past the university and Rathaus (City Hall) on the north side of the Ring, and the 2 takes you past the Stadtpark. Both leave the Ring at the opera and at Schwedenplatz.

Extending south from the Danube Canal, the first lap of the Ring is **Schottenring,** taking in the Italianate Börse or Stock Exchange and the **Votivkirche (Votive Church)** (p. 162). Running from the university, with its bookstores, bars, and cafes to Rathausplatz, the next lap of the Ring is **Karl-Lueger Ring.** The chief attraction along this stretch is the Universität Wien, dating from 1365. In the 1800s the massive new building you see today was constructed in an Italian Renaissance style.

At the end of this Ring you enter the beginning of **Dr.-Karl-Renner Ring** at the Rathausplatz. Here the Rathaus evokes a Gothic fantasy castle, the dream work of Friedrich Schmidt and a setting for frequent concerts and festivals.

Across the way is the Burgtheater or the Court Theater, constructed between 1874 and 1888 in the Italian Renaissance style. Some of the world's most famous operas, including Mozart's *The Marriage of Figaro*, were premiered here. Frescoes by Gustav Klimt, and his brother, Ernest, draw visitors inside.

Next to the city hall stands Parliament, with its elegant Grecian facade decked out with winged chariots.

Moving on, we next enter the **Burgring,** opposite the Hofburg Palace on either side of Maria-Theresien-Platz. Two of the city's largest and finest museums lie along this boulevard: The **Kunsthistorisches Museum** (Museum of Art History, p. 153) and **Naturhistorisches Museum** (Natural History Museum, p. 164).

The highlight of the next Ring, **Opernring,** begins at the Burggarten or Palace Gardens, a tranquil retreat in the heart of the city where you'll find monuments to everybody from Mozart to Emperor Franz Josef. This Ring runs to Schwarzenbergstrasse with its equestrian statue, Schwarzenberg Denkmal. The architectural highlight of this Ring is the Staatsoper (State Opera, p. 154).

Finally, the **Schubertring/Stubenring** stretch of the Ring goes from Schwarzenbergstrasse to the Danube Canal. This Ring borders the Stadtpark, which was established in 1862, the first city municipal park to be laid out outside the former fortifications. The chief architectural highlight along this boulevard is the Postsparkasse or Post Office Savings Bank, near the end of the Stubenring at George-Coch-Platz 2. This Art Nouveau building was designed at the turn of the 20th century by Otto Wagner, and it remains a bulwark of Modernist architecture.

Outside the Inner City

Kaiserliches Hofmobiliendepot (Imperial Furniture Collection) ★

A collection spanning 3 centuries of royal acquisitions, exhibits range from the throne of the Emperor Francis Joseph and Prince Rudolf's cradle to a forest of coat racks and some 15,000 chairs. At the end of World War I, the new republic inherited the collection established in 1747 that now totals some 55,000 objects.

The collection includes prized examples of decorative and applied arts; it is particularly rich in Biedermeier furnishings, which characterized the era from 1815 to 1848. Particularly stunning is Maria Theresa's imposing desk of palissander (an exotic wood) marquetry with a delicate bone inlay. Modern pieces include designs by Secession artists Adolf Loos and Otto Wagner—all housed in a century-old warehouse halfway between Hofburg and Schönbrunn Palace. Allow about 2½ hours to visit the three floors. Expect cheek-by-jowl bric-a-brac.

Andreasgasse 7. ⓒ **01/524-33570.** www.hofmobiliendepot.at. Admission 6.90€ adults, 5.50€ students and seniors, 4.50€ children 6-18. Tues–Sun 10am–6pm. U-Bahn: Zieglergasse.

Liechtenstein Museum ★★★

The rare collection of art treasures from the Liechtenstein's princely collections went on display in 2004 in the renovated family palace in the 9th District. For the first time, visitors can see the Raphaels, Rubens, and Rembrandts, of one of the world's greatest private art collections.

The renovation meant restoring frescoes, relandscaping the gardens, and rejuvenating the palace's many extraordinary details. The collection in the neoclassical Garden Palace includes works by Frans Hals, Anthony Van Dyck, and Austrians Friedrich Amerling and Ferdinand Georg Waldmüller, some 1,700 works of art in the collection, on rotating display. Works range from the 13th to the 19th centuries. Peter Paul Rubens is one of the stars of the museum, including his remarkable *Venus in Front of the Mirror* (ca. 1613). The **Hercules Hall ★** is the largest secular baroque room in Vienna. Frescoes are by Andrea Pozzo.

The palace also has two new restaurants, Ruben's Brasserie, serving both traditional Viennese and Liechtenstein fare and Ruben's Palais, offering more haute cuisine. Both restaurants have gardens in the palace's baroque courtyard.

Liechtenstein Garden Palace, Fürstengasse 1. ℂ **01/3195767-0.** www.liechtensteinmuseum.at. Admission 10€ adults, 5€ students and seniors, those up to 19 free. Fri–Tues 10am–5pm. U-Bahn: Rossauer Lände. Tram: D to Bauernfeldplatz.

Österreichische Galerie Belvedere (Belvedere Palace) ★★ Southeast of Karlsplatz, the Belvedere sits on a slope above Vienna. You approach the palace through a long garden with a huge circular pond that reflects the sky and the looming palace buildings. Designed by Johann Lukas von Hildebrandt, the last major Austrian baroque architect, the Belvedere was built as a summer home for Prince Eugene of Savoy. It consists of two palatial buildings, made with a series of interlocking cubes and an interior dominated by two great flowing staircases.

Unteres Belvedere (Lower Belvedere), with its entrance at Rennweg 6A, was completed in 1716, the **Oberes Belvedere (Upper Belvedere)** in 1723.

The Gold Salon in Lower Belvedere is one of the most beautiful rooms in the palace. Composer Anton Bruckner lived in one of the buildings until his death in 1896, and the palace was also the residence of Archduke Franz Ferdinand, the slain heir and a World War I spark. In May 1955, the peace treaty recognizing Austria as a sovereign state was signed in Upper Belvedere by foreign ministers of the four powers that occupied Austria at the close of World War II—France, Great Britain, the United States, and the Soviet Union.

Today visitors come to the splendid baroque palace to enjoy the panoramic view of the Wienerwald (Vienna Woods) from the terrace. A regal French-style garden lies between Upper and Lower Belvedere, both of which feature impressive art collections that are open to the public.

The Lower Belvedere houses the **Barockmuseum (Museum of Baroque Art).** Displays include the original sculptures from the Neuermarkt fountain, the work of Georg Raphael Donner, who dominated 18th-century Austrian sculpture, heavily influenced by Italian art. The four figures on the fountain represent the four major tributaries of the Danube. Works by Franz Anton Maulbertsch, an 18th-century painter, are also exhibited. Maulbertsch, strongly influenced by Tiepolo, was the most original and accomplished Austrian painter of his day. He was best known for his iridescent colors and flowing brushwork.

Museum Mittelalterlicher Kunst (Museum of Medieval Austrian Art) is located in the Orangery at Lower Belvedere. Here you'll see works from the Gothic period, as well as a Tyrolean Romanesque crucifix that dates from the 12th century.

Art-School Reject

One Austrian painter whose canvases will never grace any museum wall is Adolph Hitler. Aspiring to be an artist, Hitler had his traditional paintings, including one of the Auersberg Palace, rejected by the Academy of Fine Arts in Vienna. The building was accurate, but the figures were way out of proportion. Hitler did not take this failure well, denouncing the board as a "lot of old-fashioned fossilized civil servants, bureaucrats, devoid lumps of officials. The whole academy ought to be blown up!"

Outstanding works include seven panels by Rueland Frueauf portraying scenes from the life of the Madonna and the Passion of Christ.

Upper Belvedere houses the **Galerie des 19. and 20. Jahrhunderts (Gallery of 19th- and 20th-Century Art)** ★. In a large salon decorated in red marble, you can view the 1955 peace treaty mentioned above. A selection of Austrian and international paintings of the 19th and 20th centuries is on display, including works by Oskar Kokoschka, Vincent van Gogh, James Ensor, and C. D. Freidrich.

Most outstanding are the works of Gustav Klimt (1862–1918), one of the founders of the 1897 Secession movement. Klimt used a geometrical approach to painting, blending figures with their backgrounds in the same overall tones. Witness the extraordinary *Judith*. Other notable Klimt works here are *The Kiss*, *Adam and Eve*, and five panoramic lakeside landscapes from Attersee. Sharing almost equal billing with Klimt is Egon Schiele (1890–1918), whose masterpieces include *The Wife of an Artist*. Schiele could be morbid, as exemplified by *Death and Girl,* as well as cruelly observant, as in *The Artist's Family*.

Prinz-Eugen-Strasse 27. ⓒ **01/79557.** www.belvedere.at. Admission 9€ adults, free for children 11 and under. Tues–Sun 10am–6pm. Tram: D to Schloss Belvedere.

Schönbrunn Palace ★★★ The 1,441-room Schönbrunn Palace was designed for the Habsburgs by those masters of the baroque, the Fischer von Erlachs, father and son. It was built between 1696 and 1712 at the request of Emperor Leopold I for his son, Joseph I. Leopold envisioned a palace whose grandeur would surpass that of Versailles. However, Austria's treasury, drained by the cost of wars, would not support the ambitious undertaking; and the original plans were never carried out.

When Maria Theresa became empress, she changed the original plans; and Schönbrunn looks today much as she conceived it. Done in "Maria Theresa ocher," with delicate rococo touches designed for her by Austrian Nikolaus Pacassi, the palace is in complete contrast to the grim, forbidding Hofburg. Schönbrunn was the imperial summer palace during Maria Theresa's 40-year reign, and it was the scene of great ceremonial balls, lavish banquets, and fabulous receptions held during the Congress of Vienna. The empress received the 6-year-old Mozart for a performance in the Hall of Mirrors and held secret meetings with her chancellor, Prince Kaunitz, in the round Chinese Room.

Franz Joseph was born within the palace walls; it became the setting for the lavish court life associated with his reign, as well as his private austerity, and he spent the final years of his life here. The last of the Habsburg rulers, Karl I, signed the document renouncing his participation in affairs of state here on November 11, 1918—not quite an abdication, but tantamount to one. Allied bombs damaged the palace during World War II, scars since healed by restoration.

The **Gloriette** ★★, a marble summerhouse topped by a stone canopy with an imperial eagle, embellishes the palace's **Imperial Gardens** ★. The so-called Roman Ruins (a collection of marble statues and fountains) date from the late 18th century, when it was fashionable to simulate the fallen grandeur of Rome. Adria van Steckhoven laid out the park and its many fountains and heroic statues, often depicting Greek mythological characters. It is open to visitors until sunset daily.

The **State Apartments** ★★★ are perhaps the most fascinating part of the palace, both for their grandeur and their intimacy. Much of the interior ornamentation is in the rococo style, with red, white, and 23½-karat gold predominating. Of the 40 rooms that you can visit, particularly interesting is the Room of Millions, decorated with Indian and Persian miniatures. English-language guided tours of many of the palace

Schönbrunn

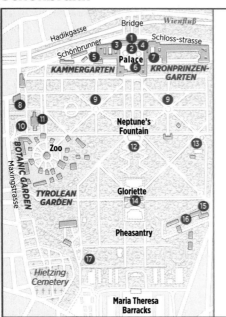

THE PARK

1 Main Gate
2 Courtyard & Wagenburg
   (Carriage Museum)
3 Schlosstheater
4 Café Restaurant Residenz ☕
5 Mews
6 Chapel
7 Kutscher Gwölb &
   Schönbrunner Stöckl ☕
8 Hietzing Church
9 Naiad's Fountains
10 Joseph II Monument
11 Palm House
12 Neptune's Fountain
13 Schöner Brunnen
14 Gloriette
15 Small Gloriette
16 Spring
17 Octagonal Pavilion

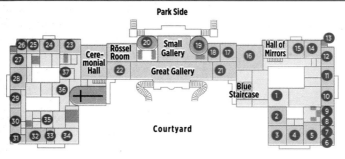

THE PALACE

1	Guard Room	
2	Billiard Room	
3	Walnut Room	
4	Franz Joseph's Study	
5	Franz Joseph's Bedroom	
6	Cabinet	
7	Stairs Cabinet	
8	Dressing Room	
9	Bedroom of Franz Joseph I & Elisabeth	
10	Empress Elisabeth's Salon	
11	Marie Antoinette's Room	
12	Nursery	
13	Breakfast Room	
14	Yellow Salon	
15	Balcony Room	
16 17 18	Rosa Rooms	
19 20	Round & Oval Chinese Cabinets	
21	Lantern Room	
22	Carousel Room	
23	Blue Chinese Salon	
24	Vieux-Laque Room	
25	Napoleon Room	
26	Porcelain Room	
27	Millions Room	
28	Gobelin Tapestry Room	
29	Archduchess Sophie's Study	
30	Red Drawing Room	
31	East Terrace Cabinet	
32	Bed-of-State Room	
33	Writing Room	
34	Drawing Room	
35	Wild Boar Room	
36	Passage Chamber	
37	Bergl-Zimmer	

rooms, lasting 50 minutes, start every half-hour beginning at 9:30am. You should tip the guide at least 1€.

Also in the grounds is the baroque **Schlosstheater (Palace Theater)** (𝄐 **01/876-4272**), which stages summer performances. The **Wagenburg (Carriage Museum)** ★ (𝄐 **01/877-3244**) is also worth a visit. It contains a fine display of imperial coaches from the 17th to 20th centuries.

The **Schloss Schönbrunn Experience** is a 60- to 90-minute children's tour. First, kids are dressed in imperial clothing, then led by English-speaking guides through rooms that offer hands-on displays.

Admission price to the palace includes a tour (the Grand Tour) of 40 state rooms with audio guide.

Schönbrunner Schlossstrasse. 𝄐 **01/811-132-39.** www.schoenbrunn.at. Admission 9.50€ adults, 8.50€ students and seniors, 6.50€ children 6–18, free for children under 6; Wagenburg Nov–March 10am–4pm, Apr–Oct 9am–6pm, 6€ adults, 4€ students and seniors, those up to 19 free. Schloss Schönbrunn Experience 4.90€ children (3–18). Apr–June and Sept–Oct daily 8:30am–5pm; July–Aug daily 8:30am–6pm; Nov–Mar daily 8:30am–4:30pm. U-Bahn: Schönbrunn.

CHURCHES

For the Hofburg Palace Chapel, where the Vienna Boys' Choir performs, and the Augustinerkirche, see earlier in this chapter; also for St. Stephan's Cathedral.

The Inner City

Deutschordenskirche The Order of the Teutonic Knights was a German society founded in 1190 in the Holy Land. The order came to Vienna in 1205, and the church dates from 1395. The building never fell prey to the baroque madness that swept the city after the Counter-Reformation, so you see it pretty much in its original form, a Gothic church dedicated to St. Elizabeth. The 16th-century Flemish altarpiece standing at the main altar is richly decorated with woodcarving, gilt, and painted panel inserts. Many knights of the Teutonic Order are buried here, their heraldic shields still mounted on some of the upper walls.

In the knights' treasury, on the second floor of the church, you'll see mementos such as seals and coins illustrating the history of the order, as well as a collection of arms, vases, gold, crystal, and precious stones. Also on display are the charter given to the Teutonic Order by Henry IV of England and a collection of medieval paintings. A curious exhibit is the Viper Tongue Credenza, said to have the power to detect poison in food and render it harmless.

Singerstrasse 7. 𝄐 **01/512-1065-214.** www.deutscher-orden.at. Free admission to church; treasury 4€ adults, 3€ students and seniors, children under 6 free. Church daily 7am–6pm; treasury Tues, Thurs, Sat 10am–noon, Wed, Fri 3–5pm. Closed Mon, Sun, and holidays. U-Bahn: Stephansplatz.

Domkirche St. Stephan (St. Stephan's Cathedral) ★★★ ☺ A basilica built on the site of a Romanesque sanctuary, this cathedral was founded in the 12th century in what was, even in the Middle Ages, the town's center.

A 1258 fire that swept through Vienna virtually destroyed Stephansdom; and toward the dawn of the 14th century, a Gothic building replaced the basilica's ruins. The cathedral suffered terribly during the Turkish siege of 1683, then experienced peace until Russian bombardments in 1945. Destruction continued when the Germans fired on Vienna as they fled the city at the close of World War II. Restored and reopened in 1948, the cathedral is one of the greatest Gothic structures in Europe, rich in woodcarvings, altars, sculptures, and paintings. The 135-m (450-ft.) steeple has come to symbolize the spirit of Vienna.

The 106m-long (352-ft.) cathedral is inextricably entwined with Viennese and Austrian history. Mourners attended Mozart's "pauper's funeral" here in 1791, and Napoleon posted his farewell edict on the door in 1805.

The **pulpit** of St. Stephan's is the enduring masterpiece of stone carver Anton Pilgrim, but the chief treasure of the cathedral is the carved wooden **Wiener Neustadt altarpiece ★★**, which dates from 1447. The richly painted and gilded altar, in the left chapel of the choir, depicts the Virgin Mary between St. Catherine and St. Barbara. In the Apostles' Choir, look for the curious **tomb of Emperor Frederick III ★★**. Made of pinkish Salzburg marble in the 17th century, the carved tomb depicts hideous hobgoblins trying to wake the emperor from his eternal sleep. The entrance to the catacombs or crypt is on the north side next to the Capistran pulpit. Here you'll see the funeral urns that contain the entrails (literally!) of 56 members of the Habsburg family. You can climb the 343-step South Tower of St. Stephan's for a view of the Vienna Woods. Called **Alter Steffl (Old Steve),** the tower, marked by a needlelike spire, dominates the city's skyline. It was originally built between 1350 and 1433, and reconstructed after heavy damage in World War II. The North Tower (Nordturm), reached by elevator, was never finished to match the South Tower, but was crowned in the Renaissance style in 1579. From here you get a panoramic view of the city and the Danube.

Stephansplatz 1. ℂ **01/515-523526.** www.stephanskirche.at. Cathedral free admission; tour of catacombs 4.50€ adults, 1.50€ children under 14. Guided tour of cathedral 4.50€ adults, 1.50€ children under 15. South Tower 3.50€ adults, 1€ children 6–14. Evening tours, including tour of the roof, 10€ adults, 4€ children under 14. Cathedral daily 6am–10pm except times of service. Tour of catacombs Mon–Sat 10–11.30am and 1.30–4:30pm; Sun and holidays 1:30–4:30pm. Guided tour of cathedral Mon–Sat 10:30am and 3pm; Sun and holidays at 3pm. Guided tour in English daily 3.45pm Apr–Oct. Special evening tour Sat 7pm (June–Sept). South Tower daily 9am–5:30pm. Bus: 1A, 2A, or 3A. U-Bahn: Stephansplatz.

Kapuzinerkirche & Kaisergruft The Kapuziner Church (just inside the Ring behind the opera) has housed the imperial crypt, the burial vault of the Habsburgs, for some 3 centuries. Capuchin friars guard the final resting place of 12 emperors, 17 empresses, and dozens of archdukes. Only their bodies are here: Their hearts are in urns in the Loreto Chapel of the Augustinerkirche in the Hofburg complex, and their entrails are similarly enshrined in a crypt below St. Stephan's Cathedral.

Most outstanding of the imperial tombs is the double sarcophagus of Maria Theresa and her consort, Francis Stephen (François, duke of Lorraine, or, in German, Franz von Lothringen, 1708–65), the parents of Marie Antoinette. The "King of Rome," the ill-fated son of Napoleon and Marie-Louise of Austria, was buried here in a bronze coffin after his death at age 21. (Hitler managed to anger both the Austrians and the French by having the remains of Napoleon's son transferred to Paris in 1940.)

Emperor Franz Joseph was interred here in 1916. He was a frail old man who had probably outlived his time and died just before the final collapse of his empire. His wife, Empress Elisabeth, was also buried here after her assassination in Geneva in 1898, as was their son, Crown Prince Rudolf, who died at Mayerling (see the "Twilight of the Habsburgs", chapter 7).

Neuer Markt. ℂ **01/512-6853-16.** www.kaisergruft.at. Admission 5€ adults, 4€ students and seniors, 2€ children up to 14. Daily 10am–6pm. Closed Nov 1, 2. U-Bahn: Stephansplatz.

Maria am Gestade (St. Mary's on the Bank) This church, also known as the Church of Our Lady of the Riverbank, was once just that. With an arm of the Danube flowing by, it was a favorite place of worship for fishermen. The river was redirected, and now the church relies on its beauty to draw people. A Romanesque church on this site was rebuilt in the Gothic style between 1394 and 1427. The western facade is flamboyant, with a remarkable seven-sided Gothic tower surmounted by a dome that culminates in a lacelike crown.

Passauer Platz. ☎ **01/5339-5940.** Free admission. Daily 7am–7pm. U-Bahn: Stephansplatz or Shottenring.

Michaelerkirche   Over its long history this church has felt the hand of many architects and designers, resulting in a medley of styles, not all harmonious. Some of the remaining Romanesque sections date to the early 1200s. The exact date of the chancel is not known, but it's probably from the mid-14th century. The catacombs remain as they were in the Middle Ages.

Most of St. Michael's as it appears today dates from 1792, when the facade was redone in neoclassical style; the spire is from the 16th century. The main altar is richly decorated in baroque style, and the altarpiece, entitled *The Collapse of the Angels* (1781), was the last major baroque work completed in Vienna.

Michaelerplatz. ☎ **01/533-8000.** www.michaelerkirche.at. Free admission. Mon–Sat 6:45am–8pm; Sun 8am–6:30pm. Information on guided tours: ☎ **0650-533-8003.** U-Bahn: Herrengasse. Bus: 2A or 3A.

Minoritenkirche   If you're tired of baroque ornamentation, visit this church of the Friar Minor Conventual, a Franciscan order also called the Minorite friars (inferior brothers). Construction began in 1250 but was not completed until the early 14th century. The Turks damaged the tower in their two sieges of Vienna, and the church later fell prey to baroque architects and designers. But in 1784, Ferdinand von Hohenberg ordered the baroque additions removed; and the simple lines of the original Gothic church returned, complete with cloisters. Inside you'll see a full-size mosaic copy of da Vinci's *The Last Supper,* by Giacomo Raffailli, commissioned by Napoleon, who abdicated before it was finished. Emperor Francis II bought it, and too large for the Belvedere, he hung it in the church. Masses are held on Sunday at 8:30am (in German) and 11am (in Italian).

Minoritenplatz 2A. ☎ **01/533-4162.** www.minoritenkirche-wien.info. Free admission. Apr–Oct Mon–Sat 8am–6pm; Nov–Mar Mon–Sat 9am–5pm. U-Bahn: Herrengasse.

Peterskirche   This is the second-oldest church in Vienna, and the spot on which it stands could well be Vienna's oldest Christian church site. It is believed that a place of worship stood here in the second half of the 4th century, and Charlemagne is credited with having founded a church on the site when he conquered what is now Vienna in 803. The present St. Peter's is the most lavishly decorated baroque church in Vienna. Gabriel Montani designed it in 1702. Hildebrandt, the noted architect of the Belvedere Palace, is believed to have finished the building in 1732. The fresco in the dome is a masterpiece by J. M. Rottmayr, painter of the frescoes in the Liechtenstein Museum, depicting the coronation of the Virgin. The church contains many frescoes and much gilded carved wood, plus altarpieces created by well-known artists of the period.

Peterplatz. ☎ **01/533-6433.** www.peterskirche.at. Free admission. Mon–Fri 7am–8pm, Sat, Sun, holidays 9am–9pm. U-Bahn: Stephansplatz.

Ruprechtskirche   The oldest church in Vienna, St. Rupert's Church has stood here since A.D. 740, although much that you see now, such as the aisle, is from the 11th century. Beautiful new stained-glass windows—the work of Lydia Roppolt—were installed in 1993. It's believed that much of the masonry from a Roman shrine on this spot was used in the present church. The tower and nave are Romanesque;

the rest of the church is Gothic. St. Rupert is the patron saint of the Danube's salt merchants.

Ruprechtsplatz. ✆ **01/535-6003.** www.ruprechtskirche.at. Free admission. Easter Monday to Oct Mon–Fri 10am–noon, Mon, Wed, Fri 3–5pm. Closed Nov–Easter. U-Bahn: Schwedenplatz.

Universitätskirche Built at the time of the Counter-Reformation, this church is rich in baroque embellishments. This was the university church, dedicated to the Jesuit saints Ignatius of Loyola and Franciscus Xaverius. The high-baroque decorations—galleries, columns, and the *trompe l'oeil* painting on the ceiling, which gives the illusion of a dome—were added from 1703 to 1705. The embellishments were the work of a Jesuit lay brother, Andrea Pozzo, on the orders of Emperor Leopold I. Look for Pozzo's painting of Mary behind the main altar. The church has a superb choir and orchestra (emigrated from the Augutinekirche) that performs classical and romantic Masses on Sundays and holy days at 10am.

Dr.-Ignaz-Seipel-Platz 1. ✆ **01/512-52320.** Free admission. Mon–Sat 7am–7pm, Sun 8am–7pm. U-Bahn: Stephansplatz or Stubentor. Tram: 2. Bus: 1A.

Outside the Inner City

Karlskirche (Church of St. Charles) The Black Plague swept Vienna in 1713, and Emperor Charles VI vowed that if the disease abated, he would build a church in thanks for Vienna's deliverance. Construction on Karlskirche was begun by Johann Bernard Fischer von Erlach in 1716 and completed by his son, Joseph Emanuel in 1737, with frescoes by J. M. Rottmayr. The green copper dome is 72m (236 ft.) high, a dramatic landmark on the Viennese skyline. Two columns, a homage to Trajan's Column in Rome, flank the front of the church, opening onto Resselpark. A sculpture by Henry Moore is mirrored in the reflection of the pool.

Karlsplatz. ✆ **01/504-6187.** www.karlskirche.at. Admission 6€ adults, 4€ students and seniors, free for children up to 10. Mon–Sat 9am–12:30pm and 1–6pm; Sun noon–5:45pm. U-Bahn: Karlsplatz.

Piaristenkirche A Roman Catholic teaching congregation launched work on the Piaristenkirche in 1716, consecrated in 1771. The plans are believed to have been drawn by von Hildebrandt, the noted architect who designed the Belvedere Palace, but many builders had a hand in its construction. This church has a fine classic facade and frescoes by F. A. Maulbertsch that adorn the cupolas.

Piaristengasse 54. ✆ **01/405-0425.** www.mariatreu.at. Free admission. Mon–Fri 9–11am; Sat 10am–noon. Tram: 2. U-Bahn: Rathaus.

Votivkirche After a failed assassination attempt on Emperor Franz Joseph, grateful subjects took up a collection to construct the Votive Church, across from the site of the attempt. Heinrich von Ferstel designed the neo-Gothic church consecrated in 1879—a magnificent facade of lacy spires and intricate sculpture.

Rooseveltplatz 8. ✆ **01/406-1192.** www.votivkirche.at. Opening hours church: Tues–Sat 9am–1pm, Sun 9am–1pm. Opening hours museum: Tues–Fri 4–6pm, Sat 10am–1pm. Admission 3.90€, 2.90[eu} students and seniors. U-Bahn: Schottenor.

MORE MUSEUMS & GALLERIES
The Inner City

Judisches Museum Wien This is the main museum tracing the history of Viennese Jewry, not to be confused with its annex at Judenplatz (see box, below). It opened in 1993 in the former Eskeles Palace, among the most elegant town houses

IN MEMORY OF VIENNA'S jewish GHETTO

Judenplatz (U-Bahn: Stephansplatz), between Wipplingerstrasse and Tuchlauben, was the heart of the Jewish ghetto from the 13th to the 15th centuries. Archaeologists excavating the square in 1995 found, as in other parts of the city, the remains of an earlier community, and a synagogue that contemporary records revealed to be one of the largest of its time, attracting renowned religious scholars to Vienna as a thriving Jewish community grew.

The opening of a Holocaust memorial on this square in 2000 by architect Rachel Whitehead honors the tradition of books and learning, as well as the closed doors on a lost culture. Around the base of the monument are engraved the names of the places in which Austrian Jews were put to death during the Nazi era. Nearby is a statue of Gotthold Ephraim Lessing (1729–81), the Jewish playwright. Together, the excavations, the memorials, and the new museum have recreated a center of Jewish culture on Judenplatz, and a place of remembrance at the center of the city's daily life unique to Europe.

Museum Judenplatz, Judenplatz 8 (© **01/535-0431**), is a new annex of Vienna's Jewish Museum. The main exhibition features a multimedia presentation on the religious, cultural, and social life of the Viennese Jews in the Middle Ages until their expulsion in 1420 and 1421. Other exhibits tell of the defining role

Viennese Jews played in all aspects of city life, from music to medicine, until a reign of terror began in 1938. The three exhibition rooms are in the basement of the Misrachi house, where an underground passage connects them to the exhibitions of the medieval synagogue. The museum is open Sunday through Thursday from 10am to 6pm and Friday from 10am to 2pm; admission is 4€ for adults and 2.50€ for children under 15, students and seniors. School classes are welcomed at no charge.

An exhibition room has been installed in the **Mittelalterliche Synagogue (Medieval Synagogue)** nearby, open during the same hours as the Jewish Museum. Built around the middle of the 13th century, it was one of the largest synagogues of its time. After the pogrom in 1420–21, the synagogue was systematically destroyed, so that only the foundations and the floor remained. These were excavated by the City of Vienna Department of Urban Archaeology from 1995 to 1998. The exhibition room shows the remnants of the central room, or "shul," the room where men studied and prayed, and a smaller room annexed to it, which might have been used by women. In the middle of the central room is the foundation of the hexagonal bimah, the raised podium from which the Torah was read. Admission is 4€ adults, 2.50€ ages 14 and under; school classes are welcomed at no charge.

in Vienna, with both temporary and permanent exhibitions. The permanent exhibitions trace the major role that Jews played in the history of Vienna until their expulsion or death in the Holocaust beginning in 1938. Displays note their extraordinary contributions in such fields as philosophy, music, medicine, and, of course, psychiatry. Sigmund Freud, although already frail, escaped to London where he died the following year. Many objects were rescued from Vienna's private synagogues and prayer houses, concealed from the Nazis throughout the war. Many exhibits are from Vienna's old Jewish Museum, which closed in 1938.

Dorotheergasse 11. © **01/535-0431.** www.jmw.at. Admission 6.50€ adults, 4€ children and seniors; school classes are free. Sun–Fri 10am–6pm. U-Bahn: Stephansplatz.

Österreichisches Museum für Angewandte Kunst The Museum of Applied Art holds a rich collection of tapestries, some from the 16th century, and the most outstanding assemblage of Viennese porcelain in the world. Look for a Persian carpet depicting *The Hunt,* as well as the group of 13th-century Limoges enamels. Exhibits display Biedermeier furniture and other antiques, glassware, and crystal; outstanding objects of the early-20th-century Wiener Werkstätte; and large collections of lace and textiles. An entire hall is devoted to Art Nouveau.

Stubenring 5. © **01/711360.** www.mak.at. Admission 9.90€ adults, 5.50€ children 6–18, free for children under 6. Free admission on Sat. Wed–Sun 10am–6pm; Tues 10am–midnight. U-Bahn: Stubentor. Tram: 1 or 2.

Naturhistorisches Museum (Natural History Museum) ☺ This is the third-largest natural history museum (after its counterparts in New York and London) in the world, and holds the oldest collections. It was established by the husband of Empress Maria Theresa (Franz Stephan von Lothringen) in 1748, who donated one of its major art objects. Located in Room no. 4 of the Mineralogy Department, and known as Der Juwelen Strauss, it's a 60cm-tall (24-in.) bouquet of flowers crafted from more than 2,000 gemstones, each of which was even rarer at the time of the object's creation than it is today.

Maria-Theresien-Platz, Burgring 7. © **01/521770.** www.nhm-wien.ac.at. Admission 10€ adults, 5€ seniors and students, under 19s free. Thurs–Mon 9am–6:30pm; Wed 9am–9pm. U-Bahn: Volkstheater. Tram: 1, 2, D, or J.

Uhrenmuseum A wide-ranging collection of timepieces—from ancient to modern—are on view at the Municipal Clock Museum. Housed in what was once the Obizzi Palais, the museum dates from 1917 and displays clocks of all shapes and sizes. Check out Rutschmann's astronomical clock made in the 18th century.

Schulhof 2. © **01/5332265.** www.museum.vienna.at. Admission 4€ adults, 2€ children. Tues–Sun 9am–4:30pm. U-Bahn: Stephansplatz.

Outside the Inner City

Heeresgeschichtliches Museum (Museum of Military History) The oldest state museum in Vienna, this building was constructed from 1850 to 1856 and is a precursor to the Ringstrasse style. Inside, exhibits delineate Habsburg military history—defeats as well as triumphs. The Sarajevo room contains mementos of the assassination of Archduke Franz Ferdinand and his wife on June 28, 1914, the event that sparked World War I. The archduke's bloodstained uniform is displayed, along with the bullet-scarred car in which the couple rode.

Arsenal 3. © **01/795610.** www.hgm.or.at. Admission 5.10€ adults, 3.30€ seniors and students, those up to 19 free. Daily 9am–5pm. Closed Jan 1, Easter, May 1, Nov 1, and Dec 24–25 and 31. Tram: 18 or D. Bus: 69A.

Sigmund Freud Museum Wien Walking through this museum, you can almost imagine the good doctor ushering you in and telling you to make yourself comfortable on the couch. Antiques and mementos, including his velour hat and dark walking stick with ivory handle, fill the study and waiting room he used during his residence here from 1891 to 1938. The museum has a bookshop with a variety of postcards of the apartment, books by Freud, posters, prints, and pens.

Berggasse 19. © **01/319-1596.** www.freud-museum.at. Admission 7€ adults, 5.50€ seniors, 4.50€ students, 2.50€ children 12–18. Free for children 11 and under. Open daily. July–Sept 9am–6pm, Oct–June 9am–5pm. Tram: D to Schlickgasse.

Wien Museum (Museum of the History of Vienna) Since the arrival of director Wolfgang Kos in 2003, the Wien Museum has burst onto the scene with one fascinating exhibition after another, interpreting the city's history, character, and complexities: On the cult of nostalgia, fashions of the Corso, or train stations to the world. There is an excellent permanent exhibit on the history of the city: Here the full panorama of Old Vienna's history unfolds, beginning with the settlement of prehistoric tribes in the Danube basin. Roman relics, artifacts from the reign of the dukes of Babenberg, and a wealth of leftovers from the Habsburg sovereignty are on display, as well as arms and armor from various eras.

Karlsplatz 4. ℂ01/505-87470. www.museum.vienna.at. Admission 6€ adults, 4€ seniors, 3€ students, those up to 19 free. Tues–Sun 10am–6pm. U-Bahn: Karlsplatz.

PARKS & GARDENS

When the weather is fine, Vienna's residents shun city parks in favor of the **Wienerwald (Vienna Woods),** a wide arc of forested countryside that surrounds northwest and southwest Vienna (p. 166). Within the city limits are more than 1,600 hectares (3,952 acres) of gardens and parks, and no fewer than 770 sports fields and playgrounds. You can, of course, visit the grounds of **Schönbrunn Park** and **Belvedere Park** when you tour those palaces. Below, we highlight Vienna's most popular parks.

The Inner City

Burggarten These are the former gardens of the Habsburg emperors. They were laid out soon after the Volksgarten was completed (see below). Look for the monument to Mozart, as well as an equestrian statue of Francis Stephen, Maria Theresa's beloved husband. The only open-air statue of Franz Joseph in Vienna is also here, and there's a statue of Goethe at the park entrance.

Opernring–Burgring, next to the Hofburg. U-Bahn: U1, U2, or U4 Opera. Tram: 1, 2, or D.

Stadtpark This lovely park lies on the slope where the Danube used to overflow into the Inner City before the construction of the Danube Canal. Many memorial statues stand in the park; the best known depicts Johann Strauss, Jr., composer of operettas and waltzes like *The Blue Danube Waltz*. Plus Franz Schubert and Hans Makart, a well-known artist whose work you'll see in churches and museums throughout Vienna. Verdant squares, well-manicured flower gardens, and plenty of benches surround the monuments. Open 24 hours daily.

Parkring. U-Bahn: U4 Stadtpark. Tram: 2, Ringtram from Schwedenplatz.

Volksgarten (People's Park) Laid out in 1820 on the site of the old city wall fortifications, this is Vienna's oldest public garden. It's dotted with monuments, including a 1907 memorial to assassinated Empress Elisabeth and the so-called Temple of Theseus, a copy of the Theseion in Athens.

Dr.-Karl-Renner-Ring, between the Hofburg & the Burgtheater. U-Bahn: U2 Herrengasse or Volkstheater. Tram: 1, 2, or D.

Outside the Inner City

The Prater ★ ☺ This extensive tract of woods and meadowland in the 2nd District has been Vienna's favorite recreation area since 1766, when Emperor Joseph II opened this imperial hunting ground to the public.

The Prater is an amusement park, fairground, and recreation area—all without barricades or an entrance gate. Its paid attractions in the *Würstlprater* are independently

TALES OF THE VIENNA woods

The Vienna Woods (*Wienerwald* in German) are often called the lungs of Vienna, a wondrous, hilly retreat of gentle paths, forests, and streams that borders the city on the southwest and northwest. It is a deeply evocative landscape somewhere between mountain and meadow, ancient hillsides, vineyards, and the occasional ruin, in whose soft contours even the angst-ridden Kafka could find love with Milena, where the troubled Beethoven, when his hearing was failing, thought the chirping of birds, the sheltering trees, and leafy vineyards of the Wienerwald made it easier for him to compose. There is something special about the light streaming in at an odd angle between the crags across a leaf-trodden lane, about the special smells of the damp earth and the crisp snap of a blue autumn sky.

A round-trip through the woods takes about 3½ hours by car, a distance of some 80km (48 miles). However, if you want to go native, head for the Wienerwald by tram, either the "D" to **Nussdorf,** the 43 to **Neuwaldegg,** or the 38 (the same ticket is valid) to **Grinzing,** home of the beloved *Heuriger* (wine taverns). At each of these, the woods are at your feet, or you can board bus no. 38A in Grinzing, and go through the Wienerwald to the top of the **Kahlenberg,** from where you can head off back down the mountain in almost any direction. The whole trip takes about 1 hour each way. You might also rent a bicycle nearby to explore the woods.

Kahlenberg is located on a hill that is part of the northeastern-most spur of the Alps (483m/1,584 ft.). If the weather is clear, you can see all the way to Hungary and Slovakia. At the top is the small Church of St. Joseph, where the Polish King Jan Sobieski stopped to pray before leading his troops to Vienna's defense against the Turks. For one of the best views, go to the right of the Kahlenberg restaurant. From the terrace of the Modul Hotel School, you'll have a panoramic sweep, including the spires of St. Stephan's. You can go directly to Kahlenberg in about 20 minutes by U-Bahn to Heiligenstadt; then take bus no. 38A.

But anywhere you find yourself in the Vienna Woods, there'll be inviting *Hütte, Beisl,* or *Heuriger* around the next bend, where you can stop for a beer or a glass of new wine, and a sausage or a spicy Liptauer cheese spread on a thick slice of *Meterbrot,* a hearty tavern loaf that comes a full meter long. Rested and restored, you can then head back out on any of the many inviting footpaths that will eventually lead you back to civilization.

For more about the Wienerwald, see chapter 7, "Lower Austria."

---

operated and maintained by individual entrepreneurs who determine their own hours, prices, and, to a large extent, policies and priorities. In addition, there are tennis clubs and riding stables, two racetracks, a golf course, a bowling alley and billiard hall, two swimming pools, bicycles, rowboats and canoes, and a soccer stadium. The vast parkland of meadows, woods, and water beyond has countless opportunities for sport and relaxation, and absorbs thousands of people without ever feeling crowded.

Few other spots convey such a sense of the pleasure in leisure that characterizes Vienna—it's turn-of-the-century nostalgia, with a touch of 1950s-era tawdriness. The Prater is the birthplace of the waltz, first introduced here in 1820.

The best-known part of the huge park is at the entrance from the Ring. Here you'll find the **Riesenrad** (ⓒ **01/729-5430;** www.wienerriesenrad.com), the giant Ferris wheel, which was constructed in 1897 and reaches 64.75m (232 ft.) at its highest point. In 1997, the Giant Wheel celebrated its 100th anniversary, and it remains, after St. Stephan's Cathedral, the most famous landmark in Vienna. Erected at a time when European engineers were flexing their mechanical muscles, the wheel was designed by British engineer Walter Basset, for the Universal Exhibition (1896–97), marking the golden anniversary of Franz Joseph's coronation in 1848. Like the Eiffel Tower a decade earlier, it was supposed to be a temporary exhibition. But except for World War II damage, the Riesenrad has been going around without interruption since 1897.

Just below is the terminus of the Lilliputian railroad, the 4-km (2½-mile) narrow-gauge line that operates in summer using vintage steam locomotives. The amusement park, right behind the giant wheel, has all the usual attractions—roller coasters, merry-go-rounds, tunnels of love, and game arcades. There is the "Volare—The Flying Coaster," which flies facedown along a 435-m (1,437-ft.) labyrinth of track at a height of 23m (75 ft.); and the "Starflyer," a tower ride where passengers are whirled around at 70m (230 ft.) above ground at speeds up to 70km/h (43 mph).

The season lasts from March or April to October, but the Ferris wheel operates all year round. Some of the more than 150 booths and restaurants stay open in winter, including the pony merry-go-round and the gambling venues. If you drive here, don't forget the no-entry and no-parking signs, which apply daily after 3pm. The place is usually jammed on Sunday afternoons in summer. Admission to the park is free, but you'll pay for games and rides. The Ferris wheel costs 8.50€ for adults and 3.50€ for children 3 to 14; infants and toddlers, free.

Prater 9. ℂ **01/728-0516.** www.prater.at. Free admission; price for rides and amusements varies. May–Sept daily 10am–1am; Oct–Nov 3 daily 10am–10pm; Nov 4–Dec 1 daily 10am–8pm. Closed Dec 2–Apr. U-Bahn: U1, or U2 Praterstern. Tram: O, 5 Praterstern, or 2 Prater Hauptallee.

ESPECIALLY FOR KIDS

The greatest attraction for kids is the **Prater Amusement Park,** but there's much more in Vienna that children find amusing, especially the performances of the horses at the **Spanish Riding School.** They also love the adventure of climbing the tower of **St. Stephan's Cathedral.** Nothing quite tops a day like a picnic in the **Vienna Woods.** Below, we list other fun-filled attractions that you and your children will enjoy. (See also "Outdoor Pursuits," below).

Schönbrunner Tiergarten, Schönbrunn Gardens (ℂ **01/87792940;** U-Bahn: Hietzing), is the world's oldest zoo, founded by Franz Stephan von Lothringen, husband of Empress Maria Theresa. Maria Theresa liked to have breakfast here with her brood, favoring animal antics with her morning Melange. The baroque buildings in a historical park landscape provide a unique setting for modern animal keeping. Admission is 12€ for adults and 5€ for children. It's open March to September daily 9am to 6:30pm, October to February daily 9am to 5pm.

Other excellent museums for children include the **Museum für Unterhaltungskunst,** Karmelitergasse 9 (ℂ **01/21106;** Tram: 21 or N), a repository of the persona that clowns and circus performers have adopted throughout the centuries; and the **Wiener Straasenbahnmuseum (Streetcar Museum),** Erdbergstrasse 109 (ℂ **01/790944900;** U-Bahn: Praterstern), a site commemorating the public conveyances that helped usher Vienna and the Habsburg Empire into the Industrial Age.

6 FOR MUSIC LOVERS

Nearly all of Vienna's great composers lived at a number of addresses during their years there. Mozart probably wins hands down with 14 ("He threw too many parties and made *much* too much noise," one of the curators confided.) Schubert was born in one where he lived a few years, and died in one where he stayed only a few months. Beethoven was far more settled with only four or so, and Strauss and Haydn actually lived established family lives. With the music everywhere, it can be fun to see the sites where it was conceived and written. But be warned: Many of these houses suffer from a bad case of museum purism—pristine, empty rooms with display cases. Only the Strauss apartment on Praterstrasse and, after much public complaint, the rethinking of the Mozart apartment on Domgasse give a real feel for the lives of the composers. The displays are interesting, but it's not the same. Still, it will help you picture the pattern of life, and you will still be able to hear their music in the concert halls and palaces where they performed and are still performed, as well as the cemeteries where they were buried.

Beethoven Pasqualatihaus (Beethoven Pasqualati House) Beethoven (1770–1827) lived in this building on and off from 1804 to 1814. Beethoven is known to have composed his Fourth, Fifth, and Seventh symphonies here, as well as *Fidelio* and other works. There isn't much to see except some family portraits and the composer's scores, but you might feel it's worth the climb to the fourth floor. At least the chamber pot by the door, which his visitors complained about, is gone.

Mölker Bastei 8. ✆ **01/535-8905.** Admission 2€ adults, 1€ children 6-18. Tues–Sun 10am–1pm and 2-6pm. U-Bahn: Schottentor.

Haydnhaus (Haydn's House) This is where (Franz) Joseph Haydn (1732–1809) conceived and wrote his magnificent later oratorios *The Seasons* and *The Creation*. He lived in this house from 1797 until his death and gave lessons to Beethoven here. The house also contains a room honoring Johannes Brahms.

Haydngasse 19. ✆ **01/596-1307.** Admission 2€ adults, 1€ students and children 10-16. Wed–Thurs 10am–1pm and 2-6pm; Fri–Sun 10am–1pm. Closed Mon and Tues. U-Bahn: Zieglergasse.

Johann Strauss Wohnung (Johann Strauss Memorial Rooms) "The King of the Waltz," Johann Strauss, Jr. (1825–99), lived at this address for a number of years, composing *The Blue Danube* waltz here in 1867. Here the wine red moiré wall coverings, paintings, and Strauss's own surprisingly small piano give a sense of his life.

Praterstrasse 54. ✆ **01/214-0121.** Admission 2€ adults, 1€ children 10-18. Tues–Thurs 2-6pm; Fri–Sun 10am–1pm. U-Bahn: Nestroyplatz.

Mozartwohnung (Mozart's Apartment) This 17th-century house is called the House of Figaro because Mozart (1756–91) composed his opera *The Marriage of Figaro* here. The composer resided here from 1784 to 1787, a relatively happy period during which he often played chamber music concerts with Haydn. Over the years he lived in 14 apartments in all, which became more squalid as he aged. He died in poverty and was buried in a pauper's grave in St. Marx Cemetery. The museum was reinvented in 2006 for the Mozart year and is now an imaginative journey into the composer's life—well worth a visit.

Domgasse 5. ✆ **01/512-1791.** www.mozarthausvienna.at. Admission 10€ adults, 7.50€ students and children. Daily 10am–7pm. U-Bahn: Stephansplatz.

Schubert Gerburtshaus (Schubert Museum) The son of a poor schoolmaster, Franz Schubert (1797–1828) was born here in a house built earlier in that century. Many Schubert mementos are on view. You can also visit the house at Kettenbrück-engasse 6, where he died at age 31.

Nussdorferstrasse 54. *C* **01/317-3601.** Admission 2€ adults, 1€ students and children 10–16. Tues–Sun 10am–1pm and 2–6pm. S-Bahn: Canisiusgasse.

ORGANIZED TOURS

Wiener Rundfahrten (Vienna Sightseeing Tours), Starhemberggasse 25 (*C* **01/7124-6830;** www.viennasightseeingtours.com), offers the best tours, including a 1-day motor-coach excursion to Budapest costing 99€ per person. The historical city tour costs 36€ for adults and is free for children 12 and under. It's ideal for visitors who want to see the major (and most frequently photographed) monuments of Vienna. Tours leave the Staatsoper daily at 9:45 and 10:30am and 2:45pm. The tour lasts 3½ hours (U-Bahn: Karlsplatz).

"**Vienna Woods—Mayerling,**" another popular excursion, leaves from the Staatsoper and takes you to the towns of Perchtoldsdorf and Mödling, and to the Abbey of Heiligenkreuz, a center of Christian culture since medieval times. The approximately 4-hour tour also takes you for a short walk through Baden, the spa that was once a favorite summer resort of the aristocracy. Tours cost 43€ for adults and 15€ for children aged 10 to 16.

A "**Historical City Tour,**" which includes visits to Schönbrunn and Belvedere palaces, leaves the Staatsoper daily at 9:45 and 10:30am and 2:45pm. It lasts about 3 hours and costs 36€ for adults and 15€ for children aged 10 to 18.

A variation on the city tour includes an optional visit to the Spanish Riding School, offered Tuesday through Saturday, leaving from the Staatsoper building at 8:30am. Tickets are 61€ for adults, 30€ for children over 13, under 12 free.

Information and booking for these tours can be obtained either through Vienna Sightseeing Tours (see above) or through its affiliate, **Elite Tours,** Operngasse 4 (*C* **01/5132225;** www.elitetours.at).

OUTDOOR PURSUITS

Biking

Vienna maintains almost 322km (200 miles) of cycling lanes and paths, many of which meander through some of the most elegant parks in Europe. Depending on their location, they're identified by a yellow image of a cyclist either stenciled directly onto the pavement or crafted from rows of red bricks set amid the cobblestones or concrete of the busy boulevards of the city center. Some of the most popular bike paths run parallel to both the Danube and the Danube Canal.

You can carry your bike onto specially marked cars of the Vienna subway system, but only during non-rush hours. Subway cars marked with a blue shield are the ones you should use for this purpose. Bicycles are *not* permitted on the system's escalators—take the stairs.

You can rent a bike for 3€ to 5€ per hour. You'll usually be asked to leave either your passport or another form of ID as a deposit. One rental possibility is **Pedal Power,** Ausstellungsstrasse 3 (*C* **01/7297234;** www.pedalpower.at). There are rental shops at the Prater and along the banks of the Danube Canal. *Note:* You can

cruising THE DANUBE

The Danube is the quintessential European river, of so many nations, and peoples from Passau, Vienna, Budapest and Belgrade, Galati and Selena all encounter each other. It was this idea of a "multi-peopled land" that was embraced by the Austro-Hungarian Empire, making it the honorable, and perhaps gentler, heir of the Holy Roman Empire. It was this river that carried ships and soldiers, courtiers and culture from one end to the other, and by the 19th century, the Austro-Hungarian army marched to commands in 11 languages. This was the river of Empire, and today it is the river of a reunited Europe, central to its new, cooperative identity as it was to the old.

Cynics aside, the Danube is really blue, at least on sunny days, and visitors to Austria will view a day cruise as a highlight of their trip. Until the advent of railroads and highways, the Danube played a vital role in Austria's history, helping to build the complex mercantile society that eventually became the Habsburg Empire.

The most professional of the cruises are operated by the **DDSG Blue Danube Shipping Co.,** whose main offices are at Handelskai 265, A-1020 Vienna (© 01/588800; www.ddsg-blue-danube.at). The most appealing cruise focuses on the Wachau region east of Vienna, between Vienna and Dürnstein. The cruise departs April to October every Sunday at 8:30am from the company's piers at Handelskai 265, A-1020 Vienna (U-Bahn: Vorgartenstrasse), arriving in Dürnstein 6 hours later. The cost is 25€ to 38€ for adults; half-price for children 10 to 15.

also rent a bike at **Bicycle Rental Hochschaubahn,** Prater 113 (© 01/7295888; www.wien.gv.at/english/leisure/bike/bikerental.htm).

One terrific bike itinerary, and quite popular as it has almost no interruptions, encompasses the long, skinny island that separates the Danube from the Neue Donau Canal. Low-lying and occasionally marshy, but with paved paths along most of its length, it provides clear views of central Europe's industrial landscape and the endless river traffic that flows by on either side.

Boating

Wear a straw boating hat and hum a few bars of a Strauss waltz as you paddle your way around the quiet eddies of the Alte Donau. This gently curving stream bisects residential neighborhoods to the north of the Danube and is preferable to the muddy and swift-moving currents of the river itself.

Along the old Danube, you'll find some kiosks in summer, where you can negotiate for the rental of a boat, perhaps a canoe, or a kayak. There are, of course, organized tours of the Danube, but it's more fun to do it yourself.

Hiking

You're likely to expend plenty of shoe leather simply navigating Vienna's museums and palaces, but if you yearn for fresh air, the city tourist offices will provide information about its eight **Stadt-Wander-Wege,** carefully marked hiking paths that originate at points within the city's far-flung network of trams.

A less structured option involves heading east of town into the vast precincts of the **Lainzer Tiergarten,** where hiking trails entwine themselves amid forested hills, colonies of deer, and abundant bird life. To reach it from Vienna's center, first take the U-Bahn (U4) to the Hietzing station, which lies a few steps from the entrance to Schönbrunn Palace. A trek among the formal gardens of Schönbrunn might provide exercise enough, but if you're hungry for more, take tram no. 60 and then bus no. 60B into the distant but verdant confines of the Lainzer Tiergarten.

SHOPPING

While traditional attire and handicrafts are part of a long-established tradition of skilled craftsmanship, Austrian design both traditional and modern is also famous all over the world. Visitors can spend many happy hours browsing antique stores, and galleries of fine art, jewelry, unique design pieces, and original fashion.

The traditional products have not lost their allure, like the *Dirndl* and *Lederhosen* that the Viennese still wear in summer and to the *Jägerball* (Hunter's Ball) each January. The traditions of the c.1900 Wiener Werkstätte designs are available at selected shops. Other favorites are petit-point linens, hand-painted Augarten porcelain, gold and silver work, ceramics, enamel jewelry, wrought-iron art, and leather goods. Shopping in Vienna is fun and most vendors know their products.

In general there are two main shopping areas. One is the inner city (1st District). Here you'll find **Kärntnerstrasse,** between the State Opera and Stock-im-Eisen-Platz (U-Bahn: Karlsplatz or Stephansplatz); the **Graben,** between Stock-im-Eisen-Platz and Kohlmarkt (U-Bahn: Stephansplatz); **Kohlmarkt,** between the Graben and Michaelerplatz (U-Bahn: Herrengasse); and **Rotenturmstrasse,** between Stephansplatz and Schwedenplatz (U-Bahn: Stephansplatz or Schwedenplatz). The side streets off the Graben, especially Dorotheergasse, are lots of fun to browse through with the high concentration of antiques stores.

Shopping Hours

Shops are normally open Monday through Friday from 9am to 6pm and Saturday from 9am to 1pm. Small shops close from noon to 2pm for lunch. Westbahnhof, Praterstern, and Süd-bahnhof shops are open daily from 7am to 11pm, offering groceries, smokers' supplies, stationery, books, and flowers.

In addition to this posher area, the real-people stretch is on **Mariahilfer-strasse,** between MuseumsQuartier and Westbahnhof, one of the longest (and often busiest) shopping streets in Europe (U-Bahn: MuseumsQuartier, Neubaugasse, Zieglergasse, or West-bahnhof). Off this boulevard there are many hidden treasures, like down the so-called "furniture mile" on Siebensterngasse or between Mariahilferstrasse and the Nasch-markt in Gumpendorferstrasse, where fine boutiques, good restaurants, and stylish hairdressers greet you at every turn.

The **Naschmarkt** itself is an international fine foods market with a lively scene every day. To visit it, head south of the opera district. It's the joiner of the Linke and Rechte Wienzeile (U-Bahn: Karlsplatz or Kettenbrückengasse; see "Noshing Your Way Through Vienna's Open-Air Markets," later in this chapter).

The larger shopping streets have elegant department stores, which are wonderful to browse in on colder days. On Kärntnerstrasse it is the **Steffl,** a glass tower from which an elevator sticks out into the street. On Mariahilferstrasse the place where you'll find everything under one roof is **Gerngross,** the renovated, century-old shopping palace (see "Department Stores", below).

Antiques

D&S Antiques ★ 🎁   Some of the greatest breakthroughs in clock-making technology occurred in Vienna between 1800 and 1840. This store, established in 1979, specializes in the acquisition, sale, and repair of antique Viennese clocks, stocking an awesome collection worthy of many world-class museums. The shop even stocks a "masterpiece" (each craftsman made only one such piece in his lifetime, to accompany his bid for entrance into the clockmakers' guild)—in this case, the work of a well-known craftsman of the early 1800s, Benedict Scheisel. Don't come here expecting a bargain—prices are astronomical and devotees of timepieces from around the world flock to this emporium, treating it like a virtual museum of clocks. Dorotheergasse 13. ✆ **01/512-5885-0.** www.ds-antiques.com.

Dorotheum ★★   Dating from 1707, this is the oldest auction house in Europe. Emperor Joseph I established it so that impoverished aristocrats could fairly (and anonymously) get good value for their heirlooms. Today the Dorotheum holds regular auctions of art, antiques, jewelry, and musical instruments. If you're interested in an item, you give a small fee to a *Sensal,* or licensed bidder, and he or she bids in your name. The vast array of objects for sale includes exquisite furniture and carpets, delicate *objets d'art,* and valuable paintings, as well as decorative jewelry. If you're unable to attend an auction, you can browse the salerooms, selecting items you want to purchase directly to take home with you the same day. Approximately 31 auctions take place in July alone; over the course of a year, the Dorotheum handles some 250,000 pieces of art and antiques. Dorotheergasse 17. ✆ **01/51560-0.** www.dorotheum.at.

Flohmarkt ★   You might find a little of everything at this flea market near the Naschmarkt (see " Noshing Your Way Through Vienna's Open-Air Markets," below) and the Kettenbrückengasse U-Bahn station. It's held every Saturday from 6:30am to 6pm, except on public holidays. The Viennese have perfected the skill of haggling, and the Flohmarkt is one of their favorite arenas. It takes a trained eye to spot the antique treasures scattered among the junk. Everything you've ever wanted is here, especially if you're seeking chunky Swiss watches from the 1970s, glassware from the Czech Republic (sold as "Venetian glassware"), and even Russian icons. Believe it or not, some of this stuff is original; other merchandise is merely knockoff. Linke Wienzeile. No phone. www.flohmarkt.at.

Galerie bei der Albertina   Come here for ceramics and furniture made during the early 20th century by the iconoclastic crafts group Weiner Werkstätte. Its members made good use of the machinery of the emerging industrial age in the fabrication of domestic furnishings and decor. The inventory incorporates decorative objects, sculpture, paintings from the Jugendstil (Art Nouveau) age, etchings, an occasional drawing by Egon Schiele or Gustav Klimt. Lobkowitzplatz 1. ✆ **01/513-1416.** www.galerie-albertina.at.

Glasgalerie Kovacek   Antique glass collected from estate sales and private collections throughout Austria takes up the ground floor of this showroom around the corner form the Dorotheum. Most items date to the 19th and early 20th centuries, some to the 17th century. The most appealing pieces boast heraldic symbols, sometimes from branches of the Habsburgs. Also here is a collection of cunning glass paperweights imported from Bohemia, France, Italy, and other parts of Austria.

The upper floor holds the kind of classical paintings against which the Secessionists revolted. Look for canvases by Franz Makart, foremost of the 19th-century historic academies, as well as some Secessionist works, including two by Kokoschka. Spiegelgasse 12. 🎁 **01/512-9954.** www.kovacek.at.

Zeitloos 🎁 This pun means both timeless (*zeitlos*) and recalls the famous turn-of-the-century architect Adolf Loos whose artistic influence still shapes the industry today. This shop has more to offer than just furniture, you'll find unique statuettes, ceramics, candlesticks and enchanting lamps. The proprietor is very accommodating and is glad to organize shipping for larger items. Kirchengasse 39/Burggasse 47. 🎁 **0676/526-1956.** www.zeitloos.at.

Art

MAK Design Shop ★ The creators of the unique pieces at the MAK (Museum für angewandte Kunst) design shop are among the best up and coming Austrian and central European designers and architects. Here you'll find everything from clothing and handbags to office decor and silverware. A formable and washable breadbasket or a magnetic bird as a paperweight, India inspired scarves to a 3D picture frame. And I guarantee that no one at home will have anything like it. 9 Stubenring 5. 🎁 **01/711-36-228.** www.makdesignshop.at.

M-ARS ★ 🎁 You stroll around with a shopping cart, selecting a future Picasso, a Matisse, or perhaps a Klimt. Well, maybe we're not that lucky, but this unique supermarket is stocked with works of fine art by Austrian artists—not groceries. And you just might find for 15€ the Gustav Klimt of 2050. Only a 5-minute walk from MuseumsQuartier, the M-ARS offers more than 1,000 paintings, sculptures, and photographs, the work of some 50 artists selected by a panel of art historians and directors from Austrian museums. 9 Westbahnstrasse. 🎁 **01/890-5803.** www.m-ars.at.

Ö.W. (Österreichische Werkstatten) ★ Even if you skip every other store in Vienna, check this one out. This fascinating and well-run shop sells hundreds of handmade art and design pieces, organized by leading artists and craftspeople around the country as a cooperative to showcase their wares. The location is easy to find, only half a minute's walk from St. Stephan's Cathedral. There's an especially good selection of pewter, along with modern jewelry, glassware, brass, baskets, ceramics, and serving spoons fashioned from deer horn and bone. Take some time to wander through this cavernous three-floor outlet, also a favorite of discriminating locals. Kärntnerstrasse 6. 🎁 **01/512-2418.** www.austrianarts.com.

Books

The British Bookshop This is the largest and most comprehensive emporium of English-language books in Austria, with a sprawling ground-floor showroom loaded with American, Australian, and English books just off the Ring next to the Marriott Hotel. Especially strong in fiction (there's a good section of audio books) and language-learning materials and phrase books for teaching English as a second language. Regular readings featuring local authors and visiting writers on Vienna and the region. Weihburggasse 24-26. 🎁 **01/512-1945.** www.britishbookshop.at.

Morawa This is the well-stocked main branch of one of Austria's largest bookstore chains, with a collection of mostly German-language, and to a lesser degree English and other foreign-language books. A fine selection, including much on contemporary life and politics. Also be sure to check out the Press Centre at the back (2nd entree on Bäckerstrasse) that carries leading newspapers and magazines in many languages from all over the world. Wollzeile 11. 🎁 **01/910-76276.** www.morawa.at.

Satyr Filmwelt 📖 Described by insiders as the best-stocked bookstore on film in Europe, this is remarkable place carries everything from histories, biographies and memoirs, to screenplays, original posters and a best-of connoisseur's DVD shop. Books and films in every relevant language, including a strong section on film music, with hard-to-find books on the great Austrian film composers. Marc-Aurel-Strasse 5 (entrance Vorlaufstrasse) **✆ 01/ 535 53 26, -27 -28.** E-mail satyr.filmwelt@netway.at.

Shakespeare & Company ★★ 📖 Established in the 1980s, this is a book lovers' haven, packed from floor to the ceiling in a creaky building charmed by age. Modelled to some degree after its older namesake in Paris, this store carries well-chosen books on Vienna and Austria, plus a general selection of fiction, and non-fiction and magazines on politics, culture and world affairs. A knowledgeable staff can guide you through the fine selection of literature from Central Europe of which Vienna is still the cultural capital. Sterngasse 2. **✆ 01/535-5053.** www.shakespeare.co.at.

Candy & Desserts

Altmann & Kühne Many older Viennese fondly recall the marzipan, hazelnut, or nougat confections their parents bought for them during strolls along the Graben. Established in 1928, this cozy shop stocks virtually nothing good for your waistline or your teeth, but it's great for the soul, and undeniably scrumptious. The visual display of all things sweet is almost as appealing. The pastries and tarts filled with fresh seasonal raspberries are, quite simply, delectable. Graben 30. **✆ 01/533-0927.** www.altmann-kuehne.at.

Gerstner Gerstner competes with Café Demel (see "Coffeehouses & Cafes," chapter 5) as one of the city's great pastry makers and chocolatiers. Some of the most scrumptious cakes, petits fours, and chocolates anywhere. Kärntnerstrasse 11-15. **✆ 01/512-49630.** www.gerstner.at.

Clothing (Modern/Traditional Austrian)

Lanz A well-known Austrian store, Lanz specializes in dirndls and other folk clothing. This rustically elegant shop's stock is mostly for women, with a limited selection of men's jackets, neckties, and hats. Clothes for toddlers begin at sizes appropriate for a 1-year-old; women's apparel begins at size 36 (American size 6). Kärntnerstrasse 10. **✆ 01/512-2456.** www.lanztrachten.at.

Mary Kindermoden ☺ Here's a store specializing in children's clothing with a regional twist. In the heart of the Old Town, near St. Stephan's Cathedral, the store has two floors that stock well-made garments, including lace swaddling clothes for christenings. Most garments are for children aged 10 months to 14 years. The staff speaks English and seems to deal well with children. Graben 14. **✆ 01/214-0213.** www.mary-kindermoden.at.

Mühlbauer ★★ Since the early 1900s, the name Mühlbauer has been synonymous with quality headwear in Vienna. Today's owner, Klaus Mühlbauer, and his sister, Marlies, took over at the dawn of the millennium and have brought the company into the à la mode styling of the 21st century, when headgear isn't what it used to be. Along with the latest creations of headgear the store has begun producing a clothing line. All over the world, the fashion elite wears Mühlbauer headwear, nearly 80% of which is exported from Vienna. The flagship store is in the 1st District. 10 Seilergasse. **✆ 01/5335269.** www.muehlbauer.at.

PARK This is where the chic Viennese of today shop. The minimalist storefront encloses brand names and sought-after young designers galore. You'll find hard-to-get combos for both men and women along with accessories and fun gift items like books on fashion or photography. Mondscheingasse 20, 1070. ℂ **01/526-4414.** www.park.at.

Popp & Kretschmer   When ball season comes to Vienna the employees of Popp & Kretschmer have their hands full dressing the world's finest ball-goers in this year's trendiest or utterly timeless gowns. The employees know their products and fit each gown to Italian shoes and delectable accessories. Off-season the fashion is not as decadent, but the light-hearted attitude translates into Pucci and Cavalli bright get-ups that will have heads turning. Three floors of dresses, along with shoes, purses, belts, and a small selection of men's briefcases and travel bags await you at this boutique opposite the State Opera. Kärntnerstrasse 51. ℂ **01/512-78010.** www.popp-kretschmer.at.

Vintage Threads

If you're looking for second-hand or vintage clothing, join Vienna's youth rifling through the racks at the year-round **Naschmarkt** (U-Bahn: Karlsplatz).

Department Stores

Steffl Kaufhaus   This five-story department store is one of Vienna's most visible and well advertised. You'll find rambling racks of cosmetics, perfumes, a noteworthy section devoted to books and periodicals, housewares, and thousands of garments for men, women, and children. If you forgot to pack something for your trip, chances are very good that Steffl Kaufhaus will have it. Kärntnerstrasse 19. ℂ **01/514310.** www.kaufhaus-steffl.at.

Jewelry

A. E. Köchert ★★★   The sixth generation of the family who served as court jewelers until the end of the Habsburg Empire continues its tradition of fine workmanship here. The store, founded in 1814, occupies a 16th-century landmark building. The firm designed many of the crown jewels of Europe, but the staff gives equal attention to customers looking only at charms for a bracelet. Neuer Markt 15. ℂ **01/512-58280.** www.koechert.at.

Frey Wille   Jewelry from this famed creator combines artistic authenticity with the highest craftsmanship. Every detail is fashioned after a piece of art history inspired by art epochs or by famous artists such as Klimt or Hundertwasser. Although there are shops all over the world, the pieces are only produced in Vienna and make a classy gift or souvenir. Stephansplatz 5. ℂ **01/513-4892.** www.frey-wille.com.

Swarovski   In Vienna, crystals are a girl's best friend. Most any self-respecting Viennese lady has a pair of Swarovski earrings, a necklace, or bracelet. Some even cover their iPods or phones in Swarovski crystals. Not only can you find the figurines of this famed enterprise all over the globe, the shop has something for everyone. From watches, belts, and crystal-covered rings to the masses of decorations, chandeliers, and collectables. The store is usually a hub of activity, and even if you don't buy anything, the sparkling display windows on Kärntnerstrasse are worth a look. Kärntnerstrasse 8. ℂ **01/512-9032-33.** www.swarovski.at.

Lace & Needlework

Zur Schwäbischen Jungfrau ★★★   This is one of the most illustrious shops in Austria, with a reputation that goes back almost 300 years. Here, Maria Theresa bought her first handkerchiefs, and thousands of debutantes have shopped here for

NOSHING YOUR WAY THROUGH VIENNA'S open-air MARKETS

Viennese merchants have thrived since the Middle Ages by hauling produce, dairy products, and meats in bulk from the fertile farms of Lower Austria and Burgenland into the city center. The tradition of buying the day's provisions directly from street stalls is so strong that, even today, it's tough for modern supermarkets to survive within the city center.

Odd (and inconvenient) as this might seem, you'll quickly grasp the fun of Vienna's open-air food stalls after a brief wander through one of these outdoor markets. Most of the hundreds of merchants operating within them maintain approximately the same hours: Monday through Friday from 8am to 6pm and Saturday from 8am to noon.

The largest is the **Naschmarkt**, Wienzeile, in the 6th District (U-Bahn:

Karlsplatz), just south of the Ring. Because of its size, it's the most evocatively seedy and colorful of the bunch, as well as being the most firmly rooted in the life of the city.

Less comprehensive are the **Rochusmarkt**, at Landstrasser Hauptstrasse at the corner of the Erdbergstrasse, 3rd District (U-Bahn: Rochusgasse), a short distance east of the Ring, and the **Brunnenmarkt**, on the Brunnengasse, 16th District (U-Bahn: Josefstädterstrasse), a short walk north of the Westbahnhof. Even if you don't plan on stocking up on produce and foodstuff (the staff at your hotel might not be amused if you showed up with bushels of carrots or potatoes), the experience is colorful enough and, in some cases, kitschy enough, to be remembered as one of the highlights of your trip to Vienna.

dresses. Come here for towels, bed linens, lace tablecloths, and some of the most elaborate needlepoint and embroidery anywhere. Service is impeccable, courtly, and cordial. Graben 26. © **01/535-5356.** www.schwaebische-jungfrau.at.

Music

Arcadia Opera Shop   This respected record store is one of the best for classical music. The well-educated staff knows the music and performers (as well as the availability of recordings), and is usually eager to share that knowledge. The shop also carries books on art, music, architecture, and opera, as well as an assortment of musical memorabilia. The shop is on the street level of the Vienna State Opera, with a separate entrance on Kärntnerstrasse. Guided tours of the splendid opera house end here. Wiener Staatsoper, Kärntnerstrasse 40. © **01/513-95680.** www.arcadia.at.

Da Caruso   Almost adjacent to the Vienna State Opera, this store is known to music fans and musicologists worldwide. Its inventory includes rare and unusual recordings of historic performances by the Vienna Opera and the Vienna Philharmonic. If you're looking for a magical or particularly emotional performance by Maria Callas, Herbert von Karajan, or Bruno Walter, chances are you can get it here, digitalized on CD. There's also a collection of taped films. The staff is hip, alert, and obviously in love with music. Operngasse 4. © **01/513-1326.** www.dacaruso.at.

Porcelain

Albin Denk ★★   The the oldest continuously operating porcelain store in Vienna (since 1702), Albin Denk's clients have included Empress Elisabeth, and the shop you see today looks almost the same as it did when she visited. The three low-ceilinged rooms are beautifully decorated with thousands of objects from Meissen, Dresden, and other regions. Graben 13. ✆ **01/512-44390.** www.albindenk.24on.cc.

Augarten Porzellan ★★ The history of one of the oldest porcelain manufacturers in Europe goes back almost 300 years. Exquisitely crafted, Vienna porcelain is famous for its delicate and graceful shape and the purity of its lines. Augarten blends time-honored tradition with contemporary art. Here, every step of production—from mixing the paste to the finishing touches—is carried out by hand. The manufacturer and shop may be a little out of the way, but the trip is worth it. You can watch the master craftsmen at work and also see the former hunting lodge of Kaiser Franz Joseph, surrounded by the beautiful Augarten park, and the Augarten Palace, home of the Vienna Choir Boys. Stock-im-Eisenplatz 3-4. ✆ **01/512-14940.** www.augarten.at.

Shopping Center

The Ringstrassen-Gallerien Rental fees for shop space in central Vienna are legendarily expensive. In response to the high rents, about 70 boutiques selling everything from hosiery to key chains to evening wear have pooled their resources and moved to labyrinthine quarters near the Staatsoper, midway between the Bristol and Anna hotels. Its prominent location guarantees a certain glamour, although the cramped dimensions of many of the stores might be a turn-off. The selection is broad, and no one can deny the gallery's easy-to-find location. Each shop is operated independently, but virtually all of them conduct business Monday to Friday 10am to 7pm and Saturday 10am to 6pm. In the Palais Corso and in the Kärntnerringhof, Kärntner Ring 5–13. ✆ **01/512518111.** U-Bahn: Karlsplatz.

Toys

Kober ★ ☺ Kober has been a household name, especially at Christmastime in Vienna, for more than 100 years. It carries old-fashioned wood toys, teddy bears straight out of a Styrian storybook, go-karts (assembly required), building sets, and car and airplane models. The occasional set of toy soldiers is more *Nutcracker Suite* than G.I. Joe. Graben 14-15. ✆ **01/533-60180.** www.kobertoys.com.

Vinegars & Oils

Gegenbauer ★★ 👜 It's true you don't have to go to Vienna to purchase more than 50 artisan vinegars and about 20 specialty oils from this unique store, as you can do so on the Internet or through such distributors as Dean & DeLuca. Running a family business—going since 1929—Erwin Gegenbauer may be the world's expert on vinegar. Ever had vinegar made from tomatoes? At this store you can purchase such, but also bottles of vinegar made from elderberry, asparagus, lemongrass, sour cherry, cucumber, and even beer. Rare oils come from fruit kernels, wine grapes, or other ingredients. Gegenbauer 14, Naschmarkt. ✆ **01/6041088.** www.gegenbauer.at.

VAT Refunds

Fortunately for non-EU visitors to Austria, the country's Value-Added Tax (*Mehrwertsteuer (MwSt)*, or VAT), which can be as high as 34% on some luxury goods, is refundable. See "Taxes" in chapter 16.

Wine

Wein & Co Since the colonization of Vindobona by the ancient Romans, the Viennese have always taken their wines seriously. Wein & Co is Vienna's largest wine outlet, a sprawling cellar-level ode to the joys of the grape and the bounty of Bacchus. You'll also find wines from around the world, including South Africa and Chile. Jasomirgottstrasse 3-5. ℂ **01/535-0916.** www.weinco.at.

VIENNA AFTER DARK

Whatever nightlife scene turns you on, Vienna has a little bit of it. You can dance into the morning hours, hear a concert, attend an opera or festival, go to the theater, gamble, or simply sit and talk over a drink at a local tavern.

The best source of information about what's happening on the cultural scene is *Wien Monatsprogramm,* which is distributed free at tourist information offices and at many hotel reception desks. *Die Presse,* the Viennese daily, publishes a special magazine in its Thursday edition outlining the major cultural events for the coming week. It's in German but might still be helpful to you.

The Viennese are not known for discounting their cultural presentations. However, *Wien Monatsprogramm* lists outlets where you can purchase tickets in advance, thereby cutting down the surcharge imposed by travel agencies. These agencies routinely add about 22% to what might already be an expensive ticket.

If you're not a student and don't want to go bankrupt to see a performance at the Staatsoper or the Burgtheater, you can purchase standing-room tickets at a cost of about 5€.

Students under 27 with valid IDs are eligible for many discounts. For example, the Burgtheater, Akademietheater, and Staatsoper sell student tickets for just 10€ on the night of the performance. Theaters almost routinely grant students about 20% off the regular ticket price. Vienna is the home of four major symphony orchestras, including the Vienna Symphony and the Vienna Philharmonic. In addition to the ÖRF Symphony Orchestra and the Niederöster-reichische Tonkünstler, there are literally dozens of others, ranging from smaller orchestras to chamber orchestras.

The Performing Arts

At 6pm, the Viennese close the office door behind them and head off into the evening. There's no time to waste! A light meal and then it's off to the theater or a concert, doll up for the opera or a festival, or dance into the wee hours; you can try your luck at roulette, or simply sit and talk over a drink at a local *Beisl.*

While the Viennese love their time-honored culture, that's far from the whole story. So take a look around; whatever you like to do, you can probably find it somewhere in this dynamic city. And like the local's favorite coffee, you can make your own "Wiener Melange."

In general the Viennese are avid partygoers; age, interests, and occupation alone play a role in choosing the venue. This selection of nightspots should give you a good foundation to chase the dawn in whichever way you enjoy most. Below we describe just a few of the highlights—if you're in Vienna long enough, you'll find many other diversions on your own.

AUSTRIAN STATE THEATERS & OPERA HOUSES

Reservations and information for the four state theaters—the Wiener Staatsoper (Vienna State Opera), Volksoper, Burgtheater (National Theater), and Akademietheater—can be obtained by contacting **Österreichische Bundestheater (Austrian Federal Theaters),** the office that coordinates reservations and information for all four theaters (✆ **01/514442959**; www.bundestheater.at). Call Monday through Friday from 8am to 5pm. *Note:* The number is likely to be busy; it's easier to get information and order tickets online. The major season is September through June, with more limited presentations in summer. Many tickets are issued to subscribers before the box office opens. For all four theaters, box-office sales are made only 1 month before each performance at the Bundestheaterkasse, Goethegasse 1 (✆ **01/514440**), open Monday to Friday 8am to 6pm, Saturday 9am to 2pm, and Sunday and holidays 9am to noon. Credit and charge card sales can be arranged by telephone within 6 days of a performance by calling ✆ **01/5131513** Monday through Friday from 10am to 6pm, and Saturday and Sunday from 10am to noon. Tickets for all state theater performances, including the opera, are also available by writing to the Österreichischer Bundestheaterverband, Goethegasse 1, A-1010 Vienna, from points outside Vienna. Orders must be received at least 3 weeks in advance of the performance to be booked. No one should send money through the mail. For more information on tickets, go to the websites of the venues listed below.

Note: The single most oft-repeated complaint of music lovers in Vienna is about the lack of available tickets to many highly desirable musical performances. If the suggestions above don't produce the desired tickets, you could consult a ticket broker. Their surcharge usually won't exceed 25%, except for exceptionally rare tickets, when that surcharge might be doubled or tripled. Although at least half a dozen ticket agencies maintain offices in the city, one of the most reputable agencies is **Liener Brünn** (✆ **01/5330961**), which might make tickets available months in advance or as little as a few hours before the anticipated event.

As a final resort, remember that the concierges of virtually every upscale hotel in Vienna long ago learned sophisticated tricks for acquiring hard-to-come-by tickets. (A gratuity of at least 10€ might work wonders and will be expected anyway for the phoning this task will entail. You'll pay a hefty surcharge as well.)

Akademietheater This theater specializes in both classic and contemporary works, from Brecht to Shakespeare. The Burgtheater Company often performs here, as it's the second, smaller house of this world-famous theater (see below). Lisztstrasse 3. ✆ **01/514444740.** www.burgtheater.at. Tickets 4€–48€ for seats, 1.50€ for standing room. U-Bahn: Stadtpark.

Burgtheater (National Theater) The Burgtheater produces classical and modern plays in German, universally accepted as the leading stage in the German-speaking world. Work started on the original structure in 1776; it moved to the Ring in 1857, was badly damaged in World War II, and reopened in 1955. Among its permanent company today are Oscar winners Klaus Maria Brandauer (*Mephisto, Out of Africa*) and Christoph Waltz (*Inglourious Basterds*), and Sonke Workmann (*Pope Joan*). Dr.-Karl-Lueger-Ring 2. ✆ **01/5144-4140.** www.burgtheater.at. Tickets 5€–48€ for seats, 1.50€ for standing room. Tram: 1, 2, or D to Burgtheater.

Volksoper This folk opera house presents lavish productions of Viennese operettas and other musicals September through June on a daily schedule. Tickets go on sale at the Volksoper itself 1 hour before the performance. Währingerstrasse 78. ✆ **01/514-443670.** www.volksoper.at. Tickets 7€–150€ for seats, 2.50€–4€ for standing room. U-Bahn: Volksoper.

Wiener Staatsoper ★★★ This is one of the three most important opera houses in the world. With the Vienna Philharmonic in the pit, some of the leading opera stars of the world perform here. In their day, Richard Strauss and Gustav Mahler worked as directors. Daily performances are given September through June. (For information on tours, see "Other Top Attractions.") Opernring 2. ✆ **9/51444-42960.** www.staatsoper.at. Tickets 10€–220€. U-Bahn: Karlsplatz.

MORE THEATER & MUSIC

Performing arts and especially music is at the heart of Vienna's cultural life. This has been true for centuries, and the city continues to lure composers, librettists, musicians, and music lovers. You can find places to enjoy everything from orchestras, chamber music and pop, to jazz, gypsy music, alternative, electro and anything else in between. You'll find small discos and large concert halls, as well as musical theaters, cabaret, clubs, and piano bars. If you tire of listening, you'll find no shortage of theater, from classical to avant-garde. Below we describe just a few of the better-known spots for cultural diversion; if you're in Vienna long enough, you'll find many others on your own.

English Lovers This group of charmers does improvizational theater every second Friday night at 10:30pm. The "Late Night Theater Jam" begins with asking the audience for a theme and characters from which they create a drama. The troupe is very gifted and is a joy to watch. If you have a good grasp of German you can see them *auf Deutsch* on the Fridays in between. Theater Drachengasse 26. Fleischmarkt 22. ✆ **01/513-1444.** www.english-lovers.at. Tickets 16€, 10€ for students. U-Bahn: Schwedenplatz.

International Theatre & The Fundus First a touring company, the International Theatre found a permanent home in 1980, continuing as a repertory company of a dozen actors who put on six to eight productions a season from the leading playwrights of British and American theater, from Noel Coward and Eugene ONeill to Lillian Hellman and Woody Allen. Their annual production of *A Christmas Carol* has become a Vienna institution. The theater's season runs September through May. Box office is open Monday to Saturday 10am to 7:30pm. Porzellangasse 8. ✆ **01/319-6272.** www.internationaltheatre.at. Tickets 20€–25€, 15 € students and seniors. Tram: D Schlickplatz.

Theater in der Josefstadt One of the most influential theaters in the German-speaking world, this institution reached legendary heights under the aegis of Max Reinhardt beginning in 1924. Built in 1776, it presents a variety of comedies and dramas. The current actor/director Helmut Lohner is also credited with leading the theater through another era of consistent excellence. Box office is open daily 10am to

---

A Note on Evening Dress

People like to dress in Vienna, a change from the informality of North America or some parts of Europe. Not only do locals don evening clothes for concerts and theater visits, they also get quite dolled up to go clubbing. No clubs require jackets or eveningwear, but you won't be let in if you don't put look together. For especially festive occasions—such as opera premieres, receptions, and balls—tails or dinner jackets and evening dresses are *de rigeur*. And while few will force the issue, it's best not to reek "tourist" in jeans and flip-flops. If you want to dress up and didn't bring the right clothes, you can rent evening wear (as well as carnival costumes) from several places. Consult your hotel concierge or the telephone classified section under "Kleiderleihanstalten," also available online at www.herold.at. It's a good idea to take a light coat when you go out in the evening, even in summer.

7:30pm. Josefstädterstrasse 26. ℭ **01/42700.** www.josefstadt.org. Tickets 3€–65€. U-Bahn: Rathaus. Tram: J. Bus: 13A.

Vienna's English Theatre This popular English-speaking theater was established in 1963. Many international actors and celebrities from Joan Fontaine, Anthony Quinn, and Princess Grace of Monaco, to Siobhan McKenna and Judi Dench have appeared on the neo-baroque boutique stage. The seasons are a mix of comedy and drama, classics and premiers, that in recent years have included Yazmina Reza's *Art,* winner of the Prix Molière, and the Austrian premiere of *Old Wicked Songs.* Box office is open Monday to Friday 10am to 7:30pm. Josefsgasse 12. ℭ **01/402- 1260-0.** www.englishtheatre.at. Tickets 20€–38€. U-Bahn: Rathaus. Tram: J. Bus: 13A.

Volkstheater Built in 1889, this theater presents classical works of European theater. Modern plays and comedies are also presented. The theater's season runs September through May. Box office is open Monday to Saturday 10am to 7:30pm. Neustiftgasse 1. ℭ **01/521-110.** www.volkstheater.at. Tickets 8€–40€. U-Bahn: Volkstheater. Tram: 1, 2, 49, D, or J. Bus: 48A.

The Club & Music Scene
NIGHTCLUBS

Aux Gazelles This place is a multi-tasker. A Turkish spa and restaurant by day, the flair of these rooms literally downstairs from the Maria Hilferstrasse is unequalled. One loud room with a dance floor is balanced by a number of side areas with lots of cushions, with Turkish lamps and alcoves for a more intimate atmosphere, and a long bar area with tables in front. Despite the foreign theme and decor, the place has become a staple of Viennese nightlife—perhaps the only place in Vienna where the Turks laid siege and succeeded! Rahlgasse 5. ℭ **01/5856645.** www.auxgazelles.at. Cover varies. U-Bahn: MuseumsQuartier.

Belmar (Havana Club) Many a twitchy behind has been set in motion by the legendary Latinpop at this watering hole. "La Vida" takes the form of everything from merengue to hip-hop. On select evenings a "professional" dancer will give salsa lessons in a very laid-back fashion, with Caipirinha in hand. The club is located a minute's walk from the Opera House behind the Ringstrassengalerien. Open nightly 7pm to 4am. Depending on the night, you might be hit with a cover charge. Otherwise, cocktails start at 8.90€. Mahlerstrasse 11. ℭ **01/5132075.** www.clubhavana.at. Cover varies. U-Bahn: Karlsplatz.

Café Leopold No one ever expected that the city's homage to Viennese expressionism (the Leopold Museum) would ever pulsate with the echo of dancing feet and high-energy music. But that's exactly what happens here every night but Sunday. The museum's restaurant fills up with drinkers, wits, gossips, dancers, and people of all ilk on the make. There's a revolving cycle of DJs, each vying for local fame and approval, and a wide selection of cocktails, priced at around 10€ each. The cafe/ restaurant section is open Sunday to Wednesday 10am to 2pm, Friday and Saturday 10am to 4pm. The disco operates only Thursday to Saturday 9:30pm till between 2 and 3am, depending on business. In the Leopold Museum, Museumsplatz 1. ℭ **01/523-67-32.** www.cafe-leopold.at. U-Bahn: Volkstheater or /MuseumsQuartier.

Chelsea ★ This is the city's hottest venue for underground music. From all over the continent, the best bands and DJs are imported to entertain the gyrating throngs who gather here in a sort of rock and pop atmosphere. The pulsating club lies in one of the arches of the old railway train tracks that divide the north of the city from the historic core. Open Monday to Thursday 6pm to 4am, Friday and Saturday 6pm to 5am, and Sunday 4pm to 3am. Lerchenfelder-Gürtel (Stadtbahnbögen 29–31). ℂ **01/407-93-09.** www.chelsea.co.at. Cover 6€–12€. U-Bahn: Josefstädterstrasse/Thaliastrasse.

Klub Kinsky ★   This gem of a location just reopened and is all about quality rather than quantity. The rooms inhabited by this classy establishment are in the Palais Kinsky, between the Graben and Schottentor. The renovation has yielded state-of-the-art technology, Italian designer furniture; in short, a private and elegant ambiance with great service. The vibes are great as the bass reverberates through the archways of this baroque palace. In Palais Kinsky, Freyung 4. ℂ **01/5353435.** www.palaisklub.at.at. Cover varies. U-Bahn: Schottentor.

Passage ★   This club has been a raging success ever since it opened its catacombs to the public in 2003. At the point where "The Ring" joins Mariahilferstrasse, literally underneath the Ringstrasse, this hot spot has a reputation for having a strict door policy—so no sneakers for gents and snazzy party attire a must for the ladies. The lighting concept is inspired and the layout of the space lets different moods all weld together in one open space, broken up only by lounge sofas and cocktail bars. Just watch your bag. This is a night spot that seems to attract sticky fingers. Even in Vienna, there are a few. Open Tuesday to Saturday 10pm to 6am. Ringstrasse at Babenbergerstrasse. ℂ **01/9618800.** www.sunshine.at. Cover 13€. U-Bahn: MuseumsQuartier.

ROCK, SALSA, JAZZ & BLUES

Jazzland ★   This is one of the oldest and probably the most famous jazz club in Austria, noted for the quality of its U.S. and central European-based performers. It's in a deep 200-year-old cellar below the Ruprechtskirche, unheard on the street. Platters of classic Viennese Beisl food, like Wiener schnitzel or spicy *cevacici* meat paddies and roulades of beef cost 5€ to 10€. Open Monday to Saturday 7:30pm to 1:30am. Music is from 9pm to 1am, in three sets. No reservations, so best to arrive by 8pm or before. Franz-Josefs-Kai 29. ℂ **01/533-2575.** www.jazzland.at. Cover 11€–18€. U-Bahn: Schwedenplatz.

Porgy & Bess ★   Its name may suggest George Gershwin's great all-black classic musical back in the States, but in Vienna this is actually the best jazz club in town. Its array of performers from Europe and around the world is absolutely first class. Established in 1993, the club became an instant hit and has been going strong ever since, patronized by Vienna's most avid jazz aficionados. The club opens Monday to Saturday at 7pm and Sunday at 8pm; closing times vary, often 3am or 4am. Riembergasse 11. ℂ **01/5128811.** www.porgy.at. U-Bahn: Stubentor. Tram: 1A to Riemerg.

Reigen ★   This Jugendstil-themed venue has been a highlight of the live music scene for 10 years, but is a little out of the way. In Hietzing, almost at Schönbrunn, this downstairs location is a must for jazz lovers. On "Session Nights" a concert is followed by an open-ended jam session, or on Saturdays you can practice your salsa moves at the Latin Club. Hadikgasse 62. ℂ **01/8940094.** www.reigen.at. U-Bahn: Hietzing.

Tunnel   Experiences like the ones created in the 1960s and 1970s by Jimi Hendrix are alive and well, if in less dramatic form, at Tunnel. In a smoke-filled cellar near Town Hall, it showcases musical groups from virtually everywhere. You'll never know quite what to expect, as the only hint of what's on or off is a recorded German-language announcement of what's about to appear and occasional advertisements in local newspapers. It's open daily 9pm to 2am, with live music beginning around 10pm. Florianigasse 39. ℂ **01/405-3465.** www.tunnel-vienna-live.at. Cover 3€–15€. U-Bahn: Rathaus.

DANCE CLUBS

Camera Club 🎁 This joint is as infamous as studio 54 when it comes to urban legend. Open since 1971, this place is cult. The sound system is very powerful and exudes house, deep house, minimal, electro, techno, drumn'n'base, on multiple levels and on two separate floors. The club is not new and although it was recently renovated not much was invested in the decor. The place is not chic, but oh, so trendy. Don't miss the craziest night of the week when "Heaven" takes over on Saturdays, letting Vienna's gay crowd rule the dance floor. Neubaugasse 2. ✆ **01/523-323063.** www. camera-club.at. Cover 10€. U-Bahn: Neubaugasse.

Flex ★ No other dance club in Vienna has a history as long, as notorious, and as "flexible" as this one. This industrial-looking venue is set between the edge of the canal and the subway tracks. With exterior graffiti that is redone every year mostly by locals, and both an indoor and outdoor chill area, it's a prime venue for post-millennium fans of electronic music. Inside, you'll find a beer-soaked, congenially battered venue. It's where the young and the restless (some of them teenagers) of Vienna go for access to music that's the rage, and the rave, in places such as Berlin, London, NYC, and Los Angeles. The cafe is open from 6pm onwards and the club from 9pm–open end. Am Donaukanal. ✆ **01/533-7525.** Cover 10€. U-Bahn: Schottenring.

Praterdome 🖐 At the entrance to the Prater amusement park, this new addition to the club scene is overwhelming—which may or may not be good. When you arrive you are given a card on which you credit your drink and pay when you leave. On the eight different floors you'll find a techno dance floor with a very impressive light show, also "house" and "soul." There is an outdoor chill area in summer months and parts of the club are theme inspired, like the castle corner or ski lodge bar. The club is very impressive, but not worth the instigated teenage bar fights and spilled long drinks that seem to be the inevitable outcome of an evening here. Am Riesenradplatz 7. ✆ **01/9081192900.** www.praterdome.at. Cover 10€. U-Bahn: Praterstern.

Pratersauna ★ As the name suggests, this location used to be a fitness club and sauna and, although the pool remains, the patrons are not there for their health. The self-dubbed "social life and art space" is the new vintage. Many complain about the inconsistent door policy, but all in all, the place is a big hit, especially for the art and fashion crowd. In the Prater. ✆ **01/729-1927.** www.pratersaunau.tv. Cover 10€–15€. U-Bahn: Messe Prater. Tram: 1 Prater Hauptalle.

U4 ★ This is one of the most famous nightclubs in Vienna, with a history going back 30 years, and a gift for reinventing itself with each new generation of night owls. Its name has even surfaced in songs by rockers throughout Europe and the world; the high-profile roster has included Kurt Cobain and David Bowie, among many others. Set on the city's western edge, it offers two floors, and a total of three fast-moving bars. There are often live acts on Mondays, and Fridays are "Addicted to Rock." Tuesday and Thursday nights are the most youth-oriented (that is, the late teen end of 20-something). A somewhat more mature crowd (20 and emotionally available 30-year-olds) is there on Saturday, when disco fever takes over for "Behave." U4 is open nightly from 10pm till around 5am, depending on demand, and closed every Sunday between June and September. Schönbrunner Strasse 222. ✆ **01/817-1192.** www.U-4.at. Cover charge 8€–11€. U-Bahn: Meidlinger Hauptstrasse.

Volksgarten Disco A favorite since the 1950s, this disco has stayed abreast of the times, offering everything today from hip-hop, to house and break-beat remixes of current hits. There is a great vibe on the dance floor and in the warm months you can step into the garden area behind the DJ where an enormous swirling bar leads you straight to a pool and lounge chairs. Also, the summer-only Volksgarten Pavillon, next door, is a garden bar and a great place to finish off a hot summer day (see "Only in Vienna," below). Friday and Saturday are the most popular nights, although the club is open Tuesday to Saturday 10pm to 5am. Inside the Ring at Volksgarten. ✆ **01/5330518.** www.volksgarten.at. Cover charge 5€–15€. U-Bahn: Volkstheater.

The Bar Scene

Vienna's bar scene clusters at the **Bermuda Triangle,** an area roughly bordered by Judengasse, Seitenstettengasse Rabensteig, and Franz-Josefs-Kai. You'll find everything from intimate watering holes to large bars with live music, a sample of which we list below. The closest U-Bahn stop is Schwedenplatz. But there are others.

Barfly's Club ★ ▮▮ This is the most urbane and sophisticated cocktail bar in town, frequented by journalists, actors, and politicians. It's got a laissez-faire ambience that combines aspects of Vienna's *grande bourgeoisie* with its discreet avant-garde. A menu lists about 370 cocktails that include every kind of mixed drink imaginable. The only food served is "toast" (grilled sandwiches). It's open daily 6pm to between 2 and 4am, depending on the night of the week. In the Hotel Fürst Metternich, Esterházygasse 33. ✆ **01/586-0825.** http://barflys.at. U-Bahn: Kirchengasse. Tram: 5.

Bar Italia The fashion and society crowd flocks here after dark to sip on cocktails, wine, or beer and look good. The intimate atmosphere of the place is part of what makes it popular, as eavesdropping is made easy. Even if you don't speak German, there is plenty to see and stylish snacks are available for small appetites. Mariahilfer-strasse 19–21. ✆ **01/585-2838.** www.baritalia.net. U-Bahn: MuseumsQuartier. Tram: 5.

First Floor ▮▮ At the bottom of the hill leading to the aforementioned Bermuda Triangle, an unassuming doorway leads you—you guessed it—to the first floor, where dimmed lighting and a fishless aquarium with swaying sea grass sets the backdrop for one of the best bars in the city. Over 200 cocktails are served by very competent but unobtrusive staff to a mixture of jazz and blues. Great place for a tête à tête or one for the road. Rabensteig 8. ✆ **01/533-8193.** www.krah-krah.at. U-Bahn: Schwedenplatz.

Krah Krah This place is the most animated and well-known beer joint in the area. An attractive, and sometimes available, after-work crowd fills this woodsy, somewhat battered space. Malt liquor is the drink of choice here, with more than 60 kinds available. Sandwiches, snacks, and simple platters, including hefty portions of Wiener schnitzel, start at 8.50€. It's open daily 11am to 2am, often with live music. Rabensteig 8. ✆ **01/533-8193.** www.krah-krah.at. U-Bahn: Schwedenplatz.

Loos American Bar ★ ▮▮ One of the most unusual and interesting bars in Vienna, this very dark, sometimes mysterious bar was designed by the noteworthy architect Adolf Loos in 1908. At the time, it was the drinking room of a private men's club. Today, it's more democratic and welcomes a mostly bilingual crowd of hip singles from Vienna's arts-and-media scene; and in these cramped quarters you can't help making new acquaintances. Walls, floors, and ceilings sport layers of dark marble and black onyx, making this one of the most expensive small-scale decors in the city. No food is served, but the mixologist's specialties include six kinds of martinis, plus five kinds of Manhattans, each 10€. Beer starts at 2.60€. It's open daily noon to 4am. Kärntnerdurchgang 10. ✆ **01/512-3283.** U-Bahn: Stephansplatz.

Onyx Bar One of the most visible and best known, though crowded, bars on Stephansplatz is on the sixth (next-to-uppermost) floor of one of Vienna's most controversial buildings—Haas Haus. Lunch is served from noon to 3pm daily; dinner is served from 6pm to midnight. The staff serves a long and varied cocktail menu from 6pm to 2am, including strawberry margaritas and caipirinhas, each priced from 10€ to 15€. Live or recorded music usually begins after 8:30pm. In the Haas Haus, Stephansplatz 12. ℂ **01/53539690.** U-Bahn: Stephansplatz.

Rhiz Bar Modern ★ Hip, multicultural, and electronically sophisticated this bar is nestled into the vaulted, century-old niches created by the trusses of the U6 subway line, a few blocks west of the Ring. Drinks include Austrian wine, Scottish whiskey, and beer from everywhere in Europe. It's open Monday to Saturday 6pm to 4am and Sunday 6pm to 2am. Llerchenfeldergürtel 37–38, Stadtbahnbögen. ℂ **01/409-2505.** www.rhiz.org. U-Bahn: Josefstädterstrasse.

Schikaneder If you're young and hot, and you want to meet locals who share those same traits, come here. Through the door past the sofa chairs, the bar atmosphere blends with cinema feeling at a 10m-long (33-ft.) bar counter. There's plenty of conversation, good drinks, and sympathetic company. You can also order various wines by the glass. The bar starts filling up by 9:30pm and by midnight it's packed, often with university students. Don't dare tell anyone in this hip crowd you're a tourist. Open daily 6pm to 4am. Margaretenstrasse 22–24. ℂ **01/5855888.** www.schikaneder.at. U-Bahn: Margaretengürtel.

Sky Bar ★ Local hipsters ridicule this place as a posh see-and-be-seen venue for Vienna's social striving *nouveaux riches*. We think the place is well designed and, under the right circumstances, can be a lot of fun, particularly when we remind ourselves that the Steffl building was erected on the site of the (long-ago demolished) house where Mozart died. Take an elevator to the top floor of the building for a sweeping view over the city. Open Monday to Saturday 6pm to 2am. Kärntnerstrasse 19. ℂ **01/513-1712.** www.skybar.at. U-Bahn: Karlsplatz.

Weinquartier ★★ Anyone who thought drinking wine in Vienna means accordion players and dirndl-clad servers has a surprise in store. This newly opened establishment is Vienna's embassy for the *Weinviertel*. Subdued lighting, chic waiters, and slightly kitschy black and whites of the vineyards whose wares you're sampling somehow fit with the location between the Opera and the Albertina. Not over-priced, although you'd gladly pay more. Hanuschgasse 3. ℂ **01/513-43-19.** www.weinquartier.at. U-Bahn: Karlsplatz.

The Wine Bar at Julius Meinl Part of its allure derives from its role as a showcase for the wine-buying savvy of Vienna's most comprehensive delicatessen (Julius Meinl) and wine shop. It's small and cozy, set in the cellar of a food shop that leaves most gourmets salivating, and accessible through a separate entrance that's open long after the delicatessen has closed. Its decor evokes the interior of a farmhouse on, say, the Austro-Italian border. You'll be amply satisfied with the dozens of wines listed on the blackboard or on the menu; but if there's a particular bottle you're hankering for in the stacks of wine within the street-level deli, a staff member will sell it to you and uncork it at a surcharge of only 10% more than what you'd have paid for it retail. Open Monday to Saturday 11am to midnight. Graben 19. ℂ **01/532-3334-6100.** www.meinlamgraben.at. U-Bahn: Stephansplatz.

Gay & Lesbian Bars

Alfi's Goldener Spiegel The most enduring gay restaurant in Vienna (p. 141) is also its most popular gay bar, attracting mostly male clients to its position near

Vienna's Naschmarkt. You don't need to come here to dine, but you can patronize the bar, where almost any gay male from abroad drops in for a look-see. The place is very cruisy, and the bar is open Wednesday to Monday 7pm to 2am. Linke Wienzeile 46. © **01/586-6608.** U-Bahn: Kettenbruckengasse.

Café Berg ★   This stylish establishment is known for hosting wild events, such as fashion shows and before and after parties surrounding the annual Life Ball AIDS gala. For 18 years it's been a staple of gay, lesbian, and transgender life in Vienna. Most notably it serves a great breakfast. Berggasse 8. © **01/3195720.** www.café-berg.at. U-Bahn: Kettenbruckengasse.

Café Savoy   Soaring frescoed ceilings and a smoke-stained beaux-arts decor make this cruisy cafe/bar an appealing setting. The clientele are mostly men and the mood is always jovial; no loud music, just a pleasant atmosphere and echoes of laughter and conversation. Open Monday to Friday 5pm to 2am, Saturday 9am to 2am. Linke Wienzeile 36. © **01/586-7348.** U-Bahn: Kettenbruckengasse.

Eagle Bar   This is one of the premier leather and denim bars for gay men in Vienna. There's no dancing, and the bar even offers a back room where free condoms are distributed. It's open daily 9pm to 4am. Blümelgasse 1. © **01/587-26-61.** www.eagle-vienna.com. U-Bahn: Neubaugasse.

Felixx ★   It's the classiest gay bar and cafe in town, thanks to a refurbishment. The decor emphasizes turn-of-the-20th-century cove moldings, a crystal chandelier that could proudly grace any Opera Ball, and a huge late-19th-century portrait of the female cabaret entertainer, Mela Mars, who introduced *lieder* (Austrian *chansons*) for the first time to a generation of wine- and coffee-drinkers. Ironically, the venue is less kitschy than you'd think, managing to pull off a lasting impression of elegance and good taste. On Saturday and Sunday breakfast is served here from 10am to 4pm. Open daily 7pm to 3am. Gumpendorferstrasse 5. © **01/920-4714.** U-Bahn: Babenbergerstrasse or MuseumsQuartier.

Frauencafé   Frauencafé is exactly what its name implies: A politically conscious cafe for women, lesbian, or otherwise, who appreciate the company of other women. Established in 1977 in a century-old building, it's filled with magazines, newspapers, modern paintings, and a clientele of Austrian and international women. Next door is a feminist bookstore loosely affiliated with the cafe. Frauencafé is open Tuesday to Saturday 6:30pm to 2am. Glasses of wine begin at 2.50€. Langegasse 11. © **01/4063754.** U-Bahn: Lerchenfelderstrasse.

Heuriger

These *Heuriger,* or wine taverns, on the outskirts of Vienna have long been celebrated in operetta, film, and song. Grinzing and Nussdorf are probably the most visited, but there are many other *Heuriger* neighborhoods including Sievering, Neustift am Walde, Stammersdorf, and Heiligenstadt, for a start.

Grinzing lies at the edge of the Vienna Woods, a short distance northwest of the center. Much of Grinzing looks the way it did when Beethoven lived nearby. It's a district of crooked old streets and houses, with thick walls surrounding inner court-yards where grape arbors shelter wine drinkers. The sound of zithers and accordions lasts long into the summer night. If you're a motorist, don't drive to the *Heuriger.* Police patrols are very strict, and you may not drive with more than 0.8% alcohol in your bloodstream. It's much better to take public transportation. Most *Heurigen* are within 30 to 40 minutes of downtown, an easy tram ride away. So start at Schottentor, and take tram no. 38 to Grinzing, no. 41 to Neustift, or no. 38 to Sievering (which is also accessible by bus no. 39A). Heiligenstadt is the last stop on U-Bahn line U4.

Der Rudolfshof ★   One of the most appealing wine restaurants in Grinzing dates back to 1848, when it was little more than a shack within a garden. Its real fame came around the turn of the 20th century, when it was adopted by the Crown Prince Rudolf. A verdant garden, scattered with tables, is favored by Viennese apartment dwellers on warm summer evenings. Come here for pitchers of the fruity white wine *grüner Veltliner* and light red *roter Bok*. Glasses of wine cost 3€ to 5€. The menu lists schnitzels, roasts, and soups, but the house specialty is shish kabob. The salad bar is very fresh. Main courses cost 10€ to 13€. Open daily 3 to 11pm. Cobenzlgasse 8, Grinzing. ☎ **01/32021-08.** www.rudolfshof.at.

Heuriger Mayer ★   This historic house was some 130 years old when Beethoven composed sections of his *Ninth Symphony* while living here in 1817. The same kind of fruity dry wine is still sold to guests in the shady courtyard of the rose garden. The menu includes grilled chicken, savory pork, and a buffet of well-prepared country food. Reservations are suggested. It's open Sunday to Friday 4pm to midnight. Closed Saturday. Live music is played every Sunday and Friday 7pm to midnight. Wine sells for 1.40€ a glass, with meals beginning at 13€. It's closed December 21 to January 15. Am Pfarrplatz 2, Heiligenstadt. ☎ **01/3703361,** or 01/370-1287 after 4pm.

Reinprecht   This staple of the *Heuriger* scene in Grinzing is a fun choice. Not only does the 300-year-old former monastery have its vintage charm, but this place has *Schrammel* music (live folk music) every day of the week. Besides the new wines that characterize every such establishment, they also have a tasty sparkling wine that is worth at least one toast. The place is utterly appealing, but the garden area is quite small. Cobenzlgasse 22, Grinzing. ☎ **01/320-6345.**

Sirbu   Some of the *Heuriger* in Grinzing can be overly touristy, but some hide the most beautiful gardens and the best wine favored by the Viennese. *Heuriger* Sirbu is one local favorite. The drive up the Nussberg, with an ocean of vineyards on every side, is sensational. Inside, the decor is simple but accommodating and the kitchen offers real specialties in the salad and cheese departments. The only catch is that it's a bit of a hike to get there. Take the 38A to the last station (Kahlenberg) and then it's a 15-minute walk downhill. Kahlenbergstrasse 210, Nussdorf. ☎ **01/3205928.**

Weingut Wolff   Although aficionados claim that the best *Heuriger* are "deep in the countryside" of Lower Austria, this one comes closest to offering an authentic experience just 20 minutes from the 1st District of Vienna. In summer, you're welcomed into a flower-decked garden set against a backdrop of ancient vineyards. You can fill up your platter with some of the best *wursts* and roast meats (especially the delectable pork), along with freshly made salads. Save room for one of the luscious and velvety-smooth Austrian cakes. Find a table under a cluster of grapes and sample the fruity young wines, especially the chardonnay, sylvaner, or *grüner Veltliner*. The tavern is open daily 11am to 1am, with main courses ranging from 8€ to 15€. Rathstrasse 50, Neustift. ☎ **01/440-3727.** www.wienerheuriger.at.

MORE ENTERTAINMENT

Casino

Casino Wien   You'll need to show your passport to get into this casino, opened in 1968. There are gaming tables for French and American roulette, blackjack, and chemin de fer, as well as the ever-present slot machines. The casino is open daily 11am to 3am, with the tables closing at 3pm. Esterházy Palace, Kärntnerstrasse 41. ℰ **01/512-4836**. www.casinos.at.

Films

Artis International   This and the Burg Kino (Opernring 19. ℰ **01/587-8406**; www.burgkino.at) are the two English-language cinemas in the 1st District. The Artis is frequented by the international community and Austrian cinema buffs who want to avoid the dubbed versions. It is quite small, but shows both blockbusters and select independent films and is 3D digital equipped. Schultergasse 5. ℰ **01/533-7054.** www.cineplexx.at. For movie listings: www.film.at/artis_international/. U-Bahn: Karlsplatz.

Filmmuseum   This cinema shows films in their original languages and presents retrospectives of directors from Fritz Lang to Richard Linklater. The museum presents avant-garde, experimental, and classic films. A monthly program is available free inside the Albertina, and a copy is posted outside. The film library inside the government-funded museum includes more than 11,000 book titles, and the still collection numbers more than 100,000. Admission costs 9.50€ for nonmembers. Membership for 24 hours costs 5.50€. In the Albertina, Augustinerstrasse 1. ℰ **01/533-7054.** www.filmmuseum. at. U-Bahn: Karlsplatz.

ONLY IN VIENNA

If the above nightspots aren't *Wien* enough for you, take a look at these establishments to get a truly Viennese experience.

Café Alt Wien   Set on one of the oldest, narrowest streets of medieval Vienna, a short walk north of the cathedral, this is the kind of smoky, mysterious, and shadowy cafe that evokes subversive plots, doomed romances, and revolutionary movements being hatched and plotted. During the day, it's a busy workaday restaurant patronized by virtually everybody. But as the night progresses, you're likely to rub elbows with denizens of late-night Wien who get more sentimental and schmaltzy with each beer. Foaming mug-fulls sell for 3€ each and can be accompanied by heaping platters of goulash and schnitzels. Main courses range from 6€ to 10€. It's open daily 10am to 2am. Bäckerstrasse 9 (1). ℰ **01/512-5222.** U-Bahn: Stephansplatz.

Pavillion   Even the Viennese stumble when trying to describe this civic monument from the Sputnik-era of the 1950s. Only open in warm weather, during the day, it's a cozy cafe with a multigenerational clientele and a sweeping garden overlooking the Heldenplatz (forecourt to the Hofburg). Come here to peruse the newspapers, chat with locals, and drink coffee, wine, beer, or schnapps. The place grows much more animated after the music (funk, soul, blues, and jazz) begins around 8pm. Platters of Viennese food are priced from 6.50€ to 12€. It's open daily 9am to 2am between April and October. Burgring 2. ℰ **01/532-0907.** U-Bahn: Volkstheater.

Phil 🎁   Whether it's a cafe where you can shop or a shop where you can order coffee and snacks is unimportant. At Phil you can take old and new books as well as the furniture home with you. Readings and live performances complete the repertoire of this unique address. Except, of course, for the conversation. Arrive early for performances, before all the chairs are bought. Gumpendorferstrasse 10-12. ℰ **01/581-0489.** www. phil.info. U-Bahn: MuseumsQuartier.

Schnitzelwirt Schmidt   The waitresses wear dirndls, the portions are huge, and the cuisine—only pork and some chicken—celebrates the culinary folklore of central Europe. The setting is rustic, a kind of tongue-in-cheek bucolic homage to the Old Vienna Woods, and schnitzels are almost guaranteed to hang over the sides of the plates. Regardless of what you order, it will be accompanied by french fries (*Pommes*), salad, and copious quantities of beer and wine. Go for the good value, unmistakably Viennese ambience, and great people-watching. Main courses cost 6€ to 10€. It's open Monday to Saturday 11am to 10pm. Neubaugasse 52 (7). © **01/523-3771.** U-Bahn: Neubaugasse. Tram: 49.

Schweizerhaus ★   References to this old-fashioned eating house are about as old as the Prater itself. Awash with beer and central European kitsch, it sprawls across a *Biergarten* landscape. Indulgence is indeed the word—the vastly proportioned main dishes could feed an entire 19th-century army. The menu stresses old-fashioned schnitzels and its house specialty, roasted pork hocks (*Hintere Schweinsstelze*) served with dollops of mustard and horseradish. Wash it all down with mugs of Czech Budweiser. A half-liter of beer costs 3.70€; main courses range from 5€ to 12€. It's open from March 15 to October 31 daily 11am to 11pm. In the Prater, Strasse des Ersten Mai 116. © **01/728-01-52.** U-Bahn: Praterstern.

Wiener Stamperl (The Viennese Dram)   Named after the unit of drink otherwise known as a "shot," this is about as beer-soaked and rowdy a nighttime venue as one can recommend. It occupies a battered, woodsy-looking room reeking of spilled beer, stale smoke, and the unmistakable scent of hundreds of boisterous drinkers. At the horseshoe-shaped bar, order foaming steins of Ottakinger beer or glasses of new wine from nearby vineyards served from an old-fashioned barrel. Make sure you take a look at the legendary urinal, a bit misogynist, but cult. The menu consists entirely of an array of coarse bread slathered with spicy, high-cholesterol ingredients, such as various meats and cheeses and, for anyone devoted to authentic old-time cuisine, lard specked with bits of bacon. It's open Monday to Thursday 11am to 2am, and Friday and Saturday 11pm to 4am. Sterngasse 1. © **01/533-6230.** U-Bahn: Schwedenplatz.

LOWER AUSTRIA

7

Enormously varied, Lower Austria is Austria in miniature, with mountain and meadowland, river and resort, and the rich cultural heritage of nearly 800 years of Habsburg hegemony in the region. You can ride the rack-railroad up to the 2,075m-high (6,808-ft.) Schneeberg, sail through the Wachau on board a Danube liner, go skiing on the Hochkar till spring, watch the glass-blowers in Brand-Nagelberg, or thrill at the dramatic landscapes, the nestled villages, and terraced vineyards of the Danube valley.

If you look at the map, the name of Lower Austria makes no sense: It is in fact the most northerly of all the federal states. It's the river that gives it its name: Lower Austria is farther south on the Danube than Upper Austria to the west (see chapter 11). Its 19,175 sq. km (7,404 sq. miles) make it the largest of the nine federal states, bordering on the Czech Republic to the north, Slovakia to the east, and the provinces of Styria and Burgenland to the south, and surrounding Vienna—the smallest.

This area was once heavily fortified, as some 550 citadels and castles testify—many, though in ruins, are still standing. The medieval Künringers and Babenbergers had their estates here. At the foothills of the Alps is Wiener Neustadt, the former imperial city. Moving west along the Danube, Dürnstein, with terraced vineyards, was where Richard the Lion-Heart was held prisoner. Many monasteries and churches, Romanesque and Gothic to the much later baroque abbeys, are also found in Lower Austria. Klosterneuburg Abbey dates from 1114, and Heiligenkreuz, founded in 1133, is the country's oldest Cistercian abbey. The province is filled with vineyards and, in summer, resounds with music and theater festivals, both classical and contemporary.

It is relatively inexpensive to travel in Lower Austria—prices here are about 30% lower than in Vienna, Salzburg, and Innsbruck—that, combined with the extraordinary beauty of the countryside, explains why many travelers choose one of the neighboring towns of Lower Austria when they come to explore Vienna.

Lower Austria is divided into quarters (or *Viertel*), the most popular of which are the *Weinviertel* and the *Waldviertel*. They contain thousands of miles of marked hiking paths and many mellow old wine cellars.

Some 60% of Austria's grape harvest is produced in Lower Austria, from the rolling hillsides of the Wienerwald to the terraces of the Wachau. Many visitors like to take a "wine route" through the province, stopping often at cozy taverns to sample the local vintages of Krems, Klosterneuburg, Dürnstein, Langenlois, Retz, Gumpoldskirchen, Poysdorf, and other towns.

Austria's pre-Habsburg history is often overshadowed by the family's claim on the region for nearly 800 years until 1918. But, even before the nomadic tribe wars and the conquests of Charlemagne, much of the territory now known as Lower Austria was occupied by the Romans, who built military bases along the Danube, keeping the land secure for their journey north. Vindobona was the base that later became Vienna, and a little further down the river to the east was Carnuntum, an army camp that was, among other things, general Tiberius's base during his campaigns against the Germanic Marcomanni. What remains of the camp can be found between the towns of Petronell-Carnuntum and Bad Deutsch-Altenburg. The **Carnuntum Archeological Park** (see below) is well worth a day trip from Vienna.

Lower Austria is also home to more than a dozen spa resorts, including Baden, the most frequented. Innkeepers welcome families with children at these resorts, which can be an inviting retreat from the city. Most hotels accommodate children up to 6 years old for free; children aged 7 to 12 stay for half price. Many towns and villages have attractions designed especially for kids. Some hotels have only a postal code for an address, as they do not lie on a street plan. (If you're writing to them, this postal code is their complete address.) When you reach one of these small towns, finding hotels is easy as they're signposted at the various approaches to the resort or village. Parking is rarely a problem in these places, and, unless otherwise noted, you park for free.

THE WIENERWALD (VIENNA WOODS) ★

The **Vienna Woods**—romanticized in operetta, literature, and the famous Strauss waltz—stretch all the way from Vienna's city limits to the foothills of the Alps to the south. You can hike through the woods along marked paths or take a leisurely drive, stopping off at country towns to sample the wine and the local cuisine, which is usually hearty, filling, and reasonably priced. The Viennese and a horde of foreign tourists, principally German, usually descend on the local wine taverns and cellars on weekends—we advise you to make any summer visit on a weekday. The best time of year to go is in September and October, when the grapes are harvested from the terraced hills.

Essentials

GETTING THERE You can visit the expansive and pastoral Vienna Woods by car or by public transportation. We recommend renting a car so you can explore some of the villages and vineyards along the way. Public transportation will get you around, but it will take much more time. Either way, you can easily reach all of the destinations listed below within a day's trip from Vienna. If you have more time, spend the night in one or more of the quintessential Austrian towns along the way.

VISITOR INFORMATION Before you go, visit the tourist office for **Klosterneuburg** at Niedermarkt 4, A-3400 (✆ **02243/32038;** www.klosterneuburg.com).

It's the best source of information for the Vienna Woods, and is open daily 10am to 7pm.

ORGANIZED TOURS **Vienna Sightseeing Tours,** Weyringergasse 28A-30, Entrance at Goldeggasse 29, A-1040 (© **01/712-4683-0;** fax 01/714-11-41; www. viennasightseeingtours.com), runs a popular 4-hour tour called "Vienna Woods— Mayerling." It goes through the Vienna Woods, past Liechtenstein Castle and the old Roman city of Baden. There's an excursion to Mayerling. You'll pay a short visit to the Cistercian abbey of Heiligenkreuz and take a boat ride on Seegrotte, the largest subterranean lake in Europe. The office is open daily for tours April to October 6:30am to 7:30pm, and November to March daily 6:30am to 5pm. It costs 44€ for adults and 15€ for children, including admission fees and a guide.

Klosterneuburg

On the northwestern outskirts of Vienna, Klosterneuburg is an old market town in the major wine-producing center of Austria. The Babenbergs founded the town in the eastern foothills of the Vienna Woods, making it an ideal spot to enjoy the countryside within easy reach of Vienna, 11km (7 miles) southeast.

Austrians and tourists gather in Klosterneuburg annually to celebrate St. Leopold's Day on November 15, with music, banquets, and a parade.

ESSENTIALS

GETTING THERE If you're driving from Vienna along the south bank of the Danube Canal (Donaulände), take Route 14 (B14) to Klosterneuburg. From Route 14 take the exit for Klosterneuburg or Stift. By public transportation, take the U-Bahn to Heiligenstadt, where you can then board bus no. 238, 239, or 341 to Klosterneuburg, or catch the S-Bahn from Franz-Josef Bahnhof to Klosterneuburg-Kierling.

WHAT TO SEE & DO

Stift Klosterneuburg (Klosterneuburg Abbey) ★ Stiftsplatz 1 (© **02243/ 4110;** www.stift-klosterneuburg.at) is one of the most significant abbeys in Austria.

SINGING monks OF HEILIGENKREUZ

The 12th-century Abbey of Heiligenkreuz takes up most of the village that bears its name, its sprawling additions a mishmash of Gothic and baroque on its Romanesque cloisters, and more relics of the Holy Cross than anywhere except Rome.

Today some 50 Cistercian monks live in Heiligenkreuz (© **02258/8703**), and make a highly reputable wine and sing God's praises each day at Matins and Even Song in the haunting resonance of Gregorian Chant. And thus it was that the Abbot Gregor Henckel Donnersmark invited his nephew, Florian, to the Abbey to work on his next film script.

Hearing the chant, Florian suggested the monks audition for film.

The monks submitted a video over YouTube and, overnight, had signed a contract with Universal Music. Suddenly, they were at the top of the UK classical charts. And Florian? His script became *Das Leben der Anderen,* winning a 2006 Oscar for Best Foreign Film.

Today, things have settled down in Heiligenkreuz, but the monks still make great wine and the music—well, it is probably the best we have on earth. In summer at noon and 6pm daily, visitors can attend the solemn choir prayers.

Lower Austria & the Wachau (Danube Valley)

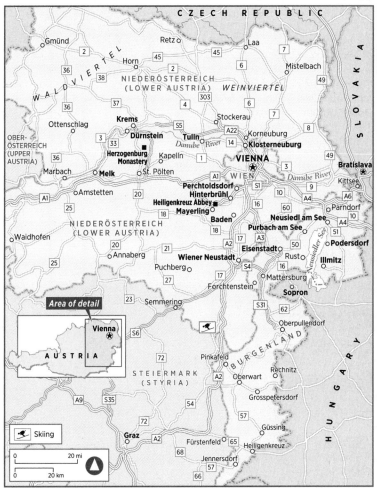

It was founded in 1114 by the Babenberg margrave Leopold III and was once the residence of the famous Habsburg emperor Charles VI.

The abbey is visited not only for its history, but also for its art treasures. The most valuable piece is the world-famous altar of Nikolaus of Verdun, created in 1181. The monastery also boasts the largest private library in Austria, with more than 1,250 handwritten books and many antique paintings. Guided tours of the monastery are given daily year-round. On the tour, you visit the Cathedral of the Monastery (unless Masses are underway), the cloister, St. Leopold's Chapel (with the Verdun altar), the former well house, and the residential apartments of the emperors.

The monastery itself remains open year-round, but the museum of the monastery is closed from mid-November to April. The museum can be visited without a guide from May to mid-November Tuesday to Sunday 10am to 5pm. Visits to the monastery itself, however, require participation in a guided tour. These are available at hourly intervals year-round daily from 9am to noon and 1:30 to 4:30pm. Except for a specially designated English-language tour conducted every Sunday at 2pm, most tours are conducted in German, with occasional snippets of English if the guide is able. The price is 8€ for adults and 5€ for children. Additional English-language tours can be arranged in advance. You can purchase a cost-effective combination ticket to the monastery and museum for 12€ for adults and 7€ for children 6 to 14.

WHERE TO STAY & EAT

Hotel Schrannenhof   Originally dating from the Middle Ages, this hotel has been completely renovated and modernized. The owners rent guest rooms with large living and bedrooms and small kitchens, as well as quiet and comfortable double rooms with showers. Right next door, the hotel's cafe-restaurant serves international and Austrian specialties. The hotel also runs the Pension Alte Mühle (see below).

Niedermarkt 17–19, A-3400 Klosterneuburg. ✆ **02243/32072.** Fax 02243/3207213. www.schrannenhof. at. 14 units. 92€–108€ double; 128€ suite. Rates include buffet breakfast. AE, DC, MC. Free parking. **Amenities:** Breakfast room; lounge. *In room:* A/C (in some), TV, kitchenette (in some), hairdryer, minibar, safe, free Wi-Fi available on request.

Park Inn Klosterneuburg   This brand new hotel is only a 5-minute drive from the center of Klosterneuburg. It's also right next to the large and well-equipped Donaupark campsite, which is popular with cyclists and a good place to meet fellow travelers. The entire hotel is a cross between an office building and a minimalist modern art museum. The rooms are spacious and echo the functionality of the early Bauhaus—primary color schemes included.

In der Au 6, A-3400 Klosterneuburg. ✆ **02243/229220.** Fax 02243/22922390. www.parkinn.de/ hotel-klosterneuburg. 130 units. 79€–89€ double. Buffet breakfast 12€ extra. AE, DC, MC, V. Free parking. Closed Dec 15–Jan 15. **Amenities:** Restaurant; bar; 24-hour front desk; air-conditioning; garden; kitchenette (in suites); room service. *In room:* A/C, TV, safe, smoke-free rooms, free Wi-Fi.

Pension Alte Mühle   A gracious and hospitable bed & breakfast that offers a bountiful morning buffet. The restaurant-cafe, Veit, is only 800m (2,624 ft.) away. Bedrooms are furnished in a cozy, traditional style, with well-maintained, if small, private bathrooms with shower units. Quaint and homey.

Mühlengasse 36, A-3400 Klosterneuburg. ✆ **02243/37788.** Fax 02243/377-8822. www.hotel-altemuehle. at. 13 units. 36€ double. Rates include breakfast. AE, DC, MC. Free parking. **Amenities:** Breakfast room; laundry service. *In room:* TV, hairdryer, minibar, safe, free Wi-Fi available on request.

Perchtoldsdorf: A Stop on the Wine Tour

This old market town with colorful buildings, referred to locally as Petersdorf, is one of the most visited spots in Lower Austria for Viennese on wine tours. You'll find many *Heuriger* here, where you can sample local wines and enjoy good, hearty cuisine. Perchtoldsdorf is not as well known as Grinzing, which is actually within the city limits of Vienna, but many visitors find it less touristy. It has a Gothic church, and part of its defense tower dates from the early 16th century. A vintners' festival, held annually in early November, attracts many Viennese. Local growers make a "goat" from grapes for this occasion.

ESSENTIALS

GETTING THERE   Perchtoldsdorf lies 18km (11 miles) from the center of Vienna (it's actually at the southwestern city limits) and 14km (9 miles) north of Baden. From

Vienna's Westbahnhof, you can take the S-Bahn to Liesing. From here, Perchtolds-dorf is just a short taxi ride away (there are cabs at the train station).

VISITOR INFORMATION The **tourist information office,** in the center of Perchtoldsdorf (© **01/536100;** www.noe.co.at), is open Monday to Friday 8:30am to 4pm.

WHERE TO EAT

Restaurant Jahreszeiten ★ AUSTRIAN/FRENCH/INTERNATIONAL Set within what was a private villa in the 1800s, this restaurant, the best in town, provides a haven for escapist Viennese looking for hints of the country life. In a pair of ele-gantly rustic dining rooms illuminated at night with flickering candles, you can enjoy such well-crafted dishes as rare poached salmon served with herbs and truffled noodles, Chinese-style prawns in an Asiatic sauce prepared by the kitchen's Japanese cooks, and filet of turbot with morels and asparagus-studded risotto. Try a soufflé for dessert. A tremendous effort is made to secure the freshest produce. Service is polite, hardworking, and discreet.

Hochstrasse 17. © **01/8656080.** www.jahreszeiten.at. Reservations recommended. Main courses 14€–20€. Set menus 30€. AE, DC, MC, V. Daily 11:30am–11pm. Closed 3 weeks in Aug.

Hinterbrühl

You'll find good accommodations and good food in this hamlet that is really no more than a cluster of bucolic homes, much favored by Viennese who like to escape the city for a long weekend. Hinterbrühl holds memories of Franz Schubert, who wrote *Der Lindenbaum* here. This tiny area is also home to Europe's largest subterranean lake (see below).

ESSENTIALS

GETTING THERE The village is 26km (16 miles) south of Vienna and 3km (2 miles) south of Mödling, the nearest large town. To reach Hinterbrühl from Vienna, take the S-Bahn from the Südbahnhof to Mödling (trip time: 15 min.) and then catch a connecting bus to Hinterbrühl, the last stop (12 min.). By car, drive southwest along the A21, exiting at the signs to Gisshubel. From there, follow the signs to Hinterbrühl and Mödling.

VISITOR INFORMATION The **tourist information office,** in Kaiserin-Elisa-beth 2, Mölding (© **02236/26727**), is open Monday to Friday 9am to 5pm.

AN UNDERGROUND LAKE

Seegrotte Hinterbrühl Some of the village of Hinterbrühl was built directly above the stalactite-covered waters of Europe's largest underground lake. From the entrance a few hundred yards from the edge of town, you'll descend a steep flight of stairs before facing the extensively illuminated waters of a shallow, very still, and very cold underground lake. The famous natural marvel was the site of the construction of the world's first jet plane and other aircraft during World War II. Expect a running commentary in German and broken English during the 20-minute boat ride.

Grutschgasse 2A, Hinterbrühl. © **02236/26364.** www.seagrotte.at. Admission and boat ride 9€ adult, 6€ children under 14 and students. Apr–Oct daily 9am–5pm; Nov–Mar Mon–Fri 9am–noon and 1–3pm, Sat–Sun 9am–3:30pm.

WHERE TO STAY

Hotel Beethoven This hotel in the heart of the hamlet boasts one of the village's oldest buildings, a private house originally constructed around 1785. In 1992, the hotel renovated most of the interior and built a new wing. It was again renovated in 2002. The average-size bedrooms are cozy, traditional, and well maintained, with good beds and adequate bathrooms equipped mostly with tub/shower combinations. There's no formal restaurant on the premises, but management maintains an all-day cafe where coffee, drinks, pastries, ice cream, salads, and platters of regional food are served daily.

Beethovengasse 8, A-2371 Hinterbrühl. (© **02236/26252.** Fax 02236/277017. www.beethoven-hotel.at. 25 units. 78€–98€ double. Rates include buffet breakfast. AE, DC, MC, V. Free parking. **Amenities:** Cafe; bar. *In room:* TV, hairdryer, minibar, safe (in some), free Wi-Fi available on request.

WHERE TO EAT

Restaurant Hexensitz ★ AUSTRIAN/INTERNATIONAL   Featuring impeccable service, this restaurant celebrates the subtleties of Austrian country cooking. Its upscale setting is a century-old building with a trio of dining rooms outfitted "in the Lower Austrian style," with wood paneling and country antiques. In summer, the restaurant expands outward into a well-kept garden. It offers daily-changing dishes such as Styrian venison with kohlrabi, wine sauce, and homemade noodles; medallions of pork with spinach and herbs; and sea bass with forest mushrooms. The traditional desserts are luscious. The kitchen personnel are devoted and professional, and the food is nearly always delightful.

Johannesstrasse 35. (© **02236/22937.** www.hexensitz.at. Reservations recommended. Main courses 12€–22€; fixed-price lunch 25€ available on Sun; fixed-price dinner 40€. MC, V. Tues 6–10pm; Wed–Sat 11:30am–2pm and 6–10pm; Sun 11:30am–2pm.

Mayerling

This beautiful spot, 29km (18 miles) west of Vienna in the heart of the Wienerwald, is best known for the unresolved deaths of Archduke Rudolf, son of Emperor Franz Joseph, and his mistress in 1889. The event, which took place in a hunting lodge (now a Carmelite convent), altered the line of Austro-Hungarian succession. The heir apparent became Franz Joseph's nephew, Archduke Ferdinand, whose murder in Sarajevo sparked World War I. Mayerling, incidentally, is only a small hamlet, not even a village.

ESSENTIALS

GETTING THERE   By **car,** head southwest on the A-21 to Alland and take Route 210 to Mayerling. Or take **bus** no. 1123, 1124, or 1127, marked ALLAND, from Vienna's Südtirolerplatz (trip time: 90 min.). From Baden, hop on bus no. 1140 or 1141.

VISITOR INFORMATION   Contact the local authorities at the **Rathaus,** in nearby Heiligenkreuz (© **02258/8720;** www.heiligenkreuz.at). It's open Monday to Friday 8am to noon and 2 to 5pm.

WHAT TO SEE & DO

Abbey Heiligenkreuz (Abbey of the Holy Cross)   Margrave Leopold III founded this abbey. It was built in the 12th century and subsequently gained an overlay of Gothic and baroque additions, with some 13th- and 14th-century stained glass still in place. The Romanesque and Gothic cloisters, with some 300 pillars of red marble, date from 1240. Some of the dukes of Babenberg were buried in the chapter house, including Duke Friedrich II, the last of his line. Heiligenkreuz has more relics of the Holy Cross than any other site in Europe, except Rome.

twilight OF THE HABSBURGS

On January 30, 1889, a hunting lodge in Mayerling was the setting of a grim tragedy that altered the line of succession of the Austro-Hungarian Empire and shocked the world. On a snowy night, Archduke Rudolf, the only son of Emperor Franz Joseph and Empress Elisabeth, and his 18-year-old mistress, Maria Vetsera, were found dead. It was announced that they had shot themselves, although no weapon ever surfaced for examination. All doors and windows to the room had been locked when the bodies were discovered. All evidence that might have shed light on the deaths was subsequently destroyed. Had it been a double suicide or an assassination?

Rudolf, a sensitive eccentric, was locked in an unhappy marriage, and neither his father nor Pope Leo XIII would allow an annulment. He had fallen in love with Maria at a German embassy ball when she was only 17. Maria's public snubbing of Archduchess Stephanie of Belgium, Rudolf's wife, at a reception given by the German ambassador to Vienna led to a heated argument between Rudolf and his father. Because of the young archduke's liberal leanings and sympathy for certain Hungarian partisans, he was not popular with his country's aristocracy, which gave rise to lurid speculation about a cleverly designed plot. Supporters of the assassination theory included Empress Zita von Habsburg, the last Habsburg heir, who in 1982 told the Vienna daily *Kronen Zeitung* that she believed their deaths were the culmination of a conspiracy against the family. Franz Joseph, grief-stricken at the loss of his only son, ordered the hunting lodge torn down and a Carmelite nunnery built in its place.

Maria Vetsera was buried in a village cemetery in Heiligenkreuz. The inscription over her tomb reads, *Wie eine Blume sprosst der Mensch auf und wird gebrochen* ("Human beings, like flowers, bloom and are crushed"). In a curious incident in 1988, her coffin was exhumed and stolen by a Linz executive, who was distraught at the death of his wife and obsessed with the Mayerling affair. It took police 4 years to recover the coffin.

Today a vital community of 50 Cistercian monks lives in Heiligenkreuz. In summer, at noon and 6pm daily, visitors can attend the solemn choir prayers.

Heiligenkreuz. © **02258/8703.** Admission 7€ adults, 3.50€ children. Daily 9–noon and 1:30–5pm (until 4pm Nov–Feb). Tours Mon–Sat 10 and 11am plus 2, 3, 4pm (also at 5pm with groups of 6 or more, reservation required). From Mayerling, take Heiligenkreuzstrasse 5km (3 miles) to Heiligenkreuz.

Jagdschloss   A Carmelite abbey, Karmeliten Kloster Mayerling, stands on the site of the infamous hunting lodge where Archduke Rudolf and his mistress supposedly committed suicide (see "Twilight of the Habsburgs," above). If it hadn't been torn down, the hunting lodge would be a much more fascinating—if macabre—attraction. Although nothing remains of the lodge, history buffs enjoy visiting the abbey.

Mayerling. © **02258/2275.** Admission 3€ adults, 1.50€ children under 14. Mon–Sat 9am–6pm (5pm Oct–Mar); Sun 10am–6pm (5pm Oct–Mar).

WHERE TO STAY & EAT

Hotel Hanner   The best hotel in town rises three stories, in a conservative but very modern format of respectability and charm. Bedrooms are streamlined, comfortable, and modern, with a color scheme that varies slightly, each from its neighbor, in its use of pastels. Guests appreciate the calm, the quiet, and the proximity to the acres of natural beauty in the surrounding region.

Mayerling 1, A-2534 Mayerling. ✆ **02258/2378.** www.hanner.cc. Fax 02258/237841. 27 units. 148€–262€ double. Rates include breakfast. AE, DC, MC, V. Free parking. **Amenities:** Restaurant; bar; fitness center; sauna; room service; laundry; dry cleaning; nonsmoking rooms. *In room:* TV, hairdryer, minibar, safe, free Wi-Fi available on request.

Restaurant Hanner AUSTRIAN Dignified, conservatively modern, and well managed, this is the best restaurant in a town not noted for lots of competition. Large windows take in a panoramic view of the surrounding forests, and dishes change with the seasons and according to the whim of the chef. Examples include fresh fish, goulash, chicken breast with paprika-flavored noodles, and filets of venison in port-wine sauce.

In the Hotel Hanner, Mayerling 1. ✆ **02258/2378.** Reservations not necessary. Main courses 15€–40€; 5-course tasting menu 98€; 7-course tasting menu 118€. AE, DC, MC, V. Daily noon–2pm and 6–10pm.

THE SPA TOWN OF BADEN BEI WIEN ★

24km (15 miles) SW of Vienna; 299km (186 miles) E of Salzburg

Around A.D. 100, the Romans were drawn to Aquae, the name they gave to Baden, by its 15 thermal springs, with temperatures reaching 95°F (35°C). You can still see the **Römerquelle (Roman Spring)** in the Kurpark, which is the center of **Baden bei Wien ★** today.

Czar Peter the Great of Russia ushered in Baden's golden age by establishing a spa there at the beginning of the 18th century. The Soviet army used the resort city as its occupation headquarters from the end of World War II to 1955, but the Russians left little mark on "the dowager empress of European health spas."

Although the spa was at its most fashionable in the early 18th century, it continued to lure royalty and their entourages, musicians, and intellectuals for much of the 19th century. This lively casino town and spa in the eastern sector of the Vienna Woods was for years the summer residence of the Habsburg court. In 1803, Franz I began annual summer visits to Baden.

During the mid- to late-19th century, Baden became known for its Schönbrunn yellow (Maria Theresa ocher) Biedermeier buildings, which still contribute to the city's charm. The Kurpark, Baden's center, is handsomely laid out and beautifully maintained. Public concerts performed here pay tribute to great Austrian composers.

The **bathing complex** was constructed over more than a dozen sulfur springs. Visitors today flock to the half-dozen bath establishments, as well as the four outdoor thermal springs. These springs reach temperatures ranging from 75° to 95°F (24°–35°C). The thermal complex also has a "sandy beach" and a restaurant. It lies west of the center in the Doblhoffpark, a natural park featuring a lake where you can rent sailboats. There's also a rose garden restaurant in the park. The resort is officially named Baden bei Wien to differentiate it from other Badens not near Vienna.

Essentials

GETTING THERE If you're driving from Vienna, head south on the A2, take exit 21 onto the B210, which leads to Baden. By train, Baden is a local rather than an express stop. Trains depart daily at 15–30-minute intervals from Wien Meidling (trip time: 30 min.). For schedules, call ✆ **05/1717** in Vienna, or check www.oebb.at. By bus, the Badner Bahn leaves every 15 minutes from the Staatsoper (trip time: 1 hr.).

VISITOR INFORMATION   The **tourist information office,** at Brusattiplatz 3 (✆ **02252/22-600-600;** www.baden.at), is open Monday to Friday 9am to 6pm, Saturday 9am to 2pm. From October to April the office is closed on both Saturday and Sunday.

Exploring Baden Bei Wien

In the Hauptplatz (Main Square) is the **Trinity Column,** built in 1714, which commemorates the lifting of the plague that swept over Vienna and the Wienerwald in the Middle Ages. Also here are the **Rathaus** (✆ **02252/86800**) and, at no. 17, the **Kaiserhaus,** Franz II's summer residence from 1813 to 1834.

Every summer between 1821 and 1823, Beethoven rented the upper floor of a modest house, above what used to be a shop on the Rathausgasse, in Baden, for about 2 weeks, hoping to find a cure for his increasing deafness. The site has been reconfigured by the city of Baden into the **Beethovenhaus,** a small museum commemorating the time he spent here, at Rathausgasse 10 (✆ **02252/868-00590**). Inside you'll find a trio of small, relatively modest rooms, furnished with one of Beethoven's pianos, his bed, several pieces of porcelain, photographs of others of his residences around the German-speaking world, some mementos, and copies of the musical folios he completed (or at least worked on) during his time in Baden. The museum is open year-round Tuesday to Friday 4 to 6pm, and Saturday and Sunday 10am to noon and 4 to 6pm. Admission is 3€ for adults, 1.50€ for students and children under 18, free for children under 6.

Among the other sights in Baden, there's a celebrated death mask collection at the **Stadtisches Rolletmuseum,** Weikersdorfer-Platz 1 (✆ **02252/48255**). The museum possesses many items of historic and artistic interest. Furniture and the art of the Biedermeier period are especially represented. It's open every day except Tuesday from 3 to 6pm. Admission is 3€ for adults and 1.50€ for children. To reach the museum from Hauptplatz, go south to Josefs Platz and then continue south along Vöslauer Strasse, turning right when you come to Elisabeth Strasse, which leads directly to Weikersdorfer-Platz.

The **Stadttheater,** at Theaterplatz 7 (✆ **02252/253253**), is a 5-minute walk from Hauptplatz, and on nearby Pfarrgasse, you'll find the 15th-century parish church of **St. Stephan's** (✆ **02252/48426**). Inside there's a commemorative plaque to Mozart, who allegedly composed his *Ave Verum* here for the parish choirmaster.

The real reason to come to Baden is the sprawling and beautiful **Kurpark ★**. Here you can attend concerts, plays, and operas at an open-air theater, or try your luck at the casino (see "Baden After Dark," below). The Römerquelle (Roman Springs) can be seen gurgling from an intricate rock basin, which is surrounded by monuments to Beethoven, Mozart, and the great playwright Grillparzer. From the park's numerous paths you can view Baden and the surrounding hills.

TAKING A BATH

As you might expect from waters that have attracted health-seekers for thousands of years, there are several different ways you can experience the local mineral baths. The **Kurhaus** (also known sometimes as the **Kurzentrum**), at Pelzgasse 30 (✆ **02252/ 48580**), in the heart of town, is a strictly medical facility, which requires doctors' appointments in advance. The less structured enterprise right nearby (at Brussatiplatz 4; **02252/45030**), is the *Römertherme,* a complex of hot mineral baths, which are open, with no reservations needed, to anyone who shows up. The *Römertherme* charges according to how long you spend inside. Two hours (the minimum charge) costs 9.50€, with each additional hour priced at 1.70€. A full day is 14€ per person, unless you opt to enter after 8pm, in which event you'll pay 4.80€. Access to any of the saunas inside costs an additional 4€, and access to the exercise and fitness area is 12.20€ per person.

Where to Stay

EXPENSIVE

Grand Hotel Sauerhof zu Rauhenstein ★   Although this estate dates back to 1583, it became famous in 1757, when a sulfur-enriched spring bubbled up after a cataclysmic earthquake in faraway Portugal. The present building was constructed in 1810 on the site of that spring, which continues to supply water to its spa facilities today. In the past, the property served as an army rehabilitation center, a sanatorium during the two world wars, and the headquarters of the Russian army. In 1978, after extravagant renovations, the Sauerhof reopened as one of the region's most upscale spa hotels.

The rooms, though comfortable and bright, have many vintage furnishings, which may be too worn for some. Expect average food from the restaurant.

Weilburgstrasse 11–13, A-2500 Baden bei Wien. ✆ **02252/412510.** Fax 02252/43626. www.sauerhof.at. 88 units. 220€ double; from 650€ suite. Rates include buffet breakfast; half-board 25€ per person extra. AE, DC, MC, V. Free parking. **Amenities:** Restaurant; bar; indoor heated pool; 2 tennis courts; fitness center; spa; sauna; salon; room service; laundry service; dry cleaning; nonsmoking rooms; solarium. *In room:* TV, hairdryer, minibar, safe, free Ethernet.

MODERATE

Krainerhütte ☺   This very zen hotel stands on tree-filled grounds 8km (5 miles) west of Baden at Helenental. It's a large A-frame chalet with rows of wooden balconies. The interior has more details than you might expect in such a modern hotel. There are separate children's rooms and play areas. The medium-size rooms and small bathrooms with tub/shower combinations are well maintained. You can dine on international and Austrian cuisine in the cozy restaurant or on the terrace; the fish and deer come from the hotel grounds. Hiking hunting, and fishing in the owner's forests, are possible. *Postbus* service to Baden is available all day.

Helenental 41, A-2500 Baden bei Wien. ✆ **02252/44511.** Fax 02252/44514. www.krainerhuette.at. 62 units. 68€–89€ double; from 89€ suite. Rates include breakfast; half-board 15€ per person extra. AE, MC, V. Free parking. **Amenities:** Restaurant; bar; babysitting; fitness center; dry cleaning; laundry service; indoor heated pool; sauna; room service; smoke-free rooms; tennis court. *In room:* TV, hairdryer, minibar, free Wi-Fi.

Parkhotel Baden   You can't beat this location. The *Römertherme,* Kurpark, and Casino are all within a few minutes' walking distance. Most of the good-size, sunny guest rooms have their own loggia overlooking century-old trees; each contains a good bathroom with tub/shower combination and plenty of shelf space. The TVs and some of the furniture are old and will hopefully be updated soon.

Kaiser-Franz-Ring 5, A-2500 Baden bei Wien. ✆ **02252/443860.** Fax 02252/80578. www. niederoesterreich.at/parkhotel-baden. 87 units. 170€ double; 280€ suite. Rates include breakfast. AE, DC, MC, V. Free parking. **Amenities:** 2 restaurants; bar; babysitting; dry cleaning; hairdryer; health club; massage; indoor heated pool; sauna; room service; laundry service. *In room:* TV, minibar, free Wi-Fi.

Schloss Weikersdorf Pure eye candy complete with vaulted ceilings, this hotel has a loggia leading out into an appealing stretch of park with a rose garden, and a courtyard arcade with a skylight. Accommodations, which include 77 bedrooms in the main house plus 27 in the annex, are handsomely furnished and very comfortable. The rooms in the newer section tastefully echo the older section's style. The rates charged on the Internet are over-priced.

Schlossgasse 9–11, A-2500 Baden bei Wien. © **02252/48301.** Fax 02252/4830-1150. www.hotel schlossweikersdorf.at. 104 units. 124€–150€ double; 250€ suite. Rates include breakfast. AE, DC, MC, V. Free parking. **Amenities:** Restaurant; bar; bowling alley; dry cleaning; laundry service; rooms for those w/limited mobility; massage; indoor heated pool; sauna; room service; smoke-free rooms, Wi-Fi available in the lobby (rates apply). *In room:* TV, minibar, hairdryer, safe, Ethernet: 10€/hr or 17€/24hr.

Where to Eat

Kupferdachl AUSTRIAN A local cornerstone since 1966, this moderately priced family favorite serves rib-sticking fare that the locals adore, everything from cabbage soup to *Apfelstrudel*. The chefs make the town's best Wiener schnitzel, served with a fresh salad and rice. The Veal cutlets with potatoes or cordon bleu are also worth trying. Expect good, old-fashioned Austrian cookery. This place is about a 15-minute drive from Baden.

Heiligenkreuzgasse 2. © **02252/41617.** www.daskupferdachl.at. Reservations recommended. Main courses 10€–14€. No credit cards. Mon–Fri 8am–6:30pm; Sat–Sun 9am–4pm.

Baden After Dark

Casino Baden The town's major evening attraction is the casino, where you can play roulette, blackjack, baccarat, poker (seven-card stud), money wheel, and slot machines. Many visitors from Vienna come down to Baden for a night of gambling, eating, and drinking; there are two bars and a restaurant. Guests are often fashionably dressed, and you'll feel more comfortable if you are, too (men should wear jackets and ties). It's open daily 3pm to 3am. A less formal casino on the premises, the Casino Leger, is open daily noon to midnight. In the Kurpark © **02252/44496.** www.casinos. at. Free admission; 25€ worth of chips for 21€.

WIENER NEUSTADT

45km (28 miles) S of Vienna; 309km (192 miles) E of Salzburg

Heading south from Vienna on the Südautobahn, the former imperial city of Wiener Neustadt is a good first stop. It was once the official residence of Emperor Friedrich III. Called *Allzeit Getreue* (forever loyal) because of its fidelity to the throne, this thriving city between the foothills of the Alps and the edge of the Pannonian lowland is steeped in history.

The town was founded in 1192, when Duke Leopold V of the ruling house of Babenburg built its castle. He had it constructed as a citadel to ward off attacks by the Magyars from the east. From 1440 to 1493, Austrian emperors lived in this fortress, in the southeast corner of what is now the old town. Maximilian I, called "the last of the knights," was born here in 1459 and buried in the castle's Church of St. George. In 1752, on Maria Theresa's orders, the castle became a military academy.

With the opening of the Austrian Southern Railway in 1841, Wiener Neustadt became an industrial town, manufacturing steam engines and railroad cars, and in 1909, was the site of Austria's first official airfield.

In 1903 Paul Daimler started building his 2-cylinder engine factory in Wiener Neustadt and in 1906 hired Ferdinand Porsch as his technical director. A half a dozen years later, the engines were purring and they began hiring young mechanical engineers from the Benz factory in Munich. One of them was Josip Broz who came down as a test driver for Daimler. He stayed, and 2 years later, at the age of 25, became the youngest sergeant major in the Austro-Hungarian army. In 1943, as Marshall Tito, Josip Broz became Prime Minister, and later President of Yugoslavia, a post he held for 37 years, and alone achieved a "non-aligned" communist option within the Soviet sphere.

Wiener Neustadt was a target for Allied bombs during World War II, probably because of its strategic position where the routes south of Vienna diverge to the Semmering Pass and to Hungary via the Sopron Gate. However, it may also have been the 200-year-old military academy that offered an added attraction to bombers; German general Erwin Rommel ("the Desert Fox"), for example, was the academy's first commandant after the Nazi *Anschluss*. The bombing leveled an estimated 60% of Wiener Neustadt's buildings. Luckily some of its most beautiful were spared.

Essentials

GETTING THERE If you're driving from Vienna, head south along the A2 and take exit 44 marked Wiener Neustadt—West onto B26. Follow B26 to Wiener Neustadt.

Trains to Wiener Neustadt leave every 10 to 15 minutes from Wien Meidling (trip time: 25–45 min.). For schedules, call ✆ **05/1717** in Vienna or check www.oebb.at.

VISITOR INFORMATION The Wiener Neustadt **tourist information office,** at Hauptplatz in the Rathaus (✆ **02622/373311**), is open Monday to Friday 8am to 5pm, Saturday 8am to noon.

Walking Around Wiener Neustadt

You can visit the **St. Georgenkirche (Church of St. George),** Burgplatz 1 (✆ **02622/3810**), daily from 8am to 6pm. The gable of the church is adorned with more than 100 heraldic shields of the Habsburgs. It is noted for its handsome interior, decorated in the late-Gothic style.

Neukloster, Neuklostergasse 1 (✆ **02622/23102**), a Cistercian abbey, was founded in 1250 and reconstructed in the 18th century. The Neuklosterkirche (New Abbey Church), near the Hauptplatz, is Gothic and has a beautiful choir. It contains the tomb of Empress Eleanor of Portugal, wife of Friedrich III and mother of Maximilian I. Mozart's *Requiem* was first presented here in 1793. Admission is free, and, while the church is always open to visitors, the abbey's office hours are Monday, Tuesday, Wednesday and Friday from 8 to 11am and 3 to 6pm.

Liebfrauenkirche, Domplatz (✆ **02622/23202**), was once the headquarters of an Episcopal see. It's graced by a 13th-century Romanesque nave, but the choir is Gothic. The west towers have been rebuilt. Admission is free, and the church is open daily from 8am to noon and 2 to 6pm.

The **Reckturm,** Babenberger Ring (✆ **02622/27924**), is a Gothic tower said to have been built with the ransom money paid for King Richard the Lion-Hearted. It's open from March to October Tuesday to Thursday from 10am to noon and 2 to 4pm, and Saturday and Sunday from 10am to noon only. Admission is free.

Where to Stay

Hotel Zentral   The best hotel in town is right on the main square. The staff are competent, very friendly and make up for the somewhat out-dated, yet comfortable furnishings. It's small, so we recommend reserving way in advance. Due to its location, parking places are scarce, but you can load and unload luggage in front of the hotel anytime and there is a parking garage 250 m away that costs 3€ per day, if you purchase your ticket at the hotel.

Hauptplatz 27, A-2700 Wiener Neustadt. © **02622/23169.** Fax 02622/237935. www.hotelzentral.at. 68 units. 150-190€ double. Rates include buffet breakfast. AE, DC, MC, V. Free parking. **Amenities:** Restaurant; bar; room service; smoke-free rooms. *In room:* TV, hair dryer, minibar, free Wi-Fi is available on request.

Where to Eat

Stachl's Gaststube ★ CONTINENTAL   Set within the city's all-pedestrian zone in the heart of town, this is one of the most popular and well-respected restaurants in the region, with a thriving catering business on the side. Food items are well presented and flavorful, served in an intimate environment that includes a busy bar area independent of the restaurant. Begin a meal here with a carpaccio of Styrian beef with wild mushrooms and arugula, or strips of marinated salmon with pesto sauce. Continue with a truffled version of mushroom risotto; Wiener schnitzel with salad; *Tafelspitz* with chive sauce and horseradish; or perhaps a filleted local lakefish (*Zander*) with herbed noodles. For dessert, consider a platter containing light and dark versions of chocolate mousse topped with berry sauce.

Lange Gasse 20. © **02622/25221.** www.stachl.at. Reservations recommended. Main courses 12€-20€. MC, V. Mon-Fri 5pm-12:30am; Sat 5pm-midnight.

THE DANUBE VALLEY ★★★

The Danube, of course, is one of the most legendary rivers in Europe, and the surrounding area is rich in scenic splendor, historic wealth, and architectural grandeur. With rolling hills and fertile soil, the Wachau, a section of the Danube Valley northwest of Vienna, is one of the most beautiful and historic parts of Austria. Throughout this part of the Danube Valley, you'll find castles, celebrated vineyards, some of the most famous medieval monasteries in central Europe, and ruins from the Stone Age, the Celts, the Romans, and the Habsburgs. This prosperous district has won many awards for the authenticity of its historic renovations.

A great way to see the area is by paddleboat steamer, most of which operate only from April to October. You can travel by armchair, lounging on the deck along the longest river in central Europe.

If you're really "doing the Danube," you can begin your trip at Passau, Germany, and go all the way to the Black Sea and across to the Crimean Peninsula in the Ukraine. However, the Vienna–Yalta portion of the trip alone takes nearly a week. Most visitors limit themselves to a more restricted look at the Danube, taking one of the many popular trips from Vienna. If you go westward on the river, your first stop might be Klosterneuburg (see "The Wienerwald/Vienna Woods," earlier in this chapter).

Essentials

GETTING THERE   If you have only 1 day to explore the Danube Valley, we highly recommend one of the tours listed below. If you have more time, however, rent a car and explore this district yourself, driving inland from the river now and then to visit the towns and sights listed below. You can also take public transportation to the towns we've highlighted (see individual listings).

VISITOR INFORMATION Before you venture into the Danube Valley, pick up maps and other helpful information at the **tourist office for Lower Austria,** Postfach 10.000, A-1010 Vienna (② **01/536-1062-00;** fax 01/536-1060-60; www. niederoesterreich.at).

TIPS ON EXPLORING THE DANUBE VALLEY The Wachau and the rest of the Danube Valley contain some of the most impressive monuments in Austria, but because of their far-flung locations, many prefer to participate in an organized tour. The best of these are conducted by **Vienna Sightseeing Tours,** Goldeggasse 29 (② **01/712-4683-0;** fax 01/714-1141; www.viennasightseeingtours.com), which offers guided tours by motorcoach in winter and by both motorcoach and boat in summer. Stops on this 8-hour trip include Krems, Dürnstein, and Melk Abbey. Prices are 61€ for adults and 30€ for children under 12, and do not include lunch, except in winter. Advance reservations are required.

Tulln: The Flower Town

Originally a naval base, Comagena, and later a center for the Babenberg dynasty, Tulln is one of the most ancient towns in Austria. Located on the right bank of the Danube, it is called "the flower town" because of the masses of blossoms you'll see in spring and summer. It's the place, according to the saga of the Nibelungen, where Kriemhild, the Burgundian princess of Worms, met Etzel, king of the Huns. A well-known "son of Tulln" was Kurt Waldheim, former secretary-general of the United Nations and president of Austria, who was plagued by his past Nazi affiliations.

ESSENTIALS
GETTING THERE Tulln lies 42km (26 miles) west of Vienna, on the south bank of the Danube, and 13km (8 miles) southwest of Stockerau, the next big town, on the north bank of the Danube. If you're driving from Vienna, head along the Danube Canal—Brigittenauer Lände/B227—and take the exit marked Klosterneuburger-Bundesstrasse/B14. Follow the B14 to Tulln.

Direct S-Bahn trains depart from Wien Franz-Josefs Bahnhof daily from 5am to 12am (trip time: 27–45 min.). You can also catch these trains at the U4 stops Spittelau and Heiligenstadt. Tulln lies on the busy main rail lines linking Vienna with Prague, and most local timetables list Gmund, an Austrian city on the border of the Czech Republic, as the final destination. For more information, call ② **05/1717,** or check **www.oebb.at.** We don't recommend taking the bus from Vienna, as it requires multiple transfers.

VISITOR INFORMATION The **tourist office** in Tulln, Minoritenplatz 2 (② **02272/67566;** www.tulln.at), is open from November to April, Monday to Friday 8am to 3pm; May to October Monday to Friday 9am to 7pm, Saturday and Sunday 10am to 7pm.

EXPLORING TULLN
The **Pfarrkirche** (Parish Church) of St. Stephan on Wiener Strasse grew out of a 12th-century Romanesque basilica dedicated to the Protomartyr. Its west portal was built in the 13th century. The Gothic overlay that followed fell victim to a baroque craze that swept the country during the 1700s. The 1786 altarpiece depicts the Saint's death by stoning.

Adjoining the church is the **Karner (Charnel House)** ★★, Wiener Strasse 20 (✆ **02272/62338**). This 11-sided polygonal structure, which was built sometime between 1240 and 1250, is not only a strikingly well-preserved example of late Romanesque, you can also visit the basement of the former bone house, where they would dump those who had outstayed their welcome in the cemetery.

In a restored former prison, Tulln has opened the **Egon Schiele Museum** ★★, Donaulände 28 (✆ **02272/64570**), devoted to its other famous son, born here in 1890. Schiele is one of the most influential Austrian artists of the early 1900s. The prison setting might be appropriate, as the expressionist painter spent 24 days in jail in 1912 in the town of Neulengbach for seducing a minor, who was probably acting as a model, and possession of what back then was regarded as pornography. While awaiting trial, he produced 13 watercolors, most of which are now in the Albertina in Vienna. The Tulln museum has more than 90 of his oil paintings, watercolors, and designs, along with lots of memorabilia. The museum is open Tuesday to Sunday, 10am to noon and 1 to 5pm, April 1 through November 1. It's also open on Mondays, which are holidays. Admission is 5€ for adults and 3.50€ for seniors, students, and children.

WHERE TO STAY & EAT

Design Hotel Römerhof　This new hotel near the river is easily accessible from the B14 and about a 15-minute walk from St. Stephan's. Its furnishings, like those of its older sister hotel, are pure functionality, but with the benefit of modern comforts. Try the dinner buffet.

CARNUNTUM

Begun as a Roman army camp in the 4th century A.D., this little-known ancient settlement became the center of the empire's fortifications for the region from Vindabona to the east. Later it became a main stop on the Amber Road, bringing this valuable resource from the Baltic Sea, crossing the Danube here and going on overland to the Adriatic, at what is now Trieste, and by ship to North Africa.

Today, the remains of the civilian settlement extend around the village of Petronell-Carnuntum, where a Roman city quarter is an open-air museum, with palace ruins, an amphitheater and arching *Heidentor,* or Meadow Gate. Built on and around real Roman ruins on the site, each house is reconstructed with contemporary materials and technology—terracotta, concrete, wood, and stone.

And inside, daily life is recreated; even the food in the kitchen is real. More than a museum, this is a chance for a visitor to feel the past as an intense present.

Parts of the site are still under construction; the large bathhouses scheduled to be finished by April 2011. Tours are available in English if arranged in advance; your chances are probably best during the week.

At various times throughout the year, the park also puts on events, from gladiators to garden parties. Once in March and once in May, you can also witness the architecture in action when the park's employees put on robes and sandals and take you on a tour of ancient life in the Danube Valley, as it was lived and preserved in these ruins.

Archäologischer Park Carnuntum ★ ☺
Hauptstr. 3, Petronell-Carnuntum
✆ 0/2163/3377-0.

Hafenstrasse 3, A-3430 Tulln an der Donau. ✆ **02272/62954.** www.hotel-roemerhof.at. 51 units. 76€–90€ double. Rates include buffet breakfast. MC, V. Free parking. **Amenities:** Dining room; bar; beer garden; sauna. *In room:* TV, minibar, hairdryer, safe, Wi-Fi available at 3€/hr.

Gasthaus zur Sonne (Gasthaus Sodoma) ★ AUSTRIAN   This is Tulln's finest and most famous restaurant. The 1940s' building, on the main street a short walk from the railway station, looks like a cross between a chalet and a villa. Under the direction of the Sodoma family since 1968, it consists of two cozy dining rooms lined with oil paintings. The menu invariably includes well-prepared versions of dumplings stuffed with minced meat, pumpkin soup, a marvelous Weiner schnitzel, onion-studded roast beef, *Tafelspitz,* and perfectly cooked *Zander* (a freshwater lake fish similar to perch) served with potatoes and butter sauce.

Bahnhofstrasse 48. ✆ **02272/64616.** Reservations recommended. Main courses 9€–27€. No credit cards. Tues–Sat 11:30am–1:30pm and 6–9pm.

Herzogenburg Monastery

A German bishop from Passau founded the Augustinian **Herzogenburg Monastery,** A-3130 Herzogenburg (✆ **02782/83113**), in the early 12th century. The present complex of buildings comprising the church and the abbey was reconstructed in the baroque style (1714–40). Jakob Prandtauer and Josef Munggenast, along with Fischer von Erlach, designed the buildings. The magnificent baroque church has a sumptuous interior, with an altarpiece by Daniel Gran and a beautiful organ loft. The most outstanding art owned by the abbey is a series of 16th-century **paintings on wood** ★; they are on display in a room devoted to Gothic art.

Entrance is 7€ for adults, 5€ for seniors and students. You can wander around alone or participate in a guided tour, departing daily at 9:30, 11am, and at 1:30, 2:30, and 3pm. The monastery is open only April to October daily from 9am to 6pm. There's a wine tavern in the complex where you can grab some Austrian fare while sampling the local grapes.

ESSENTIALS
GETTING THERE   Located 16km (10 miles) south of the Danube, the monastery is reached by taking Wiener Strasse (Rte. 1) out of St. Pölten. Head east for 13km (8 miles) toward Kapelln, and turn left at the sign along a minor road to Herzogenburg.

Krems ★

In the eastern part of the Wachau on the left bank of the Danube lies the 1,000-year-old city of Krems. The city today encompasses Stein and Mautern, once separate towns. Krems is a mellow town of old churches, courtyards, and cobblestones in the heart of vineyard country, with some partially preserved town walls. Just as the Viennese flock to Grinzing and other suburbs to sample new wine in the *Heuriger,* so the people of the Wachau come here to taste the fruit of the vine that appears in Krems earlier in the year.

ESSENTIALS
GETTING THERE   Krems is located 80km (50 miles) west of Vienna and 35km (22 miles) north of St. Pölten. If you're driving from Vienna, head north along the A22 until you approach the town of Stockerau. Here, exit onto the S5 and drive due west, following the signs to Krems.

A train with nonstop service to Krems departs daily from the Franz-Josefs Bahnhof every hour from 6:51am to 9:51pm (trip time: 60–95 min.). Trains with transfers at Absdorf-Hippersdorf or St. Pölten are available from Wien Nord (Praterstern) or Westbahnhof, respectively. For schedules, call ℂ **05/1717** in Vienna, or check **www. oebb.at**. We don't recommend traveling from Vienna to Krems by bus because of the many transfers required. Krems, however, is well connected by local bus lines to surrounding villages.

Between mid-May and late September, the Linz-based **Wurm & Köck Donau Schiffahrt GmbH** (ℂ **0732/783607;** www.donauschiffahrt.de) runs river cruises, which depart from Vienna every Sunday morning at 7:30am, arriving in Krems around 12:20pm. After a tour through the abbey at Krems, most passengers take any of the frequent trains back to Vienna.

VISITOR INFORMATION The Krems **tourist office,** at Utzstrasse 1 (ℂ **02732/82676;** www.krems.gv.at), is open Monday to Friday 9am to 6pm, Saturday 11am to 5pm, and Sunday 11am to 4pm.

EXPLORING KREMS

The most scenic part of Krems today is what used to be the village of **Stein.** Now called Stein an der Donau, its narrow streets run above the river, and the single main street, **Steinerlandstrasse,** is flanked by houses, many from the 16th century. The **Grosser Passauerhof,** Steinlanderstrasse 76 (ℂ **02732/82188**), is a Gothic structure decorated with an oriel. Another house, at Steinerlandstrasse 84, combines Byzantine and Venetian elements among other architectural influences; it was once the imperial tollhouse. Centuries ago, the aristocrats of Krems barricaded the Danube and extracted heavy tolls from the river traffic. When the tolls were more than the hapless victims could pay, the townspeople just confiscated the cargo. In the old city (*Altstadt*), the **Steiner Tor,** a 1480 gate, is a landmark.

Pfarrkirche St. Viet (ℂ **02732/857100**), the parish church of Krems, stands in the center of town at Pfarrplatz 5, where the Untere Landstrasse and Obere Landstrasse meet. The overtly ornate church is rich with gilt and statuary. Construction on this, one of the oldest baroque churches in the province, began in 1616. In the 18th century, Martin Johann Schmidt, better known as Kremser Schmidt, painted many of the frescoes inside the church.

Visit the **Weinstadt Museum Krems (The "Wine City" Museum of Krems),** Körnermarkt 14 (ℂ **02732/801567**) for a comprehensive survey of the city's cultural and commercial history. Arranged inside a restored 13th-century Dominican monastery, this collection of artifacts, from wine barrels to broad swords—frock to furniture—offers insight into the annals of this region. The museum is laid out on three levels, from the stone cellar to the upstairs art gallery, and includes a few works by the painter Martin Johann Schmidt. Admission is 4€ for adults and 2€ for children. It's open March to November, Wednesday to Saturday 10am to 6pm, Sundays and holidays 1 to 6pm.

For those interested in a more in-depth look at modern wine production, we recommend visiting **Winzer Krems,** Sandgrube 13 (ℂ **02732/85511**). You can take an informative hour-long guided tour of the winery, which includes a look at the vineyard, wine presses, the cellar (where a couple of pre-recorded ghosts talk about how to store old wine), and a short film. The tour includes three wine samples with bread. Admission is 11€ for adults and free for children under 16.

THE robber "GRASEL"

Lower Austria has its own version of Robin Hood in the person of Räuberhauptmann Grasel, who according to legend, hid out in the forests of the Weinviertel robbing from the rich to give to the poor overtaxed farmers of the district. A cherished, mythical figure, there are statues to Grasel, streets, guesthouses, and taverns named after this folk hero, about whom there are countless stories of the hapless and destitute saved at his hand.

The only trouble is, little of it is true. The real Johann Georg Grasel was in fact a pretty despicable character, from a family of thieves and swindlers, who began early and had already been jailed as a thief before the age of 10.

Not without a touch of style; he tagged along with his father who peddled drawings and paintings, burgling and picking pockets as they went. Later, they expanded petty crime to highway robbery and murder. Grasel gathered a band around him that at its peak numbered some 60 people, who terrorized the region, from southern Moravia to Hungary. Court records listed his worst crime, the murder of Anna Marie Schindlerin, on May 18, 1814.

A price of 400 Guildens was put on his head, and he was soon captured and taken to Vienna, where he was thrown in prison in leg irons and executed by hanging, on January 31, 1818. As he stood on the scaffold, he was reported to have looked out over the crowd in satisfaction, commenting, "Jesus! What a fine lot of people!"

For more of the lore, stop in at the **Graselwirtin,** in Mörtersdorf (© **02982-8235;** gasthaus@graselwirtin.at), open daily 9am to midnight. Or the **Höbarth-Madermuseum** of local folk art and artifacts (© **02982-23721)** in nearby Horn. Or yet the many castles, monasteries, and taverns in the area where Grasel surely paid a call or two during his years on the prowl.

NEARBY ATTRACTIONS

Twenty-nine kilometers (18 miles) north of Krems at St. Pölten is the Museum of Lower Austria, formerly located in Vienna. Now called **Landes Museum,** it's at Franz-Schubert-Platz (© **2742/908-090-999).** This museum exhibits the geology, flora, and fauna of the area surrounding Vienna. It also exhibits a collection of arts and crafts, including baroque and Biedermeier; temporary shows featuring 20th-century works are presented as well. Admission is 8€ for adults and 7€ for children. It's open Tuesday to Sunday 9am to 5pm.

WHERE TO STAY

Gourmethotel am Förthof ★ 🎁 This charming hotel has all the elements of a romantic country getaway. It boasts exceptional food, all from local farmers and a friendly atmosphere indicative of traditional Austrian hospitality. Each of the high-ceilinged bedrooms has a foyer and a shared balcony. Most bedrooms are fairly spacious. Bathrooms, though small, have well-kept tub/shower combinations. The hotel is entirely nonsmoking.

Donaulände 8, A-3500 Krems. © **02732/83345.** Fax 02732/833-4540. www.gourmethotel-foerthof. at. 20 units. 100€–150€ double. Rates include breakfast; half-board 25€ per person extra. AE, DC, MC, V. Free parking. **Amenities:** Restaurant; bar; outdoor pool; room service (7am–10pm); babysitting; dry cleaning; laundry service. *In room:* TV, hairdryer, minibar, safe, free Wi-Fi available on request.

Hotel Goldener Engel This family-run, multicultural bed & breakfast offers visitors a convenient base from which to explore Krems. The rooms are modest, comfortable, and well maintained. Other perks include a small outdoor swimming pool on a grassy terrace above the hotel with a view of the valley. An affordable suite with its own balcony is also available. The German-language section of the website includes a collection of panorama photographs, under "weitere Infos." All rooms are nonsmoking, but you can smoke in the courtyard and in the pool area.

Wienerstrasse 41, A-3500 Krems. © **02732/82067.** Fax 02732/77261. www.hotel-ehrenreich-krems.at. 21 units. 80€–114€ double. Rates include buffet breakfast; half-board 12€ extra per person. MC, V. Free parking. **Amenities:** Bar; outdoor pool; bike rental; laundry service. *In room:* TV, free Wi-Fi available on request.

WHERE TO EAT

Restaurant Bacher ★ AUSTRIAN/INTERNATIONAL   Lisl and Klaus Wagner-Bacher operate this excellent restaurant–hotel, with an elegant dining room and a well-kept garden. Specialties include crabmeat salad dressed with nut oil, and zucchini stuffed with fish and accompanied by two kinds of sauces. Dessert might be beignets with apricot sauce and vanilla ice cream. Lisl has won awards for her cuisine, as her enthusiastic clientele will tell you. The wine list has more than 600 selections.

Eight double and three single rooms are offered. Rooms contain TVs, minibars, phones, and radios, and each is attractively furnished with good beds and well-maintained bathrooms. Rates are 134€ to 190€ for a double with buffet breakfast. This establishment is just across the river, 4km (2½ miles) from Krems. Follow the signs from the bridge to Landhaus-Bacher.

Südtiroler Platz 208, A-2352 Mautern. © **02732/82937.** Fax 02732/74337. www.landhaus-bacher.at. Reservations required. Main courses 24€–39€; fixed-price menus 72€–99€. DC, V. Wed–Sat 11:30am–1:30pm and 6:30–9pm; Sun 11:30am–9pm. Closed mid-Jan to mid-Feb.

Dürnstein ★★

Less than 8km (5 miles) west of Krems, Dürnstein is arguably the loveliest town in the Wachau and, accordingly, draws throngs of visitors in summer. The ruins of Dürnstein Castle and the hiking paths around the mountain that indent to the left of the ruins make this an essential visit.

ESSENTIALS

GETTING THERE The town is 80km (50 miles) west of Vienna. If you're driving, take the A22 to S5 west. From Krems, continue driving west along the S5 (which becomes Route 3 or B3) for 8km (5 miles). Train travel to Dürnstein from Vienna requires a transfer in Krems (see above). In Krems, trains depart approximately every 2 hours on river-running routes; it's a 6-km (4-mile) trip to Dürnstein. For schedules, call © **05/1717** in Vienna, or check **www.oebb.at**. There's also a bus service between Krems and Dürnstein (trip time: 20 min.).

VISITOR INFORMATION A little **tourist office,** housed in a tiny shed in the east parking area called Parkplatz Ost (© **02711/200**), is open April to October 19 only. Hours are daily 11am to 1pm and 2 to 6:30pm.

A simple walk through town is special in Dürnstein; just take in the principal artery, **Hauptstrasse ★**, which is flanked by richly adorned ancient residences, many dating from the 1500s. Creamy stucco walls with heavy beam doors held

KING RICHARD'S prison TOWER

The ruins of the **castle fortress of Dürnstein,** 159m (522 ft.) above the town, accessible without restriction to hikers and families, are a fascinating destination and almost too good to be true. Here is where Richard the Lion-Hearted of England was held prisoner after having been captured in 1193 by the Babenburg Duke Leopold V, who kidnapped him on his way home from the Third Crusade. For a while, nobody knew exactly where in Austria Richard had been incarcerated. However, his loyal minstrel companion, Blondel (so the story goes) went from castle to castle, playing his lute and singing one of Richard's favorite songs. On hearing the song, Richard sang—or whistled—in reply. The discovery forced Leopold to transfer Richard to a castle in the Rhineland Palatinate. But the secret was out, and Leopold set a high ransom for the king's release, and Richard was set free. The fortifications were heavily damaged by the Swedes in 1645, but you can visit the ruins if you don't mind a short climb up from the town. It's a splendid "I capture the castle" outing for children and for adults, the view of Dürnstein and the Wachau is more than worth the effort.

together with iron studs, wide-board shutters and painted lettering, a low arch leading through a narrow alley, or a courtyard with steps down to a walled garden,—all have been well maintained through the centuries.

The 15th-century **Pfarrkirche (Parish Church)** merits a visit. The building was originally an Augustinian monastery and was reconstructed when the baroque style swept Austria. The church tower is a prominent landmark in the Danube Valley, with altar paintings by noted baroque artist Kremser Schmidt.

WHERE TO STAY & EAT

Gartenhotel Weinhof Pfeffel 🍴 This black-roofed, white-walled hotel is partially concealed by well-landscaped shrubbery. One of the best bargains in town, the hotel takes its name from its garden courtyard, where they serve tasty (but not fancy) meals. The public rooms are furnished with traditional pieces. The bedrooms are handsomely furnished with traditional Austrian motifs, with comfortable armchairs and good beds. Leopold Pfeffel, your host, serves wine from his own terraced vineyard.

Zur Himmelsstiege 122, A-3601 Dürnstein. 📞 **02711/206.** Fax 02711/12068. www.pfeffel.at. 40 units. 112€–132€ double; from 136€ suite. Rates include breakfast. MC, V. Free parking. Closed Dec–Feb. **Amenities:** Restaurant; bar; dry cleaning; laundry service; outdoor pool; room service; sauna. *In room:* TV, free Ethernet in the newer rooms, hairdryer, minibar, safe, free Wi-Fi in the older rooms.

Hotel-Restaurant Sänger Blondel ★ 🎁 Lemon-colored and charmingly old-fashioned, with green shutters and clusters of flowers at the windows, this hotel is named after the faithful minstrel who searched the countryside for Richard the Lion-Hearted. Bedrooms are furnished in a rustic style and are quite comfortable, containing small bathrooms equipped with shower units. All have good beds with fresh linens. Each Thursday, an evening of zither music is presented. If the weather is good, the music is played outside in the flowery chestnut garden near the baroque church tower. There's a good and reasonably priced restaurant serving regional cuisine.

A-3601 Dürnstein. ✆ **02711/253.** Fax 02711/2537. www.saengerblondel.at. 15 units. 92€–110€ double; 130€ suite. Rates include breakfast. MC, V. Parking 7€. Closed Dec–Feb. **Amenities:** Restaurant; dry cleaning; lounge; laundry service; free Internet in lobby. *In room:* TV, hairdryer.

Hotel Schloss Dürnstein ★★★

The perfect place for a fancy romantic dinner, this throwback villa has a stone terrace that actually overlooks the river. Elegantly furnished bedrooms come in a wide variety of styles, ranging from those that are large and palatial to others that are rather small and modern. All the bedrooms have modern bathrooms with tub/shower combinations, though sometimes in cramped conditions. The restaurant serves well-prepared dishes from the kitchen of an experienced chef.

A-3601 Dürnstein. ✆ **02711/212.** Fax 02711/212-30. www.schloss.at. 41 units. 235€–253€ double; from 338€–365€ suite. Rates include breakfast. AE, DC, MC, V. Free parking. Closed Nov 1–Easter. A pickup can be arranged at the Dürnstein rail station. **Amenities:** Restaurant; bar; 2 pools (1 heated indoor); fitness center; gymnastics center; sauna; room service; massage; babysitting; laundry service; dry cleaning, free Internet available in lobby. *In room:* TV, minibar, hairdryer, safe, Wi-Fi.

Romantik Hotel Richard Löwenherz ★★

This hotel was built on the site of a 700-year-old nunnery, originally dedicated to the sisters of Santa Clara in 1289. Its richly adorned interior is filled with antiques, Renaissance sculpture, chandeliers, stone vaulting, and paneling that has acquired a mellow patina over years of polishing. An arbor-covered sun terrace with restaurant tables extends toward the Danube. The bedrooms, especially those in the balconied modern section, are filled with cheerful furniture. The duvet-covered beds are the finest in the area. Each unit also has a beautifully kept bathroom. The restaurant offers a fine selection of local wines among its many regional specialties.

A-3601 Dürnstein. ✆ **02711/222.** Fax 02711/22218. www.richardloewenherz.at. 38 units. 166€–191€ double; 310€ suite. Rates include buffet breakfast. AE, MC, V. Free parking. Closed Nov to mid-Apr. **Amenities:** Restaurant; laundry service; lounge; outdoor heated pool; room service; free Wi-Fi. *In room:* TV, hairdryer, free Ethernet.

Melk

The words of Empress Maria Theresa speak volumes about Melk: "If I had never come here, I would have regretted it." The main attraction is the Melk Abbey, a sprawling baroque building overlooking the Danube basin. Melk marks the western terminus of the Wachau and lies upstream from Krems.

ESSENTIALS

GETTING THERE Melk is 89km (55 miles) west of Vienna. **Motorists** can follow the A1 (Link/St. Pölten), taking exit 80 to Melk. If you prefer a more romantic and scenic road, try the B3 from Krems, which parallels the Danube but takes 30 to 45 minutes longer. **Trains** leave frequently from Vienna's Westbahnhof to Melk, with two brief stops en route (trip time: about 1 hr.).

VISITOR INFORMATION The **Melk tourist office** at Babenbergerstrasse 1 (✆ **02752/52307410;** www.stadt-melk.at), in the center of town, is open April and October Monday to Friday 9am to noon and 2 to 6pm, Sunday 10am to 2pm; May, June, and September Monday to Friday 9am to noon and 2 to 6pm, Saturday and Sunday 10am to 2pm; July and August Monday to Saturday 9am to 7pm, Sunday 10am to 2pm.

WHAT TO SEE & DO

Melk Abbey ★★   The abbey and its **Stiftskirche (Abbey Church) ★** are the major attractions in Melk today. The town has been an important location in the Danube basin ever since the Romans built a fortress over this tiny "branch" of the Danube. Melk is also featured in the German epic poem, *Nibelungenlied,* in which it is called *Medelike.*

The rock-strewn bluff where the abbey now stands overlooking the river was the seat of the Babenbergs, who ruled Austria from 976 until the Habsburgs took over. In the 11th century, Leopold II of the House of Babenberg presented Melk to the Benedictine monks, who turned it into a fortified abbey. Its influence and renown as a center of learning and culture began to spread all over Austria. The Italian philosopher, Umberto Eco, no doubt aware of its reputation at the time, named the narrator of his 1980 novel, *The Name of the Rose,* after the town. The Reformation and the 1683 Turkish invasion took a toll on the abbey, although it was spared from direct attack when the Ottoman armies were repelled outside Vienna. The construction of the new building began in 1702, just in time to be given the full baroque treatment.

Most of the design of the present abbey was by the architect Jakob Prandtauer. Its marble hall, called the Marmorsaal, contains pilasters coated in red marble. A richly painted allegorical picture on the ceiling is the work of Paul Troger. The library, rising two floors, again with a Troger ceiling, contains some 80,000 volumes. The Kaisergang, or emperors' gallery, 198m (650 ft.) long, is decorated with portraits of Austrian rulers.

Despite all the adornment in the abbey, it is still surpassed in lavish glory by the Stiftskirche, the golden abbey church. Damaged by fire in 1947, the church has been fully restored, including the regilding of statues and altars with gold bullion. The church has an astonishing number of windows, and it's richly embellished with marble and frescoes. Many of the paintings are by Johann Michael Rottmayr, but Troger also contributed.

Melk is still a working abbey, and you might see black-robed Benedictine monks going about their business or students rushing out of the gates. Visitors head for the terrace for a view of the river. Napoleon probably used it for a lookout when he made Melk his headquarters during the campaign against Austria. Throughout the year, the abbey is open every day. From May to September, tours depart at intervals of 15 to 20 minutes. The first tour begins at 9am and the last is at 5pm; guides make efforts to translate into English a running commentary that is otherwise German.

Dietmayerstrasse 1, A-3390 Melk. *©* **02752/555-225** for tour information. www.stiftmelk.at. Guided tours 9.30€ adults, 5.90€ children, unguided tours 7.50€ adults, 4.10€ children; daily 9am–4:30pm (until 5:30pm May–Sept), last entry 30 min. before closing.

WHERE TO STAY

Hotel Stadt Melk ★ 🍴   Just below the town's palace, this four-story hotel, with a gabled roof and stucco walls, was originally built a century ago as a private home. It was eventually converted into this cozy, family-run hotel, and now has simply furnished bedrooms that are clean and comfortable, with sturdy beds. Well-maintained bathrooms, though small, are adequate and equipped with tub/shower combinations. Rooms in the rear open onto views of the abbey. The amiable restaurant has leaded-glass windows in round ripple patterns of greenish glass. Meals, beginning at 40€, are also served on a balcony at the front of the hotel. The food is quite good.

Hauptplatz 1, A-3390 Melk. ✆ **02752/52475.** Fax 02752/524-7519. www.tiscover.at/hotel-stadt-melk. 14 units. 93€ double; 180€ suite. Rates include breakfast. AE, DC, MC, V. Free parking. **Amenities:** 2 restaurants; bar; sauna; laundry service; dry cleaning service. *In room:* TV, minibar, hairdryer, safe.

WHERE TO EAT

Stiftsrestaurant Melk BURGENLANDER   If you're visiting Melk, this place is required dining. Sitting right at the entrance to the abbey, don't let its cafeteria-like dimensions sway you from its fine cuisine. This modern restaurant is well equipped to handle large groups—some 3,000 visitors a day frequent the establishment during peak season. From the reasonable fixed-price menu you might opt for the asparagus-and-ham soup with crispy dumplings; hunter's roast with mushrooms, potato cro-quettes, and cranberry sauce; and pretty decent *Sachertorte* for dessert.

Abt-Berthold-Dietmayrstrasse 3. ✆ **02752/52555.** www.stiftmelk.at. Main courses 10€–15€. AE, DC, MC, V. Mid-Mar to Oct daily 8am–6pm, Nov and Dec daily 10am–3pm. Closed otherwise.

BURGENLAND

Austria's easternmost and youngest province, Burgenland is a small border region created in 1921 from German-speaking areas of what was formerly Hungary. It marks the beginning of a large, flat puszta (steppe) that stretches nearly to Budapest, yet also lies on Vienna's doorstep. The province shares a western border with Styria and Lower Austria, and its long eastern boundary separates it from Hungary. Slovakia sits to Burgenland's northeast and Slovenia borders its southern edge.

One of the most fertile areas of Austria, it is considered the vegetable garden of Vienna. Burgenland is a predominantly agricultural province and is also known for its recently booming green energy sector, being home to the largest wind farm in Austria. It is noted for its vineyards, producing more than one-third of all the wine made in Austria. The province is situated where the Hungarian *puszta* gradually modulates into the foothills of the eastern Alps; forests cover 29% of its area, and vineyards compose 7% of its agricultural lands. Its Pannonia climate is known for its hot summers with little rainfall and cold winters. For the most part, you can enjoy sunny days from early spring until late autumn, one of the sunniest in central Europe.

Burgenland's population is vibrantly mixed, both historically and today. Around 2% of the population is Hungarian, while some 10% consists of Croats who settled here in the 16th century after fleeing their homes before the advance of Turkish armies. Roma also continue to reside in the area, where they live as integrated members of society. For hundreds of years, the various ethnic and national groups have lived there together, over time becoming increasingly homogenous. At the same time, Burgenland has evolved from the poorest province in Austria, eclipsed by the shadows of the Iron Curtain for nearly half a century, to a thriving region with high employment and a dynamic economy.

The ethnic diversity has produced a regional cuisine that is among the best in Europe. Its eastern neighbors, especially Hungary, provide strong influences that you will discover in goulashes and fine patisserie, as well as goose dishes. Wild game, particularly wild boar and pheasant, thrives in the wooded areas of Burgenland and is a favorite on local menus.

Eisenstadt, the small provincial capital of Burgenland since 1924, was for many years the home of Franz Josef Haydn, and the composer is buried here. Neusiedl is the only steppe lake in central Europe. If you're here in summer, exploring the lake by sailboat is the ideal experience due to the constant, gusty winds. Seewinkel, a marshy haven for hundreds of species of birds and rare flora, surrounds Illmitz, an old village near Lake Neusiedl. Like Lower Austria, Burgenland contains numerous fortresses and castles, many in ruins. The word "Burgenland" originated from the region's historical name *Vierburgenland* (land of four castles), referring to four distinct counties: Pressburg, Wieselburg, Ödenburg, and Eisenburg. Although several of these counties no longer fall within Austrian borders, the name Burgenland seemed appropriate to keep due to the many castles that remained. Accommodations in this province are limited, but they're among the least expensive in the country. You'll find a few romantic castle hotels, small guesthouses, and lakeside resorts. Parking is rarely a problem in the smaller towns, and, unless otherwise noted, you park for free. The warm months are the best time to visit Burgenland, lasting from April through October.

EISENSTADT: HAYDN'S HOME

50km (31 miles) SE of Vienna

When Burgenland joined Austria after World War I came to an end, it was a province without a capital—its former seat of government, Ödenburg (now the far-western Hungarian city of Sopron), voted in a referendum in December of 1921 to remain part of Hungary. In 1924, Burgenlanders bestowed the honor upon Eisenstadt. This small town lies at the foot of the Leitha Mountains, at the beginning of the steppe extending into Hungary. Surrounded by vineyards, forests, and fruit trees, it's a convenient stop for exploring Lake Neusiedl, 10km (6 miles) east.

Essentials

GETTING THERE While Südbahnhof remains under construction (through 2014), many of the trains departing for Eisenstadt have been rerouted to Meidling in the southwest of Vienna. This station can be reached with the U6 underground line. From Südbahnhof connections now continue directly to Eisenstadt through Neusiedl am See (trip time: 90 min.). From Meidling the connection is made at Wulkaprodersdorf. A bus from the station at Südtirolerplatz is another option, which will bring you directly to Eisenstadt's Domplatz. For schedules, call ✆ **05/1717** in Vienna, or check **www.oebb.at**.

If you're driving from Vienna, take Route 10 east to Parndorf Ort, and then head southwest along Route 50 to Eisenstadt. A more convenient, if less scenic, route takes drivers south out of the city on the A2, switching to the A3 that goes directly to Eisenstadt.

VISITOR INFORMATION The **Eisenstadt tourist office,** Schloss Esterházy (✆ **02682/67390**), will make hotel reservations for you at no charge and distributes information (in English).

Where Josef Haydn Lived & Worked

Even before assuming its new role as capital, Eisenstadt was renowned as the place where the great composer Franz Josef Haydn lived and worked while under the patronage of the Esterházys. For a good part of his life (1732–1809), Haydn divided his time between Eisenstadt and the Esterházy Castle in Hungary. Prince Esterházy eventually gave the composer his own orchestra and a concert hall in Eisenstadt in which to perform.

Every September, the **Haydn Days** festival presents an ongoing roster of the composer's works at various venues throughout town—the castle, local churches, parks—when the weather accommodates. The theme changes from year to year.

Bergkirche (also known as the Haydn Church)   If you want to pay your final respects to Haydn, follow Hauptstrasse to Esterházystrasse, which leads to this church containing Haydn's white marble tomb. Until 1954, only the composer's headless body was here. The church itself contains an architectural distinctiveness: A spiral ramp on the outside perimeter of the building leads up to the steeple, taking visitors on a tour of the passion of the Christ on the Calvary.

Josef-Haydn-Platz 1. ✆ **02682/62638.** Church free admission; Haydn's mausoleum, treasure chamber, and Kalvarienberg 3€ adults, 2€ seniors, 1€ students. Daily 9am–5pm. Closed Nov–Mar. From Esterházy Platz at the castle, head directly west along Esterházystrasse, a slightly uphill walk.

Haydn Museum   The home of the composer from 1766 to 1778 is now a museum. Reconstructed rooms give viewers an intimate perspective of Haydn's life, using personal letters and other memoirs. Although he appeared in court nearly every night, Haydn actually lived very modestly when he was at home. He was one of the more productive composers, creating over 107 symphonies and 24 operas among numerous solo pieces and concerts. Haydn also composed Germany's current national anthem, albeit unintentionally.

Joseph-Haydn-Gasse 19 and 21. ✆ **02682/7193900.** www.haydnhaus.at. Admission 4€ adults; 3.50€ children, seniors, and students. Daily 9am–5pm. Closed Nov–Mar. Pass Schloss Esterházy and turn left onto Joseph-Haydn-Gasse.

Schloss Esterházy ★   Haydn worked in this château built on the site of a medieval castle and owned by the Esterházy princes. The Esterházy clan was a great Hungarian family with vast estates that ruled over Eisenstadt and its surrounding area. They claimed descent from Attila the Hun. The Esterházys helped the Habsburgs gain control of Hungary; so great was their loyalty to Austria, in fact, that when Napoleon offered the crown of Hungary to Nic Esterházy in 1809, he refused it.

In the late 17th and early 18th centuries, it was given a baroque pastel facade. On the first floor, the great baronial hall was made into the Haydnsaal, where the composer conducted the orchestra Prince Esterházy had provided for him. The walls and ceilings of this concert hall are elaborately decorated, but the floor is of bare wood, which, it is claimed, is the reason for the room's acoustic perfection. Part of the castle provides rooms for the provincial parliament.

Esterházy Platz. ✆ **02682/6385412.** www.schloss-esterhazy.at. Admission 7.50€ adults; 6.50€ children, seniors, and students; 16€ family ticket. July–Aug daily 9am–7pm; Mar–June and Sept–Nov daily 9am–6pm; Nov–Dec Thurs–Sun 9am–6pm; closed Jan–Feb. From the bus station at Domplatz, follow the sign to the castle (a 10-min. walk).

Where to Stay & Eat

Gasthof Ohr   Although the rooms of this pleasant inn are clean and comfortable, with exposed paneling, comfortable beds, and a sense of old-fashioned charm, the place is more famous and more consistently popular as a restaurant, where main courses cost 12€ to 20€ each, and where the kitchen consistently turns out flavorful portions of *Tafelspitz,* freshwater fish dishes including zander in white wine and capers, as well as seasonal and regional delights such as wild boar and asparagus. The restaurant is open from June through September Monday 11am to 2pm and 6 to

Eisenstadt: Haydn's Home

BURGENLAND

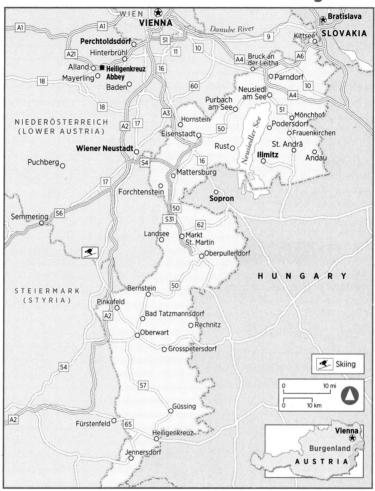

9pm. Tuesday through Saturday 11am to 3pm and 5:30 to 10pm. Sunday from 11am to 9pm. Check the website for hours during the colder months. This inn is just across from Eisenstadt's bus station.

Rusterstrasse 51, A-7000 Eisenstadt. © **02682/62460.** Fax 02682/624609. www.hotelohr.at. 40 units. 90€–145€ double. DC, MC, V. Parking 7€. **Amenities:** Restaurant; room service; babysitting. *In room:* TV, Wi-Fi.

Hotel Burgenland   This hotel opened in 1982 and quickly established itself as the best in Eisenstadt. A mansard roof, white stucco walls, and big windows form the exterior of this hotel located directly northeast of the bus station at Domplatz. The rooms have lots of light, comfortable beds, and functional furniture.

One of the best restaurants in Burgenland is the hotel's sleek and modern Bienenkorb. Bright and airy, it serves traditional Austrian dishes, Pannonia cuisine as well as dishes with a Mediterranean flair.

Schubertplatz 1, A-7000 Eisenstadt. (✆ **02682/6960.** Fax 02682/65531. www.hotelburgenland.at. 88 units. 120€–165€ double; from 200€ suite. Rates include buffet breakfast. AE, DC, MC, V. Parking 10€. **Amenities:** Restaurant; bar; babysitting (upon request); exercise room; indoor heated pool; nonsmoking rooms; room service; sauna. *In room:* TV, hairdryer, minibar, Wi-Fi.

Shopping

With a little effort, you can find some tempting shops in Eisenstadt's old town. Most appealing to visitors in our opinion is **Trachten Tack,** Hauptstrasse 8 (✆ **02682/62428**), where you'll find a family-owned shop carrying traditional *Trachten* clothing, as well as the widest selection of handicrafts in town.

Carrying an impressive inventory of wine, **Schloss Weingut Esterházy,** Schloss Esterházy (✆ **02682/6334518**), is set on the street level of Eisenstadt's famous building. Most of the wine is produced on the 60 hectares (148 acres) of vineyards associated with the castle.

Eisenstadt After Dark

Don't expect a lot, as there simply isn't much nightlife within small and sleepy Eisenstadt. You might have a quiet drink or two at such popular spots as the **Café Alex Nöhrer,** Ignaz-Semmelweisse-Gasse 1 (✆ **02682/65593**). Currently enjoying popularity are the **Mangoo Bar,** Domplatz 4 (✆ **0664/9793160**), and **Bodega La Ina,** Hauptstrasse 48 (✆ **02682/62305**). And if you want to go dancing, head for the town's only dance club, the **James Dean,** Mattesburgerstrasse 26 (✆ **2682/64249**), a trendy combination of *Mitteleuropa* and 1950s' America.

A Side Trip to Franz Liszt's Birthplace

In Raiding, a small nearby village 55km (34 miles) south of Eisenstadt, the **Franz-Liszt-Geburtshaus** contains many mementos of the pianist and composer's life, including an old church organ he used to play. The Franz Liszt Concert Hall near the museum hosts a festival in honor of the composer every October.

To get to the museum (✆ **02619/51047**), take Route S31 south of Eisenstadt; then cut east onto a minor unmarked road at Lackenbach (follow the signs to Raiding from there). It's open only from Palm Sunday to October (daily 9am–noon and 1–5pm). Admission is 3.50€ for adults and 2€ for seniors, children, and students; a family ticket sells for 7€.

NEUSIEDLERSEE ★

The region encompassing Neusiedlersee (Lake Neusiedl) is a famous getaway for the Viennese, and North Americans will find it just as desirable. The lake offers countless diversions, making it an ideal destination for families or active travelers. The geological anomaly of the Neusiedler (see "The Capricious Lake," below) and the steppe landscape make for intriguing hikes, strolls, and bike tours. Steady winds make the lake ideal for sailing, kite surfing, and windsurfing; in fact, the lake hosts a Professional Windsurfers Association World Cup competition every spring.

Neusiedl am See

On the northern shore of Lake Neusiedl lies this popular summer weekend spot where watersports prevail. You can rent sailboats, take windsurfing lessons, rent a bike, or even go for a horseback ride at a nearby stable. A watchtower from the Middle Ages still stands guard over the town with a sweeping view of the lake. Many lush vineyards cover the nearby fields. If you plan to be here on a summer weekend, be sure to make reservations in advance.

Neusiedl am See is also home to the Weinwerk, a cultural center dedicated to Burgenland's prized wineries. Here you can taste over 500 wines from 150 vinters and buy the best by the bottle. The Weinwerk can be reached at ✆ **02167/20705** and is located at Obere Hauptstrasse 31.

ESSENTIALS

GETTING THERE   Neusiedl am See lies 45km (28 miles) southeast of Vienna, 359km (223 miles) east of Salzburg, and 34km (21 miles) northeast of Eisenstadt. The town is less than an hour by express **train** from Vienna (✆ **05/1717;** www.oebb. at). If you're **driving** from Vienna, take the A-4 or Route 10 east. If you're in Eisenstadt, head northeast along Route 50, cutting east along Route 51 for a short distance. It's better to have a car if you're exploring Lake Neusiedl, although there are **bus** connections that depart several times daily from the Domplatz bus station at Eisenstadt.

VISITOR INFORMATION   The **Neusiedl am See tourist office,** Untere Haupstrasse 7 (✆ **02167/2229**), distributes information about accommodations and boat rentals. Open July and August Monday to Friday 8am to 6pm, Saturday 10am to noon and 2–6pm, Sunday 9am to noon; May and June Monday to Friday 8am to 5pm; September Monday to Friday 8am to noon and 1–5pm; October to April Monday through Thursday 8am to noon and 1–4:30pm, Fridays 8am to 1 pm.

WHERE TO STAY & EAT

Hotel Wende ★   Set at the edge of town on the road leading to the water, the hotel is almost a village unto itself. The bedrooms are well furnished, with well-maintained bathrooms containing tub/shower combinations. A swimming pool, wellness and fitness center allow guests to enjoy relaxation and activity combined.

A restaurant, bar, and daytime cafe complete the culinary setup, with a winter garden providing a bright accompaniment. The menu includes a savory soup made with fresh carp; pork cutlets with homemade noodles, bacon-flavored *Rösti* (fried potatoes); Hungarian crepes stuffed with minced veal and covered with paprika-cream sauce; and, for dessert, a strudel studded with fresh dates and topped with marzipan-flavored whipped cream.

Seestrasse 40-50, A-7100 Neusiedl am See. ✆ **02167/8111.** Fax 02167/811-1649. www.hotel-wende.at. 105 units. 140€–170€ double; 316€–320€ suite. Rates include half-board. AE, DC, MC, V. Parking garage 10€. Closed first 2 weeks in Feb. Free pickup from the Neusiedl am See train station. **Amenities:** Restaurant; bar; children's room; fitness room; Jacuzzi; indoor heated pool; massage; nonsmoking rooms; room service; sauna. *In room:* TV, hairdryer, minibar, Wi-Fi.

Landgasthaus am Nyikospark ★★   The open, contemporary apartments of Nyikospark offer a modern alternative to the conventional hotels of the area. Large glass windows allow a wide view over the town and lake, flat-screen TVs provide the

THE CAPRICIOUS lake

Neusiedler See (Lake Neusiedl) is a popular steppe lake lying in the northern part of Burgenland. But this strange lake should never be taken for granted—in fact, from 1868 to 1872, it completely dried up, as it has done periodically throughout its known history. Such behavior has led to some confusing real-estate disputes among bordering landowners. The lake was once part of a body of water that blanketed all of the Pannonian Plain. Today its greatest depth is about 1.8m (6 ft.), and the wind can shift the water dramatically, even causing parts of the lake to dry up. The lake is between 7 and 15km (4¼–9¼ miles) wide and about 35km (22 miles) long.

A broad belt of reeds encircles the huge expanse. This thicket is an ideal habitat for many varieties of waterfowl. In all, some 250 different species of birds inhabit the lake, including the usual collection of storks, geese, duck, and herons. The plant and animal life in the lake is unique in Europe. Within its slightly salty waters, alpine, Baltic, and Pannonian flora and fauna meet.

Viennese flock to the lake throughout the year; in summer to fish, sail, and windsurf, and in winter to skate. The temperate climate and fertile soil surrounding the west bank are ideal for vineyards. Washed in sun, the orchards in Rust produce famous award-winning vintages.

entertainment, and the bright colors of the rooms' decor—yellow, green, orange, and red—give a modern flair to a cozy Burgenland town. The apartments are located across the street from the restaurants, where you'll find modern versions of classic Pannonian delights such as wild duck with fig polenta and calf liver with pear pomace (10€–23€ for main courses).

Untere Hauptstrasse 59, A-7100 Neusiedl am See. © **02167/40222.** Fax 02167/7778. www.nyikospark. at. 5 units. 100€ double, 140€ suite. For breakfast a surcharge of 10€. AE, MC, V. Free parking. **Amenities:** 2 restaurants; bar. In room: A/C, TV, Wi-Fi.

Mole West ★★ INTERNATIONAL   If you want to take in the beauty of the area while having a fine meal, this is the place to go: A large wooden deck protrudes into the lake, where the setting sun can be watched in the evening. If the weather doesn't allow for outdoor dining, a glassed dining room allows the same view. The restaurant's philosophy endorses a modern international kitchen with local influences using the freshest ingredients. Wild saltimbocca with mushroom gnocchi on a bed of artichoke hearts is just one suggestion.

Strandbad Westmole, A-7100 Neusiedl am See. © **02683/20205.** Reservations recommended. Main courses 11€–26€. Jan–Mar Thurs–Sun 9am–midnight; Apr–mid Nov daily 9am–midnight. Closed mid Nov–end Dec.

SHOPPING

A fairly recent addition to the Neusiedl area, the Parndorf designer outlet center, draws shoppers from all over Austria as well as neighboring countries. It is only a short drive (5km or about 3 miles) from Neusiedl am See. Here you can find everything from Ralph Lauren to Pepe Jeans to Burberry in 150 shops, normally sold at discounts of up to 70%. Parking is free. To get there, take Neusiedler-Bundesstrasse 51 toward the town of Parndorf, exit onto Burgenland Bundesstrasse 50, and then just follow the signs.

Rust

South of Purbach, this small village prides itself on being Austria's smallest *Staturstadt,* or village with legal status. Its stork nests are perched on chimneys throughout the town. Its antiquated but charming town center is well preserved and clean, with sections dating back to the 17th century, such as the walls built in 1614 for protection against the Turks.

Rust is tucked in a rich setting of vineyards famed for the Burgenlander grape, specifically dessert wines such as the *Beerenauslese* and the *Ruster Ausbruch.* At certain times, you can go right up to the door of a vintner's farmhouse, especially if a green bough is displayed, to sample and buy wine on the spot. The town holds a wine festival in late July, called the Ruster Goldene Weinwoche, where the ancient wine cellars of the main street cater to wine-loving visitors and local craftsmen offer baskets made from lake reeds.

ESSENTIALS

GETTING THERE The village is 18km (11 miles) northeast of Eisenstadt, 71km (44 miles) southeast of Vienna, and 349km (217 miles) east of Salzburg. There's no train station, but buses connect Eisenstadt with Rust. For bus information, call the regional public transportation office (© **0810/222324**). From Eisenstadt by car, head east on Route 52. From Purbach, take Route 50 south toward Eisenstadt. At Seehof, take a left fork to Oggau and Rust.

VISITOR INFORMATION The **Rust tourist office,** Conradplatz 1, in the city center (© **02685/502**), can arrange inexpensive stays with English-speaking families. Opening hours: April and October Monday to Saturday 9am to noon and 1 to 4pm; May, June, and September Monday to Friday 9am to noon and 1 to 5pm, Saturday 9am to noon and 1 to 4pm; July and August Monday to Friday 9am to noon and 1 to 6pm, Saturday 9am to noon and 1 to 4pm, Sunday 9am to noon; November through February Monday to Thursday 9am to noon and 1 to 4pm, Friday 9am to noon.

WHERE TO STAY & EAT

Hotel-Restaurant Sifkovitz ★ Attracting summer visitors from Vienna and Hungary, this hotel consists of an older building with a new wing. Rooms get a lot of sun and are functional but comfortably furnished. There's no great style here, but the beds are firm and the bathrooms, although not large, are well maintained and equipped with tub/shower combinations. The hotel's large garden gives guests ample space to relax in the fresh air. A wine bar serves locally produced specialties, while the restaurant supplies the local fare.

Am Seekanal 8, A-7071 Rust. © **02685/276.** Fax 02685/36012. www.sifkovits.at. 33 units. 80€–130€ double. Rates include buffet breakfast. AE, DC, MC, V. Closed Dec–Mar. **Amenities:** Restaurant; bar; fitness center; nonsmoking rooms; room service; sauna. *In room:* TV, hairdryer, minibar, Wi-Fi.

Mooslechner's Burgerhaus ★ AUSTRIAN/CONTINENTAL This *gemütlich,* middle-bracket tavern in the heart of town is one of the most charming. Within a venue that dates from the 1530s, it provides plenty of old-fashioned charisma. The food, focused on traditional preparations of zander, goose, and, in-season game dishes, evokes traditional Austria at its best. The cook here is particularly proud of the terrines of goose liver that emerge from the kitchen. The venue is cozy and rather charming (seating only 60–80 diners).

Hauptstrasse 1. ✆ **02685/6416.** Reservations recommended only in midsummer. 3- 4- and 5-course menus 42€–72€. DC, MC, V. Daily noon–2pm and 6–10pm. Closed Jan–Feb.

Seehotel Rust ★   One of the most attractive hotels in the lake district, Seehotel Rust is set on a grassy lawn at the edge of the lake. This well-designed hotel remains open year-round, and offers pleasantly furnished bedrooms and clean bathrooms equipped with a shower unit. Most rooms have spacious balconies with a view over the lake. Culinary offerings in the restaurant include every type of fish from the lake as well as the hearty, meaty dishes from the land.

Am Seekanal 2–4, A-7071 Rust. ✆ **02685/3810.** Fax 02685/381419. www.seehotel-rust.at. 110 units. 166€–201€ double; from 220€ suite. Rates include half-board. DC, MC, V. Free parking. **Amenities:** Restaurant; bar; babysitting; boat rental; fitness center; indoor heated pool; spa; squash court; 4 tennis courts (2 indoor); room service; nonsmoking rooms. *In room:* TV, hairdryer, minibar, Wi-Fi.

Illmitz: A Steppe Village

This old *puszta* village on the east side of the lake has grown into a town with a moderate tourist business in summer. From Eisenstadt, take Route 50 northeast, through Purbach, cutting southeast on Route 51, via Podersdorf, to Illmitz. It's a 61-km (38-mile) drive, which seems long because traffic must swing around the lake's northern perimeter before heading south to Illmitz. There are a number of horse stables in the area, and horse-back riding on the grassy plains next to the lake has become a major tourist attraction.

NEARBY OFFBEAT ATTRACTIONS

Leaving Illmitz, head east on the main route and then cut north at the junction with Route 51. From Route 51, the little villages of Frauenkirchen, St. Andrä bei Frauenkirchen, and Andau are signposted.

Frauenkirchen has a cute pedestrian zone with a number of shops, a basilica, a Franciscan monastery, and great *Vinotheken* (wine bars). One winery from this town has risen to the ranks of the French and Italian: Weingut Umathum. The estate is located right outside the village and is open Monday to Friday 9am to 6pm, Saturdays 10am to 5pm. You can go on a tour of the vineyards and cellars and afterwards enjoy a wine-tasting.

Near the Hungarian border, the tiny village of **St. Andrä bei Frauenkirchen** is filled with thatch houses. The town is known for its basket weaving, so a shopping expedition can be planned when exploring the area.

A short drive farther will take you to **Andau,** which became the focus of world attention in 1956 during the Hungarian uprising. It was through this point that hundreds of Hungarians dashed to freedom in the west, fleeing the grim Soviet invasion of Budapest.

Starting in the late 1940s, the border with Hungary was closely guarded, and people who tried to escape into Austria were shot from the Communist-controlled watchtowers. But time has rendered the region's bleak past obsolete. In 1989, the fortifications were broken down, and before the year was out, the once-fortified border was completely opened.

The surrounding marshy area of this remote sector of Austria, called **Seewinkel,** is a large natural wildlife sanctuary. The area, dotted with windmills and reed thickets, is a haven for birds, many small animals, and some rare flora.

A newly opened spa and lodge—**St. Martins Therme Seewinkel**—is well integrated into this ecologically sensitive area. Burgenland's spas are famous in Austria due to the naturally warm water emanating from numerous springs throughout the area. The indoor and outdoor thermal pools at St. Martins allow guests to relax and recover in the invigorating waters. Day tickets are available for 20€; rooms in the adjoining lodge are also available (call **02172/20500** for further details).

WHERE TO STAY & EAT

Vila Vita Pannonia ★   This large resort is a favorite hangout for non-Austrian visitors, even during the winter months. Set in the utter calm of the *puszta,* it provides a perfect escape for those seeking tranquility and relaxation. Located about 11km (6 miles) outside Illmitz, right next to the Hungarian border, this four-star resort offers everything you need for a romantic getaway or a family trip. Outdoor activities—from horse-back riding to tennis to biking—can be organized by the staff, mostly for an extra charge, though bikes are free. Food and beverages are provided by the numerous establishments on site, including a piano bar and a cigar lounge, which will satisfy just about any taste or mood. The resort embodies the eco-friendliness of Burgenland: An on-site energy center provides 85% of the resort's energy needs.

Storchengasse 1, A-7152 Illmitz. ✆ **02175/21800.** www.vilavitahotels.com. 33 units. 150€–210€ double, from 240€. Rates include half-board (evening buffet or 4-course menu) with a surcharge of 26€. AE, DC, MC, V. **Amenities:** 3 restaurants; 2 bars; children's center; fitness center; hair salon; horse-back riding; massage; minigolf; pools (indoor heated and outdoor); spa; tennis courts (2 indoor, 3 outdoor). *In room:* A/C, TV, hairdryer, minibar, Wi-Fi.

Weingut-Weingasthof Rosenhof ★   This charming baroque hotel is surrounded by greenery. Through the arched gateway, framed by a gold-and-white facade, is a rose-laden courtyard filled with arbors. The tile-roofed building, capped with platforms for storks' nests, contains cozy, perfectly maintained bedrooms and bathrooms with shower units.

   In an older section, you'll find a wine restaurant whose star attraction is the recent vintage produced by the Haider family's wine presses. The restaurant serves Hungarian and Burgenland specialties, including wild boar cooked in a marinade thickened with regional walnuts. Locally caught fish, such as carp and the meaty zander, are in abundance. In autumn, the inn serves *Traubensaft*—delectable juice made from freshly harvested grapes that is consumed before it becomes alcoholic. In the evening, musicians fill the air with gypsy music.

Florianigasse 1, A-7142 Illmitz. ✆ **02175/2232.** Fax 02175/22324. www.rosenhof.cc. 15 units. 94€–102€ double. Rates include half-board. MC, V. Closed mid Nov–Easter. **Amenities:** Restaurant; bar; sauna. *In room:* TV, hairdryer, Wi-Fi.

Podersdorf: Best in Swimming

Podersdorf am See is one of the best places to go swimming in the lake, as the shoreline here is relatively free of reeds. Over the years, the little town has become a modest summer resort. The parish church in the village dates from the late 18th century. Check out the thatched-roof cottages where you might see storks nesting in the chimneys. The Viennese like to drive out here during the summer to go for a swim and to purchase wine from the local vintners.

   The town has been put on the map since it began hosting the Windsurfers Association World Cup competition, held every spring over 6 days in late April and early May. Windsurfers from all over the world convene in this small town for the competition, and spectators from across Austria come for the festivities. You can sit on the grass next to the lake and enjoy a delicious Austrian beer while watching the event in the warm spring sun.

ESSENTIALS

GETTING THERE   Podersdorf lies 14km (9 miles) south of Neusiedl am See. It's easiest to drive here, although buses run throughout the day from Eisenstadt via Neusiedl am See. If you're driving from Eisenstadt, head northeast along Route 50, via Purbach, cutting southeast at the junction with Route 51; you'll go via Neusiedl am See before cutting south along the lake to Podersdorf.

VISITOR INFORMATION   In summer, a little **tourist office** at Hauptstrasse 2 (✆ **02177/2227**) dispenses information daily 8am to 5pm.

WHERE TO STAY

Haus Attila   This hotel was recently enlarged so that its best rooms overlook the lake. The light-grained balconies are partially shielded by a row of trees, though a view of the sunset is still possible. Rooms are clean and comfortable, and the tiny shower-only bathrooms are well maintained. Many visitors who check in for a couple of days of lakeside relaxation never move too far, consuming their meals in the dining room of the Seewirt, less than 91m (298 ft.) away. In the basement of a nearby annex is a well-stocked wine cellar, where a member of the Karner family can take you for a wine tasting. Some of the vintages are produced from their own vineyards.

Strandplatz 8, A-7141 Podersdorf. ✆ **02177/2415.** Fax 02177/246530. www.seewirtkarner.at. 38 units. 101€–165€ double. Rates include breakfast. AE, DC, MC, V. Closed Nov 1–Feb. **Amenities:** Lounge; indoor heated pool; room service; nonsmoking rooms; rooms for those w/limited mobility; sauna. *In room:* TV, hairdryer.

Seehotel Herlinde   This favorite destination spot is on the beach of Lake Neusiedl away from the main highway. All the functionally furnished rooms have their own balconies; the best have views of the lake. Room size is only adequate; the beds are nothing special, though the mattresses are firm. The food and wine are plentiful, the latter often enjoyed on a 200-seat terrace. The hotel is entirely nonsmoking.

Strandplatz 17, A-7141 Podersdorf. ✆ **02177/2273.** Fax 02177/2430. 40 units. 106€ double. Rates include breakfast and lunch. MC, V. **Amenities:** Restaurant; bar; sauna. *In room:* TV, hairdryer, minibar.

WHERE TO EAT

Gasthaus zur Dankbarkeit BURGENLAND/AUSTRIAN   This restaurant is a favorite of the locals. The menu boasts regional specialties such as the *Seespargel* (lake asparagus) along with fish from Neusiedlersee and hearty meat dishes known and loved throughout Burgenland. The kitchen changes with the seasons, but the wine list will always offer the same beauties from the region as well as the finest from other parts of Austria. Over 50 different types of Burgenland dessert wines, such as the *Beerenauslese, Trockenbeerenauslese,* and *Eiswein* wines, are offered at the restaurant and the wine bar, which is open from 5pm Thursday through Sunday.

Hauptstrasse 39, A-7141 Podersdorf. ✆ **02177/2223.** Reservations recommended. Main courses 13€–22€; 5- and 6-course menus 50€–55€, with wine accompaniment 23€. Closed Dec–early Jan. April–Nov Mon, Tues, and Fri 11:30am–2pm and 5:30–9pm; Sat, Sun (and holidays) 11:30–9pm. Jan–Mar Fri 11:30am–2pm and 5:30–9pm. Sat, Sun (and holidays) 11:30am–9pm. Closed Wed and Thurs throughout the year.

Gasthof Seewirt Café Restaurant ★ BURGENLANDER/INTERNATIONAL
The preferred place for dining at the resort is this likable and unpretentious hotel restaurant that prepares bountiful dishes served by formally dressed waiters who are eager to describe the local cuisine. The Karner family—well-known vintners whose excellent Rieslings, red and white pinots, and *Weisburgunders* are available for consumption—are proud of their long-established traditions and a local cuisine that is infused with the Hungarian flair. A house specialty is *Palatschinken Marmaladen,* consisting of tender roast beef glazed with apricot jam, and a dessert called *Somloer Nockerl,* made of vanilla pudding, whipped cream, raisins, and nuts in a biscuit shell.

Strandplatz 1. ✆ **02177/2415.** Main courses 8€–14€. AE, MC, V. Daily 11:30am-2:30pm and 6-9:30pm. Closed Nov-Mar.

FORCHTENSTEIN

This town resembles so many others along the way that you could easily pass through it without taking much notice. However, Forchtenstein is home to one of the most famous of the Esterházy castles, which is reason enough to make it a stop on your trip.

Essentials

GETTING THERE   From Eisenstadt, take Route S-31 southwest to Mattersburg, and from there follow the signs along a very minor road southwest to Forchtenstein. Buses leave from Vienna's Südtirolerplatz and go straight to Forchtenstein (1 hr., 20 min.), and trains from Vienna's Meidling station bring you all the way to the center of town (40 min.). From Eisenstadt, take a bus from Domplatz all the way to the town center in about 30–40 minutes. For schedules, check **www.oebb.at**.

VISITOR INFORMATION   In lieu of a tourist office, the **town council,** in the mayor's office at Hauptstrasse 52 (✆ **02685/7744**), provides information Monday to Friday 9am to noon and 1 to 6pm, Saturday and Sunday 9am to noon.

What to See & Do

The castle **Burg Forchtenstein,** Burgplatz 1 (✆ **02626/81212**), 14km (8¾ miles) southeast of Wiener Neustadt in Lower Austria, was constructed on a rocky base by order of the counts of Mattersdorf in the 13th century. The Esterházy family had it greatly expanded in 1636. From its belvedere, you can see as far as the Great Hungarian Plain.

The castle saw action in the Turkish sieges of Austria in 1529 and 1683. A museum since 1815, it holds the Prince Esterházy collections, which consist of family memorabilia, a portrait gallery, large battle paintings, historical banners, and Turkish war booty and hunting arms. It's the largest private collection of historical arms in Austria. Legend has it that Turkish prisoners carved the castle cistern out of the rock, more than 137m (449 ft.) deep.

Basic admission for the castle and arms collection is 8€ for adults, 7€ for students, children. and seniors, and the price increases depending on how many of the other attractions you wish to see. The castle is open April to October daily 10am to 6pm. From November to March, tours are offered only when requested in advance. A guide shows you through.

Where to Stay & Eat

Gasthof Sauerzapf This hotel has two stories of weathered stucco, renovated windows, and a red-and-black rooftop. The updated interior is cozy and attractive, albeit simple, and is kept immaculate. Anna Daskalakis-Sauerzapf, the owner, rents modestly furnished rooms that are reasonably comfortable for the price. Their style is reminiscent of your great-aunt's house—comfortable beds and just-adequate shower-only bathrooms, inviting nonetheless. The restaurant serves good food and an array of local wines.

Rosalienstrasse 39, A-7212 Forchtenstein. ©/Fax **02626/81217.** 12 units. 48€ double. Rates include breakfast. No credit cards. Free parking. **Amenities:** Restaurant (closed Wed); lounge. *In room:* TV.

SALZBURG: CITY OF MOZART

S alzburg sits astride the Salzach River like a centurion guarding Alpine treasures. Its baroque-studded skyline is set against a pristine mountain backdrop, all on an intimate scale. Although you'll almost never be alone in this popular destination, the city and its surrounding, there is plenty to go around—splendid architecture, sweeping vistas, and serene pockets of quiet nature.

Once known as the Roman town of Juvavum, the city and river derive their names from the early residents who prospered from the region's salt mines. Despite its importance in the long-forgotten salt trade, this "heart of the heart of Europe" is and will likely forever be the city of Mozart, who was born here in 1756. The Old Town lies for the most part on the left bank of the river, where a monastery and bishopric were founded in A.D. 700, becoming an archbishopric in 798. At the height of the prince-archbishop's power, Salzburg was known as the "German Rome." On medieval maps, the little province was titled "church lands" of the Holy Roman Empire and was joined to Austria in 1816 following the Congress of Vienna.

A city of 17th- and 18th-century buildings, Salzburg is internationally known for its architectural beauty, much of it the work of the baroque masters, Johann Bernhard Fischer von Erlach and Santino Solari, the architect of the Cathedral. Several beautiful castles and palaces dot the city: Hohensalzburg Fortress, the former stronghold of the prince-archbishops of Salzburg; Residenz, an opulent palace and seat of the Salzburg prince-archbishops; and Schloss Hellbrunn, 5km (3 miles) south of the city, summer residence of the prince-archbishops. The beautifully baroque Mirabell Gardens, affording a splendid view of the townscape, were also laid out by the famous Fischer von Erlach.

The city is the setting for the Salzburg Festival, a world-renowned annual event that attracts classical music and opera lovers from all over the globe. Salzburg was also the setting for the popular film *The Sound of Music*; yes, the hills are alive with music—and reachable by tour.

ORIENTATION

Salzburg is only a short distance from the Austrian–German frontier, so it's convenient for exploring many of the nearby attractions in Bavaria (see *Frommer's Germany* or *Frommer's Munich & the Bavarian Alps*). On the northern slopes of the Alps, the city is at the intersection of traditional European trade routes and is well served today by air, Autobahn, and rail.

Getting There

BY PLANE

The **Salzburg Airport–W. A. Mozart,** Innsbrucker Bundesstrasse 95 (*©* **0662/ 8580;** www.salzburg-airport.com), lies 3km (2 miles) southwest of the city center. It has a regularly scheduled air service to Vienna, as well as to Frankfurt, Brussels, Berlin, Düsseldorf, Hamburg, London, and Zurich. Major airlines serving the Salzburg airport are Austrian Airlines (*©* **05/1766 1000**), British Airways (*©* **01/79 567 567**), Lufthansa (*©* **0810/1025 8080**), and Ryanair (*©* **0900/210 240**).

Bus no. 2 runs between the airport and Salzburg's main rail station, while no. 8 goes to Hanuschplatz and the *Altstadt* (**Old Town**). Departures are every 10 to 20 minutes (Sun and public holidays every 30 min.), and the 20-minute trip costs 2€ one-way. By taxi it's only about 15 minutes, but you'll pay at least 13€ to 15€.

BY TRAIN

Salzburg's main rail station, the **Salzburg Hauptbahnhof,** Südtirolerplatz (*©* **05/ 1717;** www.oebb.at), is on the major rail lines of Europe, with frequent arrivals not only from all the main cities of Austria, but also from other European cities such as Munich and Venice. Between 8am and 11pm, trains arrive roughly every 20 to 30 minutes from Vienna (trip time: 2½–3 hr.). A one-way fare costs 48€. There are 17 daily trains from Innsbruck (trip time: 2 hr.). A one-way fare costs 38€. Trains also arrive every 30 minutes from Munich (trip time: 90 min.–2 hr.), with a one-way ticket costing 34€.

Like those in Vienna, the Salzburg rail station is undergoing reconstruction that is slated to last until 2014. Many of the amenities have been transferred to temporary constructions on the Südtirolerplatz in front of the construction site. Follow temporary yellow signs to navigate through the site to the square. There's a **Reisezentrum** with train information, open Monday to Saturday 5:30am to 9:10pm, as well as luggage-storage lockers. There's a small tourist information office in the InfoBox on the square, along with an exhibition about the reconstruction, where you can obtain a free map, buy a more detailed city map for .70€, or make hotel reservations by paying a 2.20€ fee and a 12% deposit. The office is open daily 8:15am to 7:30pm.

From the train station, buses depart to various parts of the city, including the Altstadt (Old Town), or you can walk from the rail station to the Old Town in about 20 minutes.

BY CAR

Salzburg is 336km (209 miles) west of Vienna and 153km (95 miles) east of Munich. It's reached from all directions by good roads, including Autobahn A8 from the west (Munich), A1 from the east (Vienna), and A10 from the south. Route 20 comes into Salzburg from the north on the German side of the Salzach, and Route 158 cuts through the picturesque lake district to the southeast.

Visitor Information

In addition to the branch at the rail station, the larger **Salzburg Tourist Information Office** is located in the heart of the city's historic core, at Mozartplatz 5 (**℡ 0662/889 87-0;** www.salzburg.info). Either of these offices can book tour guides for you and dispense information about attractions and where to stay. They'll also book hotel reservations for you through their website, **www.salzburg.info**. The hours of the office on the Mozartplatz are, from October to May, Monday to Saturday 9am to 6pm; and, from June to September, daily 9am to 7pm.

City Layout

Most of what visitors come to see lies on the left bank of the Salzach River in the **Altstadt (Old Town),** although the more modern right bank offers a few old streets and shops leading up to the river. If you're driving, you have to leave your car on the right bank and enter the Old Town on foot, as most of it is for pedestrians only.

The heart of the inner city is **Residenzplatz,** which has the largest and finest baroque fountain this side of the Alps. On the western side of the square stands the **Residenz,** palace of the prince-archbishops; and, on the southern side, is the **Salzburg Dom (Salzburg Cathedral).** To the west of the Dom lies **Domplatz,** linked by archways dating from 1658. Squares to the north and south appear totally enclosed.

On the southern side of Max-Reinhardt-Platz and Hofstallgasse, edging toward **Mönchsberg,** stands the **Festspielhaus (Festival Theater),** built on the foundations of the 17th-century court stables.

STREET MAPS   You'll find handy pocket-size maps, with street indexes, all over the city at bookstores, newsstands, and hotels.

Neighborhoods in Brief

Altstadt   Most visitors head for the Altstadt, or Old Town, on the left bank of the Salzach tucked beneath the crescent-shaped Mönchsberg. This is a section of narrow streets (many from the Middle Ages) and slender houses, in complete contrast to the town constructed by the prince-archbishops across the river. The Old Town contains many of Salzburg's top attractions: The cathedral, Mozart's birthplace, and St. Peter's Cemetery.

Nonnberg   The eastern hill occupied by the dominating Hohensalzburg Fortress, Nonnberg, rises to 455m (1,493 ft.), and provides stunning views of the town and the mountains to the south. Some of the scenes from *The Sound of Music* were shot at the adjacent Stift Nonnberg, a Benedictine nunnery founded about A.D. 700 by St. Rupert.

Mönchsberg   To the west of the Hohensalzburg Fortress, this 3-km (2-mile) mountain ridge cradles the Old Town at a height of 542m (1,778 ft.), and provides walking trails with equally stunning views. The fortifications are from the 15th through the 17th centuries.

Right Bank   The newer part of town is on the right bank of the Salzach, below Kapuzinerberg, the right-bank counterpart of Mönchsberg. This peak rises 637m (2,090 ft.) and offers a lovely woodland area for long walks.

GETTING AROUND

By Public Transportation

Information about local public transportation is available at the local tourist office.

The city buses and trams provide a quick, comfortable service through the city center from the Nonntal parking area to Sigsmundsplatz, the city-center parking area. If bought from a ticket machine, a one-ride ticket is 1.90€ for adults and 1.10€ for children 6 to 15; those 5 and under travel free. Expect to pay .20€ more if you buy your ticket from the driver. Buses stop running between 11pm and midnight, depending on what part of Salzburg you're in.

DISCOUNT PASSES   The Salzburg Card lets you use unlimited public transportation and also acts as an admission ticket to the city's most important cultural sights, such as Mozart's birthplace, the Hohensalzburg Fortress, the Residenz gallery, the world-famous water fountain gardens at Hellbrunn, and more. Cards are valid for 24, 48, and 72 hours and cost 22€, 30€, and 35€, respectively, except from May through October when 3€ is added to the prices above. Children up to 15 years of age receive a 50% discount. You can buy the pass from Salzburg travel agencies, hotels, tobacconists, and municipal offices.

By Car

Driving a car in Salzburg is definitely *not* recommended. In most places it's impossible, since the monumental landmark center is for pedestrians only. Public parking areas—designated with a large P—are conveniently located throughout the city. If you're driving into Salzburg, leave your car on the left bank of the Salzach River. You'll find convenient underground parking areas like the one at Mönchsberg, from which it's an easy walk to the center and Domplatz.

However, we do recommend a car for touring around Land Salzburg (see chapter 10); relying on public transportation means a lot of travel time.

RENTALS   Car rentals are best made in advance (see chapter 3). If not, try **Avis** (© 0662/877278) or **Hertz** (© 0662/876674), both located near the train station at Ferdinand-Porsche-Strasse 7. Avis is open Monday to Friday 7:30am to 5pm; Hertz is open Monday to Friday 8am to 6pm, Saturday 8am to 1pm.

REPAIRS   Try **ÖAMTC (Austrian Automobile Service),** Alpenstrasse 102 (© 0662/639990), or **ARBÖ (Austrian Motorists Association),** Münchner Bundesstrasse 9 (© 0662/433601), day or night. The emergency number, in case of automobile breakdowns, is © **120** for ÖAMTC and © **123** for ARBÖ.

By Taxi & Horse-Drawn Carriage

You'll find taxi stands scattered at key points all over the city center and in the suburbs. The Salzburg Funktaxi–Vereinigung (radio taxis) office is at Rainerstrasse 27 (© **0662/8111** to order a taxi in advance). Fares start at 3.70€.

A "traditional taxi"—a *Fiaker* (horse-drawn carriage)—will not only provide you with a ride, but also a bit of history of the region as well. You can also rent a *Fiaker* at Residenzplatz. Four people usually pay 35€ for 30 minutes, but all fares are subject to negotiation.

By Bicycle

In an effort to keep cars out of the center, Salzburg officials have developed a network of bicycle paths, which are indicated on city maps. One pleasant bike path goes along the Salzach River for some 14km (9 miles) to Hallein, the second-largest town in Land Salzburg (see "Side Trips from Salzburg," later in this chapter).

Topbike offers bike rental at the train station from April to October (© **06272/4656**), daily from 10am to 5pm, and 9am to 7pm in July and August. An additional stand is located at the Staatsbrücke from June to September with the same opening hours. Rentals cost about 15€ per day, with a 20% discount for Salzburg Card holders.

[FastFACTS] SALZBURG

American Express
The office, located at Mozartplatz 5-7 (© **0662/8080**), adjacent to Residenzplatz, is open Monday to Friday 9am to 5:30pm and Saturday 9am to noon.

Babysitters Arrangements can be made through **Hilfswerk Salzburg,** Klessheimer Allée 45 (© **0662/434702**), at a cost of 10€ to 15€ per hour.

Business Hours Most shops and stores are open Monday to Friday 9am to 6pm. Some smaller shops shut down at noon for a lunch break, which can last 1 or 2 hours. Saturday hours in general are 9am to 5pm, but some shops may close at noon. Banks are open Monday to Friday 8am to noon and 2 to 4:30pm.

Currency Exchange
You can exchange money at the Hauptbahnhof, on Südtirolerplatz, daily from 7am to 10pm, and at the airport daily from 9am to 4pm.

Dentists For information on how to find an English-speaking dentist, call Dentistenkammer, Faberstrasse 2 (© **0662/873466**).

Doctors If you suddenly fall ill, your best source of information on finding a doctor is the reception desk of your hotel. If you want a comprehensive list of doctors and their respective specialties, which you can acquire in Salzburg or even before your arrival, contact **Ärztekammer für Salzburg,** Bergstrasse 14, A-5020 Salzburg (© **0662/871327;** www.aeksbg.at). And if your troubles flare up over a weekend, the **Medical Emergency Center of the Austrian Red Cross** maintains a hotline (© **141**), which you can use to describe your problem. A staff member will either ask you to visit their headquarters at Karl Renner Strasse 7 or send a medical expert to wherever you're staying. This service is available from 5pm on

Friday to 8am on Monday and on public holidays. For more information on medical emergencies, refer to "Hospitals," below.

Drugstores Larger pharmacies, especially those in the city center, tend to remain open, without a break, Monday to Friday 8am to 6pm and Saturday 8am to noon. Pharmacies in small towns near Salzburg and in the suburbs have similar hours but close for lunch, usually from 12:30 to 2:30pm Monday to Friday. For night service, and service on Saturday afternoon and Sunday, pharmacies display a sign giving the address of the nearest pharmacy that has agreed to remain open over the weekend or throughout the night. A pharmacy that's particularly convenient to Salzburg's commercial center is **Elisabeth-Apotheke,** Elisabethstrasse 1A (© **0662/871484**), north of Rainerstrasse, toward the train station.

Embassies & Consulates The **Consulate of Great Britain,** Alter Markt 4 (© **0662/848133**), is open in winter Monday to Friday 9am to noon, and in summer 8 to 11am. **U.S. citizens** needing business with their consulate should go to Vienna or Munich.

Emergencies For emergencies, call the following numbers: Police © **133,** fire © **122,** and ambulance © **144.**

Hospitals Salzburg is well equipped with medical facilities, including the **Unfallkrankenhaus,** on Dr.-Franz-Rehrl-Platz 5 (© **0662/65800**); and **Krankenhaus und Konvent der Barmherzigen Brüder,** Kajetanerplatz 1 (© **0662/80880**).

Internet Access The most convenient cafe with Internet capability is **Cybar,** Mozartplatz 5 (© **0662/843696**), across from the tourist office. It's open daily 9am to 10pm and charges 2€ for 10 minutes of Internet access.

Luggage Storage & Lockers Lockers are available at the Hauptbahnhof, Südtiroler-platz (© **0043/51717**), and accessible 24 hours daily. For 24 hours, you can rent a large locker for 3.50€, a medium one for 3€, or a small one for 2€. The luggage storage counter, with an attendant, is open 4am to midnight daily.

Police For the police, call © **133.**

Post Offices The main post office is at Residenz-platz 9 (© **0577/677510**). The post office at the main railway station is open Monday to Friday from 8am to 8:30pm, Saturday 8am to 2pm, and Sunday 1 to 6pm. The postal code for Salzburg is A-5020; for Anif, A-5081; and for Bergheim, A-5101.

Safety Salzburg, like all of Austria, has a low crime rate compared with most European cities, but there is still some crime here, particularly in tourist areas. Take the usual precautions here as you would elsewhere. Use discretion, of course, and common sense.

Taxes The government value-added tax (VAT) and the service charge are included in restaurant and hotel bills presented to you. For a VAT refund, see "Fast Facts: Austria," chapter 16. Other than this blanket tax mentioned above, Salzburg imposes no special city taxes.

Toilets These are identified by the wc sign and are found throughout the city in museums and at sightseeing attractions, the rail station, and the airport. You can stop at a cafe, but these establishments prefer you to be a customer, even if it's only a small purchase.

Transit Information **Stadtbus Salzburg** provides information on the bus lines crisscrossing the city. For information, schedules, and fares, visit the city transport office at Alpenstrasse 91, call © **0800/660660,** or visit **www.stadtbus.at.**

Useful Telephone Numbers For the airport, call © **0662/8580;** for train information, call © **05/1717.**

WHERE TO STAY

Some of the best places to stay, particularly the castle hotels, converted farmhouse pensions, and boarding houses, lie on the outskirts of Salzburg within an easy drive of the city during times like the Salzburg Festival (see chapter 10). But if you don't have a car, you'll probably want to stay right in the city, within walking distance of all the major sightseeing attractions.

Many hotels in the Old City must be reached on foot because of the pedestrian-only streets. However, taxis are allowed to take passengers from the airport or the rail and bus stations and deliver them to the door of a hotel. Many hotels away from the city center can be reached by public transportation.

On the Left Bank (Old Town)

VERY EXPENSIVE

Altstadt SAS Radisson ★★   This is not your typical Radisson property—in fact, its style and charm are a rather radical departure for the chain. Dating from 1377, this is a luxuriously and elegantly converted Altstadt inn. The old and new are blended in perfect harmony here, with the historic facade concealing top-rate comforts and luxuries. The cozy, antiques-filled lobby sets the tone, while a flower-lined, sky-lit atrium adds cheer even on the darkest of days. Stone arches from the medieval structure still remain. Rooms vary greatly in size but have a certain charm and sparkle, with some of the city's best beds, complemented by elegant bathrooms equipped with tub/shower combinations. Overlooking the river, the Restaurant Symphonie is one of the best hotel dining rooms in the city (see "Where to Eat," later in this chapter).

Rudolfskai 28/Judengasse 15, A-5020 Salzburg. ✆ **800/333-3333** in the U.S., or 0662/848571. Fax 0662/8485716. www.austria-trend.at. 62 units. 310€–345€ double; from 650€ suite. 22€ buffet breakfast. AE, DC, MC, V. Parking 28€. Bus: 3, 5, 6, 7, 8, or 10. **Amenities:** Restaurant; bar; room service; babysitting; laundry service; dry cleaning; nonsmoking rooms. *In room:* TV, minibar, hairdryer, safe, Wi-Fi.

Goldener Hirsch ★★★   Goldener Hirsch wins the award for the finest hotel in Salzburg; this establishment is so steeped in legend and history that any Austrian will instantly recognize its name. The hotel is built on a small scale, yet it absolutely reeks of aristocratic elegance, which is enhanced by the superb staff. Sitting in an enviable position in the Old Town, a few doors from Mozart's birthplace, it's composed of three medieval town houses joined together in a labyrinth of rustic hallways and staircases. A fourth, called "The Coppersmith's House," is across the street and has 17 charming and elegant rooms. Street-side units have double-glazed windows. All are beautifully furnished and maintained.

The formal Goldener Hirsch and the more casual s'Herzl are two of the more distinguished restaurants in Salzburg (see "Where to Eat," later in this chapter).

Getreidegasse 37, A-5020 Salzburg. ✆ **800/325-3535** in the U.S., or 0662/8084. Fax 0662/843349. www.goldenerhirschsalzburg.com. 69 units. 180€–535€ double; from 1,080€ suite. Higher rates at festival time (the first week of Apr and mid-July to Aug). AE, DC, MC, V. You can double-park in front of the Getreidegasse entrance or at the Karajanplatz entrance, and a staff member will take your vehicle to the hotel's garage for 33€. Bus: 1, 4, 8, or 10. **Amenities:** 2 restaurants; babysitting; bar; dry cleaning; laundry service; room service; nonsmoking rooms. *In room:* A/C, TV, coffeemaker, minibar, hairdryer, safe, Wi-Fi.

MODERATE

Altstadthotel Weisse Taube   Constructed in 1365 the Weisse Taube, or White Dove, has been run by the Haubner family since 1904. Rooms are, for the most part, renovated and comfortably streamlined, with traditional furnishings, and frequently renewed beds. The hotel is in the pedestrian area of the Old Town, a few steps from Mozartplatz, but you can drive up to it to unload baggage.

Kaigasse 9, A-5020 Salzburg. ✆ **0662/842404.** Fax 0662/841783. www.weissetaube.at. 31 units. 98€–186€ double. Rates include breakfast. AE, DC, MC, V. Parking 9€. Bus: 3, 5, 6, 7, 8, or 10. **Amenities:** Breakfast room; bar; lounge. *In room:* TV, hairdryer, minibar, safe, Wi-Fi.

Cityhotel Goldenes Theater   Set within a short walk of Salzburg's medieval core, this establishment contains time-share units and some conventional hotel accommodations. Most of the theatrical-looking design you'll see today derives from a radical renovation that occurred in the late 1980s, when a 19th-century shell was

Hotels in Salzburg

Altstadthotel Weisse Taube **25**
Altstadt-Hotel Wolf-Dietrich **14**
Altstadt SAS Radisson **23**
Bergland Hotel **9**
Cityhotel Goldenes Theater **12**
Der Salzburger Hof **6**
Goldener Hirsch **4**
Haus Arenberg **27**
Hotel Amadeus **15**
Hotel & Villa Auersperg **8**
Hotel Blaue Gans **3**
Hotel Bristol **18**
Hotel Drei Kreuz **11**
Hotel Elefant **22**
Hotel Goldene Krone **16**
Hotel Jedermann **10**
Hotel Kasererbräu **24**
Hotel Mozart **7**
Hotel Restaurant Gablerbräu **20**
Hotel Sacher Salzburg Hof **19**
Hotel Schloss Mönchstein **1**
Hotel Stein **21**
Hotel Stieglbräu **6**
Hotel Trumer Stube **17**
Neutor **2**
NH Hotel Salzburg **13**
Pension Adlerhof **6**
Pension Wolf **26**
Rosenvilla **28**
Salzburg Sheraton Hotel **5**

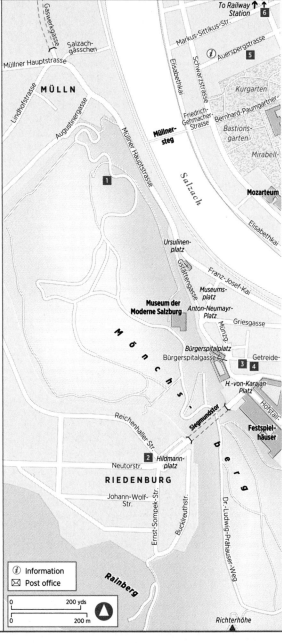

9

SALZBURG: CITY OF MOZART | Where to Stay

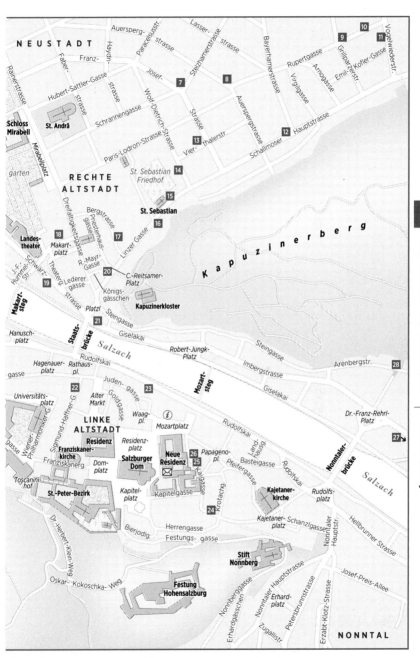

gutted and reconfigured into the vaguely Jugendstil-style setting you see today. Each accommodation is painted a pale yellow and named after a composer or a writer. All rooms are comfortable, neatly maintained, and equipped with well-kept shower-only bathrooms. As a result of its artistic theme, the hotel's clientele includes lots of singers and composers. The Barcarole restaurant serves dinner only.

Schallmooser Hauptstrasse 13, A-5020 Salzburg. ✆ **0662/8816810.** Fax 0662/88168692. www. gt-hotel-salzburg.com. 58 units. 72€–159€ double. Rates include buffet breakfast. AE, DC, MC, V. Bus: 4. **Amenities:** Restaurant; bar; babysitting; dry cleaning; laundry service; massage; room service; sauna; nonsmoking rooms; solarium. *In room:* TV, hairdryer, minibar, Wi-Fi.

Hotel Blaue Gans   The Blue Goose lies in the historic core of Salzburg, near the underground garages of the Mönchsberg, a few doors away from hotels that charge almost twice as much. Although the building is almost 700 years old, a 2002 renovation transformed the establishment into an art hotel. Each room has modern furniture and generous space, and those opening onto the courtyard are quieter than those facing the street; nos. 332 and 336 are probably the biggest. You'll register in an understated lobby, one that's so discreetly tucked away that it might be hard to identify. Within the same building is a historic restaurant and beer hall, Stadtgasthof Blaue Gans (see "Where to Eat," later in this chapter).

Getreidegasse 43, A-5020 Salzburg. ✆ **0662/8424910.** Fax 0662/8413179. www.blauegans.at. 38 units. 139€–259€ double; 259€–420€ suite. Rates include buffet breakfast. AE, DC, MC, V. Parking 10€. Bus: 1, 4, or 8. **Amenities:** Restaurant; bar; babysitting; dry cleaning; laundry service. *In room:* TV, hairdryer, minibar, safe, Wi-Fi.

Hotel Elefant   Near the Old Town Rathaus, in a quiet alley off Getreidegasse, is this well-established, family-run hotel with the Best Western stamp of approval. It, too, is one of Salzburg's most ancient buildings, more than 700 years old. The well-furnished and high-ceilinged rooms have small bathrooms and redesigned interiors with radiant color schemes. On the ground floor is the vaulted Bürgerstüberl serving Austrian and international cuisine, where high wooden banquettes separate the tables, and a wooden elephant.

Sigmund-Haffner-Gasse 4, A-5020 Salzburg. ✆ **0662/8433970.** Fax 0662/84010928. www.elefant.at. 31 units. 95€–215€ double. Rates include buffet breakfast. AE, DC, MC, V. Parking 11€. Bus: 1, 4, 8, or 10. **Amenities:** 2 restaurants; bar; babysitting; dry cleaning; laundry service; room service; nonsmoking rooms. *In room:* TV, hairdryer, minibar, safe, Wi-Fi.

Hotel Kasererbräu   In one of the Old Town's most colorful neighborhoods, a few blocks from the cathedral, the Kasererbräu has baroque and Biedermeier furniture that goes well with the oriental rugs and embellished plaster ceilings. Most double rooms are spacious and all are cozy. Some units are large enough to be classified as apartments, and are suitable for two to four persons. Guests have free access to a steam room and sauna, and on the ground floor there's a pizzeria and a cinema, one of the oldest in the country.

Kaigasse 33, A-5020 Salzburg. ✆ **0662/842445.** Fax 0662/84244551. www.kasererbraeu.at. 45 units. 118€–154€ double; 169€–229€ apt accommodating up to 5 persons. Rates include buffet breakfast. AE, DC, MC, V. Parking 12€. Bus: 3, 5, 6, 7, 8, or 10. **Amenities:** Restaurant; cafe; lounge; dry cleaning; laundry service; massage; sauna; solarium; steam room. *In room:* TV, minibar, Wi-Fi.

Neutor ★ 👜   This hotel has long been known as a meeting place for artists because of its central location, only a 3-minute walk from the famous Getreidegasse. It is close to many art events, and a frequent stopover for visiting orchestral groups, choirs, and musicians in general, especially during the Salzburg Festival.

Accommodations in two buildings are on par with each other, as all the rooms are comfortably and beautifully furnished. Because many performing artists are up late at night, the hotel offers sleep-late floors, which don't have to be vacated until 1pm. On site is the Artist's Café, decorated with local artwork.

Neutorstrasse 8, A-5020. ℭ **0662/844154-0.** Fax 0662/84415416. www.neutor.at. 89 units. 110€–188€ double; 124€–202€ penthouse units. Rates include buffet breakfast. AE, DC, MC, V. Free parking. Bus: 1, 4, 8, or 10. **Amenities:** Restaurant; bar; laundry service; room service. *In room:* TV, safe.

Pension Wolf 🌢 Ideally located near Mozartplatz, this building dates from 1429. A stucco exterior with big shutters hides the rustic and inviting interior that is decorated with a few baroque touches and often sunny rooms. Many new bathrooms have been installed, making this a more inviting choice than ever. The rooms are a bit cramped, as are the shower-only bathrooms. Still, this pension represents very good value for high-priced Salzburg. Since the hotel is usually full, reservations are imperative.

Kaigasse 7, A-5020 Salzburg. ℭ **0662/8434530.** Fax 0662/8424234. www.hotelwolf.com. 15 units. 108€–214€ double; 188€–248€ suite. Rates include buffet breakfast. AE, MC, V. Bus: 3, 5, 6, 7, 8, or 10. **Amenities:** Breakfast room; lounge. *In room:* TV.

On the Right Bank
EXPENSIVE

Hotel Bristol ★ Built in 1890, this handsome, traditional hotel lies near the Mirabell Gardens and opposite Mozart's former home, encompassing a view of the Hohensalzburg Fortress. Compared with the noble courtliness of the Goldener Hirsch (see above), this hotel can come across as stuffy, although recent renovations offset this, combining elements of sleek modernism with the late-Empire mix of classical and Jugendstil. But be warned, vigorous marketing means the Bristol is often fully booked. Rooms range from upper-class minimalism to opulently baroque, with decorated ceilings and crystal chandeliers. Most have been redecorated with antiques, chandeliers, oriental rugs, often half-canopied beds, and spacious closets. Try for a front room with a view of Mirabell Palace.

Restaurants include the Polo Lounge, seating 40, and the 80-seat Crystal Room, serving high-standard Austrian and international cuisine. The piano bar has terrazzo floors, oriental rugs, and discreet music.

Makartplatz 4, A-5020 Salzburg. ℭ **0662/873557.** Fax 0662/8735576. www.bristol-salzburg.at. 60 units. 170€–470€ double; 390€–670€ suite. Rates include buffet breakfast. AE, DC, MC, V. Self-parking 13€; valet parking 26€. Bus: 1, 3, 5, or 6. **Amenities:** 2 restaurants; bar; babysitting; dry cleaning; laundry service; massage; room service; nonsmoking rooms. *In room:* A/C, TV, hairdryer, minibar, safe, Wi-Fi.

Hotel Sacher Salzburg Hof ★★★ Built originally as the Hotel d'Autriche in 1866, this popular hotel was soon attracting guests from all over the world. It has survived the ravages of war, always keeping up with the times through renovations and expansions. Inside are big windows with panoramic views of the Old Town. The cheerful and comfortable rooms are well furnished, with excellent beds. Try to reserve a room overlooking the river. Most doubles are large; singles tend to be small.

A host of drinking and dining facilities is available, including a cozy bar with piano music in the evening; the Roter Salon, an elegant dining room facing the river; the Zirbelzimmer, an award-winning restaurant; the Salzachgrill, offering everything from a snack to a steak, with a riverside terrace; the Café Sacher, a traditional Austrian cafe, also with a riverside terrace; and a pastry shop that sells the famous Sachertorte.

Schwarzstrasse 5–7, A-5020 Salzburg. ℂ **800/223-6800** in the U.S. and Canada, or 0662/88977. Fax 0662/88977551. www.sacher.com. 113 units. 219€–398€ double; suites from 471€. AE, DC, MC, V. Parking 29€. Bus: 1, 3, 5, or 6. **Amenities:** 3 restaurants; 2 bars; babysitting; cafe; health club; laundry service; dry cleaning; lounge; massage; nonsmoking rooms; room service; rooms for those w/limited mobility; sauna; steam room. *In room:* A/C, TV, hairdryer, minibar, safe, Wi-Fi.

Hotel Stein ★★   This stunning, revitalized Bauhaus hotel lies directly on the water with a panoramic view of the historic Old Town of Salzburg. The Stein, which had grown stodgy, was refitted with a contemporary look from its animal prints to its flat-screen TVs, and the rooftop cafe has accurately been called divine. The bedrooms, ranging from beautifully furnished doubles to luxurious suites, are well appointed, with state-of-the-art private marble bathrooms. Suites have leather bedspreads, leather upholstery, and zebra-skin patterns on some of the in-room fabrics; other rooms are outfitted in either a Mozart motif (that is, vaguely rococo patterns) or the Stein design (conservatively modern) style. After a restful night's sleep, you're served a breakfast buffet on the 7th floor terrace.

Giselakai 3–5, A-5020 Salzburg. ℂ **0662/8743460.** Fax 0662/8743469. www.hotelstein.at. 54 units. 175€–230€ double; 245€–290€ junior suite; 265€–310€ suite. Rates include breakfast. AE, DC, MC, V. Parking: 19€. Bus: 1, 3, 4, 5, 6, 7, 8, or 10. **Amenities:** Cafe bar on top floor; room service; babysitting; laundry service; dry cleaning. *In room:* TV, hairdryer, safe, Wi-Fi.

Rosenvilla ★ 🛍   This gracefully proportioned 100-year-old villa is located in a residential suburb within a 20-minute walk from Salzburg's historic core. Sheathed with ocher-colored stucco and flanked with roses that climb over wrought-iron supports and a small garden, it's small-scale, personalized, conservative, and a bit sleepy. Bedrooms are more lavish than you'd expect, with wooden floors, theatrical draperies, deep upholsteries, and a decor that you might have expected in a conservative and well-mannered private home. Other than breakfast, no meals are served here. The hotel is entirely nonsmoking.

Höfelgasse 4, A-5020 Salzburg. ℂ **0662/621765.** Fax 0662/6252308. www.rosenvilla.com. 14 units. 128€–199€ double; 158€–255€ junior suite. Rates include breakfast. Children under 12 stay free in parent's room. AE, DC, MC, V. Bus: 7. **Amenities:** Laundry service; dry cleaning. *In room:* TV, safe, Wi-Fi.

Salzburg Sheraton Hotel ★★   One of the crown jewels of the Sheraton chain, this five-star, seven-story hotel opened in 1984 in a desirable location about a 10-minute walk from Mozartplatz. The Austrian architect who designed this building took great pains to incorporate it into its 19th-century neighborhood. The exterior is capped with a mansard roof, and the casement windows are ringed with elaborate trim. As you enter, the lobby opens to reveal sun-flooded views of the garden. Rooms have thick wall-to-wall carpeting and contain beds with built-in headboards. The exclusive junior, queen, and president suites are filled with elegant Biedermeier furniture. Half the rooms look out over Mirabell Park.

The cream-and-crystal Restaurant Mirabell serves a good-value luncheon buffet Monday through Friday and a dressed-up version on Saturday and Sunday. A less formal dining area, the Bistro, offers daily specials, wine, and beer. A piano bar is outfitted with burnished brass, richly grained wood, and an Art Nouveau decor.

Auerspergstrasse 4, A-5020 Salzburg. ℂ **800/325-3535** in the U.S., or 0662/889990. Fax 0662/881776. www.sheratonsalzburg.at. 161 units. 120€–255€ double; 300€–600€ suite. AE, DC, MC, V. Parking 15€. Bus: 1, 2, 3, 5, or 6. **Amenities:** 2 restaurants; bar; babysitting; laundry service; dry cleaning; indoor heated pool; sauna; room service; nonsmoking rooms; 1 room for those w/limited mobility. *In room:* TV, coffeemaker, hairdryer, minibar, safe, Wi-Fi.

MODERATE

Der Salzburger Hof A two-block walk from the railway station, close to the Mirabell Gardens, this streamlined hotel often hosts groups of central Europeans. The attractive, modern lobby is paneled with light-grained oak and is carpeted. Rooms are well-insulated refuges from the surrounding commercial neighborhood. The beds are comfortable and the bathrooms are moderate in size with tub/shower combinations. Housekeeping is a definite plus here. The hotel's thriving trio of dining rooms features Austrian, Italian, and Indian specialties.

Kaiserschützenstrasse 1, A-5020 Salzburg. ⓒ **0662/46970.** Fax 0662/4697025. www.bayrischerhof. com. 32 units. 78€–134€ double; 90€–144€ suite. Rates include breakfast buffet. AE, DC, MC, V. Free parking outdoors. **Amenities:** Restaurant; bar; babysitting; laundry service; dry cleaning; room service; nonsmoking rooms. *In room:* TV, minibar, hairdryer.

Hotel & Villa Auersperg ★ This traditional family-run hotel near the right bank of the Salzach lies only a 5-minute walk from the Altstadt. With its own sunny gardens, it consists of two buildings: A main structure and a smaller villa. The inviting rooms are warm, large, and cozy, with big windows, excellent beds, and well-equipped bathrooms, moderate in size. A 2009 renovation added a touch of sleek modernity to its old-fashioned charm. The library bar is not only convivial and informal, but also one of our favorite spots for drinking and conversation in Salzburg. On the top floor, you'll find a roof terrace offering nice views of Salzburg.

Auerspergstrasse 61, A-5020 Salzburg. ⓒ **0662/889440.** Fax 0662/8894455. www.auersperg.at. 55 units. 144€–188€ double; 205€–275€ suite. Rates include buffet breakfast. AE, DC, MC, V. Free parking. Bus: 2 from the train station. **Amenities:** Breakfast room; bar; fitness center; sauna; steam room; laundry service; dry cleaning; nonsmoking rooms. *In room:* TV, minibar, coffeemaker (some), hairdryer, safe, Wi-Fi.

Hotel Mozart ☺ ✦ Known for its unpretentious charm and welcoming hospitality, Hotel Mozart is a comfortable, family-run hotel located in the city center. Everything is homey and traditional, with oriental rugs, local paintings, and an attractive TV lounge. It's a 10-minute walk from the train station and only 5 minutes from the pedestrian area of Linzer Gasse and the famous Mirabell Gardens. Rooms are often sunny and come with all the standard extras. Most are quite spacious, with built-in furniture and twin beds, and accommodations facing the street are soundproof. Some of the guest rooms are big enough to sleep four comfortably. The courteously attentive staff provides careful service and thoughtful touches.

Franz-Josef-Strasse 27, A-5020 Salzburg. ⓒ **0662/872274.** Fax 0662/870079. www.hotel-mozart.at. 33 units. 90€–155€ double; 110€–175€ triple. AE, MC, V. Parking 10€. Closed Nov 9–26. Bus: 2. **Amenities:** Breakfast room; babysitting; laundry service; dry cleaning; room service; nonsmoking rooms. *In room:* TV, minibar, hairdryer, safe.

Hotel Stieglbräu Located in the Mirabell district, this hotel provides comfortable and contemporary accommodations within a 10-minute walk of Salzburg's historic core and a 5-minute walk from the railway station. The clean rooms have big windows and simple furniture, including comfortable beds. Bathrooms are spotless and equipped with tub/shower combinations. Owned by the brewery but separately run, the hotel has two pleasant restaurants, serving international cuisine. There are at least half a dozen cozy dining rooms, and a spacious outdoor garden-style terrace for warm-weather drinking and dining.

Rainerstrasse 14, A-5020 Salzburg. ⓒ **0662/88992.** Fax 0662/8899271. www.imlauer.com. 50 units. 173€–204€ double; 191€–247€ suite. Rates include buffet breakfast. AE, DC, MC, V. Free parking. Bus: 1,

2, 3, 5, or 6. **Amenities:** Restaurant; bar; laundry service; dry cleaning; massage; room service; non-smoking rooms. *In room:* A/C, TV, hairdryer, minibar, Wi-Fi.

NH Hotel Salzburg ☺

This welcome addition brings a successful chain format from Spain to Salzburg, although it lacks the style of the Sheraton. Unlike most Novotels, this one, like the Novotel Wien City, is centrally located, within walking distance of many major sights. Rooms, although no style-setters, are well maintained, with good beds and medium-size bathrooms with tub/shower combinations. For families, this is a favorite; and by Salzburg standards, prices are reasonable. Geared to early or late arrivals, the routine restaurant, bar, and cafe are open daily from 6am to midnight.

Franz-Josef-Strasse 26, A-5020 Salzburg. ✆ **0662/8820410.** Fax 0662/874240. www.nh-hotels.com. 140 units. 101€–186€ double. AE, DC, MC, V. Parking 15€. Bus: 2 or 4. **Amenities:** Restaurant; bar; cafe; exercise room; sauna; room service; laundry service; dry cleaning; rooms for those w/limited mobility. *In room:* TV, minibar, hairdryer, safe, Wi-Fi.

INEXPENSIVE

Altstadt-Hotel Wolf-Dietrich ★ ☺

Two 19th-century town houses were joined together to make this select little hotel. The lobby and ground floor reception area have a friendly and elegant atmosphere and bright, classical furnishings. The smallish rooms are comfortably furnished, appealing, and cozy, with excellent beds. The ground-floor "Wiener Kaffeehaus" pays successful homage to the large extravagant coffeehouses built in the former century in Vienna, Budapest, and Prague. Alpine carvings and graceful pine detailing adorn one of the two restaurants. Decorating the indoor swimming pool are mirrors and unusual murals of Neptune chasing a sea nymph.

Wolf-Dietrich-Strasse 7, A-5020 Salzburg. ✆ **0662/871275.** Fax 0662/8712759. www.salzburg-hotel. at. 27 units. 100€–230€ double; 170€–255€ suite. Children under 12 stay free in parent's room. Rates include buffet breakfast. AE, DC, MC, V. Parking 15€. Bus: 2 or 4. **Amenities:** Restaurant; bar; cafe; babysitting; laundry service; dry cleaning; massage; indoor heated pool; room service; spa; solarium. *In room:* TV, minibar, hairdryer, Wi-Fi.

Bergland Hotel ★ 📱

Cozy, personalized, and substantial, this guesthouse sits within a quiet residential neighborhood. It was bought by the grandfather of the present owner in 1912 and rebuilt after its destruction during World War II. A 15-minute walk from the train station and a 10-minute walk from the Altstadt (rental bikes are available), it is managed by the friendly English-speaking Peter Kuhn, who has decorated the *Pension* with his own artwork, oversees breakfast, and is on hand most evenings to converse with guests in the cozy bar/lounge. An outdoor terrace is also available for relaxing. There's a green *Kachelofen* (tiled stove), and decor that might remind you of a ski lodge high in the Alps. The hotel is entirely nonsmoking.

Rupertsgasse 15, A-5020 Salzburg. ✆ **0662/872318.** Fax 0662/8723188. www.berglandhotel.at. 18 units. 90€–112€ double; 140€ suite. Rates include buffet breakfast. AE, DC, MC, V. Free parking. Closed Dec 20–Jan 31. Bus: 4. **Amenities:** Breakfast room; lounge. *In room:* TV, hairdryer, Wi-Fi.

Haus Arenberg

Staying in a place like this gives you the chance to enjoy the best of the Austrian countryside while being only a short bus ride from the Old Town. On a fieldstone foundation, on a slope of the Kapuzinerberg, the two balconied stories feature white stucco and wood detailing. Parts of the interior are completely covered in blond paneling, while the scenic breakfast room is accented with hunting trophies and oriental rugs. Rooms are rather small, but the staff works hard to ensure comfort by providing well-managed bathrooms with tub/shower combinations and spotless housekeeping. Breakfast is the only meal served.

Blumensteinstrasse 8, A-5020 Salzburg. ℂ **0662/640097.** Fax 0662/6400973. www.arenberg-salzburg.at. 13 units. 129€–165€ double; 149€–176€ triple. Rates include buffet breakfast. AE, MC, V. Free parking. Bus: 6, 7, or 10. **Amenities:** Breakfast room; lounge. *In room:* TV, coffeemaker.

Hotel Amadeus The walls and foundations of this pleasing, four-story hotel date from the 15th century, and the facade from the 18th, but much of what you'll experience today is a post-millennium upgrade. The quietest rooms are those overlooking the rear, with views of the graveyard where Mozart's wife is buried. Rooms are pleasant and decorated with reproductions of country-Austrian furniture. Breakfasts are generous; the staff is helpful. The building's ground-floor cafe, the Amadeus, serves drinks and bistro-style food throughout the day and evening.

Linzer Gasse 43–45, A-5020 Salzburg. ℂ **0662/871401.** Fax 0662/8714017. www.hotelamadeus.at. 30 units. 125€–200€ double; 165€–225€ triple. Rates include buffet breakfast. AE, DC, MC, V. Parking 15€. Bus: 2 or 4 to Wolf-Dietrich-Strasse. **Amenities:** Breakfast room; cafe. *In room:* TV, hairdryer, safe, Wi-Fi.

Hotel Drei Kreuz The name *Drei Kreuz* refers to the three crosses of the nearby Kapuzinerberg, which was the site of public executions centuries ago. Once you get past the dreary bunker-like facade, you'll find a warmly decorated and inviting interior. The restaurant has some of the most massive beams we've ever seen in Austria, and a cozy bar with rustic decor. The often small rooms are tasteful and well furnished. It's about a 10-minute walk from the historic center.

Vogelweiderstrasse 9, A-5020 Salzburg. ℂ **0662/8727900.** Fax 0662/8727906. www.hoteldreikreuz. at. 24 units. 74€–94€ double; 94€–125€ triple. Rates include breakfast. AE, DC, MC, V. Free parking. Bus: 4. **Amenities:** Restaurant; bar; laundry service; dry cleaning; nonsmoking rooms. *In room:* TV, hairdryer.

Hotel Goldene Krone Our favorite part of this family-run guesthouse is the big sun terrace with ivy-covered walls, where a family member will serve you coffee after a tiring day in the city. The hotel is only a few minutes from the Staatsbrücke. Rooms range from small to medium, but furnishings, including the beds, are comfortable. A breakfast buffet is the only meal served.

Linzer Gasse 48, A-5020 Salzburg. ℂ **0662/872300.** Fax 0662/87230066. www.hotel-goldenekrone. com. 21 units. 119€–129€ double. Rates include breakfast. AE, DC, MC, V. Parking 12€. Bus: 2 or 4 to Wolf-Dietrich-Strasse. **Amenities:** Breakfast room; lounge; Wi-Fi. *In room:* TV.

Hotel Jedermann Set within a quiet, tree-lined residential neighborhood less than 1km (½ mile) north of Salzburg's medieval core, this is a respectable and decent pension that has received consistently favorable recommendations from Frommer's readers. The building was constructed as a spacious private home in the 1930s, and today it remains home to the Gmachl family, its owners and managers. Public areas contain modern and elegant furnishings that create a comfortable atmosphere. Rooms, last renovated in 2006, are modern and comfortable. Breakfast only.

Rupertgasse 25, A-5020 Salzburg. ℂ **0662/8732410.** Fax 0662/8732419. www.hotel-jedermann.com. 16 units. Low season 95€ double; During holidays and festivals 160€ double. Rates include buffet breakfast. AE, DC, MC, V. Free parking. Bus: 4. **Amenities:** Breakfast room; lounge; nonsmoking rooms. *In room:* TV, minibar, Wi-Fi.

Hotel Restaurant Gablerbräu This inviting hotel is near the Makartplatz. Rooms are furnished in a simple, modern style—an utter functionalism that deters lingering or long stays. Nonetheless, beds are frequently renewed, housekeeping is good, and the tiny shower-only bathrooms are well kept. Inside are three restaurants:

One with vaulted ceilings and murals, another covered with wrought-iron detailing, and the third—the least formal—a beer hall.

Linzer Gasse 9, A-5020 Salzburg. ② **0662/88965.** Fax 0662/8896555. www.gablerbrau.com. 52 units. Low season 79€–138€ double; summer and Advent holiday 115€–158€ double; 24€ children 10–14; free for children 9 and under. Rates include buffet breakfast. AE, DC, MC, V. Parking 13€. Bus: 1, 3, 5, or 6. **Amenities:** Restaurant; bar; room service; nonsmoking rooms; rooms for those w/limited mobility. *In room:* TV, hairdryer, safe.

Hotel Trumer Stube Originally built in 1869 as a private home, this flower-bedecked townhouse is tucked in a side street of the Old Town, well-buffered from the bustle of Linzergasse, but only a 6-minute stroll from Mirabell Gardens and the Mozart Wohnhaus. Ideal for couples and families, it's managed by the friendly Marianne Hirschbichler, who speaks English and is happy to give sightseeing tips, and make restaurant and guided tour reservations. An elevator provides access to comfortable rooms in a country style that are elegant in their simplicity, accentuated with Asian or small-town baroque touches, and equipped with spotless and efficient bathrooms.

Bergstrasse 6, A-5020 Salzburg. ② **0662/874776** or 0662/875168. Fax 0662/874326. www.trumer-stube.at. 22 units. 96€–135€ double; 154€ triple. Served breakfast available. AE, DC, MC, V. Parking 11€. Bus: 1, 3, 5, or 6 to Makartplatz. **Amenities:** Breakfast room; lounge; nonsmoking rooms. *In room:* TV, Wi-Fi.

Pension Adlerhof Conveniently located near the train station, the Pregartbauer family runs this hotel that entertained American troops stationed in Salzburg after World War II. Although built in 1900, the second and third floors contain original baroque embellishments. The high-ceilinged but cozy interior has wooden furniture with occasional painted designs, plus many folksy touches. Rooms, frequently reno-vated, are *very* snug and cozy, suitable for an overnight stay—not a long trip. Bath-rooms with shower units are a bit cramped, but housekeeping is exemplary.

Elisabethstrasse 25, A-5020 Salzburg. ② **0662/875236.** Fax 0662/873663. www.gosalzburg.com. 30 units, 28 with bathroom. Sept–June 68€–92€; July–Aug 78€–108€. Rates include continental breakfast. No credit cards. **Amenities:** Breakfast room; lounge. *In room:* TV, Wi-Fi.

At Mönchstein
VERY EXPENSIVE

Hotel Schloss Mönchstein ★★ This handsome, Teutonic-style manor house, really a small castle, stands on top of a hill above the center of Salzburg. Be warned in advance: This is a haunt of the haute bourgeoisie, many of whom return year after year, so be prepared to dress for dinner. From its elegant salons, guests can enjoy panoramic views of the city. The Schloss was constructed as a fortified tower in 1350 and wasn't transformed into a hotel until 1950. On the premises are a wedding chapel and a garden terrace overlooking a statue of Apollo in the private park. Rooms come in varying sizes and styles, but are all uniformly comfortable, with roomy closets. Some are very elegant, with oriental rugs resting on parquet floors, king-size beds, and CD players. The hotel also has a garden terrace, a cocktail bar, and a restaurant (p. 257).

Mönchsberg Park 26, A-5020 Salzburg. ② **800/44-UTELL** in the U.S., or 0662/8485550. Fax 0662/848559. www.monchstein.at. 24 units. 345€–445€ double; from 595€ suite. Rates include buffet breakfast. AE, DC, MC, V. Free parking. **Amenities:** Restaurant; bar; cafe; babysitting; access to nearby health club; laundry service; dry cleaning; in-room massage; room service; secretarial services; non-smoking rooms; tour desk. *In room:* TV, minibar, hairdryer, safe, Wi-Fi.

At Rott

INEXPENSIVE

Pension Helmhof ✦ On the northwestern outskirts, Pension Helmhof is an appealingly rustic stucco chalet with flower-bedecked balconies and a stone-trimmed sun terrace. Rooms are comfortably furnished and well kept, with small bathrooms equipped with tub/shower combinations. There is old-fashioned chalet-style comfort to this snug nest.

Lieferinger Hauptstrasse (Kirchengasse 29), A-5020 Salzburg-Liefering. ✆ **0662/433079.** Fax 0662/433079. www.helmhof.at. 15 units. 72€–78€ double; 93€–99€ triple. Rates include breakfast. AE, MC, V. Free parking. Bus: 34. Adjacent to the Salzburg-Mitte exit off A1 Autobahn. **Amenities:** Breakfast room; lounge; outdoor pool. *In room:* TV.

In Anif

MODERATE

Hotel Friesacher ★ Run by a family of the same name, this large and elegant chalet has a hipped roof, a long expanse of gables, and natural-grained wooden balconies covered with flowers. An older building a few steps away across the flowering lawn serves as a well-furnished annex. Rooms are generally spacious and well furnished, with good beds and ample bathrooms equipped with tub/shower combinations. There's a country-style dining room, one of the finest in the area, so you might want to drive out for an evening here even if you aren't staying in Anif. In summer, guests can eat on the open-air terrace. Food is served Thursday to Tuesday noon to 2:30pm and 6 to 9:30pm.

Hellbrunnerstrasse 17, A-5081 Anif. ✆ **06246/8977.** Fax 06246/897749. www.hotelfriesacher.com. 90 units. Low season 145€–190€ double. During Festspiele and holidays 165€–235€. Rates include breakfast. AE, DC, MC, V. Free parking. Bus: 25. Take Westautobahn toward Graz and exit at Salzburg-Süd. Follow signs to Salzburg and then Anif. In Anif, make a left at 1st traffic light. **Amenities:** Restaurant; 2 bars; exercise room; sauna; outdoor heated pool; nonsmoking rooms; rooms for those w/limited mobility. *In room:* TV, minibar, hairdryer, safe.

Schlosswirt zu Anif ★ This country inn on the outskirts of Anif, 6km (4 miles) south of the center of Salzburg, was founded in 1607. With its flagstone floors, Biedermeier furniture, good beds, and collection of local artifacts and hunting trophies, it has been a thriving business ever since. It's so well known that Austrians sometimes drive all the way from Innsbruck to dine here. If you're a late riser, be warned that beginning at 7am, traffic might disturb you if you're housed in the annex, which is right on the highway. There's a generous breakfast buffet of *Wurst*, cheese, and poached eggs. Dinner is an elegant experience with such menu items as soused herring with dill, wild game (in season), and duckling in rosemary sauce. A kind English-speaking hostess in regional dress will help you with translations.

Salzachtalbundesstrasse 7, A-5081 Anif. ✆ **06246/72175.** Fax 06246/721758. www.schlosswirt-anif. com. 29 units. 130€–158€ double; 220€–258€ suite. Rates include buffet breakfast. AE, DC, MC, V. Free parking. Take the Salzburg-Süd exit from Autobahn A10 and drive less than 1km (½ mile). Bus: 25. **Amenities:** Restaurant; bar; laundry service; dry cleaning; room service. *In room:* TV, minibar, hairdryer.

In Aigen

INEXPENSIVE

Hotel-Gasthof Doktorwirt ☺ On the southern edge of Salzburg, 10 minutes by bus from the Old Town, this chalet has prominent gables, a red-tile roof, and white stucco walls. The adjoining restaurant produces many of the sausages it serves, as well as a collection of tempting pastries. The decor is rustic, sunny, and pleasant, with wood detailing. The cozy rooms come in sizes ranging from singles to junior suites. The triple rooms and the family units are extremely popular, as the Schnöll clan prides itself on running a family hotel. The best rooms are the two tower units.

Glaser Strasse 9, A-5026 Salzburg-Aigen. ℂ **0662/622973.** Fax 0662/62297325. www.doktorwirt.at. 41 units. 110€–170€ double. Rates include breakfast. AE, DC, MC, V. Parking 8€. Bus: 7 from Salzburg. Exit from Autobahn A10 at Salzburg-Süd. **Amenities:** Restaurant; bar; 2 pools (1 heated indoor); babysitting; fitness center; laundry service; dry cleaning; room service; sauna. *In room:* TV, hairdryer, safe, Wi-Fi.

At Gersberg

EXPENSIVE

Romantic Hotel Die Gersberg Alm ★★ 📇   The former farmstead traces its origins back to the 16th century, and in Mozart's time it was a popular dining excursion from Salzburg. The estate overlooks the city from its mountain perch on the Gersberg, with panoramic views in all directions, yet the location is only about a 15-minute drive from the center. Today, following a restoration, modern comforts have been installed in the once-rustic precincts, yet many of the 1832 alpine architectural features were left intact. The individually decorated bedrooms are comfortably furnished and filled with much charm. From a summer garden to a blazing fireplace in winter, there is much here to lure you away from Salzburg itself.

Gersberg 37, A-5020. ℂ **0662/641257.** Fax 0662/644278. www.gersbergalm.at. 43 units. 137€–295€ double; 287€–349€ suite. AE, DC, MC, V. Bus: 151. **Amenities:** Restaurant; bar; outdoor pool; sauna; tennis courts. *In room:* TV, minibar, hairdryer, Wi-Fi.

A Castle Hotel in Oberalm

The main reason for visiting Oberalm, directly north of Hallein and also north of Golling, is to stay at the castle hotel recommended below, which lies 16km (10 miles) south of Salzburg. From Salzburg, take the A10 south; from Golling, take the A10 north. However, if you're nearby, you might want to stop to see the Romanesque **Pfarrkirche (Parish Church),** with Gothic extensions. It has a magnificent high altar from 1707 by J. G. Mohr. The church is embellished with baroque furnishings and heraldic tombstones. Be sure to see the funereal shield from 1671.

Schloss Haunsperg ★ 📇   Signposted at the approach to town, this early-14th-century castle (owned by the von Gernerth-Mautner Markhof family) is decorated with towers and interior ornamentation. A small but ornate baroque chapel adjoins the hotel. The public areas include a series of vaulted corridors furnished with antiques and rustic chandeliers, several salons with parquet or flagstone floors, and a collection of antiques. Our favorite is the second-floor music salon. Many of the accommodations, which contain period furniture, are divided into suites of two or three rooms, along with some doubles.

Hammerstrasse 51, A-5411 Oberalm bei Hallein. ℂ **06245/80662.** Fax 06245/85680. www. schlosshaunsperg.com. 8 units. 135€–170€ double; 163€–210€ suite. Rates include buffet breakfast. AE, DC, MC, V. Free parking. **Amenities:** Breakfast room; lounge; tennis court. *In room:* TV, hairdryer.

WHERE TO EAT

Two special desserts you'll want to sample while in Salzburg are the famous *Salzburger Nockerln,* a light mixture of stiff egg whites, and the ubiquitous *Mozart-Kugeln,* with bittersweet chocolate, hazelnut nougat, and marzipan. You should also try a beer in one of the numerous Salzburg breweries.

If you want to picnic, the city has a number of delis where you can stock up on supplies. The best place to eat your picnic goodies is Mirabell Gardens, on the right bank (see "What to See & Do," later in this chapter).

While Salzburg is not a late-night dining town, many restaurants stay open late, often to accommodate concert- or theatergoers. But late in this sense rarely means beyond 11pm.

On the Left Bank (Old Town)

VERY EXPENSIVE

Esszimmer ★★ FRENCH/AUSTRIAN   A star on the Salzburg's hip culinary scene, this restaurant is operated by one of the town's most inventive chefs, Andreas Kaiblinger. The interior is a funky modern designer affair, and the restaurant serves classic French cuisine with an Austrian twist. The well-chosen menu changes every week and features the best produce at the market. A glass-floor installation allows guests to look down on the Almkanal that virtually flows right through the restaurant. The best menu items include marinated trout with pumpkin *Rösti* and pumpkin-flavored vinegar; cold filet of veal with goose liver in aspic; sautéed breast of pigeon with braised leeks, crêpes, and a sweet potato purée; saddle of venison with red cabbage and polenta; and white chocolate gateau with peaches and poppy seeds.

Müllner Hauptstrasse 33. ✆ **0662/870899.** www.esszimmer.com. Reservations required. Main courses 26€–29€; 3- to 7-course meals 51€–83€; 3-course lunch menu 28€. AE, DC, MC, V. Tues–Sat noon–2pm and 6:30–9:30pm. Open Mon during 2-week Christmas holiday and Mon during Salzburg Festival.

Goldener Hirsch ★★★ AUSTRIAN/VIENNESE   Fans of this place are willing to travel long distances just to enjoy the authentic ambiance of this renovated inn, established in 1407. Don't be fooled by the relatively simple decor of this place, a kind of well-scrubbed and decent simplicity that's emulated by dozens of other restaurants in resorts throughout Austria. The venue is chic, top-notch, impeccable, and charming, richly sought after during peak season. The food is so tasty and beautifully served that the kitchen ranks among the top three in Salzburg. Specialties include saddle of farm-raised venison with red cabbage, king prawns in an okra-curry ragout served with perfumed Thai rice, and tenderloin of beef and veal on morel cream sauce with cream potatoes. In season, expect a dish devoted to game, such as venison or roast duckling.

Getreidegasse 37. ✆ **0662/80840.** Reservations required. Main courses 20€–28€; 3-course lunch 29€; 3-course dinner 34€. AE, DC, MC, V. Daily noon–2:30pm and 6:30–9:30pm. Bus: 1, 4, 8, or 10.

EXPENSIVE

Alt-Salzburg ★ AUSTRIAN/INTERNATIONAL   A retreat into old-world elegance, Alt-Salzburg is one of the most venerated restaurants in the city, a bastion of formal service and refined cuisine—and at times, snobbery. Occupying a building constructed into the side of the steep and rocky cliffs of the Mönchsberg, the wood-ceilinged interior is crafted to reveal part of the chiseled rock. The menu features main dishes such as filet of river char sautéed with tomatoes, mushrooms, and capers, and served with leaf spinach, and potatoes; and lamb chops sautéed in a herb crust and thyme sauce with zucchini and potato cakes. In August, the restaurant is also open on Sunday and Monday for lunch.

Bürgerspitalgasse 2. ✆ **0662/841476.** www.altsalzburg.at. Reservations required. Main courses 12€–24€; fixed-price menu 41€–49€. AE, DC, MC, V. Mon 6–10:30pm; Tues–Sat 11:30am–2pm and 6–10:30pm (to midnight in Aug). Closed last week in Feb. Bus: 1, 4, or 8.

Restaurants in Salzburg

Alter Fuchs **18**
Alt-Salzburg **8**
BIO Wirtshaus Hirschenwirt **15**
Café Bazar **23**
Café-Konditorei Fürst **9**
Café Tomaselli **29**
Carpe Diem Finest Fingerfood **10**
Die Weisse **17**
Esszimmer **1**
Fasties **35**
Festungsrestaurant **33**
Goldener Hirsch **12**
Hagenauerstuben **25**
Hotel Stadtkrug Restaurant **21**
K & K Restaurant **32**
Konditorei Ratzka **36**
Krimpelstätter **2**
Magazin **3**
Mundenhamer Bräu **16**
Polo Lounge **19**
Purzelbaum **34**
Restaurant M32 **5**
Restaurant Schloss
   Mönchstein **4**
Restaurant s'Herzl **13**
Restaurant Symphonie **31**
Restaurant Wasserfall **22**
Ristorante/Pizzeria Il Sole **6**
Schatz-Konditorei **27**
Stadtgasthof Blaue Gans **11**
Sternbräu **14**
Stiftskeller St. Peter **28**
Strasserwirt **7**
Zipfer Bierhaus **26**
Zum Eulenspiegel **24**
Zum Fidelen Affen **20**
Zum Mohren **30**

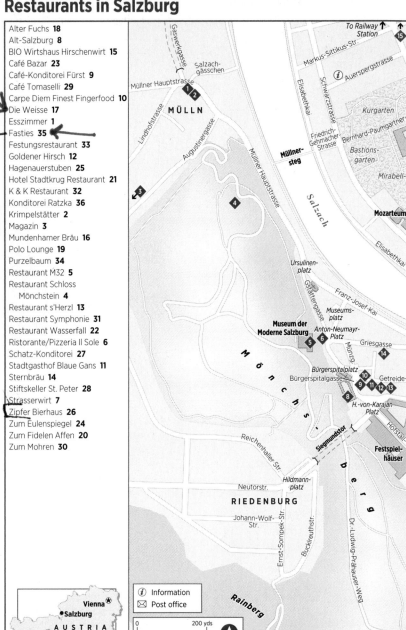

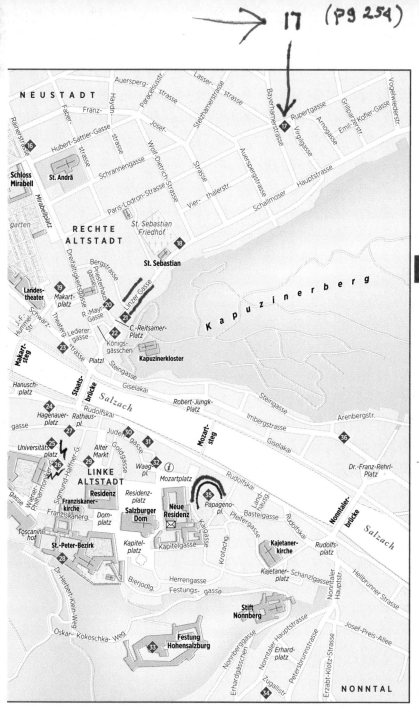

17 (Pg 254)

Café Bazar ★, Schwarzstrasse 3 (ℂ **0662/874278**; www.cafe-bazar.at; bus: 1, 3, 4, 5, or 6). This handsome Jugendstil cafe is a fixture in Salzburg's social life and has been since 1906, with a pleasingly motley assortment of regulars—artists and theater people, students, deal-makers and dilettantes. Housed in a handsome turn-of-the-century *palais* with many period features, it's located across the river from the main section of the Old Town. The interior is high-ceilinged and glistening, with lustrous wood and gleaming brass fittings. You'll still occasionally see someone with a Franz Josef mustache wearing a gray flannel Styrian suit with Loden trim, but a growing number of the patrons are young and stylish. You can order salads, sandwiches, and omelets. It's open Monday to Saturday 7:30am to 11pm, Sunday 9 to 6pm.

At the **Café-Konditorei Fürst,** Brodgasse 13, at the corner of Getreidegasse (ℂ **0662/843759**), *Mozart-Kugeln* (traditional marzipan–pistachio chocolate-dipped cookies) are sold. The owner invented this sweet in 1890 but forgot to patent the recipe. The treat is often duplicated, but here you can sample it from the authentic and original recipe. Norbert Fürst, a descendant of the original founder, still makes these fine chocolates with a recipe handed down to him by his great-grandfather. In addition to the *Mozart-Kugeln*, there's a wide range of other chocolates and truffle specialties, including such Austrian favorites as the Sachertorte, the Dobosch torte, and the inevitable *Apfelstrudel.* Open Monday to Saturday 8am to 9pm, Sunday 9am to 9pm.

Established in 1705, **Café Tomaselli** ★, Alter Markt 9 (ℂ **0662/ 844488;** www.tomaselli.at; bus: 2 or 5), opens onto one of the most charming cobblestone squares of the Altstadt. Aside from the chairs placed outdoors during summer, you'll find a room with a high ceiling and many tables (it's a great place to sit and talk), and another more formal room to the right of the entrance that houses oil portraits of well-known 19th-century Salzburgers and attracts a haute bourgeois crowd. Choose from 40 different kinds of cakes or other menu items, including omelets, wursts, ice cream, and a wide range of drinks. Of

Magazin ★★ INTERNATIONAL   This is the trendiest dining post in all of Salzburg. Somewhat hidden away, it's worth the search. Once you get here, you discover not only the town's most stylish wine bar, but a wine shop, a floral decoration store, and a restaurant in a mountainous gallery set in an architectural complex of avant-garde buildings on top of and next to each other. At this multipurpose hub for the epicurean set, you're treated to Marcus Radauer's market-fresh cuisine. The food is often as unusual as it is delicious. And with every plate, you're assured of some of the best wines in the area. The culinary creations are sometimes simple, sometimes complex, rarely mannered, and never pointless. The chef does wonders with Styrian beef, and the fish dishes are handled to near perfection. You're never certain what's on the menu but expect a surprise—a pleasant one that is.

Augustinergasse 13. ℂ **0662/841584.** www.magazin.co.at. Reservations required. Lunch main courses 6.50€–32€; dinner main courses 24€–32€; 4-course fixed-price menu 59€–62€. AE, DC, MC, V. Tues-Sat 10am–midnight. Bus: 4.

course, the pastries and ice cream are all homemade. The cafe is open Monday to Saturday 7am to 9pm; until 12am during the Festspiele.

A melody by Mozart, who was born next door, might accompany your before-dinner drink at **Hagenauer-stuben,** Universitätsplatz 14 (ⓒ 0662/ **842657;** bus: 1, 4, 7, 8, or 10). Many visitors never get beyond the street-level bar, where snacks (such as salads and goulash) and drinks are served in a 14th-century room with stone floors and a vaulted ceiling, highlighted by a changing exhibition of modern lithographs and watercolors. At the top of a narrow flight of stone steps, you'll discover an austere trio of thick-walled rooms decorated with a ceramic stove and wooden armoires. A central serving table holds an array of salads and hors d'oeuvres. The cafe is open Monday to Saturday 9am to 1am; Sunday 10am to 6pm.

The small **Konditorei Ratzka,** Imbergstrasse 45 (ⓒ 0662/640024; bus: 6, 7, or 10), 10 minutes from the center of town, is owned by its pastry chef, Herwig Ratzka. A master at his craft,

he uses the freshest ingredients to produce about 30 different pastries. Because the cakes are made fresh every day, much of the selection is gone by late afternoon, so go early. It's open Tuesday through Friday 8am to 5pm and Saturday 8am to 12:30pm and 1:30 to 6pm. Closed 2 weeks in January, June, and September. Mr. Ratzka requests that patrons don't smoke in the shop.

Almost every item sold at the old-time Austrian confectionery **Schatz-Konditorei,** Getreidegasse 3 (ⓒ **0662/842792;** bus: 1, 4, 7, 8, or 10), is made from traditional recipes. Our favorite treat is the well-known *Mozart-Kugeln* (see above), with pistachio, marzipan, and hazelnut nougat, all dipped in chocolate. You can enjoy the pastries and coffees at a table inside the cafe or take them away. Some varieties of pastry, including the *Mozart-Kugeln,* can be shipped around the world. It's open Monday to Friday 8:30am to 6:30pm and Saturday 8am to 5pm, with extended hours during the summer Salzburg Festival.

Purzelbaum ★ AUSTRIAN/VIENNESE   Located in a residential neighborhood not often frequented by tourists, this sophisticated bistro is near a duck pond at the bottom of a steep incline leading up to Salzburg Castle. A cramped corner of the bar is reserved for visitors who want to drop in for only a drink. Most guests, however, reserve a table in one of the trio of rooms containing an Art Nouveau ceiling and marble buffets from an antique bistro in France. Menu items change according to the whim of the chef and include well-prepared dishes such as turbot-and-olive casserole, a selection of wild game (in season), Styrian mountain lamb in white-wine sauce with beans and polenta, and the house specialty, scampi *Gröstl,* composed of fresh shrimp with sliced potatoes baked with herbs in a casserole. During the Salzburg Festival, the restaurant is also open on Sunday and Monday midday.

Zugallistrasse 7. ⓒ **0662/848843.** www.purzelbaum.at. Reservations required. Main courses 19€–26€; 4-course fixed-price menu 46€. AE, DC, MC, V. Mon evening–Sat noon–2pm and 6–11pm. Bus: 5, 20, or 25.

Restaurant M32 ★★ INTERNATIONAL   All day long Sepp Schellhorn, an award-winning chef, cookbook author, and president of the Austrian Hotelier Association, feeds visitors to the Museum Der Moderne Salzburg (p. 266), but in the evening the restaurant feeds even more refined palates. The setting alone, with the grandest panorama of any restaurant in Salzburg, makes it a worthy choice. But it offers so much more in the way of a cuisine that bursts with freshness and originality. But, first, you absorb the ambiance, including a tremendous light installation of 500 deer antlers by architect Matteo Thun.

Among some of the better dishes here is the *Tafelspitz* with egg noodles. Other favorites include the braised beefsteak with quail eggs or the sautéed morels with potato-based noodles and a *tapenade* of olives and Styrian tomatoes. For the *Nachspeisen* to close off a meal, there is a very nice cheese plate with red pepper strips, a white chocolate mousse, and a salad of bitter oranges with fresh berries and a vanilla-flavored cream sauce.

Mönchsberg 32. © **0662/841000.** www.m32.at. Reservations required for dinner. Main courses 13€–25€; set-lunch menu 14€. AE, MC, V. Sept–July Tues–Sat noon–2:30pm and 6–10pm, Sun 9am–6pm; Aug daily 9am–1am. Take the Mönchsberg elevator to the top.

Restaurant Symphonie ★ INTERNATIONAL   Set within a riverfront building whose origins go back to the 15th century, this restaurant evokes the kind of 18th-century country-baroque setting where a young Mozart might have given a concert. Most menu items focus on traditional Austrian specialties, including marinated fried chicken, a Viennese *Tafelspitz,* and a vegetarian specialty consisting of creamed mushrooms with rosemary and herbs. Fish dishes include filet of sole with a zucchini crust and olive purée, and crispy-roasted filet of char with parsley potatoes and salad. For dessert, consider buttermilk dumplings with marinated cherries.

In the Hotel Altstadt SAS Radisson, Rudolfskai 28. © **0662/84857155.** Reservations recommended. Main courses 19€–25€; 3-course fixed-price menu 39€; 4-course fixed-price menu 46€; 5-course fixed-price menu 52€. AE, DC, MC, V. Mon–Sat noon–2pm and 6:30–10:30pm. Bus: 3, 5, 6, 7, 8, or 10.

MODERATE

Carpe Diem Finest Fingerfood ★★ 📱 INTERNATIONAL   This establishment is one of the snazziest and most unique in town. Owned by Dietrich Mateschitz, creator of Red Bull, and launched by star chef Jörg Wörther, the two-story lounge and cafe offers a new culinary concept: Fine cuisine packed into waffle shells or cones. The chef's intricate inventions come neatly tucked in a crisp shell, at times with contrasting temperatures. Some of the dishes from the revolving menu include steak filet in mushroom cream with a dumpling, cream of avocado with carrots tempura, and, finally, turbot with fennel, chorizo ravioli, and paprika sauce. The breakfast, lunch, and dinner menus differ in selection, and the patio area teems with activity.

Getreidegasse 50. © **0662/848800.** www.finestfingerfood.com. Reservations required. Breakfast 10€–16€. Cones 4.80€–10.50€ depending on the filling. Fixed-price menus: 17.50€ 3 courses; 23.50€ 4 courses; 28.50€ 5 courses; 33.50€ 6 courses; 38.50€ 7 courses. AE, DC, MC, V. Daily 8:30am–midnight. Bus: 1, 4, or 8.

K & K Restaurant AUSTRIAN/INTERNATIONAL   Separated into about half a dozen intimate dining rooms on four floors, the K & K is decorated with wood paneling, slabs of salmon-colored marble, flickering candles, antique accessories, and a well-dressed clientele. The menu contains a medley of well-crafted dishes, ranging from the traditional to the innovative, including carpaccio of beef on basil pesto with mushroom salad and parmesan, *Tafelspitz,* and filet of butterfish on sea grass salad with potatoes and salmon caviar sauce. If you'd like to check out a cool informal hangout and witness a marvel of masonry, head down the massive stone staircase to reach the Bierkeller, a beer cellar that serves drinks and snack food to a sometimes rowdy crowd.

Waagplatz 2. ✆ **0662/842157.** Reservations required. Main courses 13€–20€; fixed-price menu 22€–44€. AE, DC, MC, V. Daily 11:30am–2:30pm and 6–11:30pm; drinks and snacks daily 11:30am–midnight. Bus: 3, 5, 6, 7, 8, or 10.

Restaurant s'Herzl ★★ 💣 AUSTRIAN/VIENNESE With an entrance on the landmark Karajanplatz, s'Herzl sits next door and is connected to the glamorous Goldener Hirsch. Good value attracts visitors and locals alike to its pair of cozy rooms, one paneled and timbered. Waitresses in dirndls serve appetizing entrees, which are likely to include roast pork with dumplings, various grills, game stew (in season), and, for the heartiest eaters, a farmer's plate of boiled pork, roast pork, grilled sausages, dumplings, and sauerkraut.

Karajanplatz 7. ✆ **0662/8084889.** www.goldenerhirschsalzburg.com/herzl. Reservations recommended. Main courses 7€–24€; fixed-price menu 13€–20€. AE, DC, MC, V. Daily 11:30am–10pm. Bus: 1, 4, or 8.

Stiftskeller St. Peter (Peterskeller) ★ AUSTRIAN/VIENNESE Legend has it that Mephistopheles met with Faust in this tavern, which was established by Benedictine monks in A.D. 803. In fact, it's the oldest restaurant in Europe, housed in the abbey of the church that supposedly brought Christianity to Austria. Aside from a collection of baroque banquet rooms, there's an inner courtyard with vaults cut from the living rock, a handful of dignified wood-paneled rooms, and a brick-vaulted cellar with a tiled floor and rustic chandeliers. In addition to wine from the abbey's own vineyards, the tavern serves good home-style Austrian cooking, including roast pork in gravy with sauerkraut and bread dumplings, braised oxtail with mushrooms and fried polenta, and loin of lamb with asparagus. Vegetarian dishes, such as semolina dumplings on noodles in a parsley sauce, are also featured. Try the apple strudel or sweet curd strudel with vanilla sauce or ice cream, and, most definitely, the famed *Salzburger Nockerln.*

St.-Peter-Bezirk 1-4. ✆ **0662/8412680.** www.haslauer.at. Reservations recommended. Main courses 12€–25€; fixed-price menus 16€–45€. AE, DC, MC, V. Daily 11:30am–2:30pm and 6–10:30pm. Closed Dec 24.

Zum Eulenspiegel ★ AUSTRIAN/VIENNESE Housed in a white-and-peach building opposite Mozart's birthplace, Zum Eulenspiegel sits at one end of a quiet cobblestone square in the Old Town. Inside, guests have a choice of five rooms on three different levels, all rustically but elegantly decorated. A small and rustic bar area on the ground floor is a pleasant place for pre-dinner drinks. Traditional Austrian cuisine is meticulously adhered to here. The menu features such classic dishes as *Tafelspitz,* Wiener schnitzel, spinach dumplings stuffed with ewe cheese in a tomato sauce and topped with parmesan, filet of pork with warm cabbage salad and bacon, and, for dessert, nutty *Mozart Knödel* with fruit topping.

Hagenauerplatz 2. ✆ **0662/843180.** www.zum-eulenspiegel.at. Reservations required. Main courses 13€–23€. AE, MC, V. Mon–Sat 11am–2pm and 6–10:30pm. Closed Feb 1–Mar 15. Bus: 1, 4, 7, 8, or 10.

INEXPENSIVE

Fasties INTERNATIONAL   This is an inexpensive, unpretentious restaurant that doesn't take itself too seriously. It specializes in "fasties," but, unlike most fast food, these meals actually contain flavor and nutrients. Set at the corner of the Papageno-platz, in one of the most historic neighborhoods of Salzburg, the restaurant has a stand-up counter and three large communal wooden tables where a staff member will serve you. When the weather cooperates, additional tables are set up on the square outside. The menu, written on a blackboard, changes daily, but invariably includes at least two soups, salads, and sandwiches. Platters are more substantial, consisting of assorted pâtés and cheeses, goulashes, roasts, and at least one vegetarian special. A second branch is in a less convenient location across the river, at Lasserstrasse 19 (✆ **0662/873876**; bus: 2).

Pfeifergasse 3. ✆ **0662/844774.** www.fasties.at. Reservations not accepted. Main courses 5€–8€. MC, V. Mon–Fri 7:30am–9pm; Sat 8am–5pm. Bus: 3, 5, 6, 7, 8, or 10.

Festungsrestaurant ★ ☺ SALZBURGIAN/AUSTRIAN   The venue of this well-known restaurant is modern, warmly decorated, and airy, perched atop the former stronghold of the prince-archbishops of Salzburg, on a huge rocky spur about 122m (400 ft.) above the Old Town and the Salzach River. From its windows, you'll have a sweeping view over the city and the surrounding countryside. The kitchen offers fish, well-prepared beef, pork, lamb, and such old-fashioned and traditional dishes as a *Salzburger bauernschmaus* (a bubbling stewpot of veal, pork, sausage, and dumplings), *Salzburger Schnitzel, Salzburger Gröstl* (a form of beef hash with potatoes and onions), and *käse Spätzle* (*spätzle* with cheese). There's also wild game dishes served in season. The Fürstenzimmer offers occasional concerts, often Mozart. For ticket information, call ✆ **0662/825858.**

Hohensalzburg, Mönchsberg 34. ✆ **0662/841780.** www.festungsrestaurant.at. Reservations required July–Aug. Main courses 10€–21€. AE, DC, MC, V. Mar–Jan 7 daily 10am–9pm. Funicular from the Old Town.

Krimpelstätter SALZBURGIAN/AUSTRIAN   This restaurant has been an enduring favorite, dating from 1548. Originally designed and constructed as an inn, with chiseled stone columns that support the vaulted ceilings and heavy timbers. Both the informal room marked GASTZIMMER and a trio of cozy antique dining rooms serve the same menu, tasty and high-quality Land Salzburg regional cuisine featuring wild game dishes. Start with the cream of goose soup or else homemade chamois sausage. Traditional main courses include roast pork with dumplings, and white sausage *Gröstl* with mustard and sauerkraut. Spinach dumplings are topped with a cheese sauce, and marinated beef stew comes with noodles in butter. Wash it all down with an Augustiner beer.

Müllner Hauptstrasse 31. ✆ **0662/432274.** www.krimpelstaetter.at. Reservations recommended. Main courses 8€–16€. MC, V. Tues–Sat 11am–midnight (open daily in Aug). Closed 3 weeks in Jan. Bus: 7 or 10.

Ristorante/Pizzeria Il Sole ITALIAN   The venue is charming and convivial, and the prices are relatively modest at this well-managed Italian restaurant immediately adjacent to the lower stage of the Mönchsberg elevator. The Austrian-born owners, the Rauzenberger brothers, are Italian by adoption, thanks to the dozens of trips south of the border for foodstuffs and decorative objects showcased in this restaurant. The tantalizing fettuccine with shrimp is highly recommended, as well as vegetable tortellini stuffed with blue cheese and spinach. Equally vibrant was a platter of chicken Il Sole, with fresh parmesan, a zesty tomato sauce, and pesto. The lemon-flavored chicken with fresh tagliatelle was a delight, as was a selection of grilled or sautéed fresh fish. Among their selection of 15 pizzas, the house brand (Il Sole, made with ham, salami, artichoke hearts, and mozzarella) is the most consistently popular.

Gstättengasse 15. © **0662/843284.** Reservations not necessary. Pizzas and pastas 6€–9€; main courses 11€–15€. AE, DC, MC, V. Daily 11:30am–2:30pm and 5:30pm–midnight. Closed Tues Mar–June and Sept–Nov. Bus: 4 or 8.

Stadtgasthof Blaue Gans AUSTRIAN   The Blue Goose consistently attracts local residents, some of whom plan their week around a meal here, and is an old-fashioned testimonial to *gutbürgerlich* (home-style) cooking. Within a timeless setting that includes vaulted ceilings originally designed in 1432 and a scattering of antique oil paintings, you can order such dishes as Wiener schnitzel, one of the best in town; *Tafelspitz*; and a braised calf of veal with mashed potatoes. Pink-roasted lamb with apples and porcini is an enduring favorite. Don't overlook this establishment's newest addition, a stone-built cellar, 500 years old, some of which is visible from above via a tempered glass plate set directly into the floor of the upstairs bar.

In the Arthotel Blaue Gans, Getreidegasse 43. © **0662/842491.** Reservations recommended. Main courses 13€–22€. AE, DC, MC, V. Wed–Mon 10am–10pm (last order 10pm).

Sternbräu AUSTRIAN   The entrance to this establishment is through an arched cobblestone passageway leading off a street in the Old Town. The place seems big enough to have fed half the Austro-Hungarian army, with a series of eight rooms in varying degrees of formality—a rustic fantasy combining masonry columns with hand-hewn beams and wood paneling. You can also eat in the chestnut tree-shaded beer garden, which is usually packed on summer nights, or under the weathered arcades of an inner courtyard. Drinks are served in the restaurant's bar, Grünstern. Daily specials include typically Austrian dishes such as Wiener and chicken schnitzels, trout, cold marinated herring, Hungarian goulash, hearty regional soups, and many other solid selections.

Griesgasse 23. © **0662/842140.** www.sternbraeu.com. Reservations not accepted. Main courses 8€–16€. AE, MC, V. Daily 10am–11pm (until midnight July–Aug). Bus: 1, 4, 7, or 8.

Zipfer Bierhaus AUSTRIAN   This longtime favorite is especially popular with the after-concert crowd. In a building dating from the 1400s, the establishment is more of a restaurant than its beer hall decor suggests. The good food is familiar if you've been in Austria for a while: Noodle casserole with ham in a cream sauce, breaded and fried filet of catfish, beef goulash with a bread dumpling, and the *Bauernschmaus* (farmer's feast) of roast pork, smoked meat, sausages, sauerkraut, and a bread dumpling. The food is well prepared and the portions are generous.

Sigmund-Haffner-Gasse 12. © **0662/840745.** www.zipfer-bierhaus.at. Reservations recommended. Main courses 7.90€–16€. AE, DC, MC, V. Mon–Sat 10am–midnight (kitchen closes at 10pm). Bus: 3, 5, 6, 7, 8, or 10.

Zum Mohren ★ AUSTRIAN   A statue of an exotic-looking Moor sits atop the wrought-iron sign at the entrance to this restaurant, in a house built in 1423. You'll have to descend a flight of stone steps to three distinct eating areas, the best right of the entrance. Replicas of Moors, gold earrings and all, provide an offbeat decor. A third area, on the left as you enter, is more cave-like, with an orange ceramic stove and a low ceiling. Meals include entrecote, Parisian style; sirloin steak with herb butter; grilled lamb chops; a good selection of cheeses; and many rich desserts.

Judengasse 9. ℂ **0662/840680.** www.restaurant-zummohren.at. Reservations recommended. Main courses 12€–21€. MC, V. Mon–Sat 11am–11pm. Bus: 3, 5, 6, 7, 8, or 10.

On the Right Bank
EXPENSIVE

Polo Lounge (aka The Restaurant in the Bristol Hotel) AUSTRIAN/ITALIAN/INTERNATIONAL   This is the dining counterpart of the upscale restaurant within Salzburg's other top-notch hotel, the Goldener Hirsch. In this case, the venue is a stately, baronial-looking area outfitted in tones of pale orange and accented with large-scale oil paintings. Menus feature freshwater crab salad with mango, tuna carpaccio with horseradish cream sauce, goose-liver parfait with apple chutney, grilled filet of beef with pinot noir sauce, roast loin of lamb with a pumpkin-flavored risotto, or perhaps grilled loin of veal with morel-flavored cream sauce. And for dessert, consider the warm chocolate mousse served with hot and sour cherries. Immediately adjacent to the restaurant is a club-style bar with the requisite leather upholsteries and well-oiled paneling.

In the Hotel Bristol, Makartplatz 4. ℂ **0662/873557.** Reservations recommended. Main courses 14€–29€. AE, DC, MC, V. Sept–June Mon–Sat noon–2pm and 6–10pm; July–Aug daily noon–2:30pm and 6–10pm. Bus: 1, 3, 4, 5, or 6.

MODERATE

Alter Fuchs ☺ TYROLEAN/AUSTRIAN   Traditional Tyrolean dishes are served along with mugs of the nearby Bavarian brew, Weininger, in a vaulted stone cellar tavern. The "Old Fox" restaurant is comfortable, the food is uncomplicated but made with high-quality ingredients, and the service is friendly and efficient. Kids are also welcome; if they're toddlers, high seats are provided for them. An array of fresh fish and such classics as Wiener schnitzel are served along with a range of food that Tyroleans have been eating for years. Portions, such as sausages, roast pork, baked ham, and dumplings, are large and will satisfy the trencherman in women and men alike. The bread is often exceptionally good, including honest-to-God pretzels.

Linzer Gasse 47–49. ℂ **0662/882022.** www.alterfuchs.at. Reservations recommended. Main courses 10€–21€. MC, V. Mon–Sat 11:30am–midnight. Bus: 4.

BIO Wirtshaus Hirschenwirt ★ 🍴 AUSTRIAN   This is a hotel dining room, but one with a difference: All of the ingredients used in its cuisine derive from organically grown ingredients, raised in Austria without chemical fertilizers or insecticides. The setting is a quartet of cozy dining rooms, each with a name that evokes a mountain chalet. There's the *Stüberl,* for nonsmokers; the *Schank,* a bar area with a handful of dining tables; the *Speisesaal,* the richly paneled main dining room; and *Hirsch Saal,* a Deer Room, with lots of memorabilia related to hunting. Menu items change with the season but might include a creamy pumpkin soup, carpaccio of Austrian beef, *Tafelspitz,* several versions of Wiener schnitzel, and about five different vegetarian dishes, the best example of which is small *Spätzle,* a pasta-like side dish in a cheese-flavored onion sauce.

In the Hotel zum Hirschen, St. Julien Strasse 23. ℂ **0662/872943.** www.biowirtshaus.at. Reservations recommended. Main courses 8€–15€. AE, DC, MC, V. Daily 11:30am–midnight. Bus: 1, 2, 3, 5, or 6.

Die Weisse AUSTRIAN   This is one of the best restaurant-cum-breweries in Salzburg. It's traditional and serves food that has been consistently popular since it opened in 1890. Carry a big appetite if you dine here, as portions are huge. Instead of butter, cold lard and cracklings are spread over dark rye bread. This is followed by the biggest Wiener schnitzel we've ever encountered in Salzburg, accompanied by a freshly made salad, potatoes, and cranberry sauce for added flavor. Other rib-sticking fare includes a platter of mixed sausages and perfectly roasted ham. Dumplings accompany main dishes. Naturally there's plenty of beer to wash everything down, along with a bakery full of pretzels and freshly baked breads. For dessert, finish off with an *Apfelstrudel*.

Rupertgasse 10. ✆ **0662/872246.** www.dieweisse.at. Reservations not required. Main courses 8€–16€. AE, MC, V. Mon–Sat 10:30am–midnight. Closed Dec 24–31. Bus: 2.

Hotel Stadtkrug Restaurant AUSTRIAN/INTERNATIONAL On the right bank of the Old Town, on the site of what used to be a 14th-century farm, the 'City Bock' occupies a structure that was rebuilt from an older core in 1458. In an artfully rustic setting, illuminated by gilded wooden chandeliers, you can enjoy good, hearty dishes including highland cattle soup with noodles; roasted lamb with parmesan polenta and spinach; grilled trout with market-fresh vegetables; and glazed cutlet of pork with caraway seeds, deep-fried potatoes, and French beans with bacon. A dessert specialty is lemon sorbet doused in strawberry sparkling wine.

Linzer Gasse 20. ✆ **0662/873545.** www.stadtkrug.at. Reservations recommended. Main courses 17€–27€. AE, DC, MC, V. Sept–June Wed–Mon noon–2pm and 6–11pm; July–Aug daily noon–2pm and 6–11pm. Bus: 1, 3, 4, 5, or 6.

Mundenhamer Bräu SALZBURGIAN/INTERNATIONAL This warm-hued restaurant near the main train station has been serving copious portions of food to Salzburgers since the 1930s. There are several different seating areas—our favorite is the big-windowed section with a view of the city park. In season, game is a specialty; also Salzburger cream schnitzel, filet of rabbit in red wine vegetable sauce, mushroom ragout, and a house specialty called Mundenhamer potpourri, a mixed grill for two. The menu is in English and the portions are large.

Rainerstrasse 2. ✆ **0662/8756930.** www.mundenhamer.at. Reservations recommended. Main courses 7.20€–16€; fixed-price menus 10€–12€. AE, DC, MC, V. Mon–Sat 11:30am–2pm and 5:30–11:30pm. Bus: 2, 3, 5, or 6.

Restaurant Wasserfall ★ 📖 ITALIAN This discovery serves some of the best Northern Italian fare in Salzburg to the sounds of quiet jazz and gurgling water from a waterfall. The restaurant extends into the rocks of the Kapuzinerberg (p. 267), the forested area on the right bank of the Salzach River, rising over the cityscape of Salzburg. Excellent local produce and some fine imported ingredients from Italy go into the creation of this fresh-tasting and well-prepared cuisine. The cookery is simple, nothing to interfere with the natural flavor of the food. The fresh fish dishes are very nice, with some lemon and fresh herbs adding flavor. Succulent pasta comes with a number of flavorful and tangy sauces. Best of all, some of their recipes are available on their website for trying out at home.

Linzer Gasse 10. ✆ **0662/873331.** www.restaurant-wasserfall.at. Reservations required. Main courses 7€–22€. AE, DC, MC, V. Mon–Sat 6–10:30pm. Closed mid-July to mid-Aug. Bus: 1, 3, 4, 5, or 6.

Strasserwirt ★ AUSTRIAN Set within a 10-minute walk south of Salzburg's historic core, this restaurant occupies three indoor dining rooms and also, during clement weather, one of the most charming gardens in town. The 200-year-old structure houses the culinary intelligence of Chef Christian Sussetz and his wife,

Alexandra, who oversees the service of the dining room staff. Celebrating the cuisine and the agrarian bounty of Austria, main courses include roasted mountain lamb from nearby high-altitude meadows, served with polenta and zucchini; roast chicken bathed in a tomato–caper ragout with homemade noodles; and fresh Atlantic char that's simply grilled and served with parsley potatoes and garlic butter. Wiener schnitzels and goulash are delightful, albeit not particularly exotic.

Leopoldskronestrasse 39. ℂ **0662/826391.** www.zumstrasserwirt.com. Reservations recommended. Main courses 9.90€–18€; 4-course set-price menu 39€ without wine, 50€ with wine. DC, MC, V. Wed–Sat 11:30am–2pm and 6–10pm; Sun 11:30am–9pm. Closed for 2 weeks in Oct and 2 weeks in Feb. Bus: 21 or 22.

Zum Fidelen Affen AUSTRIAN   Set on the eastern edge of the river near the Staatsbrücke, this restaurant is an animated and jovial pub with food service. Management allows only three tables on any particular evening to be reserved; the remainder are given to whomever happens to show up. It's best to give your name to the maître d' and then wait at the bar.

Menu items are simple, inexpensive, and based on regional culinary traditions. A house specialty is a gratin of green (spinach-flavored) noodles in tomato sauce with fresh parmesan and salad. Also popular are Wiener schnitzels, ham goulash with dumplings, and the filling Monkey Steak: Grilled pork with *Rösti* potatoes, mushrooms, bacon, tomatoes, and cheese. Dessert might be a cheese dumpling or one of several kinds of pastries. True to the establishment's name, translated as "The Merry Monkey," its interior depicts painted and sculpted simians cavorting across the walls.

Priesterhausgasse 8. ℂ **0662/877361.** Reservations recommended. Main courses 9€–16€. DC, MC, V. Mon–Sat 5pm–1am (the kitchen closes at 10:45pm).

On the Outskirts
VERY EXPENSIVE

Ikarus in Hangar 7 ★★ 🏠 INTERNATIONAL   In no other major city of Europe do we recommend that you go to the airport for fine dining. Star chef Eckard Weizigmann manages the unique Ikarus installed in Hangar 7, a glass-and-steel ellipsoid near the airport. He employs a different award-winning, international chef each month to create his specialties, each creating offering three menus. Finely crafted dishes might include rabbit with cabbage, barley, and blood orange; an oxtail ragout; halibut on a chorizo couscous and bell pepper foam; a delicacy of pear, Cassis, and chocolate; and ice cream with tonka beans, followed by an international selection of cheese. Cuisine can be combined with technology; guided tours of the on-site Flight Museum are offered at various times at Hangar 7.

7A Wilhelm-Spazier Strasse (5km west of Salzburg). ℂ **0662/219-777.** www.hangar-7.com. Reservations required. Main courses 32€–50€; set-price menus 95€–135€. AE, DC, MC, V. Daily noon–2pm and 6:30–10pm. Bus: 2 or 8.

Pfefferschiff ★ 🏠 CONTINENTAL   This treat is set in a country-baroque rectory built about 300 years ago as a home for the village priest in the suburb of Hallwang, 3.2km (2 miles) northeast of Salzburg's center. Inside, a trio of high-ceilinged, rather stiffly formal dining rooms, showcases the cuisine of owner and chef Klaus Fleishhaker. The menu changes frequently, with an emphasis on fresh regional products. The finest dishes include roasted sheatfish served with tomato and avocado salad and couscous, blood sausage with crispy jumbo shrimp in an apple–mango chutney, and a ragout of scallops and seafood in a saffron-flavored cream sauce. Desserts are sublime—especially the rhubarb tart served with buttermilk-flavored ice cream. Take a cab; or else drive along the north edge of the Kapuzinerberg in the direction of Hallwang, and then follow the signposts into Söllheim.

Söllheim 3, in the suburb of Hallwang. ⓒ **0662/661242.** Reservations required. Main courses 20€–35€; fixed-price menus 52€–80€. DC, MC, V. Tues-Fri 6–10pm, Sat noon-1:30pm and 6–10pm; open midday during Easter and the Festspiele, and the rest of the year for groups of 15 or more.

Restaurant Schloss Mönchstein ★★★ INTERNATIONAL   This is the most glamorous and prestigious restaurant in Salzburg, thanks to a historic pedigree and cuisine that defines it as one of the most appealing Relais & Châteaux members in Austria. In addition to the elegantly outfitted dining rooms, there's also an outdoor terrace open in good weather. Menu items change with the seasons and the whims of the chefs, but might include delectable king prawns with sesame oil and fresh ginger, butter-fried filets of Arctic char nestled on a purée of celery, Muscovy duck breast in a watercress sauce with braised baby leeks, or a roasted loin of lamb dredged in pumpkin seeds and served with sage sauce. In autumn and early winter, savory game dishes include medallions of venison with rosemary sauce.

In the Hotel Schloss Mönchstein, Mönchsberg Park 26. ⓒ **0662/8485550.** www.monchstein.at. Reservations recommended. Main courses 25€–50€. AE, DC, MC, V. Wed-Mon noon-2pm and 6–10pm. Limited menu available daily 2–6pm.

EXPENSIVE

Brandstätter ★ AUSTRIAN   One of the best restaurants in Salzburg is actually right outside the city limits in Liefering, lying just off the Autobahn-Mitte. It's northwest of the city, about 30 minutes by bus, or 20 minutes if you prefer to take a taxi. Brandstätter is an intimate, cozy choice for a special meal. The daily menus are seasonal so that the best and freshest produce, game, and meat are used. We recommend beginning with the crayfish *Gröstl* with curry and proceeding to the saddle of rabbit with porcini mushrooms and risotto. Some dishes might be only for the adventurous—for example, marinated calf's head with avocados and salad—but others are quite elegant, including a perfectly cooked roast pheasant breast with a bacon-and-cranberry sauce. Finish your meal with one of the homemade desserts, such as a hazelnut parfait.

Münchner Bundesstrasse 69, Liefering. ⓒ **0662/434535.** www.hotel-brandstaetter.com. Reservations required. Main courses 8€–32€. AE, MC, V. Mon-Sat 11:30am-2pm and 6–10pm. Closed 1 week in Jan. Bus: 4 from the center of Salzburg to the Fischergasse stop.

Obauer ★★ 🏨 AUSTRIAN/ITALIAN   It's worth the 45-minute train ride to the hilltop village of Werfen to sample the cuisine of Karl and Rudolph Obauer, who worked for some of the greatest chefs of Europe before opening their own little hotel and restaurant. The windows of the restaurant look out upon mountain vistas and the town's ancient fortress, and there's a lovely garden at the back.

Great care goes into the selection of the produce, including young salmon and trout from nearby streams, farmer's chicken, and even Pongau lamb and veal from nearby mountain pastures. One of our favorites is tender Werfen lamb in its pan juices with a side order of buttery Swiss chard and an onion stuffed with white polenta. For dessert, we'd recommend the Banyuls-soaked prunes topped with *ganâche*. The village of Werfen lies near the A10 (the Tauern Autobahn), 35km (22 miles) from Salzburg. The Werfen train station is only a 5-minute walk from the hotel.

Markt 46, Werfen. ⓒ **0646/852120.** www.obauer.com. Reservations required. Main courses 15€–45€; 3-course menu 58€; 4-course menu 68€; 5-course menu 88€; 6-course menu 98€. AE, MC, V. Wed-Sun noon-2pm and 7-9:30pm.

MODERATE

Gasthof Riedenburg ★ CONTINENTAL   One of the best restaurants in and around Salzburg occupies a substantial-looking white-sided villa in the suburb of Riedenburg, about 3km (2 miles) south of the city's historic core. Elegant and well-respected by virtually everyone in town, it attracts well-groomed and well-heeled members of the local bourgeoisie. Enter a trio of paneled dining rooms, each with an elegantly rustic motif of Land Salzburger charm. Menu items are urbane, sophisticated, and delicious—some of the best in town. Examples include nutmeg pumpkin gnocchi with bak choy and nuts; zander and lobster served with kohlrabi and lime risotto; veal with yogurt, saffron egg, spinach and brie *tramezzini;* Tauern lamb in artichoke risotto on verbena. Dessert might be a white chocolate mousse with mandarin oranges.

Neutorstrasse 31. (✆ **0662/830815.** www.riedenburg.at. Reservations recommended. Main courses 24€–41€; fixed-price menus 59€–79€. AE, DC, MC, V. Sept–July Tues–Sat noon–2pm and 6–10pm; Aug daily noon–2pm and 6–10pm. Bus: 1, 4, 8, or 10.

9 WHAT TO SEE & DO

Most of the Old Town lies between the left bank of the Salzach River and the ridge known as the Mönchsberg, which rises to a height of 503m (1,650 ft.). The right bank also retains a smaller, well-preserved medieval district with baroque highlights like the **Mirabell Gardens.** The main street of the left bank is Getreidegasse, a narrow thoroughfare lined with five- and six-story burghers' buildings. Most of the houses along the street date from the 17th and 18th centuries. Mozart was born at no. 9 (see below). Many of the houses display lace-like wrought-iron signs over carved windows.

You might begin your explorations at **Mozartplatz,** with its outdoor cafes. From here you can walk to the even more expansive **Residenzplatz,** where torchlight dancing is staged every year, along with outdoor performances.

The Top Attractions

Festspielhaus   Designed by Wolf Dietrich and built in 1607, this Festival Hall was once the court stables. Today it's the center for the major musical events of Salzburg, its cultural activity peaking during the August festival. The modern hall seats 2,170 spectators, and most major concerts and big operas are performed here. Tour reservations are advisable. *Note:* Tours are canceled if there is a rehearsal or performance of virtually anything, so this is no longer a major tourist stop, but rather, a grace for music buffs.

Hofstallgasse 1. (✆ **0662/8045-500.** www.salzburgerfestspiele.at. Admission to tours 5€ adults, 2.90€ children. Jan–May and Oct 1–Dec 20 daily at 2pm; June and Sept daily at 2 and 3:30pm, July–Aug daily at 9:30am, 2 and 3:30pm. Bus: 1, 4, 7, 8, or 10.

Festung Hohensalzburg (Hohensalzburg Fortress) ★★ ☺   The stronghold of the ruling prince-archbishops before they moved "downtown" to the Residenz, this fortress towers 122m (400 ft.) above the Salzach River on a rocky dolomite ledge. The massive fortress crowns the Festungsberg and literally dominates Salzburg. To get here, you can hike up one of the paths or lanes leading to the fortress, or you can walk from Kapitelplatz by way of Festungsgasse or from the Mönchsberg via the Scharten-tor. You can also take the funicular from Festungsgasse ((✆ **0662/842682)** at the station behind the cathedral. Museum tickets include admission and the funicular ride. Call the museum or the Festungsgasse number to check availability.

Work on Hohensalzburg began in 1077 and was not finished until 1681, during which time many builders of widely different tastes and purposes had a hand in the construction. This is the largest completely preserved castle left in central Europe. Functions of defense and state were combined in this fortress for 6 centuries. The elegant state apartments, once the dwellings of the prince-archbishops and their courts, are on display. Note the coffered ceilings and intricate ironwork, and check out the early-16th-century porcelain stove in the Golden Room.

The **Burgmuseum** is distinguished mainly by its collection of medieval art. Plans and prints tracing the growth of Salzburg are on display, as are instruments of torture and many Gothic artifacts. The Salzburger Stier (Salzburg Bull), an open-air barrel organ built in 1502, plays melodies by Mozart and his friend Haydn in daily concerts following the glockenspiel chimes. The **Rainermuseum** has arms and armor exhibits. The beautiful late-Gothic St. George's Chapel, dating from 1501, has marble *bas-reliefs* of the Apostles.

Visit Hohensalzburg just for the view from the terrace. From the Reck watchtower, you get a panoramic sweep of the Alps. The Kuenberg bastion has a fine view of Salzburg's domes and towers.

Mönchsberg 34. 📞 **0662/84243011.** www.salzburg-burgen.at/en/hohensalzburg. Admission 10.50€ adults, 6€ children 6-14, free for children 5 and under; family ticket 24.50€. Fortress and museums Oct–Apr daily 9:30am–5pm; May–Sept daily 9am–7pm.

Glockenspiel (Carillon) ★ ☺ The celebrated *Glockenspiel* with its 35 bells stands across from the Residenz. You can hear this 18th-century carillon at 7 and 11am, and 6pm. The ideal way to hear the chimes is from one of the cafes lining the edges of the Mozartplatz.

Mozartplatz 1. 📞 **0662/80422784.** www.salzburgmuseum.at. Bus: 3, 5, 6, 7, or 10.

Petersfriedhof ★★ St. Peter's Cemetery lies at the stone wall that merges into the bottom of the rock called the Mönchsberg. Many of the aristocratic families of Salzburg lie buried here alongside many other noted persons, including Nannerl Mozart, sister of Wolfgang Amadeus (also an exceptionally gifted musician, 4 years older than her brother). You can also see the Romanesque Chapel of the Holy Cross and St. Margaret's Chapel, dating from the 15th century. The cemetery and its chapels are rich in blue-blooded history; monuments to a way of life long vanished. You can also take a self-guided tour through the early Christian catacombs in the rock above the church cemetery.

St.-Peter-Bezirk. 📞 **0662/8445760.** Free admission to cemetery. Catacombs 1€ adults, .60€ children aged 6-15. Cemetery open daily 6:30am–7pm. Catacombs open May–Sept. Closed Mon 10:30am–5pm; Oct–Apr Wed–Thurs 10:30am–3:30pm, Fri–Sun 10:30am–4pm. Bus: 1, 4, 7, 8, or 10.

Residenz State Rooms/Residenzgalerie Salzburg ★★ This opulent palace, just north of Domplatz in the pedestrian zone, was the seat of the Salzburg prince-archbishops after they no longer needed the protection of the gloomy Hohensalzburg Fortress of Mönchsberg. The Residenz dates from 1120, but work on a series of palaces, which comprised the ecclesiastical complex of the ruling church princes, began in the late 1500s under Archbishop Wolf Dietrich and continued until about 1796. The Residenz fountain, from the 17th century, is one of the largest and most impressive baroque fountains north of the Alps.

Salzburg Attractions

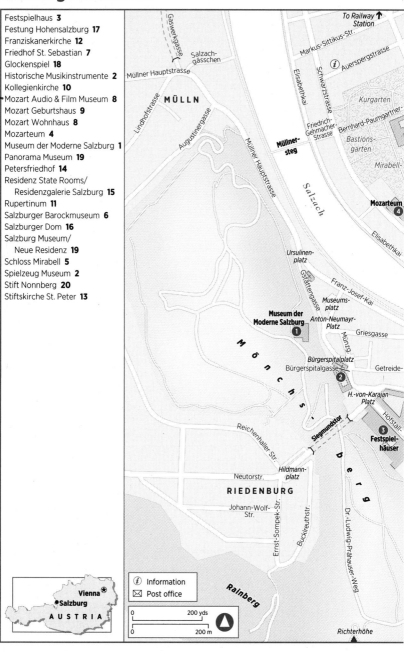

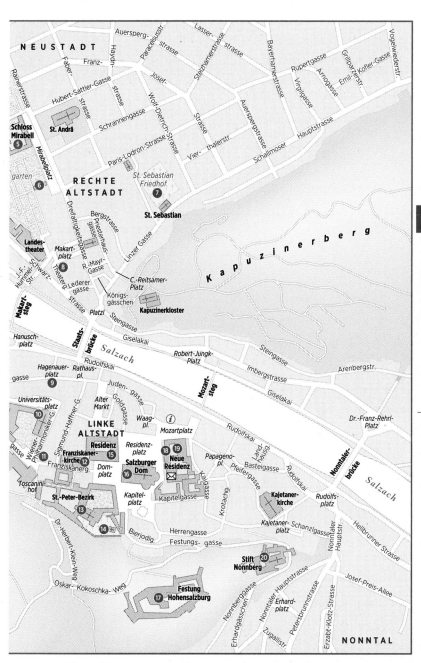

IN MOZART'S footsteps

Wolfgang Amadeus Mozart was born in Salzburg on January 27, 1756, son of an obsessive, stage-door father, Leopold Mozart, whose control he eventually fled. "Wolfi" was a child prodigy, writing music at the age of 4, before he could even shape the letters of the alphabet. By the age of 6, he was performing at the Palace of Schönbrunn in Vienna before assembled royalty and aristocrats.

But the public at home bored him: In Salzburg, audiences were wooden, he complained, no more responsive than "tables and chairs." He often struggled to make ends meet. In spite of the success of *The Magic Flute* in 1791, his career ended in obscurity; he died penniless and was buried in a pauper's grave in the St. Marx cemetery.

Today, though, Salzburg lives off the reputation of a young musician they barely paid heed to in his lifetime. Mozart's image is everywhere. In the heart of town, **Mozartplatz** bears his name, with a statue of the composer erected in 1842, the first recognition of his birth he'd received in the town since

his death. A music academy is named after him, and, of course, his music dominates the Salzburg Festival.

You can visit **Mozart Geburtshaus (Birthplace)** ★, Getreidegasse 9 (✆ **0662/844313;** www.mozarteum.at). He lived here until he was 17—that is, when he was in Salzburg at all and wasn't touring such cities as Prague, Milan, or Vienna. There are three floors of exhibition rooms, which include the Mozart family apartment. The main treasures are the valuable paintings (such as the well-known oil painting *Mozart and the Piano,* left unfinished by Joseph Lange) and the original instruments: The violin Mozart used as a child, his concert violin, and his viola, fortepiano, and clavichord.

You can also visit the restored **Mozart Wohnhaus (Residence)** ★, Makartplatz 8 (✆ **0662/87422740**), where the composer lived from 1773 to 1780. Damaged in World War II air raids, the house reopened in 1996, honoring the year of Mozart's 240th birthday. In 1773, the Mozart family vacated the cramped quarters of Mozart's birthplace for this

The child prodigy Mozart often played here in the Conference Room for guests. In 1867, Emperor Franz Josef received Napoleon III here. More than a dozen state rooms, each richly decorated, are open to the public via guided tour.

On the second floor, you can visit the **Residenzgalerie Salzburg** (✆ **0662/ 840451**), an art gallery founded in 1923, which now contains European paintings from the 16th to the 19th century, displayed in 15 historic rooms. Paintings from the Dutch, Flemish, French, Italian, Austrian baroque, and Austrian 19th-century schools are exhibited. Self-guided audio tours are included in the admission.

Residenzplatz 1. ✆ **0662/80422690.** Combo ticket for Residenz State Rooms and Gallery 8.50€ adults, 6.50€ students and seniors, 2.70€ children 6–15, free for children 5 and under. Tues–Sun 10am– 5pm. Bus: 3, 5, 6, 8, or 10.

Salzburger Dom ★   Located where Residenzplatz flows into Domplatz (where you'll see a 1771 statue of the Virgin), this cathedral is world-renowned for its 4,000-pipe organ. The original building from A.D. 774 was superseded by a late-Romanesque structure erected from 1181 to 1200. When this edifice was destroyed by fire haunt on Makartplatz. In the rooms of these former apartments, a museum documents the history of the house, life, and work of Wolfgang Amadeus Mozart. There's a mechanized audio tour in six languages with musical samples.

Both the Geburtshaus and Wohnhaus are open September to June daily 9am to 6pm and July and August daily 9am to 8pm (you must enter 30 min. before closing). A combination ticket to both costs 12€ adults, 10€ seniors and students, 4.50€ children 15–18, 3.50€ children 6–14 (free for children under 6), and 25.50€ families. Otherwise, a ticket to either costs 7€, 6€, 3€, 2.50€, and 16.50€ respectively.

Aficionados will want to stop by the International Mozarteum Foundation's **Mozart Audio & Film Museum,** Makartplatz 8 (𝄐 **0662/883454**). Here is a collection of 11,000 audio and 1,000 video titles of Mozart. There are also sections devoted to the work of contemporary Austrian composers, available at eight video and 10 audio stations, and there's a large-scale screen for groups.

The museum, which is free, is open Monday, Tuesday, and Friday 9am to 1pm and Wednesday and Thursday 1 to 5pm. The 1914 Jugendstil **Mozarteum,** at Schwarzstrasse 26 (𝄐 **0662/8894030**), can be visited by appointment and is well worth it. Most lovely is the library—a *Bibliotheca Mozartiana*—on the second floor, with approximately 12,000 titles devoted to Mozart. The wing at Schwarzstrasse 28 houses the large concert hall, where up to 800 guests enjoy concerts held throughout the year. The smaller, next door, is the Viennese Hall, for 200. The highlight is the celebratory festival *Mozartwoche,* which commemorates Mozart's birthday (Jan 27) with 10 days of concerts and operas. It's open Monday to Friday from 9am to 5pm. In the garden is the **Magic Flute House**—the little wooden structure in which Mozart composed *The Magic Flute* in 1791, shipped to Salzburg from the Naschmarkt in Vienna.

In 1971, the Mozarteum was designated as the College of Music and the Performing Arts.

in 1598, Prince-Archbishop Wolf Dietrich commissioned construction of a new cathedral, but his overthrow prevented the completion of this project. His successor, Archbishop Markus Sittikus Count Hohenems, commissioned the Italian architect Santino Solari to build the present cathedral, which was consecrated in 1628 by Archbishop Paris Count Lodron.

Hailed by some critics as the most perfect Renaissance building in the Germanic countries, the cathedral has a marble facade and twin symmetrical towers. The interior has a rich baroque style with elaborate frescoes, the most important of which, along with the altarpieces, were designed by Mascagni of Florence. In the cathedral, you can see the Romanesque font at which Mozart was baptized. The dome was damaged during World War II but was restored by 1959. In the crypt, traces of the old Romanesque cathedral that once stood on this spot have been unearthed.

The treasure of the cathedral, and the "arts and wonders" the archbishops collected in the 17th century, are displayed in the **Dom Museum** (𝄐 **0662/8047-1860**), entered through the cathedral.

South side of Residenzplatz. © **0662/844189.** www.salzburger-dom.at. Free admission to cathedral; excavations 5€ adults, 1.50€ children 6–18, free for children 5 and under; museum 5€ adults, 1.50€ children. Cathedral May–Sept 8am–7pm; Mar, Apr, Oct, Dec 8am–6pm; Jan, Feb, Nov 8am–5pm. Opens all year Sun at 1pm; museum Mon–Sat 10am–5pm, Sun 11am–6pm. Closed Jan 7–Apr 7 and Nov. Bus: 3, 5, 6, 7, 8, or 10.

Salzburg Museum/Neue Residenz ★★   A series of attractions are sheltered in the New Residence complex, which actually dates from the 1600s, when it was Prince-Archbishop Wolf-Dietrich's "overflow palace." The main part of the complex is a series of state reception rooms that marked the beginning of the Renaissance in Salzburg.

One of the highlights of the museum is the exhibitions once housed in the Museum Carolino Augusteum. Rare archaeological treasures are found here, including Hallstatt Age relics, plus fragments of ruins from the town's Roman occupation. A Celtic bronze flagon is one of the chief treasures. The museum is also noted for its collection of Old Masters, with a rich trove of Gothic panel paintings and much art work from the Romantic period. The Gothic altarpieces show fine craftsmanship, and you may want to seek out works by Hans Makart, a leading 19th-century Austrian artist, designer, and decorator of celebrity status in his day, born in Salzburg in 1840 and a major influence on Gustav Klimt.

In the basement of the Neue Residenz is the **Kunsthalle,** a multifunctional circular hall where special exhibitions are staged every year, many devoted to artists who had a special relationship with Salzburg.

Mozartplatz 1. © **0662/620808-700.** www.salzburgmuseum.at. Admission 7€ adults, 4€ students, 3€ ages 6–15. Reduced prices on Sun. Tues–Wed and Fri–Sat 9am–5pm, Thurs 9am–8pm; July–Sept also Mon 9am–5pm.

Schloss Mirabell ★   This palace and its gardens (see "Parks & Gardens," below) were originally built as a luxurious private residence called Altenau. Prince-Archbishop Wolf Dietrich had it constructed in 1606 for Salome Alt, his mistress and the mother of his children. Unfortunately, not much remains of the original grand structure. Johann Lukas von Hildebrandt rebuilt the Schloss in the first quarter of the 18th century, and it was modified after a great fire in 1818. The official residence of the mayor of Salzburg is now in the palace, which is like a smaller rendition of the Tuileries in Paris. The ceremonial marble Barockstiege-Engelsstiege (angel staircase), with sculptured cherubs, carved by Raphael Donner in 1726, leads to the Marmorsaal, a marble-and-gold hall used for private concerts and weddings.

Rainerstrasse. © **0662/80722334.** Free admission. Mon–Thurs 8am–4pm, Fri 8am–2:30pm; closed on other days. Bus: 1, 2, 3, 4, 5, or 6.

 Mozart Cycle Path

A new cycle path, **Mozart-Radweg** (www.mozartradweg.com), named after hometown boy Wolfgang Amadeus Mozart, now connects the lake district to the east, the city of Salzburg and Bavaria and its lakes, such as Chiemsee, before ending at Berchtesgaden, near Hitler's former country retreat. The route stretches more than 410km (255 miles) and is primarily flat, with just a few hills along the way. It's ideal for families. Salzburg tourist offices will provide trail maps.

More Attractions

For the many sites and attractions focusing on Salzburg's favorite son, Mozart, see the box "In Mozart's Footsteps," above.

CHURCHES

Franziskanerkirche With origins stretching back to as early as 774, the present structure was rebuilt and consecrated in 1221. It is a successful fusion of architectural periods, beginning with the somber Romanesque barrel nave lined with Gothic arches. In contrast, the heart of the edifice opens up into a translucent choir with five columns rising into late-Gothic fan vaulting that recalls a palm forest. Hans von Burghausen commenced the construction in the 1420s and Stefan Krumenhauser finished up after his death. South Tyrolean sculptor Michael Pacher, who crafted a famous altarpiece in nearby St. Wolfgang (p. 332), also constructed a late-Gothic high altar (1495–98), of which only the Madonna statue remains. Fischer von Erlach followed up with the high altar from 1708. Don't miss a curious 12th-century marble lion at the base of the pulpit's winding staircase, which is smothering a man trying to knife the beast.

Franziskanergasse 5. ℂ **0662/843629.** Free admission. Daily 6:30am–7:30pm. Bus: 1, 4, 7, 8, or 10.

Friedhof St. Sebastian Prince-Archbishop Wolf Dietrich commissioned this cemetery in 1595 to be laid out like an Italian *campo santo*. The tombs of Mozart's wife and his father, Leopold, are here. In the middle of the cemetery is St. Gabriel's Chapel, containing the mausoleum of Dietrich. The mausoleum's interior is lined with multicolored porcelain.

To reach the cemetery, walk down the Italian-style steps from St. Sebastian's Church. The original late-Gothic edifice dated from the early 16th century. It was rebuilt and enlarged in 1749, in the rococo style. Destroyed by fire in 1818, it was later reconstructed. Only the 1752 rococo doorway remains from the old church building. Paracelsus, the Renaissance doctor and philosopher who died in 1541, is entombed here. According to ancient Roman Catholic tradition, ceremonies here are carried out entirely in Latin.

Linzer Gasse 41. ℂ **0662/875208.** Free admission. Daily 9am–7pm (until dusk in winter). Bus: 1, 3, 4, 5, or 6.

Kollegienkirche Opening onto an open-air marketplace, Collegiate Church was built between 1694 and 1707 for the Benedictine university founded in 1622. The great baroque architect Fischer von Erlach had already commenced work on Vienna's Schönbrunn Palace, when he was brought to Salzburg to build churches like this. The greatest and largest of his four churches in town, its high altar by Anton Pfaffinger features delicate stucco work by Diego Francesco Carlone and Paolo d'Allio. Altar paintings in the transept are by Johann Michael Rottmayr.

Universitätsplatz. ℂ **0662/84132772.** Free admission. Daily 9am–6pm. Bus: 1, 4, 7, 8, or 10.

Stiftskirche St. Peter ★★ Founded in A.D. 696 by St. Rupert, whose tomb is here, this is the church of St. Peter's Abbey and Benedictine Monastery. Once a Romanesque basilica with three aisles, the church was completely overhauled in the 17th and 18th centuries in an elegant baroque style. The west door dates from 1240. The church is richly adorned with art treasures, including some altar paintings by Kremser Schmidt. The Salzburg Madonna, in the left chancel, is from the early 15th century.

St.-Peter-Bezirk 1. ℂ **0662/844578.** Free admission. Daily 9am–noon. Bus: 3, 5, 6, 8, or 10.

MUSEUMS

Historische Musikinstrumente (Historic Musical Instruments)   Part of the Salzburg Museum, this museum houses rare instruments, dating back to the 16th and 17th centuries, including antique keyboard, wind, string, plucked, and percussion instruments. The collection of baroque string instruments is especially fascinating, as are the wind instruments of the late baroque and classic eras. Tickets are also valid for the Toy Museum.

Bürgerspitalgasse 2. Ⓒ **0662/620808-300.** www.salzburgmuseum.at. Admission 3€ adults, 2.50€ students, 1€ ages 6-15. Tues–Sun 9am–5pm; July–Aug and Dec Mon also 9am–5pm. Bus 25, stop Hellbrunn

Museum der Moderne Salzburg ★   Built on the side of Mönchsberg mountain overlooking the city, this museum is devoted to some of the best contemporary art to come out of Austria, from Klimt via Kubin to Kokoshka. An urban landscape and a natural setting of beauty are dovetailed here in the exhibitions, which also highlight the Austrian Gallery of Photography. The design alone makes this one of the most beautiful museums of Austria. Large rotating exhibitions of international modern art are displayed in the spacious and beautifully lit exhibition salons. If you get bored with the artwork itself (highly unlikely), you can take in the views of the mountains in the distance.

Mönchsberg 32. Ⓒ **0662/842220403.** www.museumdermoderne.at. Admission 8€ adults; 6€ seniors, students, and children. Tues–Sun 10am–6pm (Wed until 9pm); summer Mon also 10am–6pm. Take the Mönchsberg elevator to the top.

Panorama Museum   This curious, but noteworthy museum is devoted to displaying one of the few remaining 360-degree panoramic paintings in the world. It shows Salzburg as it looked in the early 1800s. It was created by Johann Michael Sattler (1786–1847), covering 125 sq. m (1,345 sq. ft.) Telescopes on the visitors' platform allow a closer view of the details of domestic architecture as it existed at the time. Around the panorama, large-format paintings of motifs from all over the world are by Johann Michael Sattler's son, Hubert.

Residenzplatz 9. Ⓒ **0662/620808-730.** Admission 2€ adults, 1.70€ students, 1€ ages 6-15. Daily 9am–5pm (until 8pm Thurs); reduced hours Dec 24, 31, and Jan 1; closed Nov 1 and Dec 25. Next to the Post Office in the Old City pedestrian zone.

Rupertinum (Museum of Modern Art Salzburg)   This smaller twin of Museum der Moderne Salzburg (see above), housed in a 17th-century building, is known for its wide variety of temporary exhibits, plus a permanent collection of works by Klimt, Kokoschka, and lesser-known artists. There is also a display of photography and graphic arts. Although it's a fairly minor attraction, it's a nice stop for those interested in 20th-century art.

Wiener Philharmonikergasse 9. Ⓒ **0662/84220541.** www.museumdermoderne.at. Admission 6€ adults, 4€ students, free for children 15 and under. Tues–Fri 10am–6pm (Wed to 9pm). Bus: 1, 4, 7, 8, or 10.

Salzburger Barockmuseum   The museum in the orangery of the Mirabell Gardens (see "Parks & Gardens," below) displays 17th- and 18th-century European art, with works by Giordano, Rottmayr, Bernini, Straub, and others.

Mirabellgarten 3. Ⓒ **0662/877432.** Admission 4.50€ adults, 3.70€ students 15-18 and seniors, free for children 14 and under. Sept–June Wed–Sun 10am–5pm, Sun and holidays 10am–1pm; July–Aug Tues–Sun 10am–5pm. Bus: 1, 2, 3, 4, 5, or 6.

Spielzeug Museum (Toy Museum) ☺   Founded in 1978 and part of the Salzburg Museum, this museum shares an entrance with the Museum of Historic Musical Instruments. In fact, a ticket for that museum also entitles you to admission to the Toy Museum—or vice versa. The Toy Museum possesses the largest collection in Austria of historical European toys. Feast upon an array of antique dolls and doll houses, paper theaters, metal and wooden toys, and soft and furry toys, especially the collection of teddy bears. A Punch and Judy show is scheduled every Tuesday and Wednesday at 3pm, except in summer. An on-site shop sells a wide array of toys in the Bürgerspital or civilian hospital, which was constructed around the most beautiful Renaissance courtyard in Salzburg.

Bürgerspitalgasse 2. ✆ **0662/620808300.** www.smca.at. Admission 3€ adults, 2.50€ students, 1€ ages 6–15. Tues–Sun 9am–5pm; July–Aug and Dec also Mon 9am–5pm. Bus 25, stop Hellbrunn.

Panoramic Views

KAPUZINERBERG

This forested area on the right bank of the Salzach River rises more than 610m (2,001 ft.) above the city and is today a landscaped park. To get here, cross the Staatsbrücke spanning the Salzach to the right bank, continue walking for 2 minutes until you come to Steingasse, and cut right; after exploring Steingasse, walk through the Steintor, then climb an adjoining stone stairway, and follow the signs to Kapuzinerberg. You can also take bus no. 1, 3, 4, 5, or 6.

A Capuchin friary was built here at the very end of the 16th century, constructed inside an old medieval fortification. On the south side of the hill are Steingasse, a pretty street from medieval times, and the Steintor, which was once a gate in the walls of Salzburg. From vantage points on the Kapuzinerberg, you can see into Bavaria, in Germany.

MÖNCHSBERG

West of the Hohensalzburg Fortress, this heavily forested ridge extends for some 2km (1½ miles) above the Old Town and has fortifications dating from the 15th century. From several vantage points, including the Mönchsberg Terrace just in front of the Grand Café Winkler, you can see Salzburg.

You can get up here by taking the express elevators leaving from Gstättengasse 13 (✆ **0662/44806285**). The elevators leave daily from 9am to 1am. A round-trip fare is 2.90€ for adults and 1.60€ for children 6 to 15; it's free for children 5 and under.

Parks & Gardens

On the right bank of the river, the baroque **Mirabell Gardens ★**, off Makartplatz, laid out by Fischer von Erlach, are the finest in Salzburg. Now a public park, they're studded with statues and reflecting pools. Von Erlach also designed some of the marble balustrades and urns. There's a natural theater as well. For the best view of the gardens and also of Salzburg, pause at the top of the steps where Julie Andrews and her seven charges showed off their singing in *The Sound of Music*. Be sure to visit Zwerglgarten, a fantasy grove of marble baroque dwarfs and other figures, located by the Pegasus Fountains in the lavish garden west of Schloss Mirabell, from which you have an excellent view of the Hohensalzburg Fortress. The gardens are open daily from 7am to 8pm. In summer, free brass band concerts are held Wednesday at 8:30pm and Sunday at 10:30am.

Especially for Kids

Of the attractions already reviewed, those that children will most like include the **Glockenspiel, Hohensalzburg Fortress, Mönchsberg, the Spielzeugmuseum** and, on the outskirts, the **Hellbrunn Zoo** (see "Side Trips from Salzburg," later in this chapter). Kids will also enjoy the **Salzburger Marionetten Theater** (see "Salzburg After Dark" section, below).

ORGANIZED TOURS

The best organized tours are offered by **Salzburg Panorama Tours,** Mirabellplatz (⟨℃ **0662/8832110;** www.panoramatours.at), which is the Gray Line company for Salzburg.

The original **"Sound of Music Tour"** combines the Salzburg city tour with an excursion to the lake district and other places where the 1965 film with Julie Andrews was shot. The English-speaking guide shows you not only the highlights from the film, but also historical and architectural landmarks in Salzburg and parts of the Salzkammergut countryside. The 4½-hour tour departs daily at 9:30am and 2pm and costs 37€, and 18€ for children 4 to 12.

You must take your passport along for any of the three trips into Bavaria in Germany. One of these—the Eagle's Nest Tour—takes visitors to Berchtesgaden and on to Obersalzburg, where Hitler and his inner circle had a country retreat. The 4½-hour tour departs daily at 9am from May 15 to October 31 and costs 50€ for adults, 37€ for children 4 to 12.

The City & Country Highlights tour takes in historic castles and the surrounding Land Salzburg landscape. This 5-hour tour departs daily at 1pm and costs 50€, 37€ for children 4 to 12. Coffee and pastry at the Castle Fuschl are an added treat.

You can book these tours at the bus terminal at Mirabellplatz/St. Andrä Kirche (⟨℃ **0662/874029**).

SHOPPING

If you can't make it to Vienna, you'll find several branches of good shops from the capital, in addition to many great local businesses. Good buys in Salzburg include souvenirs of Land Salzburg (dirndls, lederhosen, and petit point) and all types of sports gear. **Getreidegasse** is a main shopping thoroughfare, but you'll also find some intriguing little shops on **Residenzplatz.**

Most stores are open Monday through Friday from 9am to 6pm, but note that many stores, especially smaller shops, take a 1- or 2-hour break for lunch. On weekends, stores are generally open only Saturday mornings.

Shopping A to Z

BOOKS & PRINTS

Eduard Höllrigl   This is the oldest bookstore in the country, dating from 1594. In addition to books, you'll find an array of maps, sheet music, and the best postcards in town. Sigmund-Haffner-Gasse 10. ⟨℃ **0662/841146.** Bus: 3, 5, or 6.

CHINA & CRYSTAL

Lobmeyr   Lobmeyr is the Salzburg branch of the famous store in Vienna's Kärntnerstrasse. Lobmeyr offers a wide range of crystal drinking sets and elegant Herend-china, as well as some of the prettiest breakfast services one can find, many made in Hungary. Schwarzstrasse 20. ⟨℃ **0662/873181.** www.lobmeyr.at. Bus: 3, 5, or 6.

CRAFTS

Lackner Gertraud   If you like wood crafts, there's no better place in Salzburg. It offers both antique and modern country furniture, especially chairs. Among the newly made items are chests, chessboards, angels, cupboards, crèches, and candlesticks. Badergasse 2. ℂ **0662/842385.** www.woodart.at. Bus: 3, 5, or 6.

Salzburger Heimatwerk In a dignified stone building in the least-crowded section of Residenzplatz, this is one of the best places in town to buy local Austrian handicrafts and original *Tracht*: The dirndls, capes, and regalia that's still worn during commemorative ceremonies and festivals. Items include Austrian silver and garnet jewelry, painted boxes, candles, woodcarvings, copper and brass ceramics, tablecloths, and alpine designs for cross-stitched samplers. A new wing offers Austrian culinary specialties. Wherever you go in this curious store, you're bound to find little treasures, so keep exploring. Am Residenzplatz 9. ℂ **0662/844119.** www.sbg.heimatwerk.at. Bus: 3, 5, 6, 7, 8, or 10.

Wiener Porzellanmanufaktur Augarten Gesellschaft This is the premier shop in Salzburg for Austrian porcelain, specializing in Augarten porcelain. Such patterns as Viennese Rose and Maria Theresa are still very popular, but its most famous item is the black-and-white coffee set created by architect/designer Josef Hoffmann. Alter Markt 11. ℂ **0662/840714.** www.augarten.at. Bus: 3, 5, 6, 8, or 10.

FASHION

Brigitte Kinder-Trachten Children up to age 14 are dressed here in plain or embroidered knit jackets, dirndls, and folk dresses that are the longtime favorite apparel of Land Salzburg. Lederhosen for boys come in full or short lengths with all the appropriate accompaniments. Although American kids often prefer their jeans, Austrian and German children (or at least their parents) sometimes like these looks. Universitätsplatz 7. ℂ **0662/841193.** Bus: 3, 5, 6, 8, or 10.

Jahn-Markl This small and elegant clothing store in Old Town has been in the same family for four generations, although its origins date from 1408. It carries lederhosen, leather skirts, and traditional Austrian coats and blazers. Leather for both women and men is also sold, including jackets, pants, and gloves. Some children's clothing is available. Less expensive items can be bought off the racks, but more expensive pieces are usually made to order in 4 weeks and can be mailed anywhere in the world for an additional charge. Residenzplatz 3. ℂ **0662/842610.** www.jahn-markl.at. Bus: 3, 5, 6, 7, or 10.

Lanz At this well-stocked store across the river from the Old Town, you'll find one of the widest collections of long-skirted dirndls in town, in dozens of different fabrics and colors. Men's clothing includes loden-colored overcoats. The store also sells dirndls for little girls and hand-knit sweaters. There's another branch along the main shopping street of Salzburg, at Kranzlmarkt 1, Getreidegasse (ℂ **0662/840300**). Schwarzstrasse 4. ℂ **0662/874272.** Bus: 1, 3, 4, 5, or 6.

MUSIC

Musikhaus Pühringer Established in 1910, this store sells all kinds of classical musical instruments, as well as a large selection of electronics (including synthesizers and amplifiers). You'll find classical and folk-music CDs and tapes. The store is only a few buildings away from Mozart's birthplace. Getreidegasse 13. ℂ **0662/843267.** www. musikinstrumente.at. Bus: 3, 5, or 6.

PASTRIES

Schatz-Konditorei ☺ This excellent pastry shop (reviewed above in the Cafes box in "Where to Eat") is one of the few in Salzburg that will mail cakes around the world. The store's specialty is the highly acclaimed *Mozart Kugeln,* a cookie of pistachio, marzipan, and hazelnut nougat dipped in chocolate. Packages of this gourmet delight can be airmailed to North America. Getreidegasse 3. ℂ **0662/842792.** Bus: 3, 5, 6, 8, or 10.

SPORTING GOODS

Sporting Goods Dschulnigg   Queen Elizabeth II and Prince Philip have been photographed on a shopping expedition at this upper-crust emporium for clothes and sporting goods. Among the items sold are many kinds of sporting goods, including guns, as well as children's outfits, overcoats for men and women both, intricately patterned sweaters, and fur-lined hats. You can get hunting rifles (but not pistols or revolvers) in Austria without a license, although the Customs officers back home might present a problem. Griesgasse 8. © **0662/8423760.** www.jagd-dschullnig.at. Bus: 3, 5, or 6.

TOYS & SOUVENIRS

Neumüller Spielwaren   In winter, this store sells children's toys. In summer, the stock changes with the tourist influx, and the shelves fill up with handcrafted souvenirs such as mugs, cowbells, and rustic art objects. Rathausplatz 3. © **0662/841429.** www. neumueller.vedes.at. Bus: 3, 5, 6, 8, or 10.

SALZBURG AFTER DARK

The annual cultural events, which reach their peak at the Salzburg Festival, overshadow any after-dark amusements such as dance clubs and beer halls. Clubs come and go in Salzburg fairly rapidly.

It's said that there's a musical event—often a Mozart concert—staged virtually every night in Salzburg. To find out what's playing, visit the **Salzburg tourist office,** Mozartplatz 5 (© **0662/889870;** www.salzburg.info), or get a free copy of *Offizieller Wochenspiegel,* a monthly pamphlet listing all major and many minor local cultural events; it's available in most hotels. The annual Mozart Week is in January.

Free Concerts & Special Events

Free concerts are frequently presented by students in the **Mozarteum,** Schwarzstrasse 26 (© **0662/8894030;** bus: 1, 2, 3, 4, or 5). In summer, free brass-band concerts are performed in the **Mirabell Gardens** on Wednesday at 8:30pm and, depending on the venue, either Saturday or Sunday at 10:30am; Sunday chamber-music concerts are held throughout the city at major landmarks such as the **Residenz.**

The second most famous music festival in Salzburg is the **Osterfestspiele (Easter Festival),** which features high-quality operas and concerts performed in the Festspielhaus. Some, but not all, of the music focuses on works associated with the resurrection of Christ as interpreted by the great 18th- and 19th-century composers. Established by Herbert von Karajan in the 1960s, the festival requires that spectators purchase tickets to the opera and each of the three concerts associated with the event. Prices for the series are anything but cheap: They range, per person, from 90€ to 720€. For information and ticket purchases, contact the **Osterfestspiele,** Herbert von Karajan Platz 9, A-5020 Salzburg (© **0662/8045361;** www.osterfestspiele-salzburg.at; bus: 1).

Christmas Eve in Salzburg is unforgettable. Traditionally, in the little chapel of Oberndorf, north of Salzburg, *Silent Night* is performed (www.stillenacht-oberndorf. at). Franz Gruber composed music for Joseph Mohr's poem and premiered the famous tune here in 1818 during his tenure as an organist.

Buying Tickets

If you don't want to pay a ticket agent's commission, you can go directly to the box office of a theater or concert hall. However, many of the best seats might have already been sold, especially those at the Salzburg Festival. Despite the availability of ticket outlets in any of the below-mentioned theaters, many visitors head for the larger umbrella ticket agency, **Salzburger Ticket Office,** Mozartplatz 5 (✆ **0662/840310**), which is affiliated with the city of Salzburg and adjacent to Salzburg's main tourist office. Open Monday to Saturday 9am to 6pm (to 7pm in midsummer) and Sunday 10am to 6pm, it's the single best source for cultural information and ticket sales in town, usually with tickets to virtually every musical event in the city on sale—except, of course, to those events that are sold out long in advance.

Curiously, though Salzburg is known as a city of music and culture, it has no famed local troupes. However, it does attract visiting guest artists with blue-chip credentials in the world of performing arts.

The Performing Arts
OPERA, DANCE & MUSIC

Festspielhaus All the premier ballet, opera, and musical concerts are performed at this world-famous citadel of Salzburg culture. The *Grosses Haus* (Big House), the larger venue, seats 2,170. The *Kleines Haus* (Small House) seats 1,323. Most performances begin at 7:30 or 8pm, although there are matinees from time to time at 11am and 3pm. Hofstallgasse 1. ✆ **0662/8045.** Tickets 8€–200€ (the higher cost is for the best seats at the Salzburg Festival); average but good seats range from 35€–80€. Bus: 1, 4, 8, or 10.

Festung Hohensalzburg (Hohensalzburg Fortress) If your visit to Salzburg doesn't happen to coincide with any of the city's annual music festivals, you can

---

THE SALZBURG festival

One of the premier music attractions of Europe, the Salzburg Festival, founded by composer Richard Strauss with director Max Reinhardt and writer Hugo von Hofmannsthal, celebrated its 90th season in 2010.

Every year, the Festival restages Hofmannsthal's adaptation of the morality play *Jedermann (Everyman),* performed in German and staged outside the cathedral in Domplatz. Concerts are usually conducted in the Rittersaal of the Residenz Palace (Mozart conducted here) and in the marble salon of Mirabell Palace (Mozart's father, Leopold, conducted here). The Salzburger Marionetten Theater (see below) also presents performances. Ballet performances are usually given by the Vienna State Opera Ballet with the Vienna State Opera Chorus and the Vienna Philharmonic. International soloists are invited annually, and the London Symphony or the Berlin Philharmonic is also likely to be invited.

Festival tickets, however, are in great demand, and there are never enough of them. Don't arrive expecting to get into any of the major events unless you've already purchased tickets. Travel agents can often get tickets for you, and you can also go to branches of the Austrian National Tourist Office at home or abroad. Hotel concierges, particularly at the deluxe and first-class hotels of Salzburg, always have some tickets on hand, but expect to pay outrageous prices for them, depending on the particular performance you want to attend. At first-night performances of the major productions, remember that evening dress is *de rigueur.*

Subject to many exceptions and variations, and without agent commissions, drama tickets generally range from 30€ to 200€. Opera tickets can begin as low as 45€, ranging upward to 300€.

For full details, contact the Salzburg Festival box office, Hofstallgasse 1, A-5020 Salzburg, Austria (✆ **0662/8045;** www.salzburgfestival.at).

always attend the concerts that are presented within the Hohensalzburg Fortress. Here, in historic and dramatic settings, you're likely to hear heavy doses of Mozart and, to a lesser degree, works by Schubert, Brahms, and Beethoven. From mid-May to mid-October, performances are likely to be held at 8 or 8:30pm every night of the week. The rest of the year, they're presented most (but not all) nights, with occasional week-long breaks, usually at 7:30pm. The box office for the events is at Adlgasser Weg 22 (℃ **0662/825858;** www.salzburg-burgen-at/en/hohensalzburg). Mönchsberg 34. ℃ **0662/84243011.** Tickets cost 10€ adults, 5.70€ ages 6–14, and 23€ family ticket. To reach the fortress, take the funicular from Festungsgasse.

Mozarteum   On the right bank of the Salzach River, near Mirabell Gardens, is the Mozarteum, Salzburg's major music and concert hall. All the big orchestra concerts, as well as organ recitals and chamber-music evenings, are presented here. In the old building at Schwarzstrasse, there are two concert halls, the Grosser Saal and the Wiener Saal. In the newer building on Mirabellplatz, concert halls include the Grosses Studio, the Leopold-Mozart Saal, and the Paumgartner Studio. Make sure to find out which hall your musical event is in. It's also a music school, and you can ask about free events staged by the students. The box office is open Monday through Thursday from 9am to 2pm and Friday from 9am to 4pm. Performances are at 11am or 7:30pm. Schwarzstrasse 26 and Mirabellplatz 1. ℃ **0662/8894030.** www.mozarteum.at. Tickets 10€–55€. Bus: 1, 2, 3, 4, or 5.

Salzburger Schlosskonzerte   The Salzburger Schlosskonzerte (Palace Concerts) are privately owned by Salzburg violinist Luz Leskowitz, who carries on the 57-year-old tradition of presenting the best ensembles. The carefully chosen programs combine with the beautiful, historic venue (Schloss Mirabell's Marmorsaal, where Mozart himself played) to create an atmosphere of perfect harmony. Mozart's music is heavily featured, but the famed music of classical Austria and Italy is also included in the repertoire. Beethoven, Mendelssohn, Schubert, Bach, Brahms, Vivaldi, Haydn—the list is endless. Unchanged since the days of Mozart, concerts are staged in the richly decorated baroque chambers. The box office is open Monday to Friday 9am to 5:30pm. Schloss Mirabell, Mirabellplatz. Booking office, Theatergasse 2. ℃ **0662/ 848586.** www.salzburger-schlosskonzerte.at. Tickets 29€–35€ adults, 16€ students. Bus: 1, 2, 3, 5, or 6.

THEATER

Although the **Salzburger Landestheater,** Schwarzstrasse 22 (℃ **0662/8715120;** www.theater.co.at; bus: 3, 5, or 6), doesn't always play for summer visitors, you can see its regular repertoire of operas (not just Mozart) and operettas if you're in Salzburg from September to mid-June. You might see a thrilling performance of Verdi's *Traviata*. Opera tickets usually range from 16.50€ to 49€. In July and August, Salzburg Festival performances are held here.

Salzburger Marionetten Theater, Schwarzstrasse 24 (℃ **0662/8724060;** www. marionetten.at; bus: 3, 5, or 6), presents shows from Easter to September, as well as special shows at Christmas and during Mozart Week, the last week of January. The puppets perform both opera (usually Mozart) and ballet, to the delight of adults and children alike. Founded in 1913, the theater continues to be one of the most unusual and enjoyable theatrical experiences in Salzburg. You might forget that marionettes are onstage—it's that realistic. Tickets are 18€ to 28€, 14€ for children under 12.

The Club & Music Scene

The best alternative music spot is **Rockhouse,** Schallmooser Hauptstrasse 46 (℃ **0662/884914;** www.rockhouse.at; bus: 1 or 4), which also has a cafe. Local and

European bands are booked to play this tunnel-like venue, which offers everything from blues and funk to jazz and techno pop. Sometimes groups from the United States or even Africa appear here. The structure itself is from the 1840s, having once been a wine cellar and ice-storage depot. Cover can range from 9€ to 30€, depending on the act. Call to see what's happening at the time of your visit.

A recently renovated American bar from the 1950s, the **Republic Cafe,** Anton Neumayr Platz 2 (✆ **0664/841613;** www.republic-cafe.at; bus: 1, 4, or 8), is a hotbed of counter-cultural activities in Salzburg. It defines itself as a cross between a bar and a cafe, with a "radical performance space." Its nerve center is a lively street-level bar and cafe, open Monday to Thursday from 8am to 1am, Friday from 8am to the early morning, depending on the event and the crowd.

The Best Bars

Augustiner Bräustübl Outside the cultural venues, the most entertaining evenings in Salzburg are here. Founded in 1621 by Augustine monks, this brewery, about a 10-minute walk from the Altstadt, is a Salzburg institution and a great place for a meal in the huge outdoor beer garden or upstairs in one of the huge beer halls. Counters sell sausages and cold cuts, cheese, pretzels, hamburgers, grilled chicken, soup, salads, boiled pork with horseradish, beef with creamed spinach and potatoes, and more. It's a crowded, noisy place, as a brewery should be. It's open Monday to Friday 3 to 11pm and Saturday and Sunday 2:30 to 11pm. Augustinergasse 4. ✆ **0662/881377.** www.augustinerbier.at. Bus: 10.

Bar Seitensprung This very hip bar spins the most recent music in a cave that's partially natural and partly dug by hand several centuries ago into the rock of the Kapuzinerberg. The bar serves a full menu of cocktails, including American-style martinis at 4.30€ each, and the even more popular roster of Austrian wine by the glass, priced at 4€. There's a limited food menu, in case you get hungry. Prosciutto with cheese and pâté platters are priced at around 8.70€ each. The crowd tends to be young, 20 to 25. It's open nightly from 9pm to at least 4am. Steingasse 11. ✆ **0662/881377.** Bus: 3, 5, or 6.

Chez Roland Roland Kübler has maintained this stylish, unusual cocktail bar since the mid-1970s. In the process, he's entertained some of the biggest names of the Salzburg Festival and nurtured an arts-conscious crowd ranging in age from 25 to 75. The bar is set within an old salt storage cellar with a vaulted ceiling that allows natural illumination. You can always order a martini, but the large majority of drinkers here opt for glasses of Austrian wine. Priced at 3€ to 5€, they include many vintages of Styrian chardonnays and sauvignons. There's also Beck's beer selling for 2.80€ and a limited menu of toasts (warm sandwiches). It's open daily 7pm to at least 4am and usually later, depending on business. Giselakai 24. ✆ **0662/874335.** www.chez-roland.com. Bus: 1.

O'Malley's With a name like O'Malley's, this could only be an Irish pub. Opened in 1998, this pub opts for authenticity by importing wooden bars created by Irish tradesmen in Belfast from the timbers of a disused 3-centuries-old church. The pub is decorated with some of the architectural details of the church, even musical instruments from the Emerald Isle. This bar, featuring live music, attracts a young crowd and has one of the most jovial atmospheres of any place in town. Beer costs from 3€. Hours are Sunday to Thursday 6pm to 2am, Friday and Saturday 6pm to 4am. Rudolfskai 16. ✆ **0662/849263.** www.omalleyssalzburg.com. Bus: 3, 5, or 6.

Stieglkeller To reach this place, you'll have to negotiate a steep cobblestone street that drops off on one side to reveal a panoramic view of Salzburg. Part of the establishment is carved into the rocks of Mönchsberg Mountain, so all that's visible from the outside is a gilded iron gate and a short stone stairway. The cavernous interior is open only in summer, when you can join hundreds of others in drinking beer and eating sausages, schnitzels, and other *Bierkeller* food. Menus cost 16€ to 21€.

On the first Sunday of the month, a *Frühschoppen*—a traditional Salzburger music fest—is presented from 10:30pm to midnight. No ticket is necessary—you pay for what you eat and drink. Likewise, no ticket is necessary to attend another musical evening, a *Happing,* staged from May to September, every Thursday from 6 to 8pm. Festungsgasse 10. ✆ **0662/842681.** www.imlauer.com. Bus: 3, 5, or 6.

Zweistein   This is the leading club for Salzburg's gay and lesbian community. Sometimes there's entertainment, but don't count on it. The contemporary art on the walls changes monthly. The international gay crowd, mostly under 35, likes the friendly, welcoming environment. On weekends, the place becomes almost overcrowded. Cocktails range from 5.80€ to 6.80€. Open Sunday to Wednesday 6pm to 4am, Thursday to Saturday 6pm to 5am. Giselakai 9. ✆ **0662/877179.** www.zweistein.at. Bus: 51.

A Casino

Casino Salzburg Schloss Klessheim   The only year-round casino in Land Salzburg occupies the soaring Schloss Klessheim, a baroque palace designed by one of the most influential architects of Austria's baroque age, Fischer von Erlach. Monday night is poker night. To enter the casino, you must present some form of identification, either a driver's license or a passport. There's also a dress code: Except during the hottest months of summer, men are encouraged to wear jackets and ties. The complex is open daily from 3pm to 3am.

To get here, drive west along highway A1, exiting at the SCHLOSS KLESSHEIM exit, about 1.5km (1 mile) west of the center of Salzburg. The casino also runs a shuttle taxi that departs, without charge, from the rocky base of the Mönchsberg every hour on the half-hour daily from 5pm to midnight. A-5071 Walzsezenheim. ✆ **0662/854455.** www.casinos.at. Cover 23€; includes 25€ worth of casino chips.

SIDE TRIPS FROM SALZBURG

The environs of Salzburg are wonderfully scenic; to explore them fully, refer to chapter 10, "Land Salzburg." The area is a setting of old castles, charming villages, glacial lakes, salt mines, ice caves, and some of the most panoramic alpine scenery in Europe. But before heading to Land Salzburg, here are a few attractions right on the city's doorstep.

A Palace, Zoo & Museum in Hellbrunn

Schloss Hellbrunn ★   A popular spot for outings from Salzburg, this palace dates from the early 17th century and was built as a hunting lodge and summer residence for Prince-Archbishop Markus Sittikus. The Hellbrunn Zoo, also here, was formerly the palace deer park. It's a 20-minute drive from Salzburg; turn off Alpenstrasse at the Mobil gas station.

The palace **gardens,** one of the oldest baroque formal gardens in all Europe, are known for their trick fountains. As you walk through, take care—you might be showered from a surprise source, such as a set of antlers. Set to organ music, some 265 figures in a mechanical theater are set in motion hydraulically.

On an adjacent hill, a natural gorge forms the **Stone Theater,** where the first opera in the German-speaking world was presented in 1617. This attraction (signposted) can be reached on foot, about a 20-minute walk from the castle. A Hellbrunn Festival is held in the gardens, palace, and theater in August.

Fürstenweg 37, Hellbrunn. ✆ **0662/8203720.** www.hellbrunn.at. Admission 9.50€ adults, 6.50€ students, 4.50€ those aged 4-18. Tours given July–Aug daily 9am–9pm; May–June and Sept daily 9am–5:30pm; Apr and Oct daily 9am–4:30pm. Bus: 25.

Volkskundemuseum   Overlooking Hellbrunn Park, 5km (3 miles) south of Salzburg, the Volkskundemuseum offers a folk collection assembled by Prince-Archbishop Markus Sittikus in 1615. The displays, spread over three floors, reflect a cross-section of local folk art and depict popular religious beliefs, folk medicine, and the traditional costumes of Land Salzburg.

Monatsschlösschen, Hellbrunn. ✆ **0662/620808500.** www.salzburgmuseum.at. Admission 2.50€ adults, 2€ students, 1€ ages 6-15. Apr-Oct 10am–5:30pm. Bus: 25.

Zoo Salzburg ☺   The beautiful landscape provides a wonderful setting for viewing the diverse animals of the Zoo Hellbrunn, located just south of Salzburg. Chamois, otter, white rhinoceros, and antelope share large outdoor enclosures. You can also see cheetahs and free-flying griffin vultures. In 2010 a new lion house was unveiled with various animals from Africa. There's a children's zoo as well.

Schloss Hellbrunn, Morzgerstrasse. ✆ **0662/820176.** www.salzburg-zoo.at. Admission 9€ adults, 8€ students, 4€ those aged 4-14, free for children 3 and under. Oct-Mar daily 8:30am–4pm; Apr-Sept Mon-Thurs and Sun 8:30am–7:30pm, Fri-Sat 8:30am–10:30pm. Bus: 25.

Hallein & The Dürrnberg Salt Mines

The second-largest town in Land Salzburg, Hallein, once a center for processing the salt from the mines of Dürrnberg, was a prize possession of the prince-archbishops of Salzburg. Today you pass through this industrial town on the Salzach River on the way to the Dürrnberg mines. The **tourist office,** Mauttorpromenade 6, A-5400 Hallein (✆ **06245/85394;** www.hallein.com) is open Monday to Friday 9am to 5:30pm.

On the north side of the Hallein parish church are the former home and tomb of the man who composed the music for Mohr's "Silent Night," Franz-Xaver Gruber, a schoolteacher who died in 1863.

The **Dürrnberg salt mines (Salzbergwerk Hallein;** ✆ **06245/835110;** www.salzwelten.at) are the big draw. This popular attraction is easily visited on a day trip from Salzburg. On guided tours, visitors walk downhill from the ticket office to the mine entrance, and then board an electric mine train that goes deep into the caverns. From here, tourists go on foot through galleries, changing levels by sliding down polished wooden slides before exiting the mine on the train that brought them in. An underground museum traces the history of salt mining back to ancient times.

To get to the mines, you can either drive to Hallein from Salzburg or take a train there from Salzburg's main railway station (they depart throughout the day at 20-min intervals). From a point just in front of the railway station at Hallein, you'll then board a bus for the ongoing 12-minute ride to Dürrnberg. (Be warned in advance that the buses are less frequent than the trains—they depart every hour, 55 min. past the hour, throughout the day.)

Tours of the salt mines and the lectures that precede them last about 90 minutes each and are conducted from April to October daily 9am to 5pm, November to March daily 10am to 3pm with tours beginning on the hour. Admission to the mines costs 18€ for adults, and 9€ for students and children 4 to 15. Children under 4 are not admitted.

If you embark upon this adventure from Salzburg's main railway station, you can buy from any ticket counter a combined ticket for round-trip transport on the train and the subsequent bus to Dürrnberg, with admission to the salt mines included, for 26€ per adult.

The Ice Caves of Eisriesenwelt ★★

Some 48km (30 miles) south of Salzburg by train is the "World of the Ice Giants," the largest known **ice caves** in the world. The caves, opening at some 1,678m (5,505 ft.), stretch for about 42km (26 miles), although only a portion of that length is open to the public. Fantastic ice formations at the entrance extend for half a mile. This underground wonderland is lined with amazing ice figures and frozen waterfalls. The climax of this chill underworld tour is the spectacular Ice Palace.

Please keep in mind that a visit to this spelunking (cave exploring) oddity is recommended only for those who are quite fit and hardy, and is not suggested for elderly travelers or small children. You'll be walking down narrow, slippery passages.

To reach the **Eisriesenwelt,** begin by heading for the hamlet of Werfen, which is located approximately 40km (24 miles) south of Salzburg. The village of Werfen is also the home of **Castle (Schloss) Hohenwerfen** (© 06468/7603), which was founded in the 11th century and frequently reconstructed. One of the most important castles in Land Salzburg, it's visible for miles around. You can get to Werfen by driving along the main A10 highway (the Tauern motorway), or by taking a train from Salzburg's Hauptbahnhof to Werfen station.

From the village of Werfen, you'll drive up a steep and narrow 6km (3½-mile) access road, following the signs to Eisriesenwelt, which leads to a high-altitude parking area. If you don't have a car, there's a local bus service (the Eisriesenwelt Linie; © 06468/5293 for information). For a fee of 3.50€ per person, it will haul you along the above-described 6-km (3½-mile) road. Service is provided only between May and October at 8:20 and 10:20am, and 12:20 and 2:20pm. It's often more convenient to pay around 11€ to hire any of the local taxis in lieu of waiting for the bus, and hardy hikers sometimes opt to walk the steep incline to the above-mentioned parking area. If you opt to hike, know in advance that the altitude from the start to the end of your climb will rise from 488 to 915m (from 1,601 to 3,002 ft.)—it is very steep indeed.

Once you reach the parking area, expect an additional, relatively easy 20-minute mostly shaded uphill hike to reach the cable car which hauls you vertiginously upward to the entrance to the caves. If you opt to avoid the cable car in favor of walking, expect to spend 90 sweaty minutes with sweeping views. Even if you do opt for the cable car, you'll face an additional 20-minute climb from the top of the cable car to the entrance to the ice caves.

There's a cafe and restaurant en route within a woodsy-looking building, the Dr.-Friedrich-Oedl-Haus, located at 1,568m (5,144 ft.) above sea level. Supervised tours of the inside of the caves generally last 75 minutes, and cost 8.50€ for adults, 7.50€ for students, and 4.50€ for ages 4 to 14. The caves are open only from May to October, with tours beginning each hour on the half-hour between 9am and 3:30pm (until 4:30pm July–Aug). A combined ticket for round-trip access on the cable car, with a tour of the caves included, costs 19€ for adults, 17€ for students, and 9.50€ for children aged 4 to 14.

From Werfen, allow about 6 hours for the entire trip. Dress warmly and wear shoes appropriate for hiking. Even if you don't want to go underground, consider the trek from Salzburg to the mouth of the cave for the scenery.

Eisriesenwelt Werfen is entered at Wimmstrasse 24 (© **06468/5248** or 0662/842690; www.eisriesenwelt.at).

LAND SALZBURG

The borders of this lofty province in the high Alps look like the handiwork of a mapmaker gone haywire. Craggy mountains, deep valleys, winding rivers, lakes, and rolling foothills, plus a little political expediency, all affected the cartographer's pen. Within this Bundesland (province) of some 7,154 sq. km (2,762 sq. miles) are some of the most dramatic landscapes in Austria, including the spectacular Krimml Falls, the highest in Europe.

10

Land Salzburg is perfect for those seeking Austria's clear alpine air and blue mountain lakes, the countryside made famous in *The Sound of Music*. You can begin by exploring the Salzkammergut lake country, a narrow corridor in Land Salzburg between Bavaria and Upper Austria. Many parts of Salzkammergut, which means "domain of the salt office," grew rich from mining salt—and also gold.

Although there are often Land Salzburg excursions leaving from the city of Salzburg, we think it's much more fun and less expensive to do it on your own. Most people involved in tourist services speak English, and you can travel through the district in security and comfort.

This is a land of summer and winter sports, with such celebrated spas as Badgastein and renowned ski resorts as Zell am See, Kaprun, Saalbach, and Hinterglemm. Relax at a lakeside resort, such as St. Gilgen, or stay at a mountain hotel where the air is crisp.

Of course, Land Salzburg is a skier's paradise. The season usually begins about 10 days before Christmas and usually lasts until Easter or beyond, depending on snow conditions. However, it is sometimes much longer, and skiing on some of the lofty plateaus is possible year-round. Kaprun, Saalbach, and Zell am See are long-established *and* expensive resorts. However, in the true spirit of the Frommer's guides, we've sought less familiar and even undiscovered places—many known only to the Austrians and an occasional German tourist.

Although Salzburg itself is flat, most of Land Salzburg is mountainous. Always inquire about local weather conditions before embarking on a day's sightseeing, particularly if you're going to be traversing one of those lofty alpine highways. The highest mountain range in Austria, the Hohe Tauern, lies on the southern fringe of Land Salzburg. The Hohe Tauern

National Park encompasses one of the most beautiful areas of the eastern Alps and remains mainly undeveloped. The park's core is formed of mighty mountains, steep rock faces, glaciers, and glacial streams, one of which feeds the Krimml Falls. Mountain meadows, alpine pastures, and protective woods comprise the park's periphery. Other natural attractions are Liechtensteinklamm, south of St. Johann in Pongau, the most dramatic gorge in the eastern Alps; Gollinger Wasserfälle (the Golling Waterfall), between the Valley of Kaprun and its powerful dams; and an ascent to the Kitzsteinhorn at 2,931m (9,616 ft.).

The Tauern Highway is one of the most important north–south roads over the Alps, passing through two tunnels: The Tauerntunnel is 6km (4 miles) long, and the Katschbergtunnel is 5km (3¼ miles) long. Because of the extensive upkeep, tolls are charged, but they're not excessive and are a fair price for the view alone. The Grossglockner Road, with its heart-thumping hairpin turns, is Europe's longest and most beautiful alpine highway. But unlike regions of Austria more devoted to serious skiing, Land Salzburg derives a good percentage of its income from midwinter travelers who appreciate the region's accessibility from the major (snow-free) highways and rail routes of Austria. Prices in August tend to be the same as in January and February, and cheaper in the off-season months of June and October. In fact, resort hotels in Land Salzburg often close completely during the gray meltdown days of early spring and the rainy days of late autumn.

Instead of staying in Salzburg, especially crowded during the Salzburg Festival months, you might reserve a room at a resort described below and commute to the province's capital city. You'll find the prices often lower and the atmosphere more laid-back. Accommodations are wide-ranging, from deluxe resorts to a mountain hut. There are a few castle hotels in Land Salzburg to suit those who have traditional tastes and don't always demand the latest in plumbing fixtures. Long cut off from the rest of the world but now accessible because of modern engineering achievements, some sections of Land Salzburg still cling tenaciously to their traditions. Old costumes and folklore still flourish in the province.

Most hotels in the district automatically price your accommodations with half-board included. Although you can always request a bed-and-breakfast rate and take your meals elsewhere, the supplement for half-board usually represents good value, sometimes allowing you to eat your main meal of the day for between 12€ and 20€ per person. You could try out the local restaurants at lunch. But hotels here generally have the best restaurants, so we suggest a hotel dining room for dinner. Parking is rarely a problem, and, unless otherwise noted, you park for free.

For information on Land Salzburg, contact the **Salzburg State Tourist Board,** P.O. Box 1, Wiener Bundesstrasse 23, A-5300 Hallwang (© **0662/66880;** fax 0662/668866; www.salzburgerland.com).

Tips for Active Travelers

Land Salzburg seems like one vast outdoor playground—from skiing in winter to canoeing, fishing, golfing, hiking, and much more in summer.

CANOEING & RAFTING   In summer, many visitors head for either the Salzkammergut or the Pinzgau regions of Land Salzburg, known for their beautiful lakes and roaring whitewater streams. Lakes here are ideal for canoeing, rafting, or kayaking because the waters aren't polluted and the government limits powerboats, making the waters safer.

One of the best outfitters is **Club Zwilling,** Waldhof 64, Abtenau (✆ **06243/3069**), and well recommended is **Motion Center,** Andreas Voglastätter, Lofer (✆ **06588/7524**), located at the edge of Lake Sallachsee.

Other centers for watersports include **Rafting Center Taxenbach,** Marktstrasse 38 (✆ **06543/5352;** www.raftingcenter.com), at the edge of the Salzach River. You can also call **Adventure Service,** Steinergrasse 9, in Zell am See (✆ **06542/73525;** www.adventureservice.at), a cheerful and well-managed outfit that offers guided excursions with instruction in rafting, whitewater kayaking, sailing, canoeing, paragliding, hiking, and mountain climbing.

CROSS-COUNTRY SKIING & DOWNHILL SKIING We've previewed in this chapter the most important ski resorts. For more options, contact one of the 120 local tourist offices for details on the dozens of ski schools in the province that provide instruction to novice and experienced skiers. For complete skiing data, write or call the Salzburg State Tourist Board (see above).

FISHING You'll find some wonderful places to fish, but you'll need a license, which you can obtain at the local tourist office where you're staying. For more information about where to fish in the province, call the Salzburg State Tourist Board (see above).

GOLF If you'd like to play a round of alpine golf, you can get a complete listing of the over 15 provincial courses from the Salzburg State Tourist Board (see above).

HIKING This is a great place to hike. The Salzburg State Tourist Board (see above) stocks a very helpful brochure called "Walking and Trekking," which surveys the countless trails in the province.

THE TENNENGAU

The Tennengau, named after the Tennen massif, is a division of the Salzach Valley, south of Salzburg, characterized by rolling hills and woodlands. Waterfalls dot the landscape—those outside the town of Golling are the most visited. Much of the Tennengau area, especially the houses with their gables and window boxes full of geraniums, will remind visitors of neighboring Bavaria.

As you leave Salzburg, going south on the left bank of the Salzach River, you'll pass through Anif, on the outskirts of Salzburg. You'll find some excellent old romantic accommodations in Anif (reviewed in chapter 9) if you'd like to stay near the provincial capital.

If you don't want to stay in the Tennengau region, you might consider a day trip from Salzburg. Its chief sight is the Dürrnberg Salt Mines outside Hallein (see "Side Trips from Salzburg," in chapter 9). However, if you'd like to stay in the district, you'll find good accommodations in Golling.

Golling

Golling was first mentioned in historical sources as a farm hamlet in the 9th century. Today residents of this quietly stylish outlying burg tend to commute to work in Salzburg. Many visitors use Golling as a base for various outdoor activities in the nearby mountains.

ESSENTIALS
GETTING THERE **Trains** heading south to Villach and Klagenfurt in Carinthia stop here, and depart from Salzburg for the 31-km (19-mile) journey at 1- to 2-hour

intervals; the trip takes 20 minutes. Railway officials refer to the village station as Golling-Abtenau. For rail information in Salzburg, call © **05/1717,** or visit **www. oebb.at**.

Buses (Postbus no. 170) depart approximately every hour throughout the day from Salzburg's main railway station (with a subsequent stop at Mirabellplatz). The trip to Golling takes about 65 minutes. For information about buses from Salzburg to the outlying regions, call the local tourist office (see below).

VISITOR INFORMATION For **tourist information,** go to Verkehrsverein, Am Marktplatz 51 (just follow the signs), in the center of town. The office (© **06244/ 4356**) is open Monday to Friday 8am to noon and 2 to 6pm, and Saturday 9 to 11am.

THE GOLLING WATERFALL ★★ & SALZACH GORGE

What draws visitors to Golling, 12km (7½ miles) south of Hallein via the A10, is the **Gollinger Wasserfall (Golling Waterfall).** It's 2km (1½ miles) west of the little resort along an unnumbered local road (look for signs saying GOLLINGER WASSERFALL), followed by a 20-minute walk from the parking area to the falls. The waterfall—between Golling and Kuchl, 27km (17 miles) south of Salzburg—tumbles down more than 153m (502 ft.) over a rock wall. Open from May to October, access to the falls costs 2.50€ for adults and 1.50€ for children.

You can also visit the rushing **Salzach Gorge** near Golling, an hour's walk from town up to Pass Lueg. It lies 3km (2 miles) south of Golling and is accessible by following Highway B159. As the entrance is not strictly regulated, you might arrive before the park attendants do (as local climbers are known to). Admission is 3€ per person. In winter, snow and ice block access, and the gorge is unsafe except for experienced rock and ice climbers. Visits both to the falls and the gorge are possible from May to October daily from 9am to 6pm; or if you're a bit adventurous, you can visit year-round at your own risk. It's best to go while attendants are on hand.

Heimatmuseum Burg Golling, Markt 1 (© **06244/4356-0**) has a chapel and an interesting folklore collection. You'll see remains of cave bears, fossils, and copies of rock drawings, plus old pictures of the village. There's also a hunting room, exhibits of regional costumes, and a chamber of torture. It's open from May to mid-October Wednesday through Sunday from 10am to noon, and 1 to 5pm. Admission is 4.30€ for adults, 1.80€ for children.

WHERE TO STAY & EAT

Döllerer's Geniesserhotel Built in the 12th century but given its present antique look in 1925, the hotel also known as Goldener Stern sits amid a row of picture-book houses in the center of the village. Rustic yet modern furniture fills the interior. Rooms are cozy and comfortable, with spotless bathrooms. The hotel even has a sauna and a solarium.

Many of the region's gourmets frequent the in-house restaurant, home of star chef Andreas Döllerer, 2010 recipient of Gault Millau's "Chef of the Year" award for Austria. Serving Austrian, French, and Italian food, its specialties include dried alpine beef, sliced wafer-thin and served with pearl onions and pickles; an Austrian version of the Italian saltimbocca (veal with ham); and seafood dishes. The distinguished wine list includes mainly Austrian and Italian vintages. Dinner is served Tuesday to Sunday 8am to midnight; reservations are suggested. There is also a deli and a wine store.

Am Marktplatz 56, A-5440 Golling. © **06244/42200.** Fax 06244/691242. www.doellerer.at. 20 units. 110€–160€ double; 150€–180€ suite. Half-board 19€ per person. Rates include breakfast. DC, MC, V.

Land Salzburg

| Dürrnberg Salt Mines **1** |
| Franz-Josefs-Höhe **7** |
| Golling Waterfall **2** |
| Grossglockner Road **6** |
| Krimml Falls **5** |
| Liechtensteinklamm **3** |
| Salzach Gorge **4** |

Amenities: 2 restaurants; babysitting; bar; laundry service; dry cleaning; nonsmoking rooms; room service; sauna; solarium. *In room:* TV, hairdryer, minibar, safe, Wi-Fi.

THE PONGAU

Badgastein and Bad Hofgastein, covered in greater detail later in this chapter, are part of an area of Land Salzburg known as the Pongau—one of several sections of an alpine valley called Salzach. The Pinzgau section (also later in this chapter) of the Salzach Valley is to the southwest.

Visitors to the Pongau most frequently go through the **Gastein Valley,** of which Badgastein and Bad Hofgastein are a part. For many centuries, the Gastein Valley has been known for its hot springs, but since World War II it has also become a winter-sports center. As a consequence, many old spas such as Badgastein suddenly find themselves overrun with skiers in winter.

The **Radstädter Tauern** region is the second most popular section of the Pongau. It sprawls across five mountains and four valleys, with a mammoth expanse of terrain from St. Johann to Obertauern. In between, you'll find that Wagrain, Flachau, Altenmarkt, and Radstadt have many places to stay. It's helpful to have a car here, although most of Radstädter Tauern can be reached by lifts and runs.

10

LAND SALZBURG | The Pongau

Goldegg

Goldegg lies on a small lake dominated by a 14th-century castle. This winter- and summer-sports resort is reached by going through Schwarzach–St. Veit at the western end of the Pongau. A 9-hole golf course is nearby.

Don't expect crystal-clear waters from the shallow lake, Goldeggersee, where waters abut the town center. Years of percolating through the surrounding moors have infused the waters with organic matter, mostly peat, and transformed them into a greenish-brown brew, resembling weak tea. Locals claim that the waters are healthy and beneficial, but only one hotel, the Hotel Gesinger Zur Post (see below), pipes the water into its in-house spa. Incidentally, the brown color of the water absorbs sunlight faster than clear water, so in summer, the water actually becomes tepid.

ESSENTIALS

GETTING THERE   Goldegg is 71km (44 miles) south of Salzburg and 389km (242 miles) southwest of Vienna. No rail lines go directly to Goldegg. **Trains** run from Salzburg to the nearby railway station at Schwarzach–St. Veit; call ✆ **05/1717,** or visit **www.oebb.at** for schedules. From here, **buses** make the 15-minute run at intervals of between 45 minutes and 2 hours throughout the day.

If you're **driving** from Salzburg, take the A10 south to the junction with Route 311. Continue west until you see the signposted turnoff to Goldegg. Then head northwest along an unmarked road.

VISITOR INFORMATION   Goldegg's **tourist information office** is at Hofmarkt 18 (✆ **06415/8131;** www.goldeggamsee.at), in the town center. It's open in winter Monday to Friday 8:15am to noon, and in summer Monday to Friday from 8:15am to noon and 1:30 to 6pm.

THE OLD CASTLE OF GOLDEGG

Count Christoph of Schernberg bought the old castle of Goldegg in the 16th century and added the Rittersaal, a big hall now decorated with paintings of the Roman–German Empire, Renaissance ornaments, Christian images, and depictions of ancient myths. In 1973, the local municipality bought the building and began renovating it. The Count of Galen still lives in the village.

In the castle is the **Pongau Folk Museum,** Hofmarkt 1 (✆ **06415/8131** for the tourist office). It displays old tools used in the everyday lives of those who once lived here, as well as local sports equipment from the past 300 years. Guided tours in German are conducted in May, June, and September on Thursday and Sunday at 3 and 4pm; July and August Tuesday, Thursday, and Sunday at 3 and 4pm; and October to April Thursday at 2pm. Hours are Monday, Tuesday, and Thursday to Saturday from 10am to noon and 3 to 5pm, Sunday 3 to 5pm. Closed Wednesday. Adults pay 3.50€, children 1€.

WHERE TO STAY & EAT

Hotel Gesinger Zur Post ★   This lakeside hotel with a mountain view consists of two interconnected country-style buildings, both with flowered balconies and window boxes. The oldest part of the building was erected in 1890. The interior is outfitted with painted regional furniture, polished pine paneling, and homelike details. The congenial hosts, Raimund and Hertha Gesinger, do everything they can to make guests comfortable. The cozy rooms are equipped with spacious private bathrooms, and usually have enclosed sleeping compartments behind full-length curtains.

Under the rafters of what was a barn, the hotel has installed a pub complete with hanging lanterns and intimate corners. The Hotel Zur Post Restaurant serves Austrian

A SPECTACULAR gorge IN THE EASTERN ALPS

Just 3km (2 miles) south of St. Johann in the Pongau is perhaps the most spectacular gorge of the eastern Alps, the **Liechtensteinklamm ★**, which attracts more visitors than any other such site. A path has been blasted through to the 1km-long (¾-mile) gorge, and over the course of a 25-minute trek you can climb up the mammoth gorge with rock walls some 305m (1,001 ft.) high. At its tiny waist, the gorge is only 4m (13 ft.) wide. A tunnel leads to the waterfall, with a drop of about 61m (200 ft.) at the gorge's end.

The wooden bridges and the footpath that runs along the bottom of the gorge were paid for by Johann II, Prince of Liechtenstein, who consequently lent his name to the site. In some areas the ravine is so narrow that the sky is barely visible from the bottom. Roaring waterfalls and swiftly flowing waters add to the site's allure.

To reach the Liechtensteinklamm, go approximately 1.5km (1 mile) by road to Grossarl. The road to the gorge is marked. From here, it is about an hour by foot. The gorge can be visited May to September daily from 8am to 6pm, October daily 9am to 4pm. Admission is 4€ for adults and 2.50€ for children 6 to 18.

and international cuisine. You might want to dine here even if you're not a guest of the hotel. The owners have a private beach on the nearby lake, available only in the summer, of course.

Hofmarkt 9, A-5622 Goldegg. ⓒ **06415/81030.** Fax 06415/8104. www.hotelpost-goldegg.at. 38 units. 134€–182€ double; 198€–214€ suite. Rates include breakfast. Half-board 11€ per person. MC, V. Free parking outside, 10€ in the garage. Closed Apr and Nov. **Amenities:** 3 restaurants; bar; babysitting; bike rentals; games room; room service; laundry service; dry cleaning; massage; nonsmoking rooms; sauna; spa. *In room:* TV, hairdryer, safe, Wi-Fi.

Hotel Seehof ★   Hotel Seehof is filled with the kind of rustic artifacts and local painted furniture that many of us spend weeks looking for in antiques shops. This hotel dates from 1449 and sits on the lake, which reflects the chalet's forest-green shutters and the flowerpots on the hotel's balconies. An outdoor terrace sports sun umbrellas. In summer, guests can enjoy the private lakeside beach, and in winter the hotel rents ski equipment for the nearby slopes. Rooms are contemporary and warm, with good beds and modern private bathrooms. Units often have private balconies and sloped, paneled ceilings.

The owner, Mr. Schellhorn, is director of the cross-country ski school of Goldegg, where you can find 58km (36 miles) of the best-groomed cross-country ski trails in Land Salzburg. He's also the director of the resort's golf course and offers hotel residents discounts on green fees.

Hofmarkt 8, A-5622 Goldegg. ⓒ **06415/8137-0.** Fax 06415/8276. www.derseehof.com. 30 units. 144€–218€ double; 390€ suite. Rates include breakfast. AE, DC, MC, V. Closed Apr and Nov. **Amenities:** Restaurant; bar; babysitting; 18-hole golf course; laundry service; dry cleaning; room service; sauna; nonsmoking rooms. *In room:* TV, hairdryer, safe, Wi-Fi.

St. Johann im Pongau

St. Johann im Pongau (there's a larger one in Tyrol) is 61km (38 miles) south of Salzburg on a sun-drenched terrace on the right bank of the river.

The winter-sports season here lasts December through April, and there are more than 52 lifts and cable cars in the tri-resort area, plus some 97km (60 miles) of prepared runs. This well-known ski-lift network in the Salzburg Mountains is called Drei-Taler-Skischaukel (Three-Valley Ski Swing).

If you're a nature lover, St. Johann is a good base for visiting the **Grossarltal (Grossarl Valley)** to the south of the town and the mouth of **Wagrainertal (Wagrain Valley)** to the east.

The town's twin-towered **Pfarrkirche (Parish Church)** was built in 1855, but a house of worship has stood on this site since A.D. 924.

ESSENTIALS

GETTING THERE St. Johann lies directly on the main rail line connecting Munich and Salzburg with Klagenfurt, Venice, and Trieste. Between 4:50am and 10:20pm, these **trains** depart from Salzburg's Hauptbahnhof no more than 2 hours apart (trip time: 1 hr. and 8 min., when no train changes en route). If the delay between trains poses an inconvenience, consider taking one of the more frequent trains between Salzburg and the important railway junction of Schwarzach–St. Veit, and then backtrack, taking a taxi or bus the 5km (3 miles) to St. Johann. For rail information in Salzburg, call ☏ **05/1717** (www.oebb.at).

Unless you're coming in from one of the neighboring villages, arriving by **bus** in St. Johann isn't practical because of the multiple transfers required from such cities as Salzburg and Innsbruck.

If you're **driving,** head south from Salzburg on the A10, and then cut southwest at the junction with Route 311.

VISITOR INFORMATION St. Johann's **tourist office** is at Hauptplatz (☏ **06412/ 6036;** www.sanktjohann.com). It's open in winter Monday to Friday 8am to 6pm, Saturday 9am to noon and 2 to 5pm, Sunday 9 to 11am; in summer Monday to Friday 8am to 6pm, Saturday 9am to noon.

WHERE TO STAY & EAT

Alpenland ★ Set in the heart of the village, this is the largest hotel in St. Johann and one of the largest time-sharing resorts in Land Salzburg. Built in the 1980s and designed like a big interconnected series of alpine chalets, it contains an excellent set of facilities and comfortable accommodations that are among the best in town. Each is furnished with vaguely chalet-style decor, a bit functional but with excellent beds and good-size bathrooms. On the premises are two restaurants (Italian and Austrian) with an attentive and helpful staff. Throughout, you'll find burnished pine and regional accessories. Meals in the most formal of the restaurants begin at 26€, although many less expensive options are available on-site. The hotel rents bicycles to anyone interested in exploring the nearby region for 12€ per day.

Hans-Kappacher-Strasse 7, A-5600 St. Johann im Pongau. ☏ **06412/70210.** Fax 06412/702151. www.alpenland.at. 144 units. Winter 136€–182€ double, 198€–270€ junior suite; off-season 110€–128€ double, 159€–186€ junior suite. Half-board 18€ per person. AE, DC, MC, V. Free parking. **Amenities:** 2 restaurants; 2 bars; nightclub; lounge; babysitting; boutiques; fitness center; Jacuzzi; laundry service; dry cleaning; massage; indoor heated pool; 2 tennis courts; sauna; room service. *In room:* TV, hairdryer, minibar, Wi-Fi.

BAD HOFGASTEIN ★

88km (55 miles) S of Salzburg; 8km (5 miles) NW of Badgastein; 42km (26 miles) SE of Zell am See

The old, established spa of **Bad Hofgastein** (elevation 869m/2,851 ft.) has long been a rival of Badgastein for the tourist euro. It's smaller than its twin 8km (5 miles)

up the valley, but almost as charming. The little resort is actually almost a satellite of the larger spa, as the radioactive waters of Badgastein are pumped to its neighbor. Some hardy visitors like to follow a marked footpath on the 2½-hour walk between the two towns. The two resorts welcome almost as many visitors as Salzburg.

Essentials

GETTING THERE   Bad Hofgastein is a major stop on the main rail lines connecting Munich and Salzburg with Klagenfurt and Venice. Most efficient are the express **trains** from Salzburg, which depart about once an hour throughout the day (trip time: 1¼ hr.). Night trains might require a transfer at Schwarzach–St. Veit, 68km (42 miles) south of Salzburg. Dozens of trains traveling from Innsbruck also stop in Schwarzach–St. Veit. Trains continue on south to Villach every 2 hours on average via the 8-km long (5-mile) **Tauerntunnel.** Call ✆ **05/1717,** or visit **www.oebb.at** for more information.

One daily **bus** runs in both directions between Salzburg's Mirabellplatz and the rail station in Bad Hofgastein, and then on to Badgastein.

If you're **driving,** take the A10 south of Salzburg, cut right onto Route 311, and continue west to the junction with Route 167, where you head south to Badgastein. Driving further south to Spittal, Villach, or Lienz will require loading your vehicle onto the *Autoschleuse,* a train that transports cars through the tunnel. Call ✆ **05/ 1717,** or visit **www.oebb.at** for details.

VISITOR INFORMATION   The **tourist information office** in the town center at Tauernplatz 1 (✆ **06432/3393260;** www.gastein.com) is open Monday to Saturday 8am to 6pm.

Spa Facilities

The thermally heated waters of Bad Hofgastein originate in the same high-altitude springs that feed the spa facilities of Badgastein, 8km (5 miles) away. Bad Hofgastein is the newer of the two, and a bit more upscale and glamorous as well. The waters are rich in radon, a controversial element that doctors once dismissed as harmful but now say is beneficial in small doses of no more than 20 minutes of immersion per day.

There are no public facilities here as in Badgastein; instead, three local hotels have built full spa facilities on their premises. You won't have to move between buildings for treatments, a bonus during cold or snowy weather.

The most complete Bad Hofgastein spa lies within the Grand Park Hotel (see below). The spa treatments are great for the foot-sore (and leg, and back, and more) traveler. You can get all types of massage, electrotherapy, aromatherapy, saunas, steam baths, and mud packs, or take part in aerobic classes or gymnastics. Less scientific "cures" include lying prone on plastic bags filled with dried flowers, or being partially buried in tubs of wet straw that have been soaked in the hot thermal waters.

What to See & Do

The **Pfarrkirche (Parish Church)** of this tiny village is late Gothic, dating from the late 15th century, although it has a baroque altar. Some sights, such as old houses with turrets, are reminders of the gold-mining days of the Gastein Valley. In the 16th century, the nearby gold mines made Bad Hofgastein rival even Salzburg in wealth. A rich mining family lived at the 15th-century Weitmoserschlössl, which has now been turned into a cafe.

The Gastein Valley and Bad Hofgastein are attracting more and more winter-sports fans. Some 50 gondolas and ski lifts provide access to more than 241km (150 miles) of well-marked and well-groomed ski runs. Thanks to the high capacity of an updated funicular, a mono-cable rotation gondola lift with cabins for six passengers, two quadruple chairlifts, and a triple chairlift, skiers don't have to wait in long lines. The Dorfgastein–Grossarl connection and the lift network from Schlossalm via the Angertal and Jungeralm ski center up to the Stubnerkogel (the largest lift interconnection in Land Salzburg) provide some of the most enjoyable ski runs in the valley. Visit www.skigastein.com for details.

Also available are cross-country skiing on well-maintained tracks, tobogganing, skating, and riding in horse-drawn sleighs.

Where to Stay & Eat

VERY EXPENSIVE

Grand Park Hotel ★★   Originally constructed in the 1920s, this five-star hotel was completely rebuilt in the early 1990s and reopened in 1994. It's a majestic, classically styled building set in its own birch-filled park, with a swimming pool and chairs on the grassy lawns around it. The elegant interior is filled with stone and polished wood, plush carpets, and shining brass. Rooms are handsomely furnished and beautifully maintained, with excellent beds and ample bathrooms. The hotel restaurant, open to nonguests, is one of the area's finest, serving Austrian and international cuisine. A pianist entertains every evening.

Kurgartenstrasse 26, A-5630 Bad Hofgastein. ✆ **06432/63560.** Fax 06432/8454. www.grandpark hotel.at. 89 units. Summer 210€–290€ double, 354€–392€ suite; off-season 258€–306€ double, 384–422€ suite. Rates include half-board. MC, V. **Amenities:** Restaurant; bar; babysitting; bike rentals; fitness center; indoor thermal pool; Jacuzzi; laundry service; dry cleaning; massage; room service; sauna; spa; nonsmoking rooms; 1 room for those w/limited mobility. *In room:* TV, minibar, hairdryer, safe, Wi-Fi.

EXPENSIVE

Kurhotel Palace ★ 🛍   Situated in a quiet, sunny spot, this first-class hotel is a few minutes' walk from the resort center. This is a surprisingly snug and cozy retreat in spite of its large size. The well-furnished rooms all have radios and balconies. Beds are about the finest in the resort, so comfortable that you might not want to get out of them; bathrooms are generous in size and well maintained. A daily program of entertainment and activities includes a lively nightclub, a Vienna coffeehouse, and bars. The Salzburger Stüberl serves Austrian, international, and vegetarian cuisine, and the Wiener Café offers homemade cakes and tarts.

Alexander-Moser-Allee 13, A-5630 Bad Hofgastein. ✆ **06432/67150.** Fax 06432/6715567. www.kur hotelpalace.at. 90 units. 168€–192€ double. Rates include half-board. AE, DC, MC, V. Parking 6€. **Amenities:** Restaurant; 2 bars; nightclub; babysitting; cafe; fitness center; laundry service; dry cleaning; indoor thermal pool; salon; sauna; solarium, spa; 2 tennis courts. *In room:* TV, hairdryer, minibar, radio, safe, Wi-Fi.

MODERATE

Hotel Astoria ★   This four-star hotel, built in the 1950s and now under new management, is a generously proportioned five-story building with a simple wood-balconied facade. The interior has been renovated in a contemporary design of streamlined furniture and warm, inviting colors. Rooms are only standard in size, but each is quite comfortable, with good beds and small bathrooms. Austrian regional specialties are served, and a country buffet is offered once a week.

Salzburger Strasse 24, A-5630 Bad Hofgastein. ✆ **06432/62770.** Fax 06432/627777. www.astoria-hofgastein.com. 73 units. 130€–170€ double. Rates include half-board. AE, MC, V. Closed Apr 23–May

26 and Nov 27-late Dec. **Amenities:** Restaurant; bar; babysitting; fitness center; laundry service; dry cleaning; indoor heated pool; spa; sauna; room service; nonsmoking rooms. *In room:* TV, hairdryer, minibar, safe, Wi-Fi.

Hotel St. Georg ★   An elegant country-house atmosphere prevails at this hotel offering attractive and well-furnished rooms and family suites designed for discerning guests. The manager and hotel staff make sure rooms, with medium-size bathrooms, are well maintained. Half-board includes a buffet breakfast and a five-course dinner. Tempting Austrian cuisine is served in the country-style restaurant, and special diets can be accommodated. Although it's not as well known as the previously recommended hotel, it has its devotees.

Dr. Zimmermann-Strasse 7, A-5630 Bad Hofgastein. ✆ **06432/6100.** Fax 06432/610061. www. stgeorg.com. 50 units. Winter 196€-252€ per person double, 229€-279€ suite for 2; summer 126€-169€ per person double, 186€-204€ suite. Rates include half-board. MC, V. Parking 3€ in summer, 6€ in winter. Closed early Nov-mid Dec. **Amenities:** Restaurant; bar; babysitting; fitness center; laundry service; dry cleaning; massage; indoor heated pool; room service; sauna; solarium. *In room:* TV, hairdryer, safe, Wi-Fi.

Hotel Sendlhof ★   The six floors here are surrounded by balconies and potted flowers, and an outdoor heated swimming pool lies across the lawn. The interior has large windows, inviting fireplaces, and extra touches such as ceramic stoves. Management sometimes provides live zither music in the evening. The elegant, cozy rooms have exposed wood, and most have private balconies. Bathrooms, although neatly kept, might be a bit cramped.

Pyrkerstrasse 34, A-5630 Bad Hofgastein. ✆ **06432/38380.** Fax 06432/3838-60. www.sendlhof.co.at. 60 units. Winter 160€-232€ double; summer 130€-196€ double. Rates include half-board. MC, V. Parking 5€. Closed Apr 20-May 22 and Oct 15-Dec 18. **Amenities:** Restaurant; bar; babysitting; fitness center; laundry service; dry cleaning; outdoor heated pool; sauna; room service. *In room:* TV, hairdryer, safe, Wi-Fi.

Kurhotel Germania ★   Beautiful Victorian antiques (including an exquisite collection of armchairs) fill some of the big-windowed public areas of this four-star hotel, which dates from around 1900. If your guest room has a balcony—and many of the pleasant and sunny rooms do—you'll have a view of the houses and barns of the valley below. Traditional alpine furnishings are somewhat functional but retain a bit of charm.

Kurpromenade 4, A-5630 Bad Hofgastein. ✆ **06432/6232.** Fax 06432/623265. www.hotelgermania. at. 70 units. Winter 140€-240€ double; summer 118€-160€ double. Rates include half-board. MC, V. Parking 10€. Closed Nov-mid Dec and Apr 16-May 13. **Amenities:** Restaurant; lounge; fitness center; laundry service; dry cleaning; massage; indoor heated pool; room service; sauna; health spa. *In room:* TV, Wi-Fi.

INEXPENSIVE

Hotel Carinthia ★   This large, solid-looking chalet has flower-filled balconies on all sides. The interior has elegant and unusual touches, such as the tucked-away corner bar and modern chandeliers in the high-ceilinged dining room. The spacious rooms are contemporary and well equipped, beds you sink into and a medium-size bathroom.

Dr. Zimmermann-Strasse 2, A-5630 Bad Hofgastein. ✆ **06432/83740.** Fax 06432/837475. www.hotel-carinthia.com. 35 units. Winter 140€-206€ double; summer 128€-146€ double. Rates include half-board. No credit cards. Closed Easter-early May and Nov. **Amenities:** Dining room; bar; babysitting; fitness center; Jacuzzi; laundry service; dry cleaning; massage; indoor heated pool; thermal pools; sauna; nonsmoking rooms; tennis and squash court. *In room:* TV, hairdryer, minibar, safe, Wi-Fi.

Kurhotel Völserhof Built in the 1960s, this hotel rises five balconied stories above a flowering garden near the edge of town. In summer, masses of red flowers bloom above the windows of the second-floor restaurant. Rooms are rather small and don't have much charm, but each is comfortably equipped with good beds. The city's recreation center is within a 5-minute walk, and the terminus of the funicular, Schlossalm Bahn, is 10 minutes away. The Lang family, your host, is very helpful in providing information about the area. One of the best times to book here is during their lowest season—the last 3 weeks in January and last 2 weeks in March—when rates are even lower than in the discounted summer season.

Pyrkerstrasse 28, A-5630 Bad Hofgastein. © **06432/8288.** Fax 06432/828810. www.voelserhof.com. 30 units. 116€–176€ double. Rates include half-board. MC, V. Closed Oct 25–Dec 7 and the first 2 weeks of May. **Amenities:** Dining room; bar; babysitting; laundry service; dry cleaning, sauna. *In room:* TV, hairdryer, minibar.

Kur- und Sporthotel Moser ★ 🍴 On the main town square, this hotel has sections dating from the 12th century, although you'd never know it from the pleasant balconied facade above the street-level awnings. The interior, however, is vaulted and cozy, with old exposed wood, heavy beams, and oriental rugs. The furnishings are rustic and regional, with homey touches such as racks of pewter in the dining room. When the weather is good, the rooms are often flooded with sunlight. All in all, the emphasis is on comfort, as reflected by the traditional furniture and duvet-covered beds. There's an intimate lounge and terrace dining, as well as a cozy cellar for dinner and dancing in winter.

Kaiser-Franz-Platz 2, A-5630 Bad Hofgastein. © **06432/6209.** Fax 06432/620988. www.dasmoser. com. 54 units. 130€–170€ double. Rates include half-board. AE, DC, MC, V. Parking 6.50€. Closed Apr and Nov 1–Dec 15. **Amenities:** Restaurant; bar; babysitting; bike rentals; fitness center; massage; indoor heated thermal pool; room service; nonsmoking rooms; sauna; spa. *In room:* TV, hairdryer, safe, Wi-Fi.

Bad Hofgastein After Dark

For your big night on the town, take a taxi from Bad Hofgastein to Badgastein to gamble at the casino (see below). In Bad Hofgastein, you can go clubbing, sit in a tavern beside an open fire, or dance to the music of a live band at one of the hotels in the winter season. The tourist office will give you the latest information on which hotels or clubs are likely to have nightlife at any given time.

One of Bad Hofgastein's busiest nightspots is the **Norica Bar,** just off the lobby of the Hotel Norica, Kaiser-Franz-Platz 3 (© **06432/8391-0**). Open every day from 5pm until 2am, it offers some kind of music act, from evergreen oompah to rock 'n' roll, in both winter and summer. There's no cover charge, and beer costs 3€ to 5€. Closing time varies, depending on business.

BADGASTEIN ★★: AUSTRIA'S PREMIER SPA

100km (62 miles) S of Salzburg; 410km (255 miles) SW of Vienna

Badgastein is not only Austria's premier spa, it's also one of the great spa towns of Europe. The local tourist industry began when Frederick, Duke of Styria, came here in the 15th century for treatment of a gangrenous wound. The duke was healed, and word spread. Badgastein had made its way onto the medieval tourist map. Royalty and aristocrats flocked here around the turn of the 19th century to "take the waters." And good waters they are—radioactive springs with healing properties.

On the north slope of the Tauern massif, this is one of the most scenic spots in Austria. The spa town is spread across steep hillsides split by the waters of the tumbling Gasteiner Ache. Hotels, many with water piped in directly from the Ache, adorn the steep slopes formed by the cascading waterfall. The spa's indoor swimming pool is carved into a rock filled with the radon waters.

Badgastein is now also a center for winter sports. With its pristine alpine air, skiing equal to that of St. Moritz in Switzerland, the finest hotels in Land Salzburg, 18 hot springs for thermal hydrotherapy, and a mountain tunnel that has been called "the world's only natural giant sauna," Badgastein is the pinnacle of mountain spa resorts.

Essentials

GETTING THERE Badgastein is a major stop on the main rail line connecting Munich and Salzburg with Klagenfurt and Venice. Express **trains** from Salzburg depart every hour throughout the day (trip time: 1½ hr.). Certain trains, especially night trains from Salzburg, might require a transfer at the railway junction of Schwarzach–St. Veit, 68km (42 miles) south of Salzburg. Dozens of trains traveling from Innsbruck also stop in Schwarzach–St. Veit. Call ✆ 05/1717 (www.oebb.at) in Salzburg for schedules.

One daily **bus** makes a 2-hour run in both directions between Salzburg's Mirabellplatz and the railway station in Badgastein. Buses from Badgastein make frequent runs into the surrounding villages.

If you're **driving,** take the A10 south of Salzburg and cut west at the junction with Route 311. At the junction with Route 167, head south.

VISITOR INFORMATION The **tourist office** (✆ 06434/25310) in the center of town is open year-round Monday to Friday 8am to 6pm. In winter, it's also open Saturday 10am to 6pm and Sunday 10am to 2pm.

What to See & Do

Along with the natural scenery of the town and the surrounding area, you can see the **Nikolauskirche,** a 15th-century church with well-preserved Gothic frescoes, a late-Gothic stone pulpit, and baroque altars and tombs.

In summer, besides swimming in thermal baths, the spa offers a host of saunas, massages, and solariums. There's also an 18-hole golf course, tennis courts, horseback riding, hiking, and a variety of excursions, perhaps in a *Fiaker* (horse-drawn carriage). Cable cars and chairlifts are not only for winter-sports crowds; in summer, take one up to the top and get a panoramic view of the Hohe Tauern.

In winter, most visitors come for the great skiing. In 1958, Graukogel, one of the main ski areas, was the site of the world championships.

Nearby Attractions

One of the region's most quirky attractions is the **Gasteiner Heilstollen,** A-5645 Böckstein (✆ 06434/3753; www.gasteiner-heilstollen.com), a labyrinth of underground tunnels carved out of the **Kreuzkogel** peak during the 18th and 19th centuries as a gold mine. It has been transformed into a small-scale health spa, where tiny cars carrying six patients are shuttled through the tunnels on a narrow-gauge railway. The 15-minute trip through the heated and mildly radioactive air (local doctors claim the effects are dispersed from the body within an hour) is cited as a cure for arthritis.

Between mid-January and early-November, you can ride through the tunnels Monday to Friday 8am to 4pm for 59.50€. The tunnels are 3km (2 miles) from Badgastein. Follow the signs from Böcksteinerstrasse, or take one of the hourly blue-and-gray Lackner buses.

The Gastein valley also offers a trio of chairlifts for summer hikers and winter-sports enthusiasts. **Graukogel** (2,508m/8,228 ft.), to the east of the valley, attracts expert skiers from all over Europe, who crowd these slopes in the afternoon. A chairlift takes skiers to the halfway station, and a double chairlift or surface lift takes them to the top. A round-trip ticket costs around 18€, while a day pass in the winter costs 35€. A mountain restaurant at the halfway station makes for a pleasant break, and is also a favorite starting point for alpine walking tours. Call ℭ **06434/2005** for ticket information. Service is daily 9am to 4pm.

On the west side of the valley rises **Stubnerkogel** (2,230m/7,316 ft.). A six-seat gondola takes you most of the way; however, it takes a chairlift and a couple of surface lifts to reach the top. There's also a mountain restaurant with a panoramic view. The gondola and the chairlift (ℭ **06434/6455**) are in service from late May to mid-October daily from 8:30am to 4pm; a round-trip ticket costs 18€ and a day pass is 41€.

The **Kreuzkogel** (2,684m/8,806 ft.) peak is at **Sportgastein,** 8km (5 miles) up the valley to the south of the village of Böckstein, site of the tunnel sauna mentioned above. This is a great place to come for high-altitude bowl skiing. It's about a 20-minute bus ride from Badgastein. A chairlift will take you to the halfway station, with a surface lift pulling you to the Kreuzkogel's top station. Besides the well-equipped skiing facilities here, including cross-country trails, you can enjoy hiking, indoor horseback riding, indoor tennis, curling, and ice-skating.

You can drive from Badgastein to Sportgastein along Gasteiner Alpenstrasse at elevations ranging from 900 to 1,454m (2,953.–4,770 ft.). The toll charge is 3€ per person by bus, 4€ if you bring your car, and free for children 4 and under. The ski-season ticket includes the road toll.

Where to Stay & Eat
EXPENSIVE
Elisabethpark ★★　This is Badgastein's premier address. The vastly improved four-star hotel has a ceiling covered with heavily textured knotty pine and rooms crowned with Moorish patterns of geometric greens and reds. The public areas stretch on and on—not surprising, since the hotel is a vast, sprawling collection of buildings with a white exterior, many balconies, and a series of hallways that are decorated with unusual paintings, hunting trophies, and regional antiques. Available in a wide variety of sizes, the rooms are traditionally furnished, often with antiques. The hotel's a la carte restaurant is one of the best at the spa, offering Austrian and international dishes alike.

Franz-Josef-Strasse 5, A-5640 Badgastein. ℭ **06434/25510.** Fax 06434/255110. www.elisabethpark. at. 119 units. Winter 208€–262€ double, 248€–282€ junior suite, from 296€ suite; off-season 136€–198€ double, 176€–228€ junior suite, from 196€ suite. Rates include half-board. AE, DC, MC, V. Parking 11€. **Amenities:** 2 restaurants; coffeehouse; bar; babysitting; indoor heated pool; fitness center; sauna; room service; massage; laundry service; dry cleaning; nonsmoking rooms. *In room:* TV, minibar, hairdryer, Wi-Fi.

Hotel Grüner-Baum ★★　This hotel is a complex of five chalets surrounding a grassy area in the Kötschach Valley on the outskirts of Badgastein. During its long history, the establishment has offered hospitality to Kaiser Wilhelm, the Shah of Iran, conductor Arturo Toscanini, and actor Charles Laughton. The oldest parts of the building are exquisitely crafted of local woods, sometimes with elaborate regional carvings, and decorated with hunting trophies beneath the beamed ceilings. Rooms are cozy and rustic, with wood paneling and a recessed sleeping alcove in some of the singles. The beds and mattresses ensure a good night's sleep.

Organized weekly activities and a bar with dancing provide the entertainment. The hotel's restaurants, Gunghoferstüberl, Rösslstube, and Hochzeitsstube, are open from 6pm to midnight in winter and from 6 to 11pm in summer, serving excellently prepared Austrian and international specialties. There's also a garden restaurant in summer.

Kötschachtalstrasse 25, A-5640 Badgastein. © **06434/25160.** Fax 06434/251625. www.hoteldorf. com. 80 units. 185€–273€ double; 237€–325€ suite. Rates include half-board. AE, DC, MC, V. Parking 8€–10€. Closed Nov. **Amenities:** 3 restaurants; bar; babysitting; bowling alley; fitness center; laundry service; dry cleaning; lounge; massage; outdoor heated pool; indoor heated thermal pool; sauna; 2 tennis courts; room service; nonsmoking rooms. *In room:* TV, minibar, hairdryer, safe, Wi-Fi.

Hotel Weismayr ★ Situated prominently in the town center between the congress hall and the casino, the Hotel Weismayr has been one of the leading hotels in the Gastein Valley since 1832. With the Alps literally in your backyard, this hotel makes an ideal starting point for outdoor activities in the valley: Golfing, horseback riding, skiing, swimming, hiking, climbing, relaxing, and more. At this cozy abode, rooms are well furnished with especially good beds. Parasols and plants dot the terrace cafe, and the elegant, high-ceilinged dining room is beautifully decorated. Austrian and international dishes are prepared with the freshest ingredients.

Franz-Josef-Strasse 6, A-5640 Badgastein. © **06434/2594.** Fax 06434/259414. www.weismayr.com. 89 units. Winter 210€–280€ double; 225€–300€ suite for 2; summer 110€–142€ double, 121€–145€ suite for 2. Rates include half-board. AE, DC, MC, V. Parking 10€. **Amenities:** Restaurant; bar; cafe; indoor heated pool; fitness center; sauna; beauty treatments; room service; massage; babysitting; laundry service; dry cleaning. *In room:* TV, minibar, hairdryer, safe, Wi-Fi.

MODERATE

Hotel & Spa Haus Hirt ★ Originally built in 1930 and completely renovated in 1997, this hotel retains touches of folkloric and old-fashioned charm that some newer hotels have a hard time matching. It's a 20-minute walk downhill from the center of town. All rooms have comfortable furnishings and neatly maintained bathrooms with tub/shower combinations. There's a bar, sweeping views over the Gastein Valley, and a sense of family-run thrift and virtue, thanks to the on-site presence of the owners. The hotel's cozily paneled dining room serves Austrian specialties that taste particularly good after a day in the great outdoors. There's even a sunny, wind-sheltered terrace that attracts many sunbathers.

Kaiserhofstrasse 14, A-5640 Badgastein. © **06434/2797.** Fax 06434/279748. www.haus-hirt.com. 30 units. Winter 174€–318€ double, 246€–376€ suite; summer 136€–254€ double, 216€–322€ suite. Rates include half-board. AE, MC, V. Closed mid-Oct to Nov and mid-Apr to May. Parking 7€. **Amenities:** Restaurant; bar; babysitting; fitness center; games room; laundry service; dry cleaning; massage; indoor heated pool; nonsmoking rooms; room service; sauna; sun beds. *In room:* TV, hairdryer, minibar, safe, Wi-Fi.

Hotel Wildbad 🔑 With its dark-yellow facade, big windows, and prominent balconies, Hotel Wildbad, in the center of the village near the indoor thermal pools and the ski lifts, stands out from the buildings around it. Renovated in 2008, the medium-size rooms have a fresh degree of comfort. Most offer panoramic valley views; some have a sitting area. There's also a terrace sun deck with chaise longues and cafe tables. Gerhard Hörtnagl, owner and manager, sees to it that excellent food is provided, with a superb salad bar and a buffet breakfast.

K. H. Waggerlstrasse 20, A-5640 Badgastein. ⓒ **06434/3761.** Fax 06434/376170. www.hotel-wildbad. com. 40 units. Winter 250€–360€ double; summer 160€–260€ double. Rates include half-board. MC, V. **Amenities:** Restaurant; bar; lounge; babysitting; fitness center; 18-hole golf course; laundry service; dry cleaning; massage; nonsmoking rooms; rooms for those w/limited mobility; room service; sauna; spa. *In room:* TV, hairdryer, minibar, safe, Wi-Fi.

Kurhotel Miramonte On the landscaped slope above town, the Miramonte offers a panoramic view of the valley. A big terrace with sun umbrellas provides a nice spot to sit and relax, whereas the comfortable and traditionally furnished rooms make for a snug retreat. Although the hotel dates from the 1950s, its accommodations have been renovated many times. The public areas are elegant yet simple.

Reitlpromenade 3, A-5640 Badgastein. ⓒ **06434/2577.** Fax 06434/25789. www.hotelmiramonte.com. 36 units. 104€–240€ per person. Rates include half-board. AE, DC, MC, V. Parking 4€. Closed Nov–Dec 7. **Amenities:** Restaurant; bar; babysitting; fitness room; Jacuzzi; laundry service; dry cleaning; massage; breakfast-only room service; sauna. *In room:* TV, hairdryer, minibar, safe, Wi-Fi.

INEXPENSIVE

Alpenblick ☺ The charms of this well-managed hotel are especially obvious in summer, when a garden with a small *kneipe* (pub) and lots of flowing water and flowering shrubs make it an alpine idyll. And, in winter, guests can ski almost to the building's front door. Its core, built around 1900, continued to grow with enlargements and renovations. This chalet has a side wing containing comfortable rooms with balconies and big windows offering mountain views. Beds are good, and the bathrooms, although tiny, are tidily kept. Well-prepared and rather hearty meals are served in the timbered and beamed dining room. In summer, a children's playground with a trampoline is featured.

Kötschachtalerstrasse 17, A-5640 Badgastein. ⓒ **06434/2062-0.** Fax 06434/206258. www. alpenblick-gastein.at. 38 units. Winter 102€–144€ per person; summer 92€–132€ per person. Rates include half-board. AE, MC, V. Closed mid-Oct to early Dec. **Amenities:** Restaurant; bar; outdoor pool; fitness center; sauna; room service; babysitting; laundry service; dry-cleaning. *In room:* TV, hairdryer, Wi-Fi.

Hotel Mozart ⚑ This unusual hotel, designed in the 19th century, has a long veranda on the ground floor and a gabled mansard roof. Inside, beautifully patterned oriental rugs cover the floor of the wood-paneled lobby area, and crystal chandeliers hang from the detailed plaster ceiling. All the comfortably furnished rooms have private, immaculate bathrooms, in addition to the thermally heated baths on each floor. Rooms aren't large, but the beds are comfortable and housekeeping is first-rate. Both traditional and innovative cuisine is served in the hotel's restaurant, the Mozartstuben.

Kaiser-Franz-Josef-Strasse 25, A-5640 Badgastein. ⓒ **06434/26860.** Fax 06434/268662. www. hotelmozart.at. 70 units. Winter 80€–108€ double; off-season 70€–92€ double. Rates include breakfast. DC, MC, V. **Amenities:** Restaurant; bar; fitness center; sauna; Jacuzzi; nonsmoking rooms; rooms for those w/limited mobility. *In room:* TV, Wi-Fi.

Villa Hubertus ⚑ Unpretentious and evocative of the final days of the Habsburgs, this two-star hotel, a 5-minute walk from the center of town, was built as a Jugendstil-inspired villa in 1908. Two rooms have private balconies; the others are simple but comfortably outfitted. The on-site restaurant is open only to residents. The room used for breakfast and resident dinners is especially noteworthy, as it is pure Jugendstil in design with an authentic turn-of-the-20th-century decor. The venue is small scale, family oriented, and kindly.

Kaiser-Franz-Josef-Strasse 24, A-5640 Badgastein. ℂ/Fax **06434/2607.** 6 units. Winter 92€–128€ double with half-board; summer 60€–69€ double. Rates include breakfast. No credit cards. **Amenities:** Winter restaurant; breakfast room; lounge.

After Dark in Badgastein

Badgastein is a hotspot at night as well, with cabaret, theater, folk events, and other activities. The center of nightlife in the winter and summer seasons—and the place to be seen—is the **Casino Badgastein** (ℂ **06434/2465**). You can play roulette, baccarat, poker, and blackjack; you'll need your passport and must be at least 18. The entrance fee is 21€, which entitles you to 25€ worth of chips. The casino is open Christmas through April 2 and early July through mid-September daily from 7pm to 2am.

At **Tanzlokal Schialm,** Böcksteiner Bundesstrasse 27 (ℂ **06434/2055;** www.schafflinger.at/schialm.php), by the light of a blazing open fireplace, young and old enjoy dance music and the romantic and very rustic-looking alpine atmosphere of this popular beer and dance hall. Nightly themes range from a cheese-and-knockwurst evening (Mon) to a recreation of a *Heurige,* complete with Austrian wines and music (Wed), to a candlelit dance (Sat). Drinks begin at 5.50€, and full meals are served daily from 6 to 9pm.

If you want more conventional dancing, head for the **Elisabethpark** (see "Where to Stay & Eat," above). This elegant nightspot is the place to go if you want to get dressed up.

THE PINZGAU

The Pinzgau section of Land Salzburg stretches east from the Gerlos Pass to the Gastein Valley, with the Salzach River flowing through. To the south lies Hohe Tauern, and to the north is the Kitzbühel alpine region.

For visitors, skiing is the reason to come. The renowned resorts of **Saalbach** and **Hinterglemm** lie at the end of a valley ringed by a horseshoe of mountains dotted with more than 40 ski lifts. The chief resort of the Pinzgau is **Zell am See** (see later in this chapter). Another outstanding ski resort in the Upper Pinzgau region is **Kaprun.** The **Grossglockner Road** also begins in Pinzgau (see later in this chapter).

Lofer ★

Ideally situated among forests, valleys, and mountain rivers is the old market town of Lofer. This is a good base for exploring much of Land Salzburg, including Salzburg itself, the Grossglockner alpine road, Krimml Falls, the dams at Kaprun, Kitzbühel, and Innsbruck, as well as Chiemsee and Berchtesgaden in Germany. There also happens to be great golfing, with three 18-hole golf courses within an hour's drive.

ESSENTIALS

GETTING THERE The nearest railway stations are at St. Johann in Tyrol and at Saalfelden. From Saalfelden, nine **buses** depart every day for the 39-km (24-mile) trek to the northwest. From St. Johann, 10 buses depart daily for the 43-km (27-mile) ride northeast to Lofer. Note that some bus routes, traversing the strip of Germany that juts into Austria at this point, travel directly from Salzburg's railway station about five times a day; the trip takes about an hour. If you choose this route, you might be asked to show your passport.

Motorists can take the A1 southwest of Salzburg into Germany; take Route 1 until it turns into Route 178 at the Austrian border.

EXPLORING LOFER

Lofer has a **Bauerntheater (Peasant Theater)** and a Gothic-style **Pfarrkirche (Parish Church),** whose tower dominates the town with its two onion-shape domes. Many houses are decorated with oriels, an architectural style inspired by nearby Bavaria.

Lofer doubles as a health resort and a ski center, offering hospitality, tradition, and rural charm. It's known for its peat-water and mud baths, as well as its Kneipp cures. The area around Lofer is nice for walking or hiking in both summer and winter. Sports facilities include a tennis court, skating rink, miniature golf course, and enclosed swimming pool.

A ski school operates here, and there are nine T-bar lifts. A chairlift will deliver you to the Sonnegg-Loderbühel at 1,003m (3,291 ft.) and the upper station of the Loferer Alm at 1,403m (4,603 ft.). Rising in the background of the town are the Loferer Steinberge and the Reiter Steinberge.

You can visit **Lamprechtshöhle** (✆ 06582/8343; www.naturgewalten.at), Austria's deepest water-bearing cave, on the road from Lofer to Weissbach (Rte. 311), about 60km (37 miles) from Salzburg by bus. A guided tour takes about 40 minutes. The cavern is open daily 8:30am to 7pm, and 5pm on weekends; admission is 3.60€ for adults and 1.80€ for children. It's closed from November through April.

WHERE TO STAY & EAT

Hotel St. Hubertus ★★   This hotel, the largest and best in Lofer, was built in the mid-1960s. The chalet windows provide great views over the Saalach River and the Loferer Steinberge mountain ranges. Rooms are well furnished, and most have balconies. The doubles are large enough to be rented as triples, and the suites (without kitchen) are big enough to house two to four guests. In summer, guests enjoy the garden with its sunny terrace. About a 5-minute walk from the village center and the cableways, it's near several walking paths and promenades. For cross-country skiers, tracks begin only 2 minutes from the hotel. Half-board includes a buffet breakfast followed that evening by a four-course meal with a large choice of desserts and cheeses. The hotel bar provides a cozy retreat.

Grisseman, A-5090 Lofer 180. ✆ **06588/8266.** Fax 06588/7465. www.hubertus-lofer.net. 56 units. Winter 132€ double; off-season 110€ double. Rates include half-board. AE, DC, MC, V. Closed late Apr to mid-May and Nov 1 to mid-Dec. **Amenities:** Dining room; bar; laundry service; dry cleaning; massage; nonsmoking rooms; breakfast-only room service; indoor heated pool; sauna. *In room:* TV, hairdryer, safe.

St. Martin bei Lofer

This tiny, quaint village, about 2km (1½ miles) south of Lofer, is visited for its pilgrimage church, a large baroque edifice called **Maria Kirchenthal.** The building was designed by the renowned baroque master J. B. Fischer von Erlach. The church's museum displays votive pictures from the 17th to the 19th centuries. About 1.5km (1 mile) west of the village, the church is reached by a toll road open only in summer, or by an hour's walk from Lofer.

Vorderkaser Gorge (✆ 06588/8527, the tourist office in St. Martin bei Lofer, www.naturgewalten.at) can be visited from St. Martin. A 2.5-km (1½-mile) road connects the gorge with the Mittelpinzgau road near the Vorderkaser bus stop. It's open to the public from the second weekend in May to October 20 daily from 10am to 5pm, and 9:30am to 6pm in July and August. Admission is 3.50€ for adults and 2€ for children.

Self-catering is a good idea here, especially with 10 grills at your disposal.

ESSENTIALS

GETTING THERE Getting to St. Martin is similar to getting to Lofer. The **buses** that originate in Saalfelden and Salzburg also stop in St. Martin. If you take a bus in St. Johann, however, you'll have to transfer to another bus in Lofer or call a taxi for the short continuation to St. Martin. If you're **driving,** continue south of Lofer along Route 311.

Saalbach & Hinterglemm ★

This internationally known tourist resort, at an elevation of 1,003m (3,291 ft.), emphasizes relaxation, recreation, and sports—both summer and winter. It's located 64km (40 miles) southwest of Salzburg, 399km (248 miles) southwest of Vienna, and 185km (115 miles) southwest of Linz.

Saalbach has seen rapid growth as a winter-sports resort in recent years. Hinterglemm, its twin, is about an 8-minute drive west on an unclassified road that's signposted at the head of the valley. Often the region is spoken of as a unit—the Saalbach–Hinterglemm ski area, and the resorts are linked by a lift system and ski bus. Several lifts are near the center of town, including one cable car big enough to carry 100 passengers, along with 40 tows and chairlifts that provide access to a variety of well-groomed slopes and deep-powder runs. The major lift, the Schattberg cableway, leaves from the heart of Saalbach, taking skiers to the top station (2,001m/6,565 ft.), where an excellent restaurant boasts a sunny terrace with a panoramic view. Of course, summer visitors can also take the cableway to enjoy the scenery.

The Glenntal Ski Pass, valid for the 60 lifts and the 193km (120 miles) of downhill runs of the Obertauern region (Saalbach, Hinterglemm, and Leogang), costs 42.50€ for 1 day, 117.70€ for 3 days, and 205.50€ for 6 days. It's sold at the bottom of the biggest ski lift as well as the **Schi-Pass Kassenbüro** on Dorfstrasse (© 06541/6271).

The Saalbach–Hinterglemm visitors' racing course is open Tuesday through Sunday from 10am to noon and 2 to 4pm, staging slalom, giant slalom, and parallel slalom. Many cross-country ski tracks also start from here. Both resorts have ski schools and provide ski-circus runs. In the winter, tobogganing is also popular, as are ski-bobbing, sleigh rides, and curling.

From spring until late in the autumn, you can take quiet walks or extended hikes along some 257km (160 miles) of well-laid-out footpaths, as well as go mountain climbing, horseback riding, or bowling, or play minigolf and tennis. A nearby lake is great for swimming and sailing. A kindergarten caters exclusively to tourist children.

Saalbach can also be a good base for exploring the neighboring resorts of Kaprun and Zell am See (see below).

ESSENTIALS

GETTING THERE The nearest **railway** line is at Zell am See (see below). Here, you'll have to transfer to one of the many **buses** that travel up the winding valley road. Buses depart from the railway station at Zell am See about every hour throughout the day, stopping first at Saalbach (trip time: 30 min.) and then continuing on to Hinterglemm (40 min.).

If you're **driving,** follow the route from Salzburg to Lofer (see above), and then cut south at the junction with Route 311.

VISITOR INFORMATION The **tourist office** (© 06541/680068; www. saalbach.com) is in the center of Saalbach but also provides information for Hinterglemm. It's open in winter Monday to Saturday 9am to 6pm, and Sunday 9am to noon; in summer Monday to Friday 8:15am to noon and 1:30 to 6pm, Saturday 8:15am to noon and 3 to 6pm, Sunday 9am to noon.

WHERE TO STAY & EAT

Most visitors dine at their hotels.

Expensive

Alpenhotel Saalbach ★   Built in 1968, this fairly large chalet-style hotel is renovated in part every 2 years. Its convenient location in the center of Saalbach is near the cable car, chairlifts, and tennis courts. The cozy, well-furnished interior includes a collection of country artifacts and several fireplaces. Your host, the Thomas family, rents comfortable rooms plus a series of suites or apartments sleeping two to six guests, suitable for extended stays. Those opening onto private balconies are the most requested.

Part of the hotel's draw is that it's a major gathering spot for the whole resort. It has five Austrian-style *Stuben*, or taverns serving hearty local cuisine to half-boarders, and a trio of alternative restaurants: The Pipamex, the Vitrine, and La Trattoria. La Trattoria, for example, is both an Italian pizzeria and a Spanish bodega. The most popular after-dark diversion is the Arena, which is also a nightclub.

Dorfstrasse 212, A-5753 Saalbach. ✆ **06541/6666.** Fax 06541/6666888. www.alpenhotel.at. 96 units. Winter 146€–316€ double, 230€–570€ suite; summer 98€–200€ double, 198€–276€ suite. Rates include half-board. AE, DC, MC, V. Parking 11€. Closed mid-Apr to mid-May and mid-Oct to late Dec. **Amenities:** 3 restaurants; 5 taverns and bars; babysitting; bike rentals; health club; Jacuzzi; laundry service; dry cleaning; indoor heated pool; room service; sauna. *In room:* TV, hairdryer, minibar, safe, Wi-Fi.

Eva Village Hotel ★★   The Unterkofler family has taken over this popular hotel—once called the Ingonda—and improved it considerably, pampering guests as never before. This hotel restaurant exudes an aura of well-established, even antique, prosperity. The hotel enjoys a status as the finest of the four-star hotels in town. In the center of Saalbach in a traffic-free zone, it is first class all the way. The hotel contains well-furnished rooms, each with a balcony, armchairs, and desk space.

Skiers appreciate the hotel's proximity to the village's three ski lifts, a 1-minute trek from the entrance on skis. In the well-recommended restaurant, guests enjoy such specialties as scampi flambéed in gin, filet of beef jambalaya, tender cuts of well-seasoned beef, and homemade strudels. If you're dropping in to dine in season, reserve a table. Aside from Eva's five-star restaurant, the social center is a rambling pine-covered bar with an intricately crafted wood ceiling and comfortable leather chairs.

Dorfstrasse 218, A-5753 Saalbach. ✆ **06541/6262-0.** Fax 06541/626262. www.evahotels.at. 73 units. Winter 178€–374€ double, 310€–490€ suite; off-season 120€–174€ double, 136€–234€ suite. Rates include half-board. AE, DC, MC, V. Parking 9.80€ in winter, free in summer. Closed Oct to mid-Dec. **Amenities:** Restaurant; bar; babysitting; indoor heated pool; fitness center; Jacuzzi; massage; room service; rooms for those w/limited mobility; sauna; solarium. *In room:* TV, hairdryer, minibar, safe, Wi-Fi.

Hotel Glemmtalerhof   This chalet-style hotel rises six stories above the village's central street. Built in 1951, it was partially rebuilt in 1992. The street level contains a few small shops. Inside, the hotel offers cozy public areas, some with fireplaces. There are public tennis courts only a few buildings away. Rooms, covered with mellow pine and invitingly lit, are medium-size and exceedingly comfortable. A *Tagesmenu* (daily menu) is offered at lunch and dinner. The hotel staff can also organize mountain or biking excursions for you.

Dorfstrasse 150, A-5754 Hinterglemm. ✆ **06541/7135.** Fax 06541/713563. www.glemmtalerhof.at. 85 units. Winter 138€–218€ double; summer 102€–150€ double. Rates include half-board. AE, DC, MC, V.

Parking 8€. Closed late Apr–May 15 and Nov 1–Dec 15. **Amenities:** Restaurant; 3 bars; cafe; nightclub; babysitting; fitness center; laundry service; dry cleaning; massage; indoor heated pool; 3 tennis courts (nearby); room service; sauna. *In room:* TV, hairdryer, safe, Wi-Fi.

Moderate

Gasthof Unterwirt   Built in 1973 as a modern interpretation of a traditional chalet, this pleasant and relaxed establishment, with its rustic decor of ceiling beams and ceramic tile stoves, is owned by the Kröll family. Rooms range from small to medium and have traditional alpine furnishings. Bathrooms are equipped with tub/shower combinations and are beautifully maintained. The international and regional cuisine is hearty and plentiful.

Unterdorf 31, A-5753 Saalbach. 🕐 **06541/6274.** Fax 06541/627455. www.saalbach-unterwirt.at. 53 units. Winter 164€–224€ double; summer 102€–110€ double. Rates include half-board. MC, V. Closed Mar 30–early May and Nov 1–Dec 10. **Amenities:** Restaurant; bar; laundry service; dry cleaning; sauna; steam bath. *In room:* TV, hairdryer, Wi-Fi.

Hotel Haus Wolf   If you're interested in ski lessons, this might be an ideal place to stay, since the local ski school is headquartered here. The hotel, right beside the Reiterkogel cable car, has wooden balconies and a first-floor sun terrace. In winter, fires burn beneath copper-sheathed chimneys, and guests congregate in one of the several bars or restaurants. A smaller annex provides comfortable but less-inspired accommodations. For a special experience (and a pretty penny), hotel owner and pilot Thomas Wolf will pick you up from Salzburg or Munich... by helicopter.

Reiterkogelweg 169, A-5754 Hinterglemm. 🕐 **06541/6346.** Fax 06541/634669. www.wolf-hotels.at. 45 units. 188€ double; 228€ suite. Rates include half-board. MC, V. Closed Apr 15–May 15 and Oct 15–Dec 20. **Amenities:** Restaurant; bar; indoor heated pool; sauna; babysitting; laundry service; dry cleaning. *In room:* TV, minibar, hairdryer, safe.

Hotel Kristiana ★ 🔶   A local favorite since it was built in 1979, this well-managed hotel lies a short walk uphill from the village center. Balconies adorn its facade, and in one corner, just above the sun terrace, an artist has executed a series of etched panels depicting the seasons. The interior is a rustic fantasy of carved beams and well-polished paneling, open fireplaces, and comfortable, well-planned rooms, most of which have fine views and individual character. Owner Johann Breitfuss and his family serve tasty meals to hotel guests only and maintain a pleasant bar.

Oberdorf 40, A-5753 Saalbach. 🕐 **06541/6253.** Fax 06541/625399. www.kristiana.at. 34 units. Winter 174€–274€ double; summer 136€–248€ double. Rates include half-board. MC, V. Closed Apr–May 15 and Oct–Dec 10. **Amenities:** Restaurant; bar and wine cellar; sauna; room service; babysitting. *In room:* TV, hairdryer, safe, Wi-Fi.

THE RESORTS AFTER DARK

Saalbach is one of the liveliest centers in Land Salzburg for nightlife. The after-skiing crowd shuttles back and forth between Saalbach and Hinterglemm, and after a few drinks, the resorts seem to merge into one.

   Hexenhäusl, Zwolferkogelbahnweg 122 (🕐 **06541/6334;** www.hex.at), is one of the busiest and most consistently popular après-ski venues in Hinterglemm. Positioned at the bottom of the Zwolferkogelbahn gondola, it combines the functions of a bar, pub, and cafe into a rowdy, sudsy, beery, schnapps-permeated mountain hut. Cozy, dark, candlelit, and moderately claustrophobic, it's a place where English and French skiers mingle with locals, some of whom aren't particularly interested in skiing at all. Beer sells for 2.50€ to 6€; snacks such as strudels, pizzas, and baguettes sell for 1.75€ to 5.50€. You'll recognize the place by the carved effigies of *Hexen* (witches) that decorate the outside and inside of this folkloric but very hip place. From May to October, it's open Tuesday to Saturday 3pm to 6am; November to April it's open daily 3pm to 6am—so late that anyone who actually remains on-site till closing will probably not venture onto the ski slopes the following day.

Since its opening in the 1950s, Hotel Glemmtalerhof (see above) has always maintained an active nightlife for both travelers and local residents in its cellar. The folksy **Glemmerkeller Nightclub** hosts a series of live bands performing everything from Bavarian oompah music to more modern (and highly danceable) tunes. It's open every night 9pm to 3am, although during ski season it's also open every afternoon for post-slopes revelry from 4 to 6pm. In winter, live dance music is usually featured at **Aprèsworld** in the Knappenhof Hotel, Dorfstrasse 140, Hinterglemm (© **06541/ 6497**), while the adjacent dance club plays recorded tunes. Sometimes Tyrolean music is interspersed with more modern sounds. Grilled specialties are offered as well as Wiener schnitzel, pizza, and Italian food, with meals beginning at 10€. The cover charge of 8€ includes your first drink. Open daily from 9pm to 4am; closed in October.

Saalfelden ★

An old market town lying in a broad valley formed by the Saalbach River, Saalfelden is set against a background of towering mountains in the Middle Pinzgau, a good base for exploring the **Steinernes Meer,** or Sea of Stone, a limestone plateau with underground rivers and caverns that the Austrian government has made a nature preserve. Saalfelden lies 64km (40 miles) south of Salzburg and 399km (248 miles) southwest of Vienna.

Although Saalfelden is primarily a summer resort, winter-sports areas in the mountains are within easy reach. The town has a **Pfarrkirche (Parish Church)** with a gothic crypt beneath the choir and a late-Gothic triptych in the presbytery.

At **Ritzen Castle** (© **06582/72759;** www.museum-saalfelden.at), which dates from 1563, the Heimatmuseum is devoted to life in the Pinzgau region. Here you'll see a rich collection of Christmas cribs by artist Alexander "Xandl" Schläffer. Another hall displays pictures and ecclesiastic art along with exhibits tracing the geology of Saalfelden, a peasant's room from the 1700s, an open-hearth kitchen, native handicrafts, and various documents on the history of the area. Admission is 4.20€ for adults; free for children under 18. It's open in July, August, and September Tuesday to Sunday from 11am to 7pm; off-season, it's open Wednesday, Saturday, and Sunday from 2 to 5pm and is closed in March, April, and November.

ESSENTIALS

GETTING THERE Saalfelden is a major stop on express and local trains from both Innsbruck and Salzburg. **Trains** from Innsbruck are usually direct, while trains from Salzburg sometimes require a change in Schwarzach–St. Veit. With transfers included, the trip from both cities to Saalfelden takes about 1⅔ hours. Trains arrive there about once an hour throughout the day. For train information, call © **05/1717,** or visit **www.oebb.at**.

Although Saalfelden is the transfer point for many **bus** routes heading into the surrounding mountains, few visitors would consider reaching Saalfelden by bus from any large Austrian city, with the possible exception of Salzburg. These buses depart from Salzburg's main railway station about six times a day, making many stops en route (trip time: about 95 min.).

Driving from Zell am See, head north along Route 311. From Salzburg, follow directions to Lofer (see above), continuing south on Route 311.

VISITOR INFORMATION The **tourist office** is at Bahnhofstrasse 10 (✆ **06582/70660;** www.leogang-saalfelden.at). It's open in winter Monday to Friday 8am to 5pm, and Saturday from 9am to noon; in summer Monday to Friday from 8am to 6pm, Saturday from 9am to noon.

WHERE TO STAY & EAT

Hotel Gasthof Hindenburg ★★ Set in the heart of Saalfelden, this hotel is one of the oldest in the region, with foundations and a reputation for hospitality that date back more than 500 years, and an alpine design that looks a lot older than the 1992 renovation that transformed it into the hip-roofed, many-gabled design you'll see today. Rooms are cozily outfitted with mostly contemporary furniture. There's a trio of restaurants, the most formal of which is the richly paneled Gaststube. An affordable range of fixed-price lunch meals is available and dinner may include brook trout filet with pumpkin cubes, leg of lamb in thyme and garlic sauce, or venison goulash. Overall, it's a worthy four-star choice with as many luxuries and conveniences as any of its competitors in Saalfelden.

Bahnhofstrasse 6, A-5760 Saalfelden. ✆ **06582/7930.** Fax 06582/79378. www.hotel-hindenburg.at. 70 units. 156€–220€ double. Rates include half-board. AE, DC, MC, V. **Amenities:** 3 restaurants; bar; babysitting; laundry service; dry cleaning; sauna; room service; solarium. *In room:* TV, minibar, hairdryer, safe, Wi-Fi.

Kaprun & Its Dams

A summer resort and a winter ski center, Kaprun is known for its high glacier skiing. The town is hardly the most attractive or the most atmospheric in Land Salzburg, but serious skiers don't seem to mind.

ESSENTIALS

GETTING THERE The nearest railway station is in Zell am See, 8km (5 miles) north. From here, about 14 **buses** a day depart for the 15-minute uphill run to Kaprun. (**Note:** Don't confuse the village of Kaprun with the more southerly and much more isolated ski hamlet of Kaprun Heidnische Kirche, which requires an additional transfer.) **Motorists** in Zell am See should head west on Route 168 to Fürth, at which point they can cut south on an unclassified road to Kaprun.

VISITOR INFORMATION The **tourist office** (✆ **06547/8643**) is in the town center. Open Monday to Friday 9am to 6pm, Saturday 9am to noon, and Sunday 2 to 6pm.

EXPLORING THE VALLEY OF KAPRUN

The name "Kaprun" conjures up imagery of stunning mountain scenery and powerful dams that display mankind's engineering prowess. Yet, the name also stands as a solemn reminder of tragedy that struck the otherwise serene valley in November 2000, when 155 travelers perished in a fire in the former funicular tunnel leading toward the Kitzsteinhorn. A long memorial made of steel and glass opposite the Gletscherbahn entrance honors the victims.

An ascent to the **Kitzsteinhorn** (2,931m/9,616 ft.) can be somewhat complicated, involving postal buses and cableways, but it's equally rewarding. Always have your routes outlined at the tourist office with a detailed map before you set forth. An English-speaking staff member can provide you with the most up-to-date information on hours, costs, types of services available at the time of your visit, and weather conditions. After mid-October, tours to the valley of the dams may not be possible. However, a visit to the Kitzsteinhorn is an attraction in all seasons.

To reach the Kitzsteinhorn, you can take a series of **Gletscherbahn** (☏ 06547/8700) cable cars—either the two *Gletscherjets* carrying 24 and 15 people, or the combination *Panoramabahn* and *Langweidbahn* for 8 and 4 people respectively—to the Restaurant Alpincenter (2,446m/8,025 ft.), where you can enjoy lunch with a view halfway up Kitzsteinhorn. At Alpincenter, change to a cable car, which swings west via the highest cable car supports in the world (113m/373 ft.), coming to a stop near the summit of the Kitzsteinhorn.

A little below the summit, you'll find the 305-m (1,001-ft.) **Panoramatunnel** (☏ 06547/86210) cut through the mountain and opening onto an incredible view of Nationalpark Hohe Tauern. On clear days, you'll be able to see Grossglockner, the highest peak in Austria, at 3,764m (12,349 ft.). Try the Aussichtsrestaurant (talk about dining with a view!), or for snow in summer, you can take a short cable car down to the glacier. Purchase a day ticket for both the cable railway and the glacier lift; 42€ for adults and 21€ for children under 15. It's open daily from 8am to 4pm.

THE DAMS

The **Kapruner Tal** ★, or the Valley of Kaprun, is visited in summer for its dams, one of the more dramatic alpine sights. Constructed in tiers, the dams were originally built as part of the U.S.-financed Marshall Plan. Experts from all over the world come here to study these hydroelectric constructions, which are brilliant feats of engineering.

Visit the hydroelectric plant, Turbinenhaus, inside the **Tauernkraftwerke** (☏ 06547/7151527). Its shafts, tunnels, turbines, and bulwarks are an interesting change of pace for most visitors. A small museum, filled with technical drawings and photographs, conveys the magnitude of the project.

If you want to explore the region and see how the dams manage to hold back up to 19 billion gallons of alpine water, the staff at Kaprun's tourist information office offers a self-guided full-day tour for 18€ that encompasses overviews of the three lakes formed by the dams and transportation. The ascent up to the dams, including the **Limbergsperre,** the **Moossersperre ★★**, and the **Drossensperre,** is via yellow post buses and a funicular. You can visit daily from 8:10am to 4:45pm from May 27 to October 9, depending on weather conditions.

WHERE TO STAY & EAT

Hotel Orgler ☺   A cream-colored house in the middle of the village and set apart from its neighbors, the Hotel Orgler offers peace, quiet, and a rustic interior of high ceilings, heavy beams, and chalet furniture. Each room has a balcony and bath. Apartments with extra beds are available for families. The hotel's dining room and restaurant are furnished in traditional alpine style, as are the cozy lounges and the bar with an open fireplace.

Schlossstrasse 1, A-5710 Kaprun. ☏ **06547/8205.** Fax 06547/7567. www.hotel-orgler.at. 37 units. Winter 162€–272€ double, 252€–322€ suite; summer 122€–154€ double, 70€–84€ per person apt. Rates include half-board. DC, MC, V. Parking 10€. **Amenities:** Restaurant; bar; babysitting; fitness center; 36-hole golf course; Jacuzzi; laundry service; dry cleaning; room service; sauna; nonsmoking rooms; solarium; tennis court. *In room:* TV, hairdryer, minibar, safe, Wi-Fi.

Sportkristall Kaprun   On the village's outskirts, this large chalet has a sloping roof and flowered balconies. Built in 1977, it has paneled ceilings, big windows, and spacious public areas. The good-size rooms are modern and comfortable, and most have a balcony. Bathrooms are carefully maintained and equipped mostly with tub/shower combinations. There's a restaurant for half-board diners, plus a pizzeria.

Schlossstrasse 32, A-5710 Kaprun. © **06547/71340.** Fax 06547/713450. www.sport-kristall.at. 60 units. 140€–240€ double. Rates include half-board. AE, MC, V. Take the cable lift to the stations at the southern exit of Kaprun. **Amenities:** Restaurant; bar; babysitting; fitness center; games room; laundry service; dry cleaning; room service; sauna; nonsmoking rooms; solarium. *In room:* TV, minibar, hairdryer, safe, Wi-Fi.

KAPRUN AFTER DARK

Kaprun has its own relatively modest nightlife, but should you ever get bored, take the shuttle bus over to Zell am See for much more excitement. Nightlife reaches its modest peak in Kaprun on Friday and Saturday nights. On other nights you might like to turn in with a good book or sit and drink around an open fire. Nearly all hotels and pensions welcome outside guests.

Café Baum Bar (© **06547/8216;** www.baumbar.at) is less than 1.5km (1 mile) north of Kaprun's center, far enough from all the hotels that the noisy crowd won't disturb anyone's sleep. Built as an outbuilding for a local cattle farm in the 1930s, this is the largest, most crowded, and most sociable watering hole in town. Although a part of it is devoted to serving pizzas, Wiener schnitzels, pastas, salads, and sandwiches, it's best known as a dance club that thumps every night of the week, summer and winter, from 9pm to 3am. Kitchen hours vary according to demand but usually last to midnight, and while you can walk, management runs minivans between Kaprun's center and the Baum at frequent intervals, although some visitors opt for a midnight walk (or crawl) to and from the site. Pizzas cost 6€ to 10€. The dance club's cover charge is 2€ to 7€, depending on the live act; it's free when there's recorded music. Beer begins at 2€ in the early afternoon but increases in price to 3€ after 9pm.

Krimml

Krimml is the best base for exploring the Krimml Falls. The village is in a heavily forested valley called Krimmler Ache, between the Kitzbühel Alps and the Hohe Tauern. Although it's mostly a summer resort, there's also good skiing at **Gerlosplatte** (1,708m/5,604 ft.), 11km (7 miles) away.

ESSENTIALS

GETTING THERE A local **train,** making more than 30 stops en route, travels from Zell am See to Krimml. Trains depart every hour (trip time: about 90 min.). Contact © **05/1717** (www.oebb.at) for rail information. About a dozen buses depart every day from the railway station at Zell am See for Krimml (trip time: about 75 min.). **Driving** from Zell am See, take Route 168 west to Mittersill, and continue west along Route 165.

VISITOR INFORMATION The **tourist office** (© **06564/7239-0;** www.krimml.at) in the town center is open Monday to Friday 8:30am to noon and 2:30 to 5:30pm, Sunday 8:30 to 10:30am and 4:30 to 6pm. Krimml lies 153km (95 miles) southwest of Salzburg.

KRIMML FALLS ★★★

This village in the far-western extremity of Land Salzburg is visited mainly for the iridescent **Krimmler Wasserfälle (Krimml Falls)** (© **06564/7212**). The highest in Europe, these spectacular falls drop 381m (1,250 ft.) in three stages. They lie to the south of the Gerlos Pass, which connects the Salzach Valley in Land Salzburg to the Siller Valley in the Tyrol.

If you drive here, you can either leave your car at the parking area at the south of the village and walk 30 minutes to the lower falls, or take the Gerlos Pass toll road costing 7.50€ for a day, open from May 1 to September 30. If you don't have a car, you can take one of the frequent buses marked KRIMML from the center of town. Get off at Maustelle Ort, where the path to the falls begins. The falls are open from mid-May to the end of October daily from 8am to 6pm; it costs 1.80€ for adults and .50€ for children.

Visitors should allow about 3½ hours to explore the entire falls area. On a sunny day, try to visit around noon when the falls are at their most dramatic. In summer, the waterfalls are likely to be floodlit on Wednesday nights, depending on weather conditions. Wear good, sturdy shoes and, if you don't want to get sprayed, a raincoat.

After you've checked out the lower falls, if you want to see the second stage, count on another 12-minute walk. From here it's only another 5 minutes to the third and final stage for viewing the cataracts. There are paths leading to two more viewing points. The middle part of the falls can be seen at the sixth and seventh lookouts. At the Bergerblick, you'll have your greatest view of the waterfalls, reached by continuing another 20 minutes from the seventh viewing point. If you want, you can go on to the Schettbrücke (1,464m/4,803 ft.) for a look at the upper cascades. The waterfalls lie under a deep ice layer during the winter.

WHERE TO STAY & EAT

Hotel Klockerhaus ♦   This peaceful two-story chalet has wooden balconies from which you can view the Krimml Falls. Located on the border of the Hohe Tauern National Park, the family hotel has well-furnished lounges. Rooms range from small to medium, each tastefully decorated and with balconies. The kitchen serves Austrian and international specialties.

Wasserfallstrasse 10, A-5743 Krimml. ✆ **06564/7208.** Fax 06564/720846. www.klockerhaus.com. 43 units. Winter 106€–190€ double; summer 88€–98€ double. Rates include breakfast. MC, V. Closed Nov. **Amenities:** Restaurant; lounge; fitness center; Jacuzzi; massage; rooms for those w/limited mobility, sauna. *In room:* TV, hairdryer.

Hotel Krimmlerfälle ☺   Sea-green shutters and wood siding cover the third and fourth floors of this pretty four-story house, built a century ago but renovated many times since. The congenial hosts, the Schöppl family, rent tasteful and comfortable rooms with balconies covered in pink and red flowers in summer. Some rooms are in a less desirable annex nearby, only functionally furnished, but they're still comfortable.

Wasserfallstrasse 42, A-5743 Krimml. ✆ **06564/7203.** Fax 06564/7473. www.krimmlerfaelle.at. 58 units. Winter 145€–190€ double; summer 123€–156€ double. Rates include half-board. AE, DC, MC, V. Closed Oct 19–Dec 12. **Amenities:** Restaurant; bar; lounge; 2 heated pools (1 indoor, 1 outdoor); spa; sauna; children's playrooms; room service; massage; babysitting. *In room:* TV, hairdryer.

THE GROSSGLOCKNER ROAD ★★★

The longest and most splendid alpine highway in Europe, and one of the biggest tourist attractions on the continent, **Grossglocknerstrasse** (Rte. 107) will afford you one of the greatest drives of your life.

The hairpin turns and bends would challenge even Grand Prix drivers. It's believed that this was the same route through the Alps used by the Romans, although this was forgotten until 1930, when engineers building the highway discovered remains of the work their road-building predecessors did some 19 centuries earlier. This engineering feat was finished in 1935. Switzerland and France copied it years later when they built their own alpine highways.

The highway runs for nearly 48km (30 miles), beginning at Bruck an der Grossglocknerstrasse at 757m (2,484 ft.), via Fusch/Grossglocknerstrasse; heading toward Ferleiten, Hochmais, and Fuschertörl, where you can branch off onto Edelweiss-Strasse, going along for about 2km (1½ miles) to the parking area at the **Edelweiss-Spitze** (2,572m/8,438 ft.). The stunning view from here encompasses mountains rising 3,048m (10,000 ft.). This is the best vantage point to take in the tremendous mountain and alpine lakes of the **Hohe Tauern National Park.** Really a massive mountain range, the Hohe Tauern covers 29 towns, 304 separate mountains, and nearly 250 glaciers. At Edelweiss-Spitze is an observation tower, going up to more than 2,577m (8,455 ft.).

Continuing south through the Hochtortunnel, where the highest point is 2,507m (8,225 ft.), one of the interesting detours along the road is to the stone terrace of the **Franz-Josefs-Höhe** ★★★. This aerie is named after the emperor who once had a mansion constructed here in the foothills of the Pasterze Glacier. The stretch from Gletscherstrasse to Franz-Josefs-Höhe (2,370m/7,776 ft.) is some 8km (5 miles) long, branching off near Guttal. This road lies above the Pasterze Glacier, opposite the Grossglockner (3,791m/12,438 ft.). The Pasterze, incidentally, is the largest glacier in the eastern Alps, 9km (5½ miles) long.

If you're traveling in spring and autumn, it might not be possible to take detours to the Edelweiss-Spitze or the Franz-Josefs-Höhe if heavy snow falls. If you do go, avoid arriving around midday. On a sunny day, the place is mobbed. It has an outstanding view of the majestic Grossglockner. From May to September you can descend from Freiwandeck to Pasterze Glacier by funicular. The service is available every hour daily 8am to 4pm.

The remainder of the route leads from Guttal to Heiligenblut (1,301m/4,268 ft.) in Carinthia. In total the actual mountain part of the road stretches for some 22km (14 miles), usually at about 1,983m (6,506 ft.), with a maximum gradient of 12%.

Many visitors opt to drive this spectacular stretch, but because of the high altitudes, the road is passable only from mid-May to mid-November, depending on weather conditions. Always check with some authority about the road conditions before considering such a drive, especially in spring and autumn. The passenger car round-trip toll is 35€ for a 15-day ticket or 28€ for a 1-day ticket collected at either Ferleiten or Heiligenblut.

You can also take a yellow-sided Austrian Postbus from Zell am See. From May to October, the buses depart from in front of the main railway station twice daily at 8:50 and 9:50am. Stopping at about a dozen small villages en route, the buses meander up Grossglockner to its most panoramic point, the Franz-Josefs-Höhe, where passengers can get out and explore for about 2½ hours before boarding the same buses (at 2:45 and 3:45pm, respectively) and returning to Zell am See. A round-trip ticket costs 25€. For information, call either the tourist office in Zell am See (© **06542/7700**) or the local bus station (© **06542/544412**).

ZELL AM SEE ★

389km (242 miles) SW of Vienna; 85km (53 miles) SW of Salzburg

Founded by monks around the middle of the 8th century, the old part of Zell am See lies on the shore of the Zeller See (Lake Zell), under a backdrop of mountains. The Zeller See is a deep glacial lake filled with clear blue alpine water. The town today is the most popular resort in the Middle Pinzgau (see "The Pinzgau," above). Zell is fashionable in both summer and winter, and a good starting point for visits to the Grossglockner.

Essentials

GETTING THERE   Zell am See sits astride the lesser used rail lines carrying passengers between Salzburg and Innsbruck. Most express **trains** between the cities pass through Rosenheim, Germany, before the Austrian junction at Wörgl. Consequently, make sure you're not on the express train, but the slower one offering quite frankly much better scenery. Trains from Salzburg take about 90 minutes and depart about once an hour as well. Frequent connections are also possible to and from Klagenfurt, although a transfer is required at the nearby railway junction of Schwarzach–St. Veit, about 34km (21 miles) to the east. Contact ✆ **05/1717** (www.oebb.at) for rail information.

If you're **driving** from Salzburg, cut south on the A10 to the junction with Route 311, at which point you head west.

VISITOR INFORMATION   The **tourist office** on Bruckner Bundesstrasse (✆ **06542/7700;** www.zellamsee-kaprun.com) is open Monday to Friday 9am to 6pm, Saturday 9am to noon, and Sunday 10am to noon.

What to See & Do

Unlike most resorts in Land Salzburg, Zell am See has some old buildings worth exploring. These include the **Kastnerturm,** or Constable's Tower, the oldest building in town, dating from the 12th century. It was once used as a grain silo. The town's **Pfarrkirche (Parish Church)** is an 11th-century Romanesque structure. Inside is a late-gothic choir from the 16th century. **Castle Rosenberg,** also from the 16th century, was once an elegant residence of the free state of Salzburg, built in the southern Bavarian style. Today it houses the Rathaus (town hall) with a gallery.

The **folklore museum** is in the old tower, the Vogtturm, near the town square. The tower is about 1,200 years old. In the museum, old costumes are displayed, and exhibited artifacts show the traditional way of life in old Land Salzburg. From May to October, the museum is open Monday, Wednesday, and Friday 1:30 to 5:30pm. Admission is 2.80€ for adults and 1.50€ for children aged 6 to 15; family ticket 4.50€.

Winter & Summer Sports

For winter visitors, snow conditions in the Zell area are usually ideal from December to the end of April. Zell am See attracts beginner and intermediate skiers, plus many nonskiers—people who like the bustling life of the winter resort even if they never take to the slopes. Even if skiing isn't your thing, take the chairlift (shoes are fine) for the alpine scenery. Skiing is possible at elevations ranging from 915 to 2,745m (3,002 to 9,006 ft.).

There is a **Zell/Kaprun Ski Pass** (www.zellamsee-kaprun.com) that covers both Zell am See and Kaprun. A 2-day pass costs 80€ and is sold at the tourist office in

Zell am See and often at the lifts. A free shuttle bus runs between the two resorts during the day from late December to mid-April every 15 minutes. If you're coming to Land Salzburg to ski, we recommend purchasing a ski package from your travel agent. A package will include the cost of all lifts and ski passes, and will be more economical than paying for each activity separately.

Sports fans gravitate to the **Kur-und-Sportzentrum,** an arena northwest of the resort housing a mammoth indoor swimming pool as well as saunas and an ice rink (sometimes in cold weather the lake is frozen over).

Zell am See also attracts visitors in the peak summer months. **Lake Zell,** which has been called the cleanest lake in Europe, is warm, maintaining an average temperature of some 70°F (21°C) in summer. The lake is 4km (2½ miles) long and 2km (1 mile) wide. Motorboats can be rented. You can go along a footpath from the town to the bathing station at Seespitz, a half-hour walk.

Going Up the Schmittenhöhe ★★

Schmittenhöhe, at 1,967m (6,453 ft.), towers to the west of Zell am See. There are four different ways to ascend the mountain, with even more options for getting down. In summer, you can climb it in 4 hours, or take the cableway. The view from here is one of the finest in the Kitzbühel Alps, the majestic glacial peaks of the Grossglockner range. You can have lunch at the Berghotel at the upper station. From the west side of Zell am See, you can also take a four-seat cableway to the middle station. From here you can connect with several lifts that will take you to the upper platform. A sun terrace at the upper station is popular in both summer and winter. Don't be surprised to see bare breasts, even in February. It's about 1.5km (1 mile) up Schmittenhöhe. Figure on at least 1¾ hours for your round-trip, plus another 18 minutes by cable car. In summer, service is every half-hour.

You can also take the Sonnalm cableway (entrance near the Schmittenhöhe terminus) to Sonnalm at 1,385m (4,544 ft.). Another restaurant is perched here. From Sonnalm, it's possible to go by chairlift to Sonnkogel (1,836m/6,024 ft.) and by surface lift to Hochmais (1,728m/5,669 ft.). From the eastern part of Lake Zell, you can take the chairlift up to Ronachkopf (1,487m/4,879 ft.).

From Zell am See, you can also take a funicular to Kaprun (see the "Kaprun" section earlier in this chapter), at the foot of the Kitzsteinhorn, for glacier and year-round skiing. In fact, some of the most spectacular excursions possible from Kaprun can be made easily from Zell am See (refer to the "Kaprun" section for more details).

Where to Stay & Eat

EXPENSIVE

Hotel Salzburgerhof ★★   Just a glimpse of the handcrafted interior of this five-star chalet-style hotel near the lake, and you know you're in for a treat. Inside, a fire blazes in an unusual stucco fireplace in the salon. The Holleis family maintains the pleasant outdoor garden with its sun terrace for summer barbecues. Evening programs include dancing, playing the zither, and telling folk tales. There are suites with private saunas and open fireplaces. Rooms are carpeted and well maintained, if lacking in style; they have generous storage space and balconies with a nice view.

The hotel's restaurant serves some of the area's finest regional specialties. A six-course fixed-price menu might include such classic dishes as cream of sauerkraut with smoked-meat dumplings, cream of black salsify (oyster plant) with truffle dumplings, and filet of jack salmon in a potato crust. Many of the chef's best dishes are fish from either the lake or the sea.

Auerspergstrasse 11, A-5700 Zell am See. ☎ **06542/765.** Fax 06542/76566. www.salzburgerhof.at. 70 units. Winter 300€–570€ double, 330€–900€ suite for 2; summer 250€–320€ double, 280€–620€ suite for 2. Rates include half-board. AE, DC, MC, V. Free parking outside. Closed Nov. **Amenities:** Restaurant; bar; babysitting; fitness center; 36-hole golf course; Jacuzzi; laundry service; dry cleaning; massage; indoor heated pool; salon; sauna; room service; nonsmoking rooms; spa. *In room:* TV, hairdryer, minibar, safe, Wi-Fi.

MODERATE

Grand Hotel ★   This is the third "grand hotel" on this site, with the present structure dating from 1986. Based on a late-Victorian model, it's a wedding cake of mansard roofs and cream-colored stonework whose elaborate cornices and moldings are reflected in the cold waters of the lake. Centrally located on its own peninsula, it has a private beach and sun terrace. Although there are other four-star hotels in town of comparable range, this one enjoys the most desirable location, jutting into the lake. Most of the suites are in the main (Grand Hotel) building; the single and double rooms are in a more lackluster annex. Accommodations come in a wide range of sizes and designs, and some have kitchenettes. Recreation instructors offer special programs in parasailing, river rafting, and glacier skiing. The indoor pool has a panoramic view overlooking the lake.

The restaurant offers fresh fish daily; equally appealing is the Imperial, a cozy bar.

Esplanade 4, A-5700 Zell am See. ☎ **06542/788-0.** Fax 06542/788305. www.grandhotel-zellamsee. at. 115 units. Winter 178€–380€ per person double, 310€–480€ per person suite; summer 150€–250€ per person double, 270€–290€ per person suite. Rates include half-board. AE, DC, MC, V. Parking 7€. Closed mid-Oct to mid-Nov and 2 weeks around Easter. **Amenities:** Restaurant; bar; babysitting; fitness room; Jacuzzi; laundry service; dry cleaning; massage; indoor heated pool; sauna; room service. *In room:* TV, hairdryer, minibar, safe, Wi-Fi.

Hotel St. Georg ★ 🏛   Hotel St. Georg, the stylish country hotel of Zell am See, is graced with flowery balconies and curved awnings. The interior has beamed ceilings, antique wrought-iron, and old painted chests. Rooms are medium-size, well kept, and nicely decorated, with bathrooms equipped with tub/shower combinations. The hotel also rents five two-bedroom apartments, a favorite with families. Depending on the season, these apartments rent for 85€ to 160€ per person. Apartments are suitable for up to five guests.

The restaurant has vaulted ceilings and a circular open fireplace. The Austrian cuisine is highly recommended. Try the marinated slices of ox with corn salad and tomato vinaigrette, or perhaps smoked salmon tartar. Main dishes might include medallions of deer in a juniper-cream sauce flavored with cinnamon, or filet of lamb in a thyme sauce with spinach.

Schillerstrasse 32, A-5700 Zell am See. ☎ **06542/768.** Fax 06542/768300. www.stgeorg-hotel.at. 36 units. Winter 178€–296€ double, 209€–319€ suite; off-season 119€–165€ double, 143€–181€ suite. Rates include half-board. AE, DC, MC, V. Free parking. Closed Apr. **Amenities:** Restaurant; bar; babysitting; fitness center; laundry service; dry cleaning; indoor heated pool; sauna; room service. *In room:* TV, hairdryer, minibar, safe, Wi-Fi.

Hotel St. Hubertushof ★ 🛎   This large, sprawling hotel is designed like a collection of balconied chalets clustered into a single unit. The sober, elegant decor attracts many repeat visitors, and the flat-roofed dance bar ranks as one of the area's top nightspots. Run by owner Josef Hollaus, the hotel is located in one of the resort's sunniest spots. The large, comfortable, and rustic rooms are a bit cramped if you have a lot of ski equipment, but they contain fine beds. The menu in the adjoining restaurant includes international specialties as well as a few regional recipes. Meals are well prepared and beautifully served.

Seeuferstrasse 7, Thumersbach, A-5700 Zell am See. ☎ **06542/767.** Fax 06542/76771. www.zellamsee.at/hubertushof. 110 units. Winter 80€–134€ double; summer 78€–116€ double. Rates include half-board. AE, DC, MC, V. Closed mid-Oct to Nov. **Amenities:** Restaurant; bar; sauna. *In room:* TV, Wi-Fi.

Hotel zum Hirschen   Members of the Pacalt family are the congenial, hardworking owners of this balconied hotel with a central location across from the post office. The snug and comfortable rooms are traditionally furnished and bathrooms are moderate in size with spotless housekeeping. Guests can use the golf course for reduced fees.

Restaurant Zum Hirschen has a rustic setting of light-grained paneling. Specialties include fresh white fish from the nearby lake, mountain game, and homemade pâté. There's also creamed chipped veal or entrecote Café de Paris.

Dreifaltigkeitsstrasse 1, A-5700 Zell am See. ☎ **06542/774.** Fax 06542/7740. www.hotel-zum-hirschen.at. 45 units. Winter 168€–220€ double, 210€–300€ suite; off-season 110€–130€ double, 150€–170€ suite. Rates include half-board. MC, V. Parking 8€. Closed mid-Apr to mid-May and mid-Oct to Dec 1. **Amenities:** Restaurant; bar; babysitting; fitness center; laundry service; dry cleaning; massage; indoor heated pool; sauna; room service; solarium; nonsmoking rooms. *In room:* TV, hairdryer, minibar, safe, Wi-Fi.

Schloss Prielau Hotel ★★ 👜   This fairy-tale castle owned by automobile tycoon Dr. Wolfgang Porsche has been restored with its turreted towers intact, and now provides the most elegant accommodations on Lake Zell. Set in a park and completely isolated, the Schloss was built in 1425 and, since then, has been modified and improved over the years. It's not so much of a castle as a country house, and is painted white with red shutters. The bedrooms are furnished beautifully and comfortably, with authentic country pieces and antiques. Fabrics are elegant and tasteful, and some of the rooms are a bit dark because the windows are small. Opposite in a country house is an award-winning restaurant, serving classic Austrian cuisine. The service is top rate, and the welcome is one of the more inviting in the area.

Hofmannsthalstrasse 10, A-5700 Zell am See. ☎ **06542/729110.** Fax 06542/7260955. www.schlosshotels.co.at. 7 units. 360€–520€ double; 480€–720€ suite. Rates include breakfast. Half-board 25€ extra. AE, DC, MC, V. Closed mid-Apr to mid-May and Nov to early Dec. **Amenities:** Restaurant; bar; babysitting; bike rentals; laundry service; dry cleaning; children's playground; sauna; solarium. *In room:* TV, hairdryer, minibar, Wi-Fi.

Zell am See After Dark

Zell am See has one of the liveliest after-ski scenes in Land Salzburg. All the clubs and taverns are very informal and, unlike some other resorts, are unpretentious. In addition to the establishments below, there are countless taverns where you can sit around an open fire and enjoy a cold pint of beer or hot-mulled wine.

The **Hotel Waldhof Keller,** Schmittenstrasse 47 (☎ **06542/775;** www.derwaldhof.at), is a rustic alpine tavern that often has a local musician, attired in lederhosen and red stockings, play for skiers, who like to dance on the small floor. A beer costs 2.95€, and a 4-course supper goes for 15€ to 32€. It's open daily from 7 to 10:30pm; closed April 15 through April 30 and October 15 through December 15.

Gasthof Alpenblick, Alte Landersstrasse 6 (☎ **06542/5433**), is a typical Austrian Bierstüberl in the satellite hamlet of Schüttdorf on the road to Kaprun. Zither music is usually played every evening in winter. There's a restaurant on the premises, popular with hikers in summer and skiers in winter. It serves food daily from noon to 9pm in summer and from noon to 10:30pm in winter. Meals here cost 11€ to 27€, and beer goes for 3.50€. The Gasthof is closed April 5 to May 5 and November 28 to December 28.

THE FLACHGAU

So far, we've been exploring sections of Land Salzburg south and southwest of Salzburg; now we'll introduce you to resorts northeast of Salzburg, on our way to Linz in Upper Austria (see chapter 11). One of the chief attractions of the Flachgau district is **Wolfgangsee (Lake Wolfgang),** which lies mainly in Land Salzburg, although its major center, St. Wolfgang, is in Upper Austria. The best-known lake in the Salzkammergut, the Wolfgangsee, is 10km (6 miles) long and 2km (1¼ miles) wide. The northwestern shores are fairly inaccessible. The major Land Salzburg resort on the lake is St. Gilgen. Many people visit Lake Wolfgang on day trips from Salzburg, as it's within easy commuting distance.

The Flachgau is a relatively flat area, dividing the Austrian province of Styria from Bavaria in Germany. Unlike the other areas of Land Salzburg, discussed above, the Flachgau is primarily a summer resort area for those who enjoy lakeside retreats.

Hof bei Salzburg

About 15 minutes from Salzburg on Lake Fuschl is this resort, once popular with Salzburg aristocrats who came for its private hunting and fishing preserves set among mountains, woods, and alpine waters.

There's a 9-hole golf course here, and you can lazily spend the day fishing for trout on the lake. From here it's easy to explore not only the Fuschlsee, but also the Wolfgangsee and the Mondsee.

Like the suburb of Anif (see chapter 9), Hof bei Salzburg is an ideal spot for traditional accommodations, especially come festival time in August, when hotel rooms are virtually impossible to obtain in Salzburg.

ESSENTIALS

GETTING THERE   There are no railway lines running into Hof bei Salzburg, but **buses** run frequently to and from the nearest railway junctions, at Salzburg and at Bad Ischl. From the railway station at Bad Ischl, about a dozen buses depart every day, each of which stops in Fuschl (trip time: 1 hr.). An equal number of buses depart from the railway station at Salzburg (trip time: 30 min.). If you're **driving,** take Route 158 east of Salzburg for 18km (11 miles). Hof bei Salzburg lies 299km (186 miles) southwest of Vienna.

VISITOR INFORMATION   The **tourist office** at Postplattenstrasse 1 (*©* **06229/ 2249**) is open Tuesday to Friday 9am to 4pm.

WHERE TO STAY & EAT

Gasthof Nussbaumer INTERNATIONAL   The decor of this old-fashioned restaurant is woodsy and folkloric, reflecting the village atmosphere of the surrounding region. But the clientele (thanks to the dormitory-style bedrooms upstairs that house workers for many of the surrounding hotels) is young, energetic, and sometimes after work—a bit raucous. Because of the youthful emphasis, it's likely to be a bit more hip and a bit more "modern" than you'd have expected from a conventional dining room. Menu items include both chicken and pork schnitzels, *Tafelspitz* (boiled beef), fondues, salads, soups, and the kind of rib-sticking fare that hard-working people appreciate in the great outdoors. On the premises is something akin to a singles bar, with rustic-looking accessories and a lot of off-duty, sometimes good-looking, and sometimes hard-drinking wait-staff.

Gitzen 13, A-5322 Hof bei Salzburg. *©* **06229/2275.** Reservations not required. Fixed-price lunch 8€; main courses 8€–15€. MC, V. Kitchen daily 10am–11pm; bar daily 8pm–2am.

Hotel Jagdhof ★★ Sheraton owns and operates this well-managed four-star hotel, in addition to the nearby (and recommended, below) Hotel Schloss Fuschl. Providing less expensive accommodations than those at its grander (five-star) neighbor, it was originally built in the 1500s as a farmhouse and has an authentic style that many Austrian hotels have tried to emulate. Rooms, renovated in 2002, vary in size and design, but each is cozily furnished and inviting with excellent beds. The hotel is well maintained and tasteful, with an accommodating staff and an excellent restaurant. A la carte meals begin at around 14€ to 18€ each. Specialties include pike terrine with green sauce, and a wide choice of fish and game dishes.

A-5322 Hof bei Salzburg. ✆ **06229/23720.** Fax 06229/2553-1531. www.hoteljagdhof-fuschlsee.at. 143 units. 175€–215€ double; from 265€–485€ suite. Rates include breakfast. AE, DC, MC, V. Free parking. **Amenities:** 2 restaurants; bar; babysitting; concierge; fitness center; games room; 9-hole golf course; Jacuzzi; laundry service; dry cleaning; massage; indoor heated pool; room service; nonsmoking rooms; rooms for those w/limited mobility; sauna; spa; tennis court. *In room:* TV, coffeemaker, hairdryer, iron, minibar, safe, Wi-Fi.

Hotel Schloss Fuschl ★★★ The main section of this castle, built in 1450, has a simple facade of unadorned windows. Its former guests have included Jawaharlal Nehru, Eleanor Roosevelt, and Nikita Khrushchev. In World War II, von Ribbentrop selected the Schloss as his headquarters; later, Mussolini came here to meet with Nazi leaders. It was the former hunting lodge of the prince-archbishops of Salzburg, who cultivated the peninsula garden jutting into Lake Fuschl. The interior is decorated with elegant fireplaces, timbered ceilings, stone columns, and handcrafted stonework. The swimming pool is dedicated to the Roman goddess Diana. You can rent either a modern, well-furnished room inside the hotel or a luxurious suite fit for a prince and studded with valuable antiques.

The wonderful food at the Schloss restaurant makes it one of the most popular restaurants in Land Salzburg. Patrons may dine in the winter garden or, in summer, on the terrace overlooking the lake. Inside are several elegant rooms, all decorated with antiques and paintings. The view encompasses much of the lake and sometimes a peek of Salzburg. On the menu are lobster terrine with caviar, summer truffles, and a host of seasonal specialties. Reservations are needed. The dining room is open daily from 12:15 to 2pm and 7 to 9pm.

A-5322 Hof bei Salzburg. ✆ **06229/22530.** Fax 06229/22531531. www.schlossfuschlresort.at. 110 units. 450€ double; from 650€ suite. Rates include breakfast. Half-board 25€ per person extra. AE, DC, MC, V. Free parking. **Amenities:** 2 restaurants; 2 bars; babysitting; fitness center; 9-hole golf course; Jacuzzi; laundry service; dry cleaning; massage; indoor heated pool; room service; nonsmoking rooms; rooms for those w/limited mobility; sauna; spa; tennis court. *In room:* TV, hairdryer, minibar, safe, Wi-Fi.

Fuschl am See

Fuschlsee, the closest lake featured here to Salzburg, lies 31km (19 miles) east of the festival city, reached by Route 158. The fact that there isn't much to do in Fuschl is the very reason it's so crowded with Salzburgers on weekends, who come to relax by the beautiful lake, and eat and drink in the taverns. Lake Fuschl is ringed by woodland, some of which comprises a nature reserve. The lake, lying to the northwest of the larger Lake Wolfgang, is only 4km (2½ miles) long and less than 1.5km (1 mile) wide. Fuschl, strictly a summer resort, is on the eastern strip of the lake, across from Hof bei Salzburg. Fuschl am See is a good alternative to Salzburg, especially worth considering during the festival season.

ESSENTIALS

GETTING THERE There are no railway lines running into Fuschl, but **buses** run frequently to and from the nearest railway junctions, at Salzburg and at Bad Ischl. From the railway station at Bad Ischl, about a dozen buses depart every day, each of which stops in Fuschl (trip time: 1 hr.). An equal number of buses depart from the railway station at Salzburg (trip time: 35 min.).

VISITOR INFORMATION The **tourist office** in the town center (© 06226/ 8250) is open in winter Monday to Friday from 9am to noon and 3 to 5pm; in summer Monday to Friday from 8am to noon and 2 to 6pm, Saturday 8am to noon, Sunday 10am to noon.

WHERE TO STAY

Ebner's Waldhof, Silencehotel ★   Opened in the late 1950s as a small inn, this first-class chalet hotel has expanded to become the largest and one of the most prestigious in the village. The interior has a crackling open fireplace. Opening onto geranium-lined balconies, each of the individually decorated and comfortable rooms is warm and inviting. Guests can sign up for guided nature walks, which often end up at the local tavern.

Seepromenade, A-5330 Fuschl am See. © **06226/8264.** Fax 06226/8644. www.ebners-waldhof.at. 75 units. 208€–284€ double; 284€–461€ suite. Rates include half-board. DC, MC, V. Closed mid-Mar to Apr and Nov–Dec 15. **Amenities:** Restaurant; bar; babysitting; fitness center; laundry service; dry cleaning; massage; 2 heated pools (indoor and outdoor); room service; salon; sauna; nonsmoking rooms; shooting gallery. *In room:* TV, minibar, hairdryer, safe, Wi-Fi.

WHERE TO EAT

Brunnwirt ★ 🍴 AUSTRIAN   Brunnwirt is one of the region's leading restaurants, serving light and well-prepared meals to traveling gourmets from as far away as Vienna. Housed in a 15th-century building thick with atmosphere, the restaurant serves cuisine inspired by regional recipes. The kitchen staff is directed by Frau Brandstätter, who insists on strictly fresh ingredients. Specialties include game dishes, veal, and lamb. The menu changes frequently, and portions are generous. Herr Brandstätter will help you select a wine.

Wolfgangseestrasse 11, A-5330 Fuschl am See. © **0664/2807192.** www.brunnwirt.at. Reservations recommended. Main courses 17€–33€. AE, DC, MC, V. Feb–June and Sept–Dec Tues–Sat 6–11pm, Sun noon–1:30pm and 6–11pm; July–Aug daily noon–2pm and 6–11pm. Closed Jan.

St. Gilgen

This leading lakeside resort lies at the western edge of the Wolfgangsee. It's easily accessible from Salzburg, just 29km (18 miles) away. Once a stronghold of the prince-archbishops of Salzburg, St. Gilgen today is the playground for the city's new aristocracy: The fashionable and wealthy who maintain mountain villas here. Parties at festival time tend to be lavish, and you're lucky if you get an invitation. In summer the resort attracts mainly Austrians and Germans to the indoor swimming pool and bathing beach.

The town has many Mozart connections. In the vicinity of the Rathaus (Town Hall) is the house in which Mozart's mother, Anna Maria Pertl, was born in 1720. After the composer's sister, Nannerl, married Baron Berchtold zu Sonnenberg, she also settled in St. Gilgen. The Mozart Fountain, built in 1927, stands on the main square in front of the Rathaus.

ESSENTIALS

GETTING THERE There are no railway lines running into St. Gilgen, but **buses** (the same line serving Fuschl am See and Hof bei Salzburg) run frequently to and from the nearest railway junctions, stopping in St. Gilgen after a ride from Salzburg (trip time: 50 min.) or Bad Ischl (trip time: 40 min.). **Motorists** should head east of Salzburg for 34km (21 miles) on Route 158.

VISITOR INFORMATION The **tourist office** (© **06227/23480;** www. wolfgangsee.at) in the town center is open Monday to Friday from 9am to 5pm, and Saturday 9am to noon.

WHERE TO STAY & EAT

Parkhotel Billroth ★ 🎁 About 1.5km (1 mile) from the resort, this hotel, standing in its own spacious grounds, was built in the 1890s and vastly revamped and enlarged in the 1960s. One wing was designed in a white-walled villa style, while the main section looks more like an overblown chalet. The view from the rooms and from the parasol-dotted sun terrace takes in the lake and the mountains beyond. Most rooms are well furnished, with oriental carpets and often several windows. The hotel has its own lakeside beach, with a floating raft ideal for sunbathing. It also allows easy access to the ski lifts.

Billrothstrasse 2, A-5340 St. Gilgen. © **06227/2217.** Fax 06227/221725. www.billroth.at. 52 units. Summer 124€–224€ double; winter 98€–130€ double. Rates include breakfast. MC, V. Closed mid-Dec to mid-Jan. **Amenities:** Restaurant; bar; babysitting; massage; nonsmoking rooms; sauna; tennis court. *In room:* TV, safe, Wi-Fi.

UPPER AUSTRIA

Often overlooked by travelers, Upper Austria is a land of plunging mountains, placid lakes, and picturesque valleys with Styria and Land Salzburg to its south and Bavaria to the west. To the north the Bohemian Forest forms the border with the Czech Republic and Lower Austria lies to the east. Its German name, Oberösterreich (Ober meaning upper) reveals it's closer to the source of the Danube than its twin, Lower Austria.

Upper Austria has three different landscapes. In the northern Mühlviertel are granite-laden hills, separated in the center of the province by the Valley of the Danube. There are also the limestone Alps and the Salzkammergut lake district, about a 30-minute drive from Linz, which crosses into Upper Austria. Here you'll find the area's most idyllic settings. You can center your activities at the Mondsee or the Attersee, Austria's largest lake. Also visit the Traunsee, one of the biggest lakes in the Salzkammergut, or the Wolfgangsee, Austria's most romantic lake.

These *Seen* (lakes) are all great for boating, but if you like to swim, know that the lake water here is not as warm as in Carinthia (see chapter 14). The lake district is dotted with farms and fruit trees, from which an excellent cider is produced that actually competes with wine for popularity among the locals.

Upper Austria is a choice for nature lovers. Most of its towns are small, and although there's a lot of industry, it leaves little imprint on the landscape. Industrial installations are often discreetly hidden away, much as they are in Switzerland. Linz, the provincial capital, harbors many historic treasures. Near Linz, the former Nazi concentration camp of Mauthausen is a tragic reminder of the horrors of World War II.

Bad Ischl, once a retreat of the imperial court, is the area's most fashionable spa. Emperor Franz Josef summered here for 60 years. From the beautiful village of Hallstatt, you can tour still-active salt mines at Saltwelten Hallstatt.

Historic abbeys abound in the province: Abbey of St. Florian, south of Linz, the province's largest abbey and an outstanding example of baroque architecture; Wilhering Abbey, west of Linz, a stunning example of rococo architecture; Lambach Abbey, outside Wels, a Benedictine abbey founded in 1056; and Kremsmünster Abbey, near Bad Hall, a Benedictine abbey from 777, noted for its famed fish pond and Hall of the Emperors.

Most of the best hotels are in the Salzkammergut region, but in every town and village are one or two moderately priced to inexpensive inns.

Abbey of St. Florian **1**
Dachstein Caves **5**
Kremsmünster Abbey **2**
Salt Mountain **4**
Schafberg **3**

There are few deluxe accommodations here, although several old castles have been turned into romantic lodges. Most hotels around the lakes are open only in the summer. Parking is rarely a problem, and, unless otherwise noted, you park for free.

May is an ideal time to visit. These areas tend to be overrun with visitors in the peak months of July and August, especially Germans. Try for another time.

Many North Americans aren't familiar with the ski areas of Upper Austria, as they lie for the most part in the southeastern corner. The **Dachstein** is a major ski area—and the **Dachstein Caves** are a spectacular natural attraction. If you like to ski and don't demand massive facilities and a big night scene, you'll find Upper Austria's emerging ski resorts far less expensive than the more popular and frequented resorts in Tyrol and Land Salzburg.

PROVINCIAL CAPITAL: LINZ ★★

187km (116 miles) W of Vienna; 130km (81 miles) NE of Salzburg; 269km (167 miles) E of Munich

Linz, the provincial capital of Upper Austria, is the third largest city in the country after Vienna and Graz. It's the biggest port on the Danube, which widens out considerably here to become a majestic thoroughfare. Three bridges connect Linz with the suburb of Urfahr, on the left bank of the river. If you enter the country from Passau, Germany, Linz will be your gateway to Austria.

Linz was the site of a Roman castle and settlement, Lentia, in the 1st century A.D. By the Middle Ages it had become a thriving center of trade because of its position on the river. Emperor Friedrich III lived here from 1489 to 1493. The city sits on a direct rail route linking the Adriatic and Baltic seas. The first large-scale metal-working company dates back to 1840 with the Linzer Schiffswerft, and afterwards Krauss, the German train-engine factory as well as textiles. A dreamy country town in the 1850s with no more than 26,600 inhabitants, Linz had a population of almost 50,000 only 20 years later. Its industrial capacity was rapidly built further after Hitler seized Austria in 1938, and the Nazis later established chemical plants here. Unfortunately, Linz's industrial boom made it a frequent target of Allied bombing; it took years to repair the destruction rained upon the city. In the Nazi era Linz settled into its role as Steel City. In 1938 the huge steelworks and armament factory "Reichswerke Hermann Göring" was built in Linz's southern precincts, necessitating the razing of the village of St. Peter. The Reichswerke were to form the basis for VOEST and Linz's chemical industry. Bindermichl, Spallerhof, and Neue Heimat, huge new developments, were built to house the tens of thousands of workers. Nor was that the end of the story: Linz also harbored three satellite camps connected to nearby Mauthausen concentration camp, whose purpose was to supply the armament industry with forced laborers.

Hitler, having chosen Linz as the place to retire, wanted to transform the city into a cultural metropolis adorned with monumental buildings and the world's largest collection of artworks. To make this happen, the Nazis looted artworks from private collections—mostly of Jews—and from museums across Europe. In view of the planning for the city's transformation, it is fortunate that only a few of the projects were realized: The Nibelungenbrücke, the so-called Brückenkopfgebäude that closed off Hauptplatz to the north, and a spate of communal housing projects.

Today Linz's Danube Port is still Austria's largest port and the largest port in the Danube's upper reach. But overshadowed by Vienna and Salzburg, Linz is a more modest destination. Still, it is interesting nonetheless as one of the cultural centers of Austria. The city's name appears in numerous Germanic songs, and many notable figures have been connected with Linz, including native son and composer Anton Bruckner. Mozart dedicated a symphony to the city, and Beethoven wrote his *Eighth Symphony* here. Franz Schubert described with pleasure his holidays in Linz. Goethe, who had a romance with a Linz *Fräulein,* dedicated one of his most lyrical works "to the beautiful girls of Linz."

Essentials
GETTING THERE
By Plane
Austrian Airlines, Lufthansa, and Air Berlin are the major connections into Linz, serving destinations like Düsseldorf, Frankfurt, and Zurich. Ryanair also connects Linz with London Stansted. **Flughafen Linz,** or Blue Danube Airport (© **07221/6000;** www.flughafen-linz.at), is 12km (7½ miles) southwest of the city, near the hamlet of Hörsching. Postbus 601 of the OÖVV (© **0810/240 810;** www.ooevv.at) connects the airport and the center of town, leaves hourly, and costs 2.60€. For rail riders, the

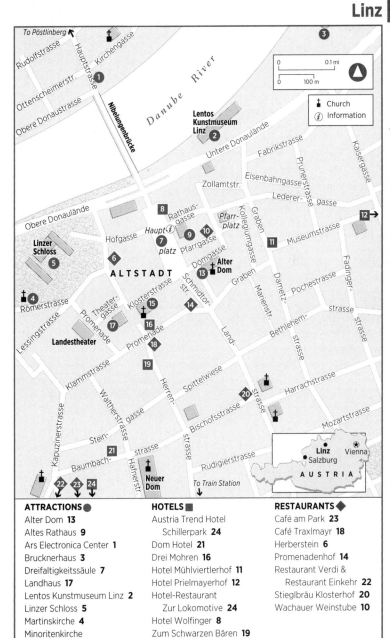

ATTRACTIONS ●

Alter Dom **13**

Altes Rathaus **9**

Ars Electronica Center **1**

Brucknerhaus **3**

Dreifaltigkeitssäule **7**

Landhaus **17**

Lentos Kunstmuseum Linz **2**

Linzer Schloss **5**

Martinskirche **4**

Minoritenkirche
(Landhauskirche) **15**

HOTELS ■

Austria Trend Hotel
Schillerpark **24**

Dom Hotel **21**

Drei Mohren **16**

Hotel Mühlviertlerhof **11**

Hotel Prielmayerhof **12**

Hotel-Restaurant
Zur Lokomotive **24**

Hotel Wolfinger **8**

Zum Schwarzen Bären **19**

RESTAURANTS ◆

Café am Park **23**

Café Traxlmayr **18**

Herberstein **6**

Promenadenhof **14**

Restaurant Verdi &
Restaurant Einkehr **22**

Stieglbräu Klosterhof **20**

Wachauer Weinstube **10**

Salzkammergut Adventure Card

Even if you're only planning to visit a couple of attractions, the Salzkammergut Card generally involves a saving. It gives up to 30% off public transport including lake ferries, mountain railways, and lifts, along with salt mines, ice caves, scenic roads, nature parks, museums, swimming, and other activities. The card costs 4.90€ a day; there's no card for children 15 and under, who simply benefit from child rates. The card is available from tourist offices, shops, and hotels. See www.salzkammergut.at for details.

airport maintains a free shuttle bus from the airport to the railway station at Hörsching; from here, you can take one of the commuter trains into Linz—there's one about every half-hour from early morning to midnight. It's more convenient to take a taxi, which will cost about 30€ one-way to virtually anywhere in Linz.

By Train

Linz sits directly astride the rail lines that connect Salzburg with Vienna, and on those that connect Prague to Graz and the major cities of Slovenia and Croatia. Trains, many of them the express Railjet, depart every 20 to 40 minutes throughout the day and night from Vienna's Westbahnhof (trip time: 1¾ hr.) and from Salzburg's main station (1¼ hr.). One train every 2 hours throughout the day departs from Graz for Linz (3½ hr.). For rail information, call © **05/1717,** or visit **www.oebb.at**. The recently rebuilt train station is located south of the city center at Bahnhofplatz.

By Bus

Linz is the center of an extensive network of bus lines carrying passengers from its busy railway station to the outlying villages and hamlets of Upper Austria. In case the train can't get you where you need to go, Eurolines (© **1/7982900;** www.eurolines. com) does offer a few connections from Linz to European destinations.

By Car

If you're driving from Salzburg, head northeast along the Autobahn A1; from Vienna, take the A1 Autobahn west.

GETTING AROUND

Most visitors limit their exposure in Linz to the city's historic core, most of which is a pedestrian zone centered on the Hauptplatz. Expect lots of shopping possibilities, lots of cafes serving the city's best-known confection (the Linzer torte), and access via tram nos. 1, 2, and 3, and bus nos. 26 and 50, any of which make access to the center from the periphery easy. Buses and trams operate daily from 5am to midnight and cost 1.80€ per ride, for access between any points in Greater Linz. For more information, contact the city tourist office. There is also a 1-day ticket valid for 24 hours, costing 3.60€.

VISITOR INFORMATION

The **Linz tourist office** is at Hauptplatz 1 (© **0732/70701777;** www.linz.at), and is open Monday to Friday 8am to 7pm (6pm in winter), Saturday and Sunday 10am to 7pm (6pm in winter).

American Express, Bürgerstrasse 14 (☎ **0732/669013**), is open Monday to Friday 9am to 5:30pm and Saturday from 9am to noon.

Linz is the first city in Austria to offer free wireless hotspots at locations like the train station, Taubenmarkt, and the Hauptplatz.

Exploring Linz's Churches & Historical Buildings

Among the four major cities of Austria, Linz is the least publicized and the least visited by foreign tourists, but its charms are many and its history as a Danube port is long and illustrious. The best way to explore the town is to hire one of the English-speaking guides provided by the **Linz tourist office,** Hauptplatz 1 (☎ **0732/ 70702009;** www.linz.at). Do-it-yourselfers can request the brochure "A Walk through the Old Quarter," which highlights the city's main attractions.

Much of the shopping offered lies along **Landstrasse,** which acts like a commercial artery running through town, and is filled with a variety of boutiques.

Hauptplatz was the original marketplace and is now one of Europe's biggest and most beautiful squares, with baroque and rococo facades surrounding it. On the east side is the **Altes Rathaus (Old Town Hall),** built in 1513. In the heart of the square stands the **Dreifaltigkeitssäule (Trinity Column),** built in 1723 to mark the city's deliverance from plague, fire, and Turkish invasions. This marble column rises 26m (85 ft.).

The **Brucknerhaus** concert hall was named in honor of Anton Bruckner, the Linz-born composer, and has an elliptical facade of glass and steel with a wooden interior. Concerts presented in this acoustically perfect hall have been transmitted throughout the world. The building was constructed from 1969 to 1973 as a cultural and conference center.

Alter Dom   The largest baroque church in the city and formerly the cathedral of Linz, the Alter Dom was constructed by the Jesuits at the end of the 17th century. You mustn't judge this church by its relatively simple exterior. The inside warms up considerably with pink marble columns, an intricately carved pulpit, and lots of statues. The high altar is bedecked with marble images. Native son Anton Bruckner was the church organist for 12 years, and the annual Bruckner Festival is centered here. Two other composers are honored at the same time—Mozart, who composed his *Linz*

THE SILICON valley OF MITTELEUROPA

Linz is not as preoccupied with its baroque and imperial past as many visitors believe. It's also home to a new generation of computer-industry whiz kids, who are transforming prosperous but staid Upper Austria into the Silicon Valley of Mitteleuropa (central Europe). Their ambitions are celebrated at Linz's **Ars Electronica** festival, held annually over a 5- or 6-day period during early September. Originating in 1979, it awards the coveted Golden Nica Prize to whichever entrepreneur or developer has created the previous year's most memorable electronic product. The festival has been called "The Oscar Awards Ceremony of the European Computer World." Previous awards have gone to the developer of the best international website and the developers of the most realistic computer game.

Symphony (no. 36) at the building now designated as the city tourist office (Haupt-platz 1), and Beethoven, who composed part of his *Eighth Symphony* in Linz.

Domgasse. ℂ **0732/7708660.** Free admission. Daily 7am–7pm. Tram: 1, 2, or 3.

Ars Electronica Center ★   Resembling a great glass and steel ship when illumi-nated at night, this museum accurately calls itself "the museum of the future." Changing exhibitions reflect the cutting edge of technology and its relationship to humans. The place will certainly give you a thrill: Expect lots of interactions with machines. For example, a full-body flight simulator takes you on a whirlwind "tour" over Upper Austria without leaving the building. Several levels allow you to enjoy a hands-on experience. In the interactive 3-D room on the ground level, you can explore "the outer reaches of space," or so it will seem. This unique museum is located across the bridge from Hauptplatz.

Hauptstrasse 2. ℂ **0732/72720.** www.aec.at. Admission 7€ adults; 4€ students, children, and seniors. Tues–Fri 9am–5pm, until 9pm on Thurs, Sat–Sun 10am–6pm. Tram: 1,2,3; Bus: 33, 33a, 38, 102.

Landhaus   One of the most important historic buildings in Linz, the Landhaus today serves as the headquarters for Upper Austria's government. The original struc-ture was built around 1570 with a gracefully arcaded courtyard surrounding a foun-tain. The complex served as the city's university during the 1600s and is still celebrated as the site where Johannes Kepler, the noted astronomer and mathemati-cian, taught and developed his theories of planetary motion.

Within the Landhaus's labyrinthine confines are the Church of the Minorite Brothers (see below) and the richly furnished apartments used by Empress Elisabeth ("Sissi") on the night she spent en route from her childhood home in Bavaria to the court of Vienna just before her marriage to Franz Josef in 1854.

Klosterstrasse 7. ℂ **0732/77200.** Free admission for views of the courtyard and the Minorite church; for more extensive visits, join one of the tourist office's organized tours. Mon–Tues and Thurs 7:30am–1pm and 2–6pm; Wed 7:30am–1:30pm; Fri 7:30am–1pm. (Hours extended for tourist office's organized tours.) Bus: 26 or 27.

Lentos Kunstmuseum Linz ★★   On the bank of the Danube River, this gallery is one of the most important repositories of contemporary painting in Linz. Many art lovers drive from Vienna to feast on these paintings—some 1,600 works in all that include pieces from Andy Warhol, Gustav Klimt, Egon Schiele, and more. The gallery also owns 850 rare photographs, including the work of Man Ray. The earliest are from the first half of the 19th century, but most of the collection is from after 1945. One of the greatest gifts came from a Berlin art dealer, Wolfgang Gurlitt (1888–1965), who amassed a stunning collection of 120 important artworks. The building itself is one of the finest examples of modern architecture in Linz, a glass-and-concrete struc-ture that lights up at night, creating a nighttime spectacle paired with the Ars Elec-tronica Center across the river.

Ernst-Koref-Promenade 1. ℂ **0732/70703600.** www.lentos.at. Admission 6.50€ adults, 4.50€ seniors and students under 26. Fri–Tues 10am–6pm; Thurs 10am–10pm. Tram: 1, 2, or 3.

Linzer Schloss ★   High above the river and a 5-minute walk west of Hauptplatz stands the castle used by Emperor Friedrich III when he and his court resided in Linz (1486–89) during Vienna's occupation by King Matthias of Hungary. At the turn of the 17th century, Rudolf II erected a new building. A catastrophic fire destroyed the south wing in the early 19th century—having been replaced in 2009 with an

A BAROQUE masterpiece: THE ABBEY OF ST. FLORIAN

The **Abbey of St. Florian** ★★, the largest in Upper Austria, is an outstanding example of baroque architecture. Augustinians have occupied this site since the 11th century, although the baroque structures you see today were built between 1686 and 1751. St. Florian was a Christian martyr who was drowned in the Enns River around A.D. 304. He is often called upon by the faithful to protect their homes against flood and fire. The abbey was constructed over his grave.

One of the most prolific composers of church music—and to some the greatest— in 19th-century Austria, Anton Bruckner (1824–96) was the organist at St. Florian as a young man and composed many of his masterpieces here. Although he went on to greater fame in Vienna, he was granted his wish to be buried at the abbey church underneath the organ he loved. You can visit the room where he lived for a decade.

The western exterior of the abbey is crowned with a trio of towers. The doorway is especially striking. As you enter the inner court, you'll see the **Fountain of the Eagle.** In the library, which contains some 140,000 books and manuscripts, are allegorical ceiling frescoes by Bartolomeo Altomonte. The marble salon honors Prince Eugene of Savoy for his heroic defense of Vienna against the Turkish Siege in 1683. The ceiling paintings here depict the Austrian victory over the "infidels."

Altdorfer Gallery is the most outstanding part of the abbey, surpassing even the Imperial Apartments. Well-known works by Albrecht Altdorfer, a 16th-century master of the Danube school of painting, are displayed. Altdorfer was a warm, romantic contemporary of Dürer, to whom he is often compared. He painted more than a dozen panels for the abbey's Gothic church, depicting, among other scenes, the martyrdom of St. Sebastian.

The **Imperial Apartments,** the Kaiserzimmer, are reached by climbing a splendid staircase. Pope Pius VI once stayed here, and a whole host of royalty has occupied these richly decorated quarters. You're allowed to visit the bedrooms of the emperors and empresses.

The **Abbey Church** has twin towers reaching 79m (259 ft.). The church is distinguished by columns of pink marble, quarried near Salzburg. Lavish stucco decoration was used in the interior, and the pulpit is in black marble. The choir stalls are heavily gilded and adorned with ornamentation and carving. You should allow about an hour for a tour.

Visitors can enter the church free, but guided tours of the monastery are 7.00€ for adults and 3€ for children under 18. Tours are conducted April through October daily at 10 and 11am and at 2, 3, and 4pm. Otherwise, you must write to the abbey for permission to visit.

The Abbey of St. Florian, Stiftstrasse 1, St. Florian (✆ **07224/890230;** www.stift-st-florian.at.), lies 19km (12 miles) southeast of Linz. It has its own exit (St. Florian) from the Autobahn linking Linz and Vienna. In addition, Postbus no. 410 runs throughout the day from Linz to St. Florian.

ultra-modern addition. Today the castle houses the **Provincial Museum of Upper Austria.** Its exhibits range from medieval art to works by the great moderns. There's an extensive arts-and-crafts department and a folklore collection. During the last few years, the permanent exhibitions have been expanded to include special exhibitions on cultural history.

Tummelplatz 10. (📞 **0732/774419-0.** www.schlossmuseum.at. Admission 3€ adults, 1.70€ students and seniors. Tues–Fri 9am–6pm; Sat–Sun and holidays 10am–5pm. Bus: 27.

Martinskirche   The finest example of Carolingian architecture in the region, St. Martin's Church, is the most ancient church in Austria still (more or less) in its original form. Constructed by Charlemagne in the 8th century, it used the ruins of an ancient Roman wall for parts of its foundation. Its interior is decorated with frescoes, several fine examples of baroque art, and a 15th-century Gothic choir. Restored in 1948, the church stands in a commercial neighborhood a 10-minute walk west of Hauptplatz. Not open to the public, a glass door permits a look inside, and the church is almost always included as part of the official tours sponsored by the Linz tourist office (📞 **0732/70701777**).

Römerstrasse. Free admission as part of tourist office's official guided tours. Bus: 26.

Minoritenkirche (Landhauskirche)   Originally built during the 1200s in the early Gothic style, the Church of the Minorite Brothers was for some time the seat of the city's municipal government until the larger Landhaus was built around it in the late 1500s. The interior was given a baroque overlay in 1758. Its masterpiece is the high altar by Bartolomeo Altomonte, depicting the Annunciation. The church also contains three red-marble side altars by Kremser Schmidt.

Klosterstrasse. (📞 **0732/772011364.** Free admission. Apr–Oct 8am–4pm; Nov–Mar daily 8–11am; hours extended for tourist office's organized tours. Bus: 26 or 27.

Where to Stay

UNDERGROUND PARKING GARAGES & CAR PARKS

A parking guidance system has been introduced to make it easier to find a parking space. The city of Linz is divided into the regions of "Urfahr" (GREEN), "Center east" (RED) and "Center west" (YELLOW). Each of the three zones is provided with characteristic colors, which can be found on the eight information boards and the 179 sign posts. This means that motorists are guided quickly and without detours to garages, where their vehicles can be parked for an unlimited time. In addition, there are parking lots located in close vicinity to tram and bus stops.

EXPENSIVE

Austria Trend Hotel Schillerpark ★★   The finest and most prestigious hotel in town, this mirror-covered structure was built around 1980 at the edge of the city's pedestrian zone, a 5-minute walk north of the railway station. This five-star hotel contains three comfortable restaurants, two bars, and a casino, open daily from 3pm to 3am. Rooms are airy, sunny, and filled with tastefully streamlined furniture. The beds are very comfortable, and the bathrooms are well equipped with robes and tub/ shower combinations. Rooms with waterbeds available on request.

Of the three restaurants within the hotel, the Rouge et Noir, serving French and Austrian cuisine, is the best; the Primo Piano offers upscale dining, serving regional cuisine; and the Café am Pair serves small meals, pastries, and coffees.

Rainerstrasse 2–4, A-4020 Linz. (📞 **0732/6950.** Fax 0732/69509. www.austria-trend.at. 111 units. 125€–322€ suite. AE, DC, MC, V. Parking 13€. Tram: 1, 2, or 3. **Amenities:** 2 restaurants; 3 bars; babysitting; casino; fitness center; laundry service; dry cleaning; room service; sauna; nonsmoking rooms; solarium. *In room:* A/C, TV, hairdryer, minibar, safe, Wi-Fi.

Drei Mohren ★★   This is one of the smallest hotels in Linz and also one of the best, for those desiring an intimate atmosphere and top-notch service. Renovations and improvements have been so drastic that the hotel was granted another star. Its name, "Three Moors," was divined after three men from the Far East were stranded in 1770 in a violent snowstorm in Linz, and liked the place so much they decided to live here. Opposite the Landhaus Park, the inn lies in the center of town, taking over a trio of buildings from the 1500s. Most of the rooms are spacious doubles with regal furnishings, plus some less lavish.

Promenade 17, A-4020 Linz. ⓒ **0732/772626-0.** Fax 0732/772626-6. www.drei-mohren.at. 25 units. 142€ double; 220€–350€ suite. AE, DC, MC, V. **Amenities:** Bar; laundry service; dry cleaning; room service. In room: A/C, TV, minibar, hairdryer, safe, Wi-Fi.

MODERATE

Dom Hotel ★   Ideally located in a quiet area in the center of town, this hotel is only a few minutes' walk from the Marienkirche, or New Cathedral. It was built in the 1970s and renovated in the late 1990s, and today it provides five floors of sub-dued decor a few steps from the cathedral. The owners maintain the hotel as a cozy stopping place. The comfortably furnished rooms have private (though small) bath-rooms, with adequate shelf space. On the ground floor is a cocktail bar, and the hotel restaurant serves international specialties and Austrian dishes.

Baumbachstrasse 17, A-4020 Linz. ⓒ **0732/778441.** Fax 0732/775432. www.domhotel.at. 40 units. 140€ double. Rates include breakfast. AE, DC, MC, V. Free parking Tram: 1, 2, or 3. **Amenities:** Restaurant; bar; babysitting; fitness center; laundry service; dry cleaning; nonsmoking rooms; sauna; solarium. In room: TV, hairdryer, minibar, Wi-Fi.

Hotel Prielmayerhof ★   This four-star hotel is housed in a distinguished-looking five-story structure, one of the few privately owned buildings constructed in Linz during World War II (in 1942); a new wing was added in 1994. Between 1945 and 1955, the hotel housed American occupation troops, who faced their Soviet counter-parts across the Danube during the early days of the Cold War. Today the hotel is owned by Franz Zihitner, the English-speaking son of the original owners, and is well run and comfortable. In the restaurant, Prielmayerhof, a *Tagesmenü* depends on seasonal availability.

Weissenwolfstrasse 33, A-4020 Linz. ⓒ **0732/774131-0.** Fax 0732/771569. www.prielmayerhof.at. 64 units. 127€ double. Rates include buffet breakfast. AE, DC, MC, V. Free parking. Less than 1km (½ mile) east of Hauptplatz. Bus: 45 or 46. **Amenities:** Restaurant, lounge; laundry service; dry cleaning; non-smoking rooms; rooms for those w/limited mobility, sauna. In room: TV, hairdryer, minibar, safe, Wi-Fi.

Hotel Wolfinger   Hotel Wolfinger is housed in a 500-year-old building on what is the largest and best-preserved baroque square in Europe. The entrance is through an arcade, a short distance from the Danube, in the middle of a pedestrian zone. A new wing was added to the hotel in 1992. Since 1975, the Dangl family, with the help of an enthusiastic staff, has run the hotel. With a respect for tradition, they have added modern comforts. Rooms are furnished with antiques.

Hauptplatz 19, A-4020 Linz. ⓒ **0732/7732910.** Fax 0732/77329155. www.hotelwolfinger.at. 45 units. 90€–126€ double; from 188€ suite. Rates include buffet breakfast. AE, DC, MC, V. Parking: 12€. Bus: 26 or 27. **Amenities:** Restaurant; bar; babysitting; lounge; nonsmoking rooms. In room: TV, Wi-Fi.

INEXPENSIVE

Hotel Mühlviertlerhof 🍴   This three-story town house, originally built in the 1740s, is maintained by the Lumpi family. Cozy and comfortable, with a convenient location about 90m (295 ft.) from Hauptplatz, the hotel offers well-scrubbed accommodations designed with both charm and efficiency in mind. The small rooms have good beds and well-organized bathrooms. About half the rooms offer views of a small garden in back. The Klosterhof Restaurant, under different management, occupies part of the building's street level.

Graben 24–25, A-4020 Linz. ⓒ **0732/772268.** Fax 0732/77226834. www.hotel-muehlviertlerhof.at. 23 units. 97€–111€ double. Rates include breakfast. AE, DC, MC, V. Parking: 12€. Tram: 1, 2, or 3. **Amenities:** Restaurant; bar. *In room:* TV, Wi-Fi.

Hotel-Restaurant Zur Lokomotive This simple, unpretentious, and comfortable place is a family-operated hostelry in a five-story building erected just before World War I. Its interior was efficiently renovated in 2003. Rooms are a bit small, as are the bathrooms, which have tub/shower combinations. A restaurant on the premises serves traditional Austrian food to many business workers throughout the day, as well as passengers departing from or arriving at the railway station, which is about a minute's walk away.

Weingartshofstrasse 40, A-4020 Linz. ⓒ **0732/654555.** Fax 0732/658337. www.hotel-lokomotive.at. 46 units. 92€–98€ double; 108€ triple. Rates include buffet breakfast. AE, DC, MC, V. Free parking. Tram: 1, 2, or 3. **Amenities:** Restaurant; bar; room service. *In room:* TV, Wi-Fi.

Zum Schwarzen Bären ✦ Set within a block of the main, all-pedestrian shopping street of Linz, this is a substantial stucco-covered building that offers a traditional-looking restaurant and *Weinstube* (wine tavern); a sense of solid, somewhat unimaginative tradition; and well-scrubbed but not overly large bedrooms. Each of them has touches of wooden paneling, or at least varnished wooden trim, a mixture of alpine and blandly contemporary furniture, and a tile-sheathed bathroom with a shower (in rare instances, there's a tub/shower combination). This was the birthplace of renowned native son, opera singer Richard Tauber (1891–1948).

Herrenstrasse 9–11, A-4020 Linz. ⓒ **0732/772477.** Fax 0732/77247747. www.linz-hotel.at. 30 units. 98€–136€ double. Rates include breakfast. AE, DC, MC, V. Parking 7€. Bus: 26 or 27. **Amenities:** Restaurant; wine tavern; laundry service; nonsmoking rooms; Wi-Fi in lobby. *In room:* TV.

Where to Eat
EXPENSIVE

Herberstein ★ AUSTRIAN/ASIAN In the center of the old city, in the historic Kremsmünsterhaus, this restaurant has been modernized and draws sophisticated foodies to its stylish precincts. Many locals patronize its lively bar. In summer you can sit outside in the inviting courtyard, perusing a limited but well-chosen menu. Count on an enticing daily special. There is always a freshly made soup of the day, plus a selection of oriental appetizers. You can follow with fish dishes such as yellow fin tuna on warmed bok choy salad or filet of pork served with gnocchi. A delicate fish tempura is a local favorite.

Altstadt 10. ⓒ **0732/786161.** www.herberstein-linz.at. Reservations required. Fixed-price 4-course meal for two on Sat 99€. Entrees 18€–23€. AE, DC, MC, V. Mon–Sat 4pm–4am, kitchen opens at 5:30pm. Bus: 26 or 27.

Restaurant Verdi & Restaurant Einkehr ★★ MODERN CONTINENTAL/ AUSTRIAN The core of this house, which has a panoramic view that sweeps out over and above Linz, was built about a century ago, but little is still recognizable. Many come here for the view, the fresh high-altitude air, and a cuisine that includes

CAFES

Linz is world famous for the Linzer torte, which looks like an open jam pie. The torte is filled with raspberry jam or preserves, while the batter, made from ground unblanched almonds, is flavored with cinnamon, cloves, and cocoa. It is cut in thin wedges and sprinkled with confectioners' sugar. You shouldn't leave Linz without trying a piece.

The **Café am Park,** in the Hotel Schillerpark, Rainerstrasse 2-4 (✆ **0732/ 6950;** tram: 1 or 3), is a great place to go on a Sunday afternoon in Linz. It's a big L-shaped room redecorated in 1994 in a streamlined modern style. You can get all the beverages and light snacks you'd expect, as well as wholesome meals priced from 8.50€ to 15€. It's open daily 6:30am to 11pm.

Another favorite, **Café Traxlmayr,** Promenade 16 (✆ **0732/773353;** www. traxlmayr.at; bus: 26 or 27), has a

pleasing period mystique. This 150-year-old coffeehouse is next to the Landhaus on a wide ornamental boulevard, in a beige-and-brown building. Its outdoor terrace is lined with thick privets and geraniums and in the fountain in front, a little stone boy is forever playing with two gurgling fish. Inside, the formally dressed waiters in black vest and white apron slide efficiently past with trays of coffee and cakes. The decor includes traditional round marble tables, big mirrors, and crystal-and-gilt chandeliers. A rack of Austrian and foreign-language newspapers completes the setting of a Viennese coffeehouse. During cold weather, hot dishes like goulash or sausages are served; pastries are priced from 3.50€, coffee starts at 3€. It's open Monday to Saturday 7:30am to 10pm, Sunday 9am to 6pm.

both conservative time-tested folkloric dishes (in Einkehr) and more experimental modern cuisine (in Verdi). Frankly, the main allure that attracts residents is Verdi, where rich-looking earth tones and leather-covered chairs create the kind of place where you can hang out for a prolonged evening meal. Menu items reflect the changing seasons and a willingness to experiment on the part of the kitchen staff.

Pachmayrstrasse 137, in Lichtenberg, A-4040 Linz. ✆ 0732/733005. www.verdi.at. Reservations recommended for Verdi, not necessary at Einkeher. Verdi main courses 21€–25€; Einkehr main courses 7€–13€. DC, MC, V. Tues–Sat 5pm–1am. There's no public bus to this place. Either take a taxi or drive north from Linz, following the Leonfelder Strasse for 3km (2 miles). On the outskirts of the village of Lichtenberg, you'll see a sign pointing to the Restaurant Verdi.

INEXPENSIVE

Promenadenhof ★ AUSTRIAN/MEDITERRANEAN   Dining here in summer is a special delight, as you can ask for a table on the roofed garden which is like a fabulous flower garden. Another feature is the wine cellar where you will be escorted to select your own bottle for the night from among one of the best selections of vintages in town. You can also request the waiter to bring you wine by the glass. Some of the town's best regional cuisine is served here, with *Tafelspitz* (boiled beef) being the chef's specialty. Daily specials are also featured based on the shopping at the market on any given day. Desserts are among the best in Linz, especially a special baked apple dumpling in wine sauce.

Promenade 39. ✆ **0732/777661.** Reservations recommended. Main courses 8€–23€. AE, DC, MC, V. Mon–Sat 10am–1am. Bus: 26 or 27.

Stieglbräu Klosterhof AUSTRIAN   Centuries ago, this building served as one of the outposts of Kremsmünster Abbey, several days' horseback ride away. Today, from a position on the edge of Linz, it functions as the town's most likable beer garden, with a sprawling outdoor terrace and a cavernous interior. A quick tour of the variety of rooms reveals where you feel most comfortable. An old-fashioned, overworked staff serves copious portions of traditional Austrian food throughout. Desserts include a Linzer torte covered with apricot jam. Many people come for just a drink.

Landstrasse 30. (✆ **0732/773373.** www.klosterhof-linz.at. Reservations recommended. Main courses 8.90€–22€. DC, MC, V. Daily 9am–midnight. Tram: 1, 2, or 3.

Wachauer Weinstube AUSTRIAN   A baroque bas-relief of an ecstatic saint adorns the corner of this historic building on a cobblestone sidewalk near the old cathedral. The smallest portion of any wine sold here is a quarter liter, about two full glasses. Wines from the Wachau region are featured, including five whites, four reds, and one rosé. There is a limited array of conventional platters served here, including wursts, salads, and the occasional schnitzel.

Pfarrgasse 20. (✆ **0732/774618.** Reservations recommended. Main courses 4.50€–11€. AE, MC, V. Mon–Sat 11am–1am. Bus: 33.

Shopping

Quietly prosperous, Linz is the regional center of the antiques trade, so if you're interested in adding a piece or two to your collection, consider dropping into **Richard Kirchmayr Antiquitäten,** Bethlehemstrasse 5 (✆ **0732/770117**), or any of the shops listed below.

Linz is home to a branch of the Vienna-based **Dorotheum,** Fabrikstrasse 26 (✆ **0732/7731320;** www.dorotheum.com/linz), an auction house that has allowed many socially prominent but impoverished families to keep their bills paid during hard times by means of discreet auctions of the family heirlooms. Auctions take place every Wednesday at 1:30pm, but there's plenty of time for viewing the objects during normal business hours in the week preceding the sale.

Less desirable objects are scattered randomly among the display tables at the **Linzer Flohmarkt (Linz Flea Market),** which takes place on the Hauptplatz every Saturday from March to mid-November from 7am to around 2pm, or until the inventories are depleted. Amid lots of junk and debris from estate sales throughout the region, it's still possible to find something charming and handcrafted.

At **O. Ö. Heimatwerk,** a gift shop and clothing store at Landstrasse 31 (✆ **0732/ 773377;** www.ooe.heimatwerk.at), you can buy local handicrafts such as pewter, intricately patterned silver, rustic ceramic pots, slippers, dresses, and dressmaking fabrics in regional patterns (lots of polka dots). The entrance to the airy, sunny store is under an arcade, although the shop windows face the busy pedestrian walkway of Linz's main shopping district.

Linz After Dark

Although the nightlife here isn't as trendy or as edgy as you'll find in Vienna—the scale is simply a lot smaller—Linz offers some very interesting theater and music venues, and enough nocturnal diversions to keep you well entertained.

CULTURAL LINZ

The city's most prestigious theater is the historic **Landestheater,** Promenade 39 (✆ **0732/76110, 0800/218000;** www.landestheater-linz.at; bus: 26 or 27). Dating from 1670 and home to the local opera company, it's the city's all-purpose venue for opera, musicals, theater, and ballet. Part of its interior is devoted to the smaller **Kammerspiele** (same address and phone), which tends to put on more contemporary and, in many cases, more experimental theater. A more modern concert venue is the one within the **Brucknerhaus,** Untere Donaulände 7 (© **0732/76120,** 0732/ 775230; www.brucknerhaus.at; bus: 26). Built in the 1970s, it presents concerts every year from mid-September to early October as part of the city's annual Bruckner Festival. While many performances are devoted to the symphonies of Linz's native son, Anton Bruckner, works by Beethoven and Mozart are also included.

Tickets to performances within any of the theaters mentioned above can be obtained directly at their box offices (Mon–Fri 9am–6pm) or by contacting the ticket agency that represents virtually everything in Upper Austria, **Kartenbüro,** Herrenstrasse 4 (© **0732/778800;** tram: 1, 2, or 3). For a rundown on what's going on in Upper Austria, ask for a copy of the monthly pamphlet "*Was ist los in Linz und Oberösterreich*" ("What's Happening in Linz and Upper Austria"). The tourist office will usually give you a copy; or buy one for 3€ at a newsstand.

THE BAR & CLUB SCENE

Don't believe the naysayers: Linz offers a burgeoning nightlife scene for whiling away the evening hours. The most happening place in town is behind the giant Ars Electronica Center in the **Stadtwerkstatt,** Kirchengasse 4 (© **0732/731209;** www.stwst.at). In the downstairs cafe **Strom,** DJs spin the latest in electronica, lounge, and underground music. This is an easy place to meet people, a crossroads of students, young professionals, active members in the arts community, and activists from various political leanings. The upstairs venue features live acts from the up-and-coming local scene or those from elsewhere in Europe just passing through. A reasonable cover charge usually applies. At **Stonewall,** Rainerstrasse 22 (© **0732/600438**), you can expect a gay and lesbian crowd, although many straights come here as well. Dancing begins Friday and Saturday at 10pm. During the week it attracts devotees to its bar.

Looking to linger over a glass of wine in Old Austria? Head for the **Alte Welt Weinkeller,** Hauptplatz 4 (© **0732/770053;** www.altewelt.at; tram: 1 or 3), where a choice of mostly Austrian and Hungarian wines are sold by the glass or the bottle in a very old, very traditional setting that, judging by the state of the wood, has been here virtually forever. It's a very mellow place, perfect for swapping life stories. At least once a week, on an iffy schedule, live bands perform or poets and writers read from their works, usually in German.

CASINO ACTION

Yes, there's a **casino** in Linz, within the Austria Trend Hotel Schillerpark (see earlier in this chapter), Rainerstrasse 2–4 (© **0732/6544870;** tram: 1, 2, or 3), but nothing so scintillating that it will tempt you to mortgage your house or spend the children's college fund. The casino contains two separate sections of differing formality. The **Casino Léger,** or "Jackpot Casino," is open daily noon to midnight, has no dress code, and houses most of the establishment's slot machines. A step away, the **Linzer Casino Classic,** open daily 3pm to 4am, is more grand, calling for a cocktail dress or business suit; no jeans or sneakers, but a supply of jackets on hand, for the unprepared. A ticket that grants admission to both sections costs 23€, but it is accompanied by gaming tokens worth 25€. You must be over 18 and present a valid passport to enter either area.

Side Trips from Linz
PÖSTLINGBERG

The most popular day trip from Linz is to Pöstlingberg, 5km (3 miles) northwest of the city on the north bank of the Danube. You can drive here via Rudolfstrasse on the left bank of the river, taking a right turn onto Hagenstrasse; or, you can take the electric railway no. 50 from Hauptplatz. One-way tickets cost 3.40€, while a return fare is 5.60€. A children's ticket is half the price.

Pöstlingberg has a **botanical garden** with exotic tropical plants, and the summit terrace is a riot of blooming flowers in summer. An old fortress tower now houses a grotto with a miniature railway, a favorite with children. The **pilgrimage church** is worth a visit for its 18th-century carved wood Pietà, but most tourists make the ascent mainly to take in the view over the Danube Valley, with Linz spread out below. The panorama stretches all the way to the foothills of the Alps and to the Bohemian Forest in the Czech Republic.

WILHERING ABBEY

Even if you're not a fan of church architecture, you'll find the 10-minute bus ride worth the trip to see a little-known but stunning display of rococo architecture. Seen by many as the masterpiece of this bombastic offshoot of baroque, the scale of decoration in the interior sharply contrasts with the simple exterior, and strikes the visitor upon entry, perhaps in a humorous way. Following an arson attack by a 12-year-old girl in 1733, a local craftsman named Johann Haslinger built the current Cistercian abbey and had the painters Martin and Bartolomäus Altomonte, and stucco artist Franz Joseph Holzinger, fill the interior with decoration. It was as if they were locked inside and not let out until every inch of wall space was covered. Martin Altomonte created the paintings for the high altar and side chapels while in his eighties, and had his nephew Bartolomäus paint the ceiling fresco. To get here, take the WILIA bus, numbers 8031 or 8032, going upstream along the Danube from the Old Town side of the Nibelungenbrücke. A one-way fare costs 1.80€.

MAUTHAUSEN: THE CONCENTRATION CAMP

You can make a sobering outing from Linz to Mauthausen, 29km (18 miles) down the Danube (southeast) from the provincial capital. The village is very beautiful in its own right and is often visited for its medieval architecture. This is overshadowed, however, by its history during World War II, when the Nazis operated a concentration camp and extermination center about 3km (2 miles) northwest of the village. Austria's Jews were slaughtered in large numbers, with estimates ranging from 35,000 to 2 million, and the camp remains a horrifying testament to the evils of Nazism. Thousands of other so-called undesirables were also annihilated here, including homosexuals and gypsies.

The Austrian government has not tried to hide this site of so many atrocities. The camp was declared a national monument in 1949, and various countries whose citizens died here have erected memorials outside the camp to honor them.

You can visit the huts where the condemned, most of whom almost surely knew their fate, were held. You are also led down the infamous "Stairway of Death," where the prisoners took their last walk. To visit the ghastly site is a very intense experience, and many come to bear witness, a reminder of the savagery people are capable of. Renovations through 2012 may result in closures of part of the camp.

To reach Mauthausen from Linz, take one of the dozen or so local buses departing from Linz's main railway station for Mauthausen (trip time: 1 hr.).

It takes about 1½ hours to take a tour of the camp. The camp is open daily 9am to 5:30pm; it's closed December 24 to 26, December 31, and January 1. For more information, call © **07238/2269,** or visit en.mauthausen-memorial.at. Admission is 2€ for adults and 1€ for children.

Stift Kremsmünster ★   The Benedictine Kremsmünster Abbey, 42km (26 miles) southwest of Linz between the emerging hills of the Alps and the Danube River, overlooking the Valley of Krems, was founded in A.D. 777. Two domed towers of the church dominate the local skyline. According to a 14th-century legend, Tassilo III, a Bavarian duke, had the abbey built to honor his son Gunther, who was killed by a wild boar during a hunt. The abbey's design was Romanesque, but in the 17th and 18th centuries, it was given the baroque treatment.

The most outstanding feature of a tour through Kremsmünster is the **Fischbehalter,** a pond designed by the noted architect Carlo Antonio Carlone. The pond has five basins, each encircled by arcades, and statues that spout water depicting figures from Samson to Neptune.

In the cluster of abbey buildings, the **Kaisersaal (Hall of the Emperors)** has a portrait collection of the Holy Roman emperors, painted by Altomonte at the end of the 17th century. One of the most outstanding works of art is the *Crucifixion,* by Quentin Massys. The abbey still owns the 8th-century chalice of Tassilo that was presented to the monks by the founding duke. It's the most ancient piece of goldsmith's work in either Austria or Bavaria, the duke's home. The library also houses the priceless *Codex Millenarius,* an 8th-century translation of the Gospels.

An observation tower, called the first skyscraper in Europe, rises nearly 61m (200 ft.) and has an exhibition on astronomy and other sciences. Many noted men have been pupils at the abbey school, including novelist Adalbert Stifter. The observatory natural science tour lasts 1½ hours and includes the fish pond.

To reach the abbey, take a train departing from the Linz Hauptbahnhof (Main Railway Station) for Graz, which leaves every 40 to 60 minutes (trip time: 45 min.), and stops at Kremsmünster. Once you exit, you'll see many signs pointing toward the Stift Kremsmünster. It's a well-marked ramble eastward for 20 minutes. From Bad Hall, buses depart from Bad Hall's railway station approximately every 90 minutes throughout the day for the 15-minute ride to Kremsmünster. Driving from Wels, take Route 138 south, and then Route 122 east to Kremsmünster.

LAKES ATTERSEE & MONDSEE

Attersee ★★

The largest lake in the Austrian Alps, Attersee comes alive in summer when a sports-loving crowd flocks to the resort town that bears the lake's name. In our opinion, the lake is too cold for swimming almost all the time (although Polar Bear Club members might disagree), but it's a great draw for boaters and sailors. You can rent sail boats or take lessons from Walter Liehmann at the **Segelschule Attersee** (© **07666/7702;** www.segelschule.at). Attersee is 50km (31 miles) east of Salzburg and 69km (43 miles) west of Linz.

Those interested in fishing will appreciate the lake's clear alpine waters, with lake trout and char, and, in little tributaries, brook trout just beneath the surface. At many guesthouses along the shore you can have the fish you caught for dinner.

THE GREAT outdoors IN THE SALZKAMMERGUT

The **Salzkammergut** is one of Europe's summer playgrounds, centered on the towns of **Bad Ischl, St. Wolfgang,** and **Hallstatt.** Soaring mountains with needlelike peaks and shimmering lakes along forested valleys are the backdrop for any number of outdoor activities, including boating, fishing, swimming, and hiking. The best known of all the Salzkammergut's 27 lakes lie to the west of Bad Ischl: The **Mondsee,** the **Attersee,** and the **Wolfgangsee.**

Biking   While most of the province's terrain is too hilly for biking, you'll find great places in the districts around the lakes, particularly around the Attersee or the Traunsee. The best cycling path is the 14km (9 miles) from Bad Ischl to St. Wolfgang; of course, biking on the back roads is more scenic. Tourist offices in either town will help you plan routes. You can rent bikes from the most visible gas station in Attersee, **Petrol Schweiger** (© 07666/7821), for around 10€ per day. For easy riders, **Arros,** Traunsteinstrasse 109, 4810 Gmunden (© 07612/71698), offers electric bike rental in Gmunden and other locations on the Taunsee for 19€ per day. If you'd like to join a local bicycle tour through and around the region, consider **Eurobike Eurofun Touristik,** Mühlstrasse 20, Obertraun am See (© 06219/7444).

Boating   Most of the lakes scattered amid the forests of Upper Austria are deep, cold, and clear, and boaters love them. If you want to rent a boat, the local tourist offices of every lakefront resort can recommend local outfitters, one of the most visible is **Wolfgangsee-schiffahrt,** A-5360 St. Wolfgang (© 06138/22320).

If you're interested in exploring the lakes while someone else worries about navigation and equipment, consider one of the Attersee tours offered by **Stern Schiffahrt,** A-4863 Attersee (© 07666/7806). From June to mid-September, a 2-hour cruise along the south shore of the Attersee is 14€; cruises depart every 2 hours from 9am to 5pm. During the same time period, a 1-hour tour along the lake's north shore costs 9€ and departs at 1-hour intervals every day from 10am to 5pm.

Canoeing/Kayaking/Sailing   Some of Upper Austria's best white water lies along the swift-flowing Traun River. The region's best recommended canoe, kayak, and sailboat rental company lies in the neighboring hamlet of Nussdorf: **Yachtschule Koller,** A-4865 Nussdorf (© 0676/3305253), where a 4-hour rental of a watercraft costs between 20€ and 50€, depending on its pedigree. Sailing lessons available.

The blue-green *See* (lake) is 20km (13 miles) long and about 2km (1½ miles) wide, with many orchards growing on its uplands. There's a road around the entire body of water. From the southern part of the lake to the west of Burgau, you can take a 12-minute walk to a beautiful gorge, the **Burggrabenklamm,** with a waterfall, one of the most scenic sights along the Attersee.

ESSENTIALS

GETTING THERE   Attersee town (called Attersee am Attersee) lies at the terminus of a small railway running from the junction of Vöcklamarkt, just less than 14km (9 miles) to the north (about a dozen trains make the short run from Vöcklamarkt to Attersee every day). Reaching Vöcklamarkt is easy, as InterCity trains stop every 2

Fishing The Salzkammergut is one of the best places to fish in all of Austria—or Europe, for that matter. The easiest way, in terms of legalities, involves buying a fishing license, valid for 1 week's fishing on the Attersee (but not in any of the swift-flowing rivers) for a one-time fee of 50€, available through any branch of the local tourist offices. Acquiring a permit for fishing in the streams of the region is much more complicated, involving permission from at least one local bureaucracy. The season lasts from April 1 to November 20. For information, contact any local tourist office.

Golf The best course is the **Salzkammergut Golfclub** at Bad Ischl (© **06132/26340**; www.salzammergut-golf.at). This 18-hole, par-71 course charges green fees of 55€ to 65€ daily.

Hiking The Salzkammergut is great hiking country, and local tourist offices not only suggest hikes, but also provide route maps. The Bad Ischl area, for example, has more than 100km (62 miles) of trails. In the Attersee area, one 35-km (22-mile) hike takes 8 hours to finish. One of the best hiking trips involves circumnavigating the region's largest lake (Attersee), which can take anywhere from 3 to 5 days, depending on your fitness level and how extensive an itinerary you want to pursue. For

more details about possible outings, the tourist office in Attersee (© **07666/7719**) will send you a booklet indicating the hiking possibilities and their estimated times. For altitude seekers, the **Alpenverein** (© **0512/59547**; www.alpenverein.at) provides keys to the unstaffed huts for a fee between 13€ and 22€ according to category.

Tennis Your best bet is the **Tennisclub Bad Ischl** in the heart of the resort (© **06132/23926**; www.tcbadischl.at). The club offers both indoor and outdoor courts along with ball-throwing machines. You can also rent rackets.

Watersports Because of their proximity to such cities as Linz and Salzburg, the lakes of Upper Austria are popular spots for water-skiing and scuba diving. If you want to go water-skiing, the reception desk at lakeside hotels can provide names and addresses of suitable establishments. One good company on the Attersee is **Häuplhof,** which operates out of the hamlet of Mühlbach, near Attersee (© **07666/7788**). And if you want to scuba-dive in waters that originated high in the Alps, head for **Reiter,** in the town of Unterach (© **07665/8034**), which specializes in year-round dives into the cold, dark waters of lakes whose depths exceed 168m (551 ft.) in places.

hours or less from Salzburg and Linz. For rail information, contact © **05/1717** (www.oebb.at). Attersee is not served by bus lines. If you're driving from Linz, head west along the A1; from Salzburg, go east on the A1.

VISITOR INFORMATION The **tourist office,** A-4864 Attersee am Attersee (© **07666/62324070;** www.attersee.at), is in the town center, open in winter Monday to Friday 9am to noon and 2 to 5pm; in summer daily 9am to 6pm.

WHERE TO STAY & EAT
In Town

Hotel Seegasthof Oberndorfer This well-established, traditional family-owned hotel sits on the shores of the Attersee. The sunny, carpeted, and comfortable medium-size rooms have balconies. From the rooms there's a good view over the lake to the Höllengebirge. Gertrude Oberndorfer serves excellent Austrian cuisine, and in warm weather meals are served on a terrace next to the lake, which is shaded by old chestnut trees.

Hauptstrasse 18, A-4864 Attersee. © **07666/78640.** Fax 07666/786491. www.oberndorfer.info. 25 units. 130€–154€ double; 200€ suite. Rates include buffet breakfast. Notify desk at reservations if you intend to use a credit card. AE, MC, V. Free parking in an area next to the hotel, 8€ in the garage. Closed Nov. **Amenities:** Restaurant; bar; babysitting; laundry service; dry cleaning; massage; room service; nonsmoking rooms; sauna; swimming lake. *In room:* TV, hairdryer, minibar, Wi-Fi.

Around the Lake

At the northern extremity of the Attersee is the small village and holiday resort of **Seewalchen am Attersee,** which offers sailing and other watersports. However, the main reason we recommend it is the Residenz Häupl (see below).

You could also base yourself at the lakeside hamlet of **Unterach am Attersee.** It's so small it doesn't appear on most maps, but it occupies one of the loveliest positions on the lake—on the right bank, across from Weissenbach—from where you can explore either the Attersee or Mondsee.

Hotel Georgshof *

Built in the early 1980s of well-preserved wood and cream-colored stucco, this cozy chalet (one of the town's two hotels) is set on a hillside about a 5-minute uphill walk from the center; it's 183m (600 ft.) higher than the town itself. Windows are embellished with regional designs and look out onto a backyard with a sun terrace. Inside is a timber-and-stucco bar area. The Hollerweger family offers spacious and tastefully furnished bedrooms. Beds are comfortable, with well-kept bathrooms.

Atterseestrasse 86, A-4866 Unterach am Attersee. © **07665/8501.** Fax 07665/85018. www.oberoesterreich.at/georgshof. 25 units. 55€–88€ double. Rates include half-board. Children under 11 stay free in parent's room. AE, DC, MC, V. Closed the last week of Nov–Dec 20. **Amenities:** Dining room; lounge; laundry service; dry cleaning; indoor heated pool; sauna. *In room:* TV, Wi-Fi.

Residenz Häupl ★★

One of the region's most elegant hotels, with some of the finest food, too, this establishment began its life as a simple inn during the 1600s. Today, it stays open year-round, unusual for these parts. It sits in the center of the village, across the street from the lakeshore. From the street side, it has a pleasant facade and a steeply sloped series of interconnected gables. The interior looks like a tastefully opulent private house. Rooms are well furnished, beautifully maintained, and often quite large.

In the rustic dining room, one of the region's best, the chef prepares such delicacies as grilled char from the lake with baby vegetables in a savory sauce, perhaps followed by a dessert of curd-paste dumplings with stewed plums. Frau Häupl, whose family has run this place for the past seven generations, inspires the culinary techniques of an able group of chefs. Except for December 24, the restaurant is open daily from 11:30am to 2pm and 6 to 9:45pm.

Hauptstrasse 20, A-4863 Seewachen am Attersee. © **07662/6363.** Fax 07662/636363. www.residenz-haeupl.at. 33 units. 90€–164€ double; 180€–250€ suite. Rates include buffet breakfast. AE, DC, MC, V. **Amenities:** Restaurant; bar; babysitting; bike rental; health club; laundry service; dry cleaning; sauna; steam room; room service; nonsmoking rooms. *In room:* TV, Wi-Fi, minibar, safe.

Mondsee ★

Mondsee (Moon Lake) is one of the warmest lakes in the Salzkammergut. Since Roman times, this crescent-shape lake has been named after the celestial body it resembles. The Salzburg–Vienna Autobahn runs along the south shores of this, the third largest lake in the Salzkammergut district. In the background you can see the **Drachenwand** and the **Schafberg** mountains.

The lake is sparsely settled, so if you need accommodations, you should head to the northwest corner for the village of Mondsee. A popular summer resort, with sailing schools and beaches, Mondsee is 270km (168 miles) southwest of Vienna, 27km (17 miles) east of Salzburg, and 100km (62 miles) southwest of Linz.

ESSENTIALS

GETTING THERE   No rail lines extend to Mondsee. Most visitors travel by train to either Salzburg or Strasswalchen, a town conveniently on the main line between Salzburg and Vienna. For rail information, contact ℭ **05/1717** (www.oebb.at). Buses depart from the railway station in Salzburg every hour throughout the day (trip time: 50 min.). From Strasswalchen, five buses head south every day for Mondsee (trip time: 35 min.). From Salzburg, drivers head east on the A1; from Linz, they go west on the A1.

VISITOR INFORMATION   The **tourist office** (ℭ **06232/4070**) is in the town center at Dr.-Franz-Müller-Strasse 3. It's open year-round Monday to Saturday 8am to noon and 1 to 6pm; Sunday 8am to 7pm in July and August.

EXPLORING MONDSEE

A Benedictine abbey was once situated in Mondsee, dating from A.D. 748. However, when Emperor Josef II ordered the abbey dissolved in 1791, the abbey church became the **Pfarrkirche (Parish Church),** still a point of interest in the village. It's a 15th-century structure with an added baroque exterior, but its crypt dates from the 11th century. The church was richly decorated by Meinrad Guggenbichler, a sculptor born in 1649, including seven of the more than dozen altars.

Part of the abbey is now the **Schloss Mondsee.** The castle, where the wedding scene in *The Sound of Music* was filmed, is adjacent to the church.

Heimatmuseum und Pfahlbaumuseum   This museum is in the former cloisters of the abbey. Local artifacts related to the province's earlier eras are displayed in the Heimatmuseum. The Pfahlbaumuseum is dedicated to prehistoric archaeology; its exhibits trace local habitation from the Neolithic dwellings on pilings in the lake. Discoveries from as early as 3000 B.C., up to the disappearance of prehistoric people in 1800 B.C., include Mondsee-Keramik pottery.

Hilfbergstrasse. ℭ **06223/2270.** Admission 3€ adults, 1.50€ children. May to end-Sept Tues–Sun 10am–5pm; mid-June to Aug 31 open until 6pm; Oct Sat–Sun only, 10am–5pm. Closed Nov–Apr.

Mondseer Rauchhaus   This rustic wood chalet flanked by outbuildings was once a smokehouse used by farmers from the district. Notice the absence of a chimney above the vaulted hearth.

Hilfbergstrasse 6. ℭ **0664/3406020.** www.museummonsee.at. Admission 3€ adults, 1.50€ children. May–Sept daily 10am–6pm (closed Mondays in Sept); Oct 15–31 Sat–Sun 10am–5pm. Closed Nov–Apr.

WHERE TO STAY

Austria Classic Hotel Leitnerbräu ★   Dating back to the 17th century, this site was a popular brewery, which closed in 1904. Since then, the place has functioned as a hotel, run by many generations of the Marschallinger family. Their house stands in the center of Mondsee opposite the famous **Pfarrkirche (Parish Church).**

Rooms are usually generous in size. Some have sitting areas and private balconies. Bikes are available at no charge. Guests enjoy hearty Austrian cuisine.

Steinerbachstrasse 6, A-5310 Mondsee. ☎ **06232/6500.** Fax 06232/650022. www.leitnerbraeu.at. 30 units. 135€–173€ double. AE, DC, MC, V. **Amenities:** Restaurant; bar; fitness center; Jacuzzi; sauna; steam room; babysitting; bike rental; laundry service; dry cleaning; massage; room service. *In room:* TV, hairdryer, minibar, safe, Wi-Fi.

WHERE TO EAT

Café Frauenschuh ★ PASTRIES/SNACKS   This famous establishment, which has flourished since the 1950s, is known by sweet-tooths throughout the region for its delectable pastries and chocolates. Set in the middle of the village, it offers racks of fruited and chocolate-covered confections, which you can eat on the spot or buy by the dozen. In midsummer, rows of tables are set up amid flowerpots outdoors. One of the most popular items, a piece of strudel with ice cream or whipped cream, costs 5.10€. Other pastries begin at 2.50€, with a coffee going for 2.75€. The cafe also offers sandwiches and salads.

Marktplatz 8. ☎ **06232/2312.** www.konditorei-frauenschuh.at. Daily 7am–7pm (until 11pm July–Aug). Closed Wed off-season.

La Farandole FRENCH   An outdoor terrace, used during good weather, provides a view of the nearby forest. Specialties change with the seasons and include a delectable *tartar* of lake fish from the Mondsee, duck confit salad with fresh seasonal greens, roast rack of lamb with garlic, roebuck with chanterelle sauce, and marinated filets of salmon. Dessert might be a heavenly symphony of dark- and white-chocolate mousses or artfully arranged truffles.

Schlösslweg 1. ☎ **06232/3475.** www.lafarandole.at. Reservations recommended. Main courses 12€–19€. MC, V. July–Aug Tues–Sat noon–2pm and 7–9:30pm, Sun noon–2pm; Sept–Feb and May–June Tues–Sat noon–2pm and 7–9:30pm, Sun noon–2pm. Closed Mar. Many guests walk the ½ mile north from the center, but the bus marked MONDSEE–ZELL AM MOOS passes nearby as well.

ST. WOLFGANG & BAD ISCHL

These two resorts in the Salzkammergut, though not far apart, could hardly be more different, the one a popular "everyman" holiday resort with the extraordinary natural beauty of a mountain lake, the other, one of Austria's most elegant.

St. Wolfgang lies on the Wolfgangsee (see "The Flachgau," in chapter 10), which also forms the boundary between Land Salzburg and Upper Austria. St. Wolfgang is 50km (31 miles) east of Salzburg, 114km (71 miles) southwest of Linz, and 13km (8 miles) west of Bad Ischl.

St. Wolfgang ★

In the mountains of the Salzkammergut, the **Wolfgangsee** is one of the most romantic lakes in Austria. St. Wolfgang, a little holiday resort on the northeastern side of the lake below the Schafberg (see below), is set among all this natural beauty. In summer, the resort is overrun with visitors.

If you drive here, there are two parking areas at the entrance to the town. You can park your car and then explore the town on foot. Late spring to early autumn, it's better to go to St. Wolfgang by boat, leaving from the landing stage at Gschwendt, on the southern rim of the lake. Departures from mid-May to mid-October are usually hourly.

Other than a cog railway, which extends from St. Wolfgang to the top of the Schafbergspitz, St. Wolfgang is not serviced by any rail lines. Its only access is by bus, taxi, or car.

ESSENTIALS

GETTING THERE Buses depart from the railway station of Bad Ischl about a dozen times a day, making stops at both the marketplace (St. Wolfgang Marktplatz) and the base of the Schafbergbahn (St. Wolfgang Schafberg Rack Railway). Trip time to either is about 40 minutes.

If you're driving from Salzburg, take Route 158 east. From Linz, head southwest on the A1; then cut southwest at the junction with Route 145 to Bad Ischl. From Bad Ischl, continue west on Route 158.

VISITOR INFORMATION The St. Wolfgang **tourist office** (✆ **06138/2239;** www.wolfgangsee.at) is in the town center. It's open in winter Monday to Friday 9am to noon and 2 to 5pm, Saturday 9am to noon; in summer Monday to Friday from 9am to 8pm, Saturday 9am to noon and 2 to 6pm, Sunday 1 to 6pm.

SWIMMING, HIKING, SKIING & MORE

In summer, swimming, watersports, and just sitting at a beach cafe are all highly regarded activities at this resort. Hiking is also possible in almost any direction.

There's skiing in the hills, usually December to mid-March, and you'll also find facilities here for skating, curling, and horse-drawn sleigh rides.

St. Wolfgang is the site of the celebrated **White Horse Inn** (see below); the landscape provided the perfect setting for Ralph Benatzky's operetta *White Horse Inn,* which brought glory to the town.

Pfarrkirche St. Wolfgang Since the 12th century, long before it was a holiday resort, St. Wolfgang was a renowned pilgrimage center. This church is said to stand on the same rocky spur of land above the lake where St. Wolfgang built a hermitage (signs from the center point the way). The church contains a magnificent Michael Pacher altarpiece (1481), pictured in many Gothic art books. Pacher's altarpiece is luxuriantly adorned with panel paintings and masterfully carved figures. The main panel depicts the *Coronation of the Virgin.* An adjoining museum in the church tower, with an entrance fee of 1.50€, contains relics and explains the history of the saint.

A-5360, St. Wolfgang im Salzkammergut. ✆ **06138/2321.** Free admission. Church May–Sept daily 8am–7pm; Oct–Apr Mon–Sat 8am–4pm, Sun 11am–4pm.

WHERE TO STAY & EAT

Gasthof/Pension Zimmerbräu 🍴 This 400-year-old house was once a local beer brewery, and for more than a century it's been a guesthouse run by the Scharf family. Set in the center of town, it doesn't open onto the lake; however, it has its own private beach cabin with a sun terrace on the lake. The traditionally furnished rooms have balconies, good beds, and ample bathrooms. Consider dining here, as the food is reasonably priced and the chef is known for his Austrian specialties, including homemade beef goulash, braised beef in red wine, deer stew, and a selection of fish. One section of the menu, called "healthy and light," has vegetarian dishes. The inn is entirely nonsmoking.

Markt 89, A-5360 St. Wolfgang. ✆**06138/2204.** Fax 06138/220445. www.zimmerbraeu.com. 26 units. 78€–134€ double. Rates include buffet breakfast. MC, V. Free parking at hotel; 7€ garage parking. **Amenities:** Restaurant; bar; lounge. *In room:* TV, Wi-Fi, coffeemaker, hairdryer, safe.

Hotel Landhaus zu Appesbach ★　Set within a 5-minute walk downhill from the center of St. Wolfgang, this gracefully proportioned lakefront inn was originally built as a private home in the late 19th century. Sometime during its tenure as a private home, the Duke of Windsor spent several weeks here, a visit that added immeasurably to the building's social gloss. Today it's a socially correct address with a scattering of antique and contemporary furnishings and frequent but vague references to the building's illustrious past. Rooms are well furnished, in a wide range of sizes, as befits a former private home. The staff is polite and charming. There's a bar and a restaurant on the premises, but both are open only to residents of the hotel and their guests.

Au Promenade 18, A-5360 Wolfgang. ℰ **06138/22090.** Fax 06138/220914. www.appesbach.com. 27 units. 155€–295€ double; 225€–322€ suite. Rates include buffet breakfast. AE, DC, MC, V. **Amenities:** Restaurant; bar; exercise room; laundry service; dry cleaning; massage; room service; nonsmoking rooms; sauna; solarium; tennis court. *In room:* TV, Wi-Fi, hairdryer, minibar, safe.

Im Weissen Rössl (White Horse Inn) ★★　This hotel was the setting used for a popular play (*Im Weissen Rössl am Wolfgangsee*) written in 1896 and adapted for the Berlin stage by a group of actors and directors who returned here to rewrite it in 1930. Actually, there has been an inn on this site since 1474, with continuous ownership by the Peter family since 1912. Much of the hotel you see today dates from 1955, when the historic core was enlarged and expanded in a style true to the original design.

This scene of the famous operetta absolutely exudes a romantic atmosphere. Its stippled yellow facade conceals a collection of carved antiques. The public areas are large and sunny, usually wood-paneled and upholstered in cheerful colors. Rooms come in a variety of sizes, but all have fine beds. There is a wide lakeside sun terrace within view of the village church and sailing, water-skiing, and windsurfing facilities along their private beach. In the evening the management usually provides live piano or zither music. The inn's two restaurants serve both Austrian and international specialties, and are among the finest in the area—but overly touristy.

Markt 74, A-5360 St. Wolfgang. ℰ **06138/23060.** Fax 06138/230641. www.weissesroessl.at. 72 units. 130€–270€ double; 260€–400€ suite. Rates include buffet breakfast. Half-board (3-day minimum) 30€ per person supplement. AE, DC, MC, V. Parking 10€. **Amenities:** 2 restaurants; bar; babysitting; 2 heated pools (1 indoor); fitness center; Jacuzzi; massage; laundry service; dry cleaning; sauna; room service; nonsmoking rooms; solarium; 2 tennis courts. *In room:* TV, minibar, hairdryer, safe, Wi-Fi.

A SIDE TRIP TO SCHAFBERG

The most popular excursion from St. Wolfgang is to **Schafberg** ★★, which offers the most stunning view in Upper Austria. Legend has it that you can see 13 lakes of the Salzkammergut from here, but we've never been able to do so. However, you're almost sure to have a good view of the Mondsee and the Attersee, and, of course, the entire Wolfgangsee. On a clear day, you can see as far as the Berchtesgaden Alps. You can also gaze at the wonderful backdrop to the lakes, the peaks of the Höllengebirge, and the glacier-capped Dachstein.

The whole trip to Schafberg takes about 4½ hours, nearly half by rack rail called **Schafbergbahn,** which operates from early May to late October. Once you're here, allow for about 30 minutes of walking. Departures are hourly: From April 24 to October 26 daily from 9:15am to 5:10pm. A round-trip fare is 28.60€ for adults and 14.30€ for children. For more information, call ℰ **06138/2232;** www.schafbergbahn.at. There's a hotel on the summit of the mountain, which rises to 1,784m (5,853 ft.).

The Spa of Bad Ischl ★

Bad Ischl is one of the country's most fashionable spas and was the summer seat of Emperor Franz Josef for more than 60 years. The town, constructed on a peninsula between the Traun River and its tributary, the Ischl, still reflects a certain imperial conceit in its architecture, much of it left over from the heyday of the Austro-Hungarian Empire. The spa establishments provide relaxing brine–sulfur mud baths, which might not be the most aromatic of experiences but supposedly are beneficial for a variety of ailments.

ESSENTIALS

GETTING THERE   Bad Ischl sits astride a secondary rail line that runs north to the major rail junction of Attnang–Puchheim and south to the equally important junction of Stainach–Irdning. At these junctions, trains connect frequently with those traveling from Salzburg, Vienna, Linz, and Graz. The trip from Vienna, with connections, takes 3¾ hours; from Graz, it's around 4½ hours. For rail information, contact ✆ **05/1717** (www.oebb.at).

Many travelers opt for one of the buses that depart every hour from Salzburg's main railway station for Bad Ischl. The trip takes about 90 minutes, and transfers are usually not required. By car, Bad Ischl can be reached from Salzburg or Munich by taking Route 158 east from Salzburg.

VISITOR INFORMATION   The **tourist office,** at Bahnhofstrasse 6 (✆ **06132/ 2775-07;** www.badischl.com), will give you complete directions and information about all the sights in the immediate vicinity if you'd like to make some day trips from the spa. It's open Monday to Friday 8am to 6pm, Saturday 9am to 3pm, Sunday 9am to 1pm.

EXPLORING BAD ISCHL

Bad Ischl has chic shopping, as you'll note if you go along **Pfarrgasse.** This street comes to an end at the **Esplanade,** a shaded promenade where wealthy salt merchants lived and the most famous figures in Europe once strolled.

The former pump room, **Trinkhalle,** where the fashionable have eaten and drunk since 1831, is in the middle of town on Ferdinand-Auböck-Platz. Many of the buildings on the square are in Biedermeier style. The 1753 **Pfarrkirche (Parish Church)** was rebuilt when Maria Theresa was empress.

Kaiservilla ★★   The most important attraction in town is this imperial villa close to the center. Emperor Franz Josef used this Biedermeier palace for 60 summers as a residence and recreation center. Highlights include the Gray Salon, where Empress Elisabeth lived and from which she left on July 16, 1898 for Switzerland, a trip that ended with her assassination. In the emperor's study, Franz Josef signed the Manifest, a declaration of war that led to World War I.

In the Kaiserpark. ✆ **06132/23241.** www.kaiservilla.at. Admission 13.50€ adults, 9€ children. May to mid-Oct daily 9:30am–5pm. Apr and Oct daily 10am–4pm. Jan to Mar Wed 10am–4pm. Dec Sat and Sun 10am–4pm. Closed Nov.

Marmorschlössl   Surrounded by the Kaiserpark, this structure, dating from the mid-1800s, houses a photo-historic collection (Sammlung Frank) documenting the history of the spa. The tiny place was once used by Empress Elisabeth as a tea pavilion.

In the Kaiserpark. ✆ **06132/24422.** Admission to museum 2€ adults, 1€ children. Apr–Oct daily 9:30am–5pm. Closed Nov–Mar.

Museum der Stadt Bad Ischl This is the house where Emperor Franz Josef announced his engagement to the Bavarian princess Elisabeth von Wittelsbach, nicknamed "Sissi." Today it's a city museum devoted to the spa's history and culture, with memorabilia not only about the emperor, but also from famous composers who vacationed or lived here.

Esplanade 10. ✆ **06132/25476.** www.museum-badischl.at. Admission 4.70€ adults, 2.30€ children. Apr–Oct and Dec Wed 2–7pm, Fri 1–5pm, Sat–Sun 10am–5pm, also open Thurs in July and Aug; Jan–Mar Fri–Sun 10am–5pm. Closed Nov.

Villa Léhar This lovely villa, now a museum, stands on the opposite bank of the Traun River. Franz Léhar (1870–1948), the composer best known for his operetta *The Merry Widow*, lived here from 1912 until his death.

Traunkai. ✆ **06132/26992.** Admission 5€ adults, 2.30€ children. May, June, and Sept Wed–Sun 10am–5pm. July and Aug Tues–Sun 10am–5pm. Closed Oct–Apr.

WHERE TO STAY

Austria Classic Hotel Goldenes Schiff ★ This hotel has a great location—central but quiet—plus a garden overlooking the Traun River and the Villa Léhar. Rooms are generally spacious and offer tiny but well-kept bathrooms equipped mostly with tub/shower combinations. The riverfront rooms contain balconies and ante-rooms, and all are well furnished with radios and wall safes. Mr. Edwin and family try to satisfy all guests in this snug retreat. In the cozy dining rooms, you'll enjoy excellent cuisine. There is a personal computer with Internet access in the lobby for hotel guests.

Stifterkai 3, A-4820 Bad Ischl. ✆ **06132/24241.** Fax 06132/2424158. www.goldenes-schiff.at. 53 units. 114€–174€ double; 160€–192€ junior suite. Rates include buffet breakfast. AE, DC, MC, V. **Amenities:** Restaurant; bar; fitness center; laundry service; massage; sauna; room service; nonsmoking rooms; solarium. *In room:* TV, hairdryer, minibar, safe, Wi-Fi.

WHERE TO EAT

Villa Schratt ★★ AUSTRIAN During the heyday of Bad Ischl, when the aristocracy of the Habsburg Empire descended on the town every summer with Emperor Franz Josef, one of the town's brightest inhabitants was the actress Katharina Schratt. Famous throughout the German-speaking world, she rose to a discreet kind of stardom as the mistress of the emperor, a relationship that lasted many years with the tacit approval of Franz Josef's estranged wife, the Empress Elisabeth ("Sissi").

Today Katharina's elegant arts and crafts villa is an attractive, upscale restaurant. Set about 4km (2½ miles) west of town, beside the highway leading to Salzburg, the house, originally built in 1610 and renovated several times, was acquired by Ms. Schratt in 1889. She occupied it every summer until the death of Franz Josef in 1916.

In the restaurant's dining rooms, where all the references to Ms. Schratt and her relationship to the Emperor are extremely discreet, the atmosphere is equally understated; here, amid the unobtrusive attentions of the staff, you can select items from a changing menu, such as a terrine of duck *en gelée,* carpaccio of salmon-trout with salad, neck of lamb with garlic sauce, filet of venison with elderberry sauce, and, for dessert, cheese dumplings with cinnamon and fruit sauce. The extensive wine list includes Austrian, Italian, and French vineyards.

Steinbrüch 43. ✆ **06132/27647.** www.villaschratt.at. Reservations required. Main courses 18€–35€. AE, MC. Thurs–Mon 11:30am–2pm and 6–9pm. Closed Feb.

Weinhaus Attwenger ★ AUSTRIAN   This is one of the region's best-known restaurants, with strong connections to musical prodigies Bruckner, who dined here frequently, and Léhar, who lived next door and shared a garden and many glasses of fine wine with the owners. The restaurant's central section was originally built in 1540, and its old-style decor is much imitated. In summer, you can dine or just savor a glass of wine or coffee on the sun terrace over the Traun River. If you want a full meal, the menu includes medallions of veal chef's style, paprika schnitzel or pork schnitzel, *Tafelspitz,* and several kinds of fresh lake fish.

Léharkai 12. (✆ **06132/23327.** www.weinhaus-attwenger.com. Reservations recommended. Main courses 8.75€–22€; 4-course fixed-price menu 29€. MC, V. Tues–Sun 11:30am–2pm and 6–9:30pm. Closed Tues Nov–Apr, and 1 month around Christmas.

AN IMPERIAL CAFE

After viewing the summer playgrounds of the Habsburg monarchs, anyone with a love of history should head to **Konditorei Zauner,** Pfarrgasse 7 (✆ **06132/2331020;** www.zauner.at), founded in 1832. The imperial court used to order pastries here, and it was said that the easiest way to tap into the pulse of the empire was to eavesdrop on a nearby table during July and August. The cafe's guest book shows a clientele as rich and diverse as the pastry offerings.

You can buy the exquisite pastries from the gold-and-white rococo showroom (which has been renovated to handle the flood of summer tourists) or eat at the small tables in a series of elegant inner rooms. Many items can be mailed as gifts. Sandwiches and salads are also on the menu. Coffee costs 2.95€, with pastries starting at 4€. It's open daily 8:30am to 6pm.

BAD ISCHL AFTER DARK

Most of the year, Bad Ischl seems trapped in its imperial past, a nostalgia that can be relaxing at best and soporific at worst. During July and August, however, the spa livens up a bit and presents a well-rehearsed operetta in whichever public building can accommodate it. As part of the **Léhar Festival** (✆ **06132/23839;** www.leharfestival. at), *Paganini* and *The White Horse Inn* are on the program for 2011 with performances almost every night of the week, usually at 8pm, but sometimes at 3:30pm. Tickets range from 26€ to 78€.

HALLSTATT ★

88km (55 miles) SE of Salzburg; 19km (12 miles) S of Bad Ischl

Hallstatt, a small market town south of Bad Ischl, looks as if it is floating on the bank of the dark, brooding lake of the same name. One of the most picturesque villages in the Salzkammergut, and in Austria for that matter, this town of some 800 inhabitants retains a sleepy mountain feel even in the height of the tourist season. It sits in the shadow of the daunting Hohe Sieg peak, site of an ancient civilization and one of the many mountains that surround the 8-km long (5-mile) and 2-km wide (1½-mile) wide Hallstättersee.

Owing its longevity to the local deposits of salt, Hallstatt is the oldest continually inhabited village in Europe, site of an early Iron Age culture dating from 800 to 400 B.C. The mining of salt from the Hohe Sieg was known among pre-Celtic tribes of 1000 B.C., died out in medieval times, was revived by the Habsburgs, and continues to flourish today.

Essentials

GETTING THERE   Traveling to Hallstatt by train is a treat, in that the tiny station is on the other side of the lake and connected to town via ferry. Boats leave right after the train arrives, and being able to watch the village drift toward you is worth the extra 2.20€. The Hallstatt station lies on the same line as Bad Ischl (for more information, see "St. Wolfgang & Bad Ischl," earlier in this chapter), and is 43km (27 miles) north of the main rail junction at Stainach-Irdning and 64km (40 miles) south of the rail junction at Attnang–Puchheim. The trip to Hallstatt from Linz, with connections, takes 2 hours; from Vienna, it takes 4 hours. For rail information, contact ✆ **05/1717** (www.oebb.at).

Around eight buses per day depart from the railway station at Bad Ischl, go through Bad Goisern, and continue on to Hallstatt proper (trip time: about 35 min.).

If you're driving, go to Bad Ischl, continue south along Route 145 until you reach Route 166, and then head south via Steeg to Hallstatt.

VISITOR INFORMATION   The **tourist office** is in the Kultur- und Kongresshaus, Seestrasse 169 (✆ **06134/8208;** www.hallstaat.net). It's open in July and August Monday to Friday 9am to 5pm, Saturday 10am to 2pm. From September to June the hours are 9am to noon and 2 to 5pm.

What to See & Do

EXPLORING THE VILLAGE

The village of Hallstatt, with its narrow and often steep streets, gave its name to one of the most important eras of prehistory. Some 2,000 graves of prehistoric people, half of them cremated, have been excavated in the area, which Austrians refer to as a "cradle of civilization." Many of the artifacts excavated here dating from Neolithic times are displayed in the **Prähistorisches Museum,** Seestrasse 56 (✆ **06134/ 828015**). The cremation graves have revealed artifacts that indicated the existence of a ruling class. Apparently the burials continued to about 350 B.C., the late Iron Age. The museum is open May to September daily 10am to 6pm, October and April daily 10am to 4pm, and November to March Wednesday to Sunday 11am to 3pm. Admission is 8€ for adults and 4€ for children.

The center of this beautifully situated village, with views of the Dachstein mountain massif, is the **Marktplatz (Market Square),** which contains some 16th-century buildings.

You can visit the **Pfarrkirche (Parish Church),** which is situated within a churchyard bordering the dark waters of the lake. The house of worship is a large structure from the latter part of the 15th century. Visitors can also go to the **Chapel of St. Michael,** a Gothic church next to the parish church. The cemetery was so small that graves had to be reused starting in the 17th century. Thus, exhumed skulls were displayed in the adjoining *Karner* (charnel house or bone house) with birth and death dates written on the decorated craniums, an eyebrow-raising sight not to be missed.

OUTDOOR ACTIVITIES

Numerous cable cars and lifts are available in town and the surrounding area to take you up the mountains, where you can take in panoramic views. If you'd like a little exercise, the Salzbergweg trail right behind the Information office makes the steep climb to the Hallstattzeitliches Gräberfeld (burial ground), where a few outdoor display cases exhibit some of the finds with their tools and ornaments. Mountain climbing is also possible on the nearby **Dachstein** massif (2,995m/9,826 ft.), and you can explore the **Dachstein Giant Ice Caves,** although the mountain is more easily reached from nearby Obertraun than from Hallstatt. For a great way to spend a morning, fish in the Hallstättersee and the Traun River, or try sailing, rowing, motor boating, swimming, or tennis. In winter, Hallstatt is also a sports center, with snow from November to April. You can go skiing, sledding, curling, and ice-skating, or hike along pleasant winter footpaths. The tourist office (see above) will provide complete details about which of these activities will be available at the time of your visit.

THE SALT MINES IN SALZBURG

High above Hallstatt is one of the most distinctive geological formations in the region, **Salzwelten/Hallstatt ★** (© 06134/8251; www.salzwelten.at), which is not to be confused with Salzburg, the city. Miners have been hauling vast quantities of salt out of the mountain for centuries; the mines are still active and visitors can tour them to get an insight into the amount of work needed to create and run a modern mine. Teams of archaeologists have accumulated many rare objects from the debris left by former miners.

To reach **Salt Mountain** from Hallstatt, take an uphill ride on the cable car that departs from the southern suburb of Lahn. In May and from mid-September to mid-October, the funicular runs daily from 9am to 4:30pm; from June to mid-September, it runs daily from 9am to 6pm. The only way you can visit the mines is on a guided tour, which is 24€ for adults, and 12€ for children aged 4 to 15, including the cable car ride; for those who make the hike up and down, the fee is reduced to 18€ and 9€, respectively. Children under 4 are not admitted. From mid-April to mid-September, tours are conducted daily at frequent intervals, from 9:30am to 4:30pm. From mid-September to the beginning of October, tours are conducted daily from 9:30am to 3:30pm. In October, the last tour is at 3pm. The mines are closed from late October to mid-April. Although tours of the mines take only 50 minutes, you should allow 2½ hours for the full experience.

There's a restaurant and snack bar with a terrace and a belvedere for taking in the view. Hikers can go all the way from here to the **Iron Age cemetery,** an approximately 1½-hour trip. If you ask, the tourist office will outline a series of hikes in the area. One that goes along the Echerntal to **Waldbachstrub,** at the top of the valley, has lovely waterfalls along the way. You can also climb to the **Tiergartenhütte,** which has a small inn, and on to the **Wiesberghaus,** 1,885m (6,184 ft.). After that, only the hardy continue to the **Simony-Hütte** at 2,205m (7,235 ft.), where there's another small inn lying at the foot of the Hallstatt Glacier. From Simony-Hütte, mountain climbers can summit the **Hoher Dachstein,** the loftiest peak in the massif (2,995m/9,826 ft.); the climb takes 3½ hours.

DACHSTEIN CAVES ★

The Dachstein Ice Caves, Dachstein Bahn, A-4831 Obertraun, are among the most spectacular natural sights of Upper Austria. To reach them, drive around the southern shore of the lake to Obertraun, 6km (3¾ miles) east of Hallstatt, where a sign in the vicinity will direct you to the lower station of the cableway that takes you to the caves. The cableway deposits you at the intermediate platform (1,351m/4,432 ft.) on the Schönbergalm. From here, it's about a 20-minute walk to the entrance to the caves.

Among the many attractions is the **Rieseneishöhle (Giant Ice Cave),** where even in summer the temperature is about 30°F (–1°C). Be sure to dress for the cold. Among the ice cave's breathtaking features are the frozen waterfalls. You'll also see the so-called King Arthur's Cave and the Great Ice Chapel. The ice cave is open from the first of May until mid- to late-October daily from 9am to 4pm; a guided tour is 10.80€ for adults and 6€ for children. If you also want to visit **Mammoth Cave,** a combined ticket is 15.80€ for adults and 10€ for children. Mammoth Cave has large galleries (subterranean passageways) cut through the rock by ancient underground torrents. It takes about 1½ hours to go on a guided tour of these caves. You're allowed to visit only a small part of the cave network, which totals 37km (23 miles) in length, with a drop of 1,180m (3,871 ft.). For information, call ✆ **06134/8400.**

From the Schönbergalm station, you can continue by cableway to the upper platform at a height of 2,111m (6,926 ft.). This is the **Hoher Krippenstein ★★,** which offers a panoramic view of the Dachstein massif. A chapel commemorates the deaths of three teachers and 10 students in April 1954 after getting trapped in a snow storm. The cableway operates every 15 minutes daily from 9am to 4pm. In summer, don't be surprised if there's a line. A round-trip ticket via the Schönbergalm to Krippenstein costs 23€ for adults and 14€ for children. If you want to take the last leg over to **Gjaidalm** (1,793m/5,883 ft.), round-trip tickets then cost 25€ and 15€, respectively.

OTHER NATURAL ATTRACTIONS

The region around Hallstatt is riddled with geological oddities, including caves, caverns, and glaciers with ice that never melts. A local cavern that's particularly easy to visit is **Koppenbrüllerhöhle (Koppenbrüller Cave).** Within, there's a raging underground stream that causes continual erosion (and enlargement) of the cavern. The local municipality views it as a natural wonder and, as such, maintains a series of underground catwalks and galleries that you can walk along.

The easiest way to reach the cave is by car or taxi, but it's also accessible via trains, about three a day, that pull into the local station, Koppenbrüllerhöhle, after a 15-minute ride from Hallstatt or a 5-minute ride from Obertraun. There's a hotel, the Gasthaus Koppenrast, nearly adjacent to the railway station, which serves as an additional landmark for motorists. From here, you have to walk for about 15 minutes across well-marked trails to reach the cave. One-hour guided tours are conducted from early May to late September daily from 9am to 4pm for 10€ for adults and 6€ for children.

A final option for natural sightseeing is to check out the view over the steep and foreboding south wall of the Dachstein, technically in Styria. For the best outlook, take the **Gletscherbahn** cable car uphill to an alpine plateau known as **Hunerkogel,** site of a hotel with its own cafe and restaurant. To reach the base of the Gletscherbahn cable car, drive for 87km (54miles) along Routes 166, 99, and 320, following the signs to Schladming (which you'll pass through) and Ramsau. The 12-minute cable car ride operates year-round daily from 8am to 5pm, with the exception of annual closings between November and Christmas and from early April to mid-May. Half-day tickets cost 30€ for adults and 16.50€ for children. At the upper belvedere (the above-mentioned Hunerkogel, 2,696m/8,845 ft. above sea level), you'll enjoy a panoramic view that includes the Grossglockner Pass and the Salzkammergut Alps, and a sweep of the Schladminger Gletscher, where some hardy locals sometimes ski on rock-strewn, granular snow even in midsummer.

Where to Stay & Eat

Gasthof Zauner ★ 🍴 In the center of the town's historic market square stands this century-old inn where you are welcomed by its mountaineering owner bedecked in traditional lederhosen. A long-enduring family-run hotel, the restaurant is a favorite of locals, for the renowned fresh fish specialties direct from Hallstatt Lake, such as the delectable white fish, the mild *Reinanke*. The wine cellar also enjoys local renown. The wooden chalet is a cliché of Austrian folkloric charm, with balconies overlooking the village, and pine-paneled rooms rustically but comfortably furnished with carved headboards.

Marktplatz, A-4830 Hallstatt. ☎ **06134/8246.** Fax 06134/82468. www.zauner.hallstatt.net. 12 units. 90€–112€ double. Rates include breakfast. DC, MC, V. Closed mid-Nov to mid-Dec. **Amenities:** Restaurant. *In room:* TV, hairdryer.

Seehotel Grüner Baum This historic and rustically elegant hotel was originally established around 200 years ago as a lakeside inn and was amply enlarged around 1900. Capped with a hipped roof of hammered copper, it has an ocher-colored facade with white, heavily bordered windows. Prices for the comfortable rooms are determined almost exclusively by the views, of either Marktplatz (the town's main square), the lake, or the street. Rooms come in a variety of sizes, including an apartment for larger parties, and all are equipped with comfortable beds. The hotel's sun terrace extends out over the water on a pier, where you can go swimming or simply relax with a drink on a chaise longue. The downstairs restaurant specializes in fish from the lake, when available.

Marktplatz 104, A-4830 Hallstatt. ☎ **06134/826344.** Fax 06134/8263-44. www.gruenerbaum.cc. 19 units. 105€–170€ double; 150€–200€ apt. Rates include breakfast. AE, DC, MC, V. **Amenities:** Restaurant; bar, lounge; babysitting; laundry service; dry cleaning; exercise room; sauna; solarium. *In room:* TV, dataport.

THE TRAUNSEE ★★

One of the biggest lakes in the Salzkammergut, the Traunsee is about 12km (7½ miles) long and some 3km (2 miles) wide at its broadest. It lies east of the two major lakes already explored: The Attersee and the Mondsee. Three mountain peaks—Traunstein, Hochkogel, and Erlakogel—form a silhouette above its eastern shore that Austrians call *Schlafende Griechin* (Sleeping Greek Girl).

To reach Traunsee from Bad Ischl (see earlier in this chapter), drive northeast along the Traun River (Rte. 145) and follow the signs. The Salzkammergut road then runs along the western edge of the lake, its most dramatic part between Ebensee, at the lake's southwestern tip, and Traunkirchen. A feat of engineering, this corniche had to be hewn out of rock. The lake itself is ringed with a number of resorts, the chief town being Gmunden. A lake steamer service provides an alternative means for viewing the lake in summer.

Gmunden ★

This is one of the most popular summer resorts in the Salzkammergut, perched on the northern rim of the Traunsee with pine-green mountains forming the backdrop. Gmunden is located 169km (105 miles) southwest of Vienna, 40km (25 miles) southwest of Linz, and 76km (47 miles) northeast of Salzburg.

ESSENTIALS

GETTING THERE All train passengers to Gmunden must transfer at the railway junction of either Attnang–Puchheim (the more convenient) or Lambach. Both sit directly on the main rail line between Linz and Salzburg, handling many express trains throughout the day.

From Attnang–Puchheim, about 64km (40 miles) to the north, about a dozen trains continue on to Gmunden's Hauptbahnhof (main railway station). From Lambach, only around three trains per day run to Gmunden's Seebahnhof (lakeside railway station). Taxis are readily available for the short trip between these two stations, although the Hauptbahnhof is more convenient to most hotels. Gmunden is the starting point for many buses heading out into the surrounding valleys. For rail information, contact ✆ 05/1717 (www.oebb.at).

To reach Gmunden from Linz by car, take the A1 southwest to the junction with Route 144, at which point you head south.

VISITOR INFORMATION The **tourist office,** Toscanapark 1 (✆ **07612/ 64305;** www.traunsee.at), is open in winter Monday to Friday 9am to 5pm, Saturday and Sunday 9am to 1pm; in summer Monday to Friday 8am to 8pm, Saturday and Sunday 10am to 7pm.

WALKING AROUND GMUNDEN

Chestnut trees line the mile-long, traffic-free **Esplanade ★**, the town's chief attraction. You can walk from **Rathausplatz (Town Hall Square)** to the **Strandbad (Lakeside Beach),** watching the many majestic swans glide serenely along the lake. In days of yore, emperors, kings, and members of the aristocracy strolled along the Esplanade and in the town's park, just as you can do today. The Welfen from Hannover, Württembergs, Bourbons, and archdukes of Austria favored Gmunden as a pleasure ground, as did Franz Schubert, Friedrich Hebbel, and Johannes Brahms, among others.

The lake beaches are some of the best in the whole area, and in summer you can enjoy a wide variety of lakeside activities, from swimming and sailing to windsurfing and water-skiing, as well as tennis and horseback riding. For the experienced, it's also possible to do a little mountain climbing. Otherwise, there are folkloric performances and dance clubs, or you can just relax in a wine tavern or an outdoor cafe. The tourist office will supply details.

Gmunden, former center of the salt trade, has long produced Gmundner ceramics, and you'll see artistic work in faience (opaque-colored glazes) and green-flamed pottery.

One of the more evocative curiosities of Gmunden is the **Schloss Ort (Ort Castle) ★**, a stately Renaissance castle that's set on a small island a few yards offshore from Gmunden's town center at the far end of the Esplanade, and home to the Seeschloss Ort Restaurant (✆ **07612/62499**). Guided tours can be arranged with several days' advance notice through the tourist office (see above), although most visitors to Gmunden opt to wander around on their own.

The region around Gmunden is rich with sweeping panoramas. From a well-marked spot close to the town center, you can take a cable car, the **Grünberg Seilbahn** (✆ **07612/64977;** www.greunberg-gmunden.net), to the top of the town's nearest mountain, the Grünberg, where you'll be able to see out over the Traunsee and the Dachstein. The cable car, hauling four persons up and downhill within each of its *Kabines*, operates only May through October; it charges 12.50€ for adults and 6.50€ for children 16 and under for a round-trip from Gmunden to the top, a 12-minute ride each way. It operates daily 9am to 5pm.

In winter, ski lifts, runs, and slopes on the Grünberg are easily reached from Gmunden. Other winter activities in Gmunden are curling, ice-skating, and walking along the lake.

WHERE TO STAY & EAT

Pension Magerl   These premises were originally built in the 1600s and converted to a farmhouse around 1900. In the 1950s, members of the Magerl family transformed it into a pleasant hotel, with an annex added in 1991. The establishment you see today sits in a grassy meadow less than a kilometer (½ mile) east of Gmunden, with a view overlooking the nearby lake. Each floor contains a residents' lounge, and rooms are simple yet comfortable. Beds are adequate, not spectacular, and the bathrooms are a bit small but equipped with tub/shower combinations. Housekeeping, however, is excellent.

Ackerweg 18, A-4810 Gmunden. ✆ **07612/63675.** Fax 07612/63675220. 70 units. 90€ double. Rate includes breakfast. DC, MC, V. **Amenities:** Breakfast room; lounge; indoor heated pool; fitness center; sauna; nonsmoking rooms; rooms for those w/limited mobility. *In room:* TV, hairdryer, safe, Wi-Fi.

Schlosshotel Freisitz Roith ★★   On foundations dating from the 15th century, this castle was built as a summer house by the Habsburg emperor Rudolf II in 1597. After centuries of private ownership, it was transformed into a hotel in 1965. One mile east of the town center, it's set amid a garden on a forested hillside, overlooking the lake. Dozens of architectural oddities include a crenellated tower with tall arched windows, wrought-iron window bars, jutting parapets over many of the balconied windows, and a stone terrace—site of a well-recommended restaurant—built into the slope of the grass-covered hill. In the grounds, a private footpath leads downhill to a beach at the edge of the lake.

The interior incorporates modern building materials with the older stone-accented design of vaulted ceilings. Rooms range from old-fashioned and dignified to contemporary yet conservatively furnished. As with most old castles, rooms come in a variety of sizes, and all are comfortable. Bathrooms have been equipped with spotlessly maintained tub/shower combinations.

Traunsteinstrasse 87, A-4810 Gmunden. ✆ **07612/64905.** Fax 07612/490517. www.freisitzroith.at. 24 units. 150€–230€ double; 230€–320€ suite. Rates include breakfast. AE, DC, MC, V. **Amenities:** Restaurant; bar; babysitting; fitness center; Jacuzzi; room service; sauna; laundry service; dry cleaning; nonsmoking rooms. *In room:* TV, hairdryer, minibar, safe, Wi-Fi.

Nearby Abbey

Benediktinerstift Lambach ★   Founded in 1056, this Benedictine abbey lies in Lambach, 16km (10 miles) southwest of Wels and about 24km (15 miles) north of Gmunden, where the Traun River meets its tributary, the Ager. Drive southwest for 16km (10 miles) along Highway 1 (referred to on some maps as Hwy. 144), following signs to Lambach.

The originally Romanesque monastery on Marktplatz (Market Square) of the old town now carries a baroque facade, while a towering marble gateway from 1693 leads into the first courtyard.

In the bell tower are some 11th-century Romanesque frescoes, long hidden, that are some of the abbey's major attractions. A 1967 restoration was a major event, hailed by the Austrian press.

The abbey's other attractions include a richly decorated library and a rather sumptuous refectory from the 18th century. The abbey church was built in the 1650s, and it is believed that its main altar was designed by the celebrated baroque architect J. B. Fischer von Erlach. The only surviving monastic theater in Austria, built in 1770, is reached by a stairway.

Marktplatz, in Lambach. ✆ **07245/28355** (Lambach tourist office). Admission 7€ adults, 4€ children. Mon–Sat 10–11am; Sun 2:30–5pm.

INNSBRUCK & TYROL: THE BEST OF SCENIC AUSTRIA

Tyrol is a region of snow and ice, dense evergreen forests, and massive glaciers. Fast-flowing rivers cut through the Alps to create narrow, lush valleys that end abruptly at the feet of daunting snow-capped mountains. Tiny villages are scattered throughout these valleys and tucked between large peaks, many that still embrace the Tyrolean traditions of the past. The mountain scenery is stunning at any time of year, with endless possibilities for exploring the area. In addition to being famous for its skiing, this spectacular alpine region offers travelers a host of other outdoor activities year-round, including hiking and mountain climbing, glacier tours, trout fishing, mountain biking, and horseback riding.

If you're heading for Tyrol and want to travel around the region, Innsbruck is the best place to use as a base. Several major roads (A12, A13, and Route 171) merge at Innsbruck, and you can easily reach most of the major ski resorts, as well as the Ötz Valley, Arlberg, and the Kitzbühel area. Parking is rarely a problem; and, unless otherwise noted, you park for free. In addition to being central, Innsbruck has a great deal to offer, including an Alpenzoo, home only to animals indigenous to the Alps, and several great palaces, including the Hofburg and Schloss Ambras.

Tyrol and its capital, Innsbruck, were centers of power at the end of the Middle Ages, when the Habsburg Holy Roman Emperor, Maximilian I, made it his capital, though many of the castles that were scattered across the medieval countryside are only ruins today.

With a population of more than half a million, occupying some 12,489 sq. km (4,822 sq. miles), Tyrol was much larger until the South Tyrol, a large wine-producing area and the wealthiest part of Tyrol, was annexed to Italy in 1919. This loss was a great blow for the Tyroleans who remained in Austria, many separated from relatives, friends, and sometimes livelihoods.

By the same post-World War I treaty, East Tyrol, whose capital is Lienz, was divided from North Tyrol, where Innsbruck is the capital. The two are separated by the portion of Tyrol given to Italy, with a strip of Land Salzburg to the east. To its west is the Austrian province of Vorarlberg (covered in chapter 13), to the north is Germany, and to the south are Italy and a small part of Switzerland. East Tyrol is bordered by Carinthia on the east, Land Salzburg on the north, and Italy.

The Valley of the Inn River cuts across the northern part of the province, and in addition to its famous mountains, the province is known for its deep blue alpine lakes, such as the Achensee and the Walchsee. The Drau River, rising in the Höhe Tauern Alps, runs through East Tyrol. The Kaisergebirge is a nature reserve of Tyrol, with coniferous forests and meadowlands. And the Ötz Valley extends for 56km (35 miles) from the south bank of the Upper Inn.

Seefeld, near Innsbruck, is one of Austria's "Big Three" rendezvous points for the international ski crowd. Kitzbühel ranks among the world's most fashionable ski resorts, and at the Kitzbühel Ski Circus, it's possible to ski downhill for 80km (50 miles). Skiers also head for St. Anton am Arlberg, on the main Vienna–Zurich rail line, and the birthplace of modern skiing techniques.

Tips for Active Travelers

There's plenty to do outdoors in the dramatic high-altitude landscapes of Tyrol. If you don't want to make plans until you arrive, no problem: Every hotel, inn, and pension in the region is well versed in where, when, and how you can fish, swim, ski, play tennis, or relax at a local spa. But if you want to plan in advance, here's a list of specialists who can help you plan your outdoor adventure and, in some cases, put you in contact with those that arrange tours.

The best outfitter for arranging specialized tours, such as mountain climbing and hiking, is **David Zwilling,** Waldhof 64, A-5441 Abtenau (© **06991/3012009;** www.outdoorconsulting.com). This outfitter will also arrange other tours including white-water rafting, biking, and even paragliding.

BIKING ★★ Many areas of Tyrol are simply too rocky and steep for recreational cycling, though mountain bikers love the area. With a bit of planning, however, you can usually limit your cycling to trips up and down valleys that separate the region's many mountains. You can arrange rentals with **Crazy Bikez** (© **0650/7957214,** www.crazybikez.com), where they will deliver the bike of your choice to your hotel, or at **Schönherr Sport,** Stubaitalstrasse 79, at Neustift (© **05226/369043;** www. schoenherr.cc).

CANOEING & RAFTING ★ For canoeing and white-water rafting, contact **Sportschule Fankhauser** (© **05266/87690,** www.tirolrafting.at), a specialist in conducting waterborne excursions. But it doesn't stop there: From climbing to canyoneering to canoeing, they offer it all, for beginners to experts. The office is located in A-6425 Haiming, 40km (25 miles) from Innsbruck.

CROSS-COUNTRY SKIING In winter, you can check with the tourist offices to find out about snow conditions. The staff will also tell you how to get to the major ski areas. One of the top outfitters is **Schischule Seefeld,** 6100 Seefeld (© **05212/2412;** www.schi-seefeld.at), just outside Innsbruck. Another is in the nearby alpine

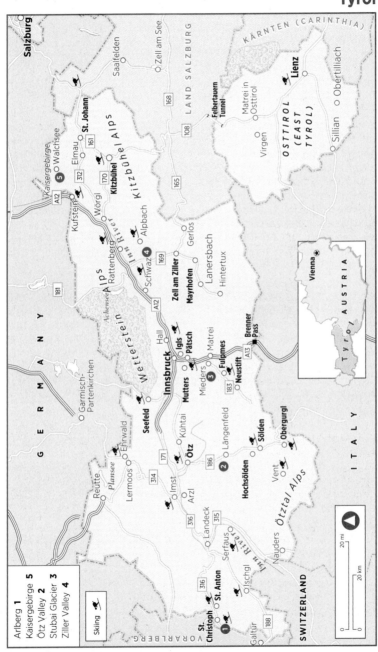

Arlberg **1**
Kaisergebirge **5**
Ötz Valley **2**
Stubai Glacier **3**
Ziller Valley **4**

Skiing

hamlet of Igls: **Schischule Igls-Patscherkofel,** Eichlerstrasse 16 (© **0512/377383;** www.snowsport-igls.com), 6.5km (4 miles) south of Innsbruck.

FISHING   Some of the best trout and carp fishing in Austria is in the streams and lakes near the town of **Kössen,** about a 30-minute drive north of Kitzbühel. A fishing license is priced at 28€ per day for the Kolhbach or Weissenbach Rivers, or 17€ per day for the Walchsee. Licenses are for sale at the **Kaiserwinkel Tourist Office** (© **0501/100**), which is open during the peak summer and winter seasons Monday to Friday 8am to 6pm, Saturday 9am to noon and 4 to 6pm, Sundays and holidays 10am to noon.

MOUNTAIN CLIMBING ★★   Austria's most dramatic mountain climbing occurs on the rocky (and sometimes icebound) slopes of Tyrol, particularly at **St. Anton, Mayrhofen, Kitzbühel,** and **Saalbach/Hinterglemm.** One of the best outfitters is Martin Ripfl-Marx, owner of **Tirolalpin Berg-Sport-Zentrum,** Seewald 11, A-6105 Leutasch (© **05214/5152;** www.tirolalpin.at). Set in a small village 5km (3 miles) northwest of Seefeld, this outfitter offers physically fit adventurers a series of climbing excursions in the Tyrolean Alps. Trips range from a half-day initiation course for beginners (42€ per person), to week-long, high-endurance exposures to rock and ice climbing and canyoneering down streambeds deeply eroded into layered bedrock. A worthy competitor closer to Innsbruck is the **Alpinschule,** In der Stille, A-6161 Natters (© **0512/546000;** www.alpinschule.com).

SAILING   If the idea of navigating the tricky and oft-changing winds from the deck of a sailing craft appeals to you, the best and most comprehensive sailing school in the region is **Segelschule Tirol,** A-6213 Pertisau (© **650/5155850;** www.die segelschule.eu). Headquartered in a lakefront town adjacent to Tyrol's largest lakes (the Achensee, a long and narrow body of water), it offers sailing instruction for all levels of sailors (beginners and advanced) as well as for children and teens. The Achensee, which measures just under 10km (6 miles) from north end to south end, lies 35km (22 miles) east of Innsbruck via the A12 superhighway.

SKIING & SNOWBOARDING ★★★   The possibilities for skiing in Tyrol are endless. The "Big Three" of Tyrol—Seefeld, Arlberg, and Kitzbühel—offer some of the world's best skiing, and frequently hold World Cup skiing events (p. 386, p. 377, and p. 396). To get an overview of some of the other resorts scattered throughout the province, check out www.ski-austria.com.

TENNIS   There are many tennis courts in Innsbruck, but since they are so popular, you should reserve court time in advance. The best courts are at **Tennis & Squash Hallen,** Fürstenweg 172 (© **0512/284364;** www.burkia.at).

INNSBRUCK ★★★: THE CAPITAL OF TYROL

489km (304 miles) SW of Vienna; 159km (99 miles) S of Munich; 360km (224 miles) SW of Linz; 190km (118 miles) SW of Salzburg; 204km (127 miles) SE of Bregenz

The capital of Tyrol, Innsbruck (elevation 573m/1,880 ft.) is one of Europe's most beautiful cities, at the junction of two important routes across the eastern Alps. Innsbruck is about 30 minutes from the Italian border and 45 minutes from Germany.

   Today Innsbruck's beauty is protected by town planners who ensure that any new structures built in the inner city harmonize with the pre-existing Gothic, Renaissance, and baroque buildings. Modern urban development exists, away from the historic areas, spreading along the Inn Valley.

The name Innsbruck means "bridge over the Inn," the fast-moving river that flows through the city. The city lies at a meeting place of the Valley of the Inn and the Sill Gorge. As long ago as 1180, a little settlement on the river was moved from the northern bank to the site of the present Altstadt (Old Town). In 1239, as part of Swabia Bavaria, it was granted its own rights and privileges as an official city, and later, Innsbruck became home of the court of the Habsburg Empire.

The city was celebrated throughout Europe under the Habsburg Holy Roman Emperor Maximilian I. Under Maximilian, whose reign (1490–1519) signaled the end of the Middle Ages, Innsbruck reached the height of its cultural and political importance (it remains the largest city and cultural center of Tyrol). The city had a second imperial zenith some 300 years later, during the 40-year reign of Maria Theresa. Much later, in 1945, Innsbruck became the headquarters of the French zone of occupation in the aftermath of World War II.

Twice in a dozen years—in 1964 and 1976—the eyes of the world turned to Innsbruck when it hosted the Winter Olympics. The city and its suburbs now combine their rich history with their reputation as a popular winter-sports center with modern facilities. Skiers who come to Innsbruck benefit twice: They stay in a cosmopolitan city called the jewel of the Alps, and ski on some of the world's most sought-after slopes. For nonskiers and summer visitors, the medieval Altstadt stands out against the stunning backdrop of daunting snow-capped peaks, a plethora of restaurants, bars and specialty shops, and the endless outdoors.

Essentials
GETTING THERE
By Plane
Innsbruck's airport, **Flughafen Innsbruck-Kranebitten,** Fürstenweg 180 (✆ **0512/ 225250;** www.innsbruck-airport.com), is 3km (2 miles) west of the city. It offers a regularly scheduled air service from all major Austrian airports, as well as from Amsterdam, Frankfurt, London, and a number of other major European cities. The frequency of flights varies depending on the time of year, with winter seeing the number of flights and departure cities increase.

The best gateways from major American hubs are Frankfurt and Vienna. Flying time from Frankfurt is 50 to 70 minutes. From the airport, bus F leads to the city center. Tickets cost 1.80€. Taxis take about 10 minutes and cost 10€ or more.

There are six car-rental kiosks at the Innsbruck Airport: Europcar (✆ **0664/ 1225995**); Megadrive (✆ **050105/4150**); Avis (✆ **0512/5717540**); Ö-rent (✆ **0512/588468**); Hertz (✆ **0512/580901**); and Sixt GmbH (✆ **0512/2929390**).

To drive from the airport to downtown Innsbruck, take the Fürstenweg (which becomes Mariahilfstrasse) for 2km (1¼ miles), following the signs to Innsbruck Zentrum.

By train
Innsbruck is connected with all parts of Europe by railway links. Trains arrive at the main railway station, the **Hauptbahnhof,** Südtiroler Platz (✆ **05/1717;** www.oebb.at). There are multiple trains from Munich (trip time: 3 hr.) and Salzburg (1 hr.) each day.

By Bus
A bus service to all Austrian cities is provided by both **PostBuses** and **ÖBB Buses.** You can take a bus from Salzburg, although the train is quicker. For information about various bus routings through Tyrol, call ✆ **05/1717.**

Innsbruck's Open Sesame Card

To attract more visitors to Innsbruck, the city has come up with the **Innsbruck Card** (www.innsbruck-tourismus.com), granting you a number of discounts to attractions, including 18 museums and all city-operated public transportation. The card even entitles you to a visit to the Swarovski Crystal Worlds (p. 355), including transport on a shuttle bus specifically designed for cardholders. Free visits to the Alpenzoo are also included. The card costs 29€ for 1 day, 34€ for 2 days, or 39€ for 3 days. The card is half-price for children under 15.

By Car

If you're **driving** down from Salzburg in the northeast, take Autobahn A8 west, which joins Autobahn A93 (later it becomes the A12), heading southwest to Innsbruck. This latter Autobahn (A93/A12) is the main artery from Munich. From the south, you can take the Brenner toll motorway.

GETTING AROUND

A network of **trams** and **bus lines** cover all of Innsbruck and its close environs, and buses and trams use the same tickets. Single tickets in the central area cost 1.80€, a booklet of four tickets goes for 5.90€, and a 24-hour ticket costs 4.10€. Tram in German is *Strassenbahn*. On the left bank of the Inn, the main tram and bus arteries are Museumstrasse and Mariahilfstrasse. On the right bank, trams and buses aren't routed into the pedestrian zone, but to their main stop in Marktgraben. For information about various routes, call the **Innsbrucker Verkehrsbetriebe** (✆ 0512/53070; www.ivb.at). Most tickets can be purchased at the Innsbruck tourist office, tobacco shops, and automated vending machines.

Buses of the Postbus system leave from the Autobushof (Central Bus Station), adjacent to the Hauptbahnhof. Here buses head for all parts of Tyrol. The station is open Monday through Friday from 7:30am to 6pm and Saturday from 7am to 1pm. For information about bus schedules, call ✆ **0512/585155.**

Taxi stands are scattered at strategic points throughout the city, or you can call a service center (✆ **0512/5311**). For a more romantic ride, you can hire a *Fiaker* (horse-drawn carriage) from a spot adjacent to the **Tiroler Landestheater,** Rennweg; slowly exploring the city to the sound of hoof beats costs around 30€ for 30 minutes.

You might consider renting a **bike** near the Hauptbahnhof. Rentals range from 17€ to 30€ per day depending on the type of bike. Bike pick-up from your hotel can be arranged for an extra fee. Rentals are available from April to early November only. For more information, call **Die Boerse** (✆ 0512/581742; www.dieboerse.at/), Leopoldstrasse 4, open Monday to Friday 10am to 6:30pm, weekends 9am to 3pm.

The center of Innsbruck is peppered with parking areas, many concealed underground. One of the largest and best positioned is at the **Tourist Center,** Salurnerstrasse 15 (✆ **0512/572353**). It charges 2.40€ per first hour and 1.20€ for each additional half-hour, day rate is 16.40€. Otherwise, parking in the city center's short-term parking zones (marked by special signs) is 1.10€ for each 30 minutes. Parking within these zones is limited to a maximum of 120 minutes. If you're parking in a limited-parking zone, you must purchase a voucher (sold at banks, gas stations, or tobacconists). Write down the time you parked the car, and place the voucher on the dashboard inside the windshield.

Innsbruck

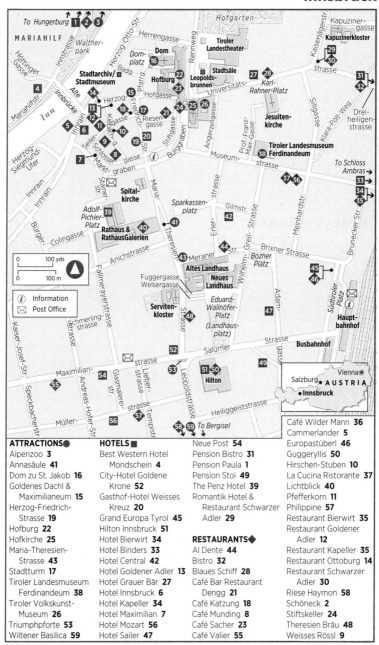

ATTRACTIONS●
Alpenzoo **3**
Annasäule **41**
Dom zu St. Jakob **16**
Goldenes Dachl & Maximilianeum **15**
Herzog-Friedrich-Strasse **19**
Hofburg **22**
Hofkirche **25**
Maria-Theresien-Strasse **43**
Stadtturm **17**
Tiroler Landesmuseum Ferdinandeum **38**
Tiroler Volkskunst-Museum **26**
Triumphpforte **53**
Wiltener Basilica **59**

HOTELS■
Best Western Hotel Mondschein **4**
City-Hotel Goldene Krone **8**
Gasthof-Hotel Weisses Kreuz **20**
Grand Europa Tyrol **45**
Hilton Innsbruck **51**
Hotel Bierwirt **34**
Hotel Binders **33**
Hotel Central **42**
Hotel Goldener Adler **13**
Hotel Grauer Bär **27**
Hotel Innsbruck **6**
Hotel Kapeller **34**
Hotel Maximilian **7**
Hotel Mozart **56**
Hotel Sailer **47**

Neue Post **54**
Pension Bistro **31**
Pension Paula **1**
Pension Stoi **49**
The Penz Hotel **39**
Romantik Hotel & Restaurant Schwarzer Adler **29**

RESTAURANTS◆
Al Dente **44**
Bistro **32**
Blaues Schiff **28**
Café Bar Restaurant Dengg **21**
Café Katzung **18**
Café Munding **8**
Café Sacher **23**
Café Valier **55**

Café Wilder Mann **36**
Cammerlander **5**
Europastüberl **46**
Guggeryllis **50**
Hirschen-Stuben **10**
La Cucina Ristorante **37**
Lichtblick **40**
Pfefferkorn **11**
Philippine **57**
Restaurant Bierwirt **35**
Restaurant Goldener Adler **12**
Restaurant Kapeller **35**
Restaurant Ottoburg **14**
Restaurant Schwarzer Adler **30**
Riese Haymon **58**
Schöneck **2**
Stiftskeller **24**
Theresien Bräu **48**
Weisses Rössl **9**

CITY LAYOUT

The main street of the **Altstadt** historic district is Herzog-Friedrich-Strasse, which becomes Maria-Theresien-Strasse, the main axis of the postmedieval **New Town.** The Altstadt developed on the right bank of the Inn River, site of the baroque and medieval buildings that give the city its architectural flair. To the south, Altstadt's boundaries end at Burggraben and Marktgraben. After 10:30am, it becomes strictly pedestrian, which is ideal as the best way to see that part of Innsbruck is on foot.

Most of your explorations will be in the Altstadt because (with a few exceptions) the younger parts of the city contain mostly residential neighborhoods. The dividing line between the old and new towns is Egger Lienz Strasse.

The Inn River divides this historic city into left- and right-bank districts, and many of the attractions, including the Hofkirche and the Goldenes Dachl, are on the right bank (in Altstadt). There are two major crossing points over the river: The **Universitätssbrücke** and the **Alte Innsbrücke.**

If you arrive at the **Hauptbahnhof (main railway station),** take Salurner Strasse and Brixner Strasse to Maria-Theresien-Strasse, which will take you into the very heart of Innsbruck.

VISITOR INFORMATION

The **Innsbruck Tourist Office,** Burggraben 3 (© **512/59850;** www.innsbruck-tourism.at), is open daily 8am to 6pm. You can stock up on printed information about Innsbruck (and other parts of Tyrol) and ask questions about virtually any touristic feature of the town.

[FastFACTS] INNSBRUCK

Babysitters For an English-speaking (or bilingual) babysitter, most hotel concierges will make arrangements for you.

Consulates Visitors from the U.S., Canada, and Australia have to use their respective consulates in Vienna. Citizens of New Zealand have to use their embassy in Berlin, Germany. British citizens can go to the **British Consulate,** Kaiser Jägerstrasse 1, Top B9 (© **0512/588320),** open Monday to Friday 9am to noon in the winter, and 8 to 11am in the summer.

Currency Exchange You can exchange money at any of the dozens of banks that line Innsbruck's commercial areas. Banks are usually open Monday to Thursday 7:45am to 12:30pm and 2:30 to 4pm, and Friday 7:45am to 3pm. There are also exchange facilities at Innsbruck's tourist office (see above) and at the Hauptbahnhof. The branch at the Hauptbahnhof maintains automated currency exchange facilities available 24 hours a day. They accept American dollars in denominations of $20, $50, and $100.

Dentists & Doctors Check with the tourist office for a list of private English-speaking dentists and doctors, or contact the **University Clinic,** Anichstrasse 35 (© **0512/504).**

Drugstores **St.-Anna Apotheke,** Maria-Theresien-Strasse 4 (© **0512/585847),** is open Monday to Friday 8am to 12:30pm and 2:30 to 6pm, and Saturday 8am to noon. As required by law, the pharmacy posts addresses of other pharmacies open on weekends or at night.

Emergencies Call © **133** for the police, © **122** for the fire department, or © **144** for an ambulance.

Hospitals Try the **University Clinic,** Anichstrasse 35 (© **0512/504).**

Internet Access There are a number of places throughout the city where you can access the Internet. Many cafes and restaurants offer free Wi-Fi to customers. In addition to this option, if you do not have a laptop there are a number of call shops throughout the city that provide inexpensive Internet access and cheap international phone calls.

Luggage Storage & Lockers At the Hauptbahnhof, on Südtirolerplatz (☎ **0512/930005445**), you can rent small lockers for 2€, medium lockers for 2.50€, or larger ones for 3.50€, for 24 hours.

Police Call ☎ **133** for the police.

Post Offices Post offices can be found

throughout the city. The post office at the **Hauptbahnhof,** Südtiroler Platz 5 (☎ **0577/6776020**), is open Monday to Friday 7am to 7pm and Saturdays from 8am to 1pm.

Restrooms (toilets) These are found at the airport, bus and rail stations, and various cafes and museums scattered throughout the city. Public restrooms (toilets) in the city center are labeled wc: Some require a .50€ coin for access to a sit-down toilet, which can be found, for example, at Maria Theresien-Strasse 18 or Museumstrasse 38, to name a couple.

Safety Innsbruck has a low crime rate, but that doesn't mean you shouldn't take the usual precautions.

Taxes Innsbruck levies no special city taxes other than the value-added tax imposed on all goods and services in Austria.

Transit Information For information about local buses and trams, call the **Innsbrucker Verkehrsbetriebe** (☎ **0512/5307500;** http://www.ivb.at/).

Useful Telephone Numbers For the airport, call ☎ **0512/225250;** for train information, call ☎ **05/1717.**

What to See & Do
EXPLORING THE TOWN

Maria-Theresien-Strasse ★★ Innsbruck's main street cuts through the heart of the city from north to south, and is a good place to begin your exploration. Once, this street was traversed by wayfarers heading over the Brenner Pass from Italy and on to Germany. Today many 17th- and 18th-century houses line the street.

On the south end of this wide street, a **Triumphpforte (Triumphal Arch),** modeled after those in Rome, spans the shopping street. Maria Theresa ordered it built in 1765 with a twofold purpose: To honor the marriage of her son, the Duke of Tuscany (later Emperor Leopold II), to a Spanish princess, and to mourn the death of her beloved husband, Emperor Franz I. Motifs representing the two events can be found on either side of the arch. From the Triumphpforte southward, the street turns into Leopoldstrasse.

Traveling north from the arch along Maria-Theresien-Strasse, you'll see **Annasäule (St. Anna's Column),** a much-photographed attraction. A statue of the Virgin Mary stands on a crescent moon atop this column, which has statues of saints Cassianus, Virgilius, George, and Anna surrounding the base. Standing in front of the 19th-century **Rathaus (Town Hall),** the column was erected in 1706 to celebrate the withdrawal, in 1703, of invading Bavarian armies during the War of the Spanish Succession.

Not far north of the Annasäule, the wide street narrows and becomes **Herzog-Friedrich-Strasse,** running through the heart of the Altstadt. This street is flanked by a number of well-maintained burghers' houses topped with turrets and gables and adorned with dormer windows and oriels. Most buildings here are overhung with protective roofs to guard them against snowfalls.

MORE SIGHTS

Alpenzoo ★ ☺ From this zoo, lying on the southern slope of the Hungerburg plateau, you'll get a panoramic view of Innsbruck and the surrounding mountains. The zoo contains only those animals indigenous to the Alps. Sheltered within are more than 800 creatures, belonging to more than 140 different and sometimes rare species, including otters, eagles, elk, rabbits, vultures, wildcats, bison, and wolves.

Weiherburggasse 37. (✆ 0512/292323. www.alpenzoo.at. Admission 8€ adults, 6€ students, 4€ children 6–15, 2€ children 4–5, free for children 3 and under. Nov–Mar daily 9am–5pm; Apr–Oct daily 9am–6pm. Tram: Hungerburgbahn (cog railway). Bus: W which starts from Marktplatz.

Dom zu St. Jakob   Based on designs by the baroque architect Johann Jakob Herkommer, the Cathedral of St. James was rebuilt between 1717 and 1724. It is roofed with domes and has a lavish baroque interior, part of which was executed by the Asam brothers, the renowned German sculptors of the late baroque era. Unfortunately, the church was heavily damaged during World War II. One of its chief treasures is the *Maria Hilf* (Mary of Succor), painted by Lucas Cranach the Elder, on the main altar. In the north aisle, look for a 1620 monument honoring Archduke Maximilian III, who died in 1618. Visits are prohibited during Mass.

Domplatz 6. (✆ 0512/583902. www.sacred-destinations.com. Free admission. Winter daily 6:30am–6pm; summer daily 7:30am–7:30pm. Closed Fri noon–3pm. Tram: 1 or 3.

Goldenes Dachl & Maximilianeum ★   The "Golden Roof" is Innsbruck's most characteristic landmark. It's a three-story balcony on a house in mid-Altstadt, its late-Gothic oriels capped with 2,657 gold-plated copper tiles. From here, Emperor Maximilian I could sit in luxury—a sort of royal box setup—and enjoy tournaments in the square below. Completed at the dawn of the 16th century, the Goldenes Dachl was built in honor of the Emperor's marriage (his second) to Bianca Maria Sforza of Milan, thus following the Habsburg tradition of expanding his territory through marriage, not conquest. Not wishing to alienate the allies of his first marriage, to Maria of Burgundy, he is depicted on the balcony standing between the two women. However, he is looking at his new wife, Bianca.

In 1996, the City of Innsbruck added a small museum, the **Maximilianeum,** to the second floor of the municipal building attached to the Goldenes Dachl. Inside you'll find exhibits that celebrate the life and accomplishments of this Innsbruck-based Habsburg emperor who bridged the gap between the Middle Ages and the Northern Renaissance. Look for costumes, silver chalices and coins, portraits, and a video that depicts his era and personality.

You can also visit the **Stadtturm (City Tower),** Herzog-Friedrich-Strasse 21 (✆ 0512/587113), nearby. Formerly a prison cell, the tower dates from the mid-1400s and stands adjacent to the Rathaus. From the top, there's a sweeping panoramic view of the city rooftops and the mountains beyond. It's open daily 10am to 5pm (July–Sept to 8pm). Admission is 3€ for adults and 1.50€ for children.

While you're here, take a look at the **Helblinghaus,** Herzog-Friedrich-Strasse, opposite the Goldenes Dachl. It's a Gothic structure to which a rococo facade was added.

Herzog-Friedrich-Strasse 15. (✆ 0512/581111. Admission to the Maximilianeum 4€ adults, 2€ seniors and students. May–Sept daily 10am–5pm; Oct–Apr Tues–Sun 10am–5pm; Closed Nov. Tram: 1 or 3.

Hofburg ★   The 15th-century imperial palace of Emperor Maximilian I was rebuilt in the baroque style (but with rococo detailing) during the 18th century on the orders of Maria Theresa. The palace, flanked by a set of domed towers, is a fine example of baroque secular architecture. The structure has four wings and a two-story *Riesensaal* (Giant's Hall) painted in white and gold and filled with portraits of the Habsburgs.

Also of compelling interest within the Hofburg are the State Rooms, the chapel, and a scattering of private apartments. You can wander at will through the rooms, but if you want to participate in a guided tour, management conducts two a day, the one at 12:30pm in a multilingual format that includes English. These tours cost 10€, which includes the price of admission. Private tours can also be arranged in advance. You must call at least a week ahead of time to schedule a tour, which lasts 30 to 45 minutes and costs 40€ plus 8€ for admission.

Rennweg 1. ℂ **0512/587186.** www.hofberg-innsbruck.at. Admission 8€ adults, free entry children under 19. Daily 9am–5pm. Tram: 1 or 3.

Hofkirche   Ferdinand I built this Gothic royal court church and tomb in 1553. Its most important treasure is the cenotaph of Maximilian I, although his remains are not in this elegant marble sarcophagus glorifying the Holy Roman Empire. He was never brought here from Wiener Neustadt, where he was entombed in 1519. This tomb, a great feat of the German Renaissance style of sculpture, has 28 bronze 16th-century statues of Maximilian's real and legendary ancestors and relatives surrounding the kneeling emperor on the cenotaph, with 24 marble reliefs on the sides depicting scenes from his life. Tyrol's national hero, Andreas Hofer—who led a rebellion against Napoleon in the early 1800s—is entombed here.

The Hofkirche has a lovely Renaissance porch, plus a nave and a trio of aisles in the Gothic style. One gallery contains nearly two dozen small statues of the saint protectors of the House of Habsburg. The wooden organ, dating from 1560, is still operational.

Another chapel, the **Silberne Kapell (Silver Chapel),** was constructed between the church and the palace in 1578. Archduke Ferdinand II of Tyrol had it constructed as the final resting place for himself and his wife, Philippine Welser. The chapel takes its name from a large embossed silver Madonna in the center of the altarpiece (made of rare wood). The silver reliefs surrounding the Madonna symbolize the Laurentanian Litany. Alexander Colin designed the sarcophagi of Ferdinand and Philippine. The Tiroler Volkskunst-Museum (see below) is reached through the same entranceway. You can purchase a combined ticket to the church and the museum for 8€ for adults and 4€ for children.

Universitätsstrasse 2. ℂ **0512/584302.** Admission 4€ adults, 2€ students or children up to 15 years, free for children 5 and under. Mon–Sat 10am–6pm, Sun 12:30–6pm. Tram: 1 or 3.

Swarovski Kristallwelten ★★★ ☺   If Disney created a magical Kingdom of Crystal, he would surely have used the fabled Swarovski Crystal Worlds as his role model. In just 15 minutes (by taking the Wattens bus from the Busbahnhof, next to the Hauptbahnhof), you are delivered to a fantasy world, a man-made hill where you'll see a giant face spouting a waterfall. Deep inside the hill is a wonder world of crystal—an underground dream world with seven linked chambers. Designed by the Viennese multimedia artist Andrew Heller, the kingdom is dedicated to the vision of Daniel Swarovski, founder of the world's leading producer of full crystal. Since it opened in 1995, millions of visitors have been drawn to the site.

After entering the giant head with its glittering eyes and waterfall, you'll immediately see a long wall of crystal with 12 tons of some of the finest cut stones in the world. In other chambers, you can wander into the Planet of the Crystals with a 3-D light show. Crystalline works of art on display were designed by artists from Andy Warhol to Salvador Dalí. In the Crystal Dome, you get an idea of what it's like being inside a crystal, and in the Crystal Theater, a fairytale world of color, mystery, and movement unfolds.

After your visit, purchases can be made from the mammoth range of Swarovski products at the on-site shop. These range from detailed crystal items such as tiny musical instruments to depictions of animals. There's also a wide selection of crystal jewelry such as necklaces and earrings, watches, home accessories, and the list goes on. The Crystal World also contains a garden with rare and indigenous plants, plus an adventure playground for children. You can easily spend several hours here taking in the surreal sights and the imagination of the creators.

Kristallweltenstrasse 1. ✆ **05224/51080.** www.swarovski.com. Admission 9.50€, free for children under 12. Daily 9am–6:30pm. From Innsbruck, take the A12 to the "Wattens" exit and then follow signs to Swarovski Kristallwelten.

Tiroler Landesmuseum Ferdinandeum ★ This celebrated gallery of Flemish and Dutch masters also traces the development of popular art in Tyrol, with highlights from the Gothic period. You'll also see the original bas-reliefs used in designing the Goldenes Dachl.

Museumstrasse 15. ✆ **0512/59489.** www.tiroler-landesmuseum.at. Admission 8€ adults, 4€ students and children (which also covers the cost of entry for the Tiroler Volkskunst-Museum and Hofkirche). Tues–Sun 10am–6pm. Tram: 1 or 3.

Tiroler Volkskunst-Museum ★★ This museum of popular art is in the **Neues Stift (New Abbey),** which dates from the 16th and 18th centuries, and adjoins the Hofkirche. The museum contains one of the largest and most impressive collections of Tyrolean artifacts, ranging from handicrafts and religious and profane popular art to furniture and national costumes. The three floors house a collection of Tyrolean mangers, or Christmas cribs, some from the 18th century. The *Stuben* (the best rooms) are on the upper floors. Displays include styles ranging from Gothic to Renaissance to baroque, as well as a collection of models of typical Tyrolean houses.

Universitätsstrasse 2. ✆ **0512/59489510.** Admission 8€ adults, 4€ children and students (which also covers the cost of entry for the Tiroler Landesmuseum Ferdinandeum and Hofkirche). Mon–Sun 10am–6pm. Tram: 1 or 3.

OUTDOOR ACTIVITIES

Ski areas around Innsbruck are excellent for winter activity or for summer mountain walks, hikes, mountain biking, and climbing. Five cableways, 44 chairlifts, and surface lifts allow access to the five sunny, snow-covered areas around Innsbruck. In winter, the city is also known for bobsled and toboggan runs and ice-skating rinks.

In summer, you can enjoy tennis at a number of courts, golf on either a 9- or an 18-hole course, and go horseback riding, canyoneering, gliding, swimming, hiking, and shooting.

The **Hofgarten,** a public park containing ponds and many shade trees, lies north of Rennweg. Concerts are often presented at the Kunstpavillon in the garden in summer.

NEARBY ATTRACTIONS

Many satellite resorts, such as Igls (see later in this chapter), are good for day trips from Innsbruck. Below we've offered highlights of those attractions on the outskirts of the city.

Bergisel

If you're driving, head out the Brenner road to Bergisel (747m/2,451 ft.), a lovely wooded section just outside Innsbruck that's ideal for leisurely strolls in warmer weather. It lies near the gorge of the Sill River on the southern outskirts of Innsbruck, about a 20-minute walk from the Wiltener Basilica. Here you'll see the ski jumps built for the 1964 and 1976 Olympic Winter Games, and there's a great panoramic view from the top of the jumps.

The hill is a historic site, scene of the 1809 battles in which Andreas Hofer led some Tyrolean peasants against French and Bavarian forces (he was later shot to death on the orders of Napoleon). Below the ski jump is the Andreas Hofer monument erected in 1893 to commemorate the battle. Tyroleans speak of this as their "field of remembrance," and it's filled with memorials and visitors. Heroic though the local deeds might be, they might not interest North Americans. Visit this place simply for the views and the relaxing walks.

Hungerburg ★★

The Hungerburg mountain plateau (872m/2,861 ft.) is one of the most beautiful spots in Tyrol, affording the best view of Innsbruck, especially on summer nights when much of the city, including fountains and historic buildings, is brightly lit. Some of the most scenic hotels in the Innsbruck area are here.

It is possible to drive to the plateau, but you can also take the **Hungerburgbahn** (© **0512/293344;** www.nordkette.com), a funicular railway that will bring you up to the plateau from the Congress, Löwenhaus, and Alpenzoo stations. A round-trip ticket from the Congress station costs 6.80€ for adults, 5.40€ for youths/seniors, and 3.40€ for children. It runs weekdays from 7am to 7:30pm, weekends and holidays from 8am to 7:30pm.

Schloss Ambras ★★

This Renaissance palace, 3km (2 miles) southeast of the heart of Innsbruck on the edge of the Mittelgebirgsterrace, was built by Archduke Ferdinand II of Austria, Count of Tyrol, in the 16th century. It's divided into a **lower** and an **upper castle** set in the remains of a medieval fortress. This was Ferdinand's favorite residence and the center of his court's cultural life. The lower castle was planned and constructed by the archduke as a museum for his various collections, including arms and armor, art, and books, all of which can be seen today. The **Spanish Hall,** one of the first German Renaissance halls, was built to house the portraits of the counts of Tyrol.

The upper castle has a small but fine collection of medieval sculpture, black-and-white frescoes on the wall of the inner courtyard, and a portrait gallery hung with dynastic paintings from the 14th to the 18th centuries. In some of the living rooms, you can see 16th-century frescoes, late-16th-century wooden ceilings, and 17th-century furniture.

After viewing the interior, walk through the castle grounds. April through October, **Schloss Ambras,** Schloss Strasse 20 (© **0152/5244802;** www.khm.at), is open daily 10am to 5pm (Aug from 10am–6pm). It's closed in November. Admission is 4.50€ for adults, 3€ for students, and free entry for children under 19, December to March; 10€ for adults, 7€ for students, and free entry for children under 19, April to October. There are no guided tours. To reach the palace, you can take Postbus no. 4134 from Innsbruck's Hauptbahnhof.

The Wiltener Basilica ★

In the southern district of Innsbruck, where the Sill River emerges from a gorge, Wilten is one of the most dramatic landscapes around the city. This ancient spot was once the Roman town of Veldidena.

Wilten's parish church, the **Wiltener Basilica,** Haymongasse 6 (© **0512/583385**), is one of the most splendid houses of worship in the Tyrolean country. Built between 1751 and 1755 in a rich rococo style with twin towers, the church did not become a basilica until 1957. Wiltener Basilica is noted for its stucco work by Franz Xaver Feichtmayr. The ceiling frescoes are by Matthäus Günther. A sandstone figure depicting Our Lady under the Four Columns has been the subject of pilgrimage since the Middle Ages. Both the church and the basilica are open daily from 9am to dusk.

Across from the basilica is a cluster of baroque buildings that belonged to an abbey founded here in 1138. The abbey church, the **Stift Wilten,** Klosterg 7 (© **0512/5830480**), merits a visit. Dating from the 1650s, the church has two stone giants guarding the porch and a grille from 1707 in the narthex (entranceway). This church was damaged by World War II bombings. To reach the site, take tram no. 1 to Stubaitalbahnhof/Bergisel.

Where to Stay

Always arrive with a reservation, as Innsbruck is never out of season. Accommodations are particularly scarce from June until the end of summer and from mid-December to mid-April. Hotel information is available at the tourist office (see "Visitor Information," p. 352).

VERY EXPENSIVE

Grand Europa Tyrol ★★ Opposite Innsbruck's railway station, in the heart of the city, the Europa is the best hotel in Innsbruck. Rooms and suites are handsomely furnished with modern conveniences and Tyrolean or Biedermeier-style decorations. Each room offers a comfortable bed and a bathroom with a neatly kept tub/shower combination. The uniformed staff is helpful in every way and will usually be willing to show you the ornate yellow-and-white Barock Saal, which the Tyrolean government uses for its most important functions. The ballroom was constructed by King Ludwig's Bavarian architects and builders. The restaurant, **Europastüberl** (p. 363), is the finest in Tyrol.

Südtirolerplatz 2, A-6020 Innsbruck. ✆ **800/223-5652** in the U.S. and Canada, or 0512/5931. Fax 0512/587800. www.grandhoteleuropa.at. 117 units. 183€–314€ double; 333€–504€ suite. Rates include buffet breakfast. AE, DC, MC, V. Parking 20€. **Amenities:** Restaurant; bar; babysitting; nonsmoking rooms; room service; sauna; solarium. *In room:* A/C, TV, hairdryer, minibar, trouser press (some), Wi-Fi.

The Penz Hotel ★★ This glittering structure that makes much use of glass may stand in the Altstadt but it has little in common with most of the district's buildings. The Penz is as modern as tomorrow, housed in the Rathausgalerie shopping center, with a panoramic American bar on its rooftop. You can drink and take in views of the old town and the Tyrolean Alps. Rooms are ultramodern and elegantly decorated, with the minimalist's eye for comfort. From the hardwood floors to the streamlined furnishings, to the discreet introduction of modern technology, everything is coordinated.

Adolf Pichler Platz 3, A-6020 Innsbruck. ✆ **0512/575657-0.** Fax 0512/575657-9. www.the-penz.com. 94 units. 180€–260€ double; 250€–420€ junior suite. AE, MC, V. Parking 15€. Bus 4125 or 4169. **Amenities:** Bar; nonsmoking rooms; room service; rooms for those w/limited mobility. *In room:* A/C, TV, hairdryer, minibar, Wi-Fi.

EXPENSIVE

Hilton Innsbruck ★ Erected in the mid-1980s and located two blocks from the railway station, this is the largest hotel and the tallest building (14 stories) in Innsbruck. Its contemporary comfort and capacity for large-scale conferences have made it very popular. Rooms, especially those on the upper floors, provide a view over the baroque spires of Innsbruck and its mountains. All contain built-in furniture and extras you'd expect of a government-rated four-star hotel. The **Jackpot Bar** provides slot fixes and drinks, depending on your whim and the time of day. Its restaurant, **Guggeryllis,** is well-recommended (see "Where to Eat," later in this chapter).

Salurner Strasse 15, A-6020 Innsbruck. ✆ **0512/59350.** Fax 0512/5935220. www.hilton.com. 176 units. 107€–194€ double; 309€–380€ suite. AE, DC, MC, V. Parking 11€. Tram: 1 or 3. **Amenities:** Restaurant; bar; babysitting; fitness center; nonsmoking rooms; room service; sauna; tour desk; 1 room for those w/limited mobility. *In room:* A/C, TV, hairdryer, minibar, trouser press, Wi-Fi.

Hotel Grauer Bär ★   This hotel, located in the center of Innsbruck, is next to the Imperial Gardens, the most interesting sights, and the shopping area. The good-size rooms are well maintained and traditionally furnished, with thick carpeting and built-in furnishings. Bathrooms have showers and tubs. Front rooms are the most comfortable and the best appointed, but they also suffer from the most traffic noise. To the side of the large lobby is the dining room, **Galerie,** with an ornate ribbed and vaulted white ceiling supported by a central stone column. Well-prepared international, Austrian, and Tyrolean specialties are served.

Universitätsstrasse 7, A-6020 Innsbruck. ℂ **0512/59240.** www.innsbruck-hotels.at/. 196 units. 175€–192€ double; 220€ suite. Rates include buffet breakfast. Half-board costs an additional 18€ per person. AE, DC, MC, V. Parking 12€. Bus 4125 or 4127. **Amenities:** Restaurant; bar; babysitting; fitness center; massage; nonsmoking rooms; room service; sauna; solarium; rooms for those w/limited mobility. *In room:* TV, hairdryer, minibar, Wi-Fi.

Hotel Innsbruck ★   This modern, streamlined, and comfortable hotel facing the Inn River is favored by upscale tourists and international business travelers. The staff is hardworking and multilingual. The furnishings in the rooms aren't remarkable, but all the beds are firm and the neatly kept bathrooms contain tub/shower combinations. The best rooms are on an upper floor and have small balconies; the dormer rooms on each floor are also superior. If you're stuck in one of the accommodations in the back, you'll do fine—in some respects, these are the coziest and most romantic rooms, opening onto vistas of the Altstadt.

Innrain 3, A-6020 Innsbruck. ℂ **0512/598680.** Fax 0512/572280. www.hotelinnsbruck.com. 109 units. 142€–215€ double. Rates include buffet breakfast. Half-board (not available year-round) with 24€ surcharge. AE, DC, MC, V. Parking 14€. Tram: 1 or 3. **Amenities:** 2 restaurants; bar; lounge; babysitting; indoor heated pool; massage; nonsmoking rooms; rooms for those w/limited mobility; room service; sauna; winter garden. *In room:* TV, hairdryer, Internet connection.

Hotel Maximilian ★   Built in 1982 and renovated in 1992, this inner-city hotel rates as one of the most attractive and up-to-date in Innsbruck. Possessing an antique charm, it offers modern and convenient accommodations. Rooms are rather small yet exceedingly up-to-date, with very firm beds. The most desirable ones look out over the back, where you'll have a close-up view of the shingled onion dome of the oldest church in Innsbruck (now used as the headquarters of a company that makes keys). Parking is sometimes available for free on the street; otherwise, it costs 13€ per day in a nearby public garage.

Marktgraben 7–9, A-6020 Innsbruck. ℂ **0512/59967.** Fax 0512/577450. www.hotel-maximilian.com. 47 units. 70€–120€ double. Rates include buffet breakfast. Parking 13€. AE, DC, MC, V. Tram: 1. **Amenities:** Bar; babysitting; laundry service; nonsmoking rooms. *In room:* TV, hairdryer, minibar.

Neue Post ★   In the heart of the city, opposite the main post office, this building began life in 1902 when it was constructed as an apartment house. Today a Best Western, it offers rooms in two different categories—standard doubles or superior or deluxe doubles. Some of its imperial architectural grandeur from the turn-of-the-20th-century remains, but everything has been modernized with all the latest gadgets. Its most elegant grace note is its Winter Garden Restaurant, serving a first-rate cuisine. The public rooms are imbued with an Art Nouveau style, and all the bedrooms, ranging from midsize to spacious, have fine furnishings, using high-quality fabrics.

Maximilianstrasse 15, A-6020 Innsbruck. ℂ **0512/594760.** Fax 0512/581818. www.hotel-neue-post.at. 50 units. 126€–190€ double; 250€ suite. AE, DC, MC, V. Parking 17€. Bus 4125, 4162, 4165 or 4176. **Amenities:** Restaurant; bar; coffee shop; room service. *In room:* A/C, TV, minibar, Wi-Fi.

Romantik Hotel & Restaurant Schwarzer Adler ★★ An appealing alternative to Innsbruck's modern hotels, the Romantik Hotel lies behind an antique facade of stucco and shutters, and a big-windowed tower. The Ultsch family, the owners, furnished the interior in an authentic style with aged paneling, hand-painted regional furniture, antiques, and *gemütlich* clutter that make for a cozy and inviting ambiance. Rooms are virtually one of a kind, each with its special character and period decor. Persian carpets cover parquet floors, and the bathrooms have dual basins, powerful showerheads, and large tubs. The two suites are even more luxurious. Restaurant Schwarzer Adler is reviewed under "Where to Eat," below.

Kaiserjägerstrasse 2, A-6020 Innsbruck. ⓒ **0512/587109.** Fax 0512/561697. www.deradler.com. 40 units. 150€–211€ double; 275€–480€ suite. Rates include breakfast. Half-board costs 27€–32€. AE, DC, MC, V. Parking 12€. Tram: 1 or 3. **Amenities:** Restaurant; bar; fitness center; massage; room service; nonsmoking rooms; spa; Wi-Fi in lobby. *In room:* A/C, TV, hairdryer, minibar, Internet access.

MODERATE

Best Western Hotel Mondschein ★ 🏅 It occupies a pink-fronted antique building that was originally erected in 1473 and that later functioned as a relay station for the Austrian (then horse-drawn) postal service. The antique integrity of its exterior has been carefully preserved, complete with its bay windows and solid proportions. Inside, however, it has been thoroughly modernized, with sturdy furniture and decor, and bedrooms that correspond to a modern international aesthetic of smooth lines, wood-grained furniture, and standardized comforts. Most have views of the Inn River or of Innsbruck's Old Town, whose northern edge lies within about 180m (591 ft.) of the hotel.

Mariahilfstrasse 6, A-6020 Innsbruck. ⓒ **0512/22784.** Fax 0512/2278490. www.mondschein.at. 34 units. 125€–182€ double; 230€–280€ apt. Rates include buffet breakfast. AE, DC, MC, V. Free parking. Tram: 1. **Amenities:** Bar; babysitting; nonsmoking rooms. *In room:* TV, hairdryer, minibar, Wi-Fi.

Hotel Central ★ One of the most unusual hotels in Innsbruck, Hotel Central was originally built in the 1860s, but from its very modern exterior you might not realize it. Throughout, you'll see a high-tech composition of textured concrete and angular windows. The comfortable rooms have an Art Deco design that evokes an almost Japanese sense of simplicity. Most are quite spacious, with excellent beds. In total contrast to the simplicity of the rest of the hotel, the ground floor contains a grand Viennese cafe with marble columns, sculpted ceilings, and large gilt-and-crystal chandeliers.

Gilmstrasse 5, A-6020 Innsbruck. ⓒ **0512/5920.** Fax 0512/580310. www.central.co.at. 80 units. 125€–170€ double. Rates include breakfast. AE, DC, MC, V. Parking 15€. Tram: 1 or 3. **Amenities:** Restaurant; bar; fitness center; nonsmoking rooms; sauna. *In room:* TV, hairdryer, minibar, Wi-Fi.

Hotel Goldener Adler ★★ Even the phone booth near the reception desk of this 600-year-old family-run hotel is outfitted in antique style. Famous guests have included Goethe, Mozart, and the violinist Paganini, who cut his name into the windowpane of his room. Rooms are handsomely furnished and vary in size and decor. Some have decorative Tyrolean architectural features such as beamed ceilings. Others are furnished more modernly. The size of your bathroom depends on your room assignment.

Herzog-Friedrich-Strasse 6, A-6020 Innsbruck. ⓒ **0512/571111.** Fax 0512/584409. www.goldeneradler. com. 35 units. 150€–210€ double; from 260€ suite. Rates include buffet breakfast. AE, DC, MC, V. Parking 11€. Tram: 1 or 3. **Amenities:** Restaurant; bar; babysitting; nonsmoking rooms. *In room:* TV, hairdryer, minibar, Wi-Fi.

Hotel Kapeller Set within a 5-minute drive east of Innsbruck's historic core, this establishment is centered on a 500-year-old house and a 1960s' four-story hotel. They're interconnected with a greenhouse-style reception area and bar. Rooms are outfitted in artfully rustic reproductions of Tyrolean-style furniture. Many overlook the mountains and the hotel's garden. The staff is attentive, English-speaking, and cooperative. Restaurant Kapeller is recommended under "Where to Eat," below. The hotel derives its name, incidentally, from a small Romanesque-era chapel that lies nearby.

Philippine-Welser-Strasse 96, A-6020 Innsbruck. ℂ **0512/343101.** Fax 0512/34310668. www.kapeller. at. 36 units. 140€ double; 165€ suite for 2–4 occupants. Rates include buffet breakfast. AE, DC, MC, V. Tram: 3. **Amenities:** Restaurant; bar; room service. *In room:* TV, hairdryer, Wi-Fi.

Hotel Sailer ★ A family-managed establishment that has stretched over five generations, this is one of the best and more affordable hotels in Innsbruck, lying a short walk west of the Hauptbahnhof. Even though it's in the city, you feel like you're in an alpine retreat because of the use of woodwork on every floor. The public rooms are warm and inviting. Guest rooms are small to medium in size and lack the character and taste of the public rooms, but they're well maintained and beautifully kept with mainly built-in pieces. The best views, as would be expected, are on the upper floors. In a series of rustically decorated restaurants, Tyrolean specialties are served, and the intimate and wood-paneled bar is a retreat after you return from the slopes. In winter, folkloric shows are often presented.

Adamgasse 8. A-6020 Innsbruck. ℂ **0512/53630.** Fax 0512/53637. www.sailer-innsbruck.at. 86 units. 220€–380€ double; 280€–460€ suite. AE, DC, MC, V. Tram: Hauptbahnhof. **Amenities:** Restaurant; bar; nonsmoking rooms; sauna. *In room:* TV, hairdryer, Wi-Fi.

INEXPENSIVE

City-Hotel Goldene Krone Near the Triumphal Arch on Innsbruck's main street, this baroque house has a green-and-white facade. Rooms are modern, comfortable, well maintained, and, for the most part, spacious with plenty of light filtering through the many windows. Most have a table with chairs, and all have firm mattresses and triple-glazed windows to cut down on noise. The hotel offers good comfort: An elevator, soundproof windows, and a Viennese-inspired coffeehouse/restaurant, the **Art Gallery-Café.**

Maria-Theresien-Strasse 46, A-6020 Innsbruck. ℂ **0512/586160.** Fax 0512/5801896. www.goldene-krone.at. 37 units. 79€–118€ double; 120€–152€ suite. Rates include buffet breakfast. Half-board 15.50€. AE, MC, V. Parking 10€. Tram: 1. Bus: A, H, K, or N. **Amenities:** Restaurant; cafe; lounge; babysitting. *In room:* TV.

Gasthof-Hotel Weisses Kreuz ★ 🔖 This atmospheric inn, located in the center of Innsbruck, has not changed much during its lifetime, with the exception of the elevator that now carries newcomers up two flights to the reception area. In 1769, 13-year-old Wolfgang Mozart and his father, Leopold, stayed here. The reception area features carved stone columns, a TV room with an arched, wood-covered ceiling, a collection of massive Tyrolean chests, and a carved balustrade worn smooth by the palms of countless visitors. Rooms are cozy and atmospheric, either small or medium in size, with comfortable furnishings. Some have private bathrooms with neatly kept shower units.

Herzog-Friedrich-Strasse 31, A-6020 Innsbruck. ℂ **0512/594790.** Fax 0512/5947990. www.weisses kreuz.at. 40 units, 31 with bathroom. 69€–79€ double without bathroom; 100€–136€ double with bathroom. Rates include buffet breakfast. AE, MC, V. Parking 12€. Tram: 3. **Amenities:** Bar; nonsmoking rooms. *In room:* TV.

Hotel Bierwirt   This hotel consists of a pair of buildings that face each other across a busy street on the southern outskirts of town, about a 15-minute walk from the historic core. The older section dates from 1615 and benefits from a 1998 renovation that brought the cozy interior up to modern standards. The restaurant and all but a dozen of the rooms are in the original building, but regardless of their location, each room has a modern bathroom with a tub/shower combination and many contemporary comforts. Restaurant Bierwirt is recommended separately in "Where to Eat," below.

Bichlweg 2, A-6020 Innsbruck. ℭ **0512/342143.** Fax 0512/3421435. www.bierwirt.com. 50 units. 127€–164€ double, breakfast included, 15€ half-board. MC, V. Parking 9€. Tram: 3. Bus: K. **Amenities:** Restaurant; bar; children's playroom; massage; nonsmoking rooms; rooms for those w/limited mobility; sauna; shuttle service; tennis court; tanning beds. *In room:* TV, hairdryer, Wi-Fi.

Hotel Binders 🍴   This is an unusual hotel, crafted and managed with a bit more imagination than equivalently priced inns within its immediate, somewhat remote, neighborhood. It presents a utilitarian, white-stucco facade to a suburban neighborhood southwest of Innsbruck's center, near the town's Olympic stadium, about a 20-minute walk from the center. Members of the Binder family recently installed an elevator in this older building; they've also renovated its public areas so frequently that not many traces remain to hint at the building's original construction. In distinct opposition to this, bedrooms run the gamut of stylishness. Most desirable are the "space-age" modern rooms, with names like Maple, Aluminum, Pink, and Turquoise. Older rooms still retain a dark-paneled, somewhat dowdy '70s version of an alpine-rustic decor.

Dr.-Glatz-Strasse 20, A-6020 Innsbruck. ℭ **0512/33436.** Fax 0512/3343699. www.binders.at. 50 units. 89€–130€ double with bathroom. Rates include breakfast. AE, DC, MC, V. Parking garage 9€. Tram: 3. **Amenities:** Bar; nonsmoking rooms. *In room:* TV, minibar, Wi-Fi.

Hotel Mozart   This recently renovated hotel has a central location and offers small rooms, including the family rooms (which have three or four beds). The beds aren't the town's most comfortable, but the prices are decent. Bathrooms are very small but do contain tub/shower combinations. You don't get a lot of frills here, but you do receive good, solid comfort at a reasonable price. From the railway station, walk down Salurner Strasse, crossing Leopoldstrasse, which leads you to Müllerstrasse and the hotel in about 10 minutes.

Müllerstrasse 15, A-6010 Innsbruck. ℭ **0512/595380.** Fax 0512/595386. www.mozarthotel.com. 42 units. 80€–95€ double. Rates include buffet breakfast. Half-board 12€. AE, DC, MC, V. Parking outdoors 6€; garage 9€. Closed Dec 13–26. Tram: 1. **Amenities:** Breakfast room; lounge; nonsmoking rooms; rooms for those w/limited mobility. *In room:* TV, hairdryer, Wi-Fi.

Pension Bistro   This is a simple but engaging government-rated two-star hotel that occupies a building from around 1955 and is located within a 15-minute walk of the city center. Rooms are relatively spacious, albeit blandly decorated. Double-paned windows block out most of the noise from the busy street, and some have views of the nearby mountains. The restaurant is recommended separately in "Where to Eat," below.

Pradler Strasse 2, A-6020 Innsbruck. ℭ **0512/346319.** Fax 0512/36025252. www.tiscover.at/hotel-bistro. 11 units. 68€–70€ double. Rates include breakfast. No credit cards. Bus: O or R. **Amenities:** Restaurant; bar. *In room:* TV, hairdryer.

Pension Paula ★ 🛏   Set on a hillside above Innsbruck and surrounded with greenery, this hotel evolved during the 1950s from the core of a 17th-century farmhouse.

Rooms are cozy but simple, with a bare-boned but comfortable ambiance that's permeated with personalized attention. Half of the rooms contain well-kept private bathrooms with shower units. The two rooms (especially no. 15) under the sloping eaves of the third floor are among the most sought-after, partially because of their sense of privacy and romance. Panoramic views are available from the porch and terrace that extend out from the two lower floors of the building, and overall there's a sense of cordiality and friendliness.

Weiherburggasse 15, A-6020 Innsbruck. © **0512/292262.** Fax 0512/293017. www.pensionpaula.at. 14 units, 7 w/private bathroom. 52€–57€ double w/shared bathroom; 62€ double w/private bathroom; 80€ triple w/private bathroom. No credit cards. Bus: D. **Amenities:** Lounge. *In room:* No phone.

Pension Stoi ☺ This pension is 3 minutes from the train station. The rooms are comfortable, with good beds and hallway showers. Because some rooms have three or four beds, this pension has long been a favorite of families on a budget. No breakfast is served, but there are several cafes nearby.

Salurner Strasse 7, A-6020 Innsbruck. © **0512/585434.** Fax 0512/585434. http://www.pensionstoi.at/. 17 units, 7 w/private bathroom. 54€ double w/shared bathroom; 65€ double w/private bathroom; 70€ triple w/shared bathroom; 75€ triple w/private bathroom. No credit cards. Tram: 1 or 3. **Amenities:** Lounge. *In room:* No phone.

Where to Eat

Finding a nice place to eat is never a problem in Innsbruck, as this alpine town has more than 200 restaurants, inns, and cafes, some of which offer evening entertainment. If you're going to be in Austria for only a short time, it might be best to stick to the Tyrolean specialties. But if that doesn't suit you, there are restaurants that serve international cuisine as well.

EXPENSIVE

Europastüberl ★★ AUSTRIAN/INTERNATIONAL The hotel that hosts this distinguished restaurant, with a delightful Tyrolean ambiance, is one of the most noteworthy in Innsbruck. Traditional regional cuisine combined with creative cooking is the chef's goal. Diners can choose from both warm and cold appetizers, such as black-and-white truffle risotto and Fine de Clair oysters. Soups include the cream of Jerusalem artichoke with lobster butter, and an array of fresh fish dishes can always be found on the menu. Four-, six-, and seven-course menus are available. Regional dishes, such as the perennial *Tafelspitz*, represent traditional Austrian cuisine. Desserts are often lavish, or you can settle for a Tyrolean apple strudel.

In the Hotel Europa Tyrol, Brixner Strasse 6. © **0512/593-01.** Reservations required. Main courses 12.50€–32€; fixed-price menu 48€–69€. AE, DC, MC, V. Daily noon–2pm and 6:30–10pm. Bus: F.

Guggeryllis SCANDINAVIAN/INTERNATIONAL Located one flight above the lobby level of a four-star hotel, this popular restaurant is a favorite of the international business community, and it's romantic enough for intimate celebrations as well. The restaurant is named after Emperor Maximilian's best-known and most popular court jester. Menu items emphasize a combination of Scandinavian, Austrian, and international foods, some of the best examples of which appear at the lunchtime buffet. A la carte items include such Nordic specialties as noisettes of reindeer with forest mushrooms and braised red cabbage, and such Austrian dishes as saddle of veal steak in a morel-studded cream sauce, and a perfectly prepared version of grilled sole with lemon butter.

In the Hilton Innsbruck, Salurner Strasse 15. ✆ **0512/5935308.** Reservations recommended. Main courses 14€–28€; lunch buffet 16€. AE, DC, MC, V. Daily noon–3pm and 6–11pm. Tram: 1 or 3.

Lichtblick ★★ INTERNATIONAL This chic dining spot on the seventh floor of the Rathausgalerie takes its name "bright spot" from the location, but also from the dining experience. The vistas over the Altstadt are especially dramatic at night. The restaurant overflows into the panoramic Café Bar Lounge 360, which you can visit even if you're not having dinner in the main restaurant. Chef Andreas Zeindlinger is a whiz, using market-fresh ingredients to concoct sublime dishes on his constantly changing menu. From poultry to beef and pork dishes, his bright ideas and sure technique are almost guaranteed to give you one of your finest meals in town.

Maria-Theresienstrasse 18, 7th floor Rathausgalerie. ✆ **0512/566550.** www.restaurant-lichtblick.at Reservations required. Fixed-price menus 39€–45€. AE, DC, MC, V. Mon–Sat noon–2:30pm and 6:30–10pm. Bus: R or F.

Pfefferkorn INTERNATIONAL The first thing you'll see within the thick walls of this 100-year-old stone building is a bar, which focuses on cocktails, a sense of conviviality, and a roster of simple, well-prepared platters. Upstairs there's a more formal and somewhat more sedate dining room, where the Austrian and international cuisine includes a wide choice of vegetarian dishes, fresh fish, pastas, and thick cuts of steaks and chops. Consider dishes from an "around the world" repertoire that includes sushi and "finger food" platters; a *pot-au-feu* of seafood served with *rouille* (spicy garlic-flavored mayonnaise); a rich assortment of meat, fish, and vegetarian fondues; *vitello tonnato* with field-green salads and parmesan-flavored vinaigrette; and eggplant cordon bleu with tomato–mozzarella sauce.

Seilergasse 8. ✆ **0512/565-444.** Reservations recommended. Main courses 11€–32€; bar platters 8€–18€; set menus 33€–57€. AE, DC, MC, V. Wed–Sat 3pm–1am, Sun 10am–1am. Closed Feb. Tram: 3.

Restaurant Goldener Adler ★ AUSTRIAN/TYROLEAN/INTERNA-TIONAL Richly Teutonic and steeped in the decorative traditions of alpine Tyrol, this restaurant has a deeply entrenched reputation and a loyal following among local residents. The menu includes hearty fare based on cold-weather outdoor life—the chefs aren't into delicate subtleties. Examples include Tyrolean bacon served with horseradish and farmer's bread, cream of cheese soup with croutons, and Tyroler *Zopfebraten,* a flavorful age-old specialty consisting of strips of veal steak served with herb-enriched cream sauce and spinach dumplings. A well-regarded specialty is a platter known as *Adler Tres,* containing spinach dumplings, stuffed noodles, and cheese dumplings, all flavorfully tied together with a brown butter sauce and a gratin of mountain cheese.

Herzog-Friedrich-Strasse 6. ✆ **0512/5711110.** Reservations recommended. Main courses 12€–25€. AE, DC, MC, V. Daily noon–10:30pm in summer; otherwise noon–2:30pm and 6–10:30pm. Tram: 1 or 3.

Restaurant Schwarzer Adler ★★ AUSTRIAN Even if you're not a guest at the richly atmospheric Romantik Hotel Schwarzer Adler (p. 379), it's restaurant is worth a visit. You will follow in the footsteps of the 18th-century Kaiser Maximilian, who housed one of his mistresses in this building and entertained her in the dining rooms. You'll have the option of dining in one of three *Stuben* (parlors), on the hotel's ground floor or within the more stately-looking cellar, beneath the vaulted ceilings of a dining room (Spiesesaal K&K—*Kaiser und Königlich*). The cuisine is elaborate and intricate; the finest examples include a salad of wild quail served with lentils, strips of braised goose liver, and a sauce that's enhanced with apple liqueur. Desserts include a selection of sorbets flavored with wild alpine berries.

In the Romantik Hotel Schwarzer Adler, Kaiserjägerstrasse 2. ℭ **0512/587109.** Reservations recommended. Main courses 15€–32€. AE, DC, MC, V. Mon–Sat noon–2pm and 6–10:30pm. Tram: 1 or 3.

Schöneck ★★★ AUSTRIAN/TYROLEAN   The cozy premises of this restaurant were once devoted to cheap but cheerful old-fashioned food. Today, within a quartet of wood-paneled dining rooms, he serves arguably the finest cuisine in Innsbruck. From at least one of these, diners appreciate a view that sweeps out over the town, bringing in the nearby peaks. Menu items change with the season and the inspiration of the chef, but might include a carpaccio of salmon; grilled octopus with fish roe and fresh noodles; and grilled sea bass with a herb-flavored vinaigrette. Dessert? Consider the chocolate-stuffed cannelloni with fresh strawberries and house-made mango sorbet.

Weiherburggasse 6. ℭ **0512/272728.** www.wirtshaus-schoeneck.com. Reservations required. Main courses 28€; set-price menus 54€–79€. AE, DC, MC, V. Wed–Sat noon–4pm and 5pm–midnight; Tues 5pm–midnight. Bus: W.

MODERATE

Cammerlander ★ AUSTRIAN/INTERNATIONAL   This is a spacious cafe/bar with several different types of kitchens on two levels, directly along the banks of the Inn River. In fair weather, nearly all guests prefer the covered terrace with its river views. Some of the best steaks in town are offered here on the main floor, especially the tenderloin or *Rumpsteak*. The all-you-can-eat lunch buffet is affordable and you can also find easy meals such as ramen noodle soups and pizzas. In the more formal first floor restaurant, you can order your choice of meats, fish, sauces, and vegetables and watch it cooked on a hot lava stone at your table. Finally, there is the tapas bar, which serves quite a selection of homemade Spanish specialties as well as a breakfast. If you are starving and can't decide which type of food to go for, this is the place for you.

Innrain 2. ℭ **0512/586398.** www.cammerlander.at. Reservations recommended. Main courses 9.50€–18€; lunch buffet 8.50€. First floor restaurant 18€ to 23€ for mixed platter. AE, MC, V. Restaurant open daily 11:30am–midnight, first floor 6pm–1am, tapas bar 8:30am–1am. Tram: 1 or 2.

Hirschen-Stuben ★★ AUSTRIAN/ITALIAN   Beneath a vaulted ceiling in a house built in 1631, this restaurant is charming and well established. You'll see hand-chiseled stone columns, brocade chairs, and a short flight of stairs leading down from the historic pavement of the street outside. The establishment, by its own admission, is at its best in spring, autumn, and winter, since it lacks a garden or terrace for outdoor summer dining. The food is well prepared, the staff is charming, and the ambiance is appropriately welcoming. Menu items include steaming platters of pasta, fish soup, trout *meunière*, sliced veal in cream sauce (Zurich-style), beef Stroganoff, pepper steak, stewed deer with vegetables, and filet of flounder with parsley and potatoes. The kitchen staff is equally familiar with the cuisine of both Austria and Italy.

> ### Impressions
>
> *The chief crop of provincial Austria is scenery.*
> —John Gunther, *Inside Europe* (1938)

Kiebachgasse 5. ℭ **0512/582979.** Reservations recommended. Main courses 9€–23€. AE, DC, MC, V. Tues–Sat 11:30am–2pm and Mon–Sat 6–10:30pm. Tram: 1 or 3.

INEXPENSIVE

Al Dente ITALIAN/VEGETARIAN   Innsbruck isn't far removed from Italy, and the cuisine is duly influenced. This modern restaurant turns out an array of reasonably priced and good-tasting Italian and Mediterranean-style dishes that are based on market-fresh ingredients. There's a beer garden and a terrace (May–Oct) for your added enjoyment. If you are in the mood for a salad, these are fresh and served with creamy dressings. You can order pastas with your choice of sauce, such as *marinara,* a creamy *carbonara,* or a *ragout.* They do not serve meat of any kind. A casual, relaxed ambiance prevails, and the trattoria is suitable for everyone from singles to families. For the most part, waiters are fluent in English.

Meraner Strasse 7. (✆ **0512/584947.** Reservations recommended. Main courses 7€–9.80€. MC, V. Mon–Sat 11am–11pm. Tram: 1 or 3.

Bistro AUSTRIAN/INTERNATIONAL   In one large paneled dining room, you'll find hints of historic charm, a loyal lunchtime clientele from surrounding office buildings, and a well-prepared menu that reflects the changing seasons. During springtime, expect creative uses of asparagus; during autumn and early winter, look for venison prepared in a variety of different ways. There's a year-round emphasis on fish that include Atlantic versions of turbot and sole, and such local freshwater varieties as *Saibling,* pikeperch, *Zander,* and trout. As its name suggests, this is an unpretentious affair with solid, generous portions.

Pradler Strasse 2. (✆ **0512/346319.** Reservations not necessary. Main courses 8€–17€. AE, DC, MC, V. Tues–Sun noon–3pm; daily 6–11pm (last order). Bus: O or R.

Blaues Schiff MEDITERRANEAN/ITALIAN   This place takes five styles and rolls them into one: Restaurant, pizzeria, pub, bistro, and bar. It's also one of the most affordable eateries in the city. What's served here is standard grub along with beer and wine. The cooks don't muck about with "nouvelle" cuisine but concentrate on crowd-pleasers such as pastas and pizza. There is also the usual repertoire of standard south-of-the-border dishes (in this case, sunny Italy).

Universitätsstrasse 13. (✆ **0512/565410.** Reservations not necessary. Main courses 5.90€–12€. AE, DC, MC, V. Daily 10am–3pm and 6pm–12:30am. Tram: 1 or 3.

Café Bar Restaurant Dengg AUSTRIAN/INTERNATIONAL   This is one of the trendiest gathering places in Innsbruck. Though it's in the old part of town, it's as contemporary as tomorrow. It has one of the most well-rounded menus in the heart of the city, with something for almost every palate. Instead of the usual spinach salad, you get additions such as pistachio nuts, squid, prawns, and a black ginger-laced sesame dressing. Dim sum arrives in steamy baskets with vegetables, or suckling pig cutlets served Cantonese-style with cabbage spring rolls. Homemade sorbets are featured along with more exotic desserts: Homemade black sesame ice cream with marinated rhubarb.

Riesengasse 11–13. (✆ **0512/582347.** www.dengg.co.at. Reservations recommended. Main courses 8.40€–22€. AE, DC, MC, V. Mon–Fri 8:30am–11:30pm. Tram: 1 or 3.

La Cucina Ristorante ITALIAN   This trattoria shows how the townspeople of Innsbruck, especially the young, are preferring the lighter and often more flavorful cuisine of Italy than more heavy Austrian dishes. This place is especially festive in summer, when action overflows onto a patio and beer garden setting. Fresh fish is always on the menu and there's also an array of fresh homemade pastas, and the pizza oven is kept busy at night. Many guests begin with one of the freshly tossed salads.

A selection of veal, poultry, and beef dishes round out the well-chosen menu, which is backed up by a varied wine list and an extensive range of beers.

Museumstrasse 26. ✆ **0512/584229.** Reservations recommended. Main courses 8.40€–22€. AE, DC, MC, V. Daily 11am–1am. Tram: 1 or 3.

Philippine VEGETARIAN/FISH/INTERNATIONAL   The inspiration for the mostly vegetarian food here derives from around the world, including India and Mexico, but the origins of its name are purely Austrian: It refers to Philippine Welser, wife of the 16th-century overlord of the Tyrol, Ferdinand II. Positioned one floor above street level, with somewhat anonymous decor, it was established as a public works project about a decade ago as a means of feeding and employing the city's homeless. All of that changed in 2000, when members of the Puffing family took over its administration and whipped it into a privately operated restaurant. The cuisine is tasty and flavorful, most of it focusing on all-vegetarian presentations of salads, lasagnas, curries, polenta, cannelloni with tofu, and pumpkin risotto. There is a limited array of fish dishes, including stir-fries of shrimp with vegetables, braised salmon with a wine-flavored herb sauce, and zander (pikeperch) with a herb-flavored butter sauce.

Templstrasse 2 at Müllerstrasse. ✆ **0512/589157.** Reservations recommended. Main courses 8€–19€. AE, DC, MC, V. Mon–Sat 11:30am–2pm and 6:30–10pm. Tram: 1.

Restaurant Bierwirt 🍴 AUSTRIAN   Antique-laden, with an architectural pedigree that goes back 300 years, this cozy alpine-style restaurant has lots of Tyrolean artifacts, carefully oiled paneling, and an excellent reputation for good food. Menu items include most of the traditional Tyrolean specialties, rib-sticking fare that goes down well in chilly weather. Examples include ragout of venison in a port-wine sauce, a savory version of *Kasfarfeln* (thick consommé with cheese, onions, chives, and dumplings), savory stews, Wiener schnitzels, *Tafelspitz*, roasts, and sausages.

Bichlweg 2. ✆ **0512/342143.** www.bierewirt.at. Reservations recommended. Main courses 7€–20€. Mon–Fri noon–2pm; Mon–Sat 5–11pm. MC, V. Tram: 3. Bus: K.

Restaurant Kapeller AUSTRIAN/CONTINENTAL   This restaurant occupies a 500-year-old house that was expanded into a hotel in the 1960s. Comfortable and welcoming, it includes three paneled dining rooms, an attentive staff, and plenty of Tyrolean knick-knacks. Menu items vary with the season, but are likely to include braised lamb with vegetables and a gratin of potatoes, duck with honey-flavored croutons and potato croquettes, and filets of sole with salmon mousse served with grape sauce and asparagus-flavored risotto. Die-hard regionalists sometimes appreciate an age-old Tyrolean dish, *Peuscherl,* composed of the tongue, hearts, and offal of beef and sheep, served with a herb-flavored sauce.

Philippine-Welser-Strasse 96. ✆ **0512/343101.** Reservations recommended. Main courses 14€–30€. AE, DC, MC, V. Tues–Sat 11am–2pm; Mon–Sat 6–10pm. Tram: 3.

Restaurant Ottoburg ★ AUSTRIAN/INTERNATIONAL   This historic restaurant, established around 1745, occupies a 13th-century building that some historians say is the oldest in Innsbruck. Inside, four intimate and atmospheric dining rooms with 19th-century neo-Gothic decor lie scattered over two different floors. Hearty dishes include venison stew, "grandmother's mixed grill," pork chops with rice and carrots, and fried trout. The international menu emphasizes Tyrolean specialties, best seen in the dessert list, which offers two kinds of strudel and several other pastries. In summer, a beer garden operates in the rear, open daily from 10:30am to 11:30pm.

Herzog-Friedrich-Strasse 1. ☎ **0512/584338.** www.ottoburg.at. Reservations recommended. Main courses 12€–25€. AE, DC, MC, V. Tues–Sun 11am–2:30pm and 6pm–midnight. Tram: 1 or 3.

Riese Haymon TYROLEAN/AUSTRIAN   Inside this 400-year-old building in the heart of the old city, you'll find an intensely Tyrolean ambiance that includes four separate dining rooms, each paneled and accessorized with old-time artifacts, plus an attentive staff. Menu items include old-fashioned but flavor-filled dishes that rely on the seasonality of the ingredients and that often come with one of the restaurant's specialties, dumplings. Look for a changing menu that usually includes such local freshwater fish as *Saibling*, pikeperch, salmon, and trout; veal and chicken dishes in wine sauce or brown stocks; Wiener schnitzel; braised liver; herb-flavored terrines of freshwater crayfish; and an especially savory version of braised oxtail.

Haymongasse 4. ☎ **0512/566800.** Reservations recommended. Main courses 9.80€–19€; fixed-price lunch (Mon–Fri only) 6.60€–8.50€; fixed-price dinner 28€–36€. DC, MC, V. Daily 11:30am–2pm and 6–9:30pm. Tram: 1 or 3.

Stiftskeller AUSTRIAN/INTERNATIONAL   The baroque detailing on this 18th-century yellow-and-white palace-turned-restaurant across from the Hofburg can be admired from the street-side beer garden (at night, lights illuminate the garden). In cold weather, you can eat inside, where there are several dining rooms. Meals are posted on a blackboard, and typical menu items include spaghetti carbonara and venison schnitzel in a pheasant-flavored cream sauce, followed by fresh homemade apple strudel. This place can get rowdy at night. During the warm summer months, folk music and oldies are played in the beer garden, starting at 7:30pm.

Burggraben 31. ☎ **0512/583490.** Reservations required. Main courses 13€–25€. AE, DC, MC, V. Daily 9am–midnight. Closed Jan 8–Feb 20. Tram: 1 or 3.

Theresien Bräu AUSTRIAN/INTERNATIONAL   There's a lot of energy, ambiance, and goodwill associated with this place, which is reflected in its popularity. It's the newest brewery in Tyrol and the only one that's based within the city limits of Innsbruck. The setting is on two floors of what was originally built in the 1940s as a movie theater. Today, you'll find all the apparatus and paraphernalia of a brewery (including big copper and stainless steel vats), positioned in full view of the bar and the dining tables. The theme of the place doesn't evoke alpine Austria, as so many other restaurants in Innsbruck rather shamelessly do. Instead, you can expect a nautical motif. All of this is peripheral, of course, to the beer, which comes in as many as four different varieties that vary with the season and the whims of the brew master.

Maria-Theresien-Strasse 51–53. ☎ **0512/5875800.** www.brauwirtshaus.at. Reservations not necessary. Main courses 12€–22€. AE, DC, MC, V. Mon–Wed 10am–1am; Thurs–Sat 10am–2am; Sun 10am–midnight. Tram: 3.

Weisses Rössl ★ AUSTRIAN/TYROLEAN   You'll enter this time-honored place through a stone archway opening onto one of Old Town's most famous streets. At the end of a flight of stairs, marked with a very old crucifix, you'll find a trio of dining rooms with red-tiled floors. One of the dining rooms (the Nebenstube) has what might be the most extensive set of stag horns (complete with the initials of the hunter and the date of the shooting) in Innsbruck. The menu is simple but classic, listing such dishes as a Tiroler *Gröstl* (a kind of hash composed of sautéed onions, sliced beef, alpine herbs, and potatoes cooked and served in a frying pan), *Saftgoulash* with polenta, several kinds of schnitzels, and a grilled platter *Alt Insprugg* for two diners.

Kiebachgasse 8. ℂ **0512/58305-07.** Reservations recommended. Main courses 18€–29€. MC, V. Mon-Sat 11:30am–2pm and 6–10pm. Closed 2 weeks after Easter and 2 weeks in Nov. Tram: 1 or 3.

CAFES

Within a Bordeaux-red decor that closely emulates the rich cafe life of its mother-lode original in Vienna, you can visit the Innsbruck branch of the **Café Sacher,** Rennweg 1 (ℂ **0512/565626;** www.sacher.com; tram: 1 or 3; bus: H or Y). Rip-offs and unauthorized copies of this chain's most famous pastry, the Sachertorte, have cost contestants millions in litigation over the years, and the holders of the original 19th-century recipe (the owners of the Hotel Sacher in Vienna) have clung ferociously to their property. You can order coffee, priced around 3.50€, and the famous pastry, at 4.95€ per slice. And if you're in the gift-giving mode, you can haul a Sachertorte, attractively boxed in a wooden container, away with you for between 10€ and 42€, depending on the size. Any of these carries a "certificate of authenticity," adding to the experience's somewhat pompous charm. The place is open daily 8:30am to midnight.

If you're tired of too-constant a diet of Austrian pastries, or if you want an insight into the way other countries create fattening between-meal treats, head for the **Café Valier,** Maximilianstrasse 27 (ℂ **0512/586180;** tram: 1). Here, within a pink, mostly Jugendstil decor, you'll choose from French and Italian (not Austrian) pastries that—according to the owners—are unique in Innsbruck.

One of the best views of the exterior of the Goldenes Dachl is available from the front terrace of the **Café Katzung,** Herzog-Friedrich-Strasse 16 (ℂ **0512/586183;** www.cafe-katzung.at; tram: 1 or 3), a time-tested cafe with an interior that was ripped apart and rebuilt during a 5-month period in 2002. The decor today is more streamlined and a bit more modern-looking than the cranky, faux-baroque decor it replaced, but the medley of international newspapers (at least 10 of them) is still available, suspended vertically on rods as you would expect to find in the cafes of Vienna. Within a decor of wooden floors and a color scheme of pale green and cream with touches of red, you'll select from a full range of whiskeys, coffees, Austrian wine, and light platters that consist mostly of sandwiches, soups, and salads. More impressively, there's an in-house pastry chef who concocts tray after tray of strudels and tortes, all the Austrian staples, priced at 3.50€ to 5€ each. It's open Monday to Saturday 8am to midnight and Sunday 9am to midnight.

On a quiet corner in the Old Town, **Café Munding ★**, Kiebachgasse 16 (ℂ **0512/584118;** www.munding.at; tram: 1 or 3), is in a comfortable-looking house built in 1720 that has baroque frescoes, carved bay windows, and Tyrolean detailing. Although it's the oldest cafe in Tyrol, the interior has been modernized, offering an interconnected series of rooms. The first thing you'll see when you enter is a pastry and chocolate shop. Food is served in the inner rooms; in addition to coffee priced from 2.75€, the menu includes typical Tyrolean dishes, *toasts* (sandwiches), plus a vast selection of wine by the glass. Hours are daily from 8am to 11:30pm in summer (until 8pm winter).

One of the most colorful and artfully ethnic cafes along Museumstrasse, **Café Wilder Mann** (ℂ **0512/583295**), was once part of a famous hotel that moved out of town, leaving only its cafe behind. Come here for tea, coffee, ice creams, pastries, and such platters of rib-sticking food as crepes stuffed with filets of pork; Greek-style gyros with herb-flavored cream sauce; piccata of turkey with spaghetti; and such vegetarian dishes as all-vegetable strudel. Dessert crepes, especially the versions with strawberries and/or chocolate, or the concoction with walnut-flavored ice cream and caramel sauce, are especially popular. This cafe is not to be confused with the more elaborate restaurant and hotel in the nearby suburb of Lans with the same name. Snacks and platters cost from 7.20€ to 11€. It's open Monday to Friday 7am to 8pm (tram: 3).

Shopping

In Innsbruck, you can buy Tyrolean specialties such as lederhosen, *Dirndls,* leather clothing, woodcarvings, Loden cloth, and all sorts of skiing and mountain-climbing equipment. Stroll around **Maria-Theresien-Strasse, Herzog-Friedrich-Strasse,** and **Museumstrasse,** ducking in and making discoveries of your own. Stores are generally open from 9am to 6pm on weekdays and from 9am to noon on Saturday. Here are a few recommendations to get you going.

Lodenbaur Lodenbaur, similar to a department store, is devoted to regional Tyrolean dress. Most goods are made in Austria, including lederhosen, coats, dresses, *Dirndls,* and accessories for men, women, and children. Be sure to check out the basement. Brixner Strasse 4. ℂ **0512/580911.** Tram: 1 or 3.

Tiroler Heimatwerk This is one of Innsbruck's best stores for handcrafted Tyrolean items such as sculpture, pewter, textiles, woolen goods, hand-knit sweaters, and lace. Do-it-yourselfers can buy regionally inspired fabrics and dress patterns, and whip them into a dirndl (or whatever). Also for sale are carved chests, mirror frames, and furniture. The store's elegant decor includes ancient stone columns and vaulted ceilings. Meraner Strasse 2. ℂ **0512/582320.** www.tiroler.heimatwerk.at. Tram: 1 or 3.

Innsbruck After Dark

If you're in luck, you'll get to attend a summer concert in the park or perhaps take in an operetta at the theater. You might retire to a beer hall to listen to brass bands and yodeling, or be lulled by zither music at a restaurant. Best of all, you can attend a Tyrolean folkloric evening or retreat to a local wine tavern offering entertainment. Many restaurants offer Tyrolean evenings (featuring evergreen music and dancing) in addition to food.

Ask the tourist office about current events. In summer, a Tyrolean brass band often parades in costume, with a concert at the Goldenes Dachl. There are also often concerts at Schloss Ambras, ecclesiastical music at Wilten Basilica, and organ concerts at the Igls parish church.

In the center of the Altstadt, across from the Hofburg, the 150-year-old **Landestheater,** Rennweg 2 (ℂ **0512/52074;** www.landestheater.at), is the major venue for theatrical or operatic presentations. The box office is open daily from 9:30am to 7pm, and performances usually begin at 7:30 or 8pm. Ticket prices are 9€ to 53€ for most operas or operettas, and 4€ to 53€ for theater seats. It's also the showcase for musicals and light operetta. For tickets, call ℂ **0512/52074-4.**

Concerts are presented at the Kunstpavillon in the Hofgarten in summer.

If you want to gamble, you have to drive to the resort of Seefeld, where the **Spiel-Casino** offers roulette, baccarat, and blackjack daily from 5pm. Or you can try your luck on the slot machines at the **Hilton Hotel Innsbruck.**

THE BAR & CLUB SCENE

Hofgartencafe Just north of Altstadt, this is perhaps the most popular place in Innsbruck. Lying in Hofgarten, it's especially packed in summer, and offers not only live music, but also indoor and outdoor seating. A lively crowd of young people is attracted to these precincts where more beer is consumed than anywhere else in town. You can opt for the home-brewed beer or else a wide selection of wines, many from such South American countries as Chile and Argentina. Long drinks cost from 7€, and you can also order platters for 7.40€ to 20€. It's open in summer daily from 11am to 4am. In winter, hours are Tuesday to Thursday 6pm to 2am, and Friday and Saturday 6pm to 4am. Hofgarten, Rennweg 6. ℂ **0512/588871.** www.der-hofgarten.at. Tram: 1 or 3.

Jackpot Bar   The attractive bar near the Hilton Hotel lobby is one of the best places in Innsbruck to meet for a drink. Beer costs 4€ and up, and there are slot machines. It's open Monday to Friday from noon to 1am. In the Hilton Hotel Innsbruck, Salurner Strasse 15. ℂ **0512/59350.** Tram: 3.

Jimmy's Bar   This bar lies in a modern building in the center of town, and is a bustling hangout in Innsbruck among young people, often university students. There's no dance floor and no live music, but it's something of an Innsbruck tradition to stop off here for a drink either early in the evening or later at night. Food is also served. The bar is open Monday to Friday 11am to 1am, Saturday 8pm to 1:30am. A large beer costs 2.50€. Wilhelm-Griel-Strasse 19. ℂ **0512/570473.** www.jimmys.at. Tram: 1 or 3.

Krah Vogel   Lying off Maria-Theresien-Strasse, this bar attracts university students in droves who crowd its tables. In winter, when some of the patrons show up in Tyrolean dress, the place seems even livelier. At the back is a small courtyard, and the overflow heads upstairs for more seating. The cafe has one of the most convivial atmospheres in town and is often crowded. Beer ranges for the most part from 2.50€ to 3.30€, with sandwiches costing from 6€. Open Monday to Saturday 10am to 2am, and Sunday 5pm to 1am. Anichstrasse 12. ℂ **0512/580149.** www.krahvogel.at. Tram: 1 or 3.

Restaurant Fischerhausel Bar   Although a lot of its business derives from its busy first-floor restaurant, the street-level bar also adds appeal. It's open Monday to Saturday from 10am to 1am and Sunday 6 to 11:30pm (closed Sun in Sept and Oct). No one will mind if you remain in the bar, quaffing schnapps or suds or whatever, but if you opt to eventually migrate up to the dining room, a *tagesmenu* (fixed-price menu) will cost 8.40€ to 20€. During warm weather, drinkers and diners tend to move out to the garden at the back back, soaking up the sunlight and the brisk alpine air. Herrengasse 8. ℂ **0512/583535.** www.fischerhaeusl.com. Tram: 1 or 3.

Treibhaus   Young people interpret this comprehensive and flexible gathering place as a combination of daytime cafe, snackish restaurant, concert hall, and dance club. Within its battered walls, you can attend a changing roster of art exhibits, cabaret shows, and protest rallies, all from a location within an alleyway about a block from Burggraben. A large beer costs 4.20€; snacks are priced from 3.20€. It's open Monday to Saturday 10am to 1am, with live music presented at erratic intervals. Angerzellgasse 8. ℂ **0512/572000.** www.treibhaus.at. Cover for live performances 10€–30€. Tram: 1 or 3.

Gay Clubs

Gay people throughout the Tyrol tend to agree that the bars and dance clubs that cater to them are bigger, more fun, and a lot more spontaneous in Vienna or even better, Berlin. If you're looking for a gay bar in the alpine fastnesses of Innsbruck, the options are extremely limited.

Bacchus   Located across the street from Innsbruck's Holiday Inn, this is a cellar-level dance club that attracts a clientele composed of about 70% gay men, 25% gay women, and 5% interested and usually well-intentioned straight people. It's open nightly 9pm to 2am or later, depending on the crowd and the night of the week. Salurnerstrasse 18. (*C* **0512/940210.** www.bacchus.tirol.at. Tram: 1 or 3.

FOLK MUSIC

Throughout the Christmas season, Easter, and the high season, from 6 to 11pm, you can visit the **Goethe Stube,** in the Restaurant Goldener Adler, Herzog-Friedrich-Strasse 6 ((*C* **0512/571111;** tram: 1 or 3), to hear authentic Tyrolean melodies, including the zither and yodelers. There's a one-drink minimum, and a large beer costs 3.50€. Meals start at 9€.

Another evening of authentic Tyrolean folk entertainment can be experienced courtesy of the shows of **Tiroler Alpenbühne/Geschwister Gundolf** ((*C* **0512/263263;** www.tiroler-abend.com), who have been performing in Innsbruck for nearly 4 decades. While you have dinner, a brass band plays along with traditional Tyrolean instruments such as an alphorn, zither, singing saw, and Tyrolean folk harp. It's big, boisterous, and definitely unique. Shows are presented daily at 8:30pm at two locations (the **Gasthaus Sandwirt,** Reichenauerstrasse 151; bus: O or R) in Innsbruck May through October. Tickets for the shows start at 27€. Dinner is optional but does complete the experience of the sounds of the region with the tastes of the region; it usually costs an additional 16€. For tickets and information, contact Tiroler Alpenbühne/Geschwister Gundolf daily from 8am to 11pm, or ask your hotel concierge if tickets are available. Tickets can be purchased on-site at both venues, but it's highly recommended that you secure a reservation. Scheduled performances are not held in November; from December to March, however, special shows will take place once a week for groups by request, in addition to Christmas concerts held every Saturday in December. If you're traveling alone or in a small group, call ahead to see if a show has been booked.

IGLS & THE ENVIRONS

This area, where events including the bobsled and luge competitions of the Olympic Winter Games of 1964 and 1976 were held, is often called "Olympic Innsbruck." The cluster of resorts just outside the city, the best known of which is Igls, is within easy reach of the Tyrolean capital. A complete system of lifts allows access to the surrounding alpine scenery for everybody, from the beginner to the most advanced skier—or the sightseer in warm weather. You might consider staying in one of these resorts instead of at an Innsbruck hotel.

Igls ★

Lying on a sunny plateau in the alpine foothills at an elevation of 877m (2,877 ft.), Igls is the resort choice of many travelers who prefer staying here and driving into Innsbruck, which is 6km (3.7 miles) north (take Rte. 82). Although its numbers swell greatly with winter and summer visitors, the town has a population of fewer than 2,000. Long known as the "sun terrace" of Innsbruck, Igls is never likely to be too hot, even on the hottest day in Austria. Because of its popularity, Igls is certainly not the cheapest resort in Tyrol.

ESSENTIALS

GETTING THERE   A streetcar from the **Berg Isel** station in Innsbruck, tram no. 6, will deliver you to Igls, 305m (1,001 ft.) higher than the capital, in about 30 minutes. It departs every 13 minutes past the hour. Bus J leaves from the Sillpark stop near the city center, departing every 15 minutes during the day, every hour in the evening. For transportation information, call 📞 **0512/561616.**

VISITOR INFORMATION   The **Igls tourist office** is on Hilberstrasse 15 (📞 **0512/377101;** www.innsbruck.info/igls). It's open Monday to Friday 8:30am to 6pm, and Saturday 9am to noon.

EXPLORING "OLYMPIC INNSBRUCK"

Although much of its world renown has been based on winter sports, Igls is also a popular summer resort where you can wander along trails, play golf, or enjoy tennis.

This is also Innsbruckers' favorite place to ski, and they're joined by throngs of visitors. Igls shared the Winter Olympics festivities and sporting competition with Innsbruck, and still boasts the bobsled, luge, and skeleton track used during the Olympics, which continues to be used for large winter-sports events such as the 2012 Winter Youth Olympics.

WHERE TO STAY

Hotel Batzenhäusl ★   Only a 2-minute walk from the center, this traditional hotel/inn began as a winery in 1893. Its name derives from the Austrian word *batzen,* a silver coin commonly used in the late 19th century. The tavern's ornate paneling is carved from what the locals call "stone pine," the glow from which beautifully complements the flowered carpets, leaded windows, and hand-worked lamps. Other sections of this comfortable hotel are crafted in a more modern style. Rooms are medium in size and well furnished, with alpine styling and wooden bed frames. Even if you don't stay here, you might want to consider having dinner in Restaurant Batzenhäusl (p. 374).

Lanserstrasse 12, A-6080 Igls. 📞 **0512/38618-0.** Fax 0512/386187. www.batzenhaeusl.at. 26 units. 92€–168€ double; 145€–210€ suite. Rates include buffet breakfast, half-board for a surcharge of 19.30€. MC, V. Free parking outdoors; 7€ garage. Closed Nov and Apr, though closing dates vary from year to year. **Amenities:** Restaurant; bar; bike rentals; children's playroom; fitness room; Jacuzzi; library; non-smoking rooms; sauna. *In room:* TV, minibar, hairdryer, Wi-Fi (for 2.40€ per hour).

Schlosshotel Igls ★★   The town's most historic and glamorous hotel, this baroque monument was built as a private castle in 1880 and converted into a small, plush hotel in the 1970s. It sits on its own grass-covered plateau at the end of a narrow street. Rooms are spacious and individually decorated with luxurious beds. Some rooms offer panoramic mountain views. If you are looking for luxury, the most renowned of the accommodations is the Lubinus Suite, with a fireplace, terrace, Jacuzzi, and steam bath. The hotel's excellent restaurant serves both traditional and international food in turn-of-the-20th-century surroundings. Guests also have access to the two tennis courts at the Schlosshotel's jointly owned hotel, the Sporthotel (see below).

Viller Steig 2, A-6080 Igls. 📞 **0512/377217.** Fax 0512/377217-198. www.schlosshotel-igls.com. 18 units. 240€–340€ double; 300€–780€ suite. Rates include breakfast buffet, half-board for a surcharge of 40€. AE, DC, MC, V. Free parking outdoors, garage 10€. Closed mid-Oct to Christmas. **Amenities:** Restaurant; bar; babysitting; fitness center; indoor heated pool; room service; sauna; tanning bed. *In room:* TV, hairdryer, minibar, Wi-Fi.

Sporthotel Igls ★   Built in 1900, the Sporthotel is a fancifully designed establishment that's a cross between a baroque castle and a mountain chalet. Its details include jutting bay windows, ornate hexagonal towers, and rows of flower-covered balconies. The spacious interior is dotted with antiques and conservative furniture, with plenty of *gemütlich* corners and sunny areas, both indoors and out. An annex handles the overflow. Rooms, which come in a variety of sizes, are cozily outfitted in the Tyrolean style, with lots of varnished pine and regional knick-knacks.

The hotel has a large dining room where dinner is served to guests on the half-board plan. It also has an attractive a la carte restaurant for nonguests. Tyrolean/Austrian cuisine is served, along with international and diet menus. In the evening, a one-man band plays in the hotel bar, and Tyrolean folkloric evenings are sometimes staged.

Hilberstrasse 17, A-6080 Igls. (*©*) **0512/377241**. Fax 0512/378679. www.sporthotel-igls.com. 75 units. Winter 136€–340€ double, 194€–404€ suite for 2; summer 150€–176€ double, 206€–236€ suite. Rates include breakfast. Half-board 22€ per person. AE, DC, MC, V. Free parking outside, 7€ garage. **Amenities:** Restaurant; bar; babysitting; fitness center; massage; nonsmoking rooms; indoor heated pool; room service; 1 room for those w/limited mobility; spa; tanning bed; 2 tennis courts located short distance from hotel. *In room:* TV, hairdryer, minibar, Wi-Fi.

WHERE TO EAT

Gasthof Wilder Mann AUSTRIAN   This place offers a breath of the Tyrolean mountains and country life in the Innsbruck suburb of Igls. Originally built in the 1600s, the building has been enlarged and modified over the years. If you appreciate architecture, you'll enjoy studying the stucco tower attached to the corner of this elongated building with a half-timbered triangular section just under the sloping roofline. The interior is spacious and rustic, with good service and a series of well-prepared traditional specialties such as wine soup, duck liver terrine with port jelly and kumquats, and venison pâté with Cumberland sauce. The dessert specialty: *Salzburger Nockerl.*

Römerstrasse 12. (*©*) **0512/379696.** http://wildermann-lans.at. Reservations recommended. Main courses 16€–30€. AE, DC, MC, V. Daily 11am–2pm and 5:30–9:30pm.

Restaurant Batzenhäusl 🍴 AUSTRIAN   In this carefully paneled antique-style dining room, the chalet chairs are intricately carved and the service is respectable. A house specialty is flambé filet steak "Didi," a popular creation prepared at your table. Other well-prepared Austrian dishes include three kinds of meat on the same platter (covered in a mushroom-cream sauce), *Apfelstrudel,* and a series of savory meat-flavored soups. A favorite local dish is venison with cranberry sauce and wild mushrooms along with potato fritters and roast zucchini. You might prefer the outdoor veranda or the garden in summer, although the dining room inside is most attractive.

In the Hotel Batzenhäusl, Lanserstrasse 12. (*©*) **0512/386180.** Main courses 9.90€–25€; fixed-price menu 18€–36€. MC, V. Mon–Thurs 11am–2pm and 6–10pm. Closed Mon and Tues, and Apr and Nov, though closing months vary from year to year.

Patsch

This small village above Igls stands on the sunny western slope of the Patscherkofel, with a clear view of the Stubai Glacier. Lying on the old Roman road below the peak, Patsch is only a short distance from the mountain's Olympics' slopes.

In winter, Patsch attracts visitors with its skiing (including cross-country runs), ice-skating, and curling; the resort offers a ski school, and horse-drawn sleighs take you along snow trails. In summer, you can go on hikes, swim, or play golf and tennis. Summer skiing is also possible on the Stubai Glacier.

The most spectacular way to spend time in Patsch involves taking a cable car, the **Patscherkofelbahn** ★ ((*©* **0512/377234;** www.patscherkofelbahnen.at), up to the top of the Patscherkofel, a panoramic site at an elevation of 1,961m (6,434 ft.). From here, you'll have access to a cafe, a restaurant, and a network of hiking and ski trails.

The cable-car ride covers a distance of 4km (2½ miles) and takes about 18 minutes. A round-trip passage for adults costs 18.40€ in summer and from 18€ in winter (depending on the time of day), and for children 9.20€ in summer and from 11€ in winter. Except for a closing during November, it operates year-round daily from 9am to noon and 12:45 to 4:30pm in summer, and daily from 9am to 4pm in winter.

ESSENTIALS

GETTING THERE There is no **train service** to Patsch, but buses depart from Innsbruck's Hauptbahnhof for Patsch usually once an hour (trip time: 20 min.). For **bus information,** call ✆ 0512/585155. If you're **driving,** you can reach Patsch by the Brennerbahn, via the Europabrücke; there's a 6€ toll. An alternate route is the road from Innsbruck going up through Vill and Igls.

VISITOR INFORMATION For **tourist information** in Patsch, call ✆ 0512/377332. The office is open Monday to Friday 8am to 12:30pm.

WHERE TO STAY & EAT

Hotel Bär Sections of this amply proportioned hotel, specifically the reception area and the well-recommended Bauernstube, date from the 1200s, when they functioned as part of a simple inn. In 1970, a modern addition was built around the original core, turning the place into an unpretentious but worthwhile three-star hotel noted for its relatively reasonable rates. Today, you'll find public areas sheathed in pinewood paneling and stone. Big panoramic windows and an antique ceramic stove add to the cozy atmosphere. The snug and traditionally furnished rooms offer plenty of comfort, from the excellent beds to the well-polished bathrooms. Maintenance and housekeeping are first-rate. Meals in the Bauernstube are served daily from noon to 2pm and 6 to 9pm. Main courses are 15€ to 18€.

Römerstrasse 14, A-6082 Patsch. ✆ 0512/38611. Fax 0512/3861141. www.baerhotel.at. 39 units. Winter 68€–114€ double; summer 54€–92€ double. Surcharge for breakfast buffet is 8€, 22€ for half-board. AE, DC, MC, V. Closed Nov and Apr, though exact dates vary each year. **Amenities:** 2 restaurants; bar; children's playroom; indoor heated pool. *In room:* TV, hairdryer, Wi-Fi (in some).

Hotel Grünwalderhof ★ 👪 Once the private hunting lodge of the counts of Thurn and Taxis, members of the Ribis family now operate this hotel. Standing on the site of an ancient Roman road, the hotel is in one of the town's prettiest chalets, with a natural-grained lattice relief under the slope of its gabled roof, striped shutters, and a modern extension stretching out the back. Inside, the decor includes a scattering of antiques, paneling, and leather-upholstered chairs in the spacious and comfortable dining room. With their alpine coziness and good housekeeping, the rooms, which come in several sizes, are among the finest at the resort; some open onto private balconies with mountain vistas.

Römerstrasse 1, A-6082 Patsch. ✆ 0512/377304. Fax 0512/378078. www.gruenwalderhof.at. 26 units. Winter 108€–138€ double; summer 116€–120€ double. Half-board 20€ per person extra. AE, DC, MC, V. Closed Apr and Nov. **Amenities:** Restaurant; lounge; babysitting; fitness center; sauna; room service; tennis court. *In room:* TV, hairdryer.

Mutters ★

On a sunny southern plateau above Innsbruck, Mutters—considered by many to be one of the most beautiful villages in Tyrol—is just 10km (6½ miles) southwest of Innsbruck. You can drive to the center of the city from here in about 15 minutes along Mutters Strasse.

Mutters is in the skiing and recreation area of the Mutterer Alm and the Axamer Lizum, which were the central bases for the 1964 and 1976 Olympic Winter Games. Mutterer Alm is the place for easygoing skiers. It can be reached by cable car; for information call ✆ 0512/548330.

ESSENTIALS

GETTING THERE The **Stubaitalbahn tram** (✆ 0512/530712 for information) departs from Innsbruck's Hauptbahnhof 18 times a day, bound for Fulpmes and stopping at Mutters en route (trip time: 28 min.).

VISITOR INFORMATION For **tourist information** in Mutters, call ✆ 0512/548410 or go to **www.innsbruck.info/mutters**. The office, located at Kirchplatz 11, is open Monday to Friday 8:30am to noon and 3 to 6pm.

WHERE TO STAY & EAT

Hotel Altenburg ★ Local archives refer to a restaurant on this site in 1622. Later it became a farmhouse and then an annex of the nearby church. In 1910, it was transformed into a flower-bedecked chalet hotel. The ground floor is sheltered by a three-arched arcade, which serves as an attractive backdrop for the nearby greenhouse-style cafe. Each snugly furnished comfortable room has a small but spotlessly clean bathroom. The hotel's elegant restaurant is filled with upholstered banquettes and conservative furniture, with big windows overlooking the mountains. The **Restaurant Altenburg** serves first-rate Tyrolean and international cuisine. Occasionally, only hotel guests can dine here, so it's best to check. Evening entertainment is sometimes provided. The Wishaber family is your host.

Kirchplatz 4, A-6162 Mutters. ✆ **0512/548524.** Fax 0512/5485246. www.altenburg.com. 34 units. 86€–132€ double. Rates include buffet breakfast. Half-board 12€ per person extra. AE, DC, MC, V. Closed end Apr to end May and Oct–mid Dec. **Amenities:** Restaurant; bar; babysitting; indoor heated pool; room service; spa. *In room:* TV, hairdryer, minibar, Wi-Fi.

Muttererhof ★ This government-rated three-star hotel, only a short walk from the village center, has a gabled roof and a dignified chalet facade—in season, its balconies are covered with flowers. The snug and comfortable rooms, in a variety of sizes, are furnished in a Tyrolean style; the best open onto private balconies with mountain vistas. The hotel has an elegantly paneled restaurant filled with carved chairs, leaded windows, and antiques, and a verdant lawn with cafe tables in summer. The restaurant is open Wednesday to Saturday 5 to 9pm, Sunday noon to 9pm.

Nattererstrase 20, A-6162 Mutters. ✆ **0512/548491.** Fax 0512/5484915. www.tec-ma.eu/muttererhof. 20 units. Summer 90€–102€ double, suite from 96€; winter 90€–140€. Rates include breakfast, half-board for a 10€ surcharge. AE, DC, MC, V. Closed Oct–mid Dec and Apr–May. Tram: STB from Innsbruck. **Amenities:** Restaurant; bar; babysitting; laundry service; dry cleaning; public Wi-Fi. *In room:* TV.

THE EASTERN SIDE OF THE ARLBERG: A SKIING MECCA

There may be no such thing as a sacred ski (and snowboarding) mountain, but if there were, it would have to be the **Arlberg.** This is where alpine skiing began in the late 1800s. On the east side of the Arlberg, 114km (71 miles) west of Innsbruck, is what's known as the cradle of alpine skiing. Here the legends and stars known to all dedicated skiers were born: The Ski Club Arlberg, the early Kandahar races, and Hannes Schneider and his Arlberg method. (The west side of the Arlberg is covered in chapter 13.)

The Arlberg range, with peaks that top the 2,745-m (9,006-ft.) mark, lures skiers with its vast network of cableways, lifts, runs stretching for miles, a world-renowned ski school, and numerous sporting amenities. Runs begin at the intermediate level, reaching all the way to the nearly impossible.

The Arlberg is the loftiest section of the **Lechtal range,** and marks the boundary between the settlers of the Tyrolean country and the **Vorarlbergers,** who live in the extreme western province of Austria. One of the Arlberg's most celebrated peaks is the **Valluga,** at 2,812m (9,226 ft.).

In 1825, a road was opened, allowing traffic to travel to the **Arlberg Pass.** A 10km-long (6-mile) rail tunnel was opened in 1884, linking Tyrol and Vorarlberg. Finally, in 1978, a new road tunnel, Europe's third longest, linked the two provinces. The toll for the **Arlberg Strassentunnel** is 8.50€ each way per car. If you're not driving, you'll find the area serviced by the well-known **Arlberg Express rail link.**

St. Anton am Arlberg ★★★

A modern resort has grown out of this old village on the **Arlberg Pass,** a place where ski history began. It also hosts some of the finest skiing in the Alps.

It was at St. Anton (1,289m/4,229 ft.) that Hannes Schneider developed modern skiing techniques and began teaching tourists how to ski in 1907. The Ski Club Arlberg was born here in 1901. In 1911, the first Arlberg–Kandahar Cup competition was held, with the best alpine skier winning a valuable trophy. Before his death in 1955, Schneider saw his ski school rated as the world's finest. Today, the ski school, still at St. Anton, is one of the world's largest and best, with about 300 instructors, most of whom speak English.

The little town is a compact resort village with a five-story limit on buildings. No cars are allowed in the business area, but sleds and skis are plentiful.

ESSENTIALS

GETTING THERE St. Anton is an express stop on the main **rail lines** crossing over the Arlberg Pass between Innsbruck and Bregenz. Just to the west of St. Anton, trains disappear into the Arlberg tunnel, emerging almost 11km (7 miles) later on the opposite side of the mountain range. About one train per hour arrives in St. Anton from Innsbruck (trip time: 75–85 min.) and from Bregenz (trip time: 85 min.). For rail information, contact ☏ **05/1717** (www.oebb.at).

Because of St. Anton's good rail connections to eastern and western Austria, most visitors arrive by train. From the city, however, many travelers take the **bus** on to other resorts such as **Zürs** and **Lech.**

St. Anton is 599km (372 miles) west of Vienna and 100km (62 miles) west of Innsbruck. If you're **driving** from Innsbruck, take the A12 toward Bregenz, then continue on to the S16 and take the exit to St. Anton. On this stretch, there are three tolls ranging from 4.50€ to 8.50€ per car.

VISITOR INFORMATION The **tourist office** in the **Arlberghaus** lies in the town center, Dorfstrasse 8 (☏ **05446/2269-0;** www.stantonamarlberg.com). In winter, hours are Monday to Friday 8am to 6pm; closed Saturday, Sunday, and holidays.

SKIING & MORE

The snow in this area is perfect for skiers, and the total lack of trees on the slopes makes the situation ideal. The ski fields of St. Anton stretch over some 16 sq. km (6 sq. miles). Beginners stick to the slopes down below, and for the more experienced skiers there are the runs from the **Galzig** and **Valluga** peaks. A cableway will take you to Galzig (2,092m/6,864 ft.), where there's a self-service restaurant. The nearby Vallugabahn will take you all the way to the peak of the Valluga, at 2,812m (9,226 ft.), which commands a panoramic view. **St. Christoph** (mentioned later in this chapter) is the mountain annex of St. Anton. Call ✆ **0544/623520** for information on the cable cars.

In addition to the major ski areas just mentioned, there are two other important sites. The **Gampen/Kapall** area is an advanced–intermediate network of slopes; its lifts start just behind St. Anton's railway station. Also noteworthy is the **Rendl,** a relatively new labyrinth of runs to the south of St. Anton that offers many novice and intermediate slopes.

In winter, St. Anton am Arlberg is quite fashionable; popular with the wealthy, there's a more conservative segment of the rich and famous here than you'll see at other posh ski resorts. There are many other cold-weather pursuits besides skiing, including ski jumping, mountain tours, curling, skating, tobogganing, and sleigh rides, plus après-ski on the quiet side.

There's so much emphasis on skiing here that there's little talk of the summertime attractions. In warm weather, St. Anton is tranquil and bucolic, surrounded by meadowland. A riot of wildflowers blooming in the fields announces the beginning of spring.

At any time of the year, you can visit the **Ski und Heimatmuseum (Skiing and Local Museum),** in the Arlberg–Kandahar House (✆ **05446/2475**), where displays trace the development of skiing in the Arlberg, as well as the region's history from the days of tribal migrations in and around Roman times. The museum, in the imposing structure at the center of the Holiday Park in St. Anton, is open from December to April and June to mid-September, daily 3 to 10pm. Admission is 4€ for adults, free for children.

The local library is also housed in the Arlberg–Kandahar House, and the park provides a variety of leisure activities, including minigolf, a woodland playground, a fishing pond, table tennis, open-air chess, and a curling rink.

WHERE TO STAY
Expensive

Hotel Alte Post ★ This rambling four-story building with ocher-colored walls, green shutters, and jutting gables was built in the 17th century as a postal station, and can easily be reached from the town's rail station. Renovations retained most of the thick-timbered beauty, and rooms combine old-fashioned paneling with tiled and timbered private bathrooms that have tub/shower combinations and sometimes very elegant accessories. Members of the Tandl family are your hosts.

The hotel contains an excellent restaurant (p. 381).

Dorfstrasse 11, A-6580 St. Anton am Arlberg. ✆ **05446/25530.** Fax 05446/255341. www.hotel-alte-post.at. 60 units. Winter 253€–437€ double, from 297€ suite; summer 160€ double, 180€ suite. For half-board, surcharge of 11.50€ in summer, 14.50€ in winter. AE, DC, MC, V. Closed May–June and late Oct–late Nov. **Amenities:** Restaurant; bar; babysitting (with advance arrangement); fitness center; Jacuzzi; massage; indoor heated pool; room service; sauna; tanning bed. *In room:* TV, hairdryer, minibar, Wi-Fi.

Hotel Post ★ In the 1990s, a large and sprawling hotel complex was divided into two smaller (and adjacent) properties, the Hotel Alte Post (see above) and the Hotel Post. Built in 1896 and noteworthy because of its sprawling dimensions and wood-and-stucco facade, it has established a reputation as one of the resort's most sports-oriented hotels. It offers appealing rooms comfortably equipped with medium-size bathrooms. Housekeeping and general maintenance here are state-of-the-art.

The hotel contains a dimly lit and woodsy series of spacious public rooms, two dining rooms, and two of the most popular nightlife facilities in St. Anton, the Post-keller and Piccadilly Pub.

Walter-Schuler-Weg 2, A-6580 St. Anton am Arlberg. © **05446/22130.** Fax 05446/2343. www.st-anton.co.at. 66 units. Winter 222€–488€ double; summer 118€–158€ double. Rates include half-board. AE, DC, MC, V. Parking 7€ per day. Closed late Apr–late July and late Sept–early Dec. **Amenities:** 2 restaurants; bar; 2 nightclubs; Jacuzzi; nonsmoking rooms; room service; sauna. *In room:* TV, hairdryer, minibar, Wi-Fi.

Hotel Schwarzer Adler ★★   In the center of St. Anton, this hotel has been owned and operated by the Tschol family since 1885. The beautiful fresco-covered building was constructed as an inn in 1570. The inn became known for its hospitality to pilgrims crossing the treacherous Arlberg Pass, and was eventually declared an officially registered hotel by Empress Maria Theresa. The hotel's interior contains several fireplaces, Tyrolean baroque armoires, and oriental rugs. Rooms are hand-somely furnished and well-equipped. All rooms have exceedingly comfortable beds. Nearly all bathrooms have big bathtubs, although a few singles offer only showers. Many patrons come to this hotel just to enjoy its food and drink (see review p. 381).

A-6580 St. Anton am Arlberg. © **05446/22440.** Fax 05446/224462. www.schwarzeradler.com. 70 units. Winter 214€–592€ double, 414€–690€ suite; summer 130€–180€ double, 220€–240€ suite. Rates include half-board. MC, V. Closed May–June and Oct–Nov. **Amenities:** Restaurant; bar; babysitting (on request); massage; indoor heated pool; room service; all nonsmoking rooms; spa. *In room:* TV, hairdryer, Wi-Fi.

Raffl's St. Antoner Hof ★★   The only government-rated five-star hotel in St. Anton, the St. Antoner Hof is a bit posher and more attentive than other hotels in town. Built in the early 1980s and run by a group of enthusiastic skiers (the Raffl family), it rises in severe dignity about a block from the resort's historic center. Rooms, in a variety of sizes, are plush and fastidiously maintained, all with thick carpeting, fireplaces, and the most comfortable beds at the resort. Guests enjoy the public rooms, each of which seems awash in Tyrolean accessories, thick tim-bers, and collections of rustic implements. Blazing fireplaces and good cuisine are all part of the experience here; the restaurant, **Raffl Stube,** is recommended on p. 380.

Arlbergstrasse 69, A-6580 St. Anton am Arlberg. ©**05446/2910.** Fax 05446/3551. www.antonerhof. at. 37 units. 350€–870€ double; 450€–970€ suite. Rates include half-board. DC, MC, V. Closed Apr 17–early Dec. **Amenities:** Restaurant; bar; babysitting; children's playroom; fitness center; Jacuzzi; mas-sage; indoor heated pool; room service; sauna; tanning bed; Turkish bath. *In room:* TV, hairdryer, mini-bar, Wi-Fi.

Sporthotel St. Anton ★   This sprawling government-rated four-star 1974 hotel sits on the main pedestrian thoroughfare of St. Anton. Ideal for shopping, it's a good choice for skiers too, since it's a 3-minute walk from the chairlifts. In winter, you're greeted at the entrance with the sight of a bar and the music of a full-time pianist, whose melodies add to the ski trip vibe and go well with afternoon cocktails. Rooms are medium-size, comfortable, and contemporary, each with a balcony. One of the hotel's restaurants, the Steakhouse, is a favorite of many St. Anton regulars (p. 381).

The Eastern Side of the Arlberg: A Skiing Mecca

A-6580 St. Anton am Arlberg. ☎ **05446/3111.** Fax 05446/311170. www.sporthotel-st-anton.at. 53 units. Winter 124€–376€ double, 295€–507€ suite; summer 102€–112€ double, 155€–168€ suite. Half-board with surcharge of 22€. DC, MC, V. Free parking outside, 10€ garage. Closed May and Oct–Nov. **Amenities:** Restaurant; bar; babysitting; massage; indoor heated pool; room service; sauna; tanning bed. *In room:* TV, hairdryer, minibar, Wi-Fi.

Moderate

Hotel Kertess ★ 🎿 Located in a quiet residential section of town called Oberdorf, this hotel lies on a hillside above the main tourist district of St. Anton, a steep 12-minute climb up the hill. You'll recognize the hotel by its country-baroque window trim. The hotel is family run, owned by Maria Kertess, a former ski instructor. Each snug and cozy room offers plenty of exposed wooden trim, functional if not stylish furniture, and, if you're lucky, a view of the Rendl ski slope. Even if you're not a guest here, consider the hotel's restaurant (p. 381). Because it's located in a residential neighborhood away from the town center, the hotel runs a shuttle bus service to St. Anton and its ski areas.

A-6580 St. Anton am Arlberg. ☎ **05446/2005-0.** Fax 05446/200556. www.kertess.com. 52 units. Winter 180€–280€ double; summer 100€–120€ double. Rates include half-board. MC, V. Closed Oct–early Dec, May–mid June. **Amenities:** Restaurant; bar; massage; indoor heated pool; spa; Wi-Fi in lobby. *In room:* TV.

Hotel Montjola Lying less than a kilometer (½ mile) west of the resort's center, about a 10-minute uphill walk, this hotel is rustically appealing. Most rooms are in a comfortable annex built in 1991, although the reception desk, restaurant, and bar are in the original core—a carefully preserved wood-and-stone structure dating from the 1930s. Rooms come in a variety of sizes, and decor ranges from traditional to contemporary; each has a good bed plus a small but efficient bathroom with a tub/shower combination. Throughout both sections, you'll see heavy ceiling beams, a stone-rimmed fireplace, rustic knick-knacks, and immaculately set dining room tables. Fondue is a specialty of the in-house restaurant.

A-6580 St. Anton am Arlberg. ☎ **05446/2302.** Fax 05446/23029. www.montjola.com. 42 units. Winter 186€–320€ double; summer 110€–134€ double. Rates include half-board. AE, DC, MC, V. Closed end Apr–mid June and mid Sept–early Dec. **Amenities:** Restaurant; bar; babysitting (on request); fitness center; massage (on request); room service; nonsmoking rooms; sauna; steam bath; tanning bed. *In room:* TV, hairdryer, safe, Wi-Fi.

WHERE TO EAT

Expensive

Raffl Stube ★★ 🎿 AUSTRIAN This restaurant was established in 1982, when members of the Raffl family enclosed a corner of their lobby at the hotel Raffl's St. Antoner Hof (see above). The dining room contains only eight tables, and in the peak of the season, reservations are imperative, especially if you're not staying here. Overflow diners are offered a seat in a spacious but less exclusive *Stube* (tavern) across the hall. The hotel has long enjoyed a favored reputation for its cuisine, and the food in the *Stube* tastes just as good. Quality ingredients are always used, and the kitchen prepares such tempting specialties as chestnut cream soup; veal filet with burgundy sunchoke and spinach; Lake Constance char with river crayfish tails in Riesling cream sauce; and the ever-popular *fondue bourguignonne*.

In the Hotel St. Antoner Hof, St. Anton am Arlberg. ☎ **05446/2910.** Reservations required. Main courses 20€–42€; fixed-price menu 68€–78€. AE, DC, MC, V. Daily 11:30am–2pm and 7–9:30pm. Closed mid-Oct to mid-Dec and mid-Apr to mid-June.

Steakhouse ★STEAKHOUSE   The Steakhouse occupies part of the street level of the Sporthotel St. Anton on the resort's main pedestrian thoroughfare. Some guests prefer to sit on a barstool; perched here, you can talk directly to the chef at the nearby grill about the preferred degree of doneness of your steak, but scattered tables provide a more secluded setting for dinner throughout the conservatively posh interior ,with richly upholstered furniture. Menu selections include Lyons-style onion soup, small and "giant" salads, grilled crayfish, filet of veal in mushroom sauce, filet of pepper steak, and, if cholesterol is a problem, sliced roast turkey with pineapple. Beer comes in foam-covered mugs, and wine is sold by the bottle as well as by the less-expensive carafe.

In the Sporthotel St. Anton, St. Anton am Arlberg. ℂ**05446/3111.** Main courses 15€–37€. DC, MC, V. Daily 11am–11pm, closed May and Oct–Nov.

Moderate

Hotel Alte Post Restaurant ★AUSTRIAN   Outsiders are welcomed into this historic establishment's five small antique dining rooms, where green ceramic stoves and intricately crafted wrought-iron lend a mellow and graceful accent. The chefs cook with flair, turning out such classic dishes as rack of lamb, filet of beef, delightful sweetbreads, venison goulash, fresh duckling, and fondue Bacchus. Although traditional, the chefs are quite skillful. They might be using old recipes, but they give you gourmet flavor deserving of its two *Toques* from Gault Millau and first-rate ingredients. You'll be guided through the menu by an attentive staff.

St. Anton am Arlberg. ℂ**05446/25530.** Reservations recommended. Main courses 15€–35€. AE, DC, MC, V. Daily 7–9pm. Closed May–June and late Oct–late Nov.

Hotel Kertess Restaurant ★★AUSTRIAN   Some of the area's finest food—some say the best in St. Anton—is served at this restaurant. It lies in the suburb of Oberdorf, high on a slope. Guests dine in one of a trio of alpine rooms, with ceramic tiled stoves, oriental rugs, and views of a snow-covered ski slope. Specialties include filet of venison in port-wine sauce, stuffed squab, salmon in Riesling sauce, and, for dessert, apple fritters in beer-flavored pastry with cinnamon. The hotel's bar, warmed by a fire in the nearby reception area, is open throughout the afternoon, but the kitchen only serves in the evening. The a la carte menu is small, but affordable.

St. Anton am Arlberg. ℂ**05446/2005.** Reservations required. Main courses 9.90€–25€. MC, V. Daily 6:30–9pm. Closed Oct–early Dec, May–mid June.

Hotel Schwarzer Adler Restaurant ★★AUSTRIAN/INTERNATIONAL   This restaurant prides itself on its Tyrolean authenticity, which reaches its zenith in one of its two wood-paneled *Stuben,* the preferred place to dine here. The darker of the two, the Tiroler *Stube,* boasts paneling said to be 4 centuries old. Here, the lighting fixtures are especially noteworthy, each designed from raw horns and fashioned into some mythical or allegorical figure from a Teutonic legend. Atmosphere aside, the main attraction is the food. The menu tempts at every turn with such dishes as homemade salmon ravioli with a chervil-flavored cream sauce or medallions of anglerfish with ratatouille. The *Tafelspitz* is another favorite. Deer and local fish are served in season.

St. Anton am Arlberg. ℂ **0512/587109.** Reservations required. Main courses 13€–27€; fixed-price menu 19€–37€. MC, V. Daily 7–9pm. A la carte restaurant only open during winter season, Dec–Apr.

Restaurant Ferwall ★★🏠AUSTRIAN/INTERNATIONAL   Set near the Arlberg Pass, this restaurant is isolated, bucolic, and very famous. It has entertained scores of guests who appreciate its nostalgia for the Tyrol of myth and legend. Some of the dining areas rely exclusively on candlelight. Menu items are based on traditional recipes that management considers a closely guarded secret. Venison frequently appears on the menu, often grilled and served with any of a wide choice of sauces, baked into casseroles, or pressed into sausages and served with sauerkraut.

You can reach the restaurant by car or taxi, though in winter many opt for a ride in a horse-drawn sleigh, which costs about 75€ each way for six occupants (inform the restaurant when you book a table, and they'll arrange the sleigh for you). Sleighs depart from the base of the Mooserkreuz hotel, 1.5km (1 mile) west of St. Anton.

Verwallwegasse 123. ✆ **05446/3249.** Reservations required. Main courses 17€–27€. DC, MC, V. Winter daily 10am–5pm and 7pm–midnight; summer daily 10am–6pm. Closed Apr–June and Oct–Nov. Take Rte. 197 to St. Christoph and the Arlberg Pass 5km (3 miles) west of the center of St. Anton.

CAFES & STUBES

The popular **Café Aquila** (✆ **05446/2217**) achieved a certain kind of fame in the ski world as the Café Tschol. Now under another name, it lies just across the street from its founder, the Hotel Schwarzer Adler. Light meals, pastries, beer, wine, tea, and several varieties of coffee are served here. Dishes include spaghetti, goulash soup, spinach-stuffed ravioli, and a self-serve buffet of appetizers. Simple, uncomplicated meals begin at 12€, although snack food is also available. It's open daily from 10am to midnight.

Café Häferl (✆ **05446/3988**), located at Dorfstrasse 20, is more animated than any of its competitors, thanks to a decor that's rich with Tyrolean artifacts and the glow of varnished pine. Inside you'll find a crowd that includes dedicated hipsters, as well as long-time seniors looking for a caffeine fix and a midmorning pastry. Don't expect full meal service—only salads, platters, and small portions of such foods as goulash soup and sandwiches are served. It's open daily from 8:30am to 10pm. Another option for a drink or snack is the **Fuhrmannstube** (✆ **05446/2921**). Conveniently located near the town church on the main street, this simple cafe and restaurant serves reasonably priced meals starting at 7.90€. It has a predictable but well-prepared array of such Teutonic specialties as *Rösti* (hash browns), *Spätzle* (cheese pasta), goulash, and venison (in season). It's open daily from 10am to midnight; closed in May, June, October, and November.

ST. ANTON AM ARLBERG AFTER DARK

St. Anton's after-dark spots are among the most frequented in Tyrol. It's most enjoyable if you know and like your fellow skiers; in season you're likely to be knocking elbows (or whatever) in most places.

Krazy Kanguruh   This restaurant/bar attracts the resort's restless and reckless. To reach it, you'll have to ski from the resort's uppermost slopes, walk up the steep hill from the village, or drive your car via the suburb of Moos along a winding narrow road. A phone call in advance will apprise you of driving conditions.

The Kanguruh serves different functions depending on the hour of the day. From 11am to 2pm, simple lunches (hamburgers, chicken wings, etc.) are served. The après-ski environment later in the afternoon is rowdy. Be sure to ask for a shot of the pear-and-plum schnapps from a local farm distillery. Prices here beat the others in the neighborhood: Lunches and small dishes begin at 5€. A large beer costs 4.80€. Open 10am to 8pm from early December to mid-April. Moos 113. ✆ **05446/2633.**

Piccadilly Pub   As its name suggests, this is an English-style pub. Lined with photos of happy revelers enjoying snow and suds, the place offers rowdy fun and loud music. Special tongue-in-cheek events such as Australia Day feature icons made of stuffed koala bears. The place is off the main pedestrian thoroughfare behind etched-glass swinging doors. A large beer begins at 4€. It's open from January to April daily, and Thursday to Saturday in December, from 9am to 2am. In the Hotel Neue Post. *℃* **05446/2213.**

Platz'l Bar   Set in the heart of town, adjacent to the Hotel Alte Post, this hangout features live music every night and creates an ambiance more sophisticated than other bars nearby. Light snacks such as pizza and pasta are available, as well as an array of international cocktails. Once the live music ends, a DJ takes over for dancing hours. Beer costs 3.80€ for a mug. The bar is open only during the ski season, December through April daily from 7pm to 2am. St. Anton. *℃* **05446/2169.**

Rodelhütte   This après-ski hangout offers the chance to combine a drink or two beside a blazing fire and finish with a bang—a downhill run by toboggan. You can reach the place only after a brisk 20-minute uphill climb from St. Anton, as it lies just shy of 1km (½ mile) from the center. It's open daily December through April from 11:30am to around 9pm, depending on business; it's at its most convivial and crowded beginning around 5pm, as night falls over the nearby mountains. It is also open in July and August daily from 9am to 9pm. At the top of the town's toboggan run.

St. Anton Bar   This place is the most popular and energetic bar in town. The bar is round, allowing drinkers to casually check out their fellow imbibers. The music is imported, and its decor makes absolutely no concessions to Tyrolean *gemütlichkeit;* instead, it's international. The professional staff adeptly handles "fancy drinks." Access is directly from Hauptstrasse, not from inside the hotel. It's open from December to April daily from 9pm to 4am. In the Sporthotel St. Anton. *℃* **05446/3111.**

Sennhütte   Cozy, charming, and artful, this wood-sided structure is most appropriately reached by ski or snowboard from higher elevations along the Galzig ski slope. Après-ski doesn't last as long here as some other venues at lower altitudes that rock on into the wee hours. (It's at its peak around 4–5pm.) Know in advance that after a day on the slopes and after some drinks here around dusk, maneuvering your way downhill on skis might do some damage. It's open in winter from 10am to 6pm, and a large beer costs 4.50€. It is also open from late June to late September, keeping the same hours, and offers a nature walk during these months, organized by the owners, free of charge. On the lower elevations of the Galzig ski slopes. *℃* **05446/2048.** www.sennhuette.at.

Vino Bar   Hidden behind the Hotel Schwarzer Adler's 400-year-old exterior frescoes lies a bar where holidaymakers can dance or enjoy a game of pool after a day on the slopes. A large beer begins at 5€. It's open daily from 8pm to 3am, but in winter only. In the Hotel Schwarzer Adler. *℃* **05446/2244606.**

St. Christoph ★★

The mountain way station of St. Anton, **St. Christoph** is linked to the St. Anton terrain by a cableway at Galzig, and at an elevation of 1,800m (5,853 ft.) is one of the highest ski villages in Austria and the eastern Alps. It's on the road to the Arlberg Pass and has essentially the same ski facilities available as St. Anton, only here you're closer to the action.

A hospice was originally established here in 1386 by a now-legendary saint-like mountain man, Heinrich of Kempten, whose self-imposed duty was to bury the remains of pilgrims who froze to death in the treacherous snowdrifts of one of the world's most unpredictable and temperamental mountain passes.

Because the Arlberg was the single most important route for commerce between northern Italy and the Teutonic world throughout the Middle Ages, literally hundreds of travelers froze to death at the pass or died of hunger, exposure, or avalanches. Kempten single-handedly founded the Order of Saint Christopher, a church-related society and monastery that has evolved into one of the most beneficent monastic orders of Europe. The monastery accumulated some famous artistic treasures, many donated by grateful merchants whose caravans were sheltered and saved.

Appropriately, the monastery was built on the uppermost heights of the frequently snowbound pass, on the Tyrolean side. The land the monastery was built on was so uninhabitable that large carts were needed to bring all the basic necessities into the community once the surrounding trees were felled for fuel.

Throughout the Age of Enlightenment, the hospice continued to recruit new members who would patrol the pass every morning and evening. The members searched for frozen bodies, assisted wayfarers in trouble, and provided desperately needed accommodations for the thousands of caravans carrying goods across the pass.

As roads, phone lines, and helicopter rescue teams made passage over the Arlberg less treacherous, the Arlberg Pass developed into one of the world's leading ski resorts. In the 1950s, the monastery, which had experienced difficulty recruiting new members, sold the complex to members of the Werner family. Under the guidance of the family patriarch, the monastery was brought into the 20th century with the addition of electricity and many of the era's comforts.

Tragically, only a few weeks after the completion of the improvements, a fire destroyed all but a portion of the ancient monastery. The fire provided the opportunity to rebuild the Arlberg Hospiz hotel, recommended on p. 384.

ESSENTIALS

GETTING THERE   Few commercial rail lines could negotiate the steep and winding slopes leading up to the Arlberg Pass and St. Christoph. Passengers usually take the **train** to St. Anton and then board one of the **buses** departing from the west terminal and traveling north over the mountain passes to St. Christoph, which leave every hour and a half from 7:30am to 5:30pm in winter (trip time: 15 min.). Contact **St. Anton's tourist office** (© **05446/22690**) for bus and train schedules.

Motorists can continue west from St. Anton am Arlberg (see above), following Route S16. St. Christoph is 8km (5 miles) west of St. Anton and 35km (22 miles) west of Landeck.

VISITOR INFORMATION   The village shares a **tourist office** with St. Anton (© **05446/2269-0**; www.stantonamarlberg.com). Winter opening hours are Monday to Friday 8am to 6pm, closed Saturday, Sunday, and holidays.

WHERE TO STAY & EAT

Arlberg Hospiz ★★★   This world-class winter-only hotel embraces mystery, legend, and romance. Many of its most charming touches were painstakingly recreated from old photographs. Visitors are welcomed into a luxurious world with more style than the medieval monks who once resided on the premises could have imagined. Rooms are beautifully maintained and have double-glazed windows, working fireplaces, walk-in dressing areas, and balconies. The beds are some of the most lavish in the area, and the spacious bathrooms have big tubs and powerful showerheads.

The Arlberg Hospiz offers superb food and an array of in-house entertainment. The party room changes its decor from year to year: Once it was transformed into an ancient Roman tavern. Even if you don't stay here, consider having a meal in the hotel's Tiroler Wirtshaus for some hearty Tyrolean dishes with a gourmet touch—like braised oxtail with fried dumplings and *pomme blanche*—but reserve in advance.

A-6580 St. Christoph. ✆ **05446/2611.** Fax 05446/3545. www.arlberghospiz.at. 99 units. 237€–351€ double; 350€–890€ suite. Rates include half-board. AE, DC, MC, V. Parking 15€. Closed May–Nov. **Amenities:** Restaurant; bar; nightclub; babysitting; games room; massage; indoor heated pool; nonsmoking rooms; room service; spa. *In room:* TV, minibar, hairdryer, Wi-Fi.

Gasthof Valluga   This is the least expensive hotel on the Arlberg Pass, a simple chalet-style guesthouse with cramped but clean rooms and impressive views from the windows of its dining room and bar. The owner, Lydia Haueis, maintains impeccably proper rooms, two that are suitable for up to four occupants. Each has thick carpeting and good beds, although the bathrooms with tub/shower combinations are a bit cramped. The restaurant is warmly accommodating, serving reasonably priced meals. It's open in winter daily 8am to 10pm. Menu items include Tyroler crusted dumplings with bacon and cream sauce.

A-6580 St. Christoph. ✆ **05446/2823.** Fax 05446/2823160. www.arlberg.com/gasthof-valluga. 10 units. 170€–280€ double. Rates include half-board. MC, V. Free parking. Closed May–late Nov. **Amenities:** Restaurant; bar; babysitting; massage; room service; sauna. *In room:* TV, hairdryer, minibar.

Hotel Arlberghöhe   Simple and unpretentious to the point of being almost bare-boned, this hotel stands across from the more prestigious Arlberg Hospiz (see above). It was built around 1940 but has been modernized several times since. Its rustic interior and heavy ceiling beams give the impression of far greater age. Most rooms are quite spacious and heavy on wood tones, and have beautiful tiled bathrooms. The wooden beds are exceedingly comfortable and cozy. The food is good and there's plenty of it—a combination of classic Austrian dishes, Tyrolean specialties, and international offerings.

A-6580 St. Christoph. ✆ **05446/2635.** Fax 05446/263544. www.arlberghoehe.at. 17 units. 202€–348€ double, 278€–410€ suite. Rates include half-board. MC, V. Closed Oct–Nov and late May to mid-July. **Amenities:** Restaurant; bar; babysitting; massage; sauna; tanning bed. *In room:* TV.

SEEFELD ★★

24km (15 miles) NW of Innsbruck

Seefeld, a member of Austria's "Big Three" international rendezvous points (along with Arlberg and Kitzbühel) for winter-sports crowds, lies on a sunny plateau some 1,052m (3,451 ft.) above sea level. Seefeld hosted the Nordic events for the 1964 and 1976 Olympic Winter Games and the 1985 Nordic Ski World Championships. Like its sister ski resorts in the region, this village was founded before the Middle Ages and had an economy deeply tied to agriculture until winter sports and tourism became the cash cow of the region.

Essentials

GETTING THERE   More than a dozen **trains** per day depart from Innsbruck for the 36-minute trip to Seefeld. Other trains leave from Munich and pass through the Bavarian resort of Garmisch-Partenkirchen before arriving in Seefeld. For rail information, contact ✆ **05/1717** (www.oebb.at).

Despite its position on several different bus routes heading up into the nearby valleys, most visitors arrive here by train. However, you can take one of the dozen or so buses departing daily from Innsbruck's Hauptbahnhof for the 45-minute trip. For **bus information,** call ✆ **0512/585155** in Innsbruck.

If you're **driving** from Innsbruck, head west along the A12 until you hit Route 177 and take the exit to Seefeld-Mitte.

VISITOR INFORMATION   The Seefeld **tourist office,** Klosterstrasse 43 (✆ **0508/800;** www.seefeld.com), is open Monday to Saturday 8:30am to 6pm, and Sunday 10am to noon during peak seasons.

Winter & Summer Sports

The slopes are served by one cable car railway, two cable cars, three chairlifts, and 14 drag lifts. The beginner slopes lie directly in the village center, and the base stations for ski lifts leading to Seefeld's main skiing areas lie less than 1km (½ mile) north of the resort (for the **Gschwandtkopf runs**) and less than 1km (½ mile) south of the resort (for the **Rosshütte/Seefelder Joch runs**). They, and virtually everything else in town, are served throughout the winter by the free shuttle buses that operate at 20- to 30-minute intervals during daylight hours. In addition to its downhill runs, Seefeld has more than 200km (124 miles) of well-maintained cross-country tracks.

Other winter activities offered here include curling, horse-drawn sleigh rides, ice-skating (**Eislaufplatz Olympia Sportzentrum;** ✆ **05212/3050**) on artificial and natural ice rinks, indoor tennis (**Håkan Dahlbo Tennis Academy;** ✆ **05212/2095**), tube sliding, indoor golf, parasailing, bowling, squash, hiking (97km/60 miles of cleared paths), fitness workouts, swimming, and spa sessions.

Summer visitors can enjoy swimming in three lakes, a heated open-air swimming pool near Seefeld Lake, or the Olympia indoor and outdoor pools. Other summer sports include tennis on 18 open-air and 8 indoor courts (Swedish Tennis School), riding (**Reitclub Seefeld;** ✆ **0664/5677906,** which also has an indoor arena), and golf on the 18-hole course, which has been rated by golf insiders as one of the 100 most beautiful courses in the world. There are 200km (124 miles) of walks and mountain paths to hike, as well as cycling, minigolf, parasailing, and rafting.

Whatever time of year it is, you can try your luck at the casino (**Bahnhofstrasse 124;** ✆ **05212/2340**), where money is gambled on roulette, baccarat, blackjack, seven-card stud poker, and slot machines.

While based in Seefeld, you'll find it relatively easy to explore part of Bavaria, in Germany (see our companion guide, *Frommer's Germany*). You may (or may not) get to see little Wildmoos Lake. It can, and sometimes does, vanish all in a day or so, and then there may be cows grazing on what has become meadowland. But the lake can return rather suddenly, and if conditions are right, it will become deep enough for swimmers. You might also visit the little German town of Mittenwald, an easy day trip from Seefeld.

For more information about these destinations, call the **tourist information** number in Seefeld (✆ **0508/800,** see opening hours on p. 386).

Where to Stay
EXPENSIVE

Hotel Astoria ★★ This lavish, government-rated five-star choice stands in a beautiful elevated position in a large park with panoramic views of the surrounding mountain ranges. It's a 5-minute walk northwest of Seefeld's center. Because of its sunny and sheltered ambiance, it's a favorite with well-heeled visitors in both summer and winter. The attractively furnished rooms have exceedingly comfortable beds and medium-size bathrooms. Saturday evenings are gala nights here, with candlelit dinners and music from the house band. Once a week, a Viennese *Heurige* (wine tavern) or a Tyrolean evening with traditional buffet is presented.

Geigenbühel 185, A-6100 Seefeld. ✆**05212/22720.** Fax 05212/2272100. www.astoria-seefeld.com. 56 units. Winter 254€–520€ double, 400€–620€ suite; summer 198€–338€ double, 294€–460€ suite. Rates include half-board. AE, DC, MC, V. Free outdoor parking; 12€ indoor parking. **Amenities:** Restaurant; bar; babysitting; fitness center; massage; indoor heated pool; outdoor pool; room service; spa; tanning bed. *In room:* TV, hairdryer; minibar, Wi-Fi.

Hotel Klosterbräu ★★★ The town's most unusual and elegant hostelry is constructed around a 16th-century cloister. The interior contains soaring vaults supported by massive columns. Rooms are encased in a towering chalet behind the front entrance, and come in a variety of sizes, but all are beautifully kept, with antiques and comfortable mattresses. Some rooms have balconies opening onto mountain vistas. In the evening, chicly dressed patrons often drop in at Die Kane nightclub, where comedians and musical revues provide a high spot in the village's nightlife. A daily afternoon tea dance in winter allows hotel guests to meet one another. Hotel Klosterbräu features two excellent restaurants; see "Where to Eat," below.

Klosterstrasse 30, A-6100 Seefeld. ✆**05212/26210.** Fax 05212/3885. www.klosterbraeu.com. 120 units. Winter 278€–758€ double, from 418€–1,600€ suite; summer 218€–398€ double, 418€–1,378€ suite. Rates include breakfast, half-board for 48€ surcharge. AE, DC, MC, V. 4.50€ outside parking, 20€ garage. Closed May and mid Oct–early Dec. **Amenities:** 2 restaurants; bar; piano bar; babysitting; fitness center; 2 heated pools (1 indoor, 1 outdoor); nonsmoking rooms; room service; spa; tanning bed. *In room:* TV, hairdryer, minibar, Internet connection.

MODERATE

Alpenmedhotel Lamm ★ The broad glass facade of this hotel opens to a dressed-down, sleek interior with black leather furniture and large abstract paintings. The rooms' walls are splashed in blues, yellows, and oranges, though some are more traditionally decorated. The best rooms are spacious and all have balconies. This hotel functions as a therapeutic getaway, with numerous spa treatments to allow for a full recovery from any type of stress. The hotel's restaurant serves only the healthiest products, which—much like the architecture of the hotel—tries to interlace traditional, international, and modern.

Dorfplatz 28, A-6100 Seefeld. ✆**05212/2464.** Fax 05212/283434. www.alpenmedhotel.com. 71 units. 180€–310€ double; 250€–380€ suite. Rates include half-board. AE, MC, V. Closed April. Parking 6€. **Amenities:** Restaurant; bar; fitness center; massage; nonsmoking rooms; rooms for those w/limited mobility; spa. *In room:* TV, hairdryer, minibar, Wi-Fi.

Karwendelhof Casino Hotel ★ The century-old Tyrolean parlors of this hotel have parquet floors, beamed ceilings, and antique accents. The personalized rooms are simple but tasteful, the suites decked out like a hunting lodge, the standard doubles more modern and less cluttered. Some have balconies with mountain views, but all are immaculately maintained and have bathrooms, some with bidets.

The hotel restaurant, Alte Stube, is completely covered in old paneling burnished to a rich, mellow glow. Dishes include well-prepared beef, veal, and pork, accompanied by fresh vegetables and followed by regional cheeses and home-baked pastries. Fixed menus are 25€ and reservations are necessary. The hotel's K-Keller is one of the village's social centers. It's open only in winter from 7:30 to 10am and 6:30 to 8:30pm. A casino in an adjoining building opens at 1pm every day in winter.

Bahnhofstrasse 124, A-6100 Seefeld. (✆) **05212/26550.** Fax 05212/265544. www.karwendelhof.at. 42 units. Winter 112€–326€ double, 156€–388€ suite; summer 114€–172€ double, 172€–230€ suite. Rates include half-board. DC, MC, V. Free parking. Closed end Oct–early Dec, and one month after Easter. **Amenities:** Restaurant; bar; babysitting; casino; room service; spa. *In room:* TV, hairdryer, minibar, Wi-Fi.

Waldhotel ☺   One of the oldest hotels in Seefeld, the Waldhotel has been fully renovated. Its location, at the edge of the resort adjoining the woods surrounding Seefeld, is about a 7-minute walk from the village center. All of the well-appointed rooms have balconies and terrific beds. The best have sitting areas; some of the smaller doubles are a bit cramped. A panoramic garden restaurant and a terrace are favorite spots for lunch or tea. Dinners include a choice of four-course menus, and breakfast is a buffet. In winter, there's a curling rink, and the hotel is just a 3-minute walk from the cable cars leading to the slopes. Year-round, the place offers a variety of entertainment, such as a live Dixieland band or Tyrolean music.

Römerweg 106, A-6100 Seefeld. (✆) **05212/22070.** Fax 05212/200130. www.waldhotel-seefeld.at. 50 units. Winter 120€–196€ double, 150€–260€ suite; summer 92€–130€ double, 110€–160€ suite. Rates include half-board. MC, V. Parking 10€ garage. Closed Nov. **Amenities:** Restaurant; bar; babysitting; children's playroom; nonsmoking rooms; rooms for those w/ limited mobility. *In room:* TV, hairdryer.

INEXPENSIVE

Hotel Christina   A 5-minute walk from the town center is this comfortable, contemporary chalet with exposed wood and a homey character. It has an indoor pool accessible through big glass doors in the cellar. Many of the comfortably furnished rooms have balconies, and, after recent renovations, the rooms are better than ever, with excellent beds.

Reitherspitzstrasse 415, A-6100 Seefeld. (✆) **05212/2553.** Fax 05212/255332. www.hotel-in-seefeld.at. 14 units. Winter 100€–120€ double, 120€–132€ suite; summer 80€–88€ double, 88€–92€ suite. Rates include buffet breakfast. DC, MC, V. **Amenities:** Breakfast room; lounge; fitness room; indoor heated pool; sauna; tanning bed. *In room:* TV, hairdryer.

Where to Eat

Most guests book into a Seefeld hotel on the half-board plan, and most of the hotels listed above have excellent dining facilities, although you should call ahead to make reservations.

Gourmet Restaurant Ritter Oswald/Bräukeller ★★ CONTINENTAL/TYROLEAN   There are two restaurants of charm and historic importance within the most legendary hotel of Seefeld. The more expensive of the two is the Ritter Oswald. Set on the hotel's lobby level and with the typical Tyrolean interior so common in the area, it's small (60 seats) and intimate. Menu items change with the seasons but might include filets of venison with a morel and port-wine sauce, strips of filet of veal served with herb-flavored cream sauce and spinach, and sophisticated variations on local freshwater trout. The less expensive and larger (150 seats) of the two is the cellar-level Bräukeller, which is capped with a 500-year-old vaulted stone ceiling that originally functioned as part of a monastery. Earthier and a bit more swashbuckling than the Ritter Oswald, it focuses on the hearty cuisine of the Austrian Alps, including *Tafelspitz*, liver-and-noodle soup, grilled lake char with seasonal vegetables, Wiener schnitzel, and braised beef with wild mushrooms. There's live Tyrolean-style music performed nightly in the Bräukeller. Whereas you might feel obliged to buy a wine with your meal in the Ritter Oswald, no one will object if you order a beer down here, and they have an extensive list of locally brewed specialties.

In the Hotel Klosterbräu, Klosterstrasse 30. ℃ **05212/26210.** www.klosterbraeu.com. Reservations recommended in Ritter Oswald, not necessary in the Bräukeller. Ritter Oswald main courses 13€–29€; Bräukeller main courses 8.50€–19€. AE, DC, MC, V. Ritter Oswald daily 7–10pm, Bräukeller 11am–11pm. Closed May and mid Oct to early Dec.

Restaurant Vorspiel ★INTERNATIONAL/AUSTRIAN   In this previously recommended hotel, Vorspiel is the casino restaurant and one of the most fashionable in town. Top-quality service and a first-rate cuisine delight visitors flocking to this chic resort. You will smack your lips over the harmonious selections that appear on the ever-changing menu, based for the most part on market-fresh ingredients. The restaurant is especially known for its fish and pork dishes, although it also does a fine turn with succulent steaks, roast duck, and the classic Austrian veal dishes. Its fixed-price menu is among the best in town.

In the Hotel Karwendelhof, Bahnhofstrasse 124. ℃**05212/2655.** Reservations required. Main courses 9€–24€. MC, V. Mon, Wed and Thurs, 6–10pm; Fri-Sun 12-2pm and 6-10pm; Closed Tues.

Seefeld After Dark

Seefeld has plenty of nightlife options to keep you entertained after a day in the mountains. If you are looking for something a little different, try having a drink at a glass-sided, oversize replica of an Eskimo's igloo, **Bar Siglu,** Klosterstrasse (℃ **05212/2621186**), where live music is presented in the early evening.

The town is filled with cafes and bars, and you can take your pick, as they are all rather similar. One particular favorite, which also serves Tyrolean dishes, is **Sportcafe Sailer,** Innsbruckerstrasse 12 (℃ **05212/2005**), which has a real local atmosphere and outdoor setting. If you like the beer, you might want to try the food. Freshly made soups are popular in winter, and the most ordered main dish—soul food to the Austrians—is *gröstli* (made with potatoes, eggs, and bacon). In summer and winter, it's open daily from 11:30am to 10pm; in the spring and autumn, daily 11:30am to 2pm and 6 to 10pm.

In season, Seefeld bustles with typical wine and beer cellars, along with nightclubs and dance clubs that come and go. However, one of the major nighttime attractions is the **Spiel-Casino Seefeld,** at the Hotel Karwendelhof, Bahnhofstrasse 124 (℃ **05212/2340**). It offers baccarat, blackjack, seven-card stud poker, a money wheel, American and French roulette, and 70 slot machines. Your admission is 21€—but that gives you the equivalent of 25€ in chips. It's open daily from 3pm to 3am.

Hotel Klosterbräu, Klosterstrasse 30, is the most sophisticated nightspot in town; its nightclub, **Die Kane,** presents an international orchestra and a floor show daily in winter and 3 nights a week in summer from 9pm to 3am. In winter, the club opens at 5pm for a *Tanztee* (tea dance), an afternoon dance session to live music where you can show off your waltzing skills.

THE ZILLER VALLEY ★★

Zillertal is the German name for this valley east of Innsbruck, where high-tech winter sports meet agriculturally oriented country folk. The scenery at first seems surreal; bright green pastures end abruptly at the feet of jagged peaks that reach skyward until snow breaks their climb. The first stretches of the Zillertal may seem unimpressive, but don't turn back. It gets more stunning as you travel deeper into the valley.

When you first enter the Zillertal during the warmer months, you'll pass rich meadowlands and healthy grazing cows. To the west are the **Tux Alps** and to the east are the **Kitzbühel Alps,** covered later in this chapter. As tempting as it might be to head for Kitzbühel, continuing farther into the Ziller Valley will bring you suddenly into narrower tracks and a more dramatic landscape.

The people of the Zillertal are known for their musical conquests: The singing culture is known throughout Austria and their skills as organ builders are equally renowned. The Zillertalers are said to be responsible for the popularity of the Christmas carol *Silent Night*. Some of the best of the little villages and resorts lie deep in the valley.

Zell am Ziller

Zell am Ziller lies 479km (298 miles) west of Vienna and 60km (37 miles) east of Innsbruck. This is the first town in the valley that deserves a stop, but don't confuse this resort with Zell am See in Land Salzburg. Zell am Ziller was founded by monks as early as 770, became a bustling gold-mining town in the 1800s, but when the gold went dry the village transformed into a trading hub. Wine was exchanged for cattle, among other transactions, by traders traveling through the Tux pass. Zell am Ziller is the major town of the lower section of the Ziller Valley, and inns here are reasonably priced.

ESSENTIALS

GETTING THERE If you're coming directly to Zell am Ziller, you can **fly** to Munich, the nearest international airport, and arrange further transportation from there.

Trains from Innsbruck travel frequently to nearby **Jenbach** (trip time: 30 min.). At Jenbach, trains depart every hour for Zell am Ziller (trip time: 45 min.). For rail information, contact ✆ 05/1717 (www.oebb.at).

Most **bus lines** servicing Zell am Ziller originate in nearby towns and villages. However, three buses per day depart from Innsbruck's Hauptbahnhof for Zell am Ziller (trip time: 1¾ hr.). For **bus information** in Zell am Ziller from other parts of Austria, call ✆ 05282/2211.

If you're **driving** from Innsbruck, head east along Autobahn A12 to the junction with Route 169, and cut south.

VISITOR INFORMATION The **tourist office** in the town center, Dorfplatz 3a (✆ 05282/2281; www.zell.at) is open Monday to Friday 8:30am to 12:30pm and 2:30 to 6pm, Saturday 9am to noon and 4 to 6pm, and Sunday 4 to 6pm. Closed on Sunday in summer.

EXPLORING ZELL AM ZILLER

Like many other Austrian villages, Zell has a parish church, the **Pfarrkirche ★**, this one dating from 1779. A huge dome tops its octagonal design.

Once this village was known only as a summer holiday site, but more recently it has also become a winter-sports resort. In 1978, the Kreuzjoch area was opened to skiers, and Zell am Ziller took its place on the ski maps of Europe. In season, a free ski bus stops at the major hotels to transport guests to the slopes.

You can travel by gondola to a restaurant with a view of the **Gründalm** (1,022m/3,353 ft.) and then continue by chairlift to **Rosenalm** (1,761m/5,778 ft.), where another restaurant opens onto a panoramic view. From Rosenalm, a surface lift can take you to a lofty citadel 2,266m (7,434 ft.) above sea level.

Another ski area, the **Geriosstein,** more than 5km (3 miles) from Zell am Ziller, also has a bus service, but not as frequently. From the bottom station, a cableway will lift you to 1,647m (5,404 ft.), where you can take a chairlift up to 1,836m (6,024 ft.).

WHERE TO STAY

Hotel Bräu   At the edge of the town's most important crossroads, this ample chalet was originally built in the 15th century, and an extra wing was added in 1985. Rising five balconied stories, its ocher-colored facade is embellished with *trompe l'oeil* frescoes. It is home to three different dining rooms (see "Where to Eat," below). Each comfortable guest room is filled with wood trim and holds the occasional Tyrolean knick-knack. Modern extras have not been ignored. Rooms are a bit small, but most have a sitting area.

Dorfplatz 1, A-6280 Zell am Ziller. ⓒ **05282/2313.** Fax 05282/231317. www.hotel-braeu.at. 36 units. Winter 128€–198€ double, 158€–218€ suite; summer 106€–114€ double, 134€–142€ suite. Rates include half-board. No credit cards. Closed Apr and Oct 15–Dec 20. **Amenities:** Restaurant; bar; massage; room service; nonsmoking rooms; rooms for those w/limited mobility; sauna. *In room:* TV, hairdryer; minibar; Wi-Fi.

WHERE TO EAT

Hotel Bräu Restaurant AUSTRIAN   Lined up side by side on the street level of the Hotel Bräu, this trio of authentic Tyrolean dining rooms competes with one another for the most regional charm. You might want to check out each of them before deciding. They're called **Speisezimmer, Bräustübl,** and **Casino.** Full meals cost around 35€ and include solid Austrian dishes, best on cold-weather days.

Dorfplatz 1. ⓒ **05282/2313.** Reservations required. Main courses 11€–28€ No credit cards. Daily 11:30am–2pm and 6–9pm. Closed Apr and mid Oct–mid Dec.

Mayrhofen ★

The road divides at Zell am Ziller, and to reach Mayrhofen, head southwest on Route 169 to this active and popular resort. It stands at 633m (2,077 ft.), enclosed by the towering Penken and Ahorn peaks and lying at the foot of the glaciers crowning the adjacent Alps, and was once home to a World Cup ski run later deemed too dangerous for the competition. It has become a winter as well as a summer hotspot due to year-round skiing possibilities on the Hintertux glacier. It has some of the best infrastructure in the valley, and also the best food. After a visit here, a trip to **Gerlos** to the southeast is recommended.

ESSENTIALS

GETTING THERE   Following the routes used to reach Zell am Ziller, travelers from Innsbruck transfer at the railway junction at Jenbach. From Jenbach, **trains** depart every hour for the 1-hour ride south to Mayrhofen. From Mayrhofen many bus lines fan out into the nearby valleys. Unless you're coming from one of those obscure valleys, it's easier to take the train. Mayrhofen is 76km (47 miles) southeast of Innsbruck. For **bus and rail information,** call ✆ **05282/2211.**

VISITOR INFORMATION The **tourist office** in the town center (✆ **05285/67600;** www.mayrhofen.com) is open Monday to Friday 9am to 6pm, Saturday and Sunday 9am to 1pm.

SUMMER SPORTS, SKIING & MORE

For decades, Mayrhofen has drawn summer holiday crowds with its endless opportunities for mountain biking, mountaineering, hang gliding, shooting, tennis, fishing, swimming in a heated outdoor pool, minigolf, and summer skiing in the **Hintertux glacier area** at the top of the valley. Mayrhofen is also a mecca for mountain climbers during the nonskiing seasons.

For the intermediate and advanced mountain biker, you will find some exhilarating trails. New single runs on the Penken, the "Himmelfahrt", and "Höllenritt" (the "Trip to Heaven" and the "Ride to Hell"), have obstacles and North-Shore elements. Bikes can be rented at **Seasonality Bikes 4 U** (✆ **0650/5517605;** www.seasonality.eu) and **Max Hürzeler Bike Station** (✆ **0664/4938361;** www.huerzeler.com). Bikes are allowed on the **Penkenbahn** cable car, which costs 10.30€ for a round trip. The cable car runs from late May to mid-October from 9am to 3pm.

In recent years, the resort village has become more a ski center. Starting from scratch, you can learn to ski at the resort school: The children's ski training is especially good here; there are several, but one of the best is **Ski- & Snowboard Schule Mount Everest,** Haupstrasse 458 (✆ **05285/62829;** www.habeler.com). Many also offer a child-care service combined with ski instruction for full or half days, which makes this an ideal family resort. Slopes for advanced skiers are available in the **Penkenjoch** section to the west of Mayrhofen, with a cableway taking you to nearly 1,830m (6,004 ft.). From the top, you'll be rewarded with a breathtaking view of the Zillertal range; there's also a restaurant, with quite a view.

You can take a cableway (departs south of Mayrhofen) up to ski in the **Ahorn** area (1,906m/6,253 ft.). There are seven surface lifts at the top, as well as another restaurant with a panoramic view.

Other winter activities include sledding on a natural toboggan run, curling, ice-skating, horse-drawn sleigh rides, horseback riding, and playing sports in an indoor arena.

After your outdoor fun, you can exhaust the last of your energy at a tea dance; just relax and enjoy the fondue. You can also hear some of that famous Ziller Valley singing at folk festivals in July and August. The dates change every year, so check with the tourist office. Another popular summer diversion is taking a ride on the narrow-gauge **steam train** between Zell am Ziller and Mayrhofen. It runs several times daily from May 1 to mid-October, during winter only between Christmas and New Year (✆ **0524/46060**).

Mayrhofen also hosts the yearly **Snowbombing** music festival, a week-long event of bands, DJs, skiing, and partying in a club made entirely from snow. It has gained in reputation among the electronic music crowds over the last decade. The event takes place in early April (www.snowbombing.com).

VENTURING INTO THE ALPS

From Mayrhofen you can venture farther into the Alps around the Zillertal, where you'll be rewarded with some of the most spectacular scenery in Tyrol. By the time you reach Mayrhofen, the trail through the Zillertal that you've been following will have split into four different parts, each of which runs through a different valley radiating off the Zillertal. Three of the valleys have the suffix *grund* (German for "ground") to their names: The **Stillupgrund,** the **Zemmgrund,** and the **Zillergrund.**

You might not have time to explore all these valleys, but if you can make time for one, make it the fourth and highest valley, the **Tuxertal,** or Tux Valley, which cuts like a deep slash through the mountains. This valley reaches its end point at several glaciers, including the **Olperer,** 3,477m (11,407 ft.) high. You can take a bus from Mayrhofen to either the village of **Lanersbach** or on to **Hintertux,** both in the Tuxertal. The road runs west from Mayrhofen for some 21km (13 miles) to the end of the valley, where ski lifts branch off in several directions.

You come first to Lanersbach, the largest village in the Tuxertal, lying in a sunny, sheltered spot. From here you can take a chairlift to the **Eggalm plateau,** which has a restaurant at 2,001m (6,565 ft.) and offers one of the most stunning panoramas the Ziller Alps has to offer.

Hintertux, your ultimate destination, lies at the top of the valley, virtually on the doorstep of the soaring glaciers. Because of thermal springs, Hintertux also enjoys a reputation as a spa. You might want to buy some woodcarvings from the skillful craftspeople here.

You can ski on the glaciers in summer. A chairlift or a gondola from Hintertux will transport you to **Sommerbergalm** (2,074m/6,804 ft.), and once here, you can take a surface lift west to **Tuxer-Joch Hütte** (2,531m/8,304 ft.).

WHERE TO STAY

Alpenhotel Kramerwirt ☺ This hotel's facade has green shutters, a painted illustration of a medieval figure, and a tower-like construction high above the roofline. The traditional interior contains a scattering of oriental rugs and antique chests. Some rooms have romantic four-poster beds and big bathrooms; others are designed in a more functional style with less spacious bathrooms. Additional but less desirable rooms are located in a 1980s' annex a short walk away. A nightclub, the **Götestube,** is in the cellar. Live musicians entertain the drinkers and diners.

Am Marienbrunnen 346, A-6290 Mayrhofen. ⓒ **05285/6700.** Fax 05285/6700502. www.kramerwirt. at. 80 units. Winter 120€–202€ double, from 200€ suite; summer 94€–150€ double, from 164€ suite. Rates include half-board. MC, V. Closed Nov 20–Dec 10. **Amenities:** Restaurant; bar; nightclub; babysitting; children's playrooms; 2 Jacuzzis; room service; sauna. *In room:* TV, hairdryer, Wi-Fi.

Elisabethhotel ★★ ☺ This stylish hotel is a 3-minute walk from the village center. Its chalet-style facade is accented with carefully detailed balconies, heavy overhanging eaves, painted designs, and a tower. Rooms, the resort's finest, have Tyrolean motifs. Bathrooms are generally spacious and equipped with charming appointments, large tubs, showers, and cosmetic mirrors. On the premises are a pleasant restaurant, Sissi Stube, and an elegant bar named after one of Mozart's most memorably comic characters, Papageno. There's also a large terrace with a coffee shop and an Italian restaurant, Mamma Mia. In winter, a dance club operates in the basement, and in summer there's a large garden as well as a children's playground.

Einfahrt Mitte 432, A-6290 Mayrhofen. ⓒ **05285/6767.** Fax 05285/676767. www.elisabethhotel.com. 32 units. Winter 240€–310€ double, from 348€ suite; summer 186€–196€ double, from 340€–580€ suite. Rates include half-board. AE, MC, V. Closed Nov and May. **Amenities:** Restaurant; bar; babysitting;

fitness center; massage; indoor heated pool; nonsmoking rooms; rooms for those w/limited mobility; room service; sauna; tanning bed. *In room:* TV, hairdryer, Jacuzzi (in some rooms), minibar, Wi-Fi.

WHERE TO EAT

Wirtshaus Zum Griena ★ 🏠AUSTRIAN/TYROLEAN   This restaurant, strong on regional charm and cuisine, sits in a meadow above Mayrhofen's main colony of hotels. The two dining rooms are covered with pinewood planks that were supposedly installed 400 years ago; the tables are an unfinished series of smoothly sanded boards. Even if you read German, you might find the menu tough going, as it's written in a little-used Tyrolean dialect. Many dishes are based on butter-and-egg mountain recipes, sometimes laden with cream from high-altitude cows. Several involve baking in a ceramic pot, including noodles layered with cream and cheese. Ever had beer soup? You might opt for the cheese platter, a bowl of polenta, or one of the meat dishes.

Dorfhaus 768. ⓒ**05285/62778.** Reservations recommended. Main courses 8€–13€. MC, V. Open daily 11am–11pm. Closed Nov, and summer hours vary. Drive uphill (north) from the town center for 10 min. to the secluded suburb of Dorfhaus; turn left at a fountain and head several hundred feet down a 1-lane road flanked with a fence.

THE KITZBÜHEL ALPS ★★★

Hard-core skiers and the rich and famous come from far and wide to this ski region, with such a dense network of lifts covering the Kitzbühel Alps that it's considered Austria's largest skiing area. The town of Kitzbühel was founded in the Middle Ages and was known as a mining hub during those ages, long before it became one of Austria's "Big Three" ski resorts. The town lies between the Kitzbüheler Horn and the Hannenkamm peaks, where one of the toughest annual runs of World Cup skiing is held. The action centers on the town of Kitzbühel, but there are many satellite resorts that are much less expensive, including **St. Johann** in Tyrol. Most visitors to the Kitzbühel Alps use Munich's international airport.

Kitzbühel ★★★

Edward, Prince of Wales (you might remember him better as the Duke of Windsor), might have put Kitzbühel on the international map with his 1928 "discovery" of what was then a town of modest guesthouses. Certainly his return a few years later with Mrs. Simpson caused the eyes of the world to focus on this town, and the upper crust of England and other countries began flocking here, placing a stamp of early elegance on Kitzbühel.

At the time of this 20th-century renaissance, however, Kitzbühel was already some 8 centuries old by documented history, and a settlement existed here much, much longer than that. Archaeological finds have shown that during the Bronze Age—and until the 9th century B.C.—copper was mined and traded in nearby mountains. The settlement *Chizbühel* is first mentioned in documents of 1165, the name derived from the ruling family of Chizzo. Kitzbühel was a part of Bavaria until 1504, when it came into the hands of Holy Roman Emperor Maximilian I of Austria and was annexed to Tyrol.

A second mining era began in Kitzbühel in the 15th century—this time copper and silver—which made the town prosperous for many decades. Numerous buildings from the mining days are still here, as are remnants of the town walls and three of the gates. In what used to be the suburbs of Kitzbühel, you'll see some of the miners' cottages still standing.

Kitzbühel

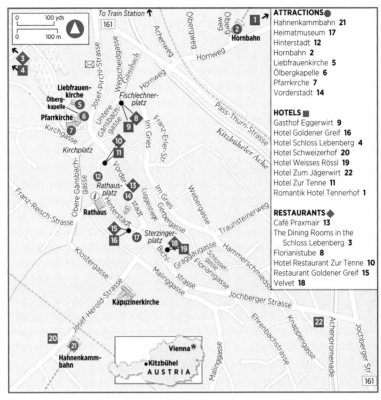

ATTRACTIONS●
Hahnenkammbahn **21**
Heimatmuseum **17**
Hinterstadt **12**
Hornbahn **2**
Liebfrauenkirche **5**
Ölbergkapelle **6**
Pfarrkirche **7**
Vorderstadt **14**

HOTELS ■
Gasthof Eggerwirt **9**
Hotel Goldener Greif **16**
Hotel Schloss Lebenberg **4**
Hotel Schweizerhof **20**
Hotel Weisses Rössl **19**
Hotel Zum Jägerwirt **22**
Hotel Zur Tenne **11**
Romantik Hotel Tennerhof **1**

RESTAURANTS ◆
Café Praxmair **13**
The Dining Rooms in the
   Schloss Lebenberg **3**
Florianistube **8**
Hotel Restaurant Zur Tenne **10**
Restaurant Goldener Greif **15**
Velvet **18**

Kitzbühel is not a cheap place to stay, but to make things easier on your wallet, the local tourist office has come up with a **Guest Card** for summer visitors. This card is valid after being stamped at your hotel or guesthouse and entitles you to discounts, some quite substantial, on the price of many activities, plus some freebies.

ESSENTIALS

GETTING THERE   Two to three **trains** per hour (many express) arrive in Kitzbühel from Innsbruck (trip time: 60 min.) and Salzburg (trip time: 2½ hr.). For rail information, contact ☎ **05/1717** (www.oebb.at).

Although it's serviced by at least nine local **bus lines** running into and up the surrounding valleys, most visitors arrive in Kitzbühel by train. The most useful of these bus lines runs every 30 to 60 minutes between Kitzbühel and St. Johann in Tyrol (trip time: 25 min.). In addition, about half a dozen buses travel every day from Salzburg's main railway station to Kitzbühel (trip time: 2¼ hr.). For **regional bus information,** call ☎ **05356/62715.**

Kitzbühel is 449km (279 miles) southwest of Vienna and 100km (62 miles) east of Innsbruck. If you're **driving** from Innsbruck, take Autobahn A12, and take exit 17

(Wörgl-Ost) toward Lofer–St. Johann. At the first roundabout, take Route 170 south to Kitzbühel.

VISITOR INFORMATION   The **tourist office,** Hinterstadt 18 (©**05356/66660;** www.kitzbuehel.com), is open Monday to Friday 8:30am to 6pm, Saturday 9am to 1pm, times vary on Sundays and holidays depending on the season.

WHAT TO SEE & DO
Exploring the Town
The town has two main streets, both pedestrian walkways: **Vorderstadt** and **Hinterstadt.** Along these streets, Kitzbühel has preserved its traditional architectural style. You'll see three-story stone houses with oriels and scrollwork around the doors and windows, heavy overhanging eaves, and gothic gables.

The **Pfarrkirche (Parish Church)** was built from 1435 to 1506 and was renovated in the baroque style during the 18th century. The lower part of the **Liebfrauenkirche (Church of Our Lady)** dates from the 13th century; the upper part dates from 1570. Between these two churches stands the **Ölbergkapelle (Ölberg Chapel),** with a 1450 "lantern of the dead" and frescoes from the latter part of the 16th century.

Heimatmuseum, Hinterstadt 32 (© **05356/67274;** www.museum-kitzbuehel. at), is the town's most visible showcase of its own culture and history. It lies within what was originally the town granary, constructed in the city's center on the site of an early medieval castle. In 1998, it was enlarged with the incorporation of the town's oldest extant tower, a 14th-century stone structure once part of Kitzbühel's medieval fortifications. Inside you'll see artifacts based on the town's legendary mines, from prehistoric times and the Bronze Age through the Middle Ages, as well as trophies of the region's skiing stars, with lots of emphasis on its 19th- and early-20th-century development into a modern-day ski resort. The museum is open from the beginning of December to Easter, Tuesday to Friday and Sunday 2 to 4pm, Saturday 10am to 6pm; after Easter until the end of October, Tuesday to Friday 10am to 1pm, Saturday 10am to 5pm. Open longer hours during the peak months of winter and summer. Admission is 5.60€ for adults and 2.10€ for those under 18.

Skiing Galore at the Kitzbühel Ski Circus
In winter, the emphasis in Kitzbühel, 702m (2,303 ft.) above sea level, is on skiing, and facilities are offered for everyone from novices to experts. The ski season starts just before Christmas and lasts until late March. With more than 62 lifts, gondolas, and mountain railroads on five different mountains, Kitzbühel has two main ski areas, the **Hahnenkamm** and the **Kitzbüheler Horn ★★.** The Hahnenkammbahnen (cable cars) are within easy walking distance, even in ski boots.

Skiing became a fact of life in Kitzbühel as long ago as 1892, when the first pair of skis was imported from Norway and intrepid daredevils began to slide down the snowy slopes at breakneck speeds. Many great names in skiing have since been associated with Kitzbühel, the most renowned being town native Toni Sailer, triple Olympic champion in the 1956 Winter Games in Cortina.

The linking of the lift systems on the Hahnenkamm has created the celebrated **Kitzbühel Ski Circus ★★★,** which makes it possible to ski downhill for more than 80km (50 miles), with runs that suit every stage of proficiency. Numerous championship ski events are held here, such as the World Cup event each January, when top-flight skiers pit their skills against the toughest downhill course in the world, a stretch of the Hahnenkamm especially designed for maximum speed. Its name, Die Strief, is both feared and respected among skiers because of its reputation as one of the world's fastest downhill racecourses. A ski pass entitles the holder to use all the lifts that form the Ski Circus.

More Winter & Summer Pursuits

Skiing, of course, is not the only winter activity here—there's also curling, ski-bobbing, ski jumping, ice-skating, tobogganing, hiking on cleared trails, and hang gliding, as well as indoor activities such as tennis, bowling, and swimming. The children's ski school, **Schischule Rote Teufel,** Museumkeller, Hinterstadt (✆ **05356/62500**), provides training for the very young skier. And don't forget the après-ski program, with bars, nightclubs, and dance clubs rocking from teatime until the small hours.

Kitzbühel has summer pastimes, too, with activities including walking tours, visits to the **Wild Life Park at Aurach** (3km/2 miles from Kitzbühel, ✆ **05356/65251**), tennis, horseback riding, golf, squash, brass-band concerts in the town center, cycling, and swimming. For the latter, there's an indoor swimming pool, but we recommend going to the **Schwarzsee (Black Lake).** This lake, about a 15-minute walk northwest of the center of town, has a peat bottom that keeps the water relatively murky. Covering an area of 6.5 hectares (16 acres), with a depth that doesn't exceed about 8m (26 ft.), it's the site of beaches and **Seiwald Bootver-leitung,** Schwarzsee (✆ **05356/62381**), an outfit that rents rowboats and putt-putt electric-driven engines in case you want to fish or sunbathe on the lake. Rowboats rent for 8€ per hour, and small-scale electric engines rent for 15€ per hour. Everything is shuttered down tight from September to mid-May when the snow rolls in.

One of the region's most exotic collections of alpine flora is clustered into the jagged and rocky confines of the **Alpine Flower Garden Kitzbühel** (✆ **05356/62857**), where various species of gentian, gorse, heather, and lichens are found on the sunny slopes of the Kitzbüheler Horn. Set at a height of around 1,830m (6,004 ft.) above sea level, the garden—which is owned and maintained by Kitzbühel as an incentive to midsummer tourism—is open from late May to early September daily from 8:30am to 5:30pm, and it's most impressive during June, July, and August. Admission is free, and many visitors see it by taking the Seilbahn Kitzbüheler cable car to its uppermost station and then descending on foot via the garden's labyrinth of footpaths to the gondola's middle station. (You can also climb upward within the garden if you are looking to get a workout.) The **Hornbahn cable car I or II** (✆ **05356/6951**), 16€ round-trip, departs from the Kitzbühel from 8:30am to 5pm during the summer months.

WHERE TO STAY

Although there's a wide range of hotels in Kitzbühel, reservations are mandatory in the high-season winter months, particularly the peak ski times such as February. As for Christmas in Kitzbühel, someone once wrote, "It's best to make reservations at birth."

Very Expensive

Romantik Hotel Tennerhof ★★★ High in the foothills of the mountains near the Hornbahn cable cars, and less than 1km (½ mile) west of the town center, this comfortable, government-rated five-star chalet hotel evolved from a 17th-century farmhouse. If you're a traditionalist, try one of the rooms in the original building, as they're the most intimate. All rooms are beautifully furnished in a style that resembles the imperial.

Griesenauweg 26, A-6370 Kitzbühel. © **05356/63181.** Fax 05356/6318170. www.tennerhof.at. 39 units. Winter 193€–421€ double, 294€–644€ suite; summer 156€–244€ double, 326€–454€ suite. Rates include breakfast, half-board with 39€–45€ surcharge. Parking 18€. AE, DC, MC, V. Closed mid Apr–late May and mid Oct–mid Dec. **Amenities:** Restaurant; bar; babysitting; massage; 2 heated pools (1 indoor, 1 outdoor); room service; spa; tanning bed. In room: TV, hairdryer, minibar, Wi-Fi.

Expensive

Hotel Goldener Greif ★   The ancestor of this hotel was built in 1271, and parts of it still remain within the massive walls of this well-known establishment. The hotel, 180m (591 ft.) from the Hahnenkamm cable-car station, has many balconies and elaborate shutters. Owner Josef Harisch (his daughter, Maria Harisch, runs the hotel now) likes traditional charm with a good dose of luxury. The public places greet you with fireplaces, antique furniture, oriental carpets, and Tyrolean paintings. The comfortable, attractive rooms have firm beds and are quite spacious with lots of wood, alcove seats, nonworking fireplaces, parquet floors, double-glazed windows, and (in some cases) a whirlpool. If you want to splurge a bit, you can request one of the deluxe suites, many with a hunting-lodge motif and their own Jacuzzis, private steam baths, and fireplaces.

The superb **Restaurant Goldener Greif** (p. 401) serves Austrian and regional cuisine.

Hinterstadt 24, A-6370 Kitzbühel. © **05356/64311.** Fax 05356/65001. www.hotel-goldener-greif.at. 56 units. Winter 156€–254€ double, 230€–292€ suite; summer 114€–146€ double, 141€–161€ suite. Rates include breakfast. Half-board available for a 25€ surcharge. AE, DC, MC, V. Free parking on street. Closed Apr–May and Oct–Nov. **Amenities:** Restaurant; bar; fitness center; massage; indoor heated pool; room service; sauna; solarium. In room: TV, hairdryer.

Hotel Schloss Lebenberg ★★   The core of this hotel is a medieval castle whose walls and turrets have been covered with stucco, and a modern extension has been added. The entire complex sits on a hill looking over the village, less than 1.5km (1 mile) from Kitzbühel, with dozens of mountain paths originating at its door. Rooms are elegant, lacking the much-loved Tyrolean clutter, and come in a range of sizes, including some spacious enough for sitting areas with wrought-iron coffee tables. Many beds are canopied and French doors lead to private patios or balconies. The dozen or so large, Gothic-style castle rooms are the most sought after. The hotel restaurant serves lunch and dinner, and provides a lavish breakfast buffet for guests.

Lebenbergstrasse 17, A-6370 Kitzbühel. © **05356/69010.** Fax 05356/6901-404. www.austria-trend. at/leb. 150 units. Rooms 225€–400€ double. Rates include half-board. AE, DC, MC, V. Free outside parking; garage parking 15€. Hotel bus picks up guests at train station. **Amenities:** Restaurant; bar; babysitting; fitness center; indoor heated pool; nonsmoking rooms; room service; sauna. In room: TV, hairdryer, Internet connection.

Hotel Weisses Rössl ★   This hotel was originally built in the 19th century as an inn for the merchants passing through Kitzbühel by coach. Today it's impeccably maintained by the Klena family. Dozens of seating niches in the public spaces give you the feeling of being in a modern loft, though parts are more classically furnished. The fourth floor contains a panoramic terrace with one of the best mountain views in town. A 2-minute walk from the ski lifts, the hotel has open rooms, most with seating areas, and neatly kept bathrooms. The newly opened a la carte restaurant Velvet is worth a visit if you want to escape the Austrian wood-paneled traditional look for an evening (p. 401).

Bichlstrasse 3-5, A-6370 Kitzbühel. ☏ **05356/71900.** Fax 05356/71900-99. www.roesslkitz.at. 86 units. Winter 230€–905€ double, from 460€–1,700€ suite; summer 270€–380€ double, from 370€ suite. Rates include half-board (7-course dinner). Parking free. AE, DC, MC, V. Closed late March to late May and mid-Sept to mid-Dec. **Amenities:** Restaurant; bar; babysitting; indoor heated pool; room service; spa; Wi-Fi in lobby. *In room:* TV, hairdryer, minibar, Internet connection (in some).

Hotel Zur Tenne ★★ A sophisticated family from Munich operates this hotel, which combines Tyrolean *Gemütlichkeit* with urban panache. The staff shows genuine concern for the clientele, who will reside in a complex created in the 1950s by joining a trio of 700-year-old houses. Rooms are as glamorous as anything in posh Kitzbühel: Wood trim, comfortable beds, eiderdowns, and copies of Tyrolean antiques. Many have working fireplaces and canopied beds for a romantic touch. In addition to intimate lounges and niches and nooks, the hotel sports the most luxurious health complex in town, complete with a tropical fountain, two hot tubs, and a hot-and-cold foot bath.

The Zur Tenne Restaurant offers international cuisine with a Tyrolean flair (p. 400).

Vorderstadt 8-10, A-6370 Kitzbühel. ☏ **05356/644440.** Fax 05356/6480356. www.hotelzurtenne. com. 51 units. Winter 193€–421€ double, from 294€ suite; summer 156€–244€ double, from 241€ suite. Rates include breakfast. AE, DC, MC, V. Free parking outdoors, 16€ in covered garage nearby. **Amenities:** 2 restaurants; bar; lounge; fitness center; Jacuzzi; sauna; room service; massage; babysitting; laundry service; dry cleaning; solarium. *In room:* TV, minibar, hairdryer, safe, Wi-Fi.

Sporthotel Bichlhof ★ Slightly more than 3km (2 miles) south of the resort's center, this 1970s' hotel offers sweeping views over most of the valley. This tasteful chalet complex surrounds you with a decor of exposed paneling and patterned carpeting. The spacious rooms sometimes look Japanese in their simplicity. The most desirable ones open onto private balconies with great views. The hotel's restaurant serves authentic Tyrolean cuisine, specializing in fish caught in its own lake. As part of its weekly programs, the hotel offers guided torchlit walks, Tyrolean buffets, and fondue evenings or barbecues.

Bichlnweg 153, A-6370 Kitzbühel. ☏ **05356/64022.** Fax 05356/63634. www.bichlhof.at. 52 units. Winter 240€–480€ double, from 310€ suite; summer 150€–260€ double, from 200€ suite. Rates include breakfast. MC, V. Parking free. Closed Apr and Nov. **Amenities:** Restaurant; bar; babysitting; fitness center; 18-hole golf course center; massage; indoor pool and outdoor pool; nonsmoking rooms; room service; spa; 2 tennis courts. *In room:* TV, hairdryer, minibar, Wi-Fi.

Moderate

Hotel Bruggerhof ★ 👥 Less than 1.5km (1 mile) west of the town center, near the Schwarzsee, is this countryside chalet with a sun terrace. Originally built as a farmhouse in the 1920s, it later gained local fame as a restaurant. The interior has massive ceiling beams and a corner fireplace. The owners, the Reiter family, run a smoothly operating hotel. Rooms are comfortable, decorated in the omnipresent Tyrolean style. All have a well-lived-in look, although housekeeping is attentive. Don't expect the smooth-running efficiency of a large-scale chain hotel, as everything here is family managed, idiosyncratic, and personalized—sometimes to the point of eccentricity. There is also the possibility of camping in the grounds. The restaurant still serves the best of the region: *Schweinshaxn* (slow roasted leg of pig), schnitzel, and also farmer buffets on certain weeks.

Reitherstrasse 24, A-6370 Kitzbühel. ☏ **05356/62806.** Fax 05356/6447930. www.bruggerhof-camping.at. 25 units. Winter 180€–240€ double, from 200€ suite; summer 180€–204€ double, from 225€ suite. Rates include half-board. AE, DC, MC, V. Closed Apr–mid May and late Sept–early Dec. **Amenities:** Restaurant; bar; babysitting; fitness center; Jacuzzi; minigolf; sauna; nonsmoking rooms; room service; tanning bed; 2 tennis courts. *In room:* TV, hairdryer, minibar, Wi-Fi.

Hotel Schweizerhof ★ ☺ This hotel is a modern version of the Tyrolean chalet, with lots of glass and less wood than the typical structure in the area. The generally light and spacious rooms have terraces and have the aura of a living room, making you want to linger instead of using it just as a crash pad. Nothing in the room can compete with the private balcony overlooking the Stein or the imposing Kaiser Mountains. The hotel restaurant's food is Tyrolean and international, and the menu is varied and interesting. On some winter evenings, the public rooms seem more like a house party than a hotel. Summer brings tables and umbrellas out on the lawns. The hotel overlooks the children's ski school next to the Hahnenkamm cableway. It prides itself on its spa, which is very much a part of its allure.

Hahnenkammstrasse 4, A-6370 Kitzbühel. ℂ **05356/62735.** Fax 05356/62735-57. www.hotel-schweizerhof.at. 42 units. Winter 200€–300€ double, from 260€ suite; summer 126€–160€ double, from 155€ suite. Rates include half-board. Parking free. MC, V. Closed 4 weeks after Easter and 4 weeks between Oct–Nov. **Amenities:** Restaurant; bar; children's playroom; massage; nonsmoking rooms; rooms w/limited mobility; room service; spa. *In room:* TV, hairdryer, Wi-Fi.

Hotel Zum Jägerwirt ★ This inn once catered to hunters, who are known in Austria for their appreciation of good food and atmosphere. The government-rated four-star hotel, smack dab in the town center, was recently enlarged and renovated. It has a bar area with hewn overhead beams. Double rooms are spacious and well furnished, while singles are rather small and might not be large enough to handle all your ski equipment. Heavy pine furniture, oriental rugs, and good beds make the place inviting, although time has taken its toll on the decor.

The hotel restaurant, Jägerwirt, serves both Austrian and international specialties. In addition to an ample breakfast buffet, guests are treated in the evening to a large salad buffet, plus a bountiful dinner. The chef can cater to special diets.

Jochbergerstrasse 12, A-6370 Kitzbühel. ℂ**05356/69810.** Fax 05356/64067. www.hotel-jaegerwirt.at. 78 units. Winter 160€–280€ double, from 230€ suite; summer 108€–132€ double, from 200€ suite. Rates include breakfast. AE, DC, MC, V. Closed mid March–late May and Oct–mid Dec. **Amenities:** Restaurant; bar; children's pool; fitness center; massage; indoor heated pool; nonsmoking rooms; room service; spa. *In room:* TV, hairdryer; minibar.

Inexpensive

Gasthof Eggerwirt ✦ Lying in Kitzbühel's lower altitudes, this lodging sits next to a gurgling stream. Today, country-baroque designs highlight the traditional stucco facade of a remodeled and enlarged hotel, with a structure that was actually built in 1658. Inside, the Gasthof is clean, with well-maintained standards of simple, solid comfort in its rooms. The decor is functional, and all rooms have neatly kept bathrooms; some units contain a private balcony. Considering the location, pricing is very good. There's a charming dining room, Florianistube (p. 402).

Goensbachgasse 12, A-6370 Kitzbühel. ℂ **05356/62455.** Fax 05356/6243722. www.eggerwirt-kitzbuehel.at. 19 units. Winter 122€–192€ double, from 140€ suite; summer 100€–125€ double, from 112€ suite. MC, V. Rates include breakfast. Parking free. Closed several weeks after Easter and Nov. **Amenities:** Restaurant; bar. *In room:* TV, minibar, Wi-Fi.

WHERE TO EAT

Many guests stay at Kitzbühel on the half-board plan. It's also fashionable to dine around, checking out the action at the various hotels. With a few exceptions, all the best restaurants are in hotels.

Expensive

Hotel Restaurant Zur Tenne ★★ INTERNATIONAL Large, elegantly paneled, accented with a corner bar, and also with plenty of deer antlers hanging from

Even before night falls, people make a mad dash for a seat at **Café Praxmair**, Vorderstadt 17 ((☏ **05356/62646**). One of the most famous pastry shops in Austria, it's known for its Florentine cookies. Later in the evening, the Praxmair Keller offers the town's most permissive nightlife. It remains open all night, summer and winter. If it's before 5 o'clock, the item to order is hot chocolate with a "top hat" of whipped cream. Coffee costs from 3€; pastries go for 2.50€ to 3.25€. The cafe is open daily from 10am to 1am; the cellar bar is open daily from 10pm to dawn.

the ceilings and walls, this is one of the village's best, also in one of its poshest hotels. Depending on the amount of sunlight, the most popular seating area is the glass-sided extension. Appetizers include fried scallops with two kinds of cauliflower and curry marinade, and citrus pepper tuna with avocado and mango salad. For main courses, turbot mussel *pot au feu* with pea–potato *croquettes*, mushrooms, and port shallots, and sole with zucchini garlic purée and lemon thyme hollandaise. If that didn't get your mouth watering, go for the *Tafelspitz* or Wiener schnitzel.

In Hotel Zur Tenne, Vorderstadt 8–10. (☏ **05356/644440.** Reservations required. Main courses 30€– 40€. AE, DC, MC, V. Daily 11:30am–1:30pm and 6:30–9:30pm.

Restaurant Goldener Greif ★★ TYROLEAN   The cuisine here is some of the best at the resort, with a menu that includes everything from a simple goulash to caviar. The dining room features vaulted ceilings, intricate paneling, ornamental ceramic stoves, 19th-century paintings, and, in some cases, views out over the base of some of Kitzbühel's busy cable cars. The ever-popular veal can be ordered, or other meaty dishes such as a pepper steak Madagascar. A "Vienna pot" is one of the chef's specials, and fresh Tyrolean trout is offered daily as a *fondue bourguignonne*. All the meats and sausages come from the hotel's own butcher.

In Hotel Goldener Greif, Hinterstadt 24. (☏ **05356/64311.** Reservations recommended. Main courses 12€–30€; fixed-price menu 16€–35€. AE, DC, MC, V. Daily 11am–2pm and 6–10pm. Closed mid-Apr to June and Oct to mid-Dec.

Velvet ★★ INTERNATIONAL   This small a la carte restaurant in Hotel Weisses Rössl is the latest addition to the gourmet scene in Kitzbühel. It is decked out in dark purple and black stained beech wood, making for a different kind of eating experience in an area dead set on Tyrolean wood panels and traditional knick-knacks. It has a limited capacity—only 20 can fit—but the menu is far reaching. Starters include Beluga caviar (if you are willing to spend 80€), and the main courses range from truffle *taglioni* with winter vegetables and haddock with yellow curry of *kefir* lime and papaya. For dessert, creamy *Zotter* chocolate mango with *beta zeta*.

In Hotel Weisses Rössl, Bichlstrasse 3–5. (☏ **05356/719200.** Reservations required. Main courses 28€–32€. AE, DC, MC, V. Kitchen open daily 6–10pm, lounge open from 4–10pm. Closed mid Sept–mid Dec and late March–late May.

Moderate

The Dining Rooms in the Schloss Lebenberg ★ AUSTRIAN/INTERNA-TIONAL   Although this hotel offers comfortable rooms, Schloss Lebenberg may be best known for its well-managed restaurant and its sense of history. Originally built in 1548, it was transformed in 1885 into Kitzbühel's first family-run hotel. The most elegant of the hotel's three dining areas is the Gobelins Room, although the other dining rooms are equally appealing and a bit less intimidating. Always reliable specialties include cream of tomato soup with gin, Tyrolean-style calves' liver, Wiener schnitzels, roulades of beef, and many desserts, which often feature mountain berries.

In Hotel Schloss Lebenberg, Lebenbergstrasse 17. ℂ **05356/69010.** Reservations required. Main courses 15€–30€; 4-course fixed-price menu 45€. AE, DC, MC, V. Daily 6:45–9pm.

Florianistube ◢ INTERNATIONAL/TYROLEAN   Named after St. Florian, patron saint of the hearth, this restaurant is in one of the less ostentatious guesthouses at the resort, and welcomes outsiders. You can dine in a Tyrolean *Stube* (tavern) or an open room with a glass ceiling, and the menu is comprehensive for an inn restaurant—it might include typical Austrian or Tyrolean dishes, or tournedos with mushroom sauce, spaghetti with clam sauce, or fondue bourguignonne. Cooking is reliable and the ingredients are fresh, but don't expect a lot of imagination from the kitchen staff or over-attentiveness in the service rituals. In summer, a lunch or dinner buffet is served outside in the rear garden.

In the Gasthof Eggerwirt, Goensbachgasse 12. ℂ **05356/62437.** Reservations recommended. Main courses 10€–22€. MC, V. Daily 11am–2pm and 6–10pm.

SHOPPING

A promenade around the resort's center reveals shops containing all the luxury goods and sporting equipment a shopper could need to satisfy even serious binges of consumerism. If you're looking for exclusive fashionable ski wear to fit into the Kitzbühel scene, check out **Sportalm,** located at Josef-Pirchl-Strasse 18 (ℂ **05356/71038**). They have everything from skiwear to traditional Austrian *Trachten*. For basic ski gear, go to **Kitz Sport,** Jochbergerstrasse 7 (ℂ **05356/62504**). **Country Classics-Driendl-Schulze Hinmüller OEG,** Jochbergerstrasse 21 (ℂ **05356/66808**), where you'll find locally handcrafted pewter, ironwork, ceramics, woodcarvings, and a small selection of traditional Tyrolean clothing for men and women. Traditional clothing for men, women, and children, as well as modern, conventional clothing for all occasions, is available at **Eden,** Vorderstadt 22 (ℂ **05356/62656**).

KITZBÜHEL AFTER DARK

If you're lucky enough to be in Kitzbühel during July or August, you can schedule your nightly promenade to coincide with the open-air concerts that begin every Tuesday, Thursday, and Friday at 8:30pm. Musicians position themselves against one edge of the Vorderstadt, whose edges are sealed off against motorized traffic. The result is an open-air all-pedestrian party with lots of folk overtones. Expect alpine folk music every Tuesday and Friday, and a roster of more international music (Dixieland or free-form jazz, or perhaps a New Orleans-style blues concert) every Thursday.

Even if you arrive when a concert isn't scheduled, you can always enjoy Kitzbühel's collection of nightlife and drinking options, most of which line either edge of the resort's two most central avenues, Vorderstadt and Hinterstadt. A site whose decor you might immediately recognize as inspired by 1950s' America (it contains an antique car and a replica of an old-fashioned gasoline station) is **Highways Pub,** Im Gries 20 (ℂ **0664/2105823**). A watering hole with a theme like that of a Victorian pub is **The Londoner,** Franz-Reisch-Strasse 4 (ℂ **05356/71427**), where hot music sometimes has late-night clients up and dancing on the tables. A conventional dance club, usually brimming with high-altitude energy, is **Python Club,** Hinterstadt 6

(© **05356/63001**). A more glamorous address, with a more aggressive policy about screening rowdies from the lines that sometimes form on weekends, is **Take Five Disco,** Hinterstadt 22 (© **05356/71300**). Here, within a mostly black and artfully lit interior, you'll find one of the biggest venues for late-night partying in town.

In winter, every Thursday from 5:30pm to around 1am, the **Alpenhotel Kitzbühel Annemarie Hirschhuber** (© **05356/64254**) sponsors live music that usually transforms the place into a fun and convivial dance. Admission is free at this party, held about 2km (1¼ miles) northwest of Kitzbühel's center, beside the lake.

Local residents who want to escape too constant a diet of evergreen music and ski-related raucousness head for the cool and quiet enclaves of Kitzbühel's most appealing piano bar, **The Piano Place,** in the Hotel Tennerhof, Griesenauweg 26 (© **05356/63181**). It features live music in winter (Dec–Apr) every Wednesday to Sunday 6pm to midnight; and in summer (late June–late Aug) every Thursday to Sunday during the same hours. The music is rather conducive to drinking. Whiskey with soda costs around 7€; beer costs 4€.

A CASINO

Casino Kitzbühel   Although it offers a less ambitious roster of entertainment options than it did in years gone by, this remains the only (legal) gambling venue in Kitzbühel. You'll be required to show a passport before entering, after which you can wander among machines and croupiers devoted to roulette, blackjack, baccarat, poker, and slot machines. There's also a bar on-site, where you might eventually search out a perch for the observation of the sometimes-sleepy gambling action at the tables.

It's open only about 6 months of the year, from July 1 to mid-September, and from about a week before Christmas to the end of March. During those periods, it's open daily 3pm to 3am. Unlike some other Austrian casinos, men are not required to wear jackets or ties. In the Hotel Goldener Greif, Hinterstadt 24. © **05356/62300.** 20€ buys 25€ of welcome chips.

St. Johann in Tyrol

St. Johann has neither the chic reputation nor the high prices of Kitzbühel. You'll save money if you stay here and travel each day to Kitzbühel, 10km (6 miles) to the south, to enjoy the facilities there. It is a surprisingly historic town; the first Catholic church was built here in the 8th century by missionaries, and the town was named after St. John the Evangelist. The copper and silver boom added to its wealth before transportation networks augmented the diversification of its economy in the 1800s.

ESSENTIALS

GETTING THERE   One **train** per hour (some express) arrives in St. Johann by way of Kitzbühel from Innsbruck (trip time: 1¼ hr.) and Salzburg (trip time: 2¾ hr.). Some trains from Salzburg require a transfer at the railway junction of Schwarzach–St. Veit. For rail information, contact © **05/1717** (www.oebb.at). You can also take one of the half-dozen **buses** that run every day between St. Johann and Kitzbühel (30 min.). For **bus or train information** in Kitzbühel, call © **05356/64055.** Buses also pull into St. Johann from Salzburg several times a day, stopping first at Kitzbühel (trip time: 1¾ hr.).

St. Johann lies 399km (248 miles) west of Vienna, 90km (56 miles) east of Innsbruck, and 90km (56 miles) southwest of Munich. If you're **driving** from Innsbruck, follow the A12 east to the junction with Route 178, which you take east to St. Johann.

The **tourist office,** Poststrasse 2 (☎ **05352/633350;** www.st.johann.tirol.at), in the town center, is open Monday to Friday 8:30am to 12:30pm and 2 to 6pm, and Saturday 9am to noon. During peak months it is open Saturday from 4 to 6pm and Sunday 10am to noon.

EXPLORING ST. JOHANN

Lying between two mountains, the **Wilder Kaiser** and the **Kitzbüheler Horn,** this village is both a summer attraction to lovers of the outdoors and a popular ski resort. In summer, it has a busy open-air swimming pool, and in winter, the good ski runs appeal to both beginners and experts. A ski school and ski kindergarten, plus cross-country ski trails, add to the attractions. The bar scene is also popular among the younger crowds.

Many old Tyrolean houses fill the little town with charm, and some of the traditional inns have frescoed exteriors, revealing its ancient roots.

The Kaisergebirge range, near St. Johann, also draws many mountain climbers.

WHERE TO STAY

Gasthof Post ★   Gasthof Post, in the town center adjacent to the village church, is about as solid a building as you'll find in Tyrol. It was first constructed in 1224, and parts of its original wooden ceiling beams are still in place. The interior is replete with stone and wood columns. Rooms range from large to intimately small and are well furnished with good beds and small private bathrooms; many open onto balconies. There's a large dining room for hotel guests and an a la carte restaurant.

Speckbacherstrasse 1, A-6380 St. Johann in Tyrol. ☎ **05352/62230.** Fax 05352/622303. www.hotel-post.tv. 45 units. Winter 114€–200€ double; summer 70€–90€ double. Rates include breakfast, half-board with surcharge of 12€. AE, DC, MC, V. Closed Apr and mid Nov–mid Dec. **Amenities:** 3 restaurants; bar; babysitting; massage; free access to nearby public indoor heated pool; 1 room for those w/limited mobility; room service. *In room:* TV, Wi-Fi.

Hotel Fischer   In the village center, this solidly built four-story chalet was erected in 1972 with wooden balconies and a sun terrace framed by cascading vines. The sunny rooms are comfortable and cozy, although in some cases they're a bit on the small side. Housekeeping rates an A. The Grander family is helpful and happy to point out nearby bars and clubs to get your night out on the town started, or you can hang out in the house cocktail lounge. Guests have free access to the local pool.

Kaiserstrasse 3, A-6380 St. Johann in Tyrol. ☎ **05352/62332.** Fax 05352/62332100. www.hotel-fischer. com. 38 units. Winter 122€–182€ double; summer 94€–112€. Rates include half-board. Parking free. DC, MC, V. **Amenities:** Bar; sauna. *In room:* TV, hairdryer, Wi-Fi.

Hotel Park ★ ☺   Well-scrubbed and appealing, this modern, government-rated four-star hotel made few attempts to emulate the chalet-style architecture of many of its competitors when it was built in 1973. The result is an angular, well-accessorized hotel that's among the least expensive, with a hardworking family staff. Skiers appreciate its easy access to the lifts, close to the larger of the town's two gondola stations. Most rooms look out over either the ski slopes or the mountains; the others overlook a pleasant garden. There's an attractive restaurant, The Park, serving Tyrolean and Austrian dishes. In summer, guests gravitate to the beer garden. The hotel is a good choice for families because it has a playground and a supply of bicycles and mountain bikes.

Spechbacherstrasse 45, A-6380 St. Johann in Tyrol. ☎ **05352/62226.** Fax 05352/622266. www.park. at. 54 units. Winter 124€–204€ double; summer 108€–128€ double. Rates include half-board. AE, DC, MC, V. Parking garage 6€. Closed mid-Oct to mid-Dec and late Mar–late May. **Amenities:** Restaurant; bar; babysitting; bike rentals; playground; sauna. *In room:* TV, hairdryer, Wi-Fi.

WHERE TO EAT

La Rustica ITALIAN   The decor is solidly elegant yet rustic, a play on both the restaurant's name and its position within a building from the 1850s in the center of the resort. But unlike many restaurants, its menu incorporates a wider-than-expected gamut of food that includes two dozen kinds of pizzas, about 20 kinds of main-course pastas, and nearly 20 hearty meat dishes that go well with the bracing mountain air. Most are inspired by the culinary tenets of northern Italy, with the exception of a pizza Margherita, whose simple tomato-with-basil-and-garlic ingredients derive from pure Neapolitan models. Desserts are made on the premises. The clientele seems about evenly divided in its preference for either Chianti or beer.

Spechbacherstrasse 31. ☎ **05352/62843.** www.larustica.at. Reservations recommended. Main courses 6€–20€. Pizza 6.50€–12€. AE, DC, MC, V. Tues–Sun 11am–2:30pm and 5pm–midnight (last order for pizza at 11:30pm, for other dishes at 10pm).

EAST TYROL ★★★

East Tyrol (known as Östtirol in German) is not geographically connected to North Tyrol. When South Tyrol was ceded to Italy in 1919 in the aftermath of World War I, East Tyrol was cut off from the rest of the province by a narrow corner of Italian land that borders Land Salzburg.

Italy, including what used to be South Tyrol, lies to the south and west, with Land Salzburg to the north and Carinthia to the east. The little subprovince, of which Lienz is the capital, is cut off from its neighbors in the north by the seemingly impenetrable Alps. The landscape is jagged and intimidating, giving a slightly different air than the green valleys and snow-capped ski resorts in "mainland" Tyrol. The nearby Dolomite range looms in the backdrop, and the transformation of the Alps into the barren and imposing mountains of northern Italy can be observed.

Because of its isolated position, East Tyrol is unfortunately neglected by the average North American tourist. The grandeur of its scenery and the warm hospitality of its people make it worth a side trip or even a longer stay. It's crowned by the towering peaks of the **Lienz Dolomites ★★**, which draw in plenty of mountain climbers and base jumpers due to the formation of the rock faces. The scenery along the **Drau** and the **Isel** valleys is spectacular. These two main valleys have many little side hollows worth exploring, especially the **Virgental.** You'll see alpine pastureland, meadows, relatively undiscovered valleys, and beautiful lakes.

The Romans occupied East Tyrol in ancient times. Later the Slavs moved into the area as settlers and made it a section of Carinthia. It has known many rulers, from the Bavarians to the French. Even Great Britain had a hand in running things here, when the Allies made East Tyrol a part of the British-occupied sector of Austria from 1945 to 1955.

Since 1967, it has been possible to reach East Tyrol by taking the 5km-long (3-mile) **Felbertauern Tunnel,** a western route through the Alps. If you're driving, you can come from the east or the west. From the **Grossglockner Road,** you take the Felbertauern Road and the tunnel. If you're driving from the north to Lienz, East Tyrol's capital, you can take the Felbertauern Road from Land Salzburg, passing through the tunnel. In summer, you might want to take the Grossglockner Road and the Iselberg Pass. This road runs along the boundary between East Tyrol and Carinthia.

It's also possible to take a train from Italy to East Tyrol. Corridor trains operate between Innsbruck and Lienz as well. As you pass through Italy on this trip, the trains are locked and you don't have to show your passport or clear Italian Customs.

Woodcarving, long a pursuit in East Tyrol, is still practiced in tranquil chalets during the long winter months. You might want to shop for some pieces while you're here.

12 Lienz ★

Don't confuse this city with Linz, the capital of Upper Austria. This **Lienz,** with an *e*, is the capital of East Tyrol. It sits at the junction of three valleys—the Isel to the northwest, the Puster to the west, and the Drau to the east. The old town of Lienz stretches along the banks of the Isel River, with Liebburg Palace, a 16th-century building, now the seat of local government, overshadowing Hauptplatz (Main Square).

ESSENTIALS

GETTING THERE   From Innsbruck, Lienz-bound travelers can take the direct **Korridorzug train,** which involves no border formalities with Italy. The **Val Pusteria** is another connection, going via Italian territory to Lienz (trip time: 3½ hr.). From Salzburg, you'll have to change trains in the rail junction at **Spittal-Millstattersee** (3½ hr.). The **railway station** can be reached by calling ℂ **05/1717** (www.oebb.at).

A confusing array of **buses** travels among the various villages of East Tyrol. One daily bus, after many stops, travels to Lienz from Innsbruck, and another travels from Zell am See. For **bus information** in Lienz, call ℂ **04852/64944.**

From Kitzbühel (p. 394), you can **drive** to Lienz by traveling southeast along Route 161, which becomes Route 108. From Salzburg, take the A10 southeast to the junction with Route 100 near Seeboden and follow the signs west to Lienz. Lienz lies 434km (270 miles) southwest of Vienna, 180km (112 miles) south of Salzburg, and 222km (138 miles) southeast of Munich.

VISITOR INFORMATION   The **tourist office,** Europaplatz (ℂ **0521/2400**), is open Monday to Friday 8am to 6pm, and Saturday 9am to noon. In July and August it's open Monday to Friday 8am to 7pm, Saturday 9am to noon and 5 to 7pm, and Sunday from 10am to noon.

WHAT TO SEE & DO
Outdoor Activities

In winter, Lienz, at an elevation of 869m (2,851 ft.), attracts skiers to its two major ski areas: The **Hochstein** and the **Zertersfeld,** serviced by chairlifts and drag lifts. The height of the top station is 2,204m (7,231 ft.).

In summer, the town fills up with mountain climbers, mainly Austrians, who come to scale the Dolomites. This is a good base for many excursions in the area. For example, from Schlossberg you can take a chairlift up to **Venedigerwarte** (1,017m/ 3,337 ft.). You can explore the excavations of **Aguntum,** the Roman settlement, 5km (3 miles) east of Lienz, or swim in **Lake Tristacher,** 5km (3 miles) south of the city.

The Dolomites, actually the northwestern part of the Gailtal alpine range, lie between the Gail Valley and the Drau Valley: Their highest peak is the **Grosse Sandspitze** at more than 2,745m (9,006 ft.).

Exploring Lienz

St. Andrä If you have time, visit the Church of St. Andrew, with its outstanding collection of 16th-century tombstones carved of marble quarried outside Salzburg. The last Gorz count is buried here. The church, consecrated in 1457, was restored in 1968. During the restoration, workmen uncovered murals, some dating from the 14th century. The church is the finest example of Gothic architecture in East Tyrol. A **memorial chapel** honors the Lienz war dead. The renowned painter Egger-Lienz is entombed here.

Patriasdorfer Strasse. Free admission. Daily 9am–5pm.

Schloss Bruck & Osttiroler Heimatmuseum The showcase of Lienz, and the focal point of its civic pride, is this former stronghold of the counts of Gorz, who controlled vast medieval estates from this strategically located castle that dominated most of the access routes to the Isel Valley. In the early 1500s, it fell to the Habsburgs. It rises impressively less than 1km (½ mile) west of the town center and contains a museum devoted to the history, culture, sociology, and artifacts of the region. The **Rittersaal (Knight's Hall)** shows how the castle looked in the Middle Ages. The **Albin Egger-Lienz gallery** contains an art collection of the outstanding native painter Egger-Lienz (1868–1926). Another section displays artifacts unearthed at the archaeological site of the Roman town of Aguntum.

Iseltaler Strasse. ℘ **04852/62580.** www.museum-schlossbruck.at. Admission 7€ adults, 5€ students and seniors, 2.50€ children under 16. May–Oct daily 10am–6pm. Closed Oct–May.

WHERE TO STAY

Gasthof Goldener Fisch ★ Well-maintained and carefully designed, this government-rated three-star hotel occupies what was originally built in the 1880s as the solid, four-story home of a prosperous local landowner. Michael and Daniela Vergeiner are the hardworking owners of a hotel whose beige-fronted facade wasn't altered during the renovations, and which, in summer, is still accented with seasonal flowers cascading from flower boxes. Bedrooms are monochromatic and painted in tones of beige and off-white, with shower stalls and a sense of cozy efficiency. An on-site cafe and restaurant, with a location less than 180m (591 ft.) from the town center encourages lots of local traffic, serves traditional platters, coffee, and drinks daily from 7am to midnight.

Kärntnerstrasse 9, A-9900 Lienz. ℘ **04852/62132.** Fax 04852/6213248. www.goldener-fisch.at. 30 units. Winter 90€–100€ double; summer 82€–92€ double. Rates include breakfast. Parking free. MC, V. Closed 3 weeks in Nov, 3 weeks in Apr. **Amenities:** Restaurant; bar; children's playground; massage; sauna. In room: TV, hairdryer, Wi-Fi.

Gasthof-Hotel Haidenhof This appealing hotel looks like a cross between an alpine chalet and a Mediterranean villa. The windows of the hotel's central section are bordered with painted Tyrolean designs, whereas on either side, symmetrical wings stretch toward the surrounding forest. Views from the balconies of the well-furnished rooms encompass most of Lienz. Rooms are exceedingly comfortable, if a bit old-fashioned, with well-maintained small bathrooms. On the premises are a sun terrace and a paneled restaurant serving regional specialties.

Grafendorferstrasse 12, A-9900 Lienz. ℘ **04852/62440.** Fax 04852/624406. www.haidenhof.at. 22 units. 140€–162€ double, 160€–180€. Rates include half-board. MC, V. Parking free. Closed Nov and several weeks in the spring. Drive 10 min. north of Lienz to the suburb of Gaimberg. **Amenities:** Restaurant; bar; lounge; massage; nonsmoking rooms; sauna; tanning bed. In room: TV, hairdryer, Wi-Fi.

Hotel Sonne This hotel's modernized mansard roof rises from one end of Südtirolerplatz. In addition to a helpful staff, the hotel has terracotta floors, oriental rugs, a roof garden, and a sun-flooded restaurant with an outdoor terrace. The reservations system is tied in to the Best Western network. The cozy rooms have modern furniture and good beds. The hotel's Restaurant Sonne is open daily 11am–2pm and 6–10pm.

Südtirolerplatz, A-9900 Lienz. © **800/780-7234** in the U.S., or 04852/63311. Fax 04852/63314. www. hotelsonnelienz.at. 62 units. 120€–140€ double. Rates include breakfast. Half-board 20€ per person extra. AE, DC, MC, V. Outdoor parking free, garage for 9€. **Amenities:** 2 restaurants; bar; nonsmoking rooms; rooms for those w/limited mobility; room service; sauna (only free during winter); tanning bed. *In room:* TV, hairdryer, minibar, Wi-Fi.

Romantik Hotel Traube ★★★   This hotel's location, in the very center of town on a tree-lined street, couldn't be more ideal. The facade is painted a vivid red, with forest-green shutters and a canopy covering part of the ground-level cafe. Furnishings in the public areas are elegant and comfortable. The hotel was demolished in World War II but rebuilt in the 1950s. The comfort level is greater here than anywhere else in East Tyrol. Beds are luxurious and the bathrooms come in a range of sizes. Many windows open onto views of the nearby mountains. The a la carte restaurant, La Taverna (see below), serves Italian and East Tyrolean favorites (see review below). A wine boutique across the street and operated by the same owners sells rarities and local specialties.

Hauptplatz, A-9900 Lienz. © **04852/64444.** Fax 04852/64184. www.hoteltraube.at. 55 units. 128€– 183€ double. Rates include breakfast. AE, DC, MC, V. **Amenities:** Restaurants; bar; babysitting; bike rental; massage; indoor heated pool; room service; spa; squash; tennis court. *In room:* TV, hairdryer, minibar, Wi-Fi.

WHERE TO EAT

La Taverna ★   AUSTRIAN/TYROLEAN/ITALIAN   Amid Tyrolean accents of flowered banquettes, gilded wall sconces, and big arched windows, this airy restaurant offers elegant meals in comfortable surroundings. The cuisine here is the best in town, based on fresh ingredients deftly handled in the kitchen. Menu items run an artful line between experimental dishes and tried-and-true Tyrolean favorites. Pasta dishes come in abundance, all using fresh homemade pasta, such as the *tagliata con rucola*. Menus change weekly.

Hauptplatz 14. © **04852/64444.** Reservations required. Main courses 9€–25€. AE, DC, MC, V. Tues– Sun 11am–2pm and 6–11pm.

SHOPPING

More energy seems to be devoted to traditional clothing in Lienz than to virtually any other product in town. Consequently, you'll find lots of outlets scattered throughout the tourist zone, one of the best of which is Trachtenstube **Krismer,** Andrä-Kranz-Gasse 4 (© **04852/62180**). The store has stacks of old-fashioned clothes (*Dirndls,* lederhosen, Loden coats, alpine hats with pheasants' feathers, embroidered suspenders) that correspond to East Tyrolean traditions. And if you're hankering for a sampling of the local breads, cheeses, sausages, and *Bundnerfleisch* (air-dried local beef that's reminiscent of beef jerky), consider dropping into any of the well-stocked local delicatessens, a particularly worthwhile example of which is **Feinkost Zuegg,** Rechter Iselweg (© **04852/66990**).

LIENZ AFTER DARK

No one ever seems to get thirsty in Lienz, where virtually every hotel and guesthouse has a *gemütlich*-looking *Stube* lined with varnished pine that's ready, willing, and eager to dispense steins of beer and locally distilled Schnapps. But if you're interested in equivalent bars that play dance music, consider **Life,** within the Dolomiten Hotel,

Dolomitenstrasse 2 (© **04852/62962**). It features a woodsy, alpine-derived decor where dozens of kegs of beer have been spilled over the years, and has been known to extend the dancing even onto the tabletops. It is open until 5am on weekends.

Incidentally, if your visit to Lienz happens to fall between early July and late September, at least part of your evening entertainment will be free. Every Saturday, Sunday, and Wednesday, beginning at 8pm, the city sponsors a 75-minute concert of traditional Tyrolean music, performed by musicians in *Trachten*, from a perch within the **Hauptplatz.** The only problem with these love fests of nostalgia is that they simply don't last long enough.

The second weekend in August in Lienz is the scheduled time for the **Stadtfest,** a public celebration of the contributions of Lienz to East Tyrolean culture. Expect kiosks scattered throughout the town's historic center selling food, wine, beer, and enough sausages to ring the city. There's also an ongoing series of afternoon and evening concerts by local singers and musicians, warbling away their odes to their heritage.

VORARLBERG

Austria's westernmost province is Vorarlberg, a land of high peaks, deep valleys, blue lakes, and meadowlands. The geographical contrasts within the small region bring visitors from the low Rhine Valley plains to glaciered alpine peaks in fewer than 37km (60 miles). The three biggest attractions are the ski slopes, the vast Lake Constance, and the lush forests of the Bregenzerwald. Vorarlberg is home to several renowned ski resorts and the high-altitude areas provide ideal conditions for skiing; one municipality, Damüls, receives the largest annual snowfall worldwide. The region's two best-known tourist centers, Lech and Zürs, are posh and expensive, but prices in the rest of the towns and resorts are quite reasonable.

13

Vorarlberg's ski slopes are linked together, offering miles and miles of trails. The Bregenzerwald (Bregenz Forest), on the northern part of the Vorarlberg alpine range, is stunning with its adventurous mountain ridges, and is home to the snowy Damuels and 21 other charming mountain villages.

Two annual special events take place in Vorarlberg during the summer: The Schubertiade in Hohenems and Schwarbenberg during the summer months, which is a music festival dedicated to the works of Franz Schubert; and the Bregenz operas, presented on an elaborately decorated stage floating in Lake Constance.

From Tyrol, you head west to reach Vorarlberg: The best gateway to the province is via the A12 from Innsbruck, or from Munich to the north on Route 96. Parking in the Vorarlberg region is rarely a problem, and, unless otherwise noted, you park for free.

THE WESTERN SIDE OF THE ARLBERG

The east side of Arlberg is discussed in chapter 12 (Innsbruck and Tyrol), so now begins the "west side story" of this massif that separates Vorarlberg from Tyrol. This part of Austria is one of the major winter sports Meccas in Europe. The leading resorts on the Arlberg massif, the highest mountain range in the Lechtal Alps, include **Lech** and **Zürs.** With an **Arlberg ski pass,** you can use the 84 ski tows, chairlifts, and cable cars located in

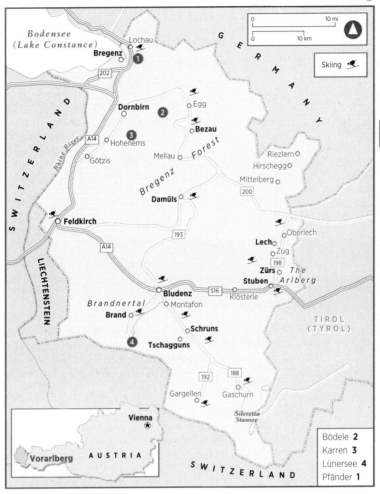

Map labels: Bodensee (Lake Constance), Lochau, Bregenz ❶, GERMANY, 202, Dornbirn ❷, Egg, Bezau, SWITZERLAND, Rhine River, A14, Hohenems, Mellau, Bregenz Forest, Riezlern, Hirschegg, Götzis, Mittelberg, 200, Damüls, Feldkirch, 193, A14, LIECHTENSTEIN, Lech, Oberlech, Zug, 198, Zürs, Stuben, The Arlberg, Bludenz, S16, Klösterle, TIROL (TYROL), Brandnertal, Montafon, Brand, Schruns, Tschagguns ❹, 192, 188, Gargellen, Gaschurn, Silvretta Stausee, Vienna ★, Voralberg, AUSTRIA, SWITZERLAND

Bödele **2**
Karren **3**
Lünersee **4**
Pfänder **1**

the entire Arlberg region. A 1-day Arlberg ski pass for this region costs 44.50€ for adults, 26.50€ for children under 16, and 40.50€ for seniors and teenagers.

Up through the **Flexen Pass,** you come to Zürs, a chic, elegant resort with skiing at **Trittkopf** and **Mahdloch.** Lech is larger, with easier skiing on the **Kriegerhorn** and **Mohnenfluh.**

SKIING IN ZÜRS & LECH   Part of Vorarlberg's popularity stems from these visible and stylish resorts. Both boast lofty altitudes that are high even by central European ski-resort standards; they enjoy access to more than 1,000m (3,281 ft.) of skiable hillside above Lech and almost 700m (2,297 ft.) of carefully maintained hillsides above Zürs, where midwinter snows accumulate in deep billowing drifts. In total, the area offers 276km (170 miles) of slopes and 180km (110 miles) of off-slope runs.

Zürs boasts straight downhill runs that have tested the skills of Olympic champions, as well as gracefully sculpted runs that pass rocky outcrops and thickets of trees. Lech, positioned in the center of a roster of north- and east-facing bowls and slopes, offers a greater number of ski options that challenge intermediate skiers as well as the experts. Although they are competing resorts, Zürs and Lech cooperate with each other. Ski passes allow access to the slopes and chairlifts and buses connect these resorts with each other and neighboring Oberlech.

Favorite ski venues around Lech include the **Kriegerhorn** and the less-popular **Rüfikopf,** which has perilously steep slopes and is subject to avalanche danger after snowstorms. In Zürs, the best skiing lies to the east of the resort, in regions known as the **Hexenboden** and the **Trittkopf,** but because of the morning glare, these slopes are most appealing in the afternoon. Morning skiers usually head out to the **Seekopf** and **Zürsersee** areas or the slopes running downhill from the **Muggengrat chairlift.**

Regardless of the resort you select, trails are usually impeccably groomed, the evening après-ski venues are the most fashionable in Austria, and Vorarlberg's scenery is among the most appealing in the world.

Zürs, Lech, and Oberlech—as well as the towns of Stubenbach and Zug—are linked by 84 lifts and cable cars (7 with heated seats), all accessible to holders of a ski pass for the area. Lifts and runs are close together, the path between Lech and Zürs can be traveled by ski, and a cable car, running daily from 7am to 1am, connects Oberlech to the heart of Lech: You can take a cable car from the heart of the resort to **Rüfikopf** (2,329m/7,641 ft.). Buses run between the towns during the day and night hours.

Lech ★★

Founded in the 14th century by émigrés from the Valais district of Switzerland, Lech still has its original **Pfarrkirche (Parish Church)** from that era. This archetype of a snug alpine ski village is practically joined to Oberlech, a traffic-free resort a little farther up the mountain. Lech stands at 1,440m (4,724 ft.); Oberlech is at 1,710m (5,610 ft.).

Zürs may be the more fashionable ski resort, but Lech is more diversified. Toboggan runs and horse-drawn sleigh rides are offered in addition to 15km (9 miles) of hiking trails. Lech offers warm-weather activities as well. Once the snow has melted, visitors come here to tour the **Upper Lech Valley,** which stretches to the scenic valley between the Lechtal and the Allgäu Alps. The high-altitude climate, fresh mountain air, quality drinking water, and brilliant scenery are favored by those looking for a relaxing trip. Demanding hiking and climbing possibilities make it an ideal spot for those seeking adventure as well. Rafting, mountain biking, and fly fishing in the surrounding trout-rich rivers make Lech and its neighbors an area of non-stop activity.

ESSENTIALS

GETTING THERE Set in the upper regions of the Arlberg Pass, Lech has no railway connections. Visitors are best advised to take the **train** to the rail stations at either end of the Arlberg Tunnel and then transfer to a bus that winds its way up the mountain passes to Lech. Passengers from either Vorarlberg or Tyrol should get off at Langen am Arlberg, the closest station to Lech. All Zurich–Vienna express trains stop here. Passengers then transfer to one of the half-dozen daily **buses** that depart for Lech (trip time: 25 min.). For bus information and schedules, call the Lech tourist office (see below).

Lech is 90km (56 miles) southeast of Bregenz, 648km (403 miles) west of Vienna, and 200km (124 miles) east of Zurich. If you're **driving** from Tyrol, take Route 198 north after you pass through the Arlberg Tunnel.

Keep in mind that hotels in Lech are adamant about not using an actual street number. As the town is small and compact, it should not be a problem to find the one you are looking for.

VISITOR INFORMATION The **tourist office** (© **05583/21610**) is in the town center. It's open in winter Monday to Saturday 9am to 6pm, Sunday 8am to noon and 3 to 5pm; in summer Monday to Saturday 8am to noon and 2 to 6pm, Sunday 8am to noon and 3 to 5pm. A 24-hour service line is also operational (© **810/966150**).

WARM-WEATHER EXPEDITIONS

From mid-June to mid-September, Lech offers an **Active-Inclusive Program.** As part of this program, any hotel guest in Lech gains automatic free access to the cable cars that run in the summer, buses, tennis courts, and a pool. Daily guided hikes (of various difficulties) covering 5–11km (3–7 miles) are also included in the program.

WHERE TO STAY
Very Expensive

Gasthof Post ★★★ Queen Beatrix of the Netherlands frequently visited this establishment, but even without its royal clientele, it's the noblest hotel in town. Behind the hotel's chalet facade ornamented with *trompe l'oeil* murals, the Moosbrugger family displays many 18th-century items, including alpine painted chests and baroque sculpture. Rooms come in a variety of sizes, but all contain rustic decorations, double-glazed windows, beamed ceilings, and excellent beds.

The hotel's convivial gathering places include a popular sun terrace and several bars. Zither and Austrian folk music is often performed in the peak winter months. Recent renovations have added 11 suites and a large spa to the facilities.

Dorf 11, A-6764 Lech. © **05583/22060.** Fax 05583/220623. www.postlech.com. 48 units. Winter 480€–640€ double, from 810€ suite; summer 220€–280€ double, from 410€ suite. Rates include breakfast. Half-board 30€ per person. MC, V. Parking 15€. In winter minimum stay of 7 days required. Closed late Apr–late June and Oct–early Dec. **Amenities:** 2 restaurants; bar; babysitting; children's playroom; fitness center; massage; nonsmoking rooms; indoor heated pool; room service; spa; tennis court. *In room:* TV, CD player, hairdryer, minibar, Wi-Fi.

Hotel Kristiania The most advanced skiers are often attracted to this tranquil retreat because it was built by the family of Othmar Schneider, the Olympic alpine ski champion. The many amenities make this a worthy government-rated 4-star hotel. Rooms facing south have balconies and mountain views, while north-facing rooms have views of the village and the valley, but no balconies. The Kristiania is a 3- to 5-minute walk above the resort's center. Most guests leave their ski equipment at the Skiraum in the center of town, where someone will wax their skis for the following day, so that they don't have to lug them uphill to the hotel. An on-site wine cellar offers diners 300 different labels, and a large terrace provides guests with a comfortable place for an afternoon drink. Kristiania's Otto Wagner restaurant received its first Wine Spectator award for service excellence in 2010.

Omesberg 331, A-6764 Lech. ✆ **05583/25610.** Fax 05583/3550. www.kristiania.at. 29 units. Winter 470€–780€ double, 840€–1,150€ suite; summer 340€–360€ double, 800€ suite. Half-board 40€ per person. AE, DC, MC, V. Parking 15€. Closed end Apr 25–end Nov. **Amenities:** 2 restaurants; bar; airport transfer (45€); babysitting; concierge; massage; nonsmoking rooms; indoor heated pool; room service; spa. *In room:* TV, CD player, hairdryer, minibar (in some), Wi-Fi.

Expensive

Hotel Arlberg ★★★   Built in 1965, the Hotel Arlberg is a sprawling chalet well equipped for an alpine trip in any season, and it's one of the only government-rated five-star hotels open during the summer in Lech. The interior offers regional antiques, crafted paneling, elegant accessories, and a baronial fireplace. Rooms are excellently furnished with antiques, luxurious carpeting, comfortable beds, and double-glazed windows. Most open onto picture windows and individual balconies. Medium-size bathrooms are done in marble with corner tubs and dual basins.

The food served in the richly outfitted dining room is as generous as the decor itself. The Schneider family directs a team of chefs who prepare Italian- as well as Austrian-inspired foods. Guests appreciate the intimate lighting in the bar after a day in the brilliant sunshine. Meals are also served, in season, on a flower-bedecked sun terrace. The hotel is entirely nonsmoking, aside from the bar.

A-6764 Lech. ✆ **05583/21340.** Fax 05583/213425. www.arlberghotel.at. 52 units. Winter 430€–700€ double, from 650€ suite; summer 550€–660€ double, from 760€ suite. Rates include half-board. MC, V. Free parking. Closed May–June and Oct–Nov. **Amenities:** 2 restaurants; bar; babysitting; fitness center; massage; 2 pools (1 indoor heated, 1 outdoor available only in summer); room service; spa; tennis court. *In room:* TV, minibar (in some), hairdryer.

Moderate

Hotel Lech & Pension Chesa Rosa   This very pleasant establishment, open year-round, is 5 minutes from the ski lifts. The interior of the two-chalet complex is handsomely paneled and accented with soft lighting. The recently renovated, medium-size rooms are comfortably furnished and have small but tidy bathrooms with tub/shower combinations. At the hotel restaurant, you can enjoy a fondue evening and a rustic dinner with Zither music (Austrian and international cuisine is served). It is open only to hotel guests. Special events include toboggan games at night, horse-drawn sleigh rides with torches, and even cocktail parties in cable cars.

A-6764 Lech. ✆ **05583/22890.** Fax 05583/2727. www.hotel-lech.info. 40 units. Winter 160€–350€ double; summer 100€–160€ double. Rates include half-board in winter, breakfast only in summer. MC, V. **Amenities:** Restaurant; bar; babysitting; massage; nonsmoking rooms; sauna; steam bath; tanning beds; Wi-Fi (2€ per day). *In room:* TV, hairdryer.

PLACES TO STAY IN NEARBY OBERLECH

Oberlech is known as the "terrace of the Arlberg mountains," where ski slopes end at your hotel's doorstep. Oberlech is a car-free village; some hardy souls struggle about a kilometer (½ mile) uphill on foot from Lech to reach Oberlech, a site of about 10 hotels and a grocery store. The best way to reach Oberlech is to ride the **Bergbahn Oberlech cable car,** which operates daily from 7am to 1am during the winter season (✆ **05583/2350** for information), from the center of Lech to Oberlech. Those with ski passes ride free. Otherwise, the round-trip ticket costs 12.80€ for adults and 7.20€ for children during the winter, 6.20€ and 3.40€ during the summer.

If your hotel is in Oberlech, park your car at the base of the Bergbahn Oberlech (the cost of which is usually included in the price of your hotel), and carry your luggage to the cable car, where the operator will phone ahead to your hotel. An employee will usually meet you at the top to assist with your luggage.

Hotel Montana ★ 👜 Above the village, this government-rated four-star hotel opens onto a large sun terrace looking out over Lech. The light-grained chalet has a stylish interior and its cafe/bar area is an attractive place for an afternoon drink. Furnished in an alpine style, the rather small rooms are exceedingly cozy on long winter nights. The bathrooms have lovely tub/shower combinations. Owner Guy Ortlieb, an expatriate Frenchman, organizes weekly farmer buffets, cocktail and gala evenings, buffets dedicated to international cuisine, and generally does everything he can to make guests feel at ease. The hotel restaurant, **Zur Kanne,** serves a high-quality French cuisine and is also known for its fondue (p. 417).

Oberlech 276, A-6764 Oberlech. ✆ **05583/24600.** Fax 05583/246038. www.montanaoberlech.at. 47 units. Winter 250€–540€ double; from 300€ suite. Rates include half-board. AE, MC, V. Parking 13€. Closed end Apr–end Nov. **Amenities:** Restaurant; cafe/bar; child entertainment; fitness center; indoor heated pool; room service; sauna, steam bath; tanning beds. *In room:* TV, minibar (in some), hairdryer.

Sonnenburg Built as one of the first hotels in Oberlech, and opening onto the village square, this large double chalet has wood-trimmed balconies, a sun terrace looking down the hillside, and a warm, intimate, woodsy decor. The newly renovated and well-maintained rooms have modern comforts, though they lack alpine charm. Nonetheless, the hotel is a welcome retreat on a snowy night, and the bathrooms, though small, are equipped with tub/shower combinations and are handsomely cared for by the bevy of maids. Hypo-allergenic rooms are also available. A short distance away—connected by an underground passage—stands the hotel's annex, Landhaus Sonnenburg, whose pleasantly furnished rooms rent for slightly less than those in the main building.

A-6764 Oberlech. ✆ **05583/2147.** Fax 05583/214736. www.sonnenburg.at. 81 units. 250€–420€ double; from 340€ suite. Rates include half-board. MC, V. Closed May–Nov. **Amenities:** 2 restaurants; 2 bars; indoor heated pool; fitness center; spa; room service; babysitting; nonsmoking rooms. *In room:* TV, minibar, hairdryer.

WHERE TO EAT
Expensive
Bauernstube/Johannisstubli ★★ AUSTRIAN/INTERNATIONAL These restaurants are the best recommended and most legendary in Lech. The older of the two, Bauernstube (its official name is the Alte Goldener Berg), is the oldest building in Lech, a weathered and nostalgically evocative farmhouse from the 1400s that serves such traditional recipes as fondues (five different kinds). The 2-*Toque* award-winning Johannisstubli lies within the main body of the Goldener Berg Hote. Here, in a setting that's among the most glamorous in an admittedly glamorous town, you can enjoy carefully prepared international dishes that change according to the season and the chef's inspiration. The most popular are the eight-course menus, serving small-sized Austrian-inspired "tapas." The two restaurants are under different roofs,

though managed by the same owner, and operate under the same theme: Only the finest local products, organic vegetables, and food that is allowed to "live" on its own.

In the Hotel Goldener Berg, Oberlech 117. ✆ **05583/2205.** Reservations required. Main courses 26€–45€. 8-course menus at Johannistube 140€–200€ with wine accompaniment. MC, V. Bauernstube daily 11am–11pm; Johannisstube 11am–2:30pm and 7–10:30pm. Both closed May–June, Oct–Nov.

Hotel Berghof Restaurant ★ AUSTRIAN/INTERNATIONAL   Peter Burger and his family run this popular government-rated four-star hotel dining room with white walls and wood trim. Big windows look out over the baby lift and the ski slopes. You might enjoy cream of cauliflower soup, saddle of lamb, *Tafelspitz*, a filet of chamois with salad greens and a red-wine dressing, or medallions of veal in calvados with curried potatoes. For dessert, perhaps you'll sample a soufflé of curd cheese. Year after year, this kitchen turns out respectable and well-prepared food that has pleased some of the most demanding palates in Europe. Fixed-course meals change on a daily basis.

A-6764 Lech. ✆ **05583/2635.** Fax 05583/26355. Reservations required. Main courses 20€–30€; 3-course menu 39€, 5-course 48€. MC, V. Daily noon–10pm. Closed end Apr–end June and end Sept–early Dec.

Post Stuben ★★ AUSTRIAN/NOUVELLE   The Moosbrugger family, owners of the previously recommended Gasthof Post hotel (see above), also presides over the restaurant, a member of Relais & Châteaux luxury hotels and gourmet restaurants. Step into an old-fashioned imperial world of antiques, alpine paneling, and tiled stoves. Many guests are on half-board, but nonresidents can select from two dining salons and an a la carte menu or, perhaps more recommendable, a fixed-price menu. The latter is pricey, but you get your money's worth in fresh ingredients prepared with care and flair. Game is featured in season, and Austrian classics, including *Tafelspitz*, are always served. Other delicacies include Trout *meunière*, Chateaubriand, venison, rabbit pâté, and an impressive dessert list.

In the Gasthof Post hotel, Dorf 11, A-6764 Lech. ✆ **05583/22060.** Reservations recommended. Main courses 26€–38€, fixed-price menu 85€. DC, MC, V. Daily 7–9pm. Closed mid-Apr to June 24 and Oct 1–Nov 30.

Moderate

Fux ★★ EUROPEAN/ASIAN   "House Fux" is home to two kitchens: One that serves Euro-Asian fusion cuisine, the other a steak house. From the former, east meets west in novel mixtures and aromas, while the latter offers everything pertaining to steak, from bison to salmon to hand-massaged Wagyu beef. Modern versions of sushi and maki are offered along with specialties such as calamari with cilantro, tomato–chili essence and artichoke, and braised lamb with coriander, yogurt, spinach, and almonds. Set menus (Vegetarian Menu and Menu of the Aromas) are offered by the Euro-Asian restaurant at reasonable prices. Bring an appetite. The jazz bar will provide the music, which opens at 4pm every day.

Omesberg 587, A-6764 Lech. ✆ **05583/2992.** Reservations recommended. Main courses 28€–85€, fixed menu 59€–72€. MC, V. Euro-Asian restaurant open daily 6–10pm, steakhouse 6pm–1am. Closed May–Nov.

Hus Nr. 8 ★ 🍴 AUSTRIAN   The building in which this restaurant is currently housed was first built in 1760 as a *Walserhaus*, a log cabin of the people from the Valais valley who settled in the region centuries ago. The building was renovated in the 1990s but still possesses its ancient charm. The owners pride themselves on the hominess of the establishment, where it is not only tasted but also experienced. What you order here is guaranteed to be truly local: *Blunzengröstl* (blood sausage *gröstl*) and *Walser Käsesuppe* (Valais cheese soup), as well as regional fondue favorites.

In the Hotel Krone, A-6764 Lech. (✆) **05583/33220.** Reservations recommended. Main courses 23€–30€. MC, V. Daily noon–2pm and 7–9:30pm. Closed end Apr–mid June, early Oct–early Dec.

Kronen Stuben ★ AUSTRIAN   Located in the previously recommended Hotel Krone, this restaurant is patronized by many nonguests. The Pfefferkorns are your charming hosts. The restaurant's two parlors have preserved their 17-century elegance. Chef specialties include goose liver tart with apricot and braised calf cheeks with Périgord truffles. One dish that invariably pleases is alpine trout from local streams prepared virtually any way you desire. Dishes are rich in flavor and texture, and the chefs try to use very fresh ingredients.

In the Hotel Krone, A-6764 Lech. (✆) **05583/2551.** Reservations recommended. Main courses 23€–30€. MC, V. Daily noon–2pm and 7–9:30pm. Closed mid-Apr to early July and mid Sept–early Dec.

PLACES TO EAT IN NEARBY OBERLECH & ZUG

Auerhahn ★ 🎁 AUSTRIAN   This restaurant prides itself on its role as the oldest dining spot in and around Lech. Set on the outskirts of town, in the hamlet of Zug, the 17th-century building was originally a farmhouse. The restaurant serves large quantities of homemade noodle dishes, four kinds of fondue (Chinese, bourguignonne, cheese, and in summer, chocolate for dessert), game dishes (such as venison in red-wine sauce), plus wine and beer. Desserts tend toward traditional favorites such as strudel smothered in vanilla sauce. The kitchen seems immune to passing fads and fancies in cuisine, and turns out consistently reliable dishes based on tried-and-true methods.

Zug Nr. 12, A-6764 Zug. (✆) **05583/2754.** Reservations recommended. Main courses 15€–30€. No credit cards. Winter Mon–Sat 11am–midnight; summer Tues–Sun 11am–midnight. Closed mid Sept–mid Dec and end Apr–mid July.

Gasthof Rote Wand ★ AUSTRIAN/INTERNATIONAL   Lying in the hamlet of Zug (3km/2 miles north of Lech) near the onion-domed village church, this pleasantly old-fashioned place serves meals in an unpretentious *Beisl* (bistro) tradition. A specialty of the house is *Spätzle* (egg noodles) with cheese; roast veal and pork, warm cabbage salad, and *Tafelspitz* (boiled beef) are also available. Some diners come for the fondue bourguignonne or *chinoise*, which could be followed by a soup made from venison purée. If you're up for dessert, the hot curd strudel is heavenly.

The Gasthof Rote Wand now offers 26 rooms and in 1998 they built 12 apartments. A standard double room costs 330€ to 470€ including half-board, 250€ in the summer. Suites cost 380€ including half-board for two (265€ in summer). Family suites and suites for larger groups are also available.

A-6764 Zug. (✆) **05583/3435.** Reservations required. Main courses 18€–36€. MC, V. Mon–Sat 6–9pm. Closed late Apr–end Nov.

Zur Kanne FRENCH/ALSATIAN/AUSTRIAN   This restaurant is run by Alsace-born Guy Ortlieb, who operates the previously recommended Hotel Montana (p. 415) and sets very high standards, and was rewarded for his efforts with two toques from Gault Millau. It is known for serving the best fish in the valley, including a filet of freshwater *fera* from Lake Constance. Offerings include homemade foie gras, and filet of roebuck in red-wine sauce. The waiter presents a menu with no prices—the fixed-price menus are best. Many customers prefer to dine on the sun terrace, even during the chilly winter months when electric heaters are strategically placed.

In the Hotel Montana, Oberlech 276. ℭ **05583/2460.** Reservations required for dinner. Main courses 28€–38€; fixed-price dinner 46€–58€. MC, V. Daily noon–6pm and 7–9:30pm. Closed Apr 27 to the end of Nov.

SHOPPING

Most of the shops in Lech are found along the resort's main thoroughfare, the **Hauptstrasse,** and all steadfastly refuse to identify themselves with an individual street number. Lech offers sporting equipment from almost every important manufacturer in Europe. Three of the most impressive shops include **Sportalp** (ℭ **05583/ 2110), Sporthaus Strolz** (ℭ **05583/23610**), and **Pfefferkorn** (ℭ **05583/2224**), all on Hauptstrasse. If you're interested in souvenirs or folkloric clothing, Sporthaus Strolz and Pfefferkorn both offer Austrian handicrafts, lederhosen, and *Trachten* (traditional Austrian clothing).

LECH APRÈS-SKI & AFTER DARK

Lech has the most vibrant après-ski scene in Vorarlberg, and if you ever get bored here, you can check out the action at the satellite resorts or head over to Zürs.

The evening begins with a tea dance at the **Hotel Tannbergerhof** (ℭ **05583/ 2202**), where Veronica Heller welcomes you; later in the evening you can enjoy disco music. It's open from December to April 14 daily from 9pm to 5am. Beer starts at 4.50€; hard drinks start at 10€.

Oberlech's **Red Umbrella,** operated by the December-to-April **Petersboden Sport Hotel** (ℭ **05583/3232**), is the most famous afternoon rendezvous for skiers in the Lech area. The hydraulically operated red umbrella, approximately 11m (36 feet) wide, is set on an elevated wooden deck. It's raised at 10am each morning and lowered each afternoon at 4 or 5pm, depending on business. Under the umbrella there's a circular bar where you can sit on a stool and order drinks such as *Jägertee* (laced with rum) or vodka *feigen* (with floating figs). Of course, in the cold, schnapps remains the favorite drink. The food here is simple and filling; a popular item is *Germknödel,* a jam-stuffed steamed dumpling covered with poppy seeds.

Stuben

This little village and winter resort is almost a suburb of Lech, lying on the southern fringes of the larger village on the west side of the Arlberg Pass. Stuben was first established as an imperial post office, and mail-coach drivers' last rest stop before crossing the Voarlberg Pass. It can be reached by bus, but the most romantic way to go from Lech is by horse-drawn sleigh.

The hamlet has been a way station for alpine travelers for many centuries, but in recent years, it has become a modern ski area with its own lift station on **Albona.** (It was the birthplace of Hannes Schneider, the great ski instructor.) Lacking the glitz and glamour of Zürs, its prices are much more reasonable and its location is preferred by those more interested in skiing than socializing. Stuben has links with St. Anton in Tyrol, as well as with Lech and Zürs.

Stuben is especially geared for family enjoyment, with children's ski courses, special meals, and hosts who help the small fry feel at home.

The helpful tourist office (℃ **05582/399**) is inside the Hotel Post (under separate management) in the village center. The office is open in winter daily 9am to noon and 3 to 6pm; in summer Monday to Friday 9am to noon.

ESSENTIALS

GETTING THERE   Although a casual glance at some maps might lead newcomers to believe that Stuben lies on the main rail lines between Innsbruck and Bregenz, this is not the case. Stuben-bound passengers must get off the **train** at the tunnel's western mouth, **Langen am Arlberg,** and then take one of the dozen or so daily **buses** that wind their way upward during the 5-minute ride to Stuben. For rail information, contact ℃ **05/1717** (www.oebb.at).

Drivers should follow the directions to Lech and then follow signs to Stuben, which is 10km (6 miles) south of Lech and 24km (15 miles) east of Bludenz.

WHERE TO STAY

Hotel Mondschein ★★   This building dates from 1739, when it was constructed as a rambling private home near the village church. Today it's the second-oldest hotel in Stuben, and its antique accents include forest-green shutters and weathered siding. The snug and cozy rooms have alpine accents and comfortable beds. Crackling fires add to the ambience (and warmth), and secondary heating is provided by traditional ceramic-tiled stoves. The hotel is a well-recommended government-rated three-star choice. The hotel's mountain hut, about a 10-minute walk from the main building, throws a lively après-ski party every Thursday evening.

A-6762 Stuben. ℃ **05582/511.** Fax 05582/736. www.mondschein.com. 33 units. 160€–270€ double, from 190€ suites. Rates include half-board. MC, V. Parking 8.50€. **Amenities:** Restaurant; bar; babysitting; nonsmoking rooms; indoor heated pool; sauna. *In room:* TV, hairdryer.

Hotel Post ★   When it was built in 1608, this comfortable, government-rated three-star hotel served as a shelter for tired mail-coach drivers. Most of the rustically attractive public rooms have fireplaces and deep-seated chairs. On the premises are a dining room and two old *Stuben*, or taverns, where people can drink and dine a la carte. In 1997, a third *Stube* was added to the existing two, using old timbers and antique panels removed from an older site for authenticity. The hotel is just at the edge of the village. Accommodations are spacious and decorated in a bright alpine style. Rooms at the nearby Hunting Lodge Post, or Jägdhaus (which is part of the hotel), cost the same but are slightly less desirable.

A-6762 Stuben. ℃ **05582/761.** Fax 05582/762. www.hotelpost.com. 70 units. Winter 140€–280€ double; summer 94€–130€ double. Rates include half-board. One week minimum stay in winter. MC, V. Parking free outside, 9€ garage. Closed May–mid June and Oct–Nov. **Amenities:** Restaurant; bar; infrared cabins; massage; nonsmoking rooms; 2 saunas; solarium; steam bath; Wi-Fi. *In room:* TV, hairdryer, Internet.

Zürs ★

An immaculate resort lying 4km (2½ miles) south of Lech in a sunny valley, Zürs (1,708m/5,604 ft.) consists of about 1km (½ mile) of typical white stucco Vorarlberger buildings with carved-wood balconies. The resort, really a collection of extremely expensive hotels, is reached via the scenic **Flexen Road.**

Zürs is strictly a winter resort, and nearly all hotels close in summer. Because of its location, Zürs is avalanche prone, but these potential snowslides do not deter the loyal Zürs clientele.

A chairlift east of Zürs takes you to **Hexenboden** (2,349m/7,707 ft.), and a cable lift goes to **Trittkopf** (2,402m/7,881 ft.), which has a mountain restaurant and sun terrace.

In the west, a chairlift will take you to **Seekopf** (2,188m/7,179 ft.), and from the windows and terrace of the restaurant here, you can see the frozen **Zürser Lake.** A chairlift travels from Seekopf to the top station at 2,451m (8,041 ft.).

The year-round population of Lech is 1,000 people, but the year-round population of Zürs is just 100: Zürs is almost dead in the summer. Guests to Zürs are smug about returning season after season, some for as many as 30 years in a row, and it seems like everyone knows everyone else. Every hotel in Zürs has facilities that let guests ski directly up to a point near the hotel's entrance.

ESSENTIALS

GETTING THERE   The **buses** described in the Lech section (p. 413) stop in Zürs about 10 minutes before their scheduled arrival in Lech. Likewise, if you're driving, follow the same directions for Zürs as for Lech (p. 412). Zürs is 90km (56 miles) southeast of Bregenz, 34km (21 miles) east of Bludenz, and 43km (27 miles) west of Landeck in Tyrol. If you're arriving at the Zurich airport, as many do, Zürs is 240km (149 miles) east. Many of the hotels offer a shuttle bus service from the airport to Zürs.

The nearest **railway station** is in the town of **Langen,** 14km (9 miles) away. Several direct trains a day arrive from Innsbruck (trip time: 1¼ hr.). For rail information, contact ☎ **05/1717** (www.oebb.at). From Langen, yellow postal buses (a 25-min. ride) and taxis make frequent runs to and from Zürs.

VISITOR INFORMATION   The **tourist office** (☎ **05583/2245**) is in the town center, 6763 Zürs. It's open Monday to Friday 10am to 2pm, and a 24-hour **hotline** will answer your questions when the office is closed (☎ **810/966150**).

WHERE TO STAY

Zürs is one of the most expensive ski resorts in the world—*prices are lethal.* If you're seeking bargains—and want to avoid celebrities—other resorts in the area offer the same quality alpine skiing environment without the excessiveness.

Very Expensive

Central Sporthotel Edelweiss ★   One of the genuinely picturesque hotels of Zürs, with balconies and an old-fashioned look that corresponds to its role as one of the oldest hotels in town, this hotel has kept up with modern tastes and a kind of urban-hipster mode that corresponds well with upscale clients from Munich and Vienna. Bedrooms are spacious yet cozy and brightly painted, with handsome furniture and comfy beds. The hotel has an elegant dining room reserved for residents on half-board, as well as two additional eateries, the ultra-upscale gourmet venue known as Chesa, with seating for a maximum of only 30 diners at a time, and the more democratic (and cheaper) Flexenhäusl, a mountainside affair specializing in fondues, which is open to the general public.

A-6763 Zürs. ☎ **05583/2662.** Fax 05583/3533. www.edelweiss.net. 60 units. 300 €–600€ double; from 500€ suite. Rates include half-board. MC, V. Parking free outdoors, 13€ garage. Closed May–early Dec. **Amenities:** 2 restaurants; bar; nightclub; babysitting; boutiques; fitness center; massage; room service; sauna. *In room:* TV, minibar, hairdryer, safe, Wi-Fi.

Hotel Zürserhof ★★   An exclusive and private world unto itself, this hotel—the most luxurious of mountain refuges—consists of five interconnected chalets in the shelter of the valley. This self-sufficient hotel has been cited as one of the best in central Europe, with virtually everything under one roof.

Accommodations consist of private apartments, many of which have stone fireplaces, bars, double-glazed windows looking out onto mountain views, and other opulent comforts. The spacious bathrooms have plenty of shelf space, robes, and tub/shower combinations. Suites have Roman-style baths.

Live music is offered almost every night in the cellar bar, and the hotel's restaurant (p. 422) is open to the public.

A-6763 Zürs. (☎) **05583/2513.** Fax 05583/3165. www.zuerserhof.at. 81 units. 430€–850€ double; 490€–4,200€ suite. Rates include full board. MC, V. Free parking. Closed mid-Apr to early Dec. **Amenities:** Restaurant; bar; babysitting; fitness center; massage; indoor heated pool; room service; spa; 4 tennis courts. *In room:* TV, minibar, hairdryer, Wi-Fi.

Expensive

Hotel Enzian ★ Set above the bustle of Zürs, this hotel's newer rooms are more luxurious and have more amenities than those in the older core. Bathrooms are spacious, with towel warmers and most with tubs. The hotel is at the edge of the village, on a hill behind a church and near the cable-car station—you can ski from the front door to all the lifts. You'll enjoy a glass of *Glühwein* in the alpine *Stube*. On the premises are two dining rooms, a cozy bar, and a sun terrace with waiter service.

A-6763 Zürs. (☎)**05583/22420.** Fax 05583/3404. www.hotelenzian.com. 32 units. 300€–360€ double; from 320€ suite. Rates include half-board. MC, V. Parking free outside, 10€ garage. Closed May–Nov. **Amenities:** 2 restaurants; bar; babysitting; badminton courts; fitness center; games room; massage; nonsmoking rooms; room service; spa; squash court. *In room:* TV, hairdryer, Wi-Fi.

Hotel Erzberg ★★ 🏨 Within its category, this is one of the most appealing hotels in Zürs. The hotel's location, close to the ski lifts, is ideal. Built in 1972, the comfortable interior features wrought-iron, soft lighting, and softly burnished paneling crafted from local pines. Rooms are cozy and warm, and each contains a good bed and a well-equipped private bathroom.

Although there's a separate restaurant on the premises that's open to the public, hotel residents eat in their own dining room. Regardless of where it's consumed, the food is well prepared, flavorful, and served in generous quantities. The day begins with a buffet breakfast, and dinner is four courses, including a big salad buffet. Sometimes the hotel arranges special events, such as candlelight dinners and welcome cocktail parties.

A-6763 Zürs. (☎) **05583/26440.** Fax 05583/264444. www.hotel-erzberg.at. 26 units. 190€–390€ double; from 300€ suite. Rates include half-board. MC, V. Free parking outdoors, 13€ in covered garage. Closed mid Apr–Nov. **Amenities:** Restaurant; bar; babysitting; infrared cabin; massage; nonsmoking rooms; room service; sauna; steam bath; tanning bed. *In room:* TV, hairdryer, Wi-Fi.

WHERE TO EAT

Hotel Hirlanda ★ AUSTRIAN This hotel, originally built as a small inn in the 1920s, houses a popular restaurant frequented by ski instructors. The kitchen prepares hearty Vorarlberg fare as well as more delicate Mediterranean dishes. Spicy seasoned filet steaks are prepared on the wooden charcoal grill. Barbary goose with orange sauce is another delectable main course. The pastry chef concocts different surprises every night, perhaps Málage sabayon with mango slices. The owners keep the fireplace blazing to take the chill off the coldest winter night.

Twenty-nine cozy, alpine-style bedrooms are also rented. On the half-board plan, doubles cost 280€ to 385€, and suites are 345€ to 466€. Parking costs 12€ for the indoor garage, outdoor parking for free.

A-6763 Zürs. ✆ **05583/2262.** Reservations required. Lunch main courses 17€–30€; dinner main courses 22€–35€. MC, V. Daily 11:30am–11pm. Closed mid-Apr to early Dec.

Hotel Zürserhof Restaurant ★★ INTERNATIONAL   A rich and famous clientele dines here, occasionally in black tie in season, especially for the Sunday galas (evening dress required). The dress codes have been relaxed for the rest of the week (only jackets for men), but the glamour of this hotel may still only be desirable for those wishing to see and be seen. Even the unpretentious cuisine of rural Austria is expensive here (although well prepared). Main courses might include a delectable roast suckling pig, Viennese roast chicken, roast veal, bratwurst, and roast pork. Many guests prefer to dine in the *Stube,* which has a traditional alpine decor. The kitchen also prepares the most beautiful cheese buffet in town. The gala nights offer an extensive dessert buffet, with farmer buffets and fondues offered during the week.

A-6763 Zürs. ✆ **05583/2513.** Reservations required. Main courses 25€–35€. MC, V. Daily noon–2pm and 7:30–9pm. Closed mid-Apr to Oct.

Restaurant Chesa INTERNATIONAL   This sporty, elegant enterprise is decorated in Kaiser gold, yellow, and green, and its ambiance is stimulating on a winter's night. Main courses include zander filet with a warm vinaigrette sauce, or beef filet stuffed with goose liver and served with a sabayon of chives and sautéed vegetables. The cheese board is impressive, as is the wine list. A fresh salad buffet is offered daily, along with wholefood selections for health-conscious guests. After dinner, many guests head to the basement dance club for late-night entertainment.

In the Central Sporthotel Edelweiss, A-6763 Zürs. ✆ **05583/2662.** Reservations required. Main courses 15€–30€. MC, V. Tues–Sun noon–2pm and 7–9:30pm. Closed May–Nov.

ZÜRS AFTER DARK

After dinner, many hotel guests retreat to their hotel bars—or even up to their rooms—for privacy and R&R before braving the wilds of the Voralberger Alps for another day of skiing. But if you're tempted to go dancing, the resort's two dance clubs are **Vernissage,** in the Robinson Club Alpenrose (✆ **0676/84070777**), and the **Disco Zürserl,** in the Hotel Edelweiss (✆ **05583/2668**). Neither charges any cover; beers cost around 4.50€ each. Of the two, Vernissage is likely to be more crowded because of its location within the largest hotel in Zürs. Both open for business at 9pm daily during the peak season and continue until the last client staggers home. Disco Zürserl is closed on Sundays and Mondays during the slower months.

THE MONTAFON VALLEY ★★

Montafon is a high alpine valley known for its sun and powdery snow. It stretches some 42km (26 miles) at the southern tip of Vorarlberg, with the Ill River flowing through on its way to join the Rhine. The valley, filled with mountain villages and major winter recreation areas, is encircled by the mountain ranges of Rätikon, Silvretta, and Verwall. Ernest Hemingway hiked to this area in 1925, attracted by the beauty of the area and the copious amounts of alcohol in local bars. He wrote *The Sun Also Rises* during his time spent in Schruns.

Montafon has been called a "ski stadium" because of its highly integrated ski region. One ski pass covers unlimited use of 70 cable cars, chairlifts, and T-bars in all four of the valley's main ski areas, as well as transportation among the resorts.

Hochjoch-Zamang offers skiing in the back bowls and down the front, and is the main mountain at Schruns. Tschagguns has **Grabs-Golm** for some easier runs. **Silvretta-Nova** at Gaschurn and St. Gallenkirch is a superb ski circus on several mountains, and the **Schafberg** of Gargellen is secluded in a side valley.

Exploring Schruns & Tschagguns ★

Schruns is the largest resort in the Montafon Valley, lying on the right bank of the Ill River. Tschagguns (a smaller resort) is on the left, and the hamlets are so close (less than 1.5km/1 mile apart) that they can be treated as one.

Although known for their winter sports, these towns are also popular in summer. The warm-weather allure here revolves around walking, hiking, and climbing in the alpine majesty of Vorarlberg. Locals pride themselves on the nearness of **Pizbuin,** the highest peak in Vorarlberg (3,312m/10,866 ft. above sea level). Throughout the Montafon Valley, yellow-and-black signs point out natural attractions and destinations, and how long it will take to get there. For more information about climbing, hiking, canyoneering, glacier climbing, and other outdoor adventures, call **Bergführer Montafon** (© 066443/11445 from 1–8pm weekdays; www.montafon.bergfuehrer. at), a local climbing club. Ski lift passes are also sold in the summer (for hiking and climbing, not skiing). These passes include unlimited lift rides as well as free access to all the valley's public pools. For more information, call the tourist office (see below).

Above Tschagguns, at Latschau, you can take a cable railway or chairlift to **Grabs-Golm** at 1,388m (4,554 ft.), a small but fascinating ski region with several lifts, including a four-person lift going up to 2,135m (7,005 ft.). These slopes attract both beginners and experts alike, and are known for World Cup races. While you're at Golm, you can stop at a rustic little restaurant or a modern self-service one, and then take the surface lift to Hochegga at 1,587m (5,207 ft.).

Essentials

GETTING THERE Almost two dozen **trains** depart from Bludenz every day for Schruns (trip time: 20 min.). Schruns is the last stop on this line, and several buses head into the nearby valleys from Schruns. For rail information, contact © 05/1717 (www.oebb.at).

From the railway station in Schruns, several trains and about a dozen buses per day make the 4-minute trip to Tschagguns's main square, **Dorfplatz.** If you are laden with luggage, you might want to take a taxi.

Schruns is 698km (434 miles) west of Vienna and 63km (39 miles) southeast of Bregenz. From Bregenz, **drive** southeast along Autobahn A14 until you reach Bludenz. At Bludenz, follow the MONTAFON signs and head up the valley until you reach Schruns.

VISITOR INFORMATION The **tourist office** at Schruns is located at Silvretastrasse 6 (© 05556/721660), in the village center of Schruns. Open mid-December to mid-April and mid-June to the beginning of October, Monday to Friday 8am to 6pm, Saturday 9am to noon and 3 to 6pm (winter) and 9am to noon and 4 to 6pm (summer), and Sunday 10am to noon. Outside of these months, opening hours are Monday to Friday, 8am to 5pm. In Tschagguns, the **office** is located at Latschaustrasse 1, open

Monday to Friday 8 to noon, 1:30 to 6pm (during the peak seasons), Saturday during the winter 9am to noon, 3 to 6pm, and in summer 9am to noon and 4 to 6pm. Open Sundays from 4 to 6pm. In the off season, open weekdays 8am to noon, and 1:30 to 5pm.

Where to Stay & Eat
IN SCHRUNS

Hotel Krone 🍴 Owned by members of the Gmeiner family since 1847, this yellow baroque building has white trim, black shutters, and a hipped roof with a pointed tower. It's one of the few baroque structures in a resort loaded with chalets. The hotel has a shaded beer garden, a collection of rustic artifacts, and ornate paneling whose rich glow is reflected in the leaded windows. Rooms are pleasantly furnished, comfortable, and snug, with excellent beds and small shower-only bathrooms. The in-house restaurant, the Montafoner Stube, offers well-prepared and beautifully served cuisine. It's open daily for lunch and dinner, and welcomes all patrons.

Ausserlitzstrasse 2, A-6780 Schruns. ☎ **05556/722550.** Fax 05556/7225522. www.austria-urlaub. com. 12 units. Winter 200€–350€ double; summer 160€ double. Rates include half-board. MC, V. Closed last 2 weeks of Apr. **Amenities:** Restaurant; bar; room service; sauna. *In room:* TV, minibar, hairdryer.

Löwen Hotel Schruns ★★★ Built in 1974, this is the most lavish hotel in Schruns. The hotel's creative designers decided to give guests the best of both the alpine and modern worlds. The rambling chalet sits back on a large lawn in the center of town. The shrub-dotted lawn, however, actually rests on top of a modern steel, glass, and concrete construction. In many ways, this is a town social center and, except for outdoor recreation, it provides almost everything you need. Rooms are imaginatively designed and well furnished, with good, comfortable beds and small bathrooms. The recently added spa is fully equipped and considered one of the best in Austria.

The hotel is home to the upscale Restaurant Edel-Weiss, which serves nouvelle cuisine, and the more casual and *gemütlich* Restaurant Barga.

Silvrettastrasse 8, A-6780 Schruns. ☎ **05556/7141.** Fax 05556/73553. www.loewen-hotel.com. 83 units. Winter 260€–420€ double, from 370€ suite; summer 250€–315€ double, from 350€ suite. Rates include half-board. AE, DC, MC, V. Parking 6.50€. Closed mid Apr–mid May and late Nov–mid-Dec. **Amenities:** 2 restaurants; bar; babysitting; fitness center; massage; nonsmoking rooms; 2 heated pools (1 indoor, 1 outdoor); room service; rooms for those w/limited mobility; spa. *In room:* TV, hairdryer, minibar, Wi-Fi.

IN TSCHAGGUNS

Hotel Montafoner Hof ★★ This government-rated four-star hotel is the premier resort at Tschagguns. A striking peach color on the outside, the Montafoner Hof is decorated inside with Austrian woods to lend it an authentic alpine atmosphere. All

The Gathering Place of Town

Café Feuerstein, Dorfstrasse 6, Schruns (☎ **05556/72129**), is the best-known place in town for ice cream and pastries. Housed in an antique building in the town center, the establishment serves attractively decorated pastries—some are miniature works of art. Coffee begins at 2.50€, pastries start at 2.60€, and individual pizzas range from 6€ to 12€. It's open noon to 9pm. Closed Easter to June and late October to mid-December, and closed Thursday during the summer.

of the well-furnished rooms come with good beds, lounge corners, and balconies with mountain views, plus small but well-organized bathrooms with ample shelf space and tub/shower combinations.

The Montafon Stube offers a rather glamorous fixed-price menu and serves on the large terrace in good weather. This is a popular après-ski venue.

Across the street, less expensive meals are served in the 4-century-old **Gasthof Löwen,** operated by the hotel's owner and closed mid-June to July 7. The day's menu costs 16€ and because of its reasonable prices, the restaurant is also popular with local residents.

Kreuzgasse 9, A-6774 Tschagguns. ⓒ**05556/71000.** Fax 05556/71006. www.montafonerhof.com. 50 units. Winter 222€–362€ double; summer 130€–250€ double. Rates include half-board. MC, V. Closed one week after Easter–end May and end Oct–mid Dec. **Amenities:** Restaurant; bar; Jacuzzi; nonsmoking rooms; indoor–outdoor heated pool; room service; rooms for those w/limited mobility; sauna; Wi-Fi in lobby and bar. *In room:* TV, hairdryer, minibar.

Schruns & Tschagguns After Dark

Be aware that Schruns offers a wider range of nightlife than the smaller and sleepier Tschagguns, where a drink or two beside a flickering fire in any of the resort's hotels might be the most popular after-ski activity.

In Schruns, one of the favorites is **Café Astoria,** embracing the old-English pub style, often with DJs playing live sets (ⓒ **0650/3385882**), located at Kronengasse 2. The Zimba Alm, found at Hotel Zimba at Veltlinerweg 2 (ⓒ **05556/72630**), has consistent live dance music during the peak season. If you are looking for something more on the wild side, the **Blue Moon Table Dance Bar** (Gantschierstrasse 4, ⓒ **05556/72710**), is an erotic night club with style, and stays open until 5am. A calmer, more contemplative bar that's undeniably cozy is the Löwen Hotel's **Kamin Bar.**

THE BRAND VALLEY ★★

Often visited from Bludenz, the Brand Valley (Brandnertal in German) is one of Austria's most scenic valleys, a place of rare beauty surrounded by glaciers. The valley runs for about 15km (10 miles) before reaching Brand, and along the way are romantic little villages and lush pastureland set against a panoramic alpine backdrop. This valley offers a wealth of inns and hotels, especially at Brand, and skiers are drawn to the mountain ranges, namely **Niggenkopf** and **Palüd.**

Essentials

GETTING THERE   No rail lines run into Brand. The easiest way to reach the resort is by taking the **train** to Bludenz, from which about a dozen **buses** per day make the 25-minute trip to Brand. Each bus makes at least five different stops in Brand, where the city limits sprawl for several miles beside the valley's main highway.

Brand is 69km (43 miles) south of Bregenz, 10km (6 miles) southwest of Bludenz, and 171km (106 miles) east of Zurich. To reach it by **car** from Bregenz, drive southeast on the A14 to Bludenz and then cut southwest along the road that's marked BRAND.

VISITOR INFORMATION   The **tourist office** (ⓒ **05559/555**) is in the town center, Mühledörfle 40. It's open in winter Monday to Friday 8am to noon and 2 to 5pm. Hours may differ during the slower months, so it is best to call in advance.

Exploring Brand

A few centuries ago, exiles from the Valais, in Switzerland, settled this village at the mouth of the Zalimtal, near the Swiss border. At an elevation of around 1,010m (3,314 ft.), Brand has long been a popular mountain health resort spread out along a mile-long stretch at the base of the Scesaplana mountain range. It's now a much-visited winter-sports center, the main resort of the **Rätikon district** of Vorarlberg.

You can take a cableway to the top of the **Tschengla**, at 1,250m (4,101 ft.), as well as a chairlift to **Eggen**, at 1,270m (4,167 ft.). From Eggen, it's easy to make connections to **Niggenkopf**, at 1,600m (5,249 ft.).

About 6km (4 miles) south of Brand, beside the only road leading south of town (it's an extension of the Hauptstrasse and is marked LÜNERSEE), you'll find the **Lünersee Talstation.** Here, hardy souls can start a 1-hour climb leading steeply uphill to the **Lünersee (Lake Luner)** ★★, a glacial lake, which has increased in size with the construction of a dam—its western edge abuts the frontier of Switzerland. The lake is surrounded by a nature park, which makes it ideal for climbers and hikers. If you find the climb daunting, you can take a cable car, **Lünerseebahn.** It operates from late May to mid-October, every half hour from 8am to noon, and then from 1:30 to 4:30pm (☎ **05556/70180412**). The round-trip cost for adults is 9.30€, 6.10€ for children. Remember that the last cable car downhill departs shortly before 5pm.

Where to Stay & Eat

Hotel Scesaplana ★   In the resort's center, this hotel has been tastefully modeled after a chalet, with wood accents, accommodating sun terraces, and balconied extensions. The hotel offers attractively furnished rooms, many with balconies. There are three restaurants, a pub, and a cigar bar named Havana. A range of other sports is within easy reach, including riding, fishing, skiing, a 9-hole golf course, and carriage drives (many of them at an additional fee). The hotel restaurants are quite pleasant, and guests on the half-board plan receive a wide choice of specialties included with the evening meal. The a la carte restaurant offers Austrian favorites—*Rostbraten, Tafelspitz,* and schnitzel—along with less locally influenced cuisine such as prawns in herbed pasta. Prices are reasonable, from 12€ to 23€.

A-6708 Brand. ☎ **05559/221.** Fax 05559/445. www.s-hotels.com. 62 units. Winter 140€–290€ double, suites from 206€. Rates include half-board. DC, MC, V. Free parking. Closed late Apr–mid May. **Amenities:** 3 restaurants; 2 bars; babysitting; 9-hole golf course; massage; nonsmoking rooms; 2 heated pools (1 indoor, 1 outdoor); room service; spa; 4 outdoor and 2 indoor tennis courts. *In room:* TV, hairdryer, minibar.

EN ROUTE TO BREGENZ: FELDKIRCH & DORNBIRN

If you're heading for Bregenz—Vorarlberg's capital—the Bregenz Forest, or Switzerland, a stop at Feldkirch and Dornbirn along the way is highly recommended. Arrive in Feldkirch in the morning, wander through the old town and castle, and stay the night before continuing on to Bregenz.

Feldkirch ★: The Gateway to Austria

This venerable town, "the gateway to Austria," lies on the western edge of Vorarlberg. Feldkirch was once a fortified town that grew up at the "heel" of Schattenburg Castle, on a tributary of the Ill River. The town's architecture reveals Gothic influences as well, as shown by the St. Nikolaus cathedral.

ESSENTIALS

GETTING THERE Feldkirch sits atop an important junction in the Austrian railway network, with lines to Innsbruck and Bregenz, as well as a line running into Liechtenstein and Switzerland. Dozens of **trains** arrive every day from Innsbruck (trip time: 1¾–2½ hr.) and Bregenz (trip time: 30–45 min.). It's easier to get there by train, but many local bus lines connect in Feldkirch. For rail information, contact ℭ **05/1717** (www.oebb.at).

Passengers who opt to fly to a point near Feldkirch usually land in Zurich. From the **Hauptbahnhof** in Zurich, trains depart every 2 hours, stopping at Feldkirch en route to either Innsbruck or Vienna.

By car, Feldkirch is 35km (22 miles) south of Bregenz (take the A14 south to reach it) and 121km (75 miles) east of Zurich (the nearest airport), from which it can be reached by taking Swiss motorway N13 to the Feldkirch exit.

VISITOR INFORMATION The **tourist office** (ℭ **05522/73467**) is at Schlossergasse 8. It's open year-round Monday to Saturday 8am to 6pm.

EXPLORING THE OLD TOWN & CASTLE

The **Old Town ★**, which can be explored in about an hour, is the attraction here—the New Town lies to the northeast. The heart of the Old Town is **Marktgasse (Market Street),** a rectangle with arcades. Many of the old houses facing Marktgasse are graced with oriels (large bay windows) and frescoed facades. A popular wine festival is held here on the second weekend of July, and the town fills with revelers.

Among the curiosities of the Old Town is the **Katzenturm,** or Tower of the Cats, named for a defense cannon adorned with lion heads. The **Churertor (Chur Gate)** is another Feldkirch landmark. Sights include the **Domkirche,** a cathedral known for its 15th-century double nave, where you should stop in and see the *Descent from the Cross,* a 1521 painting by Wolf Huber of the Danube school.

The **Schattenburg (Schattenburg Castle),** in Neustadt, can be reached by car (by heading up Burggasse), or you can climb the steps by the **Schloss-Steig.** The castle was once a fortress, and parts of it date from the turn of the 16th century. It's now a museum and restaurant. From the castle precincts, you have a panoramic view of the Rhine Valley.

The **Heimatmuseum** (ℭ **05522/71982;** www.heimatmuseum.com), inside the Schattenburg, exhibits a wealth of furnishings of the region, ranging from those you might have found in a farmer's shack to pieces that graced noblemen's halls. Also displayed are large collections of art and armor. From April to October, the museum is open Monday to Friday 9am to noon and 1:30 to 5pm. Weekends and holidays from 10am to 5pm. During November and December, open on weekends and holidays from 11am to 4pm, and January to March Tuesday to Friday 1:30 to 4pm, weekends and holidays 11am to 4pm. Admission is 6€ for adults, 4.5€ for students and seniors, and 2.50€ for children.

WHERE TO STAY & EAT

Hotel Alpenrose ★ ▮▮ In the heart of the Old Town and only a few minutes' walk from the pedestrian precinct, this hotel appeals to traditionalists. With a history going back 5 centuries, it has been run by the Gutwinski family since 1896. The nonsmoking accommodations come in various sizes and are quite stylish, with most containing small private bathrooms with shower units. Run with charm and flair, the hotel has an elevator, and there's a Biedermeier lounge for guests. The hotel's featured restaurant, Rosenbar, serves regional cuisine and is open Monday through Friday noon to 2pm and 6 to 10pm, Saturdays 6 to 10pm.

Rosengasse 4–6, A-6800 Feldkirch. (✆ **05522/72175.** Fax 05522/721755. www.hotel-alpenrose.net. 27 units. 126€ double; 144€ suite. Rates include buffet breakfast. Free parking outside, garage for 4€. AE, DC, MC, V. **Amenities:** Restaurant; bar; lounge; massage; room service; 1 room for those w/limited mobility. *In room:* TV, hairdryer, minibar, Wi-Fi.

Dornbirn

In the heart of Vorarlberg, Dornbirn, the "city of textiles," is the province's largest town and commercial center. Only 11km (7 miles) south of the provincial capital, it sits on the outskirts of the Bregenz Forest, at the edge of the broad Rhineland Valley.

The city center, Marktplatz (Market Square), is graced by a 19th-century neoclassical parish church and by the Rotes Haus (Red House), a 1639 building that is now a restaurant.

ESSENTIALS

GETTING THERE Dornbirn is an express stop on the rail lines connecting Innsbruck with Bregenz. **Trains,** both local and express, arrive from either direction at 30-minute intervals throughout the day. For rail information, contact (✆ **05/1717** (www.oebb.at). It's easier to get here by train, but there's also a **bus** that travels from the railway station at Bregenz to Dornbirn about nine times throughout the day (trip time: 26 min.).

If you're **driving** from Bregenz, head south along the A14 until you reach the signposted junction with Route 190, where you'll head east for Dornbirn.

VISITOR INFORMATION There's a **tourist office** (✆ **05572/22188**) in the center at Rathausplatz 1. It's open year-round Monday to Friday 9am to noon and 1 to 6pm, Saturday 9am to noon.

WHAT TO SEE & DO

If you're a car buff, you shouldn't pass up a visit to the **Rolls-Royce Museum ★**, 11A Gütle (✆ **05572/52652;** www.rolls-royce-museum.at), the world's largest museum dedicated to the world's most illustrious cars. Rolls-Royce collector Frank Vonier assembled the collection, and many of the swanky cars were once owned by celebrities, including such pop icons as John Lennon as well as less-loved individuals like Generalissimo Francisco Franco, the long-time Spanish dictator.

Take the A14 motorway to Dornbirn, exiting at Dornbirn Süd. Drive along Lustenauerstrasse, passing the Dornbirn Hospital, and follow the signs to Gütle. By public transport, take bus no. 4 from the center of Dornbirn. Admission is 8€ for adults and 4€ for ages 6 to 16. From April to October, it's open from 10am to 6pm; November through March from 10am to 5pm; closed during the Christmas holidays and most of January.

The most exciting excursion in the area is to **Karren** (976m/3,202 ft.), about 2km (1½ miles) from the heart of town. If you're pretty fit, you can make the climb in about 2 hours, but you can also take the **Karrenseilbahn** cable car and get there in 5 minutes, operating during the summer 9am to 11pm (9am to midnight on Saturdays) and 10am to 11pm most days in the winter (call (✆ **05572/22140** for details). From Karren, you can hike down to the **Rappenloch Gorge ★**, one of the largest gorges in the eastern Alps, with the Ache River flowing through it.

WHERE TO STAY

Gesundheitszentrum Rickatschwende ★ This large, modern, renovated hotel lies on a steeply sloping hillside overlooking Dornbirn. It's composed of two interconnected buildings; one houses the restaurant, the other contains the bedrooms. The atmosphere here is calm and quiet, and guests opt for walks in the nearby forest or in grassy meadows, or for any of the various spa cures offered by the on-site health therapists. A full range of medicinal therapies is offered, along with homeopathic cures, and beauty and cosmetic programs are available as well. Rebuilt in 2000, the building has rooms outfitted with warm colors, exposed wood, big windows, balconies, excellent beds, and small but efficiently arranged bathrooms with tub/shower combinations.

Rickatschwende 1, A-6850 Dornbirn. ☏ **05572/25350.** Fax 05572/2535070. www.rickatschwende. com. 50 units. 160€–260€ double; from 472€ suite. Rates include breakfast. Free parking. V. From the center of town, drive west toward Bödele for 5km (3 miles). Closed Nov 29–Jan 4. **Amenities:** Restaurant; bar; fitness center; massage; nonsmoking rooms; indoor heated pool; room service; 1 room for those w/limited mobility; spa. *In room:* TV, hairdryer.

WHERE TO EAT

Das Rotes Haus ★★ AUSTRIAN/VORARLBERG No other restaurant in the region offers such a historic setting for a meal. It was originally built in 1639 as a tavern and has functioned in the same role ever since. Its owners proudly define it as the oldest building that's open to the public in the Austrian Rheintal and strenuous efforts are made to preserve and protect the antique quality of its setting. You'll dine within one of five cozy dining rooms, each with a slightly different decor: The Jagdstube is outfitted with hunting trophies, while the Ammanstube displays political memorabilia. Local menu items include schnitzel, *Tafelspitz, Käsknöpfle,* and a rich selection of steaks. A note about the building's facade: In the 17th century, cow's blood was mixed with binders to create the dark red that—with some assistance from modern paint—still adorns the building's facade today.

Marktplatz 13, A-6850 Dornbirn. ☏ **05572/31555.** www.roteshaus.at. Reservations recommended. Main courses 10€–25€. AE, DC, MC, V. Apr–Sept 11:30am–midnight; Oct–Mar 11:30am–2pm, 5:30pm–midnight and closed Mondays.

BREGENZ ★★

658km (409 miles) W of Vienna; 130km (81 miles) E of Zurich; 11km (7 miles) S of Lindau (Germany)

Bregenz, the capital of Vorarlberg, sits on terraces rising above the water at the eastern end of Bodensee (Lake Constance). It was first settled by the Celts in 400 B.C., and later conquered by the Romans to become the camp of Brigantium. Bregenz is now a major tourist spot with both modern and historic attractions. The modern part of town lies along the lake's shore, with the old town rising above it. In summer, the promenade along the Bodensee's shoreline is a popular hangout, and cruise ships and cable cars departing from the town allow for gorgeous views of the lake. The town has become particularly well-visited by opera-goers and music lovers who flock to the Bregenzer Festspiele (Bregenz Music Festival) in July and August every year.

Essentials

GETTING THERE Bregenz is the most important railway station in western Austria, where dozens of **trains** arrive from Zurich, Munich, Innsbruck, and Vienna

THE BREGENZ music FESTIVAL

Bregenz is at its liveliest during the annual **Bregenz Music Festival.** This festival, held during a 4-week period in mid-July to mid-August, was established in 1946. Open-air and indoor concerts are given (some at the acoustically sophisticated Festspiele-und-Kongresshaus), but the most appealing productions are the lavish operas, operettas, and musical comedies. The more elaborate shows—with their ornately dressed actors and singers—are presented on a stage floating on the Bodensee, which is equally elaborately decorated. The audience looks on from a shoreside amphitheater that seats 6,500. Some of the latest productions have included *Aida* by Giuseppe Verdi and *André Chénier* by Umberto Giordano. Tickets, from 28€ to 288€, are available at the **Bregenzer Festspielhaus,** Platz der Wiener Symphoniker 1 (*©* **05574/4076;** www.bregenzerfestspiele.com).

throughout the day. The trip from Innsbruck takes about 3 hours and occasionally requires a change of train at Feldkirch. Although it's easier to arrive here by train, several bus lines make the trip to Bregenz. For **train and bus information,** call *©* 05/1717 (www.oebb.at).

If you're **driving** from Innsbruck, take the A12 west into Vorarlberg, and then follow the S16 west until you hook up with the A14 Autobahn going north.

VISITOR INFORMATION   At the **tourist office,** Bregenz-Tourismus, Rathausstrasse 35a (*©* **05574/49590**), you can pick up a map for a walking tour of the Old Town. It's open from January to mid-July, Monday to Friday 9am to 6pm, Saturday from 9am to noon; from mid-July to late August, Monday to Saturday 9am to 7pm; from late August to end December, Monday to Friday 9am to 6pm, Saturday 9am to noon.

What to See & Do

You can travel the Bodensee district by boat, venturing into Germany and Switzerland, which share Bodensee with Austria. For a panoramic view of the lake and the town, with Switzerland looming in the background, take a cable car to **Pfänder** (see "Up the Mountain to Pfänder," below).

The **Unterstadt (Lower Town)** is Bregenz's shopping district, with traffic-free shopping centers along the shore. In spring, the flower beds along the quays of the Unterstadt blaze with color.

The Upper Town is called both **Oberstadt** and **Altstadt.** Once the stronghold of the counts of Bregenz and Montford, this area is great for history buffs. If you're driving from the Lower Town, head up Kirchstrasse, Thalbachgasse, and Amstorstrasse; park; and then stroll back into the Middle Ages as you wander through the old quarter's quiet squares and narrow streets.

The **Pfarrkirche (Parish Church),** dedicated to St. Gall, stands on a hill south of the Upper Town. This 15th-century sandstone structure has a sunken nave from the 18th century.

Martinsturm   On the upper floor of the 13th-century Tower of St. Martin is a local military museum. St. Martin's Chapel (founded in 1362), at the base of the tower, features 14th-century murals. Far more interesting than the art, however, is the view of the surrounding area from the top of the tower, which is capped with one of the largest all-wood cupolas in Austria.

Martingasse 3b. ⓒ **05574/46632.** Admission 1.50€ adults, .50€ children. Apr–Oct daily 10am–5pm, closed Monday.

Where to Stay

For the most luxurious accommodations in the area, stay at Deuring Schlössle (see p. 431 in "Where to Eat").

Hotel Mercure Near the Festspielhaus, this hotel, a member of a popular French hotel chain, is one of the town's most state-of-the-art. And it's in the same building as the local casino. The small rooms are of the bland hotel-chain variety but are comfortable. Some have balconies. The hotel's specialty restaurant, Symphonie, also operates an inexpensive cafeteria. Summer guests enjoy sitting out on the large umbrella-shaded terrace for drinks and food.

Platz d. Wiener Symphoniker 2, A-6900 Bregenz. ⓒ **05574/461000.** Fax 05574/47412. www.accor hotel.com. 94 units. 198€–338€ double. Rates include buffet breakfast. Half-board 20€ per person extra. AE, DC, MC, V. **Amenities:** Restaurant; bar; babysitting; fitness center; 18-hole golf course; non-smoking rooms; rooms for those w/limited mobility; room service; sauna; tanning bed; Wi-Fi. *In room:* TV, hairdryer, Internet, minibar.

Schwärzler Hotel ★ One of the best hotels in Bregenz, the elegant Schwärzler Hotel is a 5-minute drive east of the town center. Most of the handsomely furnished rooms are spacious and have balconies. Bathrooms are small but efficiently organized with a shower. The restaurant, **Schwärzler,** is one of the most respected in the area, serving Swiss, Austrian, and international dishes. The hotel is known for its candle-light dinners and farmer buffets.

Landstrasse 9, A-6900 Bregenz. ⓒ **05574/4990.** Fax 05574/47575. www.schwaerzler-hotels.com. 80 units. 136€–280€ double. Rates include breakfast. Half-board 28€ per person extra. AE, DC, MC, V. Free parking. **Amenities:** Restaurant; bar; babysitting (on request); bike rental; massage; nonsmoking rooms; indoor heated pool; room service; sauna; tanning bed. *In room:* TV, hairdryer, minibar, Wi-Fi.

Where to Eat

Deuring Schlössle ★★ AUSTRIAN In the center of Bregenz, at the highest point in the Old Town, this restaurant is one of Austria's finest. The imposing, ivy-covered 600-year-old castle has provided exceptional food (and hotel rooms) since 1987. The establishment contains half-timbered detailing, a Renaissance-era fireplace, and an impressive wine list. Menu items are seasonal, varied, and thoughtful, such as cream soup with exotic fruits and poached Lake Constance char with spinach *tagliolinis* and mangold.

Some guests opt to spend the night in one of the 15 rooms. Accommodations are spacious and contain antiques, Persian carpets, parquet floors, and panoramic views of the lake. Modern comforts have been added, and rooms come in a variety of sizes, with great beds and luxurious bathrooms with both tubs and showers. Doubles run from 196€ to 222€, suites from 286€ (for half board including a five-course gourmet dinner, a surcharge of approximately 60€ per person is added). Rooms have minibars, TVs, and phones.

Ehre-Guts-Platz 4, A-6900 Bregenz. ⓒ **05574/47800.** Fax 05574/4780080. Reservations required. Main courses 24€–38€; fixed-price menus 78€–95€, wine accompaniment 48€–58€. AE, DC, MC, V. Mon–Sat 6–10pm, closed February.

Goldener Hirschen ★ AUSTRIAN   One of the most folklorically conscious dining rooms in town occupies an old-world building that was originally built as a tavern around 1800 and has functioned in that capacity ever since. Inside, you'll find one very large dining room where the seating expands during nice weather onto an outdoor terrace, with views extending out over the other historic buildings of Bregenz's historic core. Come here for the kind of cuisine that many Austrians associate with their grandmothers. Examples include giant Wiener schnitzel; *Tafelspitz*; local fish served with herbs and a white-butter sauce; roasted beef with onions; and creamy goulash. A particular specialty favored by locals is *kisselfleisch*, composed of roasted pork served with sauerkraut, braised onions, and herbs.

Kirchstrasse 8, A-6900 Bregenz. (℃ **05574/42815.** Reservations recommended. Main courses 10€–24€. AE, DC, MC, V. 10am–midnight, Wed 4pm–midnight, closed Tues.

Shopping

Nose-to-the-grindstone Bregenz doesn't have a lot of shopping options, but you'll find a scattering of outlets within the Lower Town that might appeal to you. Noteworthy for traditional alpine clothing—lederhosen, *dirndls,* and woolen clothing suitable for men, women, and children in any season—is **Sagmeister,** Römerstrasse 10 ((℃ **05574/ 4319011**).

Bregenz After Dark

If you're in Bregenz on a summer night, you will hardly crave a dark smoke-filled bar: Few clubs could compete with a walk along the lakeshore and a visit to a cafe. However, if you'd like another diversion, you can visit the **Spiel-Casino Bregenz,** Platz der Wiener Symphoniker 3 ((℃ **05574/45127;** www.casinos.at), where roulette, baccarat, and blackjack are played daily from noon to 3am (Fri to Sat until 4am). Parking in the garage is free. For 29€, you receive access to the casino bar, one free cocktail, and 25€ worth of chips. Men must wear jackets and ties. The in-house **Casino Restaurant** offers a fixed-price four-course menu (it includes the admission charge) for 57€.

Up the Mountain to Pfänder

Almost 300,000 visitors a year make the uphill trek to the mountain observation station of Pfänder, west of Bregenz. Pfänder is accessible by road (a meandering distance of 10km/6½ miles) or via the **Pfänderbahn cable car** (a straight-line transit of 4km/2½ miles) from the center of Bregenz. Operating year-round daily from 8am to 7pm, it departs from its lowest station, about 460m (1,509 ft.) east of the **Kornmarkt 1 Bregenz,** and takes about 7 minutes to reach its summit. The round-trip fare is 10.80€ for adults or 5.40€ for children. Call (℃ **05574/421600** for information about departure times.

At the summit, you'll find a scattering of shops and restaurants along with the **Pfänder Alpine Wildlife Park** ((℃ **05574/421840**). The owners emphasize that it is not a zoo. The park's large fenced-in areas are devoted to herds of red deer, wild boar, mountain goats, and wild sheep. Access to the Wildlife Park is free; it takes about 20 minutes to wander through its 10 hectares (26 acres) of rocky terrain. A section for children shows marmots, pot-bellied pigs, rabbits, and pygmy goats in a semi-natural habitat.

To get to this alpine complex by car from Bregenz, travel east of town (toward Lindau, Germany) along a narrow, twisting road through the mountains. Turn right, toward Lochau, where you'll pass a parish church, and turn right onto a secondary

If you're passing through the valley on a Sunday, you'll see an occasional Vorarlberger going to church in his or her traditional garb. The headdress of the women is often striking, ranging from small crowns to wide-brimmed black straw hats. Unlike most of the rest of Europe, the people of this area wear white for mourning rather than black.

road leading to Pfänder. Cars usually park at a large area near the summit. From here, you'll walk about 10 minutes to reach the panorama from the Berghaus Pfänder. From the Berghaus, an additional 5-minute walk up the mountain leads to another, much smaller, alpine house with its own simple restaurant and a different panorama, **Gasthaus Pfändersptize,** located between the Sendeturm and the Gipfelkreuz.

THE BREGENZ FOREST ★

From Bregenz, you can make one of the most remarkable scenic excursions in Vorarlberg—or in Austria, for that matter—deep into the **Bregenzerwald,** or the Bregenz Forest. It is divided between the lower area near the Rhine Valley and the upper region that transcends altitudes of 2,000m (6,561 ft.), and has a different dialect to go with each.

The forest takes up the northern part of the Vorarlberg alpine range. A state highway splits the valley of the Bregenzer Ache River, making driving easy, but the true charm of the forest lies off the beaten path in the little undiscovered valleys cut by the river's tiny tributaries. Don't expect a proliferation of trees in the Bregenz Forest: The Austrians have cleared a lot of the woodlands to make meadows, where you'll see contented cows grazing and the Alps towering in the background.

One of the most frequented areas for sports and recreation is the **Bödele,** which lies between the Valley of the Ache and the Valley of the Rhine. Skiers are drawn to the highlands in winter.

Bezau

The best-known village of the Bregenz Forest, Bezau, is surrounded by a landscape that's scenic in any season. Be careful not to confuse Bezau with a village nearby, at the end of the neighboring valley, named Bizau.

In the spring, summer, and autumn, you can hike, climb, swim, go mountaineering, fish for trout, or play tennis or minigolf. In winter there's alpine skiing, with the **Hinter-Bregenzerwald ski ticket** covering a range of more than 50 lifts and cable railways. There are some 56km (35 miles) of cross-country ski trails, and you can also go tobogganing. A cableway from here will take you to the **Baumgartenhöhe,** at 1,632m (5,354 ft.).

ESSENTIALS
GETTING THERE   Bezau has no railway connections. From Dornbirn, a 15-minute ride south of Bregenz, around 20 **buses** depart every day for Bezau, which takes about 45 minutes. Buses destined for Bezau also leave from Bregenz, which takes about an hour.

13

VORARLBERG

The Bregenz Forest

If you're **driving** from Bregenz, head south on Route 190 to the junction with Route 200. Cut east along this winding road to Bezau, which lies 36km (22 miles) from Bregenz.

VISITOR INFORMATION   The **tourist office,** Platz 39 (© **05514/2295**), is in the center of town. It's open year-round Monday to Friday from 8:30am to noon and 2 to 6pm, Saturday 8:30am to noon.

WHERE TO STAY & EAT

Gasthof Gams ★   This dignified hotel has a facade of cedar shingles, white stucco, gables, and balconies. Although the core was built in 1648, guests will find an abundance of modern comforts, including a big garden and several antique-style sitting rooms. Rooms are well furnished and come in a variety of sizes; each year a few units are renovated. The most desirable rooms open onto private balconies with scenic views. Beds are first-rate, and the small bathrooms have tub/shower combinations. The restaurant specializes in game, particularly venison. You'll also be offered seafood, such as a well-prepared filet of sole, along with filet steak, curry dishes, and desserts with fresh mountain berries. A variety of multi-course menus are available, some served with wine and champagne to your rooms, for various additional charges. Perfect for the romantic getaway.

Platz 44, A-6870 Bezau. © **05514/2220.** Fax 05514/222024. www.hotel-gams.at. 70 units. 226€–220€ double; from 320€ suite. Rates include half-board (5-course dinner) with a 19€ surcharge. AE, MC, V. **Amenities:** Restaurant; bar; lounge; fitness room; massage; outdoor heated pool; room service; spa; tanning bed. *In room:* TV, fireplace (in suites), hairdryer, minibar (in some).

Damüls

At an elevation of 1,427m (4,682 ft.), this town is one of the best places to ski in the Bregenz Forest. The village was recently awarded the title of snowiest town in the world; it receives over 9m (more than 30 ft.) of snow each winter. Skiers who come here every season describe it as a place for ski connoisseurs. Hotels organize weekly après-ski programs, so check to see what's going on during your stay. The loftiest village in the forest, Damüls, is an area of great scenic beauty, so a summer visit is also pleasant.

ESSENTIALS

GETTING THERE   From Bregenz, visitors should take a southbound 15-minute **train** to Dornbirn and then board one of the **buses** to Damüls. Buses depart around six times a day (trip time: 1½ hr. to 2 hr.).

To get to Damüls from Innsbruck, you have to take a 2-hour train ride west to Bludenz and then board one of the nine daily buses that depart for the 90-minute ride to Damüls.

Damüls is 60km (37 miles) southeast of Bregenz, and a long 698km (434 miles) west of Vienna. To get to Damüls by **car** from Bezau, drive southeast along Route 200 until you come to the junction with Route 193, and head southwest to Damüls.

VISITOR INFORMATION   The **tourist office** (© **05510/620**) is found at Kirchdorf 138, at the edge of the village center. It's open year-round Monday through Friday from 8:30am to noon and 1:30 to 6:30pm; in winter it's also open Saturday 10am to noon and 4 to 6pm, Sunday 10am to noon.

WHERE TO STAY & EAT

Hotel Damülser Hof   This collection of modern chalets, each connected by covered passageways, sits in an alpine meadow a 5-minute walk uphill from the village church. Built in 1963 and partially renovated virtually every year since then, it boasts an elegant interior with enough variety in its decor to please most guests. The cozy public areas have intimate niches, soft lighting, and several fireplaces. Rooms are medium-sized, comfortable, and well furnished, if rather impersonal.

A-6884 Oberdamüls. ⓒ **05510/2100.** Fax 05510/543. www.damuelserhof.at. 50 units. Winter 150€–210€ double. Half-board included for a 10€ surcharge. MC, V. Parking free outdoors, 8€ garage. Closed Nov and mid April–mid May. **Amenities:** Restaurant; 2 bars; bowling alley; fitness center; massage; nonsmoking rooms; indoor heated pool; room service; rooms for those w/limited mobility; spa; tanning bed. *In room:* TV, hairdryer, Wi-Fi.

CARINTHIA

Many who know the dramatic landscapes of Carinthia will say, without blushing, they think it the most beautiful place in the world. It's hard to disagree: The sweeping wooded hills and plunging mountains with idyllic lakes and villages make this lush province a thrill. Bordering on Italy and Slovenia to the south, the Mediterranean influence is strong in the architecture and the cuisine of Carinthia and in the gentle lowland climate of Klagenfurt and the Wörtersee. High in the mountains, though, the air never loses the crisp, breathtaking clarity and its geographical position also makes for a good stopping point on your way south.

14

The high mountains surrounding Kärnten, the province's German name, create natural borders like a gigantic amphitheater, with mountainous Upper Carinthia to the west, and the Lower Carinthia Basin sloping to the east. The province is bisected by the eastern-flowing Drau River, which becomes the Drava when it enters Slovenia. Klagenfurt is the capital of Carinthia, and Villach, 40km (25 miles) to the west, is the biggest road and rail junction in the eastern Alps.

If you're athletic, climb the *Nocken*, the gentle lowland hills, or head for the more demanding mountains. The region glories in more than 200 warm, crystal-clear lakes and sparkling, cold mountain streams that are wonderful for fishing. The lower lake district of the Wörthersee, Ossiachersee, and Millstattersee is often called the "Carinthian Riviera," where the balmy summers and astonishing natural beauty have long attracted elite, who have built fantasy castles and summer cottages and boat houses along the shores. The Weissensee, another big lake, is less well known and less developed—protected by its higher elevation and cooler temperatures that make it the ideal choice for hikers and climbers. The best way to see the lakes is to take one of the boats that operate from April to mid-October.

If you want to enjoy the lakes, visit Carinthia from mid-May to September, although the first 2 weeks in October are ideal, too. Flocks of Austrians swoop down here in July and August, so make reservations in advance if you plan on visiting during those months.

Although the warm lakes are Carinthia's main attraction, the province also has some fine ski areas that draw the cognoscenti to its mountains in winter. The relatively mild winters—both a blessing and a curse—here don't always deliver the best ski conditions, though, and the ski season lasts only from December to March. The good news: As a ski center, this province is much more affordable than Tyrol or Land Salzburg. If you do your research, you can find yourself skiing in shirtsleeves in February. Regardless of the season, parking is rarely a problem: Unless otherwise noted, you park for free.

This is a very old part of Austria; archaeologists have established human settlements in Carinthia far before recorded time. Roman legions marched into the area to conquer alpine Celtic tribes in the kingdom of Noticum, establishing it as a Roman province in 15 B.C., ruling the area for the next 500 years. The Carinthian Alps formed a natural boundary for the Romans between their southern dominions and their newer ones in the north, and through them, an all-important trade route developed bringing spices, silks, glass, and wine to the north, and furs, salt, and iron to the south.

For centuries, this area was home to ethnic groups from Slovenia, belonging to the kingdom of Germany and Avar-dominated Slavs from the east. Hoping to fend off invasions, the populace eventually invited Bavaria to become Carinthia's protector, making it part of the Holy Roman Empire.

When the Habsburgs took Kärnten as part of their rapidly expanding empire, it was a duchy of the Holy Roman Empire under the Bohemian aegis. To secure his control over the area, the Habsburg Ferdinand I, soon to become emperor, married the heiress to Bohemia and made Carinthia an imperial duchy. Later, Carinthia was designated a province of Austria.

The Yugoslav Republic claimed southern Carinthia after World War I, with some territory ceded to Yugoslavia and more to Italy, all later restored. After the collapse of the Habsburg Empire, the Slovenian minority in the south voted in 1920 to remain with Austria. Today, a sizable minority, about 4.5%, of Carinthia's population is Slovenian.

Tips for Active Travelers

If you spontaneously decide to spend a day boating, bicycling, or fishing, the staff at any local hotel should be able to tell you where to go. Here's a list of outfitters who can help with advance planning and, in some cases, hook you up with a choice of specialized tours.

BIKING   Carinthia's gentle contours are great for cyclists. The tourist office in the **Rathaus** (✆ **0463/5372223**) in Klagenfurt rents bicycles for 10€ per day.

BOATING   The reception staff at virtually any lakeside hotel can arrange boating lessons and boat rentals, but two local favorites are **Segel-und-Surfschule Wörthersee/Berger,** Seecorso 40, Velden (✆ **04274/26910**), and **Flaschberger Georg,** Seeuferstrasse 130, Pörtschach (✆ **04272/2743**). These two outfits or any of the dozens of other *Bootsverleih* (boat-rental agencies) can help you arrange windsurfing, canoeing, or sailing, and, where it's allowed, even rent you a motorized craft for fishing.

FISHING   Any local tourist office can provide you with the worthwhile pamphlet "*Kärnten Fischen,*" which explains the rules and procedures involved in a fishing expedition. Some hotels adjacent to important lakes offer fishing packages that include rooms, boat rentals, guides, and equipment in one price.

GOLF   Some of the most appealing golf games in Austria are held close to Carinthia's beautiful lakes. From May to October, Carinthian golf is in full swing. The best of the district's golf courses include **Golfanlage Moosburg-Pörtschach,** A-9062 Moosburg (✆ **04272/83486;** www.golfmoosburg.at). A nearby golf academy, **Golfakademie Moosburg-Pörtschach,** A-9062 Moosburg (✆ **04272/82302**), offers

Carinthia

Skiing

20 mi
20 km

Bad Kleinkirchheim **4**
Hochosterwitz Castle **3**
Magdalensberg Excavations **2**
Maria Saal **1**

STEIERMARK
(STYRIA)

Völkermarkt

Lake Klopeiner

A2

Brück

Eisenkappel

92
82
85

Friesach

317
S37
82
91

Strassburg
Gurk
93
St. Veit
an der Glan

3
2

Klagenfurt
1
Krumpendorf
Pörtschach
Maria Wörth

A2

Drau River

Feldkirchen
94
Ossiach
Velden

Lake Wörther

A11

Radenthein
4

Lake Ossiacher
Annenheim

Villach
A2

SLOVENIA

Lake
Millstatter

Millstatt
A10
Gmund
Trebessing

A10

CARNIC ALPS

Seeboden
Spittal

Lake Weissen

Hermagor

ITALY

99
A10

LAND
SALZBURG

Obervellach
Kolnitz
Mallnitz
106

Techendorf

100
Dellach

Drau River

107

Heiligenblut

Kötschach
Mauthen

OST-
TIROL
(EAST
TYROL)

AUSTRIA
Vienna
Carinthia

438

lessons on the same course. Another fine course is **Golfclub-Austria Wörthersee,** Golfstrasse 2, A-9062 Moosburg (℡ **04272/83486**). Each of the courses mentioned above has 18 holes, a par of 72, and green fees of 65€.

HIKING In summer, Carinthia hosts hordes of hikers. Every lakeside resort has kilometers of marked trails. The Ossiacher See area is especially suited for hiking, as are Hochosterwitz and Friesach. The towns of **Bad Kleinkirchheim, Feld am See,** and **Millstatt** have the best in the region. Ask at the local tourist office for information and maps.

SKIING Carinthia doesn't have Tyrol's mountains or Vorarlberg's skiing facilities, but **Friesach** is emerging as a major ski area, attracting cross-country skiers in particular. The top ski resort is Bad Kleinkirchheim.

SWIMMING & WATERSPORTS All the major lakes contain public beaches, and the waters are among the purest in Europe. You can drink from them safely, although we don't recommend it. In late summer, lake temperatures reach about 75°F (24°C), making them ideal for swimmers. If you'd like to combine your swimming with more serious watersports, get in touch with **Segel-und-Surfschule Wörthersee/Berger,** Seecorso 40, Velden (℡ **04274/26910**), or **Flaschberger Georg,** Seeuferstrasse 130, Pörtschach (℡ **04272/2743**).

TENNIS Most major resorts have their own courts; we particularly like Villach and its satellite areas. Try **Tennisplätz-ASKÖ, Landskron, Süduferstrasse** at Villach (℡ **04242/41879**), or **Tenniscamp Warmbad** at Warmbad-Villach (℡ **04242/ 32564**).

KLAGENFURT

61km (38 miles) NE of Italy; 31km (19 miles) N of Slovenia; 309km (192 miles) SW of Vienna; 140km (87 miles) SW of Graz; 209km (130 miles) SE of Salzburg

Klagenfurt, a university town dating from 1161, is the provincial capital and cultural center of Carinthia, with a population of 89,000—a sort of Graz in miniature, at about one-third the size. It's perhaps a sleepy city, but nonetheless appealing, gently paced, where the ancient streets of Renaissance and baroque buildings of the Altstadt are rarely more than three or four stories, leaving its pleasant squares flooded with sunlight. Arrive in Klagenfurt, get settled, and wander around the city's historic center, stay the night, perhaps taking in an opera or concert at the lovely, 100-year-old Stadttheater, and then use Klagenfurt as the base for your explorations to **St. Veit, Hochosterwitz Castle,** the **Cathedral of Gurk,** and the region's lakes (see later in this chapter).

Destroyed by fire in 1514 and rebuilt as the duchy's capital in 1518, the city was fortified with walls torn down during the Napoleonic invasions in 1802. The center is now rimmed with wide streets where the city's walls once stood. In this quadrangle is the **Neuerplatz,** presided over by the cast-iron statue of the Lindwurm, a ferocious dragon and the city's symbol. Believed to have haunted the city, Nessie-like, before the swampland was drained to allow it to expand, scientists later found the scull of a now-extinct wooly rhinoceros on the site.

It can get very hot in the peak of summer, but if you're here, do as the Klagenfurters do and retreat to the nearby **Wörthersee (Lake Wörther)** in the western sector of the city.

Essentials

GETTING THERE

Austrian Airlines serves Carinthia from Vienna, arriving at the **Klagenfurt Airport** (✆ **0463/41500** for flight information; www.klagenfurt-airport.at), northeast of the city, several times a day. Because Klagenfurt is a popular summer lakeside resort, **Austrian Airlines** adds summer flights from Zurich, Rome, London, Berlin, and Frankfurt.

Klagenfurt, located on the lines connecting Vienna with Venice, Italy, and Zagreb, is the most important railway junction in southern Austria. It's also the focal point for several smaller rail lines whose passengers are eventually transferred to larger lines to Salzburg, Innsbruck, and Bregenz. **Trains** arrive from several different directions at intervals of 30 minutes or less throughout the day; call ✆ **05/1717** for schedules.

It's easier to take the train, but from Klagenfurt at least 20 different **bus** lines fan out into the surrounding region. For regional **bus information,** call ✆ **0463/54340** in Klagenfurt.

If you're **driving** from Vienna, head south on the A2. Take exit 308-Klagenfurt–Flughafen toward Klagenfurt. At Josef Sablatnig Strasse take a left and follow the signs to Klagenfurt. Take a right onto Sankt Veiter Strasse and at the next roundabout take the second exit into town.

VISITOR INFORMATION

The **tourist office** is in the **Rathaus,** or city hall (✆ **0463/5372223;** www. klagenfurt.at); to reach it from the rail station, head down Bahnhofstrasse. Open May to September Monday to Friday 8am to 8pm, Saturday 10am to 7pm, Sunday 10am to 3pm. From October to April, hours are Monday to Friday 10am to 6pm, Saturday and Sunday 10am to 1pm.

If you're driving into Klagenfurt there are specially marked "blue zones," where you can park for 90 minutes, so called because of blue lines on the road. You'll need a parking voucher that can be purchased at banks, gas stations, or tobacconists. When you park, you must write in the time you arrived and display the voucher on the dashboard, inside the windshield.

Exploring Klagenfurt

Alterplatz, both a broad thoroughfare and a square, is lined with many baroque mansions. It's a pedestrian zone that's the center of the **Altstadt (Old Town),** and many crooked, narrow little streets and alleys open off the square.

The **Trinity Column** on Alter Platz dates from 1681; it was built to commemorate those who died from the plague. One of the most interesting buildings on the square is the 17th-century **Altes Rathaus (Old Town Hall).** It has a three-story arcaded courtyard. The **Haus zur Goldenen Gans (House of the Golden Goose),** on Alter Platz, dates from 1599.

The **Domkirche (Cathedral) of Klagenfurt** stands to the southeast of Neuerplatz. Construction on this building began in 1578, and the interior is richly adorned with stucco and has ceiling frescos from the 18th century. Next door to the cathedral, **Diözesanmuseum** ★, Lidmanskyg 10 (✆ **0463/577701064**), is a small, often overlooked, museum containing a remarkable collection of **religious art** ★★ from the 12th to the 18th centuries. Sculpture, tapestries, jewelry, artwork, and stained glass are on display here, including the oldest stained-glass window in the country, a portrait of Mary Magdalene from 1170. Some works of art in the museum are truly remarkable, including one-of-a-kind pieces such as a rare processional cross made of iron with traces of gilt dating from the 12th century. Diözesanmuseum is open June 1–14 and from September 15 to October 15, Monday to Saturday 10am to noon; from June 15 to September 14, Monday to Saturday 10am to noon and 3 to 5pm. Admission costs 4€ for adults and 2€ for children.

The cultural jewel of Klagenfurt is the **Stadttheater** (see "Klagenfurt After Dark," below) that celebrated its 100th anniversary in September 2010, a highly successful melding of late imperial and Jugendstil design by the Vienna firm of Fellner and Helmer, designers of a number of other regional theaters at the time. Its excellent acoustics and intimate charm, make it as suitable for solo and chamber concerts as for opera or orchestra.

Landesmuseum ★ At this provincial museum, you can see ancient artifacts (many Roman) gleaned from excavations in Carinthia. The most outstanding feature is a display of ecclesiastical art. See the skull of a rhinoceros, said to have been a model for the renowned Dragon Fountain in Neuerplatz.

Museumgasse 2. ℂ **050536/30559.** www.landesmuseum-ktn.at. Admission 7€ adults, 5€ seniors and children. Tues–Fri 10am–6pm (until 8pm on Thurs); Sat, Sun, and holidays 10am–5pm. Closed Mon.

Landhaus Originally an arsenal and later Carinthian state headquarters, this structure now houses the offices of the provincial government. Building began in 1574 and finished in 1590. The courtyard of the present building has two-story arcades, and the set of staircase towers has bulbous caps. Its **Grosser Wappensaal (Great Blazon Hall),** dating from 1739, was handsomely decorated by Josef Ferdinand Fromiller. The painting on the hall's ceiling depicting 665 heraldic shields is executed in *trompe l'oeil.*

Landhaushof 1. ℂ **0463/577570.** Admission 3€ adults, 2€ ages 6–18. Apr–Oct 9am–5pm. Closed Nov–Mar.

Where to Stay

Arcotel Hotel Moser Verdino ★ This hotel's elaborate pink-and-white facade, originally built in 1890, now looks as new as ever after considerable renovations. For more than a century, it has been the town's leading hotel. The most popular cafe in town, Café Moser Verdino, is near the oak-trimmed lobby.

Domgasse 2, A-9020 Klagenfurt. ℂ **0463/57878.** Fax 0463/516765. www.arcotel.at. 71 units. 131€–180€ double. AE, DC, MC, V. **Amenities:** Restaurant; bar; dry cleaning; laundry service; rooms for those w/limited mobility; room service. *In room:* TV, hairdryer, minibar, safe, free Wi-Fi.

Goldener Brunnen 🍴 If you love the color yellow, this is your hotel. Set nearly adjacent to Klagenfurt's cathedral, in an antique building that still belongs to the local Catholic diocese, this hotel took most of its present form around 2000, when a team of entrepreneurs upgraded the then-creaky building's interior into a streamlined collection of bedrooms. Come here for solid dependability and its boutiquey style—there's nothing flashy about the place.

Am Domplatz Karfreitstrasse 14, A-9020 Klagenfurt. ℂ **0463/57380.** Fax 0463/516520. www.goldener-brunnen.at. 26 units. 110€–140€ double; 160€ junior suite. Rates include breakfast. Free parking. AE, DC, MC, V. **Amenities:** Cafe; bar; limited room service; nonsmoking rooms. *In room:* TV, minibar, safe, Wi-Fi.

Hotel Sandwirth ★ All Austrian presidents elected since 1945 have stayed in this hotel. The neoclassical building was first constructed in the 1650s and maintains a mixture of modern pragmatism and traditional charm. Rooms vary widely in style and size, but are usually high-ceilinged and full of period charms, with the more modern maintaining a tasteful link with the past. Most contain double beds, and each is equipped with a tub/shower bathroom.

Pernhartgasse 9, A-9020 Klagenfurt. ✆ **0463/56209.** Fax 0463/514322. www.sandwirth.at. 40 units. 150€–180€ double. Rates include buffet breakfast. AE, DC, MC, V. Free parking. **Amenities:** Restaurant; bar; cafe; fitness center; rooms for those w/limited mobility; sauna; smoke-free rooms. *In room:* A/C, TV, minibar, free Ethernet.

Palais Porcia ★★★   This pocket of posh is installed in a former town palace dating from the 1700s that once belonged to Italian princes. Filled with baroque embellishments and Biedermeier antiques, the hotel is so opulent you'd think the nobles were still in residence. Modern hotel comforts have been discreetly installed. The spacious bedrooms are lavishly decorated, filled with artwork that probably belongs in a museum, and much use made of four-poster beds, velvet sofas, and brocaded wallpaper. The most spectacular bedroom is called Himmelbett Room or "Heaven's Bed," although the Rose Room and the Blue Room are also very appealing.

Neuerplatz 13, A-9020 Klagenfurt. ✆ **0463/511590-0.** www.palais-porcia.at. 35 units. 113€–197€ double; 197€–349€ suite. AE, DC, MC, V. Parking 11€. **Amenities:** Bar; indoor heated pool; sauna. *In room:* A/C, minibar, hairdryer, safe, free Wi-Fi.

Roko-Hof ★ 🏠   A very small corner of this cozy, yellow-fronted hotel dates from the 1600s, when the site was used as the headquarters for a Venetian merchant. About 70 years ago, a small hotel was established on the site, but much of what you'll see now dates from the late 1990s, when Roswitha Reichmann-Kollman expanded her premises. Bedrooms are quite standardized looking, but comfortable, all with a nearly identical color scheme of browns, yellows, and blues. The in-house restaurant serves well-prepared continental and Austrian cuisine, and the lakefront is about 1km (0.6 miles) away.

Villacherstrasse 135, A-9020 Klagenfurt. ✆ **0463/21526.** Fax 0463/2152634. www.hotel-rokohof.at. 58 units. 130€–150€ double. Rates include breakfast. AE, DC, MC, V. Free parking. Bus: 10, 11, or 12. **Amenities:** Restaurant; cafe/bar; room service; laundry service; dry cleaning. *In room:* TV, hairdryer, free Wi-Fi (or Ethernet).

Salzamt Palais Hotel Landhaus   An offbeat boutique hotel of considerable charm, this restored palace in the heart of Klagenfurt dates from the Renaissance era and is protected under Austria's historic preservation laws. Until 1935, it was the "Salzamt" or town salt tax office. Today, it has emerged as a fashionable hotel with touches of camp in some bedrooms, where you are likely to find red velvet, gilt, or leopard skin. There is much comfort here, ranging from the heavenly beds with the padded headboards to the equally luxurious bathrooms, some with whirlpool baths. In a small but comfortable spa area, overlooking the rooftops of the city, you can use the Finnish sauna, a vapor bath, or take a hot and cold Kneipp shower.

Landhaushof 3, A-9020. ✆ **0463/590959.** Fax 0463/590-9590-9. www.landhaushof.at. 27 units. 200€–230€ double; 300€ junior suite; 390€ suite. Rates include breakfast. Parking 15€. AE, DC, MC, V. **Amenities:** Restaurant; bar; laundry service; room service; spa. *In room:* A/C, TV, minibar, safe, free Ethernet.

Where to Eat

Hamatle ✔ CARINTHIAN   There's been a popular restaurant in this century-old building since the 1950s, and present management, in place since around 1995, does everything it can to preserve the nostalgia. The result is a cozy restaurant with grandmother-style cuisine and an obvious allegiance to the traditions of Carinthia. (Its name is the equivalent, in local dialect, of *heimat,* which translates as "homeland.") There are two dining rooms, one on each of the two floors, outfitted in Austrian country style. Menu items focus on noodles (usually in a creamy sauce and dotted with, among other things, ham, onions, and/or mushrooms); braised trout with butter sauce and herbs; succulent schnitzels of pork, chicken, or veal; and beefsteaks.

Linsengasse 1.(✆ **0463/555700.** www.kaerntnerhamatle.at. Reservations recommended. Main courses 10€–20€. AE, DC, MC, V. Tues-Sat 10am-11pm; Sun 10am-6pm.

Maria Loretto ★★ SEAFOOD   Eat here at sundown. This is the kind of established restaurant where a local family might come for a breath of fresh air, a view of the lake, and a well-prepared roster of fish dishes. Menu items include a small selection of meats (especially Wiener schnitzels and grilled filet steak), and lots and lots of fish. Raw ingredients are hauled in from the North and Mediterranean seas, the Atlantic Ocean, and the freshwater lakes and streams of the surrounding regions. Most of these are prepared in the simplest way possible: Lightly grilled and seasoned with a garlic-flavored butter sauce, served with salad and boiled new potatoes, and accompanied with a young and fruity white wine, preferably Austrian or Italian.

Lorettoweg 54. (✆ **0463/24465.** www.maria-loretto.at. Reservations recommended. Main courses 11€–24€. V. Daily 11am-10pm. Closed Jan 6-Feb 28. From Klagenfurt's center, take bus marked STRAND-BAD KLAGENFURT/KLAGENFURT SEE.

Villa Lido—I Ragazzi ★ ITALIAN/MEDITERRANEAN   Under new management since 2008, Villa Lido now houses one of the best pizzerias in the country. The fish are as fresh as they come, the tomato sauce is made that morning, and the meats are all cut with a hand-operated slicker, which many chefs say preserves their flavor. Three kilometers (2 miles) west of the town center, beside the road leading to Villach, it offers painstakingly well-prepared fare, in a welcoming atmosphere right on the Wörthersee.

Friedelstrand 1. (✆ **0463/210712.** www.villa-lido.at. Reservations recommended. Main courses 20€–25€. AE, DC, MC, V. Daily 11:30-11:00pm. Closed 3 weeks in Nov.

Klagenfurt After Dark

The largest, grandest, and most formal theater in Klagenfurt is the **Stadttheater,** Theaterplatz 4 (✆ **0463/540640;** www.stadttheater-klagenfurt.at), which presents opera, classics of German theater, and chamber and orchestral music, often performed by visiting groups. Built in 1910, this handsome building went through a 2-year renovation (ending in 1998) that has given it new state-of-the-art facilities adapted to the elegant late imperial–Jugendstil design.

If you're lucky enough to arrive in Klagenfurt between mid-July and late August, take an evening stroll around the neighborhood of the **Pfarr-platz,** where you'll find most of Klagenfurt's nightlife options. The best of the lot includes **Bar Gallo Nero,** Pfarrhofgasse 8 (✆ **0463/512780**), where there's live music that never dips into anything too loud, too metallic, or too abrasive. Nostalgic references to Ireland pour out of **Pub Molly Malone,** Theatergasse 7 (✆ **0463/57200**), where pints of Irish, German, and Austrian beer make the often multi-lingual conversations flow more smoothly.

CATHEDRALS, CASTLES & MORE: SIDE TRIPS FROM KLAGENFURT

St. Veit an der Glan

The capital of Carinthia from 1170 until 1518, St. Veit an der Glan was where the dukes of Carinthia held power when the province was an imperial duchy. In the 15th century, high walls were built to fortify the city. To reach the town from Klagenfurt, drive 14km (9 miles) north on Route 83.

The **Trinity Column,** erected in 1715 to mark the town's deliverance from the plague, stands on the rectangular **Hauptplatz (Main Square).** Also in this square is the fountain called **Schüsselbrunnen.** It is believed that the bottom part of this fountain was excavated at the old Roman city of Virunum. A bronze statue crowning the fountain depicts a 16th-century miner, which St. Veit has adopted as its symbol.

The **Rathaus (Town Hall)** has a baroque exterior, although the building dates from 1468, and an arcaded courtyard. Guided tours are conducted through the great hall Thursday to Tuesday 8am to noon and 1 to 4pm, and on Wednesday 8am to noon (closed Sat–Sun Nov–Apr).

WHERE TO STAY & EAT

Kunsthotel Fuchspalast ★★★ 🏠 This is Carinthia's first art hotel, designed by Ernst Fuchs, doyen of Austria's Fantastic Realists. With a Tiffany-glass exterior, it's a luxurious establishment. This former ducal town has long needed accommodations to match its charm, and now it has a suitable hotel, which is often a venue for seminars and conferences.

The public rooms are filled with fine art, and each of the bedrooms is decorated in a different color scheme. All bathrooms come with new fittings, each with a shower unit. The restaurant offers impressive Styrian and continental cuisine, and there is grand comfort throughout the place.

Prof. Ernst Fuchs Platz 1, A-9300 St. Veit an der Glan. ⓒ **04212/4660.** Fax 04212/4660660. www. hotel-fuchspalast.at. 60 units. 90€ double. MC, V. **Amenities:** Bar/cafe; babysitting; dry cleaning; 1 room for those w/limited mobility; room service; smoke-free rooms. *In room:* TV, minibar, hairdryer, safe, free Wi-Fi.

Hochosterwitz Castle ★

St. Veit an der Glan stands at the center of the most castle-rich section of Austria, with more than a dozen of the fortress complexes lying within a 10-km (6½-mile) radius. The best known and most visited is **Hochosterwitz Castle** in Laundsdorf-Hochosterwitz (ⓒ **04213/2020**), about 10km (6¼ miles) to the east of St. Veit. The castle was first mentioned in documents of 860; in 1209, the ruling Spanheims made the Osterwitz family hereditary royal cupbearers and gave them the castle as a fiefdom. When the last fell victim to a Turkish invasion, the castle reverted to Emperor Frederick III, who bestowed it upon the regional governor, Christof Khevenhuller. In 1570, Baron Georg Khevenhuller purchased the citadel and fortified it against the Turks, providing it with an armory and adding the gates in 1586. Since that time, the castle has been the property of the Khevenhuller family, as noted a marble plate in the yard dated 1576.

Hochosterwitz Castle is open from Easter to October daily 8am to 6pm. Admission is 7.50€ for adults and 4.50€ for ages 6 to 18. A regional cafe and restaurant are located in the inner courtyard.

The Excavations at Magdalensberg ★

You can also strike out from St. Veit and head south, back to Klagenfurt, on Route 83. If you turn left after 6km (4 miles) on a road marked MAGDALENSBERG and travel east, you'll reach the **Ausgrabungen (Excavations) at Magdalensberg (℃ 04224/ 2255)**. About 14km (9 miles) from St. Veit, Magdalensberg was a Celto-Roman settlement site and the oldest Roman habitation north of the Alps. The Romans built a town here when they came to trade in the final century before the birth of Christ. In 1502, a farmer found a bronze statue, now called the **Magdalensberg Youth** (on display in Vienna), the earliest evidence of settlement. It was not until the late 19th century that excavation work began, with collectors in search of valuable Roman art objects. Serious archaeologists began more detailed excavations during the Allied occupation of Austria after World War II.

As you explore the ruins, you can see the foundations of a temple, as well as public baths and some mosaics. Tours are conducted only May to October daily 9am to 7pm. Admission is 5€ for adults and 3€ for children under 16.

A celebrated ritual (which has pagan origins), the "Four Hills Pilgrimage," starts from here every April. Participants race over four hills with burning torches, and must complete the run within 24 hours.

At the summit of the mountain, the Austrians have erected a shrine honoring two saints: Mary Magdalene and Helen. From it, a panoramic view of the encircling mountain range and the Klagenfurt basin unfolds.

Strassburg

Returning once more to St. Veit, you can head northeast along the B 94, which becomes the B 317. When you reach the junction with B 93, turn west along the upper Gurk Valley road, passing through the hamlet of Strassburg, which was a walled town in the Middle Ages. There is a Gothic **Pfarrkirche (Parish Church)** here, and the **Heilig-Geist-Spital Church,** dating from the 13th century, has some well-preserved frescoes. Dominating the village is a castle built in 1147, but it's changed over the centuries. This once was the headquarters of the powerful prince-bishops of Gurk. It has been turned into a local museum.

The Cathedral of Gurk ★★

A major pilgrimage site lies 3km (2 miles) to the west of Strassburg: The **Cathedral of Gurk Pfarramt Gurk (℃ 04266/8236)**. The cathedral is the principal feature of the little market town of Gurk, and from 1072 until 1787, this area was the bishop's see. The *dom* (cathedral) is a three-aisled basilica erected between the mid-12th and early 13th centuries, and it's one of the best examples of Romanesque ecclesiastical architecture in the country. A set of towers with onion-shaped domes rises nearly 43m (140 ft.).

The cathedral is rich in artwork, including the **Samson doorway ★**, an excellent example of Romanesque sculpture dating from 1180. Some **16th-century carved panels ★** tell the story of St. Emma, an 11th-century countess who was canonized in 1938. The main 17th-century altar has dozens of statues, and there's a **1740** baroque pulpit ★. In the bishop's chapel you can see **Romanesque murals ★**—other than the main altar, these are the most important art objects in the cathedral.

The cathedral is open daily 9am to 6pm. There is a guided tour in English of both the cathedral and the crypt for 4.60€. For 6.20€, you can include a visit to the bishop's chambers. Tours are conducted at 10:30am, 1:30, and 3pm daily.

Friesach

After visiting the Cathedral of Gurk, you can take the same road east, back through Strassburg. Back on the E7, and depending on your time and interest, you can either turn north to visit the town of Friesach or else travel south again, passing through St. Veit en route to Klagenfurt.

If you opt for the Friesach detour, you'll find an interesting old town worth exploring. If you came from Vienna, Friesach might be your gateway to Carinthia. This is an ancient town whose first mention in historic annals occurred in the mid-9th century. The town once belonged to the prince-archbishops of Salzburg, who held on to it until the beginning of the 19th century. Lying in the broad Valley of Melnitz, this was a stopover for traders between Venice and Austria's capital.

In the historic center of town, you can see part of the 12th-century town walls and the remains of a water-filled moat. The Romanesque **Stadtpfarrkirche (Town Parish Church),** Wiener Strasse, was constructed in the 13th century and is noted for its stained glass in the choir. The town has a number of other interesting buildings, including a **Dominican monastery** from 1673, built on the site of a much older structure and containing a 14th-century church. The monastery lies north of the moat, and in summer, open-air plays are performed here. You can also visit the 13th-century **Heiligblutkirche (Church of the Holy Blood),** south of Hauptplatz.

West of Friesach, a 1.5km-long (1-mile) road or footpath takes you to the hill **Petersberg,** where the 10th-century **Church of St. Peter** stands. Here you can see 12th-century frescoes in the watch tower, and the ruins of a castle that belonged to the prince-archbishops of Salzburg. North of the town, on **Geiersberg,** is a second 12th-century castle, partially reconstructed but still mostly in ruins.

Maria Saal ★

Just outside of Klagenfurt, you can visit the pilgrimage church of **Maria Saal,** on a hill overlooking the Zollfeld Plain, some 10km (6¼ miles) north of the provincial capital along Route 83.

Maria Saal was first built by Bishop Modestus around the mid-8th century. The present church, which dominates the valley with its twin towers made of volcanic stone, dates from the early part of the 15th century, when a defensive wall was constructed to ward off attacks from the east. In the latter part of that century, the Magyars tried to take the fortress-church, but, like the Turks in later years, they were unable to conquer it.

One of the church's most outstanding features is a "lantern of the dead" in the late-Gothic style. There are some marble Gothic tombstones on the church grounds, and there's the *karner* (charnel house), an octagonal Romanesque building with two tiers of galleries. The church has many *objets d'art,* but it's the 1425 image of the Virgin that has made it a pilgrimage site.

An excursion to take from Maria Saal is to the Herzogstuhl, or Carinthian Ducal Throne, 1.5km (1 mile) to the north. A double throne on this ancient site was constructed from stones found at the Roman city of Virunum. The dukes of Carinthia used the throne to grant fiefs in medieval days.

Lake Ossiacher

Follow the B95 northwest of Klagenfurt, passing through Moosburg and Feldkirchen to reach Ossiacher See (Lake Ossiacher). This body of water, some 11km (7 miles) long, is the province's third largest lake, with summer temperatures only slightly cooler than that of Wörthersee—a comfortable 79°F (26°C).

The lake is ringed with little villages that have become resorts by attracting summer visitors, mainly Austrians, who come to enjoy the sun and the water.

Our first stop, **Feldkirchen,** is an old town that once belonged to the Bamberg bishops. Located at a major crossroads, Feldkirchen grew and prospered from traders passing through the area, and pieces of the Middle Ages live on here, especially in the patrician houses and narrow streets. Visit the old quarter to see the Biedermeier facades added early in the 19th century. The village has a Romanesque **Pfarrkirche (Parish Church)** with a Gothic choir and frescoes from the 13th century. Some small lakes nearby are worth visiting, if time permits.

Ossiach, a resort on the lake's south side, is small (pop. 650), but it's still the biggest settlement on the Ossiacher See. Ossiach has an 11th-century Benedictine abbey that was reconstructed in the 1500s. The monastery was dissolved a century or so ago, and **Carinthian Summer Festival** special events take place here.

On the lake's north shore are the **Sattendorf** and **Treffen** resorts, which are open year-round. Here you can breathe the pure mountain air and wander across alpine meadows deep into the forest. Travelers can splash around in Ossiacher See or in indoor pools.

From the lake, you can make several easy excursions; take the **Kanzelbahn cable car** (10 min. from the resort) or drive to either Italy or Slovenia (20 min. to either destination), or make day trips to Klagenfurt (p. 439) or Villach (p. 450).

The little lakeside resort of **Annenheim** is on the north side of the Ossiacher See, near the end of the lake. From here, a cable car, the **Kanzelbahn,** takes you to **Kanzelhöhe** at 1,488m (4,882 ft.), where an observatory tower offers a panoramic view of the surrounding country.

LAKE WÖRTHER

The province's biggest alpine lake, 15km (10 miles) long, is the Wörthersee, lying just west of Klagenfurt and linked to the city by a channel. In summer, it's a mecca for watersports enthusiasts.

This lake's waters are quite warm—their temperature often exceeds 80°F (27°C) in midsummer. Beginning in May, Austrians swim here, something that rarely occurs in the alpine lakes of other provinces. The little villages around Wörthersee are flourishing summer resorts, especially **Maria Wörth** and **Velden.**

Velden ★★: The Heart of the Austrian Riviera

Velden, at the western end of the Wörthersee, is the most sophisticated resort in Carinthia and the heart of the Austrian Riviera. The resort has many landscaped parks that sweep down to the shore, and from most hotel rooms you'll have views of the sparkling blue water with the peaks of **Karawanken** in the background.

ESSENTIALS

GETTING THERE Velden sits astride the main routes that connect Klagenfurt with Villach, Salzburg, and Innsbruck. Dozens of trains stop throughout the day, and the trip from Klagenfurt takes 14 to 21 minutes. For information about **train schedules,** call ⓒ 05/1717 (www.oebb.at).

Velden has bus lines extending north and south, into small nearby villages, and east and west, paralleling the railway tracks to Klagenfurt and Villach. For **bus information,** call ⓒ 0463/54340 in Klagenfurt.

Driving from Klagenfurt, head west along Route 83 for 23km (14 miles).

VISITOR INFORMATION The **tourist office** in the village center (ⓒ 04274/2103) is open Monday to Thursday 8am to 6pm, Friday and Saturday 8am to 8pm, and Sunday 9am to 5pm.

WHAT TO DO IN VELDEN

Naturally, the big attraction here is watersports, ranging from swimming in the warm alpine lake to surfing. The long swimming season begins May 1 and continues until the end of October. Instruction is available for all water activities. The most respected watersports outfitter in Velden is **Segelschule und Surfschule Berger,** Seecorso 40, Velden (ⓒ **04274/2691**). They rent equipment—windsurfers, small boats, and canoes or kayaks—and give instruction. Many resort hotels have tennis courts, and you can also play golf at an 18-hole course 6km (4 miles) from Velden in a hilly landscape.

Most guests spend their time playing in the lake during the day and dancing the night away. Five o'clock tea dances are popular, and you can also trip the light fantastic to the orchestral music on the lake terraces. Summer festivals are often staged in Velden, and balls and beauty contests keep the resort's patrons amused. Contact the tourist office for more information about events and schedules. Also, this is a fine area for taking scenic country drives.

WHERE TO STAY & EAT

Golf Parkhotel ★★ This grand establishment attracts Viennese celebrities, members of the Saudi royal family, tennis and ski stars, and film crews shooting movies at the region's historic monuments. Originally built in 1968, the hotel sits in its own park beside the lake, offering peace, quiet, and impressive views of the valley below. Rooms are tastefully modern, each well furnished with comfy beds.

The heart and soul of the hotel is the restaurant, where a verdant terrace opens up in warm weather. The chef concocts a tempting array of frequently changing specialties, which might include a mousse of smoked trout with caviar in a champagne-flavored gelatin, river crayfish in a dill-flavored yogurt, and a supreme of freshwater char with tarragon and fresh asparagus.

Seecorso 68, A-9220 Velden. ⓒ **04274/22980.** Fax 04274/22989. www.hotelgolf.com. 90 units. 198€ double; from 228€ suite for 2. Rates include half-board. AE, DC, MC, V. **Amenities:** Restaurant; bar; indoor heated pool; 9-hole putting course; 3 tennis courts; fitness center; sauna; massage; babysitting; laundry service; dry cleaning; solarium. *In room:* TV, minibar, hairdryer, safe, free Wi-Fi.

Hotel Alte Post-Wrann ★ For many years, this hotel was the provincial headquarters for the postal routes from Vienna to Venice. Unlike many of the region's hotels, this one is open year-round. The sunny rooms are comfortable and conservatively furnished, and come in a variety of sizes—some quite large. All beds are excellent. Bathrooms generally have tubs or showers.

The entrance to the hotel's **Wrann** restaurant is marked by massive beams; during summer, seating is in the garden. Here, under a canopy of trees, you can order a range of traditional Austrian and regional recipes. The summer-only restaurant, **Vinoték,** is fashioned after a Viennese *heurige* (wine tavern) and specializes in local wines.

Europaplatz 4-6, A-9220 Velden. ℂ **04274/2141.** Fax 04274/51120. www.wrann.at. 36 units. 110€–146€ double; 144€–190€ suite. Rates include buffet breakfast. Half-board 17€ extra. AE, DC, MC, V. Parking 9€. **Amenities:** Restaurant; bar; dry cleaning; babysitting; fitness room; laundry service; room service; sauna; smoke-free rooms. *In room:* TV, hairdryer, minibar, safe, free Wi-Fi.

VELDEN AFTER DARK

The most visible and (on weekends) busiest nightlife spot is the **Casino Velden,** Am Corso 17 (ℂ 04274/2064). There are also two bars and a restaurant where you can lick your wounds after losing at the gambling tables.

You must be at least 18 years old and present your passport to enter; men must wear a jacket and tie. The complex is open daily from noon to 3am. Games of chance include blackjack, *baccarat, chemin de fer,* stud poker, and American and French roulette, as well as slot machines. You pay 23€ at the door, but you're granted 30€ worth of chips, so entrance is essentially free.

Don't think, however, that you have to enter the precincts of the casino to be amused and entertained. The **American Bar** (also known as the **Schinackl Bar,** Am Corso 10; ℂ **04274/51233**) is the de facto social centerpiece of the town. Here you'll see virtually everyone, either drinking at the bar with you or during their promenades up and down the lakefront. Set almost adjacent to the casino, it's open May to mid-September nightly from 8pm to 4am, features both indoor and outdoor areas, and presents live music from Monday to Saturday beginning at 10pm. A *schinackl,* incidentally, is a vernacular name for a style of rowboat used to catch fish in Carinthia.

If you're young at heart, you might enjoy the **Crazy Bull Disco,** Klagenfurter Strasse 17 (ℂ **04274/2034**), where high-volume music, sometimes heavy metal, brings influences from faraway London and Los Angeles to otherwise sleepy Velden. The Crazy Bull is open nightly 10pm to around 4am, usually at no charge.

Maria Wörth ★

Maria Wörth is one of the best bases for visiting Carinthia's largest alpine lake, the Wörthersee. Part of this village, on the southern side of the lake across from Pörtschach, juts out into the lake on a rocky peninsula, providing a good view of the area. In addition to enjoying the lake, you can visit the golf courses in the nearby hamlet of Dellach.

The village's Gothic **Pfarrkirche (Parish Church)** has a baroque interior and a Romanesque crypt. It's noted for its 15th-century main altar. The circular *Karner* (charnel house) in the yard was built in 1278.

Nearby is another noted church, the **Rosenkranzkirche,** from the 12th century, often referred to as "the winter church." It has some Romanesque frescoes of the Apostles from that century.

ESSENTIALS

GETTING THERE To reach Maria Wörth, take the **train** to either Velden or Klagenfurt, and then board one of the dozens of buses that depart throughout the day for Maria Wörth (trip time: 25–45 min.). For rail information, contact ℂ **05/1717** (www.oebb.at). For bus information, call ℂ **0463/54340** in Klagenfurt. If you're **driving** from Klagenfurt, head south on the B91 and turn right onto Südring. Turn left onto Wörthersee Südufer Strasse, the road running along the southern tier of the lake, and follow it to MARIA WÖRTH. The drive takes about 15 to 20 minutes.

VISITOR INFORMATION The **tourist office** in the town center (☏ **04273/ 2240**) is open Monday to Friday 8am to 12:30pm and 1 to 5pm, and Saturday and Sunday 10am to 12:30pm and 1:30 to 4pm.

WHERE TO STAY & EAT

Aenea ★★★ This startlingly modern hotel is designer chic. In all of Carinthia there is nothing as stylishly minimalist, as trend setting—rising five floors in a glass-and-concrete structure that evokes an avant-garde museum of art. The location is spectacular, in the village of Reifinitz, opening onto the southern tier of Lake Wörthersee, 3km (2 miles) from Maria Wörth.

Inside, the hotel is designed for complete relaxation, the management boasting "maximum individual freedom—with no preordained hotel rhythm." On the fourth floor is a sun terrace with a Finnish sauna, aroma steam bath, solarium, fitness center, massage room, and even a tennis court, plus a panoramic pool. An elevator takes you down to the lake pavilion with its bathing beach. Bedrooms, created by Rodolfo Dordoni, are stunning and the bathrooms are by Philippe Starck. Each room is a suite with a good-size terrace opening onto Wörthersee.

Wörthersee-Süduferstrasse 86, A-9081 Reifinitz (Maria Wörth). ☏ **04273/26220.** Fax 04273/26220-20. www.aenea.at. 15 suites. July–Aug 550€ suite; off-season 350€ suite. Rates include breakfast. AE, DC, MC, V. Closed Nov–Mar. **Amenities:** Restaurant; 2 bars; bathing beach; steam bath; fitness center; laundry service; massage; pool; room service; sauna; solarium; spa; sun terrace; tennis court. *In room:* A/C in some, TV, hairdryer, safe, free Ethernet.

VILLACH

48km (30 miles) W of Klagenfurt; 140km (87 miles) SE of Salzburg

Villach, at the center of the Carinthian lake district in a broad basin along the Drau River, is a great place from which to explore the rest of the district. It's also the gateway to the south, and it's easy to make day trips to Slovenia or Italy from here. If you were planning on continuing south anyway, this is also a good stopover point. A settlement since Roman times, Villach belonged to the bishops of Bamberg (a distant lake near Nürnberg, Germany) from the 11th century until Maria Theresa acquired it for the Habsburgs. Today it's an industrial town.

Essentials

GETTING THERE Villach is a railway junction for four different lines connecting central and southern Austria with Italy, and **trains** arrive throughout the day from Vienna (trip time: 4½ hr.) and Klagenfurt (trip time: 25 min.). Although it's easier to take the train, several different bus lines fan out into the surrounding countryside. For **train information,** call ☏ **05/1717;** for **bus information,** call ☏ **04242/ 44410.** If you're **driving** from Klagenfurt, Villach is about 56km (35 miles) west on the A2.

VISITOR INFORMATION The **tourist office,** Rathausplatz 1 (☏ **04242/ 2052900**), is open Monday to Friday 9am to 6pm, and Saturday 10am to 5pm.

Exploring Villach & the Villacher Alps ★

At the center of the Altstadt (Old City) is **Hauptplatz (Main Square).** There's a bridge over the Drau at Hauptplatz's north end, and the **Pfarrkirche (Parish Church)** is at the south end. The church is a mixture of styles, with a baroque altar

THERMAL waters TO STAY YOUNG

From the heart of the Old Town in Villach, it's a 4-km (2½-mile) drive to **Warmbad-Villach,** a town known for its thermal swimming pools and mineral springs. This spa, on the southern fringe of Villach, is the only place where visitors can swim at the source of the thermal waters, which are supposed to counteract the aging process.

The warm springs at Warmbad were used by the ancient Romans, and there was a road that passed through Warmbad en route to Italy. During the Middle Ages, Villach became a thriving market town. Beginning with Europe's spa craze in the late 19th century, a handful of spa hotels sprung up around Warmbad-Villach, the first of which was the Kurhotel Warmbaderhof. We've recommended a few spa hotels below.

Hotel Warmbaderhof, Kadischenallée, Warmbad Villach (✆ **04242/30010;** fax 04242/30011309; www.warmbad.at), is the largest and most dignified of the hotels that have sprung up near Warmbad's famous springs. Built 200 years ago, and enlarged and modernized since, it boasts a covered passageway leading directly to the town's spa facilities. Set amid gardens in the town center, the hotel offers its own heated swimming pool with a ceiling like a continuous barrel vault, and an angular outdoor pool connected with the indoor pool. The two hotel restaurants serve well-prepared food. Most of the 116 rooms and 12 suites are in a modern wing attached to the establishment's historic core and are conservatively furnished. The double rate is 246€ to 402€; a suite runs 460€ to 490€. Rates include half-board, and there's free parking. The hotel is closed 3 to 4 weeks in November and December.

Standing in a large park, **Der Karawankenhof,** Kadischenallée (✆ **04242/300220;** fax 04242/30022061; www.warmbad.at), offers a battery of health and spa facilities. The "bath world," as they call it, consists of whirlpools, indoor and outdoor swimming pools, rapids, a fitness center, a gym, a sauna, massage treatments, and other facilities. The restaurant serves excellent food. This sizable four-star modern hotel, open all year, rents 70 well-furnished rooms and 10 suites; the double rate is 150€ to 184€ or 216€ in a suite. Rates include half-board.

Josefinenhof Hotel ★, Kadischenallée 8 (✆ **04242/30030;** fax 04242/30033089; www.warmbad.com), has its own spa, fitness, and conference facilities. Although much of this hotel was built in the 1960s, its original core dates from the 1700s as a hospital, and its terrace stretches toward the hotel's private park. You can enjoy treatments at the hydrotherapy and beauty center, or dabble in a host of health and medical services. The 52 comfortable rooms and nine suites have rows of sun-flooded windows and balconies. Bathrooms are well equipped with robes and hair dryers. The double rate is 135€. Rates include full board, and parking is free.

Getting There Warmbad, no more than a cluster of buildings on routes heading into Italy, is 4km (2½ miles) south of Villach, and the spa defines the town. A **red bus** (marked WARMBAD when it goes to Warmbad and BAHNHOF as it returns to Villach) runs at 30-minute intervals all day long; the trip takes 10 to 12 minutes. In Villach, the railway station acts as the stop for the red bus, although it stops almost everywhere else in between the towns. There are also trains from Villach's main station at 30-minute intervals. For schedules and fares, call ✆ **05/1717.**

and Gothic choir stalls. Like most towns of its size, Villach has a **Trinity Column,** dating from 1739, commemorating deliverance from the plague.

In the **Schillerpark,** on Peraustrasse, there's a large panoramic relief of the province, the **Relief von Kärnten,** that's on view from May 2 to the end of October (except Fri, Sun, and holidays) from 10am to 4:30pm.

Villach is a good center from which to explore the Carinthian lake district, including the **Villacher Alps,** an 18-km (11-mile) journey via the Villacher Alpenstrasse toll road (12€ each way). There are panoramic views in many directions, and the best spots are marked. At the end of the road a chairlift will take you to the summit of **Dobratsch** (2,166m/7,106 ft.), which offers one of the most famous views in Austria. At the top, a network of hiking paths fans out.

If you're in Villach in summer, you might want to drive southeast to **Faakersee (Lake Faaker),** a small body of water that's popular with swimmers and water-skiers. This lake's waters frequently reach 79°F (26°C) in July and August. From Villach, follow the signs to Faak.

Where to Stay

Romantik Hotel Post ★★   Rich in history, this hotel was built in 1500, and some original elements have been incorporated into the updated design. The facade is a Teutonic fantasy of carved stone detailing, Ionic columns, and intricately patterned wrought-iron. Between 1548 and 1629, this was the town palace of one of Carinthia's richest families, when it hosted an emperor, a king, an archduke, and an empress (Maria Theresa). Later still, a nephew of Napoleon I dropped in and signed a registration slip. A host of elegantly furnished rooms open onto an arcade, shielded from the sun by ancient chestnut trees.

The establishment offers traditional cuisine in its most refined form, including *Tafelspitz;* schnitzels and recipes with local venison, including soups, pâtés, and stews, as well as lighter, more health-conscious cuisine. In summer, piano music and candlelit dinners are offered in the garden courtyard.

Hauptplatz 26, A-9500 Villach. ✆ **04242/261010.** Fax 04242/26101420. www.romantik-hotel.com. 63 units. 70€–195€ double; 190€–280€ suite. Rates include buffet breakfast. Half-board 25€ extra. AE, DC, MC, V. **Amenities:** Restaurant; dry cleaning; fitness center; laundry service; massage; sauna; smoke-free rooms; solarium. *In room:* TV, minibar, hairdryer, free Wi-Fi.

Where to Eat

Stadt Restaurant ★★ AUSTRIAN/CARINTHIAN   Acclaimed for its cuisine and highly rated in European gourmet guides, this restaurant is a traditional favorite. Wolfgang Puck was an apprentice chef at The Post before heading to Los Angeles, where he eventually opened his well-known restaurant, Spago. In summer, tables are placed outside in fair weather in a part of the hotel known as The Orangerie, with its wild roses and climbing ivy. If there's a celebrity visiting in summer, chances are you'll find them dining here. The menu is seasonally adjusted, including freshly caught fish, grilled to your preference. Many traditional Carinthian specialties are also served here, including *Kärtner Käsnudeln,* which are large, round ravioli stuffed with savory cheese. In summer the herbs used in many of the dishes come straight from the hotel garden, as do many of the fresh vegetables. In the evening, live piano music entertains diners.

Hauptplatz 26. ✆ **04242/261010.** Reservations required. Main courses 15€–24€. AE, DC, MC, V. Daily 11:45am–2:30pm and 6:30–10:30pm.

LAKE MILLSTATTER

The second largest lake in the province, Millstatter See is 13km (8 miles) long, 2km (1 mile) wide, and 140m (459 ft.) deep. This beautiful blue lake, east of Spittal, is set against a backdrop of the forested **Seerücken** (866m/2,841 ft.) to the south and **Nockberge** to the north.

Millstatt am See

About midway along the lake's northern rim, **Millstatt am See** and **Seeboden** are the principal lake resorts. Most hotels here are open only during the warmer months, and prices are highest in July and August, when reservations are mandatory. Prices are often reduced in late spring and early autumn, when it's easier to find a room. An **organ-music festival** is held May to September.

ESSENTIALS

GETTING THERE   Because Millstatt has no train connections, most travelers take a **train** to Spittal an der Drau from Klagenfurt (trip time: 1 hr.) or Salzburg (trip time: 2 hr.). (On many maps and timetables, this railway junction is referred to as Spittal–Millstattersee.) From Spittal's railway station, passengers catch one of the **buses** that depart around 16 times a day for the 20-minute trip to Millstatt am See.

Millstatt is 299km (186 miles) southwest of Vienna and 90km (56 miles) west of Klagenfurt. To **drive** here from Villach, head northwest along the A10, bypassing Spittal. At the turnoff for Seeboden, head east along the northern perimeter of the lake, following Route 98.

VISITOR INFORMATION   The **tourist office** in the village center (© **04766/2022**) is open daily 9am to 7pm.

VISITING THE ABBEY

Other than the lake, Millstatt's main attraction is the *Stift* (Abbey) ★, which was founded in 1080 as a Benedictine monastery. Near the end of the 15th century, it was taken over by Jesuits. One part of the monastery has been used as a hotel (the **Hotel Lindenhof**) since 1773, and it was once the mansion of the Grand Master of the Knights of St. George.

In the Abbey courtyard stands a 1,000-year-old "Judgment" lime tree. The cloister, which has Gothic vaulting and Romanesque arches, is reached from the east side of the court. The abbey contains a fresco of the Last Judgment, a masterpiece of Austrian Renaissance art. The Stiftskirche (Abbey Church) has a Romanesque doorway that is the complex's major architectural attraction.

WHERE TO STAY & EAT

Hotel Alpenrose ★ 🎁   Enjoying a splendid scenic setting with a view of the valley and the mountains, the Hotel Alpenrose is in the tiny alpine village of Obermillstatt, 2km (1½ miles) from the center of Millstatt. This is the first "biohotel" to open in Austria, whose proprietors, the Theuermanns, are involved in holistic medicine, macrobiotic diets, and yoga. They run a good hotel, largely tech-free, and restaurant in a chalet-inspired building that contains well-furnished rooms, each with a balcony. Smoking is not permitted.

Obermillstatt, A-9872 Millstatt am See. © **04766/2500.** Fax 04766/3425. www.biohotel-alpenrose.at. 30 units. 96€–111€ per person. Rates include half-board (vegetarian option available). No credit cards. **Amenities:** Restaurant; lounge; heated outdoor pool; spa; sauna; laundry service; dry cleaning; rooms for those w/limited mobility. *In room:* Hairdryer, bath robe, fruit.

Hotel am See Die Forelle ★   This attractive, four-story hotel has a history dating from around 1900, when a private villa and an unpretentious guesthouse were combined. Today, much enlarged and improved over the years, the hotel has a lakeside terrace sheltered by chestnut trees and a reputation as one of the finest hotels on the Millstattersee. The hotel's interior contains bright, medium-size rooms (all but 10 have lake views) equipped with good beds. The small bathrooms have tubs or shower stalls. There's a big, well-maintained lawn that leads down to the lakefront beach. The Aniwanter family serves excellent cuisine, with fixed-price four-course meals and a la carte dishes.

A-9872 Millstatt am See. ⓒ **04766/2050.** Fax 04766/205011. www.hotel-forelle.at. 136€–280€ double. Rates include half-board. MC, V. Closed mid-Oct to early Apr. **Amenities:** Restaurant; bar; outdoor heated pool; whirlpool; Jacuzzi; sauna; room service; smoke-free rooms. *In room:* TV, hairdryer, safe, Ethernet at 5€/hour.

STYRIA

I n Styria, the "green heart of Austria," forests cover about half the region, and grasslands and vineyards blanket another quarter. This is one of Austria's bargain provinces—even its top hotels are moderately priced. Trout fishing, mountain climbing, and hiking are popular summer activities, and, though it has a long way to go before it will rival Salzburg or Tyrol, in the past decade Styria has been emerging as a ski area and Schladming-Rohrmoos will be hosting the 2013 FIS Alpine World Ski Championship.

Styria ("Steiermark" in German) is the second largest province in the country. It borders Slovenia as well as the Austrian provinces of Burgenland, Lower Austria, Upper Austria, Land Salzburg, and Carinthia. Northwestern Styria includes the alpine ranges of the Salzkammergut, while its eastern section resembles the plains of Hungary.

Throughout history, this rich land of valleys, rivers, mountain peaks, and glaciers has been sought after. It was greedily attacked by Huns, Hungarians, and Turks, and even in Celtic times people knew that the mountains of Upper Styria were a valuable source of iron ore, which the tribes used for weapons and other tools. The Romans also exploited the rich deposits, and the Crusaders used armor made from Styrian iron to fight the "infidel" in the East. Iron resources shaped Styria's economy, and today it's Austria's leading mining province.

Styria is a province deeply steeped in tradition, and the costume that some of the men still occasionally wear demonstrates this point. Derived from an original peasant costume, it's made of stout greenish-gray cloth with Styrian green material used for the lapels and the stripe along the side of the pant legs.

Graz, the capital of Styria, is the second largest Austrian city, and in imperial times it was known as the place to which state officials retired— the city even acquired the nickname Pensionopolis (City of the Retired). Home to six universities, Graz is also a lively student town, with plenty of nocturnal activity to go around (see Graz After Dark, below).

Other interesting areas to visit in Styria include Bad Gleichenberg, the most important summer spa in South Styria, set among parks and mineral waters; and Bad Aussee, an old market town and spa in the heart of the lush Salzkammergut. Also worth a visit are Murau, a winter ski region and a good center for driving tours of the surrounding countryside, and Mariazell, Austria's pilgrimage center. If you're driving around this area, you should know that parking is free unless otherwise noted, and is rarely a problem.

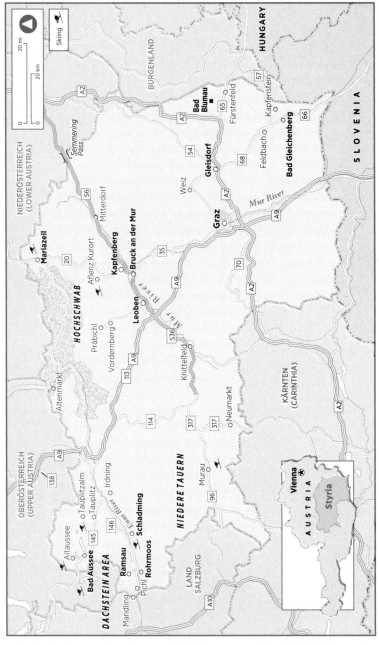

Tips for Active Travelers

Styria's Salzkammergut and steppe country, which resembles that of the Great Hungarian Plain, is a conglomerate of river valleys, mountain peaks, glaciers, and verdant sun-drunk vineyards that's a great place for outdoor activities. Graz serves as a good base for stockpiling supplies and planning your excursions. Here are a few tips on where to plan an outdoorsy trip in Styria.

BALLOONING   Styria is home to several hot-air ballooning outfits. Ask a local entrepreneur to take you up for a 90- to 120-minute escapade over the region's rooftops and lakes, preferably with a bottle of champagne and a good companion. The oldest outfitter in Styria (established in 1976) is **Johann Alma's Union Aeronautic Styria,** A-8182 Puch bei Weiz 100 (✆ 06642001916; www.ballonclub-apfeldorf-puch.at). Located in a village adjacent to the Stubenbergsee (a local lake), 40km (25 miles) east of Graz, it maintains six balloons. Excursions cost 220€ per person for the first flight and 150€ for subsequent flights. Flights can be conducted, weather permitting, in any season. Each balloon holds a pilot and up to three passengers.

BIKING   Cycling enthusiasts will be pleased by Styria's terrain. The gentle undulations of the eastern plain and the historic scenery make for a pleasant ride. You can rent a bike through an independent operator, **Bicycle,** Körösistrasse 17 (✆ 0316/8213570; www.bicycle.at), near Graz's town center for 18€ per day. Contact **Eurobike,** Mühlstrasse 20, A-5162 Oberturn (✆ 06219/7444), to arrange bike tours through some of the most scenic regions of Austria and Italy. A particularly appealing trip is an excursion known as "Wine and Wellness in Styria," a popular week-long trek along the Mur River. The average age of participants is from 50 to 60, with costs between 700€ and 850€, depending on the hotel you choose. Overnight accommodations, some meals, equipment rental, and luggage transfers are included in the price. You pay extra, however, for breakfast and dinner, costing 115€ per person.

BOATING   The region's many lakes are great places for experienced and novice boaters alike. Go to Michael **Hampl** for boat rentals, Bräuhof 61, A-8993 Grundlsee (✆ 0676 4828991). His sailing school is open from May to September. He charges 15€/hour for rentals. **Hotel Backenstein,** just up the hill at Bräuhof 156, A-8993 Grundlsee (✆ 0664/4419637; www.backenstein.at), rents small quiet apartments for one to three people at affordable rates (57€–63€ per room per day plus 1€ extra per person). The living rooms have tiled wood stoves and balconies with lovely views of the lake.

CANOEING   Whitewater enthusiasts will be enchanted by the clean, crisp waters of the glacial runoff. Although water temperatures can be brisk, any hearty rafter will tell you the best way to stay warm is to paddle furiously. **Sportagentur Strobl,** Ausseer Strasse 2–4, A-8940 Liezen (✆ 03612/25343; www.rafting.at).

FISHING   If you want to spend an afternoon fishing, cast your luck with one of the guide services that can be arranged for you by the **Tourismusverband Ausseerland,** Bahnhofstrasse 132, A-8990 Bad Aussee (✆ 03622/54040; www.ausseerland.at), or Tourismusverband **Murau Kreischberg,** Bundesstrasse 13A, A-8850 Bad Aussee (✆ 03532/2720; www.murau-kreischberg.at).

GOLF   Styria's gently undulating landscapes are well suited for golf courses, many of which allow nonmembers to reserve tee-off times if the course isn't too busy. Two of the region's most appealing golf courses are **Golfclub Gut Murstätten,** A-8403 Lebring (✆ 03182/3555; www.gcmurstaetten.at), half an hour's drive south of Graz;

and the **Golfclub Murhof,** Adriach 53, A-8130 Frohnleiten (✆ **03126/3010;** www.murhof.at), a 30-minute drive north of Graz. Additionally, any hotel or tourist office can point you to other golf courses.

HIKING   Those of us who toil for our highs will want to experience some of the climbs in the Dachstein–Tauern region. It's best to scale the steep rock faces of the Alps with an experienced guide. A guide (or, if you'd prefer, just some climbing buddies) can be located for you by **Bergführerbüro Ramsau/Dachstein,** Vorberg 237, A-8972 Ramsau (✆ **0664/5220080;** www.bergsteigerschule.net).

SKIING   The Dachstein glacier enables year-round skiing in Styria. Cross-country skiers will find this a great diversion in summertime. For general and booking information, contact **Tourismusverband Ramsau** (✆ **03687/81833**). The Dachstein–Tauern (see later in this chapter) and Salzkammergut regions have winter ski facilities.

TENNIS   If you want to get your match on, **Sporthotel Matschner** in Ramsau (✆ **03687/81721**) offers guests hotel and tennis packages, as do many other hotels with courts (see hotel reviews throughout this chapter).

GRAZ ★★

200km (124 miles) SW of Vienna; 138km (86 miles) NE of Klagenfurt; 285km (177 miles) SE of Salzburg

Graz, Styria's capital, began at a ford in the Mur River next to a steep rocky hill. Over the centuries, Roman, Slavic, and Bavarian cultures all had a hand in shaping the town that the EU chose as the European Capital of Culture 2003.

Fearing floods, early settlers established fortifications on the steep dolomite hill overlooking the river's ford. The city's name is derived from the Slavic word *gradec,* meaning "little fortress." A small castle was built on the hill, which is now the Schlossberg. Many governments have ruled Graz, including German, Bohemian, and Hungarian, not to mention the Babenbergs and the Habsburgs.

The medieval town developed at the foot of the Schlossberg and some of the structures from the late-Gothic period remain, built when Emperor Frederick III used Graz as a capital after the Hungarians forced him out of Vienna. The castle and the cathedral, along with the city's narrow-gabled roofs and arcaded courtyards, all contribute to its charm.

When the Habsburg inheritance was divided into Austrian and Spanish branches in 1564, Graz became the prosperous capital of "Inner Austria" and the residence of Archduke Carl, who ruled Styria, Carinthia, and Italian Habsburg lands. Carl had the town's fortifications strengthened in the Italian style, with bastions and moats.

A Jesuit college and Lutheran school were both active by the end of the 16th century. The astronomer Johannes Kepler (1571–1630) began his teaching career at the Lutheran school. Fine arts and commerce flourished in Graz, bringing honor and riches to the city, and that prosperity is reflected in palaces and mansions built during that period. Italian Renaissance architects were making their impact here around the time Emperor Ferdinand II moved his court to Vienna in 1619.

The city walls were demolished in 1784, and the slopes they'd stood on were planted with trees. Napoleon's armies made three appearances here, and Austria's defeat by his forces at the Battle of Wagram (1809) resulted in a treaty that forced Graz to level the Schlossberg's battlements. The citizens of Graz were able to save the **Uhrturm (Clock Tower)** and the **bell tower** by paying a high ransom. The Schlossberg became the beautiful park you see today.

During World War II, the city saw much bombing and devastation. However, in 1945, Graz was allotted to the British, and reconstruction began.

Today, Graz has some 290,000 inhabitants, and it supports thriving breweries, machine factories, trading companies, and service industries. The **Graz Fair** is an important commercial and industrial event in southeastern Europe. Graz's three universities, opera house, theater, museums, concert halls, and art galleries comprise Styria's cultural center.

Graz is a great place to stay because it's easy to make day trips into the countryside from here, and there's plenty to see and do. Visit the Schlossberg (castle), go hiking or hot-air ballooning, or visit one of the museums. If you're here in the autumn, you might want to attend the **Steirischer Herbst (Styrian Autumn)** festival, which features contemporary art, music, and literature. The arts festival has a reputation as avant-garde, presenting everything from jazz to mime.

Essentials

GETTING THERE

By Plane

Austrian Airlines (✆ **05176/67200**) offers daily flights from Vienna to **Thalerhof International Airport** (✆ **0316/2902;** www.flughafen-graz.at), 18km (11 miles) south of Graz. **Tyrolean Air** and **Lufthansa** also serve the airport. There are public GVB buses (see below) that leave from the airport 2–3 times an hour, coincident with the arrival of incoming flights, but, due to scheduling changes, the trips aren't always frequent enough. The much more convenient cab ride from the airport to the city center (for up to four passengers) costs around 20€.

By Train

Graz is Austria's southern center for rail lines between Vienna and Slovenia. It's also the junction for secondary rail lines that extend to Budapest and a series of valleys in western Styria. Trains depart from Wien Meidling every hour from 6am to 9pm. Through connections, it's easy to get here from other Austrian cities such as Innsbruck, Salzburg, and Klagenfurt. In addition, about one local train per hour arrives in Graz from minor rail lines in western Styria's isolated valleys and from the more populated areas of eastern Styria and the Hungarian border. For **rail information,** call ✆ **05/1717** (www.oebb.at).

By Bus

Graz is also the departure point for about 100 different bus lines, most of which head toward hamlets and small villages. For bus information, call ✆ **0316/5987.** Because of its excellent train connections, however, most travelers arrive by rail.

By Car

If you're driving from Vienna, take the A2 south (Süd Autobahn). Exit at Knoten Graz Ost (Exit 179).

GETTING AROUND

Graz City Transport (GVB), Andreas Hofer Platz 15 (✆ **0316/8870**), operates streetcar and bus services throughout the city. **Jakominiplatz,** on the river's eastern bank, and **Hauptplatz,** on the western bank, are the points where most streetcar lines intersect. **The GVB Mobilität Zentrum** office at Jakoministrasse 1 is open Monday to Friday 8am to 6pm, Saturday 8am to 1or pm.

AUSTRIA
Vienna
Graz

Universität
Techn. Universität

ATTRACTIONS ●
Burg **29**
Domkirche **30**
Griesplatz **2**
Hauptplatz **16**
Island in the Mur **5**
Jakominiplatz **23**
Kunsthaus **4**
Landesmuseum Joanneum **20**
Landeszeughaus **18**
Landhaus **19**
Mariahilferkirche **6**
Mausoleum of Emperor
 Ferdinand II **12**
Platz am Eisernen Tor **22**
Rathaus **17**
Schlossberg **8**
Uhrturm **13**

HOTELS ■
Augartenhotel **24**
Grand Hotel Wiesler Graz **3**
Hotel Drei Raben **1**
Hotel zum Dom **26**
Romantik Parkhotel **31**
Schlossberg Hotel **7**

RESTAURANTS ◆
Aiola Upstairs **9**
Altsteirische
 Schmankerlstub'n **15**
Café Harrach **11**
Café Leinich **25**
Das Wirtshaus Greiner **10**
Hofkeller **28**
Iohan **27**
Krebsenkeller **14**
Landhaus-Keller **21**

For information on Postbuses, contact the **Graz City Tourist office,** Herrengasse 16 (② **0316/80750**).

The city's largest underground parking area is the **Tiefgarage Andreas-Hofer-Platz,** on the Andreas-Hofer-Platz (② **0316/829191**). Parking costs 40€ for a full day or 4€ per hour. Within the city's historic center, you can park in the blue zones—indicated by a blue line painted beside the curb—for up to 3 hours. Parking costs .60€ per half-hour. You can either put coins in a parking meter or buy parking vouchers from tobacco shops or post offices. To use the voucher, fill in the blanks with the date and the time you parked in a spot, and leave it on the dashboard so it's visible through the windshield.

Major car-rental agencies in Graz (all also represented at the airport) include **Avis,** Schlögelgasse 10 (② **0316/812920**); **Budget,** Europaplatz 12 (② **0316/722074**); and **Hertz,** Andreas-Hofer-Platz (② **0316/825007**). These offices are open Monday to Friday 8am to 5pm, Saturday 9am to noon.

Taxis can be hailed on the street, lining up at any of the city's clearly designated taxi stands (the largest is in front of the main railway station), or called ② **878,** which gains access to the biggest company in Graz; also ② **983,** or ② **889.**

CITY LAYOUT

The **Altstadt (Old Town)** lies on the left bank of the Mur, centered on **Hauptplatz (Main Square).** To the south of this landmark plaza looms the **Rathaus (Town Hall).** Southeast of Hauptplatz is **Herrengasse,** a pedestrian area used by local shoppers, which comes to an end at **Platz am Eisernen Tor,** with its column mounted by a 17th-century figure of the Virgin.

At the eastern end of the **Opernring** is the municipal park, **Stadtpark,** dating from the 19th century. The Grazer **Burg,** a 15th-century imperial stronghold, stands northeast of Hauptplatz. South of the Burg rises the late-Gothic **Graz cathedral,** and south of the cathedral is the baroque **mausoleum** of Emperor Ferdinand II. Rising above the Altstadt is the **Schlossberg,** which can be reached by the cable railway.

VISITOR INFORMATION

The **Graz City Tourist Office,** Herrengasse 16 (② **0316/80750;** www.graztourism us.at), book hotel rooms throughout Styria and provide information about the area. It's open September to June, Monday to Sunday 10am to 5pm; July and August10am to 6pm.

[FastFACTS] GRAZ

Babysitters Most hotels can arrange for qualified babysitters, or you can call **UNIKID,** Harrachgasse 32 (② **0316/3801064;** http:// www.kfunigraz.ac.at/ unikid/).

Currency Exchange The best rates are offered at the main post office (see below).

Doctors & Dentists You can get the names of English-speaking doctors and dentists on call for local emergencies from your hotel or by calling the local hospital, **Landes-krankenhaus,** Auenbrugger-platz 1 (② **0316/3850**).

Drugstores The most central is the **Adler-Apoteke,** Haubtplatz 4 (② **0316/830342**). Hours are Monday to Friday 8am to 6pm and Saturday 8am to 12:30pm.

Emergencies Call ② **133** for the police (Polizei), ② **122** for the fire department (Feuerwehr), or ℂ **144** for an ambulance (Krankenwagen).

Hospitals   The two best medical facilities in Graz are the **Krankenhaus der Elisabethinen,** Elisabethinergasse 14 (ℂ **0316/ 70630**), and the larger **Landeskrankenhaus,** Auenbruggerplatz 1 (ℂ **0316/ 3850**). Both have emergency rooms, and many staff members speak English.

Internet Access   The most convenient location is **Café Zentral,** Andreas-Hofer-Platz 9 (ℂ **0316/ 832468**), open Monday to Friday 7am to 10pm, Saturday 7am to noon. It charges 4.50€ per hour.

Luggage Storage   There are storage facilities on the main floors of both the railway station and the bus station. Depending on the size of your luggage, you can either store it at the storage office for 3€ per day, or you can rent lockers for 2€–5€. The service is available daily 6am to midnight.

Police   Call ℂ **133** for the police.

Post Office   The main post office, **Neutorgasse** 46 (ℂ **0316/8808425**), is open Monday to Friday 8am to 8pm and Saturday 8am to 1pm. There's also a post office next to the Hauptbahnhof (main train station).

Restrooms (toilets)   Restrooms (toilets) in the city center are labeled WC. You can also find toilets at bus, railway, and air terminals; at major museums; and in cafes, where it's polite to buy a small item such as coffee if you want to use the restroom (toilet) facilities.

Safety   Graz traditionally has been one of Europe's safest cities. However, crime is rising, so take the usual precautions.

Taxes   Graz imposes no special city taxes other than the value-added tax on all goods and services in Austria. Standard V.A.T. is 20%.

Transit Information   Call ℂ **0316/88700.**

Useful Telephone Numbers   For the airport, call ℂ **0316/2902;** for train information, call ℂ **05/1717.**

What to See & Do
EXPLORING THE TOWN

Much of Graz's Old Town is well preserved, and many visitors take tours through here. The **Hauptplatz (Main Square),** in the heart of the city, began as the main market square around 1160—a function it still maintains to this day. It is surrounded by an array of buildings, many with medieval to late Gothic structures and sporting Biedermeier or baroque facades. The **Luegg House,** at the corner of Sporgasse, stands out with its round arch arcades and ornamented facade dating from the 17th century.

At the opposite end of the square, down Herrengasse, one of the largely pedestrian main streets, you'll find the **Landhaus,** the city's first Renaissance building, which houses the world's largest original armory, the **Landeszeughaus.**

In 1623, the Emperor had the city walls widened to accommodate a massive surge in population. The **Paulustor (Paul's Gate),** is the last remaining piece of the city's 17th-century fortification.

For a look at another side of Graz, visit the little-known neighborhood of **Gries,** lying across the River Mur from the old town. This is where the majority of immigrants have settled, forming Graz's multi-ethnic sector. The center of Gries is the aptly named **Griesplatz,** where vendors sell mainly handicrafts from countries such as South Korea, Vietnam, Thailand, China, and the Philippines. There's also a large Turkish and Lebanese population. You can grab a box of fried chicken and veggies at an Asian eatery, or a cup of thick Turkish coffee in one of the many cafes and, depending on where you are, enjoy diverse musical styles from Balkan folk to Arab pop.

Burg One of the most visible buildings in town, the castle was built in 1499 for Emperor Maximilian I. The Burg is devoted exclusively to offices of the Styrian government and is not open to visitors. However, it does contain an unusual double staircase, the **Wendeltreppe,** whose helix shape is a marvel of medieval stonework. The concierge will usually allow visitors in for a peek.

Northeast of Hauptplatz in the Old Town. Free admission. Mon–Fri 9am–5pm. Tram: 3 or 6.

Domkirche This cathedral was originally the Romanesque Church of St. Aegydius. It was a fortified structure outside the town walls that was first referred to in a late-12th-century document. In the 15th century, Frederick III had the church converted into a spacious parish church in the late-Gothic style, although it ended up with a wooden turret instead of a gothic spire. Archduke Carl of Inner Austria attached the church to his residence, the Burg, and later entrusted it to the Jesuits. After the dissolution of that order in Austria, it became the cathedral church of the bishops of Seckau. Inside you'll see two shrines (ca. 1475) made in Mantua, and a baroque high altar, the 18th-century creation of Franz Georg Kraxner.

Burggasse 3. ⓒ **0316/821683.** Free admission. Mon–Sat 6:30am–7:45pm; Sun 7am–7pm. Tram: 3 or 6.

Island in the Mur ★ This wonderfully fluid structure is a memento of Graz's designation as Europe's Cultural Capital in 2003. The **Island in the Mur** (ⓒ **0660/5566771**) appeals to locals and visitors alike, and houses an amphitheater, a children's playground, and a cafe/bar, called *Insel*. In the words of its Brooklyn-based architect, Vito Acconci, the island "takes the city into the river and the river into the city." The entire building looks like it jumped off the page of a Jules Verne novel. The cafe/bar, for example, is submerged under a water roof and can only be reached through a spiraling pathway that includes two access ramps and tubes linking the island to both riverbanks. See it at night, illuminated. Murgasse 1, near the Kunsthaus.

Kunsthaus ★★ The denizens of Graz call it the "Friendly Alien." Even its British architects, Colin Fournier and Peter Cook, dubbed it a "Spacelab." One art critic said the building resembled "nothing so much as a bodily organ that's outgrown its hosts," with 16 tubercles or light nozzles illuminating the art galleries inside. Regardless of what the building looks like—and there's nothing like it in all of Austria—the Kunsthaus is a showcase for modern art on the banks of the River. Look for a series of ever-changing and often cutting-edge exhibitions. Titles have included "Videodreams: Between the Cinematic and the Theatrical" and "Living in Motion: Design and Architecture for Flexible Dwelling." The current exhibition, "Robot Dreams," looking at the interaction between Man and Machine, is well worth a visit.

Corner of Südtirolerplatz and Lendkai. ⓒ **0316/80179200.** www.museum-joanneum.at/de/kunsthaus. Admission 7€ adults, 5.50€ seniors, 3€ students, 14€ family ticket. Tues–Sun 10am–6pm (Thurs until 8pm). Closed Dec 24–25. Tram: 1, 3, 6, or 7 to Station Kunsthaus Graz.

Landesmuseum Joanneum This museum is currently in the process of moving its offices, library, and many of its collections to new locations. Because of this, certain collections are closed until autumn 2011/2012 (see website for details). The Old Gallery, however—with works from medieval to 18th-century painting—has already reopened at **Schloss Eggenberg,** Eggenberger Allée 90 (see below). Here you'll also find the **Archaeology Museum,** including an extensive collection of Roman reliefs and various ancient artifacts, and the **Münzenkabinett,** a fascinating, comprehensively displayed coin collection.

Departments at various addresses. Admission 7€ adults, free for children under 14, if accompanied. Old Gallery Apr-Oct Tues-Sun 10am-6pm; Nov-Mar Tues-Sun 10am-5pm. Tram: 1 and 7. Bus: 33 (Franz-Steiner-Gasse) to the main museum; shuttles from there to other locations.

Landeszeughaus ★   Graz has a long history as a military center, and for more than 2 centuries it was a bulwark against the Ottoman Turks. Between 1642 and 1645 workers built the city's armory to house the massive supply. Statues of war deities Mars and Minerva flank the early baroque gate, created by Giovanni Mamolo. The cannon hall on the ground is vaulted, while the original wooden-beam ceilings separate the building's four upper floors.

The Landeszeughaus now contains thousands of harnesses, coats of mail, helmets, swords, pikes, muskets, pistols, and other instruments of war. In 1749, Empress Maria Theresa, in recognition of the Styrian military's service and Graz's strategic significance, allowed this arsenal to remain when the others throughout her empire were dismantled. This is also part of the Landesmuseum Joanneum (see above).

Herrengasse 16. ⓒ **0316/80179810.** www.museum-joanneum.at/de/landeszeughaus/. Admission 7€ adults, 5.50€ seniors, 3€ students, free for children under 6. Apr-Oct Mon-Sun 10am-6pm; Nov-Mar Mon-Sat 10am-3pm. Sun and holidays 10am-4pm. Tram: 3 or 6.

Mariahilferkirche   Our Lady of Succor, which sits on the right bank of the Mur River, was built for Franciscan Minorites who had begun settling here in the 13th century. Giovanni Pietro de Pomis, who also designed Schloss Eggenberg (see below), carried out Our Lady's reconstruction in the early 17th century and painted the celebrated altarpiece depicting St. Elizabeth interceding with the Virgin Mary. This painting has made the church a pilgrimage site.

Mariahilferplatz 3. ⓒ **0316/713169.** Free admission. Daily 7am-8pm. Tram: 3 or 6.

Mausoleum of Emperor Ferdinand II   One of Graz's most remarkable buildings. Begun in 1614 and completed in 1638, this structure was intended as a tomb for the emperor and his first wife. The Katharinenkirche (church), with a crossing cupola and a vaulted tomb chapel, is one of the best examples of mannerism in Austria. The interior contains work by J. B. Fischer von Erlach.

On Burggasse. ⓒ **0316/821683.** Admission 4€ adults, 3€ children. May-Oct daily 10am-noon and 1-4pm; Nov-Apr daily 10:30am-noon and 1:30-3pm. A 6-minute walk from Hauptplatz.

Schlossberg   This formerly fortified hill rises above Graz to a height of 473m (1,552 ft.) above sea level. As mentioned above, in 1809 the fortifications were leveled as part of the terms of Austria's treaty with Napoleon. You can take a **cable railway** (ⓒ **0316/887413**) to the restaurant on top of the hill, or you can climb the winding stairs. From the top, you'll be able to look down on the city and its environs. Guided tours of the citadel start from the bell tower opposite the upper station of the cable railway. Although you can visit the Schlossberg year-round, no guided tours are offered from November to April.

During the summer, concerts are held on a wooden stage constructed within the castle's ramparts. Tickets start at 12€ and go up to around 75€. Upcoming concerts are announced every season. For more information about schedules, call the tourist office.

The **Uhrturm (Clock Tower)** is a curiosity, rising high above the walls of the former **Citizens' Bastion.** It acquired its appearance between 1555 and 1556, when the original Gothic tower was redone in a more contemporary Renaissance style. The builders added a circular wooden gallery with oriels and four huge clock faces.

15

Graz

STYRIA

0316/8724902. Round-trip cable car fare 3€ adults, 1€ children under 16. Admission to tours 3€ adults, 1.50€ ages 6–15, free for children 5 and under. Cable car operates Apr–Sept daily 9am–11pm; Oct–Mar daily 10am–10pm. Tours given daily on the hour 9am–5pm. No tours Nov–Apr. Take the Zahn-radbahn from Kaiser-Franz-Josef-Kai 38; departs every 15 min. The ascent takes 5–10 min.

NEARBY ATTRACTIONS

Piber Stud Farm   The most important stud farm in Austria lies some 24km (15 miles) west of Graz. Lipizzaner horses are bred and trained here, and the result is quite magnificent. General Patton rescued these horses and their very special lineage from doom during a daring raid to retrieve them from behind Soviet lines at the end of World War II. When their early training is complete, the horses raised on this farm are sent to the Spanish Riding School in Vienna.

Piber Bundesgestvet, Piber, near Koeflach. *03144/3323.* www.piber.com. Admission 12€ adults, 11€ seniors, 7.50€ students, 3€ children age 3–6. 75-minute tours given Nov–Mar daily 2:30pm; Apr–Oct daily 11am. Drive west from Graz on B70 (Packer Bundesstasse/Kärtnerstrasse) until the marked turnoff onto an unclassified road to Piber. Call for an appointment before visiting and verify times.

Schloss Eggenberg   About 3km (2 miles) west of the center of Graz, this square 17th-century palace has towers at its four corners and an accentuated facade over the main gate. The building sits in a large park that's now used as a game reserve. The four wings of the baroque structure surround a large court with arched arcades and two smaller courts separated by the palace church. You can take guided tours of the baroque state apartments on the second floor.

The ground floor of the south wing houses the Landesmuseum Joanneum's (see above) Old Gallery, plus the Archaeology Museum, with a good collection of Styrian antiquities and coin collections.

Eggenberg Allée 90. *0316/5832640.* Admission 7€ adults, 5.50€ students and seniors, free children under 14. Palace tours Apr–Oct daily 10 and 11am, noon, and 2, 3, and 4pm; no tours Nov–Mar. Landes-museum collections daily 9am–1pm and 2–5pm. Tram: 1.

Where to Stay

Accommodations range from first-class hotels to camping sites. There are many rea-sonably priced family hotels and inexpensive lodgings in Graz, and even the top hotels will seem surprisingly inexpensive.

EXPENSIVE

Grand Hotel Wiesler Graz ★★   A few minutes' walk from the Kunsthaus along the Mur, this Jugendstil hotel is the most trendy in town. Rooms at the front have views of the baroque spires on the opposite side of the river. The tastefully decorated medium-size rooms come with cool colors, wide, firm beds, thick carpeting, and wooden furnishings, many of which date from around 1910. The Wiesler's restaurant, Speisesaal, offers international dishes and artsy, thrift-store furnishings. If you are just looking for a base before hitting the town, the in-house canteen, Senf & Söhne (Mus-tard and Sons), serves up meaty snacks all week from 10am–7pm.

Grieskai 4–8, A-8010 Graz. *0316/7066-0.* Fax 0316/706676. www.hotelwiesler.com. 97 units. 79€–199€ double; 139€–399€ suite. Children under 6 stay free in parent's room. Children 6–12 pay 11.50€. AE, DC, MC, V. Parking 10€. Tram: 1, 3, 6, or 7. **Amenities:** Restaurant (from 5pm); bar; barber; laundry ser-vice; room service; sauna; smoke-free rooms; free Wi-Fi. *In room:* A/C, TV, minibar, hairdryer, trouser press (some), safe, free Ethernet.

Schlossberg Hotel ★★   Housed behind a beautifully embellished cerulean facade, this 15th-century baroque inn is both unusual and charming. It has more atmosphere than the Grand Hotel Wiesler Graz. The owner's wife decorated this formerly decrepit rooming house herself in 1982 with 19th-century furniture. There's an early Biedermeier ceramic stove in the bar area, several pieces of baroque sculpture set in well-placed niches, and a courtyard with a lion's-head fountain. Many of the rooms open onto private balconies.

Guests can enjoy drinks 24 hours a day on a terrace with a panoramic view of Graz from the banks of the river. Breakfast is the only meal served, and it's offered in a beautiful winter garden.

Kaiser-Franz-Josef-Kai 30, A-8010 Graz. ✆ **0316/80700.** Fax 0316/807070. www.schlossberg-hotel. at. 54 units. 170€–265€ double; 235€–380€ suite. AE, DC, MC, V. Parking 16€. Breakfast 17€ extra. Tram: 4 or 5. **Amenities:** Breakfast room; bar; dry cleaning; fitness center; laundry service; massage; outdoor heated pool; room service; sauna; smoke-free rooms; solarium. *In room:* TV, hairdryer, minibar, safe, free Wi-Fi.

MODERATE

Augartenhotel ★★   For those of you with a soft spot for streamline Swedish furniture, this is the place for you. Only a few steps from the heart of town, the Augarten offers both regular doubles and apartments with kitchens for those planning a longer stay. Its rooftop terrace with panoramic views of the city is reason alone to like this place. If it's available, ask for room 501, which offers the most spectacular views. You'll find wooden floors and warm interiors in the beautiful bedrooms, which are also decorated in part with glass, grays, silvers, and whites. The restaurant, adorned with modern art, serves light cuisine with an emphasis on fresh fish and vegetables produced in the region. The hotel is both sophisticated and down-home friendly.

Schönaugasse 53A, A-8010 Graz. ✆ **0316/208000.** Fax 0316/2080080. www.augartenhotel.at. 56 units. 140€ double; 180€ apt. AE, DC, MC, V. **Amenities:** Restaurant; bar; indoor pool; gym; sauna. *In room:* A/C, TV, minibar, hairdryer, Wi-Fi.

Hotel zum Dom ★ 📭   In the medieval heart of town, close to the cathedral, this former palace has been turned into a funny little hotel with individually designed bedrooms. Each room has its own name and unique totem propped on the door. Furnishings appear to have been pulled together from different decades. You can breakfast in the winter garden, or patronize Restaurant MOD, with its sophisticated elegance, specializing in such dishes as shrimp-stuffed sole.

Bürgergasse 14, A-8010 Graz. ✆ **0316/824800.** Fax 0316/8248008. www.domhotel.co.at. 29 units. 170€–220€ double; 227€–332€ suite. Rates include breakfast. AE, DC, MC, V. Parking 12€. Bus: 30. **Amenities:** Restaurant; wine bar; 24-hr. room service; laundry service; dry cleaning; nonsmoking rooms; rooms for those w/limited mobility. *In room:* TV, minibar, coffeemaker (some), hairdryer, iron, safe, free Wi-Fi.

Romantik Parkhotel ★ 📭   Although housed in a 1574 building, this hotel looks much newer due to frequent renovations. It's within a 10-minute walk east of the city center, near the opera house. The interior is filled with baronial accessories, suits of armor, hanging tapestries in the beamed dining room, and a scattering of antiques. Rooms are comfortable and traditionally furnished with double-glazed windows, plush carpeting, antiques, good beds, and small bathrooms. A garden at the back provides a midsummer escape.

Leonhardstrasse 8, A-8010 Graz. ✆ **0316/36300.** Fax 0316/363050. www.parkhotel-graz.at. 71 units. 140€–200€ double; 200€–350€ suite. Rates include buffet breakfast. AE, DC, MC, V. Tram: 1, 3, 6, or 7. **Amenities:** Restaurant; bar; dry cleaning; fitness room; laundry service; indoor heated pool; room service; sauna. *In room:* TV, hairdryer, minibar, safe (in some), Wi-Fi at 3€/24hr.

INEXPENSIVE

Hotel Drei Raben ♦ This five-story hotel was originally built as an apartment house around 1900, and was later modernized and transformed into a hotel. Within a 5-minute walk from the railway station and a 10-minute walk from the Old Town, it offers modern comfort and well-furnished, medium-size rooms. There's a local franchise of Wienerwald, a chain restaurant specializing in all-day dining, roast chicken, and reasonable prices aimed at the family trade.

Annenstrasse 43, A-8020 Graz. ℗ **0316/712686.** Fax 0316/7159596. www.dreiraben.at. 50 units. 190€ double. Rates include buffet breakfast. AE, DC, MC, V. Parking 9.60€. Tram: 3 or 6. **Amenities:** Restaurant; bar, free Wi-Fi. *In room:* TV, hairdryer, free Wi-Fi.

Where to Eat

The variety of restaurants in Graz is enormous. Prices in even the top restaurants are moderate. You can dine in the hotels (which have some of the best food in town) or in intimate pubs and bistros.

We suggest skipping typical international cuisine and concentrating on genuine Styrian specialties such as *wurzelfleisch,* a kind of stew, or the different kinds of *sterz,* a German version of kasha (made with cracked buckwheat or corn). The homemade sausages are generally excellent. Vienna is noted for its *hendl* (chicken) dishes, but Graz chefs also do chicken extremely well.

The art of beer brewing is cultivated in Graz. Residents especially like the local Puntigam or Reininghaus beer, as well as the Gösser beer, brewed in Upper Styria.

You might want to try Styrian wine, made from grapes that grow on steep, sunny slopes. Important varieties such as Welschriesling, Muskat-Sylvaner, Traminer, and the Schilcher (from a limited area in West Styria) have received international recognition. Many wine restaurants provide background music in the evening.

EXPENSIVE

Iohan ★★ CONTINENTAL/NEW AUSTRIAN Although it's set on the ground floor of a medieval building behind the Rathaus (Town Hall), you might get the feeling that you're in an underground cellar here, thanks partly to a majestic-looking vaulted stone ceiling and some very impressive masonry. Long, narrow, vaguely monastic, and permeated with a sense of the Middle Ages, it's the premier and most stylish restaurant of Graz, with a clientele whose names appear in the society section of the local newspaper. Its sophisticated touches of postmodern design put the place firmly in the 21st century. There's an elongated bar—almost 30m (100 ft.) of it—crafted from beechwood, theatrical lighting, and food that's on the nouvelle side of the culinary equation. The best examples, depending on the time of year you arrive, include a breast of wild goose glazed with Pinot Grigio and a confit of goose liver; a mixture of sweet potatoes, Jerusalem artichokes, and poached carp dumplings; and filet of beef with crabmeat, roast onions, and white-bread dumplings.

Landhausgasse 1. ℗ **0316/8213120.** Reservations required. Main courses 16€–23€; 3-course menu 33€. AE, DC, MC, V. Tues–Sat 6pm–1am. Tram: 1, 3, 4, 5, 6, or 7.

Landhaus-Keller ★ AUSTRIAN This 16th century restaurant is in one of the most historic buildings in Graz, in the city center near the casino. (Its entrance is at the rear side of the Landhaus, just by Zeughaus, the Armory.) In summer, the staff set up outdoor tables in a flowered courtyard with a view of a baroque church's arcade. A dimly lit corridor passes three rustic and authentically Teutonic dining areas (there are six if you count the nooks and crannies), ranging from the Hunters' Room to the Knights' Room.

A wide and well-prepared selection of seafood, veal, beef, pork, and chicken dishes is served. Specialties are usually based on old Styrian recipes. You might begin with sour-cream soup with scorched polenta, meatballs with sauerkraut, or Styrian cheese dumplings in beef broth. Two chef specialties are Styrian beef with chanterelles and smoked *Saibling* (speckled trout) with horseradish sauce.

Schmiedgasse 9. ℂ **0316/830276.** www.landhaus-keller.at. Reservations recommended. Main courses 11€–25€; fixed-price menu 35€–45€. DC, MC, V. Mon–Sat 11:30am–midnight. Closed holidays. Tram: 1, 3, 4, 5, 6, or 7.

MODERATE

Das Wirtshaus Greiner AUSTRIAN   About 1.5km (1 mile) north of the town's center, this cozy and historic setting occupies an old-fashioned building, with foundations that date back to the early 1600s. Inside, you'll find a light and well-maintained set of dining rooms where the staff prepares meticulous parfaits of venison with orange and pistachio marmalade; roasted quail with alpine berries; filet of zander with a wine, butter, and herb sauce; and roasted goose with caramelized onions.

Grabenstrasse 64. ℂ **0316/685090.** www.wirtshaus-greiner.at. Reservations recommended. Main courses 11€–20€. MC, V. Mon–Fri 11:30am–2pm and 6–10pm. Tram: 4, 6, or 7.

Hofkeller ★★ MEDITERRANEAN   The best of Graz's new crop of hip and trend-conscious restaurants contains only 40 seats, each laid out under the ocher-painted 400-year-old vaults of a historic building in the town center. Your host is chef Norbert Kabelka, a 40-something wunderkind who attracts whatever Austrian celebrities happen to be visiting Graz at the time, along with a regular crowd of food-loving locals. Menu items vary with the seasons, but are usually devoted to a local reinterpretation of the classics of the Mediterranean world. The finest examples include a succulent grilled sea bass with lemon sauce and fresh spinach; and a tempting array of pastas—one of the best of which is a deceptively simple version prepared with fresh tomatoes, olive oil, herbs, and capers.

Hofgasse 8. ℂ **0316/832439.** www.hofkeller.at. Reservations recommended. Main courses 10€–19€. DC, MC, V. Mon–Sat noon–2pm (last order) and 6pm–midnight. Bus: 3 or 6.

INEXPENSIVE

Altsteirische Schmankerlstub'n ★ STYRIAN   The most authentic recipes of the Styrian kitchen are served here, the cuisine often compared to "granny's home cooking." The *stube* is the local favorite, using local products of good quality for classic meals. Theresia Oberländer and her daughters launched this restaurant in 1995, dedicating it to the serving of traditional family-style meals in a friendly, inviting atmosphere. Their salads are the best in town, perhaps because they use local pumpkin seed oil, which comes from a nearby mill at Leitinger where the Oberländer family was born. Their organic juices are also from a local farmer. The chef's specialty is *Rinderschulterscherzl*, boiled beef served with a pumpkin purée. Desserts are made fresh daily and are among the best in town.

Sackstrasse 10. ℂ **0316/833211.** Reservations recommended. Main courses 7.90€–19€. No credit cards. Daily 11am–11pm.

Krebsenkeller 🗡 AUSTRIAN/INTERNATIONAL   Many diners select this restaurant as much for its architecture as for its simple, wholesome food. Built in 1538,

Krebsenkeller's entrance lies beneath a covered passageway that ends in an enclosed courtyard. Cafe tables spill from beneath a grape arbor into the courtyard-style garden. There's ample seating indoors in a series of dining rooms, including an underground *keller* (cellar), a street-level *stüberl* (tavern), and a *gemütlich* room known locally as the Osteria. Menu items include grilled dishes prepared in varying degrees of spiciness, a variety of homemade soups, fresh salads, fresh fish, and wild game. For dessert, the best choice is a crepe stuffed with marmalade, chocolate, or ice cream and covered with a hot strawberry or cranberry sauce.

Sackstrasse 12. (© **0316/829377-0.** Reservations recommended. Main courses 8.90€–18€; fixed-price menus 9€–21€. DC, MC, V. Daily 10am–midnight. Tram: 1, 3, 4, 5, 6, or 7.

Cafes

Aiola Upstairs ★, Schlossberg 2 (© **0316/818797**), is a trendy bar in Graz, attracting the young, the beautiful, and the successful to its precincts with its striking architecture and its inventive menu. Its greatest asset is a spectacular view of Graz. "Our guests come here to enjoy chill-out grooves," the manager told us. When the weather allows, the cafe turns into one large patio. The location is beside the Uhrturm and elevator. The food is mainly Italian, with a typical meal of pasta, wine, and coffee costing less than 20€. Open Monday to Saturday 9am to 2am, Sunday 9am to midnight.

Café Harrach, Harrachgasse 26 (© **0316/322671**), is the most arts-oriented cafe in Graz, attracting lots of students. Because Styria is known for its wine, more spritzers are consumed here than beer. Harrach is like an old Viennese coffeehouse, and local cafe culture at its best is seen here. Many patrons come here and make a night of it. It's open Monday to Friday 9am to midnight, Saturday 5pm to midnight, and Sunday 4pm to midnight.

With a view looking over the open-air market (perfect on a summer day), the popular **Café Leinich,** Kaiser-Josef-Platz 4 (© **0316/830586;** tram: 3 or 6), has served good coffee and homemade pastries (rich concoctions using an abundance of fresh fruit and berries) since 1891. Coffee and pastries start at 2.90€. It's open Monday to Friday 7am to 7pm and Saturday 7am to 2pm.

Graz After Dark

One of the most visible and frequently showcased buildings in Graz is the **Opernhaus (Opera House),** Opernring (© **0316/8000-0;** www.buehnen-graz.com; tram: 1 or 7). It's the year-round home of Graz's opera company, of which local residents are justifiably proud. The faux-baroque theater was designed "in the style of Fischer von Erlach" at the end of the 19th century. Recent performances have included *Lucia de Lammermoor, Cavelleria Rusticana, Tosca, Rigoletto,* and even Broadway musicals. Depending on the event and your seat, tickets are 10€ to 75€.

THE BAR & CLUB SCENE

Sometimes restaurants combine dancing and nightclub shows, so you might be able to spend an entire evening at one address. The cafes often have music as well.

The area around **Farbergasse-Mehlplatz** is the most popular place for people from all walks of life, and the city's greatest cluster of bars and restaurants is here. Locals refer to it as their *Bermuda Dreieck* (Bermuda Triangle).

The city often offers some excellent jazz; but performances are not always rigidly scheduled, and certainly not every night of the week. It's best to call to find out if a jazz program is being presented at the time of your visit. Your best bet is **Das Neue Wist,** Mosterhofgasse 34 (© **0316/8366660**).

Gamlitzer Weinstube   This is the most visible *weinstube* (wine tavern) in town, established 300 years ago. The food is plentiful, inexpensive, and designed to accompany the wines (many from Styria) served here. Meals begin at around 6€ each, and wine sells for 2.80€ and up per glass. In summer, most of the establishment's business is conducted at tables and chairs outdoors. It's open Monday to Friday 9am to 11pm. Mehlplatz 4.© **0316/828760.** www.gamlitzer.com.

M-1   One of the most desirable bars in Graz, M-1 is located behind large glass windows on the rooftop of a historic building in the town's nightlife district. Views from the comfortable chairs encompass a postmodern design and breathtaking scenery. The crowd is congenial, and recorded music evokes the bar's big-city style. Beer costs 4€. It's open daily from 9am to 2am. Färberplatz 1.© **0664/3924729.**

Orpheum   The local theater/concert hall hosts everything from pop/rock to Punch and Judy to stand-up comedy. The Orpheum belongs to a cultural venue collective that also includes the **Schlossbergbühne Kasematten,** a stage set up inside the ruins of the old city walls. This open-air location puts on jazz and classical concerts all summer. Orpheumgasse 8.© **0316/80089000.**

Stargayte ★   You don't even have to be gay to appreciate the fun patrons at this club. It has the best drag shows in town and even fetish parties to bring out the leather set, some of whom wear knee-high black boots and nothing else. A waiter tells guests to dress "like a bitch or a pimp—or perhaps an Austrian soldier—to enjoy the fun more." This is a bar, lounge, and dance club, and every Thursday night it's for women only. Open Monday to Thursday and Sunday 8pm to 6am, Friday and Saturday 8pm "until the last customer leaves" long after sunrise. Keesgasse 3.© **0664/5162522.** www.stargayte.at.

BAD GLEICHENBERG ★

195km (121 miles) S of Vienna; 64km (40 miles) SE of Graz

The oldest and most important summer spa in South Styria (with a history of water treatments dating from Roman times), Bad Gleichenberg lies southeast of Graz. The countryside here, near Slovenia's border, is relatively flat, a low-altitude setting of rolling hills and vineyards. This is one of the most interesting and least-known parts of Austria to explore.

Untersteinmark, or Lower Styria, where this spa is located, was much larger in the days of the Habsburgs. Much of its territory was lost to Yugoslavia following the breakup of the empire after World War I.

Bad Gleichenberg sits in a scenic valley opening to the south. In the area's landscaped parks you'll see exotic plants, including the giant sequoia. You can partake of the mineral waters of the Emma, Konstantin, and Johannisbrunnen springs and even take a bottle home with you. The spa has flourished for 160 years, longer than any other spa in Styria. The clientele here tends to be middle-aged or elderly, and there's an emphasis on low-key activities. The calm is punctuated with an entertainment program and special tours in the environs. Hotels ring the spa facilities, which mark the resort's center. Mud baths and long soaks in the thermally heated waters are big here, along with rest and relaxation.

Essentials

GETTING THERE

By Train

Bad Gleichenberg lies at the end of a minor rail line stretching eastward from Graz. Passengers board an eastbound train in Graz and head toward the Hungarian border town of Szentgotthárd, changing trains at Feldbach (trip time: 50–60 min.). From Feldbach, about five trains a day continue to the Bad Gleichenberg. Fortunately, because rail connections from Feldbach to Bad Gleichenberg aren't always convenient, passengers can also board one of the eight Bad Gleichenberg-bound buses that depart from Feldbach's railway station every day. The trip from Feldbach to Bad Gleichenberg by bus or train takes an additional 30 to 35 minutes. For rail information, contact ✆ **05/1717** (www.oebb.at).

By Bus

There's one early-morning bus, departing daily at 7:30am for Bad Gleichenberg from Vienna's Wien Mitte bus station (trip time: 3 hr.). From Graz, four buses depart Monday through Saturday at 8:25 and 10:30am, 12:15 and 4:35pm from in front of the main railway station for Bad Gleichenberg (trip time: 2 hr.).

By Car

If you're driving from Graz, take the A2 east to the junction with B68, which you take south to the junction with B66. Continue south on the B66 to Bad Gleichenberg.

VISITOR INFORMATION

The **tourist office** in the town center (✆ **03159/2203;** www.bad-gleichenberg.at) is open Monday to Friday 8am to 5pm and Saturday 9am to noon.

Where to Stay & Eat

Hotel Gleichenberger Hof ★ ♨ This cozy 1970s' chalet is set in a forested area with a masonry sun terrace stretching below the facade. It's located in the town's center near the spa facilities. The interior has rustic yet modern accessories, including a piano bar and an open fireplace, and all rooms have balconies. The medium-size rooms are furnished tastefully and comfortably. Bathrooms are small but tidily maintained, with tub/shower combinations and adequate shelf space. The restaurant is open to nonguests for lunch only.

Bergstrasse 27, A-8344 Bad Gleichenberg. ✆ **03159/2424.** Fax 03159/29556. www.gleichenbergerhof. at. 25 units. 120€–150€ double; 147€–177€ suite for 2. Rates include half-board. Closed Dec 8-27 and Jan 10-27. **Amenities:** Buffet; room service; laundry service; dry cleaning. *In room:* TV, minibar (in suites), hairdryer, safe.

Schloss Kapfenstein ★ 🏨 As an alternative to staying in Bad Gleichenberg, you can go east to Kapfenstein and its Schloss hotel near the Slovenian border. The 10-km (6-mile) trip takes 20 minutes. Drive south from Bad Gleichenberg along Highway 66, and then cut east along the unnumbered *bundesstrasse* (provincial highway) that's marked KAPFENSTEIN. This solidly built castle has a hipped roof and a curving extension that's almost as old as the main building itself. Set in the middle of forests and rich fields, the castle offers rooms filled with antique furniture and all the modern comforts.

If you want, you can dine on the castle's terrace, which offers a view of the village below. Specialties are based on regional dishes such as roast hen, homemade *blutwurst* (blood sausage) and other sausages, and apple strudel. The Winkler family makes its own wine, a very delicate and famous vintage.

A-8353 Kapfenstein. ⓒ **03157/300300.** Fax 03157/3003030. www.schloss-kapfenstein.at. 15 units. 132€–184€ double. Rates include breakfast. AE, DC, MC, V. **Amenities:** Restaurant; room service; free Internet at reception. *In room:* TV, hairdryer, minibar, safe.

MARIAZELL ★

150km (93 miles) SE of Vienna; 140km (87 miles) N of Graz

Mariazell is the most celebrated pilgrimage center in Austria. Due to its extraordinary alpine location, it also attracts hordes of athletes every winter.

Essentials

GETTING THERE

By Train

Mariazell is at the terminus of a secondary train line that originates in the capital of Lower Austria, St. Pölten, 84km (52 miles) to the north. St. Pölten, which sits astride the main rail lines connecting Vienna and Salzburg, receives dozens of trains from Vienna (trip time: 45 min.) and Salzburg (trip time: 2½ hr.) throughout the day. From St. Pölten, about half a dozen trains head south to Mariazell (trip time: 2½ hr.). For rail information, contact ⓒ **05/1717** (www.oebb.at).

By Bus

About half a dozen buses depart every day from Vienna's Wien Mitte bus station for their final destination at Mariazell (trip time: 2¼–4 hr. for the express or local).

If the train schedule between St. Pölten and Mariazell is inconvenient, you can take one of the several daily buses that parallel the same route (trip time: 1½ hr.). In addition, two buses depart daily from the Graz railway station to Mariazell (trip time: 3 hr.). For bus information, call ⓒ **0316/820606.**

Finally, buses depart several times a day for Mariazell from the important railway junction of Mürzzuschlag (trip time: 1½ hr.), which is set on the main rail lines between Vienna and Graz.

By Car

If you're driving from Graz, head north along Autobahn A9 until you reach the junction with the S35 north. Continue north to the junction with Route 20, which leads into Mariazell.

VISITOR INFORMATION

The **tourist office,** Hauptplatz 13 (ⓒ **03882/2366;** www.mariazell.at), is open Monday to Friday 9am to 5:30pm, Saturday 9am to 4pm, and Sunday 9am to 12:30pm. It is closed on Sunday in October and November.

What to See & Do

SEEING THE SHRINE

The pilgrimage destination **Mariazell Basilica,** on Hauptplatz (ⓒ **03882/2595**), dates from the early 13th century. Criminals used to come here after a secular court imposed a "Zellfahrt" (Journey to Zell) as atonement. Hundreds of thousands come to pray and make votive offerings to the statue of the Virgin, which is mounted on the altar.

BAD BLUMAU: AUSTRIA'S purest SPA

Imagine trees sprouting out of grass-covered rooftops, tilted towers topped with onion domes, hallway floors like river beds, and a lake-size pool with hidden fountains randomly spraying thermal waters. Welcome to **Bad Blumau ★★★**.

This spa/hotel came from the drawing board of Austria's favorite naturalist architect, Friedensreich Hundertwasser, who also designed many other funny-looking buildings around the country, including the popular Kunsthaus Museum in Vienna (see "Other Top Attractions," in chapter 6).

Hundertwasser's playful rejection of architectural norms lends itself beautifully to a place dedicated to downtime. Light Easter-egg pastels cover the outer walls. The rooms are comfortable and uncluttered, with minibars and safes; bathrooms include tub/shower combos. The suites have just about the only level floors in the place.

The therapies here tend to lean toward the New Age. Although you can get your fill of shiatsu and Swedish massage, try having an attendant dip you in mare's milk, whey, or the essence of evening primrose, and then suspend you in a heat box for a good half-hour. The 3-hour "resurrection therapy" session involves gongs, a box of pebbles, hypnotism, and more than a few euros.

The saunas are co-ed and naked—don't be ashamed, no one else is. You can choose from Roman and Finnish saunas, Turkish baths, the Aromasauna, and the Bio-sanarium, which involves gassy peppermint and blinking lights. Likewise, in the health areas, you're apt to receive treatments from an attendant who is young, of the opposite sex, and utterly professional. The pool has lockers for day-trippers and overnight guests alike.

You'll eat well. Not taking the health factor to the extreme, thankfully, the buffet is full of meats and cheeses, all delicious. The a la carte menu offers a decent selection of international dishes.

The spa also offers child-care, shopping, a hairdresser, laundry service, and parking. Conference and fitness rooms are also available. Blumau and the baths, A-8283 Blumau 100, are about 130km (81 miles) south of Vienna and 50km (37 miles) east of Graz (© **03383/51000;** fax 03383/5100805; www.blumau.com). Rates are 250€ to 288€ double and 380€ to 404€ suite; half-board is 25€ extra. Rates include half-board and free use of all thermal bath and sauna facilities, service charge, and tax. Spa treatments and visitor tax are not included.

To get from Graz to Bad Blumau, take the Autobahn A2 east and follow the signs to the spa (it's well marked).

The church was originally constructed in the Romanesque style, and then a Gothic choir was added in the late 14th century. The bulbous domes are baroque, a style added to most of Austria's churches in the 17th century. Both Fischer von Erlachs, senior and junior, aided the Mariazell transformation. The grave of the world-famous Hungarian Cardinal Mindszenty is in the church; there's also the Mindszenty Museum. In 1983, Pope John Paul II visited Mariazell and the cardinal's burial place.

In the treasury are votive offerings accrued over some 600 years. The Chapel of Grace is the national shrine of Austria. Miracles are attributed to its statue of the Virgin, giving rise to fame that has spread all over Europe. The altar on which the statue is mounted was designed by the younger von Erlach. In summer, large groups gather on Saturday night for torchlight processions to the church.

The treasury is open May to October Tuesday to Friday from 10:30am to noon and 2 to 3pm, and Saturday and Sunday from 10am to 4pm. Admission is 3€.

OUTDOOR ACTIVITIES

Mariazell is a winter vacation center for the whole family. Here you'll find all the components of a modern winter-sports and recreation center: avalanche-controlled grounds for skiers of all skill levels, a cableway, a chairlift, numerous surface lifts, a natural toboggan run, a skating rink, a ski school, and a ski kindergarten.

Its high altitude and good, brisk climate also make this a favored summer vacation site. You can go walking on some 200km (125 miles) of footpaths or go mountaineering, swimming, rowing, sailing, windsurfing, canoeing, fishing, horseback riding, glider flying, and camping. You can also play tennis or golf.

For the area's most dramatic views, you can take the **Seilbahn Mariazell-Bürgeralpe,** Wienerstrasse 28 (℡ **03882/2555**), to the Bürgeralpe at 1,270m (4,167 ft.). Leaving from the center of town, cable cars depart about every 20 minutes. They run in July and August daily from 8:30am to 5:30pm; in September daily until 5pm; in May, June, October, and November daily 9am to 5pm; in December to April daily from 8am to 4pm. A round trip costs 11€.

Where to Stay & Eat

Hotel Goldene Krone   Next to the basilica is a well-managed hotel that was established as an inn in the 1300s. Rebuilt several times and renovated again in 1991, the Goldene Krone is in a substantial old Styrian house with stone trim. The interior has a contemporary bar area with decorative masonry. Rooms are a bit small, but they're well maintained and equipped with good, firm beds and small bathrooms. The restaurant, which serves Austrian national dishes along with Styrian specialties, is open to non-guests daily from 7am to 11pm.

Grazerstrasse 1, A-8630 Mariazell. ℡ **03882/2583.** Fax 03882/258333. 22 units. 78€ double. Half-board 12€ per person extra. Cash only. **Amenities:** Restaurant; dry cleaning; laundry service; lounge; room service, sauna. *In room:* TV. Mo: 8 to 11pm, kitchen open 11 to 2pm and 6 to 9pm.

BAD AUSSEE ★

196km (122 miles) NW of Graz; 299km (186 miles) SW of Vienna; 80km (50 miles) SE of Salzburg

Surrounded by a lake, mountains, and woods, **Bad Aussee** is an old market town and spa in the "green heart" of the Salzkammergut. Unlike spa towns such as Bad Gleichenberg, Bad Aussee became a resort relatively recently, with little emphasis on the medical/recuperative therapies that are all the rage at other resorts. Instead, most of the clientele comes here for its high altitude—650m (2,133 ft.) above sea level, nearly twice that of Bad Gleichenberg—and its profusion of hiking trails that are clearly marked with green-and-white signs. Guests here tend to be younger and perhaps more vigorous than those at the more sedentary Bad Gleichenberg. But it has also been a favorite of musicians and writers, including Gustav Mahler, the Busch brothers of the Budapest String Quartet, and the Austrian–American pianist Rudolf Serkin. And more recently, actor Klaus Maria.

Despite the relative lack of interest in spa rituals here, Bad Aussee does emphasize the saltwater and freshwater springs that are tapped by many of the town's hotels. Waters from the Bad Aussee Glaubersalt spring are said to be effective for losing weight, partly because a pint or so will usually manage to curtail the most stalwart of appetites. Salt mined in the nearby hills is added to bathwater, and said to relieve aches and pains.

Bad Aussee, at the confluence of a pair of upper branches of the Traun River, is the capital of the Styrian section of the Salzkammergut. Only 5km (3 miles) north is the lake Altaussee, with the spa town of the same name on its shore.

One of Austria's most beautiful areas, the town is a good center for walking and climbing in summer. Visitors shouldn't miss the 3-day Festival of Narcissus (**Narzissenfest,** www.narzissenfest.at), the largest Flower Festival in the country, which takes place annually. There is music, dancing, food and drink, and a parade with floats. Although Bad Aussee has long been known as a summer spa resort, it has also developed into a winter ski center. Several ski lifts are located nearby, making it attractive to ski enthusiasts.

Essentials
GETTING THERE
By Train
Bad Aussee sits astride a secondary rail line running between the Austrian junctions of Stainach–Irdning (which services passengers arriving from Graz and Vienna) and Attnang–Puchheim (which services passengers arriving from Salzburg and Linz). The trip from Graz to Stainach–Irdning takes about 2½ hours. At Stainach–Irdning, passengers transfer onto any of a dozen northbound trains for Bad Aussee (trip time: 40 min.).

Passengers starting in Salzburg or Linz can take any of the dozens of daily trains to Attnang–Puchheim and then transfer to a southbound train. This train passes through several resorts in Upper Austria—most notably Bad Ischl and Bad Goisern—before reaching Bad Aussee (2½ hr.). For rail information, contact ✆ **05/1717** (www.oebb.at).

By Bus
Because of its good (albeit a little complicated) rail connections, most visitors arrive in Bad Aussee by train. The most useful of the handful of bus lines running into Bad Aussee, however, is the one that runs from Styria across the border of Upper Austria into the resort of Bad Ischl several times a day (trip time: 45 min.).

By Car
Driving from Graz, take Autobahn A9 northwest and continue in the same direction as it becomes Route 113. Follow that highway's extension, which becomes Route 146, and cut west at the junction of Route 145 toward Tauplitz.

VISITOR INFORMATION
The **tourist office** in the village center at Bahnhofstrasse 132 (✆ **03622/540400;** www.ausseerland.at) is open Monday to Friday 9am to 7pm and Saturday 9am to 4pm.

Where to Stay & Eat

Erzherzog Johann ★★   This hotel in the town's center is the resort's finest. The conservatively designed building has stone detailing, and its rustic interior offers fireplaces, beamed ceilings, and comfortable furniture. Rooms are a bit small, with a balcony, good beds, and small bathrooms. Housekeeping gets high marks. The hotel restaurant serves a sampling of excellent Austrian and international dishes, with fresh ingredients used whenever possible. Main courses are served daily from noon to 2pm and 6:30 to 9:30pm. The area's sporting facilities are easily accessible from here.

Kurhausplatz 62, A-8990 Bad Aussee. ☏ **03622/52507.** Fax 03622/52507680. www.erzherzogjohann. at. 62 units. 180€–202€ double. Rates include half-board. DC, MC, V. Free parking. Closed Nov 14–Dec 5. **Amenities:** Restaurant; bar; indoor heated pool; fitness center; spa; sauna; room service; massage; babysitting; laundry service; dry cleaning; nonsmoking rooms; free Wi-Fi (in the bar). *In room:* TV, hairdryer, minibar, free Ethernet.

Hotel-Pension Villa Kristina ★ 🗝 This charming and personal establishment was built in 1892 as a simple inn for the many hunters who frequented the region. Friedl Raudaschl bought the place in the 1970s, updated its plumbing and electricity, and named it after his wife, Krista, who continues to manage it with him today. The hotel lies on ample private grounds beside the River Traun and the road leading to Altaussee, about a 10-minute walk from Bad Aussee. Inside and out, the steep-roofed, wood-trimmed house is loaded with handcrafted details. Medium-size rooms are filled with a certain eastern Austrian charm, although modern luxuries, including efficiently organized bathrooms, are present. The best rooms have private balconies with great views. The hotel has a home library and a piano, and meals are served only to guests who request them in advance.

Altauseerstrasse 54, A-8990 Bad Aussee. ☏/fax **03622/52017.** www.villakristina.at. 10 units. 88€–98€ double. Rates include breakfast. AE, DC, MC, V. **Amenities:** Free Internet in the Stüberl. *In room:* TV, free Wi-Fi (in some rooms).

15

DACHSTEIN–TAUERN

The province's major ski area, Dachstein–Tauern, lies in northwest Styria. The Dachstein in the Salzkammergut is a gigantic alpine mountain range cutting across Land Salzburg, Upper Austria, and Styria, with mammoth glaciers lying between its peaks, with the Enns River separating the Dachstein and the Tauern massifs. Championship ski races are held here, and it's a great place for powder skiing.

Schladming & Rohrmoos

To see more of West Styria, stay in either Rohrmoos or Schladming, south of Bad Aussee, as a center for exploring the alpine mountain range of Dachstein–Tauern.

ESSENTIALS

GETTING THERE This skiing center is in the Dachstein–Tauern recreation and winter-sports area on Route 308 and the Vienna–Bruck/Mur–Graz rail line. It's easy to reach. The center of Rohrmoos is 2km (1 mile) south of the center of Schladming, but the edges of the two resorts touch one another; for most practical purposes, they are considered one.

At least one **train** per hour reaches Schladming from Graz (trip time: 2½ hr.) or Salzburg (trip time: 1¼ hr.). Some trains from Graz might require a transfer at Selzthal, and some trains from Salzburg require a transfer in Bischofshofen. For rail information, contact ☏ **05/1717** (www.oebb.at).

Many **bus routes** begin in Schladming and wind into the surrounding hills and valleys; many of the town's residents use these buses. Rohrmoos has no rail connections, but many buses travel along the northeast to southwest stretch of the valley between Schladming and Rohrmoos, making frequent stops at the hotels that line the valley's main road.

In the northwestern corner of Styria, Schladming/Rohrmoos is often visited by people **driving** from Land Salzburg. To get here, take the A10 south from Salzburg to the junction with Route 308, heading east. Schladming is 299km (186 miles) southwest of Vienna and 203km (126 miles) northwest of Graz.

VISITOR INFORMATION   The **tourist office** in Schladming (📞 **03687/23310;** www.schladming-dachstein.at) is open Monday to Friday 9am to 6pm and Saturday 9am to noon.

SKIING, HIKING & MORE

Schladming is an ancient town in the upper valley of the Enns River, lying between Dachstein to the north and Schladminger Tauern to the south. It was a silver- and copper-mining town in medieval times. Old miners' houses are still standing. The **Pfarrkirche (Parish Church)** is late Gothic, and the town's 1862 church is the largest Protestant church in Styria.

The **Planai** (1,900m/6,234 ft.) and the **Hochwurzen** (1,850m/6,070 ft.) have fast downhill runs and ski slopes, equipped with a cableway, five double chairlifts, a connecting three-seat chairlift, ski buses, and 15 surface lifts, at all altitudes. Some 22,000 people per hour can be transported.

Miles of winter footpaths also make for good, invigorating walking. You can enjoy horse-drawn sleigh rides, tobogganing, ski-bobbing, curling, game-feeding trips, and many other winter activities. Cafes and bars offer lively après-ski activities, as do the hotels. In summer, you'll enjoy mountaineering, swimming, tennis, bowling, and top-quality entertainment, along with warm Styrian hospitality. Golf, rafting, and parasailing are available in nice weather.

WHERE TO STAY & EAT IN THE AREA

Alpenhotel Schwaigerhof ☺   Located on a hillside with a mountain view, this five-story chalet, built in stages from 1975 to 1981, is attractively embellished. The comfortably furnished rooms, decorated with modern pieces, are either small or medium in size. A host of sporting facilities is available nearby.

Schwaigerweg 19, A-8970 Rohrmoos. 📞 **03687/614220.** Fax 03687/6142252. www.schwaigerhof.at. 42 units. Winter 134€–140€ double, 146€–190€ suite; summer 142€–154€ double, 154€–206€ suite. Rates include half-board. DC, MC, V. Parking 10€. **Amenities:** 2 restaurants; bar; indoor heated pool; fitness center; Jacuzzi; sauna; children's playground; massage; laundry service; dry cleaning; nonsmoking rooms; solarium; rooms for those w/limited mobility. *In room:* TV, minibar, hairdryer, safe, Wi-Fi.

Hotel Alte Post ★★   This chalet-style hotel has a center-of-town location, a history that dates from 1618, and a popular restaurant with a nouvelle/traditional Austrian cuisine menu. Rooms are among the finest in town, furnished with many modern touches. Bathrooms, though small, are neatly arranged with shower/tub combos. In the restaurant, hot food is served daily from 11:30am to 2pm and 6 to 10pm. Less-formal meals and afternoon snacks are available in the rustic Knappenstube. Even if you're staying at the hotel, reservations in the formal dining room are advised.

Hauptplatz 10, A-8970 Schladming. 📞 **03687/22571.** Fax 03687/225718. www.alte-post.at. 42 units. Winter 158€–270€ double; summer 120€–170€ double. Rates include half-board. AE, DC, MC, V. Closed Nov and 2 weeks in Apr. **Amenities:** Restaurant; bar; dry cleaning; Jacuzzi; laundry service; room service; sauna; smoke-free rooms. *In room:* TV, hairdryer (in some), minibar, free Wi-Fi.

FAST FACTS: AUSTRIA

Area Codes   The Country Code for Austria is 43; and 1 for Vienna. Within the country, dial 01 from any phone. In Vienna, 01 is necessary from a cellphone, and no code is necessary from a landline. Each other city or town has its own code. See "Staying Connected" for info, p. 70.

ATM Networks/Cashpoints   See "Money & Costs," p. 53.

Business Hours   **Banks** are open Monday to Friday from 8am to 3pm, and 5pm on Thursday; closed 12:30 to 1:30pm. **Government Offices** are generally open Monday to Friday from 8 or 9am to 12, 2, or 3pm. **Other Offices** are open either 8 or 9am to 6pm, often closed at 12 or 12:30 for an hour. Regular **shopping** hours are Monday from 9 or 10am to 6pm, sometimes later at Christmas; and Saturday from 9am to 5pm in the central shopping areas, noon or 1pm elsewhere.

Car Rentals   See "Airline & Car Rental Websites," p. 483 or "Getting Around" in chapter 3.

Cellphones (Mobile Phones)   See "Staying Connected," p. 70.

Drinking & Drug Laws   Upper Austria, Salzburg, and Tyrol prohibit the consumption of distilled beverages below the age of 18, while Carinthia and Styria prohibit drinks containing more than 12 or 14% of alcohol respectively in this age bracket. Carinthia additionally requires adolescents to maintain a blood alcohol level below 0.05%, while Upper Austria prohibits "excessive consumption," and Salzburg prohibits consumption that would result in a state of intoxication. Prohibitions in Vienna, Burgenland, Lower Austria, and Vorarlberg apply only to alcohol consumption *in public*. Enforcement of purchases in supermarkets is quite strict, while in restaurants and bars enforcement is quite lax, especially for beer and wine.

Possession of narcotics is a felony and depending on the amount, you may be arrested or even deported. For small violations (consumption, possession of small amounts) fines are usually the maximum penalty.

Driving Rules   See "Getting There & Getting Around," p. 46.

Drugstores   In Austrian cities, at least one pharmacy (*Apotheke*) is always open 24 hours. If a particular pharmacy is closed, a sign on the door will list the address and phone number of the nearest one that is open.

Electricity   As in most of Europe, Austria uses 220 volts AC (50 cycles), compared with 110–120 volts AC (60 cycles) in the United States and Canada. Many Austrian hotels stock adapter plugs but not power transformers.

Bring a **connection kit** of the right power and phone adapters, a spare phone cord, and a spare Ethernet network cable—or find out whether your hotel supplies them to guests.

Embassies & Consulates   The main building of the Embassy of the **United States** is at Boltzmanngasse 16, A-1090 Vienna (✆ **01/313390;** http://austria.usembassy.gov). However, the consulate of the **United States** is at Parkring 12, A-1010 Vienna (✆ **01/5125835**). Lost passports, tourist emergencies, and other matters are handled by the consular section. Both the embassy and the consulate are open Monday to Friday 8 to 11:30am. Emergency services 8:30am to 5pm.

The Embassy of **Canada,** Laurenzerberg 2, A-1010 Vienna (© **01/531383000**), is open Monday to Friday 8:30am to 12:30pm and 1:30 to 3:30pm.

The Embassy of the **United Kingdom,** Jauresgasse 12, A-1030 (© **01/716130;** http://ukinaustria.fco.gov.uk), is open Monday to Friday 9am to 1pm and 2 to 5pm.

The Embassy of **Australia,** Mattiellistrasse 2–4, A-1040 Vienna (© **01/506740**), is open Monday to Friday 8:30am to 4:30pm.

The nearest Embassy of **New Zealand** is located in Berlin, Germany, Friedrichstrasse 60 (© **030/206210**), and is open Monday to Friday 9am to noon, however there is a consulate in Vienna at Salesianergasse 15/3. Hours vary (© **01/3188505**).

The Embassy of **Ireland,** Rotenturmstrasse 16–18, A-1010 Vienna (© **01/7154246**), is open Monday through Friday 8:30 to 11am and 1 to 4pm.

Emergencies Emergency phone numbers throughout the country (no area code needed) are as follows: © **133** for the police (or © **112,** for the Europe-wide emergency service), © **144** for the accident service, © **122** to report a fire, and © **120** to report a car breakdown on the highway.

Gasoline See "Gasoline," p. 52.

Holidays Public holidays in Austria are as follows: January 1, January 6 (Epiphany), Easter Monday, May 1, Ascension Day, Whitmonday, Corpus Christi, August 15 (Assumption), October 26 (*Nationalfeiertag;* Austrian National Day), November 1, December 8 (Feast of the Immaculate Conception), and December 25 and 26. Check locally when you arrive in Austria. Some of these holidays fall on different days every year. Also see "Austria Calendar of Events," in chapter 3.

Hospitals Two hospitals with an emergency service in Vienna are the **Allgemeines Krankenhaus Wien,** Währinger Gürtel 18–20 (© **01/404-00-0;** www.akhwien.at; U-Bahn: U6 Michaelbeuern/Allgemeines Krankenhaus), A-1090 Vienna; and the **Krankenhaus der Barmherzigen Brüder,** Johannes von Gott Platz 1 (© **01/21121-1100;** www.barmherzige-brueder.at; U-Bahn: Nestroyplatz, tram: 2 Karmeliterplatz), A-1020 Vienna. The Barmherzigen Brüder, the Merciful Brothers, is run by a catholic order and will accept all emergency cases without insurance at no charge. For information on hospitals in the rest of Austria, there is a list with contact information online: **www.medlink.at/spitaeler.html**.

Insurance For travel overseas, most U.S. health plans (including Medicare and Medicaid) do not provide coverage, and the ones that do often require you to pay for services upfront and reimburse you only after you return home. As a safety net, you may want to buy travel medical insurance.

Canadians should check with their provincial health plan offices or call **Health Canada** (© **866/225-0709;** www.hc-sc.gc.ca) to find out the extent of their coverage and what documentation and receipts they must take home in case they are treated overseas.

Travelers from the U.K. and Ireland should carry their **European Health Insurance Card (EHIC),** which replaced the E111 form as proof of entitlement to free/reduced-cost medical treatment abroad (© **0845/606-2030;** www.ehic.org.uk). Note that the EHIC covers only "necessary medical treatment."

When traveling, any number of things could go wrong—lost luggage, trip cancellation, a medical emergency—for information on traveler's insurance, trip cancellation insurance, and medical insurance while traveling, please visit www.frommers.com/tips.

Internet Access Many hotels, coffeehouses, and other businesses offer Internet access, either Wi-Fi or with online computers. Often the Wi-Fi connection in cafes is free if you order something. The dedicated Internet cafe business seems to be dying out. However, although there's no definitive directory for cybercafes—these are independent businesses, after all—two places to start looking are at **www.cybercaptive. com** and **wwws.cybercafe.com**.

Language   Austrians speak German, but English is taught in schools from the early grades. Not everyone will speak English fluently, but definitely anyone providing tourist services should be able to, whether a hotel receptionist, waitperson, or store clerk in prime shopping areas (cabdrivers might be another story). Austrians will be flattered if you try to speak German and also think Anglophone accents are cute. The Collins *German Phrasebook and Dictionary* should get you started in the right direction. Certain Austrian minorities speak Slavic languages, and Hungarian is commonly spoken in Burgenland. See chapter 17 for a glossary of common and useful German words and phrases.

Legal Aid   The police are allowed to levy on-the-spot fines for traffic offenses, but they are obliged to provide a receipt. If you are accused of a more serious offense, say and do nothing before consulting a lawyer. Here the burden is on the state to prove a person's guilt beyond a reasonable doubt, and everyone has the right to remain silent, whether he or she is suspected of a crime or actually arrested. Once arrested, a person can ask the police to make a telephone call to a lawyer, or in the case of international visitors, your embassy or consulate. For help and assistance, get in touch with your country's embassy (see above), which can often intercede for you in matters relating to your legal status in the country. An EU site gives a good explanation of the options: **http://ec.europa.eu/civiljustice/legal_aid/legal_aid_aus_en.htm**.

Mail   Post offices (*das Postamt*) in Austria are usually located in the heart of the town, village, or urban district they service. If you're unsure of your address in any particular town, correspondence can be addressed care of the local post office by labeling it POST-LAGERND. If you do this, it's important to clearly designate the addressee, the name of the town, and its postal code. To claim any correspondence, the addressee must present his or her passport.

The postal system in Austria is, for the most part, efficient and reliable. You can buy stamps at a post office or from the hundreds of news and tobacco kiosks, designated locally as *Tabac/Trafik*. Mailboxes are painted yellow, and older ones are emblazoned with the double-headed eagle of the Austrian Republic. Newer ones usually have the golden trumpet of the Austrian Postal Service.

Newspapers & Magazines   Most useful for English speakers are the *International Herald Tribune, The Guardian,* **or the** *Financial Times,* widely available in central newsstands, and for an inside view on Vienna in English, ask for *The Vienna Review* at any *Tabak/Trafik* or newsstand. You can buy some English-language news and fashion magazines, but only in select shops in the center of town.

Passports   See "Embassies & Consulates," above, for whom to contact if you lose your passport while traveling in Austria. For other information, contact the following agencies:

For residents of Australia   You can pick up an application from your local post office or any branch of Passports Australia, but you must schedule an interview at the passport office to present your application materials. Call the **Australian Passport Information Service** at *℡* **131-232,** or visit the government website at www.passports.gov.au.

For residents of Canada   Passport applications are available at travel agencies throughout Canada or from the central **Passport Office,** Department of Foreign Affairs and International Trade, Ottawa, ON K1A 0G3 (*℡* **800/567-6868;** www.ppt.gc.ca).

For residents of Ireland   You can apply for a 10-year passport at the **Passport Office, Setanta Centre, Molesworth Street, Dublin 2** (*☏* **01/671-1633;** www.irlgov.ie). Those under age 18 and over 65 must apply for a 12€ 3-year passport. You can also apply at 1A South Mall, Cork (*☏* **021/494-4700**) or at most main post offices.

For residents of New Zealand   You can pick up a passport application at any New Zealand Passports Office or download it from the website. Contact the **Passport Office** (*☏* **0800/225-050** in New Zealand or 04/474-8100; www.passports.govt.nz).

For residents of the United Kingdom   To pick up an application for a standard 10-year passport (5-year passport for children under 16), visit your nearest passport office, major post office, or travel agency, or contact the **United Kingdom Passport Service** (*☏* **0870/521-0410;** www.ukpa.gov.uk).

For residents of the United States   Whether you're applying in person or by mail, you can download passport applications from the U.S. State Department website at **http://travel.state.gov**. To find your regional passport office, either check the U.S. State Department website or call the **National Passport Information Center** toll-free number (*☏* **877/487-2778**) for automated information.

Police   Dial *☏* **133** anywhere in Austria to summon the police.

Restrooms (toilets)   The most important thing to remember about restrooms (public toilets) in Vienna, apart from calling them *Toiletten* (twa-*lett*-en) or "WC" (*vay tsay*) and not restrooms, is not the usual male/female (*Herren/Damen*) distinction (important though that is), but to pay the person who often sits at the entrance and keeps the facility clean. He or she has a saucer in which you're supposed to deposit your donation. If you don't, you may get an evil look at the least.

All airport and railway stations have restrooms (toilets), rarely with attendants. Bars, nightclubs, restaurants, cafes, and hotels have facilities as well. You'll also find public toilets near many major sights.

Smoking   A new antismoking ban went into effect throughout Austria on January 1, 2009, making it one of the last European countries to restrict lighting up in public spaces—including hotel rooms. Sill, this being Austria, the ban has many exceptions for bars and eateries that are allowed to divide the space. Bars and restaurants under 60 sq. meters (645 sq. ft.) can decide either/or. In general, Vienna is one of the last smoking havens in Europe, so don't be surprised that most bars and clubs are smoker-friendly. If having a smoking area (or being in a smoke-free establishment) is important to you, be sure to call ahead and inquire.

Taxes   In 1993, all countries belonging to the European Union became a single market by enforcing the Single European Act and merging into a common customs and Value Added Tax (V.A.T.) zone. V.A.T. is a special tax applied to goods and services alike. The rates vary from country to country; in Austria the rate is 20%.

You can arrange for a refund of V.A.T. if you can prove that the goods on which you paid tax were carried out of Austria. To get the refund, you must fill out form U-34, which is available at most stores (a sign will read TAX-FREE SHOPPING). If you plan to get your money at the border, arrange through the ÖAMTC (Austrian Automobile and Touring Club) for a quick refund. Check whether the store gives refunds itself or uses a service. Sales personnel will help you fill out the form and will affix the store-identification stamp. You show the V.A.T. (*MwSt*) as a separate item or state that the tax is part of the total price. Keep your U-34 forms handy when you leave the country, and have them validated by the Viennese Customs officer at your point of departure.

Know in advance that you'll have to show the articles for which you're claiming a V.A.T. refund. Because of this, it's wise to keep your purchases in a suitcase or carry-on bag that's separate from the rest of your luggage, with all the original tags and tickets, and the original receipts nearby. Don't check the item within your luggage before you process the paperwork with the Customs agent. In some instances, if your paperwork is in order, you'll receive a tax refund on the spot. If your point of departure is not equipped to issue cash on the spot, you'll have to mail the validated U-34 form or forms back to the store where you bought the merchandise after you return home. It's wise to keep a copy of each form. Within a few weeks, the store will send you a check, bank draft, or international money order covering the amount of your V.A.T. refund. Help is available from the ÖAMTC, which has instituted methods of speeding up the refund process. Before you go, call the Austrian National Tourist Office for the ÖAMTC brochure "Tax-Free Shopping in Austria."

Telephone   See "Staying Connected," p. 70.

Time   Vienna is on Central European Time (CET), which is Coordinated Universal Time (UTC), or Greenwich Mean Time (GMT), plus 1 hour. Clocks are moved ahead 1 hour for daylight-saving Central European Summer Time (CEST) between the last Sunday in March and the last Sunday in October. For example, when it's 6pm in Vienna, it's 9am in Los Angeles (PST), 7am in Honolulu (HST), 10am in Denver (MST), 11am in Chicago (CST), noon in New York City (EST), 5pm in London (GMT), and 2am the next day in Sydney.

Tipping   A service charge of 10 to 15% is often included on hotel bills, but it's a good policy to leave something extra for waiters and 2€ per day for your hotel maid. Railroad station, airport, and hotel porters get 1.50€ per piece of luggage, plus a 1€ tip. Your hairdresser should be tipped 10% of the bill, and the shampoo person will be thankful for a 1.50€ gratuity. Toilet attendants are usually given .50€, and hatcheck attendants expect .50€ to 1.50€, depending on the place.

At restaurants, waitstaff carry wallets with them and when paying Austrians usually round up by approximately 10% and to the nearest euro.

Visas   Citizens of the U.S., Canada, the European Union, Australia, and New Zealand need only a valid passport if visiting Austria for under 90 days. In the case of visitors who reside in most other E.U. countries, a valid identity card from that country is sufficient. Citizens of other countries should be sure to check travel regulations before leaving. You can get these in English at **www.visahq.com**.

Visitor Information   Before you book your tickets to go, gather information about the country and travel options from the **Austrian National Tourist Office** (www.austria. info). We also recommend you contact a local Austrian tourism Agency at one of these locations:

In the **United States** contact the Austrian National Tourist Office, P.O. Box 1142, New York, NY 10108-1142 (✆ **212/944-6880;** www.austriainfo.com).

In **Canada,** you'll find offices at 2 Bloor St. E., Suite 3330, Toronto, ON M4W 1A8 (✆ **416/967-3381**).

In **Great Britain** and **Ireland,** contact the Austrian National Tourist Office at 14 Cork St., W1X 1PF (✆ **0845/101-1818**).

Water   Tap water in Vienna, piped in from mountain springs, is not only safe to drink but tastes very good and is automatically served with coffee and red wine. Many people also drink bottled mineral water, generally called *Mineralwasser.*

Wi-Fi   See "Staying Connected," p. 70.

AIRLINE & CAR RENTAL WEBSITES

MAJOR AIRLINES

Aeroméxico
www.aeromexico.com

Air France
www.airfrance.com

Air India
www.airindia.com

Alitalia
www.alitalia.com

American Airlines
www.aa.com

British Airways
www.british-airways.com

China Airlines
www.china-airlines.com

Continental Airlines
www.continental.com

Delta Air Lines
www.delta.com

EgyptAir
www.egyptair.com

El Al Airlines
www.el.co.il

Finnair
www.finnair.com

Iberia Airlines
www.iberia.com

Japan Airlines
www.jal.co.jp

Lufthansa
www.lufthansa.com

Northwest Airlines
www.flynaa.com

Olympic Airlines
www.olympicairlines.com

Qantas Airways
www.qantas.com

Swiss Air
www.swiss.com

Turkish Airlines
www.thy.com

United Airlines
www.united.com

U.S. Airways
www.usairways.com

BUDGET AIRLINES

Air Berlin
www.airberlin.com

EasyJet
www.easyjet.com

CAR RENTAL AGENCIES

Auto Europe
www.autoeurope.com

Avis
www.avis.com

Budget
www.budget.com

Dollar
www.dollar.com

Enterprise
www.enterprise.com

Hertz
www.hertz.com

Kemwel (KHA)
www.kemwel.com

LANGUAGE LESSONS

17

English is widely spoken throughout Austria, at least at a functional level, especially in cities such as Vienna and Salzburg and at all the major resorts. Children are taught English in school. However, when you encounter someone who doesn't speak English, the following might be useful. Even attempting to use a little German is a nice sign of respect toward your hosts. When it comes to articles it's the masculine "der," the feminine "die," or the neutral "das." The plural always uses "die." That is the definite article or "the" in English. To use the indefinite or "a/an," say "ein" for "der" and "das" and "eine" for "die." Also, nouns are always capitalized.

BASIC PHRASES & VOCABULARY

English	German	Pronunciation
Hello	Guten Tag	**goo-ten-*tahk***
How are you?	Wie geht es Ihnen?	**vee *gayt* ess ee-neen**
Very well	Sehr gut	**zayr *goot***
Thank you	Danke schön	**dahn-keh-*shern***
Good morning	Guten Morgen	***guu-ten* morgen**
Good evening	Guten Abend	***guuten*-abend**
Good night	Gute Nacht	***guuten* nacht**
Goodbye	Auf Wiedersehen	**owf *vee*-dayr-zayn**
Please	Bitte	***bit*-tuh**
Yes	Ja	**yah**
No	Nein	**nine**
Do you speak English?	Sprechen Sie Englisch?	***shprekhen zee Eng-lish***
Excuse me	Entschuldigen Sie	**en-*shool*-di gen zee**
I'm sorry	Es tut mir Leid	**es *toot* meer *leid***

English	German	Pronunciation
Give me	Geben Sie mir	*gay*-ben zee meer
May I?	Darf ich?	*darf*-ikh
I need	Ich brauche...	*ikh brow-khuh*
Is/are there?	Gibt es?	*gibb-et* ess?
Where is . . . the airport the station? a hotel? a restaurant? the toilet?	Wo ist . . . der Flughafen der Bahnhof? ein Hotel? ein Restaurant? die Toilette? das WC?	*voh* eest dayr *floog*-hafen dayr *bahn*-hoft ain *hotel?* ain *res-tow-rahng* dee twah-*let*-tuh dahs *vay* tsay
Is it near here?	Ist es ganz in der Nähe?	*ist ez gans in der nye?*
To the right	Nach rechts	nakh *reshts*
To the left	Nach links	nakh *leenks*
Straight ahead	Gerade aus	geh-*rah*-deh-ows
I would like . . . to eat a room for one night	Ich möchte . . . essen ein Zimmer für eine Nacht	ikh *mersh*-ta *ess*-en ain *tzim*-mer feer *ai-neh* nakht
How much is it?	Wieviel kostet das?	vee-*feel* kaw-stet dahs
When?	Wann?	vahn
Yesterday	Gestern	*geh*-stern
Today	Heute	*hoy*-tuh
Tomorrow	Morgen	*more*-gen
Tomorrow morning	Morgen früh	*mor*-gen fruh
Next week	Nächste Woche	*nex*-tuh *voh*-khuh

RESTAURANTS

English	German	Pronunciation
Is service included?	Ist die Bedienung inbegriffen?	Ist dye bedden-ung inbegriffen?
The check, please	Die Rechnung, bitte	die reck-nung, *bit-tuh*
Do you have a table?	Haben sie einen Tisch?	haben see I-nen tish?
Menu	Speisekarte	*space-kart*
Do you have...?	Haben sie?	haben see?
Breakfast	Frühstück	*free*-shtick
Lunch	Mittagessen	*mi*-tahg-gess-en
Dinner	Abendessen	*ah*-bend-ess-en

EMERGENCIES

English	German	Pronunciation
It's an emergency	Das ist ein Notfall	**dahs ist ighn *noht*-fahl**
I'm sick	Ich bin krank	***ikh bin krahnk***
I'll call the police	Ich rufe die Polizei	**ikh *roo*-fuh dee poh-lee-*tsigh***
I need your help	Ich brauche deine/Ihre Hilfe	**ikh *brow*-khuh *digh*-nuh/ ee-ruh *hill*-fuh**
I'm lost	Ich habe mich verirrt	**ikh *hah*-buh mikh fer-*irt***
Help!	Hilfe!	***hill-fuh!***

DAYS OF THE WEEK

English	German	Pronunciation
Monday	Montag	***mawn*-taag**
Tuesday	Dienstag	***deens*-taag**
Wednesday	Mittwoch	***mit*-vokh**
Thursday	Donnerstag	***do-ners*-taag**
Friday	Freitag	***frai*-taag**
Saturday	Samstag	***zams*-taag**
Sunday	Sonntag	***zon*-taag**

NUMBERS

In German, numbers above 20 are inverted. So instead of "*zwanzig-eins*," (twenty-one) it's "*ein-und-zwanzig*" (one and twenty), "*zwei-und-zwanzig*," etc.

English	German	Pronunciation
one	eins	**eyntz**
two	zwei	**tzvai**
three	drei	**dry**
four	vier	**feer**
five	fünf	**fewnf**
six	sechs	**zex**
seven	sieben	***zee*-ben**
eight	acht	**akht**
nine	neun	**noyn**
ten	zehn	**tzayn**
eleven	elf	**ellf**
twelve	zwölf	**tzvuhlf**
thirteen	dreizehn	***dry*-tzayn**
fourteen	vierzehn	***feer*-tzayn**
fifteen	fünfzehn	***fewnf*-tzayn**
sixteen	sechzehn	***zex*-tzayn**
seventeen	siebzehn	***zeeb*-tzayn**
eighteen	achtzehn	***akh*-tzayn**

English	German	Pronunciation
nineteen	neunzehn	*niyn*-tzayn
twenty	zwanzig	*tzvahn*-tzik
thirty	dreißig	*dry*-tzik
forty	vierzig	*feer*-tzik
fifty	fünfzig	*fewnf*-tzik
sixty	sechzig	*zex*-tzik
seventy	siebzig	*zeeb*-tzik
eighty	achtzig	*akht*-tzik
ninety	neunzig	*noyn*-tzik
one hundred	hundert	*hoon*-dert

MENU TERMS

SOUPS (SUPPEN)

die Erbsensuppe pea soup
die Gemüsesuppe vegetable soup

die Gulaschsuppe goulash soup
die Kartoffelsuppe potato soup

MEAT (WURST, FLEISCH & GEFLÜGEL)

der Aufschnitt cold cuts
das Brathuhn roast chicken
die Ente duck
die Gans goose
das Geflügel poultry
das Kalb veal
das Lamm lamb

die Leber liver
das Rindfleisch beef
der Rindsbraten roast beef
der Schinken ham
der Schweinebraten roast pork
der Truthahn turkey

FISH (FISCH)

die Forelle trout
der Hecht pike
der Karpfen carp

der Lachs salmon
die Makrele mackerel
die Seezunge sole

EGGS (EIER)

hart gekochte Eier boiled eggs
Rühreier scrambled eggs

Spiegeleier fried eggs
pochierte Eier poached eggs

VEGETABLES (GEMÜSE)

der Blumenkohl cauliflower
die Erbsen peas
grüne Bohnen string beans
die Gurke cucumber
die Karotten carrot
der Kohl cabbage
das Rotkraut red cabbage

der Salat lettuce
die Kartoffel potato
der Spargel asparagus
der Spinat spinach
die Tomate tomato
Note: In Austrian dialect tomatoes are
often called "Paradeiser" and potatoes are
called "Erdäpfel."

FRUITS (OBST)

der **Apfel** apple

die **Orange** orange

die **Banane** banana

die **Birne** pear

Erdbeeren strawberries

Kirschen cherries

Weintrauben grapes

die **Zitrone** lemon

BEVERAGES (GETRÄNKE)

das **Bier** beer

ein **dunkles** a dark beer

ein **helles** a light beer

die **Milch** milk

eine **Tasse Kaffee** a cup of coffee

eine **Tasse Tee** a cup of tea

das **Wasser** water

CONDIMENTS & TABLE ITEMS

das **Brot** bread

Brötchen rolls

die **Butter** butter

das **Eis** ice (or ice cream)

der **Essig** vinegar

die **Gabel** fork

das **Glas** glass

der **Knödel** dumpling

der **Löffel** spoon

das **Messer** knife

der **Pfeffer** pepper

der **Teller** plate

der **Reis** rice

die **Sahne** cream

das **Salz** salt

der **Senf** mustard

der **Zucker** sugar

COOKING TERMS

blutig rare

gebacken baked

gebraten fried

gefüllt stuffed

gekocht boiled

geröstet roasted

gut durchgebraten well-done

heiss hot

kalt cold

Index

INDEX

NOTES